Praise for
O'Neill: Son and Playwright

"An indispensable work." —*Los Angeles Times*

"Fifteen years in the making and clearly it's a monumental labor of love." —*Publishers Weekly*

"An extraordinary book. . . . I thoroughly enjoyed [it]." —Brooks Atkinson, *New York Times* theater critic

"A refreshing departure from the heavily academic school of literary biography. . . . A formidable and minutely detailed narrative which at times is as dramatic . . . as O'Neill's plays. . . . An exciting and potent work." —Edmund Fuller, *Wall Street Journal*, author of *Boswell's Life of Johnson* and *John Milton*

"O'Neill's passionate intentions became his talent—a rude, almost barbaric thrust that can seize a blasé Broadway crowd and wring it dry, half from fatigue, half from an emotional buffeting that no other American playwright ever inflicted on an audience. O'Neill could do what only a major artist can do: make his public share in the life of his private demons. . . . The accumulated O'Neill agonies still produce a power beyond themselves, just as they do in his plays." —*Time*

"A wonderfully lively narrative, filled with penetrating insights. . . . [Sheaffer] writes beautifully. . . . It is all first-rate." —*St. Louis Post-Dispatch*

"This impressively documented work links hundreds of lines of dialogue from O'Neill's plays to persons and events in his troubled life. Sheaffer's research goes to exhausting lengths, but his literary style is earthbound. . . . The result is an almost unbelievably intimate acquaintance with the man who freed the American theater from the shackles of unreality. . . . Sheaffer's narrative carries O'Neill through the first years of his life [and his relationships with] a brother whom he alternately loved and disliked, and a mother for whom he felt guilt because she first had been administered morphine at his birth. . . . [This is a fruitful] study of the roots of O'Neill's plays in his own troubled life." — William Leonard, *Washington Post Book World*, drama critic for the *Chicago Tribune*

"The author has found hitherto untapped sources to develop his study of the man whose characters and plays reflected much of his own relationships with his parents and brother." —*America*

"Sheaffer's experiences as a journalist, reviewer, and worker in the theater have paid off magnificently." —Alan Downer, editor of *American Drama and Its Critics*

"[This is] a model of what biography should be. . . . [Sheaffer's work] ought to prove spellbinding for O'Neill buffs and theater addicts, and scarcely less so for readers who enjoy biographies." —*Publishers Weekly*

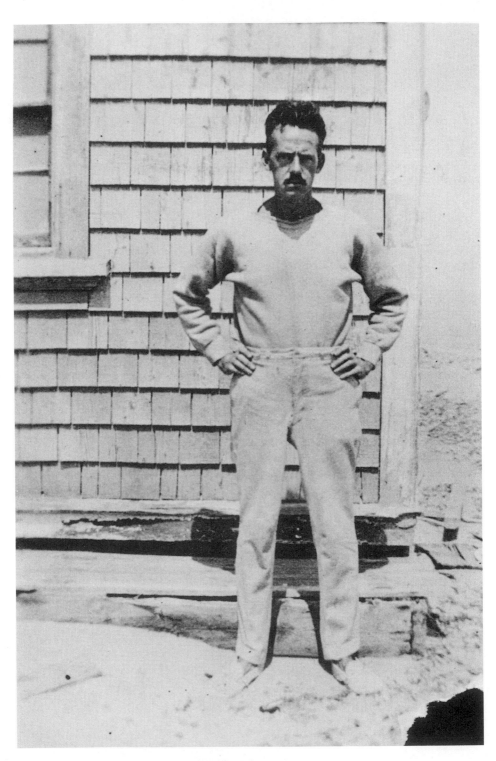

O'Neill in Provincetown

O'NEILL

SON AND PLAYWRIGHT

VOLUME I

by LOUIS SHEAFFER

with photographs

Cooper Square Press

Acknowledgments for permissions to quote copyrighted material appear in "Acknowledgments" on pages 522–23.

First Cooper Square Press edition 2002

This Cooper Square Press paperback edition of *O'Neill: Son and Playwright* is an unabridged republication of the edition first published in Boston, Massachusetts in 1968. It is reprinted by arrangement with the Estate of Louis Sheaffer.

Published by Cooper Square Press
A Member of the Rowman & Littlefield Publishing Group
200 Park Avenue South, Suite 1109
New York, New York 10003-1503
www.coopersquarepress.com

Distributed by National Book Network

Library of Congress Cataloging-in-Publication Data

Sheaffer, Louis.
    O'Neill, son and playwright / Louis Sheaffer.—1st Cooper Square Press ed.
      p. cm.
Originally published: Boston: Little, Brown, 1968.
Includes bibliographical references (p.) and index.
ISBN 0-8154-1243-6 (pbk.: alk. paper)
    1. O'Neill, Eugene, 1888–1953. 2. O'Neill, Eugene, 1888–1953—Family. 3. O'Neill, Eugene, 1888–1953—Childhood and youth. 4. Dramatists, American—20th century—Biography. I. Title.

PS3529.N5 Z797 2002
812'.52—dc21

                    2002073617

©™ The paper used in this publication meets the minimum requirements of American National Standard for Information Sciences—Permanence of Paper for Printed Library Materials, ANSI/NISO Z39.48–1992.
Manufactured in the United States of America.

For my mother, Ida Slung

One's outer life passes in a solitude haunted
by the masks of others; one's inner life passes
in a solitude hounded by the masks of oneself.

EUGENE O'NEILL, "Memoranda on Masks"
The American Spectator, November 1932

Foreword

IN the main this biography does three things: it adds new pages, if not
chapters, to O'Neill's history; it gives a portrait of the man different in
some respects from the customary image, chiefly concerning his feelings
toward his parents; and it offers both new information and some fresh
thoughts on his plays, particularly in regard to their autobiographical
content. Such a critical approach to his writings is, I realize, more or
less unfashionable today as a result of the ascendancy of the New
Critics, with their insistence that a text should be examined in a vacuum
as it were, without any account taken of its author. Undoubtedly their
credo has merit, for in the final analysis a work must stand on its own,
yet O'Neill was one of the most autobiographical playwrights who
ever lived, and knowledge of his life cannot but contribute to our understanding of his plays. Moreover, we can gain some insight into the
workings of the creative mind, into the nature of creativity itself, by
studying O'Neill's usage of his subjective raw materials, the liberties he
took with the clutter of reality in his endeavor to reveal some of its inner
truths.

O'Neill defies fathoming in any depth, it seems to me, unless one
comprehends his relations with his parents, his predominant feelings
toward each of them. A man, the Bible said with vision antedating Freud's
by several thousand years, "shall leave his father and his mother, and shall
cleave unto his wife." Unfortunately for O'Neill the man, but fortunately for O'Neill the writer, he never really "left" his mother and
father. The evidence is to be found again and again in his writings,
ultimately most clearly, most hauntingly in the posthumously released *A
Long Day's Journey Into Night*. Hence my stressing of this element of
his make-up, as reflected in the title *O'Neill, Son and Playwright*.

[ix]

The first of what is to be a two-volume biography, this book ends in 1920 with the production of *Beyond the Horizon,* O'Neill's launching on Broadway. Since one of my primary concerns is to trace relations between his life and his work, the book, though more or less chronological, looks ahead from time to time to consider aspects of his plays as they originate in his personal history: i.e., an inside story about a famous anarchist case, which he hears around 1917, will provide him with one of the main strands of his 1939 play *The Iceman Cometh;* two artists whom he meets in 1916, Charles Demuth and Marsden Hartley, are to serve as the chief models for Charles Marsden, "good old Charlie," in *Strange Interlude.* Where my first volume occasionally jumps ahead in time, the second one will, at appropriate moments, look back, as an O'Neill increasingly Proustian attempts to recapture the past.

The present book, like the one to follow, is based almost entirely on primary research and primary sources, and many if not most of the sources have hitherto been untapped by O'Neillian biography. A glance at the section "Acknowledgments" will indicate the wide range of my research; it was as thorough as a consuming interest could make it. In covering his one year at Princeton (1906–1907), for example, I wrote to all one hundred and eighty surviving members of O'Neill's class, and heard from slightly over a hundred. With those who had any recollections, however minor, I established a correspondence until I had learned apparently everything they could remember. A second round of letters to all who had disregarded my first query brought replies from about half. In addition to all this correspondence, I interviewed the half-dozen or so of his fellow students who had the most to tell.

O'Neill's four years at Betts Academy (1902–1906) in Stamford, Connecticut, posed a more difficult problem; whereas Princeton supplied me with the current addresses of its alumni, all I had as a starting point for Betts, which burned down in 1908, was a list of its former students and their home towns compiled nearly sixty years ago. It would require pages to tell of the detective work entailed in trying to locate O'Neill's classmates, for the great majority had moved elsewhere or died, but I finally succeeded in tracking down nearly forty. In their reminiscences we can trace his development from a boy painfully shy into a young rebel and sport, prematurely cynical, trying to emulate his hard-living older brother.

Since knowledge of the child is essential to an understanding of the man, I have likewise been at pains to reconstruct his earliest years. Drawing on several sources newly discovered, this book contains the first detailed portrait of Sarah Jane Bucknell Sandy, O'Neill's nursemaid the first seven years of his life and, in effect, his second mother. Next to his parents and, possibly, his brother, Sarah played a greater role than anyone else in shaping him; everything we can learn about her helps to shed some light, if indirectly, on her young charge. In addition this book, again for the first time, presents O'Neill's own view of his childhood as summarized in a diagram he once drew up — intended solely for his own eyes — outlining his feelings toward his mother, father, and Sarah Sandy from his first years into adolescence. Still other glimpses of the boy are afforded in the recollections of classmates at his first two schools, St. Aloysius Academy (1895–1900), just outside New York City, and De La Salle Institute (1900–1902), in the city.

In one of the most fertile lines of my research I spent months in New London, Connecticut, reading every issue of its newspapers, the *Day* and the *Telegraph*, from the mid-1880s, when the O'Neills began to vacation there, until late 1919, when the father sold their summer place, the nearest thing to a home they ever had. This day-to-day perusal of the papers gave me a detailed over-the-years picture of the milieu in which O'Neill spent a large portion of his formative and growing-up period; New London, as I illustrate in my narrative, provided him with more material for his writings than is yet realized. The search eventually uncovered several hundred news items of lesser or greater importance containing a fund of fresh information for his history.

I was particularly careful in reading the *Telegraph* during the three months of 1912 when Eugene was on its staff, and found a number of stories that, while unsigned, bear his signature in some way — stories that serve to contradict the usual account of him as a reporter. After he had become famous some of his early associates gave the impression that his career had set a new low in journalistic history; in fact one of them wrote a newspaper article, now widely quoted, entitled "The World's Worst Reporter." Yet the writer, who claims to have "run his legs off" doing double-work because O'Neill never turned in a story, was actually working at the time, I discovered, for the other newspaper, the *Day*.

This book, needless to say, makes use of all the standard sources — O'Neill's letters (including a large number new to his biography), published interviews, the memoirs of his contemporaries, biographical and critical studies, and so forth. However, I found no small amount of error in the written record. Unless he has been misquoted in his interviews, O'Neill himself was responsible for some of the misinformation; apparently, being an instinctive dramatist, he could not resist touching up and revising his past, but in some instances it seems that he went out of his way to confuse biographers who would one day try to retrace his trail. Part of the error in the record, though, can be attributed to writers insufficiently informed who made faulty deductions and suppositions but expressed themselves categorically.

For a long time all that we knew of O'Neill's several years as a seaman and water-front drifter, a period he later drew upon heavily for his writings, was what he had chosen to tell interviewers. In the course of more than seven years' research I have amassed data from various sources — private individuals (including men who had sailed with him), shipping lines, official archives both here and abroad, maritime and consulate authorities in Argentina, England and Norway — that document, alter and measurably augment the existing record of this period: his different trips as a sailor, his many months "on the beach" in Buenos Aires, his stay in England during the Great General Strike of 1911, his touching bottom at "Jimmy the Priest's." Who was Jimmy the Priest, what was his real name, where was his saloon and flophouse located, what did the place look like? When and from what ship did Driscoll jump overboard in mid-ocean? Was Chris Christopherson really as the playwright pictured him in *Anna Christie?* These are but a few of the questions answered in this book, and some of my findings disprove things universally accepted as part of O'Neill's history. It is not true, for instance, that he was a crew member of the Norwegian barque that carried him to Buenos Aires (he paid for his passage). Or that he met some of his Coras, Pearls, and Anna Christies at Jimmy the Priest's (Jimmy's saloon, which had no "family entrance" and separate back room, was for men only). Or that the suicide of James ("Jimmy Tomorrow") Byth had anything to do with Eugene's own suicide attempt (Byth killed himself more than a year after O'Neill's attempt and his return from the depths).

O'Neill's chroniclers have always been interested, understandably enough, in his seafaring days and their reflection in his writings, but surprisingly little attention has been given to certain other aspects of his life and his literary output. When and under what circumstances, for example, did he acquire his familiarity with and feeling for life on a farm? Until this book no one had attempted to account for the real-life experience that underlay his writing such plays as *The Rope, Beyond the Horizon* and, most notably, *Desire Under the Elms.* Neither, for that matter, has any biographer heretofore dealt more than passingly with the question of the playwright's preoccupation with insanity — the subject figures in five or six of his plays. (The usual offhand judgment is that he had a bent for "strong" subject matter.) As I illustrate in my narrative, his interest in insanity was apparently familial and personal in origin,

[xii]

stemming from a fearful phase of his boyhood. Finally, to cite one more instance, it seems to me that his first long plays — "Bread and Butter," *Servitude*, "The Personal Equation"—have been unduly neglected by his biographers and critics. A writer's first works, as Leon Edel says in his *Literary Biography*, are generally his most transparently autobiographical. While this is not true of O'Neill, for *Long Day's Journey*, patently, borrows most directly from his life, his early efforts do afford some insight into the man and the playwright.

Other aspects and stages of O'Neill's life covered in this book include the decisive effect on him of *Monte Cristo*, his father's perennial vehicle; his stay in a sanatorium for the tubercular; his year in Professor Baker's playwriting course at Harvard; his efforts to write for the movies; his period of drift in Greenwich Village; the start and early years of his association with the Provincetown Players; his first two marriages; his development as a playwright, and the prolonged ordeal of his Broadway debut. The reader will find new and, I trust, significant material on all these matters.

L.S.

Contents

Contents

Illustrations

O'NEILL

SON AND PLAYWRIGHT

1

Apprehensive Mother

H IS BIRTH proved calamitous to the family. Although things were not right with the O'Neills even before Eugene was born, they were far worse afterward.

The story of what happened, the quintessential story, is told in one of his last works, the autobiographical *A Long Day's Journey Into Night*, his "play of old sorrow, written in tears and blood." O'Neill was born in 1888, the play is set in 1912, yet its principals — the author himself, his mother, his father, his brother — are still haunted by his birth, by something his birth had set in motion.

The mother: "I was so healthy before Edmund was born. But bearing Edmund was the last straw. [Though O'Neill used in the play the actual given names of his parents and brother, he called himself "Edmund," after a brother who had died in infancy.] . . . It wasn't until after Edmund was born that I had a single gray hair. Then it began to turn white. . . . He has never been happy. Nor healthy. He was born nervous and too sensitive. . . . I was afraid all the time I carried Edmund. I knew something terrible would happen."

The father: "It was in her long sickness after bringing him into the world that she first —"

That she first took morphine. *Long Day's Journey* is a play the author placed under seal and lock almost as soon as he had written it, a play he had wanted withheld from the public until twenty-five years after his death. In it he revealed his mother as one of the most tortured of drug addicts, a shy devout soul whose Catholicism served but to deepen her shame and sense of degradation. His father he portrayed as miserly, his brother as a cynical alcoholic, corrupt and corrupting. The play was written, according to the author's foreword, with "deep pity and understanding and forgiveness." But his words are refuted by the play itself, an inextricable tangle of love and hostility, of compassion and bitter resentment, of accusation and apology, of self-pity and self-hatred; the play itself discloses that the wounds inflicted on him by the family relations remained all his life raw and bleeding. Here at last we find the matrix of his tragic outlook on life, the source of the anguish that throbs through so much of his writings.

· Though time failed to soften the playwright's memories, it apparently had a muffling effect on Ella Quinlan O'Neill's. In one of her rare extant letters, written to Eugene in 1919, she was stirred to reminiscence: "I am one of the happiest old ladies in New York tonight to know I have such a wonderful grandson but no more wonderful than you were when you were born and weighed eleven pounds [her underscoring] and no nerves at that time. I am enclosing a picture of you taken at three months. Hope your boy will be as good looking." She ended the letter with love. to his wife, baby, "and the biggest baby of the three, You."

Whether Eugene was "born afraid," as *Long Day's Journey* has it, or without "nerves," as his mother said, eleven pounds is a large infant, especially for an apprehensive woman who had been against having another child; his entrance into the world, according to stories that came down in the family, was achieved with difficulty. Shortly after his reluctant debut on October 16, 1888, a day that began fair but turned gray and showery, he was appraised by one of his mother's cousins, Lillian Brennan, a blunt-spoken woman, who took a dubious view of his large head. In describing his appearance to other relatives, she pronounced judgment on him in words she was to repeat for years: "He'll either be an idiot or a genius!"

The setting of his birth, eminently fitting for one destined to become America's foremost playwright, was in the heart of the district he was to stir up, bewilder and excite. He was born in the Barrett House, a family-style hotel at the northeast corner of 43rd Street and Broadway, in what was then Longacre Square; sixteen years later, as an odd-shaped skyscraper began to loom at the southern end of the square, the area was renamed Times Square. Though only a short distance southward the city boiled with traffic and crowds of people, life poked along quietly, leisurely in Longacre Square, predominantly residential. Behind the Barrett House nearly half of the block's expanse was given over to the tree-shaded back yards of homes and other dwellings. A few blocks north, at 50th Street, the air was farmlike with the smell of hay, horseflesh and manure from the stables of the Broadway and Seventh Avenue horsecar lines. In several years playhouses would begin to invade Longacre Square, but at the time they were concentrated between Union Square and

Herald Square; even in infancy Eugene O'Neill was ahead of the theater of his day.

The week of his birth, a lively one for the New York stage, brought seven openings, including such importations as the "ever youthful Lydia Thompson and own burlesque company of British beauties," a distinguished troupe from Paris in repertory, headed by M. Coquelin, and a new Gilbert and Sullivan work, *The Yeomen of the Guard.* Among the home-grown productions was a melodrama about an "honest old Vermont farmer, whose pretty, guileless daughter is lured away at the instance of a grasping, though not wholly unscrupulous old miser."

It likewise was a busy period for James O'Neill. A few weeks earlier he had begun, as reluctantly as his son was to be born, his sixth consecutive season in *Monte Cristo.* The romantic actor, giving around this time his fourteen-hundredth performance in the Dumas dramatization, felt almost as much prisoner as Edmond Dantès during his eighteen-year imprisonment in the grim Château d'If. Night after night, touring in New England, he emerged from a billowing canvas sea, after escaping from the Château, and clambered onto a rock (actually, a stool); when the rattling thunder subsided and the lightning flashes ended, the calcium light shone on his wild eyes and roughly bearded face as he exulted: "Saved! Mine, the treasures of Monte Cristo! The wor-rld is mi-n-ne!" Thunderous applause. Curtain.

Night after night, Manchester, Newport, Lowell, Worcester, until he would receive word that his latest child was imminent. For all his chafing under the too familiar role and his worries over his wife, his emotional state was well masked; on Monday evening, October 15, he gave in Brockton an "excellent performance to a large house." That night word came. It is unknown whether James arrived in time for the event, but he spent only Tuesday with his wife and newly born son. Immediately afterward, tied to his bookings and forever driven by fear of poverty, he returned to the road. On Wednesday in Fall River there was a "large house to see the familiar *Monte Cristo.*" Around the same time a weekly theatrical journal relayed word from its correspondent in Holyoke: "James O'Neill says that he is heartily tired of *Monte Cristo*, but that the managers won't take anything else. As long as it continues to prove such a veritable bonanza, he would be foolish to drop it." A more sympathetic chronicler, in Springfield, said that his perennial vehicle "makes one feel glad and regretful at the same time; glad that Dumas's ever popular role has among its many interpretations at least one praiseworthy reproduction, and sorry that the Count's irresistible monetary fascination is fast smothering O'Neill's versatility."

In ensuing years he would make numerous attempts to escape: Shake-

*Ella Quinlan O'Neill around the time
of her marriage in 1877*

In the early 1880s

James O'Neill in 1875

In 1869　　　　　　　　　　　　　　　　　*Circa 1915*

speare, new plays, rewritings of old successes, lavish revivals of former hits. None of them drew for long, his public turning out in large numbers only when James was running the gamut as Edmond Dantès, the trusting young sailor; the despairing prisoner of the Château, the kindly Abbé Busoni; and the mysterious, fabulously rich Count of Monte Cristo. A quarter of a century and some three thousand more performances after he had begun to weary of the play, James O'Neill, by then in his mid-sixties, crawled up on the rock for the final time and declared, "The wor-rld is mi-n-ne!" (He often told friends that this was the line in the play he most disliked.)

Fortunately, in the late 1880s he could not foresee his professional fate as he began seeking other vehicles, roles that would enable him to resume his climb toward lasting glory and a niche among the immortals of the American stage. Meanwhile, *Monte Cristo*. In Hartford, a "large and well pleased audience." In Bridgeport, a "very large house." In Waterbury, "Neither the star nor the play seems to have lost any of their popularity. The house was crowded with an enthusiastic audience."

Concerned over his wife's slow recovery, James would catch the first train for New York after a Saturday night's performance to spend the weekend with his family. Two weeks after the birth of his third son he took time off from touring to participate in a family event that was particularly important to his devout, convent-educated wife. Whatever forebodings and fears Ella had had about her latest child, she must have nursed mystical hopes that the day's sacrament would set everything right. On a warm November 1, during a brief spell of Indian summer when fall clothing felt burdensome, Mr. and Mrs. O'Neill, several close friends, and a nursemaid who was carrying the infant boarded carriages at the Barrett House for a short ride southward to Holy Innocents, a church on 37th Street near Broadway, where the child was baptized and christened Eugene Gladstone O'Neill.

The name reflected his father's pride of origin. Though James was a faithful member of the church, his religion was almost as much Irish nationalism as Catholicism. That centuries of English oppression had left his native land a land in ruin was to him not simply a fact of history but a lasting grievance, a matter of emotional concern. His eyes would grow misty whenever he spoke of Ireland's fate. And for all his love of America, his deep gratitude for the opportunities it had given him to rise in the world, he could never forget what he in common with his countrymen had encountered over here, not only poverty but prejudice and discrimination; in nineteenth-century America the Irish were widely scorned as drunkards, brawlers, thickheaded louts good only for digging ditches and other manual labor. When it was suggested to James, after he had turned actor, that he ought to take a less identifiable name, he declared that if the name O'Neill had been good enough for "kings of Ireland," it certainly was good enough for him. The anti-Irish prejudice, leading him to overcompensate, simply intensified his feeling about his ancestry and the "Ould Country," about everything Irish.

To his first-born, he had given his own name. The second he called Edmund Burke after the Dublin-born statesman who, though a Protestant, had bravely fought the Crown's harshness toward Ireland and the Catholic populace (most people, unaware of the child's middle name, thought he was named for Edmond Dantès). In calling his third child Eugene, he presumably had in mind Eoghan, a noted figure in ancient Ireland and the ancestor of the latter-day O'Neills; but James erred, for "Eoghan" is Gaelic not for Eugene but for Owen. With the child's middle name the father paid his respects to Gladstone, the "Grand Old Man" of British politics and sometime prime minister; Gladstone, to the detriment of his career, had stoutly championed home rule for Ireland.

Even had James been inclined to forget the past, the day's occurrences prevented it; the past was the present. Trouble between the Homeland and England, as well as between opposed Irish factions, was forever boiling up — political sniping, charges and countercharges, rumors of impending revolt in Ireland, agitation in England for repressive measures, arguments and even outbreaks of violence in Parliament. The trouble was always well covered in the American press, in some papers with pro-Irish bias, with Anglophile leanings in others. The day after Eugene's birth a dispatch from London told of a special commission investigating charges that Parnell and his lieutenants had conspired in the "promotion of and inciting to commission of crimes and outrages, boycotting and intimidation," all with the goal to "establish the absolute independence of Ireland as a separate nation." Scarcely a day passed during the years Eugene was growing up without something in the newspapers about "the Irish problem" and its repercussions among Irish-Americans. The following headlines, taken at random, tell the story:

"Irish Tenants Rebel. . . . Orangemen Armed/With the Intention of Offering Resistance to Home Rule. . . . Dynamite Plots Arranged in America/London's Scare. . . . Cheers for Gladstone/Home Rule in First Place. . . . Irish Members Corrupted by Government. . . . Sword to Free Ireland/Chicago Convention Calls Loudly for Revolution. . . . Belfast Riots. . . . Irish Societies Condemn Queen. . . . Irish Bleed in English Commons/'Nineteen Policemen for One Irishman' Cry the Taunting Nationalists. . . . Ireland Won't Welcome King. . . . An Insult to England/Disgraceful Scene at the Lafayette Guard Picnic in New York/British Flags Torn Down/Then They Were Cursed, Trampled Underfoot and Torn to Atoms by Infuriated Mob."

One dispatch, headlined "Old Irish Problems," began: "Now that the Boer War is practically finished, the question that promises to bring most trouble for the British Lion is the old, old one of the Emerald Isle. This land of perpetual unrest is again threatening political if not actual revolt."

With his father an emotional sounding board for the disturbances on the other side, Ireland was never far away throughout Eugene Gladstone O'Neill's formative years. "One thing that explains more than anything about me," he once said, "is the fact that I'm Irish." Paying other tribute to his ancestry, he changed his family's name in *Long Day's Journey* to "Tyrone," after County Tyrone (Tir-Eoghan or Tir-Owen), the original domain of the O'Neill clan and a region where they held sway for centuries.

But more immediately, ever present, there was the theater. Almost from Eugene's first breath he breathed the air of the theater, his father's theater. Though he would grow up to deride its heroes whiter than white and villains of blackest black — he would indeed wield the foremost shovel in America in burying that theater — he owed it much. He absorbed from it, all the while unconscious of absorbing, the fundamentals of stagecraft, of telling story in dialogue and action, of how to reveal character through a character's own mouth, of what makes a scene "go," of how to touch people's feelings and transform them, a group of individuals, into one receptive body, an audience. O'Neill stood on his father's shoulders in attaining his eminent position in the theater.

Yet various circumstances had to be right — in this case the "right" circumstances were more or less traumatic — to give him a dramatizing cast of mind, a need to verbalize his deepest feelings. Undoubtedly he would have grown up a different kind of person, perhaps no writer at all, had he had a more stable and reassuring childhood. As it was, his formative years planted and fostered in him a deep sense of insecurity.

He was early initiated as a trouper, virtually from birth, for neither of his parents could bear being long separated from one another and his mother almost always toured with her husband. Yet marriage to an actor had proven sadly different from what the convent schoolgirl had dreamed. Her awakening as Mrs. James O'Neill came quickly. Most of her former schoolmates, with the social outlook of the day (actors, regardless of what they might be like individually, simply were not quite respectable), dropped the actor's wife; they made her feel déclassée. Fastidious, timid — at bottom less a wife and mother than a man's daughter and a woman's woman — Ella dearly missed the orderly way of life, solid and cushioned, she once had known. In place of a regular home, a succession of anonymous hotel rooms where she felt she would die of isolation and loneliness. In place of her own kind of people, the hyperthyroid folk of the theater with their instant camaraderie, their worldliness and glib talk, their indulgent moral code. From the audience she had found the theater enchanting; close up, it was grimy and sleazy, anything but glamorous, her husband's associates everything except compatible. Rather than hang around backstage, she would remain in the lonely hotel rooms; but not infrequently her husband would return late, well after the performance had ended, smelling of whiskey.

Ella learned that he had a weakness for liquor while they were still, she later used to charge, on their honeymoon. She had always known that he took a sociable glass, but she had not been aware of his daily thirst, of his regular need for alcohol, preferably amid the cigars, male talk, and conviviality of a barroom. While it is true that James drank more heavily than most men, his tastes and habits were characteristic of the day, of a general social pattern. The womenfolk would visit one another at home, while the men were accustomed to gather in clubs strictly stag and in bars. In her naïveté Ella had thought James different, but to her sorrow she learned differently. (Some of O'Neill's thoughts about his mother are embodied in the romanticizing heroine, named Emma, of one of his early plays, *Diff'rent.*)

Less than three months after her marriage, while still trying to adjust to a way of life she found repugnant, Mrs. James O'Neill suffered a new blow, the most shattering of all. One of James's sweethearts, claiming him as husband and the father of her child, sued in Chicago for divorce. According to Nettie Walsh, who petitioned the court under the name of Nettie O'Neill, his relationship with Ella was not marriage but adultery. Nettie said that James became her lover when she was fifteen and living in Cleveland, where he kept her in "the most rigid seclusion," and that during this period he married her. Intent on presenting him with a maximum of unsavory publicity, she characterized him as "parsimonious in his habits and disposition," estimated that he was worth around fifteen thousand dollars, and asked for suitable alimony. According to James, who denied everything except that they had been lovers, she was not a "chaste and virtuous woman" when they first met; he challenged her to produce legal evidence of their marriage.

That Nettie had slight chance of establishing her claim and was simply hoping for a settlement from the prospering actor did not relieve matters any for Ella. What increased her anguish was that the newspapers in

Chicago, where James was performing at the time, handled the scandal with levity; he in turn needed all his ability as an actor to reply in kind. At first, before he had a grip on himself, his eyes filled with tears at the newsmen's questioning about Nettie. "She was not my wife," he insisted, according to the Chicago *Tribune* on September 8, 1877. "There is only one woman in the world that I ever asked to become a wife to me . . ."; then he broke down, unable to finish. When reporters later pressed him for further comment, urging him to "open up," he parried them with "Supper is served at the Clifton House about six. I shall open my mouth there."

Emulating her actor husband, the shaken bride began to mask her feelings and was able to withstand even the direct approach of a former schoolmate: "Oh, Ella, what on earth can you do about this woman?" Ella looked at her stolidly, no expression in eyes a dark brown, almost black, and gently said, "What woman, honey?"

This was the second of James's romances to end unhappily; the first had been, especially for the woman, even more unfortunate. For several years his leading lady, as well as mistress, was a serious, dignified actress named Louise Hawthorne whose make-up concealed from audiences a long purplish scar on her face — a disfigurement that probably contributed to her intense personality and to the depth of her feeling for James. At any rate the two, after appearing together on the West Coast, came to a parting of the ways when he was signed by the famed Union Square Stock Company of New York, which was about to open an engagement in Chicago. Miss Hawthorne, who was visiting in Chicago at the time, saw her former lover's debut with the Union Square troupe in *The Two Orphans;* feeling ill, it was afterward said, she saw only part of the play before returning to her hotel. That night James, who was staying at the same place, visited her briefly and, as it turned out, was the last person to see her alive. Several hours later her body, smashed and bloody from a fall from her sixth-floor room, was found in the inner court of the hotel. Though the coroner called it "accidental death," it was generally believed in the profession that she had killed herself out of frustrated love for handsome Jimmy O'Neill.

First the Louise Hawthorne tragedy, now the unsavory mess over Nettie Walsh — James inevitably felt on the defensive with his wife. Yet it was a position he had already prepared for himself. From the outset he had placed Ella on a pedestal, considering himself fortunate to have the opportunity to protect and love her; he had accepted her aversion to theatrical life as a natural response of her fine-grained soul and felt apologetic about subjecting her to such a milieu. The scandal in Chicago, the guilt feelings it spurred in him, intensified his worshipful attitude, his feeling that he had married above himself.

Though her parents and his had fled practically barehanded from Ireland to escape chronic hunger, if not slow death by starvation, in the Great Potato Famine of the late 1840s and early fifties, their fortunes had differed in America. The O'Neills had suffered many bitter years over here, especially after the father, homesick and superstitious, afraid of dying in an alien land, had abandoned his wife and eight children to return to Ireland. A half-century later James O'Neill could still become emotional to the point of tears when he thought of his childhood in the slums of Buffalo and Cincinnati, of his mother slaving as a charwoman, the family always ill-fed and poorly clad, he himself going to work when but ten years old for fifty cents a week.

The Quinlans, however, had fared quite well. Though they made out just passably in New Haven, where Mary Ellen was born (she later chose to be known as "Ella"), they had prospered in Cleveland, where she grew up. Her father, besides accumulating real estate, became half-owner of a thriving liquor and tobacco shop that was a hangout for actors from the nearby Academy of Music. It was through the shop that James O'Neill came to know Thomas J. Quinlan. The ambitious, hard-working young actor and the self-made Quinlan, recognizing in one another a kindred spirit, were soon friends. James was then in his mid-twenties, while Mary Ellen was around fourteen. To him she was simply the daughter of a friend, a pretty youngster he enjoyed teasing, though gently, for she blushed easily; but she, overwhelmed by his looks and personality, began to daydream about the actor.

Long Day's Journey, revising fact, has them first meeting when she was several years older and her father took her to the theater. She wept, her counterpart reminisces in the play, when Tyrone was cast into prison and then was worried that her face would be reddened, for her father had promised to take her backstage and introduce her to him. Far from being disenchanted when they met in his dressing room, as the play tells it, she found him "different from all ordinary men," handsome and fascinating and yet at the same time modest and gentle, and instantly fell in love.

Her strain of romanticism, her desire that life should live up to her daydreams, was to be her undoing. By temperament, by upbringing, by education, Mary Ellen Quinlan, the only daughter of a devoted father (there was also a son), was suited to be a homebody, the sheltered wife of a solid conventional citizen — anything except an actor's wife. Whereas James had gone to work while still but a child, she had enjoyed advantages beyond those of most girls of her day. Her father, remembering his early hardships, wanted both his daughter and son to have a privileged start in life. After she graduated from a parochial school in Cleveland, he sent her to St. Mary's Academy in Notre Dame, Indiana, one of the finest such institutions in the country. A number of Protestant and Jewish parents also sent their daughters there because of the scarcity of schools of higher learning for women.

At first Mary Ellen was homesick at school, unhappy at being separated from her father (she never felt close to her mother, a narrow, censorious woman); but before long she fell contentedly into step with the academic routine, delighting in the calm metronomic perfection of its day, in its measured pursuit of culture and learning. Indeed, the atmosphere of St. Mary's so appealed to Miss Quinlan's virginal nature that she thought of becoming a nun; at the same time, having some talent for the piano, she also used to daydream about becoming a professional musician, a goal in which she was encouraged by Mother Elizabeth, founder and head of the school's excellent music department. English-born Mother Elizabeth, a lineal descendant of the organist at Winchester Cathedral in Elizabethan times, had led a full life, including marriage and widowhood, before being converted to Catholicism. She was a person of insight and seasoned judgment. Accurately appraising the greenness of Mary Ellen's character, the Mother urged her to wait a year or two after graduation, to go out into the world and try its pleasures, before deciding whether to take the veil.

In *Long Day's Journey* O'Neill called his mother "Mary" rather than by her preferred name of Ella, which she used most of her life. He probably was motivated by thoughts of St. Mary's Academy, of the Virgin Mary, and by the feeling that Mary Ellen Quinlan, instead of marrying, should have been a nun. If she had, her playwright son, whose writings and personal history reflect a strong death-wish, would never have known this world and this life. Calling himself in the play "Edmund," after the brother who had died in infancy, and giving the dead child his own name is but one of many indications of what Brooks Atkinson termed his "infatuation with oblivion."

Most likely Ella's history would have been different had her father lived longer; it is doubtful that he would have allowed a romance to develop between her and James O'Neill, still less have given his blessing to their marriage, no matter how much he liked James himself. But her father died while she was still in school. After being a teetotaler all his years Mr. Quinlan at forty developed a great thirst, especially for champagne (possibly in rebellion against a moralistic wife to whom champagne symbolized sinful living), drank himself into poor health, and finally fell victim to tuberculosis. The Cleveland *Plain Dealer* on May 26, 1874, called him a "man of genial disposition [whose] death will be regretted by a large number of friends." His daughter, who had adored him, was brokenhearted; always reserved, she took on a deeper quiet, covering her grief with intensified piety and greater application to her music studies. At the graduation exercises, where she played Chopin's Polonaise, Opus 22, she was awarded the gold medal in instrumental music.

For all her diffidence she could be stubborn when her heart fixed on something, and she was determined to quit Cleveland for New York. Whether her home town held too many painful reminders of her father, whether she hoped for a musical career in the big city, whether she nursed romantic dreams of James O'Neill, now a leading figure with the Union Square Stock Company, whatever her primary reason for favoring New York, the important thing is that she finally succeeded in winning over a reluctant mother. And once in the city she lost little time getting in touch with the actor who loomed so brightly in her thoughts. Aroused by her shy beauty and her evident interest in him, James, around thirty, accustomed to more worldly women, fell in love with Ella, ten years younger, whom one of her classmates had described as a "tall, superb creature with a kind of burnt-gold hair in profusion and deep brown eyes. Her cheeks were pink and her lips red and her little mouth seldom smiled." The tinge of sadness in her personality aroused James's protective feelings, while her aura of respectability and genteel tastes appealed to him as one familiar with the harsh side of things, with an actor's catch-as-catch-can existence; she in short represented a finer, more stable kind of life. On her side Ella found him all her romantic heart could hope for, a man, moreover, her beloved father had liked; she probably felt, if unconsciously, that in James she recaptured something of her father.

Each feeling certain that they were made for one another, plans went ahead for their marriage, over the doubts and reluctance of Ella's mother. Mrs. Bridget Quinlan, besides taking a dim view of all actors, even one Irish and a good Catholic, realized that her daughter was ill-suited for the uncertainties and rigors of theatrical life. But nothing and no one, especially Mrs. Quinlan, could dissuade Ella. She suspected that her mother had always been a little jealous of her because of her father's indulgence, that in fact her mother would have liked her to become a nun. The marriage took place on June 14, 1877, at fashionable St. Ann's on East 12th Street, with Mrs. Quinlan as one of the witnesses. In spite of its being a small family affair, Ella, who loved fine clothes, had a costly and elegant bridal gown: the finest satin, small ruffles of old duchesse lace around the neck and sleeves, the lace also worked in with folds for a bustle effect in back.

In time the gown became to her a symbol of innocence, of girlish dreams and transient bliss, as well as a focus of bittersweet memories. Whenever the present weighed too heavily on her, she used to unfold the gown and dwell with mournful pleasure on each fold of satin, every placement of lace; but finally she stored it away in a trunk in the attic, where it remained untouched for years. The memories it aroused had made her weep too often. Her son would eventually exploit it with poignant effect in the final moments of *Long Day's Journey* as the mother, fathoms deep in morphine, trails the now bedraggled gown on the floor while she rambles on vaguely about seeking something she had lost.

Not long after the painful Nettie Walsh episode James's career took him and Ella to San Francisco, where he was a favorite son from previous long stays. They remained there nearly two years, a period of relative tranquility for the O'Neills and among the happiest they were to know in their entire married life. Ella began to be inured to playful newspaper items, such as: "[James O'Neill] had prospered in Boston, stood in the foremost rank in New York, been claimed in Chicago by three or four wives, and finally comes back to us as handsome, as talented, and as well mustached as ever." Edging out of her shell, Ella warmed to some of his old friends and their families, among them such respected figures of the community as Henry M. Black, a carriage manufacturer. Yet haunted by memories of lonely hotel rooms, she greeted the birth of her first child on September 10, 1878, in the home of friends with more than ordinary happiness; she so rejoiced in him, poured on him so much loving care, bound him to herself with such indissoluble ties that she was the only woman James O'Neill, Jr., could ever love.

The pleasant stay in San Francisco, where Ella was able to provide her first-born child with a homelike atmosphere, where she enjoyed a normal life and had women friends of her own interests, only made her ensuing existence on the road less bearable. In a St. Louis hotel in the fall of 1883 she gave birth to another son. Looking after the infant Edmund and five-year-old Jamie kept her too busy to brood over being cut off from the society of nice people, but it was also hard on her. The proper care of two small children on the road in the 1880s — coping with laundry, finding the right food, constantly shifting from hotel rooms uncertainly heated to dusty railroad cars either overheated or freezing — would have been difficult for a woman stronger, more resourceful than Ella; for Ella, though a nursemaid traveled with her, it was beyond her endurance. Since she and James could not bear long separations, she felt torn between husband and children. The only solution, always temporary, was for her to attend to the youngsters in their New York apartment until her longing for her husband became intolerable. Then, leaving her mother in charge, she used to join him on tour until maternal feelings and anxiety, not unmixed with a sense of guilt, drove her back home.

Early in 1885, yielding to her husband's letters and her own desire — with, she often said later, sharp misgivings — Ella joined him in the West. Several weeks after she had left her children and mother at their "flat" in the Richfield on West 43rd Street, Jamie contracted measles and, disregarding orders to stay away from the baby, passed it along to his brother. Word reached the parents in Denver of the children's illness, and Ella, shaken with fear, wracked by guilt feelings, packed immediately to catch the earliest possible train. Before she could leave, a telegram arrived with the dread news that Edmund had died. With James tied to *Monte Cristo*, she had to make the long trip homeward alone, companioned only by her thoughts and her grief. Somehow James managed not only to fulfill his professional obligations but to get conviction into his portrayal. The reviews in Denver were uniformly enthusiastic, but one article raised tears in his eyes, touching him more deeply probably than anything else written about him during his half-century on the stage. He preserved the newspaper clipping to the end of his life:

AN ACTOR'S SAD BEREAVEMENT

The glitter of the stage display and the glamor which is thrown around the life of a successful actor are all that the audience sees. . . . It knows nothing of the drudgery of an actor's life, nor the anguish which wrings the heart, though the actor seems to be free from care. . . . The inexorable demands which an actor's life imposes were never better or more painfully exemplified than at last night's performance of *Monte Cristo*. The vast audience did not know that poor Jim O'Neill, who lived as Monte Cristo, was heartbroken. It did not know that at that moment his little child lay dead in far distant New York, and that the agonized mother had just taken a tearful farewell of him to attend the burial of the dear little one. It laughed and clapped its hands and gave no thought but to the actor's genius and dreamed not of the inward weeping that was drowning his heart. But actors are actors and they must strut upon the stage though their hearts break. God pity them; their lot is a hard one.

That autumn Mr. and Mrs. O'Neill enrolled their only child in the Minim division — a special grouping for boys under fourteen — at Notre Dame, only a mile or so from St. Mary's, where Mary Ellen Quinlan's seriousness and piety had made her a favorite of the nuns. St. Mary's always had a strong hold on Ella; whenever James's touring brought them close to the area, she used to make side trips to her old alma mater for a few blessed hours of peace. Wandering about the familiar grounds, quietly reveling in the cloistered atmosphere, she liked to imagine that she was still one of the students. St. Mary's and Notre Dame were to her a hallowed little world. Her child would be safe in such surroundings, well looked after by Sister M. Aloysius, the superior in charge of "Minims," while she herself would feel free to travel with her husband, her mind at ease. Everyone knew that Sister M. Aloysius, a daughter of County Limerick with blue eyes, a sweet brogue and a "green thumb," had a gift for blending outdoor work and book learning to bring out the best in a boy; besides fostering scholars, she made little gardeners of her charges.

How seven-year-old Jamie felt about boarding school may easily be imagined, for his life's story points in only one direction: school meant exile from his beloved mother. Though he knew that she supported the move, he blamed the father, since it was his travels that took her away. Over and beyond the natural conflict between sons and fathers, the relationship here was sharpened by special conditions. The child viewed the father through his mother's complaints — as so often happens, her sense of grievance was more articulate than her love — and had come to regard himself as her ally against her husband. The school-enforced separation, clearly proving that her husband came first, rocked his young soul and sealed his lifelong enmity to the father. Loneliness, self-pity, betrayal, he felt all this; most of all, aware that "Mama" blamed him for Edmund's illness and death, he felt judged and condemned.

Yet Jamie was resilient and bright enough to make out exceptionally well at Notre Dame; his parents had reassuring, indeed heartening reports about him. He scored high in all his classes, was prominent in the literary and dramatic societies, and proved good at sports; he struck everyone as an all-around fine lad with much of his father's outgoing charm. Those years, while the need to exonerate himself and impress his mother were driving him to excel, his parents were confident that he would grow up a great credit to them. Perhaps, James liked to think, as a lawyer or in politics — and why not both?

Had James's state of mind depended upon his son's progress at school and his own in the theater, he would have been well content, outside of a lingering sorrow over Edmund. After more than two years of *Monte Cristo* under salary, working for John Stetson, whose mangling of the language and rough treatment of actors were legendary, he was his own boss. He had succeeded in buying from Stetson the Dumas dramatization, along with the costumes, props, scenic devices, everything, all this for only two thousand dollars. Stetson in one of his rare business miscalculations had thought the play "squeezed dry." Now that James was master of his own fortunes, he redoubled the voltage of his portrayal to the delight of electrified audiences around the country. He began to pile up money, clearing after all expenses, around twenty-five thousand a year; he was going to be wealthy.

Only one thing prevented him from really enjoying life — his wife's chronic low spirits. Augmenting her old unhappiness from lonely hotel rooms and the near-isolation of endless train rides, she could not keep from brooding over Edmund; she blamed herself for having deserted the child, her husband for persuading her to join him, Jamie for passing his illness on to the baby. (Her sense of loss and guilt would never leave her. In 1912, over a quarter-century after Edmund's death, a nurse who was unaware of Mrs. O'Neill's drug addiction was summoned to look after her, and found her sitting up in bed, weeping, hair in wild disarray, lost to all but drug-induced fantasies. "My son, my son, my poor dead baby, my son, my little son," she kept repeating with slight variations, all the while wringing her hands and rocking back and forth, until she fell asleep hours later from exhaustion. The nurse, who had known Mrs. O'Neill as a quiet, dignified lady, was not only shocked by her appearance and emotional state but perplexed that a woman of her age should be mourning an infant son.) For all Ella's piety, her faith in a merciful Jesus, she could not help feeling that the child's death was a judgment upon herself: she did not deserve to have children, an actor's life was all wrong for them, she would have no more babies.

In his concern Mr. O'Neill hoped his wife would derive some benefit from their summers in New London, Connecticut. First drawn to the old river town because Ella's mother had moved there to live with a sister, they had decided on it as their summer base when James quickly succumbed to its vintage charm. Once a center for the whaling fleet, busy and ringing with the building, repairing and stocking of ships, the town had responded to the decline of whaling in the mid-nineteenth century not with Yankee enterprise but with New England conservatism. Those who had drawn their wealth from the sea made no effort to find other sources of income; their heirs in turn were content to nurse the family fortunes and quietly enjoy the emergence of New London as a summer resort for people of means. By the 1880s New London presented a drowsy face alongside the Thames River, its life quickened only in summer by a host of vessels on the broad, well-trafficked river, by an influx of tourists and part-time residents. The life of the town otherwise drifted along peaceably in street after street lined with overarching elms; elms flanked even State Street, the chief business artery, as it climbed away from the river and the railroad station.

Everything about New London and the surrounding countryside was pleasing to James: the fat dairy farms, the empty old warehouses still faintly redolent of whale oil, the semirural charm and sea-flavored air of the Pequot, a fashionable section bordering both the river and Long Island Sound that had pretensions as another Newport; the Crocker House with its hospitable long bar, the growing Irish community, the large element of old established wealth, the beer and clambake outings of the Naumeag Engine Company, which James soon joined; roadways paved with crushed oyster shells; the ferries running to Groton and the steamers to Block Island, the atmospheric lighthouse with its hoarsely assertive foghorn, the stories handed down of a valiant stand in the American Revolution against the British, the picnics and patriotic uproar on the Fourth of July, the schooners, yachts and sailboats on the Thames (pronounced with the "*h*," not like *that* river in England).

New London offered James attractive soil in which to put down roots, and he responded with an Irishman's love of the earth, an Irishman's hunger for land. He began buying real estate, not only for summer quarters but as an investment, while Ella, more in a spirit of acceptance than with enthusiasm, went along with her husband. He established a summer residence on desirable Pequot Avenue, the nearest thing to a home the family would ever have (it would inspire the setting for the somber *Long Day's Journey Into Night*); purchased a horse and carriage, which he used to leave winters with Father Joynt, the well-loved pastor of St. Mary's Star of the Sea, and proceeded to become one of the town's most popular figures, a genial country squire in the summer. Since he liked New London so well, New London reciprocated. Ella, whom the town found reserved and ladylike, regarded it as home partly because her mother was there but primarily because there Edmund was buried.

In 1887, after a few summers in New London had failed to benefit his wife, Mr. O'Neill took her to Europe for the Grand Tour, hoping this would spur her toward a better frame of mind. Now that he could afford it, there were two places in particular he wanted to see — the Château d'If, just off Marseilles, which figures so importantly in *Monte Cristo*, and Oberammergau, Bavaria, home of the *Passion Play*. Since the pageant was not being given that summer, James had to content himself with the sight of the bearded and biblical-looking villagers, who trained their hair in keeping with their once-in-a-decade roles. James made the trip to Bavaria both out of professional interest and with a sense of pilgrimage. A few years previously he had become the first actor in America to impersonate the Christus when *The Passion* — not the Oberammergau version but an original work — was staged in San Francisco amid religious controversy and great excitement. James, as well as many others, would never forget that performance.

However much the O'Neills enjoyed Europe, whatever lift in spirit it gave Ella, the glow was short-lived. On returning home they learned of a new death in the family, that of Mrs. Bridget Quinlan. Ella was inconsolable, for the latest death brought back memories full force, sharpening the old grief over her unfortunate father and poor Edmund. She felt more than ever dependent upon James for her sustaining strength, but as ever his professional life was against her.

Once more the hotel rooms and catching trains at all hours; another season of *Monte Cristo*, to James's growing unease. But while he found it difficult to alter the course of his career, he came up with an answer to their personal unhappiness: another child. Apart from his desire for a larger family, he thought it would be good for Ella; she would be so busy taking care of the infant she would have little time to brood over the past, over things that had happened and could never be undone.

Instantly rejecting her husband's suggestion, Ella was upset at the thought of another child blurring her memories of Edmund and replacing him in her heart; she felt it her duty, as a form of penance, to keep the dead child forever enshrined in her thoughts. At last yielding to James's persistence, Ella hoped that her next child would be a girl. She could fuss more over a girl, a girl eventually would give her feminine companionship, someone with whom she could exchange woman's talk and confidences; and, perhaps best of all, through a daughter she could vicariously relive her early years, those innocent and wonderful years before marriage. And yet, despite such thoughts, it was with mounting anxiety that Ella endured the long months of pregnancy, haunted by fears of some new disaster awaiting her. Then she gave birth to her third child, and reality proved not only to match but to surpass her worst apprehensions.

"When you're in agony and half insane," the mother cries out in *Long Day's Journey*, "[the doctor] sits and holds your hand and delivers sermons on will power! . . . He understands nothing! And yet it was exactly the same type of cheap quack who first gave you the medicine. . . . I hate doctors! They'll do anything . . . to keep you coming to them. They'll sell their souls! What's worse, they'll sell yours, and you never know it till one day you find yourself in hell!"

Behind her outburst can be found the sorest point of contention in the O'Neill family — Ella's charge that James was primarily responsible for her drug addiction, that instead of engaging a competent doctor to attend her in childbirth he, to save a few dollars, had called in a "cheap quack," an incompetent practitioner who first gave her "the medicine." The accusation, echoed bitterly by the sons, was always hotly denied by the father.

Whether James O'Neill was really miserly is a difficult question to answer, for the evidence available to us is mixed — a result, it seems, of opposed drives in his make-up. Undoubtedly he had a parsimonious side, an almost pathological fear of poverty, born of his wretched childhood, that led him to pinch pennies at home. At the same time he could be generous with his family, for he saw to it that Ella always had fine clothes, he gave her costly pieces of jewelry, and he certainly never stinted on his sons' education.

As to his part in Ella's drug addiction, James in all probability was guiltless. In view of his feeling for Ella, whom he loved to the end, it seems most doubtful that he would have entrusted her to the care of a third-rate doctor. Another, more substantial factor tends to exonerate him: a great many doctors of the day and still later, not "cheap quacks" but men of standing, were much too free in prescribing addictive drugs. The practice continued quite widely in fact until the Harrison Act of 1914, which placed the dispensing of narcotics under strict federal control. But even in the nineteenth century some voices sounded an alarm; one of them, a lecturer, used to tell her audiences:

"The increase of the morphine mania may well fill us with shame for the folly and weakness of our sex and should moderate our boast about the progress and enlightment of the age. Culture is of little value if it permits votaries to fall victims to a degrading vice which reduces them to the level of the most ignorant crone that ever sought refuge from poverty and care in gin. . . . The medical men are to some extent responsible for this pernicious practice by too indiscriminately prescribing morphine injections."

The lecturer was only a woman, though, in an era when women were supposed to have little knowledge other than of housework, the preparation of meals, the rearing of children. Few heeded her warning, certainly not the doctors, not the lawmakers; Mrs. James O'Neill was among those innocently trapped.

Since she had a difficult delivery and was slow in recovering from the ordeal, her physician found it advisable to give her morphine. All Ella knew was that it freed her from pain, from any feelings of loneliness and anxiety, and made life endurable. Little wonder, then, that she continued on her own to take such an efficient, wonderful medicine. From what was later whispered among her relatives, it seems that she was ignorant of the nature of the medication, of the hold it was gaining on her, until too late. As for James, he ascribed her spells of dreaminess and detachment to the lingering effects of childbirth, to the change of personality some women undergo afterward; it was long before he discovered that his wife was a drug addict.

Ella's frequent drifting out of touch with reality, out of consciousness of those around her, could scarcely have had a beneficial effect on her child. According to authoritative present-day thought, an infant's environment, above all his relationship with his mother, starts molding his personality and character practically from birth. Thus Eugene O'Neill's first weeks, his earliest months, began dictating the story of his haunted, insecure life. The baby was not physically neglected, however, for his parents had hired a nursemaid to look after him, an Englishwoman named Sarah Jane Bucknell Sandy. Sarah, becoming part of the family, would remain with the O'Neills seven years, on the road and in New London, until Eugene was deposited at boarding school. Plump and just a bit over five feet, Miss Sandy had grayish-blue eyes, a fair complexion that freckled easily, and hair of a color suited to her name, being reddish-blond. She was neat, well-spoken, capable, apparently a perfect "nanny," and made a pleasing picture in the traditional white outfit and headdress with flowing ribbons.

Sarah, who had come to America alone when sixteen to enter domestic service, was thirty-four when she took charge of Eugene — around the same age as his mother. A good Episcopalian, she found Mrs. O'Neill rather fanatical in her Catholicism, but being discreet reserved this opinion to herself and a few intimates. She was fond of children and knew how to manage them; under her quiet manner were firm convictions as to how they should behave. A friend once observed her collar two boys scuffling in fun outside a church; holding them apart, she inquired whether they had just come from a wrestling match or from Sunday School, and when the boys said school, she replied, "Well, I suggest that until you reach home, you behave as though you've just been to Sunday School." Mrs. O'Neill came to lean heavily on Sarah; Eugene, to regard her as his second mother.

However long Ella suffered from the effects of childbirth, she had recovered sufficiently in several months to rejoin her husband and make a trip to introduce ten-year-old Jamie to his new brother. The Notre Dame *Scholastic* of January 12, 1889, reported: "Master Eugene Gladstone O'Neill, son of Mr. James O'Neill of Monte Cristo fame, is with his amiable mother visiting his brother Jamie of the Minim Department. He is a beautiful child and promises to do honor to his name. The admirers of the 'Grand Old Man' gave young Gladstone a very cordial welcome."

This was not his first press notice. Several weeks after his birth the Pittsburgh *Press*, in an item that gives some idea of Mr. O'Neill's jubilant mood at the time, reported that he "is the proud father of a junior Monte Cristo and says the world is entirely too small for him now." Around the same time a New London paper carried an item the parents preferred, for self-evident reasons, to ignore: "James O'Neill, the celebrated actor, was recently made a father for the fourth time [an innocent error that aroused unpleasant memories of Nettie Walsh and her child in Chicago]. It is a boy, and will certainly be called Monte, and probably Monte Cristo."

Whether, as Mrs. O'Neill said in her 1919 letter, he was born with "no nerves," he developed into a nervous child. He was "always getting upset and frightened about nothing at all," according to *Long Day's Journey*, while O'Neill has recorded elsewhere that into late childhood he was terrified of the dark unless his mother, Sarah, or one of the nuns at his first school was close by. He was prone to nightmares, and his father, following an old Irish peasant practice, used to soothe him with a few drops of whiskey in some water — a practice O'Neill eventually came to believe had some bearing on his serious drinking problem.

In evaluating the early forces that shaped Eugene O'Neill it would be difficult to overestimate the importance not only of his mother's drug addiction but of the rootless way of life inherent in the father's profession. It was a bewildering world the child was born into, one forever changing, dissolving, melting into something else — hotel, railroad station, train, hotel, railroad station, train, backstage of theater, hotel, railroad station, train, Syracuse and Louisville, Cincinnati and Boston, hotel, railroad station, train, Portland, Pittsburgh and Rochester, Seattle, Atlanta and San Francisco, hotel, backstage, train, hotel, railroad station, train. The only constants in this inconstant world were his mother, Sarah, whom he equated with his mother, and his father; but the father himself could be a bewildering element as he changed to strange clothes and his familiar face disappeared behind other faces, now bearded and wild-looking, now benign and clerical, now stern, aristocratic. "Usually a child has a regular, fixed home," O'Neill said in 1932, "but you might say I started in as a trouper. I knew only actors and the stage. My mother nursed me in the wings and in dressing rooms."

Like his mother, he developed a lifelong aversion to trains and to that symbol of transient living, the hotel. Except for the cottage in New London, the family knew only hotel rooms. In later years, telling of the various hotels where they had resided, O'Neill, instead of saying that they had "lived" or "stayed" at such-and-such place, used to say that they had "stopped" there. Shortly before his death in Boston, he emerged from a semistupor, struggled up on his elbows, and cried: "I knew it, I knew it! Born in a goddam hotel room and dying in a hotel room!"

As far back as he could remember, his great pleasure, his refuge in a whirling existence, was reading. From being read to by Sarah, he laboriously, doggedly, began with her help to read for himself at an early age. He took to the world of books as passionately as he would later take to the water, a semiamphibious man with the desire to have been born not human but one of the lower order, without human feelings and vulnerability.

In *A Long Day's Journey Into Night* he tells his essential story in a few words: "It was a great mistake, my being born a man, I would have been much more successful as a sea gull or a fish. As it is, I will always be a stranger who never feels at home, who does not really want and is not really wanted, who can never belong, who must always be a little in love with death!"

2

※

Actor and Peasant

CHANCE, plain luck, James O'Neill used to say, landed him on the stage. While playing billiards one evening in the mid-1860s next door to the National Theater in Cincinnati, he and a friend were approached by the stage manager. The latter, in need of supernumeraries, asked the two if they would like to take part in the performance, with the result that James and his companion, after daring one another, turned actors for the night at twenty-five cents a head. Sometimes in telling about it James said that he made his debut in *The Colleen Bawn*, a popular work of the day by Irish-born Dion Boucicault; other times, that he first appeared as a spear carrier in *Virginius*, supporting the great Edwin Forrest in one of his famous impersonations. The best available evidence points to *Colleen Bawn*, surely a suitable launching for an actor named O'Neill.

"Today," he wrote some fifty years afterward, "I remember photographically the details of that night — the mystery of the scene-setting, the peculiar smell, mingled of paint and smoke of gas and canvas, characteristic odor of the stage the world over, the lights, the wrong-side-outedness of it all captured my fancy and stirred my imagination . . . to me fell the most resplendent attire in the theater — velvet breeches, satin embroidered coat, ruffles at wrist and throat with a perfect Golconda of diamond knee buckles and shoe latches. . . . The stage manager offered me a small part in this and coming productions and I accepted with a brave alacrity and a feeling that Poetry and Art had come stepping softly into my life never more to leave me."

Expressed with Celtic extravagance, with an actor's penchant for self-dramatization, yet his plumed words only dress up the plain truth. The novice was immediately fascinated by the working theater and, for all the trials, frustrations and disappointments he was to experience, remained stage-struck all his life.

In the same magazine article he also rhapsodized on a personal theme: "It was Kilkenny, smiling Kilkenny, where I was born one opal-tinted day in October, 1847. Were I permitted to choose a birthplace for any Irishman's child, be he dreamy-eyed son of Erin with star fire in his heart or laughing gossoon with song on his lip and roguery in his eyes, 'twould be that same little town in old Leinster. . . . Not long, however, did I breathe in the air of drama and romance that fills the valley of the Nore, for while I was still a bit of a lad in skirties my parents emigrated to America and settled in Buffalo. In 1857 we removed to Cincinnati, where I grew up. [They were] careless young years, when spare evenings were spent poring over a Shakespeare given me by an elder sister, or losing myself in the land of romance at the theater where I was an established gallery god."

And so forth, for a quite charming picture. But this is James O'Neill at the mellow age of seventy talking of the long ago. Now listen to his son's version of what he used to say, as recapitulated in *A Long Day's Journey Into Night:* "Twice we were evicted from the miserable hovel we called home, with my mother's few sticks of furniture thrown out in the street, and my mother and sisters crying. I cried, too, though I tried hard not to, because I was the man of the family. At ten years old! . . . I worked twelve hours a day in a machine shop. . . . A dirty barn of a place where rain dripped through the roof, where you roasted in summer, and there was no stove in winter, and your hands got numb with cold. . . . And my poor mother washed and scrubbed for the Yanks by day, and my older sister sewed, and my two younger stayed at home to keep house. We never had clothes enough to wear, nor enough food to eat."

Since Eugene O'Neill has often been charged with reveling in gloom, with painting things darker than they are, his account of the father's childhood may be suspect; but certainly this time, according to all evidence, he was telling only the truth. The "air of drama and romance" that James bestowed on his early years was pure fantasy; and he also took liberties with other details of his past. That he was born in 1846, rather than in 1847, and made his stage bow several years earlier than the 1867 he claimed (he was already listed as an "actor" in the Cincinnati directory of 1866) is of no consequence; actors often grow younger as the years lengthen, and modify their chronology to suit their chosen age. But Mr. O'Neill's self-told history, scattered over countless published interviews, contains puzzling gaps and substantial contradictions.

There is no apparent reason for doubting that he was born in Kilkenny, Leinster, though a recent search of the parish archives in that area failed to uncover records of his birth or anything about his parents, Edward and Mary O'Neill (or O'Neil, as the name was then generally spelled).

However, some kind of family trouble or mystery is suggested by the erroneous impression he gave that he had three sisters, in addition to two brothers, when actually there were five sisters. The five, according to a surviving relation in Kentucky, were Mary, Stacia, Annie, Josephine and Margaret, all of whom led obscure lives. The names of his brothers are unknown; he told Eugene only that both, older than himself, went off to shift for themselves at an early age, that one was wounded in the Civil War and shortly afterward died. "I know little about my father's parents," Eugene once said. "Or about his brothers and sisters. . . . He had three sisters, all dead now, whom he never saw except when a theatrical tour brought him to the middle West where they lived."

If one of James's interviews can be relied on, life turned easier when he was around fourteen, thanks to an older sister and her husband, who had a thriving business in military uniforms in Norfolk, Virginia, during the Civil War. James worked for him three years, helping in the shop by day and studying with a "tutor" in the evenings. "He was a man of liberal tastes," James said, "and, liking the theater, he took me with him twice a week. . . . It was then that I formed my taste for the theater. When the war was over my brother-in-law sold out his business and moved back to Cincinnati, and I went with him." Perhaps all this was true; perhaps, instead, the brother-in-law exploited the boy and there was no tutor and regular theatergoing. Various evidence and circumstances — the apparent lack, for instance, of a close relationship between him and any of his sisters — cast some doubt on the pleasant Norfolk interlude. What is certain is that he suffered a rough childhood and as a young actor, like so many others, underwent a rough time.

James entered the theater in a transitional period. There were still managers around like the one who, when asked whether a certain actor was good, replied: "I should say he is. You can hear him 'way out on the sidewalk!" Such views were fading, however, under the influence of Edwin Booth's quiet, sensitive art. For decades the American stage had been dominated by Edwin Forrest, a barrel of muscle with a voice but slightly lower than Niagara's roar, and Charlotte Cushman, firm-jawed, commanding, an actress whose masculine-like power electrified audiences and intimidated all save the most stouthearted of leading men. But now Booth, not only a great actor but an innovator, a revolutionary force, was leading the stage away from the thundering tones and larger-than-life technique exemplified in Forrest and Cushman. While the trumpeters of the old school found his style tame and colorless, the young players were patterning themselves on the reigning new star.

As young Jimmy O'Neill served his apprenticeship, advancing from supernumerary to captain of the "supers" to general utility man to walking gentleman, he became familiar with the underside of the profession and once, when the company manager skipped town with the week's proceeds, knew the "hunger and horror of being stranded without funds." Another time, in St. Louis, he and an actor friend "found a few of our clothes tied in bundles on the floor. Our trunks had been replevined for our room rent." The landlady, a Mrs. O'Neill, told him that "even if she and I bore the same name and came from the same part of Ireland that would not pay the rent."

Yet, whatever his early trials and misfortunes, he had a good deal going for him as an actor — a quick mind, a strong graceful body, and handsome dark looks that gave him an immediate advantage with the ladies. He was an impressionable student, though one critic noted that this was "not always to his advantage, for while striving to secure the best features of other people's playing, he unconsciously absorbs their mannerisms, also." Again, though his voice was pleasing, it was encumbered with a brogue. A reviewer once praised his acting as a Scottish monarch, then crushed him with his final words: "But young Mr. O'Neill must be reminded that King James was not an Irishman." He used to laugh ("Oh, that brogue!") as he told the story on himself.

Thirstily soaking up instruction from the gifted and experienced around him, he worked hard, he learned to fence with professional grace, he cultivated his aptitude as a "quick study" in wrapping up new roles, he worked particularly hard on eliminating his accent. In a few years, self-trained, self-polished, climbing away from himself as an unschooled immigrant boy with shamrocks in his mouth, he began to advance steadily — leading man for John Ellsler's stock company in Cleveland, where he became friends with Thomas J. Quinlan and his pretty daughter, Mary Ellen; leading man for the famed McVicker's Theater in Chicago, the same berth at a higher salary for Hooley's company, a rival to McVicker's. Beneath his air of dashing romanticism, he had an alert eye for business. While attached to Ellsler's troupe, he persuaded the manager to add matinées to the schedule. Though an experiment with matinée performances had failed several years previously, the new attempt flourished, with James becoming the idol of half the feminine population of Cleveland. Schoolgirl Mary Ellen Quinlan felt lost among his legion of admirers.

So eager was he to make good that the strain sometimes showed. "Superfluity," said one critic, "is Mr. O'Neill's besetting sin. . . . He is over-anxious not to lose a point. . . . if he quivers with emotion at the words 'Good morning,' how is he adequately to say 'I love you'? He is

As Pierre in
The Two Orphans *in 1876*

In the title role
of Virginius *in 1907*

As D'Artagnan
in The Musketeers *in 1899*

driven to superhuman efforts to make a fair contrast and this makes him gasp and otherwise tear himself to tatters. When he has overcome these faults, he will be a charming actor on the high road to fame."

James redoubled his efforts. He learned when and when not to emphasize a point, how to invest one gesture with the value of three, and strove for greater naturalness. Without help ("I worked it out in my room, never had a lesson in vocal culture in my life"), he permanently lowered his register and invested it with such a warm, cello-like tone that eventually many came to regard him as having the finest voice in the theater. He had unlimited opportunity to grow as he appeared week after week in a different production — melodrama, costume pieces, parlor drama, Restoration comedy and contemporary farce, Shakespeare as well as claptrap. Often the theater where he was a member played host to a visiting star, and at such times, instead of a weekly change of bill, the tempo would quicken to a different program each night so that the visiting Personages could parade all their celebrated roles.

Taking fire from their genius, James was usually at his best in supporting the great stars. When England's lovely Adelaide Neilson, the Juliet of the century, appeared at McVicker's, she was heralded in the Chicago press as the "object of probably the largest amount of praise and admiration that has been lavished upon any dramatic artist in America within the recollection of the oldest inhabitant." Yet James succeeded in making his own impression: "Miss Neilson is fortunate in so excellent a Romeo . . . [he] looks and reads the part with admirable taste." When she turned to Rosalind, his Orlando was found "most admirable throughout in looks, action and reading." Alternating with Edwin Booth in *Othello*, his Iago was "deserving of warm encomium," and when he switched to the title role, the Chicago *Tribune* said: "It is not often that a star is as well supported by the actor playing Othello [O'Neill] as Mr. Booth was. . . . [The Moor's] passion, jealousy, and suspicion of Iago are admirably rendered and bring down a round or two of applause in the middle of the scene."

He even held his own against Charlotte Cushman. It was said of her Lady Macbeth that she "was wont to bully her royal husband in a way that tempted one to call in the police," while the actress herself used to complain that the actors who played her consort were "such *little* men I have to look down at them." Despite all this, one excited Chicago reviewer hailed James for "meeting the demands of Macbeth with a readiness absolutely astonishing."

Though the young actor kept his head, he might easily have grown conceited. Neilson, who found him the best of all her Romeos, urged him to accompany her on the rest of her American tour and was later to tell reporters, "When I played with other Romeos, I thought they would climb up the trellis to the balcony; but when I played with Jimmy O'Neill, I wanted to climb down into his arms." Edwin Booth, watching from the wings one night, said, "That young man plays Othello better than I ever did." Cushman, feeling that he had great potentiality, urged him to "work, work, work!" Those years he was justified in thinking that some day not far off he would take his place with the great ones, an expectation that was shared by many. Yet after the long Chicago period of admirable growth and high promise, his career began to level off. He became a prime favorite in San Francisco during several long engagements, and won praise as a leading member of the eminent Union Square Stock Company of New York, but without fulfilling the hopes he once had raised.

When he finally did arouse some excitement it was, ironically, in the most controversial appearance of his career, a performance in San Francisco that won him as many enemies as admirers. The vehicle in question was *The Passion*, a new work patterned on the *Passion Play* of Oberammergau, with James O'Neill as the Christus. At first, though under a term contract, he refused the assignment for fear of committing sacrilege, then consented on learning that the leading Catholic prelate of California had read and endorsed the script. James was so overwhelmed at the thought of playing the Son of God that he was blind to the hopeless inadequacies of the work. While part of it was sublime, the part lifted intact from Scripture, the author's contribution was solemn parody, prosaic and turgid.

In a raw vital city rich in colorful individuals, author Salmi Morse was among the most colorful — a tall, dignified man with long gray hair and soulful eyes who went about enveloped in an air of mystery. Whatever his deficiencies as a writer, he could tell the tallest tales about himself with an air of complete sincerity. He told of performing heroic deeds in the Crimean War and being decorated by the Sultan of Turkey, of Santo Domingo declaring a national holiday in honor of his services to that country — services he modestly forbore to describe; of sojourning twenty years in the Holy Land doing research for *The Passion*. As one of the chief sources of his inspiration, he would flourish an ancient-looking parchment covered with alleged Chaldean, Arabic and Roman symbols; it was unearthed, he used to confide, in a Maltese monastery. He was so determined to make his mark in the theater that, although himself of Jewish parentage, he never realized that in *The Passion* he had written something that gave comfort to anti-Semites.

Another self-dramatizing figure connected with the production was young David Belasco, stage manager, actor, playwright; but in his case he had talent, the kind of pseudo-grand talent that could make the most, the best, and the worst of Morse's blueprint for pageantry. Belasco at work on *The Passion* seemed to be everywhere. To absorb some ideas for its scenic effects, he stood for hours in the Mechanic's Mercantile Library in respectful contemplation of two paintings depicting Salome's dance and the Last Supper (his vigil was respectfully noted by the public). He also scurried around town recruiting a hundred nursing mothers with their infants, every unemployed actor for the mob scenes, and such Barnum-like features as a flock of sheep, to follow Joseph and Mary down the mountainside, and a contingent of Oriental dancers. Belasco's great hour had come.

The preparations moved ahead against a growing uproar set off by Protestant spokesmen (the Catholic authorities remained silent) and echoed in the press. One divine invoked "the thunders of Sinai to destroy the Grand Opera House." Even the national theatrical weeklies, fearful that the presentation would fan the old prejudice against the stage, took up the cry. "The production of such a play," the *Dramatic Mirror* said on March 1, 1879, "will strike most people as a flagrant piece of blasphemy, for which there is no shadow of excuse. . . . It is a monstrous and a shameless wrong, and it should consign everyone engaged in it to immediate ostracism from the stage." James O'Neill was hopeful, however, that the opposition would melt away, that in fact the hostile would be won over, once the production had opened. He immersed himself in learning his role, in achieving the proper exalted spirit. Normally gregarious, be began to avoid all social life, gave up cigars and liquor, and at rehearsals came to have an overawing effect on his fellow players; their jokes and small talk died away whenever he appeared, looking inspired, transfigured. But though he seemed unconcerned about the mounting agitation, he was greatly worried and Ella was becoming panicky. "I was uncertain up to ten minutes before I went to the theater," he later told a friend, "whether I should not give up the whole thing. My wife threw herself upon her knees at my feet and pleaded with me to send word that I would not go on. She said the people would kill me."

Opening night, for all their fears, went off almost without incident as a house generally respectful quickly shushed a few potential troublemakers in the gallery. The first entrance of Christ was electrifying, for in appearance and feeling James O'Neill seemed the living embodiment of all the familiar portraits, especially da Vinci's, of the Saviour. To the open-minded the evening was impressive, due to Belasco's handling of mob scenes and flair for pictorial splendor, to the reverential mood evoked by a score of Bach's "Passion" music, and, above all, to James's portrayal: no apparent striving for effect but, instead, all grace, serenity and boundless compassion. The antagonistic, however, found themselves justified in the production and redoubled their efforts to force its closing.

At following evenings, rough-looking miners fell to their knees and prayed at the sight of Christ, while women fainted when He was crowned with a ring of thorns and dragged before Pontius Pilate. Nevertheless, the audience began to dwindle after the first few nights because of all the publicity against the production. Capitulating after a week, producer Tom Maguire withdrew the spectacle and resumed offering conventional fare; but when none of his new presentations won favor with the public, he reopened *The Passion*. This time the city authorities were ready for him. Acting on a new ordinance that forbade the theatrical impersonation of sacred figures, the police closed the Morse work and carted its male principals off to jail. After a trial that drew nation-wide attention, James was fined fifty dollars; the minor miscreants who had impersonated the Apostles, including Judas, only five dollars. Thus ended *The Passion* in San Francisco, though neither Salmi Morse's dream of fame nor James O'Neill's desire to continue in the part. "My wife," he said, "likes to associate me with the character."

Attracted by the notoriety, a leading Eastern manager decided to sponsor the biblical work, but New York was no more ready for it than the West Coast; the new uproar was, if anything, even more heated. The manager, after spending thousands, canceled the production, James turned to other things, while the author, not to be cheated of fame, persisted in seeking new sponsors. After several years of tragicomic struggle, of numerous brushes with the clergy and the law, he ran out of hope. His body was found floating in the Hudson River, just off 88th Street; on his person were a signet ring, a breast pin of rubies and emeralds, a pair of spectacles, a black-handled knife, four Hebrew shekels, and forty-one cents.

"Poor old Salmi!" James said later. "He was not bad at heart, but he would spin such yarns and tell such whoppers! When [someone] staked him to bring out *The Passion* at the converted 23d Street Theatre, I was travelling; but Morse promptly telegraphed me a proposition to take a ten years' engagement, on my own terms. . . . Poor deluded old gentleman! I hope he's in heaven!"

Though the hapless author never achieved his dream of glory, his associates never forgot the West Coast presentation, particularly the central portrayal. "To O'Neill," William Seymour said, "that performance was not acting, it was devotion. He spoke the lines with all due reverence to their sacred meaning and the whole performance was in the nature of a great Biblical lesson." Belasco, going even further, said: "I have produced many plays in many parts of the world, but never have I seen an audience awed as by *The Passion*. The greatest performance of a generation was the Christus of James O'Neill."

Like his wife's taking refuge from present unhappiness in memories of convent school, James used to recall the praise he had won from Booth, Neilson and Cushman, as well as the sensation created by his Christus (though he also thought the notoriety had injured his career). Unlike his wife, James leaned on the past to help him meet the present, to reassure himself of his talent and his future. Not that he lacked cause for hope. For years he seemed on the verge of greatness and in fact was sometimes hailed for achieving it; but if he ever touched greatness, that was as far as he could reach — to touch it, not grasp it firmly and prove it part of himself. Perhaps the same fear of poverty that drove him to success prevented him, through overcaution, from climbing to the heights; or possibly he lacked that extra dimension, that indefinable quality to be found in the unquestionably great. Wherever the fault lay, he, ignoring that his career had lost momentum before his debut as Edmond Dantès, eventually came to believe that only *Monte Cristo* had prevented him from establishing himself among the legendary stars of the American stage.

His son would one day take up the same refrain. "It's too bad," he told an interviewer, "my father ever got started playing in *Monte Cristo*. He was too successful. It ruined his life. If it hadn't been for *Monte Cristo*, he might have gone ahead and taken Booth's place, as everybody expected him to." O'Neill voiced this regret not once or twice but almost every time he reminisced about his actor father, and finally gave him the chance to deliver his own epitaph, with keening emotion, in *Long Day's Journey*:

"That God-damned play I bought for a song and made such a great success in, it ruined me with its promise of an easy fortune . . . and by the time I woke up to the fact I'd become a slave to the damned thing and did try other plays, it was too late. I'd lost the great talent I once had through years of easy repetition. . . . Yet before I bought the damned thing I was considered one of the three or four young actors with the greatest artistic promise in America. I'd worked like hell. . . . I was wild with ambition. I read all the plays ever written. I studied Shakespeare as you'd study the Bible. I would have acted in any of his plays for nothing, for the joy of being alive in his great poetry. I felt inspired by him. I could have been a great Shakespearean actor, if I'd kept on. . . ."

His phenomenal record in *Monte Cristo* suggests that the production was a sensation from the outset; virtually the opposite was true. When he first turned up in the romantic melodrama in 1883, it already was an old story to both the reading public and theater fans. Initially staged in this country in 1848, it satisfied public taste without arousing any particular enthusiasm, finally scoring a triumph in the late 1860s as newly adapted and played by the Anglo-French Charles Fechter, the leading romantic actor of the time. A good friend of Charles Dickens, who advised him to try his fortunes in America, Fechter was unhappily an enemy to himself — a man of spend-thrift folly, as though actually possessing Monte Cristo wealth, a man of uncontrollable temper who in the next breath would be all apologies and self-recrimination. Because of his unstable personality, his career ended prematurely; he died a recluse and in poverty in 1879 at his small farm in Pennsylvania.

The auction in New York of his theatrical effects, to raise funds for a tombstone, drew a crowd of bargain-hunters and wits. When a pair of lackey's breeches were shown, obviously much too small for the late actor, someone shouted, to ensuing laughter, "Did Fechter ever get into those?" The swords, the wigs, the armor all found eager buyers, but the manuscripts "were passed for want of adequate bids. Someone asked what was wanted for *Hamlet* and was told $100, at which everyone roared, and the sale went on." The Fechter dramatization of *Monte Cristo*, among the scripts ignored, was later acquired by producer John Stetson, coarse-grained, shrewd, enormously successful, and widely disliked.

Few if any who saw James O'Neill perform that night of February 12, 1883, at Booth's Theater could have guessed that old *Monte Cristo* would be a success; certainly no one could have imagined that this particular combination of actor and familiar vehicle would develop so late in the day into one of the great money-makers of the century. The opening performance, a near-fiasco, appeared to cap Stetson's ill-starred season at the Booth, and to be another mark against the hard-luck theater which Edwin Booth had built and in a few years lost through mismanagement.

Stetson's troubles began with his first bill, *The Corsican Brothers*, when his leading man for the series, popular Charles Thorne, Jr., fell fatally ill. While *Brothers* faltered along with a stopgap player in the lead, the impresario opened negotiations with James O'Neill. The latter was touring in his own production of *An American King*, an emotional affair about a true-as-gold miner who strikes it rich and is woefully misused by false friends. Though James was not faring well with the play, he preferred to work for himself; at the same time he was prepared to listen if Stetson's money spoke loudly enough. When they finally came to terms, the scheduled première of *Monte Cristo* was fast approaching, and James urged the manager to postpone it a week. Instead, Stetson promised to notify the critics that James had been rushed into the part, but in the opening-day confusion Stetson forgot about it.

An underrehearsed performance that lasted four hours left the reviewers in no mood to be lenient. The New York *Tribune:* "It is a mechanical, business-like reproduction of an old and unusually tiresome play." The *New York Times:* "The performance last night was tedious and awkward. . . . Mr. O'Neill failed to make an impression of strength because he applied to broad and dashing romantic acting the restrained method of realism. His intensity at the closing scenes of the play was, nevertheless, dramatic and somewhat magnetic." The New York *Sun:* "Mr. O'Neill is especially disappointing, because he bears a well-earned reputation as an emotional actor. . . . [He] fails where Fechter was great. He depicts patient suffering far better than a raging thirst for revenge."

Years afterward, recalling that night, James said: "The critics were right that time. I was bad. I knew it. But I got at the play with hammer and tongs. I rehearsed all day in my room. By the end of the week the play was going well. The public saved the life of that play."

Even after he had hit his stride, not all was praise. Most people who had seen Fechter refused to be impressed by the new portrayal; those with some pretension to culture were condescending about the play itself. They were, however, isolated voices among the general enthusiasm for the production. A gentleman on the Boston *Advertiser* neatly summarized the Dumas work's wide attraction: "Youthful love and simplicity, the betrayal of innocent manhood to shield treachery and intrigue, a weary imprisonment, a vision of fabulous wealth, an escape from an ocean tomb, a return to life and limitless riches, and the unwearying, pitiless pursuit of three treacherous friends, until the death of each ends the vendetta — could material more opulent be imagined? And to this are to be added the pathos and the anxiety which come from the hero's ignorance of the existence of his own son, and his nearness to the commission of a frightful murder [of the son]. It is not a play for the old, the blasé, the hypercritical or any of Mr. [Henry] James's Anglo-American gentlemen, but for all who are young, romantic, not too scrupulous about dramatic logic, and sufficiently indifferent on the subject of probability, it is a drama in a thousand."

James O'Neill's playing of *Monte Cristo* more than a quarter-century, on and off, would be of no interest today save for one thing: it left an enduring mark not only on himself but on his playwright son. Thinking of his father's capitulation to popular taste, Eugene once said, "That's

Circa 1885

*as Edmond Dantès
the innocent sailor*

*the prisoner in
the Château d'If*

the Abbé Busoni

*As the Count of Monte Cristo in the gala 1900
production of the Dumas work*

The famous "world is mine" scene, from a souvenir program
in the late 1880s

what caused me to make up my mind that *they* would never get me. I determined then that I would never sell out."

Monte Cristo had a greater effect on Eugene O'Neill and in more ways than he probably ever suspected. From childhood on he knew the entire play as well as he knew his Catechism; it was bred into his bones, it was part of his blood stream, part of his breathing. Its characters were not simply figments of Dumas's imagination, so far as young Eugene was concerned, but a familiar part of his life, with Edmond Dantès virtually a fifth member of the O'Neill family. In Eugene's earliest extant letter, written in 1904 when he was nearly sixteen, he expressed regret at having to quit New London at summer's end — "especially my 'Island of Monte Cristo' and the delightful moonlight rows."

O'Neill would come to look down on the Dumas story as childish nonsense, yet this noted exponent of twentieth-century drama had his roots in the nineteenth-century theater, particularly as embodied in *Monte Cristo*. A protagonist unjustly treated by fate, the most character-istic figure in O'Neill's writings, has a counterpart in Dumas's young sailor. Behind the noble, long-suffering wives in O'Neill's plays is, among other things, the image of devoted, long-enduring Mercédes. Brothers in conflict with one another, buried treasure, scenes on the water, tavern scenes, a sympathetic character who drowns his troubles in drink, a son unaware of the identity of his real father — all these elements in the Dumas story figure in the works of Eugene O'Neill, though, it should be added, in sophisticated form and to serious purpose. After *The Emperor Jones* and *The Hairy Ape* critics felt that the author of the multiscene plays had been influenced by the movies and the fragmented narratives of expressionism; but he had been exposed to an earlier influence in *Monte Cristo* — five acts and six scenes. Again, the style of dialogue in the Fechter version — largely a matter of brief phrases peppered with exclamation marks — is evident in much that O'Neill wrote. And cer-tainly the old play's unabashed theatricality, its succession of "strong" scenes, left an impression. Robert Benchley, expressing the view of many, said of *Dynamo* that the "royal blood of the Count of Monte Cristo, which is always with Mr. O'Neill . . . gives him the power to throw a dramatic spotlight on all his works so that the lurid glow of theater lies over even his dullest passages." The same critic, appraising *Mourning Becomes Electra*, imagined the ghost of James O'Neill looking on proudly as the drama unfolded and exulting, "That's good, son! Give 'em the old Theater!"

But to appreciate the most important effect of *Monte Cristo* on him one should realize above all that it is a story of retribution, that its hero is a man grievously wronged and determined to avenge himself. Like the Ugly Duckling, like the Sleeping Princess, like Jack the Giant-Killer — there are in fact elements of all these archetypal creatures in the Dumas protagonist — Dantès has the appeal of myth; he answers to the eternal child and primitive being in man. This was among the primary factors behind the durable fascination of the absurd, ramshackle dramatization. There was nothing in the play, however, to teach young Eugene that while vengeance is human, there is a higher morality. It would be over-emphasis, if not plain foolishness, to maintain that *Monte Cristo* gave him a bent for revenge, but surely it would encourage such a bent in one who grew up feeling aggrieved at life. Both in his plays and in his personal life O'Neill would, unconsciously, try to avenge himself on a world he distrusted and feared. "Revenge," he said in 1946 in almost the last interview he ever gave, "is the subconscious motive for the individual's behavior with the rest of society."

Is it too fanciful to imagine that O'Neill, in persuading audiences to accept plays that dug for beauty among the dregs, plays with semi-brutish protagonists, plays that made bewildering use of masks, plays uncompromisingly tragic, plays of infanticide, incest and insanity — that in all this the playwright was not only trying to even his own score with life but in some part of his being was avenging his father's long bondage in a work of hokum?

Originally, though, instead of sympathizing with his father, he used the Dumas work to attack him, criticizing him for exploiting a sure-fire thing, something easy. As a writer, O'Neill always aimed high in the feeling that whatever was easy was not worth doing; indeed, "easy" was among the most damning words in his personal lexicon — his scorn unconsciously heightened, if not initially inspired, by his grievance against a mother with a diabolically "easy" escape from burdensome reality. Eugene found various ways to bedevil his father with *Monte Cristo*. Once, in a mood of drunken mockery, he carved the letters "M C" on the bottom pillar of the balustrade in their New London home, the initials so placed as to catch one's eye when one entered the house. Another time, also taking a sideswipe at his father's chauvinism about the Irish, he poured green paint over some souvenir figurines of Edmond Dantès.

From the son's critical attitude one would never guess that Mr. O'Neill began as early as 1888, the year of Eugene's birth, to try to free himself from, as he called it, his "Old Man of the Sea." His attempts to discard the play were spurred not only by his own sense of frustration but by mounting criticism in the press. "Before *Monte Cristo* built a wall round James O'Neill," the prestigious *Dramatic Mirror* said, "that little man laid way over foreign romantic actors." A Boston paper, after terming him "one of the best actors in the country," called his perennial vehicle "the artistic sepulchre of his ability." Again, the critic of the St. Louis *Spectator:* "I hate to see a good, clean-cut intelligent versatile actor spoiled. Therefore I regret to see James O'Neill spending the best years of his life playing Monte Cristo. . . . He is making of what might be an all round star of fine capabilities and achievement a one-part actor. The playing of one part induces slovenliness and the playing of a highly romantic part, such as Edmond Dantès, invites affectation and unnaturalness. It is to be hoped that Mr. O'Neill will soon conclude that he has a fair enough share of wealth and will try something worthier of his powers."

The friendly advice and criticism had an ironic ring to James; he had tried to persuade theater managers around the country to book him in something else, but they had refused, contending that the public was eager to see him only as the Dumas hero. Accordingly, another season of being tossed into the sea, of mounting the familiar rock, of once again proclaiming the line he so detested. Then another season.

Finally, after more than seven years of playing nothing but *Monte Cristo*, he broke away. "It was on account of the tiresome, even weary feeling, that accompanied so much sameness that I gave it up," he said. "I might say that I was forced to do so. . . . I believe that I should have lost my memory and mind altogether had I continued to keep up the strain."

Mr. O'Neill, who began in 1883 and finally called it quits in 1912, when sixty-five years old, portrayed the Dumas hero around 4000 times. He used to say that he had played the role over 6000 times — it must have seemed that much — but a survey of his career points to the lower figure.

In 1890 he was confident that he had found a successor to Dumas in *The Dead Heart*, a tale of self-sacrifice in the French Revolution, which Henry Irving was playing in London to crowded houses. Trying to assure its American success, James sent his director to England to study the performance, confer with Mr. Irving, and soak up everything possible for a duplication of the London production. He mounted the play in handsome style and with spectacular effects ("The storming of the Bastille is highly effective," said a Boston reviewer, "the surging masses of color, glitter of weapons, grime and fume of smoke, and yells of vengeance uniting to a very exciting whole"). But it all went for little; most of the critics found it gloomy, reminiscent of both *A Tale of Two Cities* and *Monte Cristo*, though nowhere near as good.

While playing the one, James began rehearsing another, a new American work entitled *The Envoy*, which he regarded well enough to present in New York. It was a mistake, the reviews were savage. One called the play "dreadful nonsense," and another paper, which had roasted him on every possible occasion since his presuming to impersonate the Christus in *The Passion*, called him a "thoroughly bad actor."

Indignant, worried about the future, James lashed back: "New York does not seem to want good plays or good acting. I made an honest effort, and it failed to respond. I secured the best play and the best company that money could get. . . . New Yorkers want buffoonery so I shall not play again in New York. . . . New York is the town of towns for fads, skits and horse-play. The dramatic outlook is black." The following season he was again declaiming to crowded theaters: "The wor-rld is mi-n-ne!"

One evening in the early 1890s in Lawrence, Massachusetts, he had a backstage visitor, a young fellow named Robert Frost, whom he had last seen as a child in San Francisco; James, who had been friendly with the youth's parents, invited him to supper after the performance. Years later, recalling the evening, Mr. Frost said: "In those days I didn't know what I wanted to do. I'd been to college for a year, worked in a mill, taught for a while, and I asked Mr. O'Neill how it was for a young fellow entering the theater, how he went about it, his chances for success. He said a newcomer should join any barnstorming company and be prepared for hell, rough times and high water. He was not encouraging. He was pleasant to me but bitter about the theater; maybe bitter's too strong a word. Let's say he wasn't happy because he wanted to do something better but the public demanded him in *Monte Cristo*.

"It was the same thing that happened with Vachel Lindsay. Audiences always wanted him to do 'The Congo,' and he was sick to death of it. I think that's the thing that killed him. One time at a birthday party in Baltimore for Lizette Woodworth Reese, the poet — Mencken was there — Vachel wasn't in the mood, but the crowd wanted the usual 'Congo,' and he got up there trying to work himself into the mood. Lizette covered her eyes, and I whispered to her, 'We're sitting in the front row, he can see us.'

"People want to do that to me, and I have to watch out. They want the same poems all the time, 'The Hired Man,' 'Birches.' . . . Partly to save the poems and partly to save myself, I don't do the same things all the time in my readings. And [here his watered-down blue eyes, once a vivid sky-blue, brightened with a shrewd, humorous gleam] I always talk for fifteen to twenty minutes, that takes up to a third of the time. I tell them 'This is extemporaneous free verse.' "

Apparently with James O'Neill again in mind, Mr. Frost ended by telling his visitor: "When I was in England and saw *Fanny's First Play*, someone told me it had played five hundred times. All I could think of was how the actors must hate it."

The sort of thing Robert Frost heard once, Eugene O'Neill would hear many times: "Almost the first words of my father I remember are, 'The theater is dying.' " Though James was already worried about his career by the time Eugene was born, he maintained in public a look of hearty self-assurance and in his words to the press radiated confidence. Between bouts with *Monte Cristo* he was to offer over the years a succession of new productions, always predicting that his latest would outshine the Dumas work, almost invariably finding that he had to dust off Edmond Dantès to assure himself a profitable year. As he pursued his limited course, he watched with mounting envy the steady ascent of another actor, ten years younger than himself, versatile, brilliant, arrogantly sure of himself, the protean Richard Mansfield. Only Mr. O'Neill's family knew and just a few intimates had some notion of the intensity of his feelings about Mansfield. Mansfield was a running rebuke to James, proof that new plays of merit were to be found, that Shakespeare could draw crowds, that an actor could demand of himself his best and yet achieve popular success.

A character actor rather than a romantic type, Richard Mansfield out of costume and role was physically unimpressive; he had thinning hair, small deep-set eyes that at first glance appeared beady and opaque, and off stage wore pince-nez glasses that added to his air of severity. The long black ribbon attached to his glasses was generally flying to the rear, for he always walked briskly, almost at a run, giving the impression that he found life too short to accomplish all he had in mind. Of mixed parentage, he was born in Berlin to a German opera singer; his father was said to have been an English wine merchant named Mansfield, but, according to rumor, the son had no legal right to the name. A martinet to his supporting players, he was always on his dignity with his peers. He would die in his early fifties, worn out from driving himself too hard, from being at once impresario, director and star.

Virtually unknown before, Mansfield won overnight fame in 1883 — around the same time that James opened so inauspiciously in *Monte Cristo* — with a lip-smacking portrayal of an old roué in *A Parisian Romance*, an importation that shocked and titillated New Yorkers with its picture of low life among the highly placed. (James used to boast that *his* plays were inoffensive to the most innocent.) Mansfield went on to impress audiences with the quality and range of his art. The romantic hero of *Prince Karl*, the dual role of *Dr. Jekyll and Mr. Hyde*, the pathetic figure in *Monsieur*, an original interpretation of Richard III — he embodied all these and more in the seven years that James O'Neill was playing nothing but Edmond Dantès. Unlike James's public, Mansfield's would have been disappointed had he repeated himself. To both critical praise and popular acclaim, he appeared as Beau Brummel, Shylock, Henry V, the Reverend Arthur Dimmesdale in *The Scarlet Letter,* Ivan the Terrible and, probably his finest achievement, Cyrano de Bergerac. As Bluntschli in *Arms and the Man,* and Dick Dudgeon in *The Devil's Disciple,* he introduced Shaw to America, and was among the first over here to play Ibsen. Not only a success, he was sometimes the craze; his Beau Brummel created a new vogue among the bloods of the town for the old bell-shaped hat. When he played Rostand's hero, a columnist said: "New York City is just now suffering from an imported disease which may be designated Cyranesis. It has attacked every man, woman and child here who [are] patrons of the theater."

While Mansfield was hailed as the country's finest actor, James O'Neill was reprimanded by the press for returning so often in *Monte Cristo,* for appearing in plays unworthy of him. It was an unhappy day for James when the other actor, with his wife and child, began summering in New London; Mansfield, allowing himself to be taken up by the "best people," was wined, dined and catered to as a national celebrity. Not that James gave a tinker's dam for lawn parties and tea dances, that he envied the other's social success, but he could not help comparing his career with Mansfield's, his worrisome family life with the other man's, his modest home with the fine estate Mansfield established in the Pequot, not far from the O'Neills. James himself was well contented with the Monte Cristo cottage, as he had named his summer place, but his wife and sons were critical. One day as he and Eugene were sitting on their porch, Mansfield's schooner sailed by, with the star standing near the bow. "Look," said the actor father, "at that damn fool posing there!"

Considering James's frustrations and worries, he might easily have become embittered; yet, though scarred, he remained unbroken. In *Long Day's Journey* his son says of him: "He is by nature and preference a simple, unpretentious man, whose inclinations are still close to his humble beginnings. . . . There is a lot of stolid, earthy peasant in him."

Peasantlike, James O'Neill endured.

3

⬧

New London Summers

EUGENE O'NEILL'S earliest years were all of a pattern: eight to nine
months a year touring with his parents, the summers in New London,
with Sarah Sandy always looking after him. Under conditions of the
road and with the family forever on the move, arriving and departing
at all hours, it was sometimes impossible to feed him properly. As a result
he suffered for a time from rickets — a disease generally confined to
children of the poor — that left him with a "rachitic flare" to his ribs.
He gave his parents and Sarah other worrisome moments. One winter
night in Chicago the company's advance man, an eager young chap
named George C. Tyler, was routed out of bed by a rush call from
a panicky Mrs. O'Neill; she thought the baby was dying. Tyler feared
the same when he found him "sort of black in the face and gasping and
raising Cain," but the doctor he brought running assured them, after
a quick examination, that it was only a "routine case of colic." When
Eugene was a little over one he had measles, and when around two,
typhoid fever, the usual childhood illnesses but scarcely under usual
living conditions.

Those years of continual move and change, of improvised living,
remained an unhappy memory all his life. In the 1940s a doctor, after
listening to his history, made the notation: "Strenuous childhood gave
him a difficult start. The constant migration became intolerable. He
dreaded moves."

The summers were different, of a reassuring monotony, the comfortable feeling of going to sleep and awaking always in the same bed surrounded by the same familiar walls, the comforting sameness of the quiet
house shaded on nearly all sides by trees, the comforting sameness of a
little world made up of the lawn stretching down toward the river, the
white gazebo in front where Sarah read to him by the hour and to which

his mother sometimes retreated for solitude; boats of all sorts gliding up and down the river, sea gulls loafing overhead, peace, stability and sunshine — sunshine, that is, save for the days when the mysterious fog closed down. That was peaceful, too, all outdoors vanishing into milky nothingness as life shrank to the dimensions of the house and the now shrill, now muffled sound of boat whistles and the hoarse braying of the foghorn.

The family's summer place and their mode of living were one thing; what the public read about them was another. Since James O'Neill was an actor and actors employ press agents and press agents are dedicated to improving on plain truth, stories with small grounding in reality were foisted on the public — stories that in recent times have been given fresh circulation as fact by O'Neill chroniclers. Most of the fabrications were the work of a particularly imaginative press agent named A. Toxen Worm. One of his tales, in the New York *Herald* on December 9, 1900, told of a play-size railroad, large enough to carry Eugene and a friend, that ran on hundreds of yards of track around the house on Pequot Avenue. Eugene, twelve at the time, must have found the story — designed to impress everyone with Mr. O'Neill's Monte Cristo munificence toward his son — an interesting piece of fiction. The railroad originated, and remained, in Mr. Worm's mind.

In a breathless communiqué to the press he announced that Mr. O'Neill "is now having prepared the plans and specifications for a magnificent library which he is to present to New London. The estimated cost of this projected temple of literature will be not far short of a million dollars." The New London *Telegraph* ran the story on January 3, 1900, under the headline: News That Is False.

Once, while James was appearing in Hartford, Connecticut, the press agent sent out a story that the actor nearly "drowned" on stage — he lost his way under the canvas waves of the Château d'If scene and almost suffocated. The Hartford *Post*, poking fun at the alleged accident, reported on January 12, 1901, that the doctor said to have "revived" him was actually out of town at the time; but the story was widely printed in the New York and New England press under such headlines as O'Neill's Mishap and Monte Cristo in Peril, leaving an impression among those who knew of James's fondness for liquor that he was drunk that night. Unfortunately, no one thought to forewarn Ella, who was then in New York, and she was badly frightened by the publicity hoax.

Another of Mr. Worm's stories, this one in the Boston *Sunday Journal*, told of a residence Mr. O'Neill had built next door to the Monte Cristo cottage because the old place "became too small for his needs. . . . The new house is an elegant two-story structure, and an ideal spot for rest and recreation. . . . Mrs. O'Neill's artistic ideas are manifested in the taste with which the interior is arranged. It is hard to go into any room in which there is not a cozy nook. . . . Flowers and piazzas surround the house. The piazzas are so wide that when Mr. O'Neill's friends come to see him, they do not have to go to the hotel to dance, but an impromptu 'hop' is arranged on the porch." And so forth.

Actually, except for an occasional year when James had failed to rent out the Pink House, as the new place was called, the family continued to summer in the Monte Cristo cottage at 325 Pequot Avenue, which a local paper once described as "quaint, picturesque but old-fashioned and plain." Unlike the Pink House, the cottage was never a new structure as a whole but at a cost of a few thousand dollars was put together, with additions, renovations and other alterations, from several buildings already on the site — a combination store-and-dwelling and an abandoned schoolhouse. Although without charm or style, the gray frame cottage was solidly built and had fine hardwood floors, tile fireplaces, heavy sliding doors between the ground floor rooms, and a handsome balustrade leading up to the bedrooms. The furniture and other furnishings were for the most part more serviceable than attractive. With elms, pine and maples hugging the house on several sides and the old schoolhouse annex, attached to the rear, also shutting out light, the cottage was largely in shade. Ella, who found the trees oppressive, disliked the house not only because of its gloom but because she thought it below their means and the station in life they should maintain. Jamie, who tended to see things through his mother's eyes and who, like her, had a streak of snobbery, was forever comparing their mode of living with the elegant establishments of the Pequot, particularly Richard Mansfield's.

But the house loomed importantly in Eugene's imagination, not only in childhood but always. So much had happened there, so many things that haunted his thoughts. In 1931, on his return from living abroad for several years, he visited New London to see the old place, and immediately regretted his pilgrimage. He stood looking at the house for only a short time, and left without going inside; it was much smaller than he had remembered, shabby and saddening. Years later he met a New Londoner who said she thought of him every time she passed by the place. "And whenever you do," he told her, "give it my love."

Perpetuating it finally by the only means within his power, O'Neill used it as the setting for two of his plays, two that could hardly be more different from one another: *Long Day's Journey Into Night,* a round-robin of accusation and self-torment as the family members flagellate one another, apologize almost instantly, and apply to themselves the whip until the next accusation, and *Ah, Wilderness!*, a humorous account of yesteryear family life, a sunny picture of Fourth of July festivities, apple-pie dinners, and calf love in small-town America, marked by a few passing clouds, misunderstandings between children and parents, but all of it suffused with affection.

Ah, Wilderness! came as a great surprise, accustomed as everyone was to O'Neill writing of frustration, violence, and sudden death. To the question immediately raised, the playwright replied that it was not autobiographical except for a few wisps of reminiscence; it was, rather, the sort of adolescence he would like to have had. "The truth is," he added, "that I had no youth."

For all the difference between the two plays, the parlors in which the Millers of *Ah, Wilderness!* act out their comedy and the Tyrones of *Long Day's Journey* live out their tragedy are strikingly similar in layout and furnishings — double doors, bookcases, large round table with green-shaded reading lamp, inoffensive rug, ordinary-looking couch, desk, chairs. O'Neill seems to have exercised a writer's license in creating two sharply contrasted atmospheres, one sunny and fresh, the other somber, brooding, within the same room. Yet actually the cottage, facing eastward, did have to some extent a Jekyll-Hyde personality: the early morning sunshine, slanting under the porch roof and streaming through large window-doors — also through red-glass panels atop the windows that dyed the rays still more cheerfully — bathed the pink tile fireplace in a rosy glow and brightened the parlor for a while, until the sun moved on and the trees closed in.

His mother's feelings about the trees and the house, her disheveled weeping appearance at times, when in the throes of morphine, seem to have been in the playwright's mind, strangely intermingled with elements of his imagination, when he described the now famous farmhouse setting in *Desire Under the Elms:* "Two enormous elms are on each side of the house. They bend their trailing branches down over the roof. They appear to protect and at the same time subdue. There is a sinister maternity in their aspect, a crushing, jealous absorption. They have developed from their intimate contact with the life of man in the house an appalling humaneness. They brood oppressively over the house. They are like exhausted women resting their sagging breasts and hands and hair on its roof, and when it rains their tears trickle down monotonously and rot on the shingles."

Another feature of the O'Neill property, in addition to the hovering trees, that would contribute to the tone and imagery of *Desire Under the*

Elms was an old wall, a massive "dry" wall several hundred feet long, that had been constructed from rocks and boulders of the area. The area was still strewn with them, in fact, when the O'Neills began living there, and an early photograph of Eugene shows him seated on a large boulder near his home. The deep impression made on the boy by these rude outcroppings of the terrain and by the wall became activated years later when he bought an estate in Ridgefield, Connecticut, containing a wall similar to the one behind the Monte Cristo cottage. He wrote *Desire Under the Elms* while living in Ridgefield, by which time the walls had come to symbolize to him the meager, flinty life of the New England farmer. "Here — it's stones atop o' the ground — stones atop o' stones — makin' stone walls," says one of the sons in *Desire*. And old Cabot expresses the same line of thought: "Stones. I picked 'em up an' piled 'em into walls. Ye kin read the years of my life in them walls, every day a hefted stone, climbin' over the hills up and down, fencin' in the fields that was mine. . . ."

O'Neill in later years could rarely find a good word for New London. A newspaperman who once tried to prod him to reminisce about it could extract only, "It wasn't a friendly town." He could never forget things that had happened there (especially the night his mother ran out of the house, half-crazed from lack of morphine, and wanted to throw herself into the river), or his old unhappiness over his inability to "belong." The feeling of not "belonging," always hardest to bear in youth, was particularly hard in a place where everybody knew everyone else and he felt himself under suspicious scrutiny.

Although he considered himself above such concerns as social status — and part of him was fiercely above it — his family's equivocal position in the community disturbed him more than he cared to admit, even to himself. He was forever running down the solid burghers and social leaders of the town, such people as the Chappels, whom he would deride under the name of "Chatfield" in *Long Day's Journey* as "big frogs in a small puddle." After he had begun to write and dream of monied fame, he told a friend, Dr. Joe Ganey, that he looked forward to returning one day with a "flock of painted whores, hiring a tally-ho of six horses, and having the girls ride up State Street and throw dimes to the crowd." He would laugh, he said, as the bigwigs and their ladies scrambled for the coins.

Yet, in spite of his words, the old harbor town had a lasting grip on him; he was, with feelings of love and hate, forever going home again. Six of his plays are set in their entirety or in part in towns modeled on New London, while three others take place elsewhere in Connecticut. New London people, his thoughts and feelings about them, their transformed images, bits and pieces of them, figure constantly in his work. Some of them: the affable McGinley family, newspaper editor Fred Latimer, Maibelle Scott, and poor "Hutch" Collins, athlete, actor, would-be poet, who died pathetically young in Greenwich Village (all *Ah, Wilderness!*); Edward Keefe, art student turned architect ("Bread and Butter" and *The Great God Brown*); round-bellied Tom Dorsey, realtor, drinker and town character (*Long Day's Journey*); Adam Scott, bartender and Baptist Church elder (*The Emperor Jones*); "Dirty" Dolan, pig farmer and shrewd Irish clown (*A Moon for the Misbegotten*), while multimillionaire Edward S. Harkness and wealthy Edward C. Hammond "sat" for an unflattering composite portrait in *Moon*.

An artist can find nourishment for his art wherever he happens to grow up, but some places are more fructifying than others. Eugene used to complain about the provincialism of New London, its spiritual and cultural poverty, yet it would be difficult to find another community in all New England that could have served his writings better. New London was just large enough to be town and close enough to its roots to be like country; it was both the conservatism and reserve of the old families, now static or declining, and the color and vitality of the upsurging Irish immigrants, both the puritanism and Calvinism of the one and the Catholicism of the other. The contrast, clash and intermingling of the two cultures would supply O'Neill with a major theme of his later writings.

Events that had happened well before he was born became part of his living heritage through New London's penchant for looking back, through the longevity of many of its residents (something in the soil and climate of the area fosters a hardy old age). While he was growing up, there were still a good many in the community who had served in the Civil War, men who sat around reminiscing. If O'Neill felt contemporaneous with the war as he wrote *Mourning Becomes Electra*, his feeling owed something to the atmosphere of his childhood. Moreover, on Huntington Street, once the town's most fashionable street, is a row of stately houses with Grecian columns — "whalers' row" the townspeople call them in tribute to those who had built them; in all likelihood the mansions were in the playwright's mind when he conceived of the neo-Grecian abode of the Mannons, forbidding with pillars, in *Electra*.

When gold was discovered in the Klondike region in the late 1890s, the New London papers were full of stories not only about the present strike — a number of local men chartered ships and sailed for the Klondike — but about the "forty-niners" a half-century earlier; quite a few New Londoners had likewise taken part in the California gold rush. Thus

The Monte Cristo cottage in New London in 1937

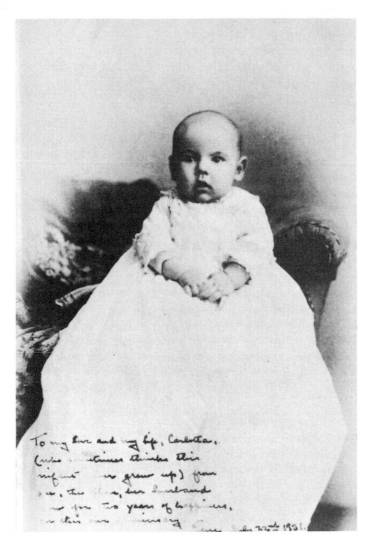

Eugene as an infant. In 1931, inscribing the photograph to his wife Carlotta Monterey, he wrote: "To my love and my life, Carlotta, (who sometimes thinks this infant never grew up). . ."

Sarah Jane Bucknell Sandy in 1910. Miss Sandy was O'Neill's nursemaid and in effect his second mother the first seven years of his life

an event in the American past was not mere history to O'Neill but part of his early memories when he wrote in *Desire Under the Elms* of the two brothers setting out for the California gold mines; he felt that he too had lived through the period.

New London was not only quintessentially New England but typically American. Few places could have celebrated the Fourth of July with more enthusiasm than the town on the Thames, as a story in the New London *Telegraph* on July 4, 1902, suggests: "Well, it is here: the Glorious Fourth, with its powder smell, its din, its litter of fireworks rubbish, its ecstatic small boy and his headachey, worried parents; its burned fingers, its excursions, its baseball fêtes and its sleepy eyes: its jags, its tin horns and its million and one detonations of greater or less degree; it is here to be suffered or enjoyed, according to temperament and years; to harass horses and make glad the street car conductors; to put dollars into the pockets of the purveyors of fun and noise and to keep the doctors busy; to fill the air with the smell of brimstone and the stomach of the small kid with soda water."

The same kind of noises and excitements crackle in the background of *Ah, Wilderness!* as the Miller children rush out to celebrate and their parents worry whether they will return intact, with all fingers, or sick from too much candy and popcorn. From his summers in New London, O'Neill was able to memorialize in all its charm and humor an aspect of American life that has lost much of its old innocence and fun.

The town did still more for him. One foot in the soil, the other in the Thames which shortly flows into Long Island Sound and thence becomes one with the open sea, New London made O'Neill feel at home on the water, helped inspire in him a dream of faraway places. It afforded him, through the saloons, seamen's dives and whorehouses of wide-open Bradley Street, a preview of the raw life he would later know in Buenos Aires, on the New York water front, and still later would write about. New London gave him a more rounded initiation in life, more material for his writings, than he ever acknowledged and perhaps ever realized.

All that would come with time. In the early years there were simply the family, the house that stood back from the road, the river's ever-changing spectacle, and a procession of comforting days, each more or less like the other. Often street musicians — two or three Germans with wind instruments or an Italian with a mechanical piano on wheels — would wander through the neighborhood, providing some of the most cherished moments of Eugene's childhood; he loved the strolling music-makers and early developed a passion for the player piano that became, if anything, still stronger in time. Yet not even the summers were free of disturbing elements. Under the sway of his romanticizing mind, stimulated by tales Sarah read to him of ladies in distress and other dream heroines, Eugene worshiped his mother, beautiful with her pale skin, large wistful dark eyes and, despite her graying hair, girlish manner. On her side she was anxiously loving, and immediately became apprehensive about his health if he showed the slightest indisposition. But there were other times when she seemed a stranger off in another world, without thought or feeling for him. "She used to drift around the house like a ghost," he later said. "I didn't know what was wrong and kept trying to reach her."

In awe of one parent, bewildered by the other, the child had no choice in the direction he took: unable to emulate hearty outgoing James O'Neill, he could only model himself on his quiet, shy mother. Since she could be remote and keep him at a distance, he in self-defense became remote, all the while hungry for reassurance and love, for a mother who would always be there when he wanted her. Locked within himself, full of fears, he envied brother Jamie's blithe, knowing manner and air of being on top of the world (a brother who viewed practically everyone and everything, his mother alone excepted, with deepening cynicism, who at a relatively young age became a determined drinker, who at bottom always held it against "the Kid," along with loving him, that his birth had triggered their mother's drug addiction).

Inevitably, Eugene's relations with Sarah Sandy were close. From evidence that has come down, she loved the child and was genuinely devoted to him; after they were separated she continued to send him Christmas gifts, usually bound volumes of the *St. Nicholas* magazine, and was glad to have him stay with her during holidays from school, whenever his mother was touring with her husband or in a sanatorium. Able, pleasant-mannered, affectionate, Sarah seemed a quite perfect governess. An omnivorous reader, especially fond of Dickens, she helped instill in her young charge a similar passion for books, one that remained a major solace all his life. But Sarah was not all that she appeared — serene, uncomplicated, content with her lot; she was a cozy-looking teapot that contained a brew stronger than tea.

Cornish born and bred, she had grown up in a corner of England rich in cromlechs, druidical circles and other relics of prehistoric man. It is the region of Merlin the magician, a region that, as one writer says, "belongs somehow to the mists of time. . . . Its winding ways, its narrow lanes, its inaccessible heights, its terrific depths, are haunted by the glamor of strange tales. There is weirdness even in its open moors, rolling on and on." Sarah Sandy, plump, blondish, was a true daughter of old Cornwall with a taste for the macabre and the supernatural. She was also a person with a grievance against life; the oldest of four children of a hard-pressed tin miner, she had had to leave home at an early age for distant America, not only to make her own way but to save money and help bring over the rest of the family. Her brother became an engineer, one of her sisters a schoolteacher, while Sarah, who never married, remained a governess. She always regretted not having a better start in life — a grievance that possibly sharpened her appetite for images of fear and violence.

If she delighted the child with *A Christmas Carol* and such unclouded pleasures as visits to the zoo, the aquarium, and the American Museum of Natural History, she also read to him Dickens's ghost stories and Edgar Allan Poe, another of her favorites, and introduced him to the Horror Chamber of the Eden Musée. O'Neill was nearly forty when he talked about Sarah for the first time to an interviewer, the latter reporting: "She had a penchant for horrible tales, whether culled from the newspapers or her imagination, and for hours she would regale little Eugene with the sordid episodes, from the latest murder to the farthest terror that her whimsy could contrive. To supplement this the nurse would often take little Eugene to those ghastly museums where were displayed the wax effigies of criminals and malformed dummies. She delighted in this sort of thing and chortled in a sort of sadistic glee when the little lad winced at the things he saw and heard. Yet I did not hear that this woman was unkind to her charge. I gathered an impression quite the reverse."

O'Neill himself, however, despite what the interviewer thought, had mixed feelings about Sarah Sandy. In an attempt at self-understanding he once drew up a diagram, designed solely for his own eyes, in which he outlined his changing attitudes from infancy into adolescence toward his parents and Sarah. Following are some of the first entries in his diagram: "Mother love — meaning — Nurse love. . . . World of reality practically unrealized — in background — terror of it emphasized by the nurse's murder stories — terror of dark alone but delight in it when feeling protecting influence (Mother-Nurse-Nuns) about."

Here, in but a few words, he summed up his conflicting views of Sarah Sandy: she was a substitute mother, her stories intensified his fear of the world, yet she also represented a "protecting influence." Her effect on him, it appears, could hardly have been more basic, complex, and contradictory. Weighing one thing against another, it is difficult to decide whether her role in his development was more beneficial or harmful. In either case, she scarcely gave him a reassuring picture of life and his fellow man; undoubtedly her Gothic tastes helped shape and darken the imagination that eventually would spill out in violent tales for the theater.

The child's withdrawn nature was apparent on sight. A New London newspaper editor named Frederick P. Latimer, who used to see him around town with his father or nursemaid—the mother was rarely in public view—long afterward recalled him as a "bashful little boy with brown shoes and a big flowing straw hat with a string under it and great dark eyes that seemed like they had been stolen from a frightened deer."

In one respect his appearance was deceptive. Though he was every-thing he seemed—shy, apprehensive on approach, tremblingly sensitive to the world—he had a streak of stubbornness that partook of both his father's peasant durability and his mother's inflexible nature. Like her he cherished his wounds and hoarded his grievances; when a dog he had left in a cousin's care was run over by a carriage and killed, he did not speak to the woman for two years. A touching photograph of him when around five conveys at once his vulnerability and his resolute side: rounded chin set quite firmly, lips pressed together and at the ends turned downward, an expression in the eyes that suggests his thoughts are far away. The solemn face appears out of keeping with his festive dress, a wide lace collar and a large bow with flowing ribbon; the over-all impression is one of determination, bafflement and brooding. In another photograph, taken several years later, the boy in the Eton cap, short jacket and pants is seated with sketch-pad and pencil on a hillside near his home, in the background the river. The pencil is poised over the pad as the youngster, head slightly forward in concentration, studies his off-camera subject. What he was drawing may be surmised from an inscription he later wrote on the photo: "Not addicted to drama then but an implacable sketcher of trees and ships."

The O'Neills on first taking up summer residence, a few years before Eugene's birth, had been welcomed as additions to the growing number of well-known people who spent their vacations in New London. They shortly, however, came to occupy a separate place in the community, somewhere vaguely in the middle, neither part of the fashionable summer colony, with its dinner parties, musicales, croquet games and thés dan-sants, nor of the town's everyday existence. As a family group they isolated themselves except for their churchgoing and contacts with some relatives of Mrs. O'Neill on her mother's side, the Sheridans and the Brennans, plain, hard-working people of limited means. The town ac-cepted the fact, without giving it particular thought, that the actor's wife was retiring and that the family practically never entertained. James himself was widely liked and esteemed, not least for his open delight in New London, for his optimism about its future; and he backed up his view by investing extensively in local real estate.

At a time when the Irish were generally looked down on as hard-drinking riffraff, James was among the first of his countrymen invited to join the Thames Club, the all-male sanctum of the town's leading citizens. But he enjoyed himself less in the Club's discreet, monied atmosphere than at the Crocker House bar, a democratic oasis for local politicos and traveling salesmen, sports and businessmen, as well as an occasional Morgan, Astor, or Vanderbilt, whose yacht was anchored at the moment in the Thames. Almost every afternoon James could be found at the hotel bar talking real estate, town affairs, politics — as a good Irishman he was a staunch Democrat — and telling tales of the theater. With a few under his belt, he was apt to launch into Shakespeare, most often Othello's defense of his marriage: "Most potent, grave, and reverend signiors . . ." (His son would one day write a play about a Negro whose marriage to a white girl concludes disastrously; the father's fondness for quoting *Othello* was probably among the unconscious factors behind the writing of *All God's Chillun Got Wings*.)

Mornings, James liked to putter around the grounds of his home, raking leaves, pushing the lawn mower, clipping the tall hedge in front, while wearing his oldest clothes, a handkerchief tied around his neck to catch the sweat. Those pleasant chores accomplished, he used to head for Captain Nat Keeney's fish market on nearby Scott's dock. He enjoyed the tale-spinning of the old seamen who hung out there but most of all he enjoyed Keeney himself, a contented soul at peace with himself and the world, a man comfortably, fluently ribald. "Hotter today than a whore's armpit," he would say to man, woman or child. "Nat," James used to tell him, "we'd make a fortune if I could put you on the stage just as you are."

Keeney once thrust a woman's bathing suit, a spoon from the Crocker House, and a man's cap down the gullet of a shark he had caught, then waited until friends were around to cut open the fish. This set off a flood of neighborhood talk and speculation and was written up in the local press. A socialite customer complained to him that his assistant had used strong language and told her, "Keep your shirt on," when she was annoyed about a late delivery. Nat exploded: "Why that foul-mouthed son of a bitch! I'll blankety blank blank the goddam blankety blank out of him!" — all the while unaware of his own language, it came so naturally to him. "Thank you," the lady said weakly. No one, not even the most fluttery spinsters, could take offense at Nat; with eyes as serenely blue as a baby's, frequent nips of "cough medicine," and eternal tobacco-chewing, his jaw wagging happily, there was something innocent about him. James O'Neill, though his wife used to criticize his taste in friends, spent some of his most enjoyable hours at Nat Keeney's fish market.

Sometimes he hitched up the family's horse and took his sons for a ride in one of their two vehicles, generally the light oak "dog cart." In a high collar, his head held erect, James, the picture of a dignified paterfamilias, used to tell Eugene, "Straighten up, get the hump off your back — you look like Richard the Third."

As the summers piled up, Eugene began to venture alone across Pequot Avenue, not to join his father at Keeney's place but to wander along the wharf, the domain of Captain Thomas A. Scott. Now old and white-bearded, Captain Scott, wrecker and onetime diver, had performed valiant underwater deeds in earlier years, particularly during the hazardous construction of Race Rock Lighthouse. It's a toss-up whether the child was more fascinated by the old mariner — three hundred pounds of commanding energy, despite his age — or by the dock itself, forever busy from the movement of dredging equipment, lighters and scows. The place was a treasureland for a boy drawn to the sea, a sprawl of wharf, warehouse and sheds littered with anchors and spars, windlasses and sails, ships' wheels and rusting old rudders, all salvaged from vessels Scott's men had brought in safely or redeemed piecemeal from the floor of the sea. The large warehouse was full of odds and ends of ships' furnishings, while its outside north wall, in plain view of passers-by on Pequot Avenue, bore the signboards of vessels that had left their bones on reefs of the neighboring coast and off-shore islands. The boy never tired of Scott's dock, of dreaming over its harvest from the sea.

He became a "fish, a regular water rat, forever playing around in the water," according to Margaret Kiley, who lived next door to the O'Neills for years; but it was a different story, she recalls, with his brother Jamie, for she never saw Jamie in swimming or messing around the boats. There were, however, other pleasures to his liking, such as drinking and hanging out in the saloons. He was inclined to look down on New London as a "hick town," but came to view it more respectfully after learning that traveling salesmen rated it as having the liveliest, most wide-open red-light district between New York and Boston. Generously gifted by nature — personable, quick-witted, ripe in Irish charm and blarney — he had a premature man-about-town air that put off some girls but that attracted more, especially those out for a good time. He had no need to settle for commercialized sex, yet at a relatively early age became a regular patron of the brothels of Bradley Street, particularly Addie Burns's place (in *Long Day's Journey* she is called "Mamie Burns"). Essentially, Jamie was a troubled young man in a hurry to become jaded with life.

Boat Day was another thing he liked, the annual event when con-

Eugene around five years old

*James O'Neill, Jr.,
around six years old*

Eugene sketching near his home. Years later, inscribing the photograph for a friend, he wrote: "Not addicted to drama then but an implacable sketcher of trees and ships."

Eugene, his brother, and their father on the porch of the Monte Cristo cottage in 1900

tingents of Yale and Harvard men took over the town, coloring it blue and crimson with partisan flags, balloons and streamers, packing the Crocker House, headquarters for the race, crowding State Street to the overflow of side streets, and cheering on their heroes in the four-mile run of the racing shells down the Thames. Jamie could always be found in the thick of things, his straw hat tilted at a cocky angle. While he made derisive cracks about the do-or-die rivalry — it would not have been Jamie otherwise — he enjoyed the carnival spirit that swept the town, the swarming of yachts, sailboats and motor launches, the bands blaring away at "Fair Harvard" and "Boola, Boola," the con men with their shell games, the high-spirited thousands that jammed the observation trains on both banks of the river, the general hell-raising.

The New London papers invariably called the Thames a "forest of masts" on Boat Day and in their reportage worked themselves into a lather of lyricism. From a typical account: "The shells had not travelled half a mile when, by the merest chance, they presented a beautiful spectacle. Harvard was still rowing at 36, and Yale had dropped her clip to the same figure, and with perfect rhythm the two crews fell into strokes at unison. The sight was one never to be forgotten. The eighteen brown backs came forward and backward together. The reach, the catch, the heave and the recover were simultaneous in both shells, and as the two craft sped on with noses and rudders exactly even they looked as if they might be mechanically connected and propelled by identical machinery."

The color and excited rivalry of Boat Day gave O'Neill the inspiration for a climactic scene in *Strange Interlude*, the yacht-deck episode in which the heroine's husband collapses. All the event ever brought Jamie, aside from hang-overs, was a bloody head, a page one story, and heated words from his father. The *Telegraph* reported: "Collegiate exuberance inordinately dampened started a free-for-all fracas in front of the Crocker House before midnight last night. When the row ended, James O'Neill, Jr., had a nasty gash in his head and James Dennison of New York a beautiful black eye. . . . In the party with them were several young men who got into an argument and began fighting. O'Neill, it is said, stepped between them, but before he could separate them, somebody hit him over the head with a chair. He fell to the sidewalk and his assailants fled. When O'Neill came to, he could remember neither about the fracas nor who hit him."

Alone in the family Ella took no pleasure from their summers, other than their being a respite from endless train rides and a thousand anonymous hotel rooms. Every year, though, she came to find New London almost attractive as the season ran out; it was an unhappy occasion to her — and to Eugene — when the actors appeared and began rehearsing. The troupe would first head into upper New England, ahead of the cold and snow, then to points south and west, all over the country. Train, railroad station, hotel . . .

No matter how dispirited Eugene felt whenever their travels began, he felt far worse when, his life changing, he was left behind. The summer of 1895 was marked by the foulest weather in many years: rain on and off for weeks, for days on end the fog, accompanied all the while by hoarse blasts from New London Light, at the end of Pequot Avenue, and faint mournful lowing from the offshore Race Rock Lighthouse. Even the murder news that Sarah read to him seemed more frightening than ever: the "black sheep" of a prominent Brooklyn family was accused of bludgeoning to death his miserly father, with the "good son" suspected of being his accomplice — a case that reminded Sarah of the Lizzie Borden mystery several years earlier; a New York woman was arrested for slaying her wealthy mother with poisoned clam chowder; a French marquis went on trial for killing his wife's extramarital child; a Chicago doctor was charged with turning his home into a "castle of death" where a half-dozen persons were murdered, including the husband and children of his paramour; a woman in Ireland, thought bewitched, was tortured to death by her husband, father and other relatives trying to exorcise her evil spirits.

Everything threw a pall over this summer, and time seemed to run out faster than ever because each day brought Eugene closer to his dreaded new life; despite his pleas and tears, his father had decided it was time he should enter school. As one who had gone to work in childhood and had always regretted his lack of an education, James was determined that his sons should have all the academic advantages. Eugene would be seven, the same age as Jamie when enrolled at Notre Dame; though the father knew that the two boys were of different natures, he felt that since the youngster was always curled up with a book, he should make out equally well at school.

While arrangements were under way for closing the summer place and efforts being made to allay the boy's apprehensions — Sarah assured him that they would remain in close touch — James was rehearsing to open his season at the town's Lyceum Theater. Things were going according to schedule when something happened that temporarily superseded all other concerns, including Eugene's over being sent away.

The accident occurred as Mr. O'Neill, William F. Connor, his business manager, and Jamie were on their way to the Lyceum to see James J. Corbett in *In a Big City*, a trumpery work with the sole merit of offering

"Gentleman Jim" in a display of his championship boxing style. While they were taking a short cut on an elevated railroad trestle, James slipped and fell, a twenty-foot drop to the street. When he was carried into the house, Ella in a panic called both the doctor and Father Joynt, their pastor and a close friend. The doctor found, almost incredibly, no broken bones or other serious injury, only bruises and a sprained ankle. The priest congratulated the patient: "God was certainly with you that moment, James." The latter, back in form after the good news, replied, "I wish God had been with me a moment before and kept me from falling!" His riposte went all over town, with Father Joynt, a good-humored soul, among those spreading the story. In a few days James, limping, was up and around with the help of a cane; preparations were resumed for his season — it would open several weeks later than scheduled — and for depositing Eugene at school.

On October 18, two days after his seventh birthday, the child began a new existence within the confines of the Academy of Mount St. Vincent in Riverdale, just outside New York City. Thirty years later, to an interviewer he found understanding and sympathetic, Elizabeth Shepley Sergeant, he poured out an account of his feelings on being packed off to school each fall — he was there five years.

"O'Neill," she wrote, "has acute memories of the outbursts of hysterical loneliness that overtook him on every return to his rigid Christian exile. Gazing afar upon a stage where a heroic figure strutted, towards a lovely distant mother to whom he stretched his arms in vain, he conceived the world in which he was at the mercy of his affections as disastrous."

In O'Neill's diagram of his earliest years, the first listing of his father is favorable: an "indefinite hero — not dangerous rival." The next comment, referring to the father's practice of giving him a few drops of whiskey in water after a nightmare, ends: "This whisky is connected with protection of mother — drink of hero father." Then his attitude changed sharply: "Resentment and hatred of father as cause of school (break with mother)."

Summarizing the period, he wrote: "Reality found and fled from in fear — life of fantasy and religion in school — inability to belong to reality."

4

※

Eugene in Exile

SIXTY years after Eugene entered the school he remained to Sister Mary Florentine a distinct memory. She could still picture him not only because there was just a handful of boys and it was her first teaching assignment, when her impressions were freshest, but because he was "different, the quietest of the lot, always reading he was, and I remember he had an occasional twitching of the head." (So had Ella O'Neill.) He was not surly, Sister Mary recalled, but polite and reserved, one who kept his thoughts to himself; he always came to life and displayed interest, however, when the boys, under a nun's supervision, were led to a roped-off area in the adjoining Hudson River for wading and swimming.

If James O'Neill had ever considered the Minim division at Notre Dame for Eugene, the school in Riverdale was a concession to the child's anxiety at being sent away. He was only several miles from Jamie, now enrolled at St. John's College and Preparatory School (it grew on the same site into Fordham University), and he was accessible to visits from Sarah Sandy, with whom he was to spend the Christmas holiday. But Mr. O'Neill had his own sentimental reasons for favoring Mount St. Vincent; the estate had originally belonged to one of his early idols, Edwin Forrest, the bugle-mouthed actor whose blasts of Shakespeare had thrilled generations of playgoers. Forrest had intended the place, dominated by a granite castle of Norman and Gothic inspiration (eventually, the school library), as a fitting residence for his wife and himself; before it was completed, however, they separated amid unsavory charges and countercharges that long titillated the country. The litigious, embittered actor lived there sporadically for a few years until he sold the estate for one hundred thousand dollars to the Sisters of Charity for a school.

Though Mount St. Vincent was a girls' academy, similar to the one in

[65]

Indiana where Mary Ellen Quinlan had wavered between dreams of nunhood and musical fame, it also maintained St. Aloysius, a small school for boys aged seven to twelve. St. Aloysius was chiefly for the convenience of families that had both sons and daughters and wanted them in the same place, but as much as possible the sexes were kept apart. The boys' life centered on the onetime caretaker's lodge, a two-story stone cottage not far from the entrance to the grounds, where they were both quartered and taught.

The campus of sixty-five acres included a farm with livestock and cultivated land which, under the management of one John Crowley, provided most of the school's food. An affable sort who liked youngsters, Crowley allowed them to lend a hand in the work—feeding the chickens, rounding up the cows, cutting hay—but Eugene was seldom among them. In good weather, while the other boys were playing at farming, climbing trees, sailing boats of paper and wood down stone-lined gutters, he was generally reading, his back against a tree trunk, or gazing with a faraway look at the Hudson River, at the vessels gliding by, and following the flight of sea gulls.

But even though he usually appeared oblivious to the farming activities that were part of the daily life around him, he absorbed more than his manner suggested. The child was litmus paper, a sponge, soaking up impressions all the while he seemed lost within himself—a receptivity he was never to lose. Carlotta Monterey, his third wife, tells a revealing story about him. Once, while they were on an automobile trip in France, they saw coffins from an old cemetery being moved to a new site, carried in a religious procession, with the participants stopping every few feet to kneel in prayer. In contrast to his wife, who was stirred, O'Neill seemed indifferent to the spectacle, preoccupied with his thoughts; months later, however, he alluded to the procession and went on to recall it in minute detail. The same sort of thing was already true of him at school; but in addition to being uncommonly impressionable and having a photographic memory, he had a strong element of primitivism in his make-up that made him responsive to the natural world, to the sea and the land. Instinctively, without apparent effort or manifest interest in his surroundings at Mount St. Vincent, he began acquiring a familiarity with and a feeling for farm life that would inform his writing of certain plays, especially *Beyond the Horizon* and *Desire Under the Elms*.

In yet other plays, most notably in *Dynamo* and *The Great God Brown*, O'Neill would almost apotheosize women of a placid, maternal, rather bovine nature, endowing them with great compassion and instinctive wisdom. This tendency in the playwright may have originated at Mount

St. Vincent, where a herd of cows was a particularly peaceful feature of the scene. At any rate, in referring to Mrs. Fife of *Dynamo*, who weighs over two hundred pounds, O'Neill said that she is "not formless [or] flabby [but] suggests, rather, an inert strength"; and at one point her husband says, with affectionate exasperation, "I might as well be married to a cow." Again, Cybel of *The Great God Brown* is, in O'Neill's words, "full-breasted and wide-hipped, her movements slow and solidly languorous like an animal's. . . . She chews gum like a sacred cow forgetting time with an eternal end." There is, however, another character, in this case a man, who more clearly reflects the playwright's almost mystical feeling for the animal. Old Ephraim Cabot of *Desire Under the Elms* is, considering his rock-ribbed character, strangely attached to the cows on his farm; it is practically the only indication of tenderness in his nature. After he comes to feel that the farmhouse is "cold . . . it's oneasy," he decides to go "down whar it's restful — whar it's warm — down t' the barn. I kin talk t' the cows. . . . They'll give me peace."

Like his brother ten years earlier among the Minims at Notre Dame, Eugene at Mount St. Vincent felt abandoned, unloved, betrayed by those dearest to him; but where Jamie had striven to excel in all directions in order to regain his mother's favor, Eugene burrowed into himself. In the depths of his being, below all conscious thought and decision, he began to armor himself against love. Love left one open to being hurt; rejection was too painful to be endured again. At the same time he began in his desolation to fantasy an ideal love that would enfold and cradle him from loneliness and protect him from the world. Some of this feeling was behind a recurrent vision that he would describe years later to his second wife, Agnes Boulton: "It was a dream of my childhood — when I had to dream that I was not alone. There was me and one other in this dream. I dreamed it often — and during the day sometimes this other seemed to be with me and then I was a happy little boy. But this *other* in my dream, this other I never quite saw. It was a presence felt that made me complete."

Thus he resorted to imagination, as his mother did to morphine, to escape reality. From his readings, from things discussed in the classroom — mystical matters given strange interpretation in his child's mind — he fashioned spiraling dream-worlds to shut out the everyday world pressing in upon him. Absorbing the nuns' teachings about the love of God, the peace of God, he tried to find in this infinitely merciful, all-knowing Jesus a substitute for his mother and Sarah. But for all his prayers and faithful observances, he found that this mysterious unseen Being could not console him for the loss of their comforting presence; in a moment of despair he told classmate Joseph A. McCarthy, "Religion is so cold."

Memories of his early quest seem to have been in the back of his mind when he has Nina in *Strange Interlude* say: "The mistake began when God was created in a male image. We should have imagined life as created in the birth-pain of God the Mother. Then we would understand why we, Her children, have inherited pain, for we would know that our life's rhythm beats from Her great heart, torn with the agony of love and birth." A maternal God, she says, would be more comforting than a male God whose chest is "too hard for tired heads." Tired heads — the echo from childhood is unmistakable.

Until entering school Eugene had rarely been around other children. While touring with his parents he had led the life of an isolated only child, and even during the New London summers had had but limited contacts with other youngsters. In the Sheridan family, his mother's cousins, there was a boy named Philip of his own age, but the two saw little of one another. "It was no fun," Phil Sheridan once said, "going over to his house. He didn't want to play ball or anything; all he wanted to do was read." Since Eugene was practically always among grownups during his most impressionable years, he found it difficult to communicate with other youngsters, and under his reserve felt uneasy with them. They would always remain to him a separate race, unfamiliar and without interest. As a father, he felt at a loss with his own children, once confessing to a friend, Kenneth Macgowan, "I don't know how to talk to them." Not surprisingly, virtually all the children in his plays are stillborn manikins.

Life for the St. Aloysius boys was not only austere but, most of the school year, rigorous; there was no central heating system or indoor plumbing in the gray stone cottage, where the boys were taught and fed on the ground floor and quartered on the second. Long afterward Stephen Philbin, one of Eugene's classmates, retained sharp memories of the long frigid trek to the outhouse, some forty feet distant, and of how the boys welcomed at breakfast the steaming mounds of Irish oatmeal which they lathered with butter and soaked in thick fresh cream — warming and very nourishing it was. The day began early, with the boys routed from bed at six-thirty; classes lasted from eight to three-thirty, after which the boys were left to their own devices until bedtime at nine. Sundays were still longer for those serving as altar boys at 6 A.M. Mass, as they did regularly by turn, at the Chapel of the Immaculate Conception on the campus.

Eugene had plenty of leisure to lose himself in daydreams and reading, his favorite books being Kipling's sea-drenched *Captains Courageous* and the *Jungle Books,* exotic, lushly green, full of fantastic adventure. Often, when wintry winds tore up and down the Hudson Valley and life pressed drearily at school, he was far away on the Grand Banks, helping to haul in nets of fish, or on the other side of the world with Mowgli and his friends—Baloo the bear, the black panther Bagheera, and Mowgli's benefactress, Mother Wolf, who saved him from the Bengal tiger and reared him with her cubs. Eugene dreamed of becoming a sailor when he grew up, of visiting distant lands, and, according to schoolmate Joseph McCarthy, was fond of quoting a line from *Monte Cristo* regarding the sea.

A subdued youngster who had early lost both his parents, McCarthy gravitated toward Eugene as a kindred spirit. In line with Sister Mary's memories, he later recalled O'Neill as a "thin lad, quiet, even tempered, little interested in games and sport, but always reading." Neither he nor Stephen Philbin, both of whom often served with Eugene as altar boys, gained an impression of spiritual turmoil and seeking. "He didn't seem particularly religious to me," McCarthy said. "He went to church every Sunday because we all had to go. Whatever his inner feelings may have been, he showed little interest in the things they taught us, no great feeling about them." O'Neill's mask was already on and securely fastened.

The orphaned McCarthy, two years older, assumed a big brother's attitude toward O'Neill and would intervene on his behalf if a fight threatened. But since Eugene more accepted than returned his friendship, he was surprised at an invitation to spend an Easter holiday in New London; he was even more surprised by his host's behavior—no attempt at entertaining him, not even companionship. Eugene, after giving him the run of his father's library, occupied himself the entire week with reading. Some thirty years later McCarthy spent an evening with O'Neill, their first reunion since school, and afterward observed: "He hadn't changed much. He was always the lone wolf."

Ella, at times accompanied by one of her New London cousins, a Sheridan or Brennan woman, found her visits to Eugene a disturbing pleasure. The short train ride from New York to the Mount St. Morris station was also a long journey in time that landed her back in earlier years. The black-habited nuns with their pink or old-ivory faces, the schoolgirls in neat Sunday dress, the shrine of Our Lady of Lourdes set in the middle of a small lake, all of it so like the peaceful scene at her beloved St. Mary's, aroused thoughts both sweet and saddening. Ella, forever yearning for the past, could see herself in the demure, untouched schoolgirls at the same time that she was aware of the gulf that separated her from them. It all reminded her of the contrast between her life at school and the way things had turned out, between her expectations of marriage to James O'Neill, a girl's dream hero, and what that marriage had become, but most painful of all, of the contrast between her former self and her present being, her descent into guilt-ridden and despairing drug addiction.

Edging away from such thoughts, she would reminisce to her son about her years at convent school, about Mother Elizabeth, whom she had loved and looked up to as the mother of her spirit, about the Holy House of Loreto, a replica of the Santa Casa in Italy, where she had often prayed to the Virgin Mary for comfort and guidance, particularly after her father's death. With a writer's natural preference for what he knows at firsthand over something he has been told, O'Neill would substitute the shrine at Mount St. Vincent for the one in Indiana when he has the mother in *Long Day's Journey* reminiscing of her life at school.

For all her habitual reticence Ella could be almost voluble about the fulfillment of life under orders, a subject she frequently brought up in talking to Eugene, for she was trying to plant in him the thought of entering the priesthood. Ella probably was concerned not only with the special grace that would enter his life but, if unconsciously, with her own salvation; by giving her son to Jesus, she hoped to expiate some of her guilt and gain new strength to conquer her addiction. More than once she told Mrs. Kiley, a neighbor in New London, that she hoped Eugene would become a priest. Far from ever fulfilling her dream, he broke away from the Church at an early age, when around fifteen; but though his mother failed in her objective, she helped foster in him a sense of commitment that, unfulfilled, was to haunt him all his life. During long drunken nights in Greenwich Village, in the back room of a saloon known as the "Hell Hole," he was fond of reciting Francis Thompson's *The Hound of Heaven*:

> *I fled Him, down the nights and down the days;*
> *I fled Him, down the arches of the years;*
> *I fled Him, down the labyrinthine ways*
> *Of my own mind. . . .*

> *. . . and a Voice beat*
> *More instant than the Feet —*
> *"All things betray thee, who betrayest Me."*

Ella used to visit her son whenever in New York and she felt up to the trip — the boys were confined to the school except at Christmas and

Easter — but most of the time she was on the road with her husband; occasionally, too, in a sanatorium for "the cure." Though Eugene rarely showed any warmth toward McCarthy, he felt a kinship with the orphan and under his air of detachment used to envy classmates surrounded of a Sunday by their families. The Christmas holidays, which for most of the boys meant parties, presents, festive meals and gatherings of the clan, were especially painful to him, even though his parents always sent him plenty of gifts, and Sarah Sandy once more, for the holiday period, took him under her wing. His feeling against the holiday never diminished; throughout his life he would become depressed, even less communicative than normally, as Christmas approached.

From an early age he had taken refuge in books; at school he came on another solace. Writing to his parents, to brother Jamie, to Sarah, he began to find some relief from his feelings of isolation in expressing himself on paper. He deluged all of them with letters and, still unsatisfied, corresponded gratefully with an older girl in San Francisco named Anita Black, whose family was among his parents' friends. More than thirty years after St. Aloysius he wrote another member of the California clan: ". . . of Anita I have a very clear recollection of her coming to see me when I was sick in bed in San Francisco. . . . I promptly fell in love and Anita was my first 'best girl.' I suppose I must have been five or so — maybe less! I also remember how kind she was later on when I had gone to school and she used to let me write her letters and answer them so promptly — which must have been a great bore to her."

Later, during his courtship of a girl in New London, he wrote her once or twice a day, not mere notes but pages, though she lived only a few houses away and they were together almost daily. When he went off to a sanatorium for the tubercular, he wrote copiously to a young nurse who had looked after him at home; there was nothing romantic between them, she once said, just his desire to remain in contact with someone he had found sympathetic. Even in his most intimate relations it became second nature for him to bare himself more readily on paper. Carlotta Monterey recalls that he almost never said he loved her but, instead, used to leave ardent notes where she would be certain to find them.

The stream of letters from a child at school, filled with more than he could endure without some outlet, was the beginning: the letters marked the embryonic stage in the birth of Eugene O'Neill, playwright, a man who found relief from his ghosts, things both known and nameless that tormented him, in writing himself out.

O'Neill always said that he never had any literary ambition until he was grown, and generally ascribed the great turning point of his life — his decision to become a writer — to a period of ill-health. At different times he told interviewers: "I just drifted along till I was twenty-four and then I got a jolt and sat up and took notice. Retribution overtook me and I went down with T.B. It gave me time to think about myself and what I was doing — or, rather, wasn't doing. I got busy writing one-act plays. . . . If I hadn't had an attack of tuberculosis, if I hadn't been forced to look at myself, while I was in the sanatorium, harder than I had ever done before, I might never have become a playwright." But another time he said: "No, it isn't exactly true that my first urge to write came at the San. Previous to my breakdown I had done quite a lot of newspaper work . . . and this experience started me."

O'Neill was less than frank, however. Almost as far back as he could remember he had always wanted to be a writer, not a playwright, not a novelist or a short-story writer, but a poet. This was, to use one of his favorite expressions, the "hopeless hope" of his life. Long before he turned to the theater and long after he had become famous — virtually to the end, in fact, of his writing days — he made repeated attempts to express himself in the distilled language of poetry.

As early as Mount St. Vincent, finding letters inadequate to his need for unburdening himself, he began struggling with rhyme and meter. When around ten years old he became friendly with a youngster in New London of similar ambition, Guy Hedlund, and the two used to encourage one another's dream. In preparatory school and at college his classmates, though they never got a chance to read any of his efforts, gathered the impression that he was constantly turning out verse. In the winter of 1908–1909 he and two young artists spent a month at an old farmhouse in New Jersey; while the other two braved the outdoors to paint snowy landscapes, Eugene labored by the fireplace over, in his words, a "series of sonnets, bad imitations of Dante Gabriel Rossetti." He used to give a ribald picture of his life in Buenos Aires, of his hand-to-mouth existence among the seamen, prostitutes, pimps and bully-boys of the wide-open water front; one thing he never mentioned was that during this period of hard living and drinking he was trying to express himself in verse. After a chance meeting in a café with one Charles Ashleigh, an English journalist and poet, the two young men wore away many nights over beer-slopped tables reading their poems to one another between discussions of Byron, Baudelaire and Dowson. Later, in Greenwich Village, at a time that he seemed half-determined to drink himself to death, he sat in the back room of the Hell Hole writing poems with such titles as "The White Night" and "Dirty Bricks of Buildings," "Revolution" and " 'Tis of Thee," "The Eyes," "The Ghost" and "In That Last Hour."

Since his verse fell markedly short of his hopes, he generally made light of it, but there are glimpses of how he really felt. Barrett H. Clark, his first biographer, has reported: "Judge Latimer [the New London newspaper editor] told me Eugene didn't like it when he was told that his forte was prose, but O'Neill says that what he wrote for the paper was hardly ever serious verse . . . he has written a good deal in verse form that means something to him. He has a large notebook of poetry, written at odd times over a fairly long period."

Again, in the last interview O'Neill ever gave, he told Hamilton Basso in 1948: "Richard Dana Skinner has written a book about me. It's called *Eugene O'Neill: A Poet's Quest*. I don't agree with many things he says, but that just about sums it up. It *has* been a poet's quest."

While Eugene had from an early age his sustaining dream, his brother, unconcerned with justifying his life under the discipline of art, had the anodynes of sex and liquor. In the Minim division at Notre Dame and afterward at St. John's Preparatory School he had so acquitted himself that everyone had predicted for him a brilliant future, probably in law. But now, although maintaining a commendable record at St. John's College, he was a source of great concern to his parents, not alone because of his dissipations but because of increasing signs of disrespect toward his father.

His rebellion had been heating up for years, ever since he was packed off to Notre Dame. It had been on a hotter flame since the day he was shattered to learn, as Eugene would be in turn, that his mother was a drug addict; he learned about her in the worst possible way, when he was around fifteen, through chancing on Ella in the act of injecting herself with a hypodermic needle. At last he understood her periods of strange withdrawal and why she spent so much time in sanatoria. What made it even harder for Jamie was that her addiction had begun with Eugene's birth — the child she had borne to make up for the loss of Edmund. If Jamie had ever succeeded in forgetting his role in Edmund's death, he would never be able to forget it now. But instead of holding this against his mother, his love for her was, if anything, intensified. He more than ever saw her as a victim of her husband: living in trains and hotels, without a real home, without her own kind of friends — no wonder she had succumbed to temptation, no wonder she had fallen. The father was to blame. Circumstances might force on Jamie an occasional truce, even arouse in him feelings of pity for the father, but his lifelong vendetta would never really end until his enemy's death.

Toward Eugene his feelings were hopelessly ambivalent, almost evenly divided between love and hostility, the scales dipping now one way, now another. He knew that it was unfair to blame "the Kid" for what had happened, and tended to pity him for his decisive role in the family tragedy. All the same, Jamie could never forget that it *was* his brother's birth that had led to the mother's downfall. His feelings toward Eugene, whether he happened at the moment to feel close to him or resentful, were generally masked under a tone of mocking affection, just as his sniping at "the Old Man" usually took place — from fear of alienating the mother — under the guise of good-humored ribbing.

In 1897, when Jamie was eighteen, an old scandal returned to plague the family. Since Ella was forever raking up past grievances when under the influence of morphine, he already knew something about the Nettie Walsh trouble shortly after his parents' marriage. Although it scarcely led him to regard his father more favorably, he had accepted it as ancient history; but it was another thing when the unpleasant past intruded on the present. The story broke in the press on March 9, 1897, that Nettie's son, who went by the name of Alfred Hamilton O'Neill, had filed suit to have James O'Neill declared his father, and was also seeking financial restitution. He claimed that his mother had lost her divorce suit through the actor's machinations and from being "misled by designing people." He charged that by "the most outrageous fraud upon the court, the defendant, James O'Neill, procured a decree to be entered in said court finding that no marriage ever existed between Nettie and the defendant." He asked the court to restrain James from leaving the state of Illinois — the latter was performing at the time in Chicago — and to appoint a receiver for his property.

After dragging on for several years, the suit finally was dismissed in 1900 when the alleged son failed to make a counter-reply to the defendant's answering papers. The two parties had apparently reached a settlement out of court; prior to the suit Alfred had been employed by a soap factory, but afterward set himself up as a soap manufacturer. This was not his last intrusion on the family. In 1922, two years after Mr. O'Neill's death, Eugene received a letter: "I am writing you as the attorney for Mr. A. H. O'Neill, the son of James O'Neill, of New London, Connecticut, by his first wife, to inquire when you expect to close up the Estate of said James O'Neill and make distribution to the heirs," etc.

Though Jamie gave the impression of taking the fresh notoriety in his stride, man-of-the-world fashion, he was more affected than he would admit. Whether he was primarily resentful about the reflection on the family's name or pleased at what had happened — it showed up his father, it suggested that Jamie had inherited his wayward tastes — his behavior became more reckless after the scandal broke. Now he could say, when James upbraided him, he was merely sowing *his* wild oats. Ella was not the only one distressed by the relationship between son and father. Eugene, an emotional seismograph for the least disturbance within the family, was pained by the growing acrimony. Since he had his own grievances, particularly over his exile at school, he sided with his brother and increasingly tended to see their father not only through his own eyes but through Jamie's.

Yet Jamie continued to give his parents cause for hope. In spite of his drinking bouts, his womanizing, his growing negligence about attending classes, he had such a quick mind that he maintained a good scholastic standing. It appeared that he might still straighten himself out and enter law, but this prospect ended when his behavior at St. John's went beyond bounds. The authorities, after learning that the "sister" he had escorted to a school affair was actually a prostitute, expelled him in December 1899, only a few months before he was to have graduated.

Eugene's life at St. Aloysius, instead of becoming tolerable with time, remained burdensome. In after years he made joking references to it in letters to McCarthy, his old classmate ("Do you ever think of Sister Martha who used to knuckle us on the bean?"), and to critic George Jean Nathan, pretending that they had been "little convent boys" together ("Remember how Sister Mary used to paddle your behind to the chime of the Angelus and never miss a beat?"). But, like a true Irishman, he was simply glossing over an unhappy past with farcical exaggeration.

His father was the unwitting cause of one of his most unpleasant experiences, one that still rankled thirty years later as he told R. D. Skinner, a Catholic writer, about it. In the spring of 1899 James O'Neill, whose many years of *Monte Cristo* had dimmed his reputation, joined forces with the vigorous new firm of Liebler & Co. to spur his lagging career. The driving power behind Liebler's was a cherubic-faced, cigar-chewing little dynamo named George C. Tyler, the same who had been Mr. O'Neill's advance agent and had run for a doctor the night the infant Eugene had seemed to be dying. The eupeptic Mr. Tyler chose for the veteran actor another Dumas dramatization, this time, as the play was called, *The Musketeers.* Though James was already in his fifties and, as several critics noted mildly, a trifle mature for the role of d'Artagnan, he was among the theater's crack swordsmen and could still cut a romantic figure, full of the spirit of derring-do. His seasoned finesse, a strong supporting cast, and a lavish production carried the day, turning the old Dumas tale into a new Broadway hit.

After Eugene had taken some of his classmates to a matinee, the boys improvised swords from tree branches and lunged at one another like musketeers. One day a nun, who tended to be of a censorious nature, came along and, learning of the origin of their new game, lectured them on the temptations and evils of the theater, her pale eyes fixed all the while on Eugene.

O'Neill resented, he told Skinner, her criticizing an innocent child's game, but most of all he resented it as a personal attack on his actor father, who was a good Catholic. This, according to O'Neill, was among the things that began his disenchantment with Catholicism. Whether or not it actually affected him as much as he later thought, he was, in his last year or so at school, being pulled in opposite directions. He was both starting to question his ancestral faith and, unnerved by the feeling this gave him of being adrift, trying with renewed fervor to believe in a benevolent, omnipotent God.

An important factor in his dawning uncertainty was his brother's skepticism, which the latter bothered less and less to conceal; Jamie held it against the Church that all his mother's piety, all her prayers, had failed to save her from her "curse." But even without Jamie's example, Eugene was being influenced by his omnivorous reading. In his father's library, among the pages of Shakespeare, Dumas and Victor Hugo, histories of Ireland and England, classics of poetry and the theater, *The World's Best Literature* in fifty volumes, he had found things that raised disturbing questions — anticlerical passages, voices of doubtful, troubled souls. The boy not only read practically everything in his father's library but reread much of it. During long summer days in New London he was a familiar sight to passers-by on Pequot Avenue as he sat for hours on the porch or in the large swing on the front lawn, always hunched over reading.

Whatever his burgeoning doubts, they were swamped by a surge of religious feeling in spring 1900 as he prepared for the second of the two principal sacraments — his baptism was the first — that would bring him into union with the Saviour, assure his salvation and eternal life in Jesus Christ. On May 24, Ascension Thursday, after confession, penance, and mortification to prepare himself for a state of grace, he received for the first time the sacrament of Holy Communion. It all was familiar to him through his regular attendance at Mass, his countless times as an altar boy: the Offertory preparations, the solemn Canon with the elevation of the Sacred Host and the chalice, the ringing of the bell, the "Memento" for the dead and "Nobis quoque peccatoribus" for the living, all climaxed in the Communion. But for all his familiarity with the ancient prayers and rituals, they took on a new solemnity and mystical significance this day as he first partook of the Eucharist, the sanctified bread and wine that had been transmuted into the Body and the Blood of the Redeemer. He was now one with Christ.

Since he would be twelve in the fall, beyond the age for St. Aloysius boys, his first Communion marked the virtual end of his five years at the school. He had entered as a frightened child of seven; he was leaving as a gangling youngster with an overlarge head, apprehensive still in the depths of his being and struggling to find permanent answer in his ancestral faith. The day of his first Communion the school had given him a small black-covered copy of Thomas a Kempis's *The Following of Christ* (as this particular edition was called), with the hope that he would try to live up to its injunctions. The boy read it carefully and, full of spiritual resolve from his new initiation into grace, marked a number of passages for special attention. Some of the passages:

"And when we meet with any small adversity, we are too quickly dejected, and turn away to seek after human consolation." — "If we strove like valiant men to stand up in the battle, doubtless we should see our Lord help us from heaven." — "Therefore should a man so establish himself in God, as to have no need of seeking many comforts from men." — "As long as we live in this world we cannot be without tribulaton and temptation." —"Hence it is written in *Job:* 'The life of man upon earth is a temptation.' " — "But often something lies hid within, or occurs without, which drags us along with it."

5

❋

End of Innocence

ALL his life people found Eugene O'Neill an enigma. One of his contemporaries in New London, voicing a common view, recalled that "you couldn't get close to him, he was always off somewhere on cloud nine." An employee of the town's Lyceum Theater, who saw him over the years from childhood on, said: "He was a deep one — even when you knew him, you didn't know him." Former schoolmates found it hard to believe that the dreamy bookish youngster of their acquaintance had grown into someone who went to sea, roughed it on the water front, and wrote about prostitutes, brutish characters, the dregs. Elizabeth Shepley Sergeant wrote an article subtitled "Man with a Mask" which begins: "Eugene O'Neill has ever walked alone, and seemed a stranger to those about him."

Even those closest to him found him elusive. Agnes Boulton, his second wife, asks rhetorically in her memoir, *Part of a Long Story:* "What made you what you are, what were the hidden stigmata that had wounded you, and at times bled with drops of bitterness?" Carlotta Monterey, his third wife, scoffed at talk of his being enigmatic yet ended in contradicting herself. At different times she told one biographer: "Don't sentimentalize him. He was not a sweet little boy searching for a mama or a young man ever so polite. He was a black Irishman, a rough tough black Irishman. . . . He could have that smile that made him appear so young; other times he'd be as old as an old oriental. . . . He was a simple man. They make a lot of nonsense and mystery out of him. He was interested only in writing his plays. . . . He was the most stubborn man I've ever known. . . . He was nine or ten men in one." Russel Crouse, the noted theater man, expressed the view of many when he summed up his feelings: "O'Neill is one of the most charming men I know, and I've known him for twenty-five years, but I can't say I understand him. His face is a mask.

I don't know what goes on behind it, and I don't think anyone else does."

The curious thing in all this is that O'Neill is among the most autobiographical of playwrights. In the history of the theater perhaps only Strindberg, one of his idols, told as much about himself as this lapsed Catholic, who so often stepped into the confessional to write his plays. It was not, however, until *Long Day's Journey Into Night* that one had the essential clues toward understanding him, or that the heavily autobiographical cast of his work became evident. Again and again in his plays he wrote about himself and his family, drawing his own and their portraits under various guises, exploring their relations with one another, dramatizing his varying, indeed conflicting feelings toward the others. Of course a great many writers have made literary capital of their personal histories, of their families, but this is more common with novelists, and even among them few have been so obsessive about it as O'Neill.

Tracing relationships between O'Neill's life and his work, viewing one through the other, throws fresh light on both, though not with equal strength. Since his plays originated not only in outward circumstance, in things that had happened to him, but in his inner self, the plays tell us more about the man than his personal history tells us about the plays. His history yields external manifestations for the most part, only occasional glimpses of the inner man; it was the inner man, the essential O'Neill, who wrote the plays. Care is of course imperative in reading him for autobiography: under the functioning of the creative imagination and a writer's opposed drives for self-disclosure (self-justification) and self-concealment (born of self-doubt and guilt feelings), the inner flux and outward reality of his life have undergone transformation, are interwoven with fiction. But it is there, the autobiography, as bed-root throughout his writings.

O'Neill has often been charged with exploiting murder, suicide, the obviously dramatic, a tendency the critics generally attribute to his upbringing, to the influence of his father's melodramatic theater. Unquestionably the old-time theater did have a great effect upon his writings, even though he grew to regard it with contempt. Yet O'Neill was too serious a playwright, too intent on expressing himself, to indulge in story matter primarily because of its theatrical effectiveness. If he so often wrote about violent things, it was not primarily because of their shock value but because of great violence within him; if he dealt in insanity, the subject itself, not merely its dramatic possibilities, interested him.

Insanity figures in a number of his plays. In *Ile* a whaling captain's wife is driven mad by her isolated life in Arctic waters. In *Where the Cross Is Made*, a short work, and *Gold*, a full-length treatment of the same story, a sea captain with murder on his conscience becomes hopelessly obsessed by a dream of buried treasure. In *Strange Interlude* the heroine resorts to adultery to have a child on learning of hereditary insanity in her husband's family. In *The Iceman Cometh* a man who has slain his wife teeters on the edge of lunacy. In *More Stately Mansions* a fastidious soul at odds with reality ends in self-willed madness, while her son, who is at war with himself, narrowly escapes her fate. In *All God's Chillun Got Wings* a young wife breaks down and imagines herself a child again.

Such a listing indicates only that the author was preoccupied with the subject of mental aberration; but one of the plays, *All God's Chillun*, points to an autobiographical factor at the root of his interest. The story of a white girl who takes refuge in insanity from her marriage to a Negro, a kind, hard-working man trying to better himself, *All God's Chillun* dramatizes some of the playwright son's feelings about the union of Ella Quinlan, gently reared, and James O'Neill, who struggled up from the meanest poverty. The girl in the play is named Ella; her husband, Jim.

While Eugene was growing up, bewildered by his mother's recurrent strangeness, he was haunted by the fear that she was mentally unstable. What else could he think? Could he imagine that his mother, his gentle pious mother, was a dope fiend, the sort of person they wrote about in dime thrillers? His attempts to question his father and brother only reinforced his suspicions, for they always tried to cut off the conversation or replied evasively that "Mama" suffered from a kind of sickness. So far as the boy could see, everything pointed to mental illness as the answer, for she obviously found life, her present life, too much for her. There was her constant comparing of her early happy years with her lot as an actor's wife, her frequent complaints about the hardships of the road, particularly the isolation from her own kind of people (a refrain that one day would be sounded by Ella Harris, feeling lost in a world of Negroes, in *All God's Chillun*). Echoes of the boy's old fear can be detected more than once in *Long Day's Journey*. Says Jamie on hearing the mother approach, "The Mad Scene. Enter Ophelia!" Again, Tyrone to his wife: "Up to take more of the God-damned poison, is that it? You'll be like a mad ghost before the night's over!"

What made the situation particularly hard on Eugene was that he harbored not only suspicions about his mother but fears for himself, fears that he might have inherited her weakness. Everyone said that he took after her, that he had the same kind of sensitive nature. The weight and anxiety of these years, as well as the bewildering confusion of the still earlier period when he was being trundled all over the country, left an enduring mark on him. Many persons, among them Hamilton Basso, would be struck by the piercing sadness of his large dark eyes. Basso was reminded of "the legend that the people of Ravenna always gave Dante a wide berth when they passed him on the street. The Ravennese, among whom Dante spent his last years, felt that the poet's burning, baleful eyes had actually looked upon the horrors of hell and that his dark complexion was the result of his being scorched in its sulphurous, overheated atmosphere. That's the way I sometimes feel about O'Neill. . . . We'll be talking, and he'll go into one of those long staring silences of his, and I'll half expect him to turn to me and say, 'You're not a bad fellow, as far as I know, but if your eyes had seen what *these* eyes have seen, you'd go on home to your wife and children and not expect me to be nice.' "

Before Eugene learned what was wrong with his mother he was haunted by one kind of fear; afterward, there was the constant apprehension that their neighbors might discover the family's secret, that her addiction might become a matter of common gossip. James O'Neill, who had lived so long with the problem, used to tell New Londoners that his wife was of delicate health, to explain her semirecluse existence and why the family occasionally summered elsewhere, generally in the Catskills or the Adirondacks. "The mountains," he said, "are better for my wife's health." Actually, whenever they vacationed in other parts, it was because James had yielded to Ella's dislike of the gloomy gray cottage on Pequot Avenue and the town itself, with its frequent sieges of fog and wailing foghorn.

It would be a mistake, however, to assume that Eugene O'Neill grew up perpetually unhappy, that he found life one long uninterrupted ordeal. For all that was weighing on him — suspicions about his mother, anxiety over himself, concern over the hostility between his brother and father — he had resilient stuff in him. "His quietness," Jamie says in *Long Day's Journey*, "fools people into thinking they can do what they like with him. But he's stubborn as hell inside." Though Jamie was talking of his brother as a grownup, the child, as the poet said, "is father to the man."

The boy, developing compensations, found channels of escape he could always turn to: the hospitable waters of the Thames, almost at the O'Neills' doorstep, where he felt so at home and could forget everything; books, through which he could lead many lives and explore other worlds while shutting out his own; words to play with, half-formed poems in mind to develop on paper; a dream of happiness in voyaging some day to strange golden places under faraway skies. There were, furthermore, periods when his mother behaved more or less normally, generally after being away in a sanatorium, and the family atmosphere lightened, became almost jubilant.

It was a relatively happy youngster who entered De La Salle Institute in midtown Manhattan in the fall of 1900; not only was he a day student and living at home, the loneliness of Mount St. Vincent behind him, but his mother had been well for some months. Without his knowing it, he himself was primarily responsible for her improvement. Watching him receive Holy Communion had given Ella almost as much pain as joy, finally firing her with renewed determination to try to overcome her "curse." When Eugene had first gone off to boarding school, she had had mixed feelings of loss and relief. Now that she was trying to save herself, she welcomed having him at home; it shored up her new resolve, besides giving her more chance to talk to him about the priesthood. Other than both schools being Catholic, De La Salle was the opposite of St. Aloysius; where one was small, countrylike and feminine in personality, the other was large, busy, located in the heart of things — the building ran from 58th to 59th Street, near Sixth Avenue — and entirely masculine. Operated by the Christian Brothers, it had a good-sized faculty, a lively athletic program, and a full curriculum. After the quiet isolation of his first school, Eugene felt confused by the size and all the activity of De La Salle, which had around one hundred and fifty students. But he was more than content with the change; home, a hotel apartment on West 68th Street, just off Central Park, was only a pleasant walk from school.

Things in general were looking up for the O'Neills. Jamie, whose expulsion from St. John's had shocked and saddened his parents, was making an effort to settle down and regain his mother's favor. Attracted by the semibohemian life of newspapermen, he had considered becoming a reporter but finally had gone to work as a traveling salesman for one of his father's New London friends, a wholesale lumber dealer named Sweeney. He came and went at the apartment, impressing his young brother with his businesslike air and talk of big commissions.

James O'Neill himself, after years spent almost entirely on the road, was also thriving. *The Musketeers* had had a good run in New York, a season in other large cities, and now he was preparing to make a new bid for public favor in his old role of Edmond Dantès. After first resisting the prospect, he had been talked into it by George Tyler. Impressed by the manager's optimism that the times were ripe for a gala *Monte Cristo*, the veteran star forgot his weariness at escaping from the island prison, claiming the world as his own, and holding up a stern finger to tick off his enemies ("One! . . . Two! . . . Three!") as he dispatched them from life one, two, three.

Intent on surpassing its *Musketeers* production, Liebler's poured twenty-five thousand dollars into the revival, a handsome figure for the day, while press agent A. Toxen Worm, ever inflationary, announced that seventy-five thousand had been spent. He also churned out advertising copy and publicity awash with superlatives: "The grand staircase on which Monte Cristo makes his entrance is 28 feet high, fifty steps high. . . . An expenditure of over $30,000 in the grand ballroom scene . . . The very perfection of science and of art have been combined to make the world behind the scenes as complete as Nature itself. Here Vulcan forges the thunderbolts, and Jove hurls them. . . . From the front the ocean looks to be a sullen, roaring monster that dashes its anger in waves fearful to behold. . . . Scenically Superb! . . . Massive, Magnificent and Miraculous!"

When the "new" *Monte Cristo* opened in Boston the production was so burdened with full-rigged ship, candelabra thirty-six feet high, and a Château d'If "all solid and nearly built up to the proper dimensions" of the actual prison that the action, as one critic noted, was "fearfully slow." Yet it was a hit; as the stagehands became adept at shifting whole villages and forests, enabling the story to move faster, crowds flocked to enjoy the swordplay and extravagant stage pictures. Following weeks in Boston, the show moved on to New York, shortly after Eugene had entered De La Salle, and settled down for a run. For the first time in years the boy found himself in the middle of things at Christmas, his family all together just like other families, with Sarah Sandy, a frequent visitor at the apartment, sharing in their holiday.

All this fall and winter Eugene felt particularly close to his mother, primarily because she was making a particular effort to reach him. One day she took him to a special matinee of Yeats's *The Land of Heart's Desire* and Robert Browning's *In a Balcony;* afterward, with her gangling twelve-year-old still in tow, she went backstage to compliment a young actress Liebler's was grooming for stardom, Eleanor Robson (later, Mrs. August Belmont). Though Ella kept her distance from most people of the theater, she found Miss Robson exceptional, a girl of refinement and quiet charm. While the two women chatted, Eugene, despite his shyness, could not keep from staring at the young actress, she was so beautiful. Finally mustering some courage, he managed to palm one of her ornamental hairpins without being observed and slipped it into a pocket close to his heart. Long afterward Mrs. Belmont remembered that the boy had hovered silently on the edge of the conversation and recalled the mother as "frail, gentle, very sweet." Ella actually was well-proportioned and quite tall, but her low voice and shy manner often left an impression of fragility.

It was a quite peaceful time in the family. Whatever the ripples, they generally were set off by Jamie's sniping at his favorite target. He could always find something with which to needle his father. When all else failed, there was the Irish; the Irish were constantly in the news.

The relative tranquility for months, the closer relationship Eugene had established with his mother, only made the aftermath harder for him. She had behaved normally for so long that he was beginning to hope for a permanent recovery, but one day he returned from school to find her acting strangely again, off in her own private world. No one was around for him to turn to; his father was on the road with *Monte Cristo*, and Jamie was traveling in New England for the lumberman. All the boy could think of, since his mother was ill-suited to look after him, was that he would be sent to boarding school again. As he feared, so it came about: in the fall of 1901 he was enrolled among the boarding students at De La Salle, a small group consisting chiefly of orphans, boys whose parents traveled a good deal, and a handful from other countries, chiefly Cuba, Mexico, and Santo Domingo. It was the "rigid Christian exile" all over again, sharpened by his closeness to home, the apartment on 68th Street, where the family came and went.

Jamie's existence also changed this fall. Whether he had become bored with being a traveling salesman or had proven unsatisfactory to the lumber dealer, the upshot was that he turned actor in his father's company. In later years he would complain that James had forced him into the theater, that he had never wanted to be an actor, yet his new situation had for him one great compensating factor — his mother's presence with the troupe.

While Eugene was again adjusting to life at a boarding school, Jamie made his debut in Boston with a bit part in *Monte Cristo*, at the same time serving as a stand-by for Albert de Morcerf, Dantès's son. His first performance may charitably be described as inadequate. Long afterward, when he could joke about it, he used to entertain friends with a story of his panicky exit after delivering a line or so. "I made my way across the stage," he once recalled, "turned up right-center, then left-center, and in the confusion of rights and lefts brought up with a jolt against the wall. Then I veered off until I hit the curtain, which gave way, rather marring the scene, but giving me the chance to get out of sight."

Once his stage fright had passed, he began to display an aptitude for acting, as might have been expected of one who had been giving a performance most of his life. Within months of his debut, after the actor playing Dantès's son had proven inadequate, Jamie was installed in the role and his salary raised from twenty to fifty dollars a week. His father, still hopeful that he might settle down, felt that he could get somewhere in the theater — not as far as he himself of course, but far enough to reflect credit on his heritage. At first the father's cautious optimism seemed justified. Eager to look good in his mother's eyes, Jamie gave his best to his assignments and won cordial words from the reviewers. Gradually, though, after he had displayed some talent, after he felt he had proved that acting was less difficult than the father maintained, he lost interest; the quality of his performance depended on his mood at the time, and the amount he had drunk before going on stage.

Said the Florida *Times-Union:* "James O'Neill, Jr., has inherited none of his father's histrionic ability. Several of the climaxes were almost absolutely ruined by his stiffness, his lack of fire, his characterless speaking of his lines. When the part of the father ceases to cloud the judgment of the actor and artist, James O'Neill, Sr., will drop James O'Neill, Jr." Nettled by the criticism, Jamie buckled down and shortly afterward gave a performance that won him praise from the Pittsburgh *Leader:* "He is a manly looking chap and did excellent work." From one night to the next the father never knew how his namesake would perform.

Ella accepted his going on the stage as necessity — he had to do something to earn a living — and was glad to have him around so long as he was behaving himself and not over-drinking. Resigned to the tedious grind and patchwork existence of the road, she felt less lonely with Jamie accompanying them. Whether or not he made a name for himself in the theater was of no real consequence to her; all her hopes were pinned on Eugene's becoming a priest.

When Eugene was packed off to Mount St. Vincent, he had blamed only his father; at De La Salle, though he still held James primarily responsible for his being at boarding school, he began to develop a sense of grievance against his mother, too. If only she had been capable of taking care of him, if only she had been stronger and more adaptable, more in fact like Sarah Sandy . . . It was inevitable that he should come to compare the two, his real and his surrogate mother, and that Sarah's sturdy character should throw Ella's shortcomings into sharper relief. From an outsider's view, the nursemaid's quiet firmness in handling youngsters, an approach that would discourage the normal and healthy rebelliousness of a growing child, probably had an inhibiting effect on Eugene's personality during his most impressionable period. Still, in his fragmented early years she had been someone to cling to, someone he could always depend on.

In several years he would pull away from Sarah (he later decided that this constituted a repudiation of her as a "mother value"); it was less easy to root her out of his unconscious. Something of perdurable Sarah was behind an image of Indomitable Woman that came in time to loom in O'Neill's fantasy-world; and absurd though it may sound, the dream figure probably drew also on Mother Wolf, who shelters Mowgli from harm in *The Jungle Book*. The image would haunt not only O'Neill's writings — his plays contain a number of dauntless mother-figures and noble, all-enduring wives — but his personal life. He would always look up to women of strength and eventually would marry one strong enough to stand between him and the world, one who was to him at once wife, mistress, secretary, nurse and, above all, mother.

As a boarding student at De La Salle, Eugene had more freedom than at Mount St. Vincent; he used to spend an occasional weekend with Sarah and, if his parents were in town, at their hotel apartment. His life, otherwise, centered bleakly on the school and its Spartan dormitory on the top floor — a series of wooden partitions curtained in front, each alcove austerely furnished with cot and wardrobe. Though the youngsters by and large came from well-to-do families, De La Salle, like his first school, favored plain living.

Since Eugene was retiring, most of his classmates had only the sketchiest impressions of him afterward: "A dreamy youngster, generally lost in himself . . . polite but taciturn and withdrawn . . . not interested in sports or any of the school activities but always reading . . . no youthful outbursts." Of all the day students who thronged the place the only one with whom O'Neill became friendly was a physically handicapped youngster named Victor F. Ridder, later a newspaper publisher. "I was lame and he was quiet," Ridder once said; "we were pushed aside by the livelier boys. De La Salle was great for sports, football, baseball, floor hockey, but Eugene never showed interest in any of them."

His closest friend among the boarding students was Ricardo Amezaga, a bright, warmhearted youngster from Havana, whose cubicle was next to Eugene's. "I liked him the first time we met," Amezaga recalls. "We both were studious and well-behaved, complying with our religious duties. I still treasure fond memories of Gene; he was always kind and understanding. One time he took a few of us to see *Monte Cristo* — we had a box — and afterward backstage to meet his father, who was friendly and very gracious. Occasionally we'd go over to Central Park for ice skating, under a Brother's supervision, but I can't remember Gene ever going. In the fall and spring we'd go boating on the lake, and he generally went with us then. I remember his reading *Don Quixote* and asking Frank Dumois, another boy from Havana, and myself how to pronounce the Spanish expressions. He wanted exact information; when we told him how to pronounce the title, he wanted to know if Cuban and Spanish pronunciation were the same.

"In later years when he became famous and I read about the kind of plays he wrote, about his going to sea and bumming around, I thought it must be another O'Neill. I couldn't believe that the gentle and delicate-in-health Gene [his thin build and quiet, his disinterest in competitive sports, gave others a misleading impression about his health] had grown to this until I read that he had gone to De La Salle. Last year my wife and I went to see *The Iceman Cometh* in Greenwich Village — a wonderful performance of a great play. But we left the theater with heavy hearts after so much misery and vice of the lower stratum of humanity. It saddens me to think that O'Neill went through so much physical and moral suffering in his path through life."

Eugene made out well at the school, ranking sixth in a class of twenty-two. His best subjects were history (average grade of 88), English (87) and religion (84), while algebra and geometry (both 57) were his poorest. Save for keeping so much to himself, he was a model student — polite toward everyone, conscientious in his studies, and obedient to the Brothers, most of them elderly and white-haired. Behind his quiet demeanor, however, he was undergoing a spiritual crisis, because of his mother. If for all her faith and piety, Jesus would not or could not save her, what good was Catholicism, what sort of God was this? Surely no all-powerful God of love and infinite compassion. At the same time fearful of the consequences and of lessening the chance of divine intervention, he struggled to purge himself of all doubt as he prayed for his mother's redemption. He thought, if this might save her, of even vowing to become a priest. The inner struggle went on for months while his schoolmates and teachers found him polite and detached. He looked forward to Sundays, when the boarding students attended Mass at St. Patrick's Cathedral on Fifth Avenue; surrounded by the sacred images and symbols, the tall stained-glass windows and soaring pillars of the church named for the patron saint of the Irish, the boy felt in closer touch with God.

Thirty years later O'Neill, freely revising his actual history, dramatized the essential points of his crisis in *Days Without End*, the story of an embattled Catholic apostate named John Loving. To point up the civil war within his protagonist, O'Neill split him in two, literally, as a Faust ("John") and a Mephistopheles ("Loving") who is visible only to this Faust. John is the suffering half that hungers for salvation; Loving, the voice of his enmity to life and God. Often in the play the two selves talk in contrapuntal fashion, one as a troubled human being, the other as the devil's subaltern.

The dual protagonists, referring to John Loving in the third person, alternate in telling of the steps that led to his apostasy: "He grew up as devout as his parents. He even dreamed of becoming a priest. . . . Oh, he was a remarkably superstitious young fool! And then when he was fifteen, all those pious illusions of his were destroyed forever! Both his parents were killed! . . . That is, they died during a flu epidemic — and he was left alone — without love. First, his father died. The boy had prayed with perfect faith that his father's life might be spared. . . . But his father died. And the poor simpleton's naïve faith was a bit shaken! . . . Then his mother was taken ill. And the horrible fear came to him that she might die, too. . . . It drove the young idiot into a panic of superstitious remorse. . . . But he still trusted in His love. . . . So the poor fool prayed and prayed and vowed his life to piety and good works! *If* his mother were spared! . . . His mother died. And, in a frenzy of insane grief . . . No! in his awakened pride he cursed his God and denied Him, and, in revenge, promised his soul to the Devil — on his knees, when every one thought he was praying!"

In life the climax came not at St. Patrick's or any other church but at home in New London, under circumstances more dramatic than those recounted in *Days Without End*. When the year ended at De La Salle with no sign of his mother's recovery, then ended Eugene's prayers and hopes for a miracle, his faith in Catholicism and a benevolent God. Stubbornly set against continuing at parochial school, but without divulging the reason, he told his parents that he was too unhappy at De La Salle, that if he had to go away, it should be to a regular boarding school; one way or another, with Jamie backing him, he countered their suggestions of Notre Dame, St. John's, any other Catholic school. The father in frustration turned on Jamie and accused him of planting the idea in the boy's mind, but finally had to yield. Once the boy had made up his mind on something, the father was starting to realize, it was virtually impossible to budge him.

His parents were still unaware of his loss of faith when in the fall of 1902 he entered Betts Academy, a nonsectarian preparatory school in Stamford, Connecticut. Grateful at getting his own way, Eugene continued to attend Mass with the family, to go through all the motions of outward observance. It was the following year, as he was approaching fifteen, that events came to a head and fired him into open revolt.

The summer of 1903 began inauspiciously with constant rain and fog. Captain Field of the New London Light had many occasions for his stock comments: "The fog is almost thick enough to cut and place in cold storage. . . . Only way a ship could get out of the harbor would be for a snow plow to go ahead and shovel away the fog." Making things worse in the Pequot, the lighthouse had recently installed a new foghorn, far more powerful than the old one, that grated on everyone's nerves. One night, after a stretch of bad weather had kept Ella marooned in the house so long that she had exhausted her supply of "medicine," the torment, the craving for relief, was beyond her endurance. Dashing out of the house in her nightdress, she tried to throw herself into the river, but her sons, with her husband panting after them, stopped her.

"It was right after that," O'Neill says through Edmund in *Long Day's Journey*, "Papa and Jamie decided they couldn't hide it from me any more. Jamie told me. I called him a liar! I tried to punch him in the nose. But I knew he wasn't lying. (His voice trembles, his eyes begin to fill with tears.) God, it made everything in life seem rotten!"

After that night, after what Jamie had told him, he was through with religion and all hollow obeisances. The following Sunday as he and his father were descending the stairway bound for Mass, he pulled back and declared that he was not going to church, that he was never going again, never! The two fought down the stairs as Mr. O'Neill sought to take him along forcibly, the boy squirming and stormy-faced under the other's superior strength, his shirt torn in the struggle. The father, realizing it was useless, at last desisted, the boy all the while glaring at him like one possessed. He told his son they would talk about it later, straightened his clothes and, assuming his usual dignified manner, left for church.

The prospect of remaining there all summer seemed unbearable not only to Ella, who had always disliked the gray house with the dark trees pressing close, but to them all. Jamie took a berth with a stock company in Massachusetts. Mr. O'Neill shipped his horses and carriages to New York, told friends he and his family were going to the Adirondacks, and they left town. Possibly the three of them did go to the mountains, perhaps the mother instead entered a sanatorium for another "cure." But it is certain that the thoughts of all four strayed often that summer to the house where the lawn ran down toward the water. For his parents and brother, that night remained a painful memory; for Eugene a catastrophe. "God, it made everything in life seem rotten!" If his birth had landed his mother in hell, she finally had taken him with her, to a hell of guilt feelings he could never escape.

6

Birth of a Rebel

Betts Academy, after Eugene's seven years of Catholic schooling, was a new kind of life. Here the overriding concern was not a student's spiritual welfare but his capacity for learning; here, unlike the authoritarian atmosphere of his other schools, the boys fraternized with their teachers, competed with them in sports, and thought nothing of addressing them by nicknames. But much as Eugene welcomed his new freedom, he clung to his shell, the other boys and his instructors finding him, as so many people had, quiet and withdrawn. Someone, most likely Jamie, had given him a gramophone as a going-away present and it could often be heard from his room, playing the same few records over and over, when he was not in class. One of the older boys, Ralph deGolier, has an isolated memory of him in his first weeks. DeGolier, handy at the piano, recalls "a shabby parlor, an ancient upright where I sat laboriously digging out accompaniments for our French master, 'Lavvy' Lavertee from Maine, who spoke French-Canadian and had some pretensions as a baritone. Suddenly an apparition peered between ancient magenta portieres — large dark eyes dominating the face, knee breeches, a sailor blouse with a wide white collar — and vanished without a word."

Although it was some time before Eugene felt at home in his new surroundings, he began to relax once he became used to "Billy" Betts, the headmaster, and realized that his bark was never followed by a bite. Betts was a devout Yale man who, quite appropriately, resembled Yale's traditional mascot: short, squarish, an outthrust jaw, tenacious in character, a conversational style of emphatic spurts more like barking than speech. In sum, he looked like a bulldog with a brushy mustache, and had something of a bulldog's personality. "Now you going to remember it?" he would say as he glared at a youngster, after pounding home a point. Brusque, impatient, he used to leapfrog over chairs in his way — though then in his

mid-fifties — and his hands were generally dirty from using them, wet
with spit, to wipe off a blackboard. The school motto, "What we do, we
do well," was but a genteel echo of his personal code. He was all-fired
determined that every boy should achieve the best within him and he
wanted them all — especially the better students and athletes — to go on
to Yale. A good man, an innocent, in a rush to improve his little corner of
the world.

The school, founded over a half-century earlier by his martinet of a
father, was located on Strawberry Hill in a choice residential section of
Stamford, Connecticut. By now, after being added to over the years, it
was a rambling two- and three-story yellow frame building, screened in
front by tall evergreens. Board and tuition, with extras, came to around
six hundred dollars, several hundred dollars less than at top-ranking prep
schools; classes were small, rarely more than six or seven, and the boys
received virtually individual attention. Under Billy's drive, the school
enjoyed a good reputation but, like the headmaster himself, who tore
around in old clothes and shapeless felt slippers, it was short on style.
Billy was a fervent advocate of higher education and equally enthusiastic
about competitive sports, particularly football. A sound mind, he was
fond of saying, in a sound body. He chose his instructors as much for
their football prowess as for their academic ability, the varsity backfield
being all-faculty, and kneaded not only a first but a second and a third
team from a student body of fifty to sixty.

Sport flourished the year around, baseball in spring, tennis and golf in
good weather, tobogganing on snow-covered slopes of the campus, ice
skating at the bottom of Strawberry Hill, where a meadow honeycombed
with brooks afforded in winter an impromptu rink; but the big thing was
football, the games on brisk Saturdays in fall against the Yale freshmen,
Hotchkiss, Lawrenceville, et al. While the athletic program was optional,
nearly everyone responded to pressure and joined in. Eugene, one of the
few nonbelievers, played only some pitch-and-catch and an occasional
game of tennis; his favorite exercise was taking long walks in the surrounding countrylike area, at times with one or two others, more often
alone. In the words of classmate T. G. Treadway, "He sat along the sidelines of fun, enjoying it in a semi-absent way."

Even Arthur ("Algie") Walter, an instructor everyone liked, found it
difficult to draw him out. "During the evening recreation hour when
other boys would be urging me to start games and play them with all
their heart," Walter once said, "O'Neill would listlessly enter if he were
coaxed, but would show no interest or enthusiasm to be the winner. If he
was at the foot, it was all right with him." He did display interest,

however, in a student who seemed to have psychic powers. Blindfolded, the youngster could lead another boy to a hidden article if the latter had concentrated on its hiding place. "Week after week," Walter said, "Eugene tested the boy and had to admit that he never failed, except when Eugene purposely didn't concentrate."

Most boys spent just a year or two at the Academy, cramming for college; Eugene was to remain four years. He initially was so reserved he made almost no impression on his classmates. When he returned for a second year, after that night in New London, the night his mother tried to drown herself, a rebel began to emerge and attract attention. His misdeeds were more or less typical schoolboy pranks — smuggling a snake into an instructor's bed, leaving Limburger cheese on the radiator in another teacher's room, squirting a syringeful of ink at a classmate — yet he had always been so subdued that what in someone else would have been simply youthful exuberance represented in him a radical change. Like others, he used to slip up on the roof for a forbidden cigarette, take off after nine o'clock bed-check to venture downtown, have midnight snacks in his room, read by candlelight to escape detection, generally books of a racy nature; but where most boys acted contrite when caught at something, he would question regulations. He seemed determined to have his own way. Betts Academy saw the beginning of his quarrel with authority.

He liked to shock the other boys, once declaring, for example, that illegitimacy had advantages — you didn't have to bother with a family and relatives. One year he decorated his room with photographs of chorus girls in tights and put up an argument when the headmaster, ordering their removal, told him he would awaken with healthier thoughts if he hung pictures of horses and dogs. Eventually he was assigned to a room opposite Algie Walter's quarters, the latter being under instructions to keep an eye on young O'Neill.

"He was a fine student when he wanted to be," says schoolmate Elliott Mott. "His work in history and English was outstanding, and he enjoyed writing the weekly essays on authors we were studying. But he was always ready to argue with the teachers on anything."

Although Betts and Walter had between them a nearly perfect record of injecting mathematics into the most reluctant mind, Eugene represented to them a semidefeat. "What's the use of studying that stuff?" he used to tell the other boys. "What good will it do me?" Walter later said, "He hated mathematics. I got him past algebra into geometry but could never get him into trigonometry. He was stubborn. He had a very determined mind of his own."

For all his developing contentiousness, he remained detached. "He would never become actively angry," Walter said, "but would withdraw into himself and sulk. In fact he generally seemed lost in himself." Years later classmates said they could still hear a teacher saying, "Wake up, O'Neill!" or "O'Neill, snap out of it!" His manner of speech also set him apart. "He never said much," Harold M. Green recalled, "but when he did he used fine English and seemed to weigh every word. It took him a long time to get something out." This slow, ruminative manner marked him all his life and, indeed, developed to such an extreme degree that people would cut in on him, thinking he had finished, as he lingered among his thoughts and groped for words.

Mr. O'Neill, a frequent visitor at the school to check on his son's progress, thought well of Mr. Betts and backed him in whatever measures he saw fit to employ with Eugene. He always came alone, for Ella still felt strongly against the boy's enrollment in a non-Catholic school; also, she was ill at ease around him now that he knew of her addiction. To cover up his wife's seeming indifference, James told the headmaster that she was a semi-invalid. The story later became garbled in the memories of José Pessino, a student from Havana, who had been concerned over Eugene's withdrawn nature. Recalling a discussion he had had with Mr. Betts's secretary, Pessino said long afterward: "He told me there was trouble in the family. I can't remember whether he said the mother had died or the parents were divorced or what, but it was some kind of family trouble. It must have had a tremendous influence on Eugene's character. He talked very little and he seldom smiled. He would sit in the room of one of the boys who had a piano, listen for a long time, and walk out without saying a word."

Despite his manner, Eugene developed a strong affection for the place. Where he had once looked on boarding school as exile from those dear to him, he regarded Betts as a refuge from family life. Decades later a doctor, summarizing O'Neill's account of his youth, wrote in his case history: "He dreaded the passing of each day because it brought him closer to the end of the school term and the end of the welcome monotony of the school environment." A negative sort of tribute, but positive testimony is also available. "I was tickled to death to get your letter and also an old Betts book," he wrote Billy in 1923. "The photos in the latter made me feel quite aged, and a bit melancholy thereat – but it wasn't an unpleasant sadness. My memories of Betts are all delightful ones – which, speaking for myself, is more than one can say of most memories."

He was at Betts from age fourteen to nearly eighteen, a trying period under the best of circumstances as a man struggles to be born within a boy's awkward and apprehensive frame; in his case, with his brother officiating as cynical midwife, the process was more than normally difficult. He was not only older than his age, as his schoolmates came to think, but younger, a vulnerable soul who would always be vulnerable. "Why am I afraid to live," says the hero, patently autobiographical, of *The Great God Brown*, "I who love life and the beauty of flesh and the living colors of earth and sky and sea? Why am I afraid of love, I who love love? . . . Why must I pretend to scorn in order to pity? Why must I hide myself in self-contempt in order to understand? . . . Why must I live in a cage like a criminal, defying and hating, I who love peace and friendship? Why was I born without a skin, O God, that I must wear armor in order to touch or to be touched? (His voice becomes bitter and sardonic) Or rather, Old Graybeard, why the devil was I ever born at all?"

At Betts he was struggling not only to grow up but, since nature abhors a vacuum, to fill the void left by his apostasy. After the loss of faith in his mother and in Catholicism (he tended unconsciously to equate her with Catholicism, just as he equated his father with the Irish), he was launched on a lifelong quest for something to believe in. He read books beyond his years, seeking some meaning to life, and when he tired of looking for answers, read to escape himself. Under Jamie's guidance he began to soak up the unsettling wine of the pre-Raphaelite brethren, including that "libidinous laureate of a pack of satyrs," that "unclean fiery imp from the pit," as one critic described Swinburne. The panting sensuality of Swinburne's alliterative swoonings, his hymns to "the roses and raptures of vice," his pseudo-pagan scorn of morality, restraint and authority — it all was to Eugene, as to generations of rebellious youth, a heady draught. Other teachers followed, Dowson, Fitzgerald, Wilde, Baudelaire, champions of the disinherited, consoling voices for the weary of heart and the self-raped. The *Rubáiyát*, *Flowers of Evil*, *The Ballad of Reading Gaol*, these became his new Scriptures, his new articles of faith: "Ah, make the most of what we yet may spend, before we too into the dust descend. . . . Harlots and Hunted have pleasures of their own to give, the Vulgar can never understand. . . . For who shall change with prayers or thanksgiving/The mystery of the cruelty of things. . . . I Myself am Heav'n and Hell."

After a weedy adolescence during which his high forehead, thin neck and slender body had given him a top-heavy look, all arms, legs and head, Eugene had developed into a handsome youth, tall, generally well-tanned, distinctive-looking. What one noticed about him above all was his eyes, large, dark, luminous, of an extraordinary intensity. They were unforgettable. They gave the feeling that he was searching into one's depths, of seeking out one's essential identity. Who are you, what are you? they seemed to say. Are you honest, are you true? When he smiled (he was practically never known throughout his life to laugh aloud), his face became transformed, radiant, his eyes seemed literally to sparkle. But his appearance, depending on his mood, could vary to a striking degree. If he were in low spirits, a resentful mouth, sagging at the edges, would predominate and he looked quite ordinary.

Since both his parents had large dark eyes, he resembled both, but in spite of having his father's nose, left an impression of looking more like Ella, primarily because they shared a quality of quivering sensitivity. He dressed neatly and well and was starting to emulate Jamie's man-of-the-world air, though it was a strain for him to look poised; his long slender hands used to twitch and he was forever fussing with his necktie, a nervous mannerism so marked that Billy Betts used to keep after him about it.

Jamie, on the other hand, resembled only the father, but without being nearly as handsome as the latter in his prime. Though slightly taller and weighing less, Jamie would come to seem heavier from lacking the other's erect bearing; and where the father's profile put one in mind of an ancient Roman coin, his nose was rather aquiline. From eying the world with cool appraisal he gave the impression his head was slightly behind his body; but in telling one of his off-color stories his face hovered close and his voice dropped to a confidential stage whisper as he swept his listener into cynical rapport. When he came to the point of a story, the ends of his lips would quiver from suppressed laughter, for he too practically never laughed out loud. But he wanted attention, unlike Eugene, and used to enter barrooms with a cheery cry of "What ho!" Always sharply dressed and with a ready flow of gab, he was popular with women, particularly "fast" women. When he smiled without cynicism, an Irish charmer, suddenly young-looking, appeared. Men enjoyed him as a ribald wit and raconteur until — in a tendency that grew with time — he turned nasty with drink. His tongue could be positively surgical; he had a gift for detecting a person's weaknesses and seemed to derive satisfaction from making one feel small.

Generally masking his animus toward his father under a bantering tone, he used to belittle him with an air of joking. Once, when Mr. O'Neill fell to reminiscing about his hardships as a young actor, particularly the constant ordeal of learning a new part each week while playing another, Jamie made light of it. "You call that work?" he said, and ended by betting ten dollars that he could memorize all four hundred and thirty lines of Goldsmith's *The Deserted Village* in a week. Eugene also became involved in the wager, undertaking Macbeth's role. The two boys, each of whom had an actor's memory, won their bets handily. "After our week was over," Eugene once recalled, "James and I stood before my father. My brother ran through *The Deserted Village*, collected his money, and then my father started to cue me my lines as Macbeth. I gave them back to him without a hitch. My father closed the book and looked at me. 'You certainly have a good memory,' he said, 'and I see you've worked hard, but never go on the stage.' " O'Neill grinned at the thought as he ended the story. He, an actor! Getting up before hundreds of strangers and sounding off!

Looking back on his life, he once said: "We were a very close family, perhaps *too* close." However he meant it, he could not have been thinking of his brother and father, for their relationship was at best a truce. The father never knew what his namesake might perpetrate, not only off stage but on. There was a scene in *Monte Cristo* in which Jamie, dressed in doeskin tights and a Hussar's jacket, had to kneel for a blessing from Abbé Busoni, one of Dantès's impersonations. Sometimes as he kneeled Jamie would tear a piece of muslin, hidden beneath his jacket, to make it sound as though his tights had split. Mr. O'Neill, whose face reddened beneath his make-up each time this happened, used to storm afterward, "One of these days it's really going to happen. Your tights are too small, you're putting on weight from all your boozing." Even more disturbing to his father, and to women in the audience, were the times Jamie wore the tights without undergarments, leaving his genitals clearly defined.

Whenever he sensed that he had about exhausted his father's patience, he would behave more or less properly for a time. His mother's presence had a restraining effect on him, but she increasingly remained behind. Sometimes she stayed with the Sheridans, her cousins in New London, generally when James was touring in New England and could spend weekends with her, or she would remain at the New York apartment if he was playing near the metropolitan area. There were also the times she was in a sanatorium — times Jamie was usually at his worst. The family had some idea, from things she said, of the hell she went through during a "cure."

On the road Jamie often stayed not at a hotel but in a whorehouse; returning the compliment, the madam and girls would attend a matinee, generally sitting in a box next to the stage, conspicuous with their painted mouths, colorful boas and other bright plumage. Mr. O'Neill on catching sight of them from the wings would mutter that he could dispense with their patronage, as company members nudged one another. If the company settled anywhere for a week or so, Jamie and a kindred spirit among the actors would find lodgings separate from the others, for greater freedom to enjoy themselves.

Not infrequently his good times led to repercussions. Once, after a New Year's Eve party at the St. Francis Hotel in San Francisco, Jamie and an actor named Bouton staggered off to their lodging house, had more drinks and finally dropped off to sleep, but not before their quarters was a shambles; Jamie had gone berserk. An angry landlady appeared at the stage door the following day and was referred to stage manager John O. Hewitt. After listening to her tale of destruction and conferring with Mr. O'Neill, Hewitt paid her the eighty dollars she loudly demanded. A few minutes later as father and son were standing in the wings, the former slowly eyed his namesake from head to foot and — alluding to his birth in that city — said in a measured voice to those nearby: "Ladies and gentlemen . . . you see before you . . . my son of the golden West!" He ended with what is known today as a Bronx cheer, and marched off to his dressing room.

His outburst was unusual. He would stand in the wings, watching Jamie perform, and shake his head: "I can't understand a son of mine being such a poor actor." He would complain to old friends like William Connor, his advance man for years, and George Tyler; but in public, even within the confines of backstage, he showed little reaction to his first-born's provocations. He gave the impression that he retained a much-tried fondness for his son, and in interviews would generously refer to him as "very talented." Hewitt, a member of the company for three years, was surprised at Mr. O'Neill's forbearance, often wondering why he did not assert himself, but James knew it would be useless. Hewitt, under standing orders to check Jamie's quarters whenever the troupe was leaving town, often found him still sleeping off his night's drinking and bundled him onto a train with only minutes to spare.

The stage manager's worst time came in St. Louis when the reigning favorite of a lavishly appointed ten-dollar brothel — the usual fee was two — fell in love with Jamie and he claimed to be serious about her; she was going to set him up in business, he said. Every night after the performance her barouche, with coachman, was waiting for him, and toward the end of the week he told Hewitt that he was going to remain behind. He finally agreed to leave with the troupe if arrangements were made for her to join him several weeks later in Kansas City. By the time they reached there, Hewitt recalled, he had forgotten his "redheaded Zaza

Eugene, left, at Betts Academy in 1905

O'Neill and Earl C. Stevens en route to Honduras, photographed October 16, 1909, O'Neill's twenty-first birthday

Kathleen Jenkins O'Neill, the playwright's first wife

from St. Louis" in a new infatuation. When in his cups he was apt to reel off something from the fin-de-siècle poets, especially Wilde's "The Harlot's House" or the well-known Dowson verse:

Surely the kisses of her bought red mouth were sweet;
But I was desolate and sick of an old passion,
When I awoke and found the dawn was gray:
I have been faithful to thee, Cynara! in my fashion.

There was a Cynara in his life: his mother. While this was not evident in his years of dissipation, it would be proven by time. A heavy drinker since youth, he quit cold right after his father's death, once he had his mother to himself, and never touched a drop until she lay dying; at that point he began drinking more heavily than ever, determined, probably unconsciously, to drink himself to death as early as possible. But other than Eugene eventually, practically no one saw the desperate soul behind the jaunty mask.

He always came off the road with stories for his favorite audience, his brother; Jamie, lips twitching with silent laughter as he told of his escapades, Eugene grinning with his eyes, were a familiar picture when they got together. "Thick as thieves," the father used to say. He envied their relationship, for he could never get close to either, and resented it; he suspected that he was generally the butt of their stories. Beyond all this, however, he was concerned over his older son's influence on the other; it was evident Eugene was patterning himself on Jamie.

Where he had once been among the shyest at Betts, the other youngsters now found him quite a sport, as a sampling of their memories indicates: "If he was not much older than the rest of us, he certainly was more mature. He had a dry sense of humor and used to talk amusingly about his weekends in New York. He was moody sometimes and could be quite cynical, but mostly I remember his humorous way of talking. . . . He was reading books about sex, plays that were pretty frank about marital problems. . . . He used to tell us about visits to Rector's, Sherry's, Churchill's, and liked to recite risqué verse — at least it seemed risqué then. . . . He once invited me to visit him in the city, but I was only a country boy and knew I wouldn't fit in. He was just too fast for me, and I was sure my family would never let me go. In fact, I never asked them."

Eugene began drinking, he told a friend, at fifteen, leaving the impression he meant not an occasional glass but serious drinking; it was shortly before he reached fifteen that he learned of his mother's addiction. He displayed little interest in Stamford girls of his own age, seeming in fact rather abashed around them, yet impressed his schoolmates by talking familiarly of chorus girls and actresses. The other boys got the idea he liked his women mature.

As the son of a prominent actor he had free access to almost all the Broadway shows — "professional courtesy" was in those days a general practice. And through Jamie, who seemed acquainted with nearly everyone in the theater, he met a good many performers socially, among them Lotta Faust, a toast of the town for her "Sammy" song in *The Wizard of Oz*, and Elphie Fay, a comedienne, who was having an affair with Jamie under the impression that his intentions were honorable. "Yes," she told a reporter, "we are thinking of matrimony, but so far we have not summoned up nerve to break the news to Papa O'Neill. I don't know how he will take it but we are both serious, and that will help some, don't you think?"

As Eugene tagged along with Jamie and his sporty friends on their rounds of the smart dining places, in an atmosphere of crystal chandeliers, soft music and well-dressed patrons, he felt that he was making rapid strides toward manhood. Actresses and other women around Broadway, touched by his youth and polite manners, made much of him. He later said of this period, "While other boys were shivering themselves into a fit of embarrassment at the mere thought of a show girl, I really was a wise guy." But it is closer to the truth that he *worked* at being a "wise guy." He could never enter wholeheartedly into the pursuit of pleasure; he was in fact less sophisticated than his schoolmates — and he himself — imagined, less receptive at bottom to his brother's tutelage than he appeared.

Glossing over his mode of living, Jamie liked to think of prostitutes as "fascinating vampires," a view he tried to implant in his brother. Eugene, once he had overcome his native fastidiousness, tended to think of them as victims of society, as evidence of the injustice and cruelty of life. The second play he ever wrote was about a tubercular prostitute at the mercy of a pimp; the opening lines of *The Web*, a revealing title in itself, tell the story: "Gawd, what a night — and me out walking the streets with this cough. What a chance I got! And he'll make me go, too, damn him!"

The battered heroine of *The Web* was the first of many such outcasts he would write about. In the process he went from one extreme to the other: he drew them realistically as both exploiters and exploited, he sentimentalized them, he turned mystical over them, he portrayed them as harpies, he even, once or twice, virtually apotheosized them. Though writers have always been fascinated by fallen women, few have been so obsessed by the subject, few have rung so many variations on the theme as O'Neill.

His sexual initiation was traumatic. Though Jamie once said, "Gene learned sin more easily than other people. I made it easy for him," the latter had other thoughts on the score. His initiation at a time his mind was full of Swinburne was more truly Swinburnean than he could have known; the English poet, an unhappy soul whose torrid dactyls and lascivious anapests were born of a famished love life and an orgiastic imagination, would have sympathized with the Betts schoolboy. On one of his weekends in New York, Jamie, deciding it was time his brother became a man, took him to a whorehouse. Decades later the memory was still painful to Eugene as he talked about it to his wife, Carlotta Monterey. "Gene told me it wasn't even one of the better houses," she recalls. "The girls were such terrible creatures they forced whiskey down his throat, with Jamie helping them, and they tore off his clothes — he was fighting them. He wasn't ready for that. He was reading a lot of poetry in those days. But later on he made himself at home in them, in the whorehouses."

His unhappy experience was on his mind apparently when he set Charlie Marsden of *Strange Interlude,* an overly fastidious writer, to thinking about his introduction to sex: "Ugh! . . . always that memory! . . . prep school . . . Easter vacation . . . Fatty Boggs and Jack Frazer . . . that house of cheap vice . . . why did I go? . . . Jack, the dead game sport . . . 'Take her!' . . . daring me . . . I went . . . miserably frightened . . . what a pig she was! . . . pretty vicious face under caked powder and rouge . . . lumpy body . . . slums of Naples . . . 'What you gawkin' about? Git a move on, kid' . . . I *was* only a kid! . . . sixteen . . . test of manhood . . . ashamed to face Jack again unless . . . fool! . . . I might have lied to him! . . . But I honestly thought that wench would feel humiliated if I . . . oh, stupid kid!"

After Eugene's reluctant initiation he went on to lead a sex life more active, more uninhibited than that of most of his generation. His excesses were an expression not only of youth but of his general rebellion against society, of his drive to free himself from conventional attitudes. Yet there would always remain in him a residue of puritanism, of regarding sex as immoral, a result to some extent of his Catholic indoctrination. Catholicism, with its veneration of the Virgin Mary, its idealization of virginity and emphasis on woman as mother, fosters guilt feelings about the flesh; and of all the national expressions of Catholicism, Irish Catholicism is perhaps the most puritanical. But an even stronger influence on O'Neill was his personal environment. The prevailing tone of the

O'Neills' family life, despite their contact with the sensuous, permissive world of the theater, was set by Ella's virginal personality. Ella, from all indications, was sexually inhibited and lacking in sensuality; her drug addiction clearly signaled a retreat from the responsibilities and obligations of her position, including those as a sex partner.

In *The Great God Brown,* in one of the most touching passages in all of O'Neill, the autobiographical Dion Anthony reminisces about his mother: "I remember a sweet, strange girl, with affectionate, bewildered eyes as if God had locked her in a dark closet without any explanation. I was the sole doll our ogre, her husband, allowed her and she played mother and child with me for many years in that house until at last through two tears I watched her die with the shy pride of one who has lengthened her dress and put up her hair. . . . She lived long and aged greatly in the two days before they closed the coffin. The last time I looked, her purity had forgotten me, she was stainless and imperishable, and I knew my sobs were ugly and meaningless to her virginity."

Eugene derived one kind of education from his nocturnal excursions with Jamie; he began another kind on the day, wandering in midtown Manhattan, he decided to explore a shop at 502 Sixth Avenue, just off 30th Street. He was always poking around bookstores but this one was different, justifying its name — the Unique Book Shop. Though its frontage was only six feet and the interior far from capacious, it was the outlet, Benjamin R. Tucker claimed, for "the largest collection of advanced literature in the world." He ran the place not for profit but to advance his cause. A deceptive-looking man whose dignified manner and conservative dress suggested a bank president or a stock broker, Tucker, in his fifties when Eugene met him, was one of America's leading radicals, the chief spokesman of "individualist anarchism."

Tucker, according to O'Neill, greatly influenced his "inner self." An American original, born in Massachusetts of Quaker and Colonial stock, Tucker could read fluently at two and, one of his biographers reports, was only four when he discovered that the Episcopal Prayer Book had misquoted Scripture. After such a beginning it was inevitable that he should grow up an independent soul; before turning eighteen he had been, in his words, "an atheist, a materialist, an evolutionist, a prohibitionist, a free trader, a champion of the legal eight-hour day, a woman suffragist, an enemy of marriage, and a believer in sexual freedom." His conversion at eighteen to anarchism "dissipated some of [his] old beliefs and confirmed others." Far from considering himself unpatriotic, he held that anarchists were "simply unterrified Jeffersonian democrats."

His brand of anarchism favored education and propaganda over force and violence to achieve its aims. "Neither the ballot nor the bayonet is to play any great part in the coming struggle," he wrote. "Passive resistance is the instrument by which the revolutionary force is destined to secure in the last great conflict the people's rights forever." Generally hard pressed for funds until he came into a moderate inheritance, he nevertheless managed from an early age to spread himself wide and noticeably; as writer, speaker, publisher, book dealer, translator, he was virtually a one-man revolutionary movement. Always quick to speak out for the individual, he earned Walt Whitman's gratitude when the latter was under fire. "Tucker did brave things for *Leaves of Grass*," the poet said, "when brave things were rare. I could not forget that. . . . I love him: he is plucky to the bone."

His reputation was largely based on his own magazine, *Liberty*, the first number of which stated: "This journal will be edited to suit its editor, not its readers. He hopes that what suits him will suit them; but, if not, it will make no difference." And he held to that stand throughout the journal's twenty-odd years of irregular existence — it appeared whenever he was in funds — and original format. Bernard Shaw, who was first published in America by Tucker, once observed that his magazine "appeared to be in verse because the lines were not 'justified' [made the same length by the printer] to save needless expense." But if it looked amateurish, it was well written, much of it by the editor himself, and had an influence on adventurous minds well beyond its limited circulation, never more than six hundred subscribers.

One of the first things Eugene noticed on entering the shop was a sign which read: "Aggressive, concise anarchistic assertions and arguments, in sheets, gummed and perforated, to be planted everywhere as seed for thought. There is no better method of propagandism for the money." The stickers were only three cents a hundred if bought in lots of more than two hundred.

Finding the atmosphere to his liking, the Betts schoolboy proceeded to make himself at home and soon learned the layout of the place: books and pamphlets in English on the counter down the center, writings in German against one wall, French and Italian authors on the other side. Proudhon, John Stuart Mill, Thoreau — his "The Duty of Civil Disobedience" in pamphlet cost ten cents — Tolstoi, Gorki, Zola, Ingersoll, Kropotkin, virtually all shades of advanced thought were represented, not only concerning government, economics and religion but about sex, marriage and eugenics. As part of his faith, Tucker believed in free love, and he lived as he thought; in middle age he fell in love with a girl somewhat younger, fathered a child by her and remained devoted to her to the end of his long life, but never married her. Marriage, he held, was unjustly imposed by society, by the established force known as government. He was for similar reasons an atheist: belief in a divine being entailed obedience to an authority outside himself.

At bottom, beneath his espousing the views of Proudhon et al., he essentially was a utopian Yankee; launched into life in a milieu of self-reliance and self-improvement, nurtured on the "very radical preaching" of a Unitarian minister in New Bedford and the brave tenets of Phillips, Garrison and Emerson, he felt that man is inherently good. Despite his clear view of the way the world wags, he thought that man, left to his own devices, could create a paradise on earth, a stateless society. Liberty, he maintained, was a "sure cure for all vices." He advocated among other things "the right of the drunkard, the gambler, the rake, and the harlot to live their lives until they shall freely abandon them." He had little doubt that the errant souls, once free of all censure and restraint, would see the light and reform.

Eugene regularly dropped into the shop during his weekends in New York, not only to buy some of the literature but, haunted by his Catholic-bred conscience and nagged by guilt feelings, to take heart from the other's dauntless spirit. Eugene was only one among many, for Tucker attracted the idealistic, rebellious young; his assured personality and solid fatherly appearance lent weight to his radical views. A journalist who looked over the shop noted that most of the patrons were "well dressed, seemingly well educated young men, whose mental processes have led them into out of the way or unconventional intellectual channels."

On one of his visits Eugene picked up a copy of Shaw's *The Quintessence of Ibsenism*, his interest in the author aroused by a current uproar over *Mrs. Warren's Profession*. The play, part of a Shaw series starring Arnold Daly, had been blasted by the press (Smells to Heaven . . . Nasty . . . A Disgrace . . . The Limit of Stage Indecency) and closed by the police after one performance. The O'Neill boys, always on the alert for something with which to bait the father, were jubilant that Liebler & Co., James's producers, had sponsored the series. Carrying home the controversy, which raged for weeks as the leading actors awaited trial, the two had a fine time defending the writer to their father. Eugene read his book with rising excitement, for the Irish iconoclast said in accents of certainty and irreverent humor all the things that the boy, trying to root out his conventional, Catholic heritage, wanted to hear.

Promulgating rather the quintessence of Shavianism than of Ibsenism, the book attacked obedience: "Every step of progress means a duty repudiated and a scripture torn up." Attacked organized religion: ". . . only reductions of the relations between man and God to the basis of the prevalent Commercialism, showing how God may be cheated, and how salvation can be got for nothing through the blood of Christ by sweaters, adulterators, quacks, sharks, and hypocrites." Attacked the economic order: ". . . poverty is mainly the result of organized robbery and oppression (politely called Capitalism)." Attacked the glorification of family life: "The family as a beautiful and holy natural institution is only a fancy picture of what every family would have to be if everybody was to be suited, invented by the minority as a mask for the reality, which in its nakedness is intolerable to them."

As Eugene read *Quintessence* he marked in red ink everything he agreed with and ended with a book in which every page was aflame with color. The book sharpened his disdain for, among other things, his father's theater — a theater, he once said, in which "virtue always triumphed and vice always got its just deserts. . . . A man was either a hero or a villain, and a woman was either virtuous or vile." From Shaw he learned that Ibsen had written plays in which a woman brings tragedy on herself and her son through her adherence to the standard moral code (*Ghosts*); in which a woman acts nobly, in the playwright's view, by walking out on her husband and small children (*A Doll's House*); in which a heroic idealist causes "more intense suffering by his saintliness than the most talented sinner could possibly have done with twice his opportunities" (*Brand*); in which a doctor trying to protect the community is denounced by all as "an enemy of the people." Ibsen further, he learned, trafficked in such daring subjects as incest, venereal disease, and marriages in which husbands and wives destroyed one another.

Small wonder, then, that Eugene's schoolmates found him old for his years and sophisticated: he was parroting not only the life-weary tones of the fin-de-siècle poets but the radical ideas he picked up through Tucker's bookshop. His father considered his favorite authors a dangerous, corrupting influence, and urged him to stick with the classics, above all with Shakespeare; everything worth knowing, he maintained, was already "nobly" said in Shakespeare. Eugene instead made the acquaintance of Emma Goldman through her new magazine, *Mother Earth*, and to his father's anxiety began echoing her views.

To James O'Neill, as to all right-minded citizens, Emma Goldman was anathema. A Russian-born Jewess who had early rebelled against her dictatorial father, she was passionately committed to economic justice and social freedom for all; as a labor organizer, as a strike leader, as a writer, as a speaker — she was an emotional, inspiring speaker — she was one of the most notorious women in public life, feared by the vested interests and hounded by the authorities. A soldier who previously had been decorated for bravery was court-martialed and sentenced to five years in prison for merely shaking hands with her at a public meeting. Among Emma's great offenses was that in a time when people worked sixty and seventy hours a week she dared to advocate an eight-hour day. At a rally in New York during a period of mass unemployment she told her followers: "[The powers that be] will go on robbing you, your children, and your children's children, unless you wake up, unless you become daring enough to demand your rights. . . . demonstrate before the palaces of the rich; demand work. If they do not give you work, demand bread. If they deny you both, take bread. It is your sacred right." After this speech, she was charged with inciting to riot (the meeting had been orderly) and sent to Blackwell's Island for a year. But nothing cooled her ardent spirit. Once out of prison, she went on organizing, writing, agitating.

Emma Goldman became one of O'Neill's idols, though without Tucker's blessing, for he and Emma were archrivals, leaders of opposing schools of anarchism; where the New Englander advocated a calm, reasoned approach to revolution, she plumped for strikes, demonstrations, direct mass action. Their feud went back to the early 1890s, when her lover, Alexander Berkman, was sent to prison for attempting to slay Henry C. Frick, the steel magnate; Berkman had wanted to avenge the workmen killed during the bloody lockout at Homestead Steel. Emma never forgave Tucker for his refusal to support the campaign to free her comrade and, a still worse grievance, for his editorial stand: "The hope of humanity lies in the avoidance of that revolution by force which the Berkmans are trying to precipitate. No pity for Frick, no praise for Berkman — such is the attitude of *Liberty* in the present crisis."

Life at school seemed pallid and futile to Eugene, the precepts on which he had been reared, timid, false and hypocritical, compared with the things he learned from Tucker's bookshop and Emma Goldman's magazine. Later in two plays he was to give glimpses of himself during this period. In *Days Without End* the hero's uncle, a kindly, understanding priest (he bears some resemblance to James O'Neill), recalls his nephew's youth with affectionate mockery: "First it was Atheism unadorned. Then it was Atheism wedded to Socialism. But Socialism proved too weak-kneed a mate, and the next I heard Atheism was living in free love with Anarchism, with a curse by Nietzsche to bless the union." In *Ah, Wilderness!*, set in summer 1906, seventeen-year-old Richard Miller (Eugene's age at the time) arouses both concern and amusement in the Miller household with his radical sentiments: "I don't believe in this silly celebrating the Fourth of July — all this lying talk about liberty — when there is no liberty! No, you can celebrate your Fourth of July. I'll celebrate the day the people bring out the guillotine again and I see Pierpont Morgan being driven by in a tumbril!" Mr. Miller: "Son, if I didn't know it was you talking, I'd think we had Emma Goldman with us."

For all the exaggeration and broad humor in the portrait there is a distinct parallel between young Miller and O'Neill at the same age, just as the play's bachelor uncle, a genial alcoholic, is a softened image of Jamie. Like his fictional counterpart, Eugene was full of ill-digested revolutionary theory and critical of his elders, but here the resemblance ends; unlike Richard, Eugene inspired little mirth in his parents, particularly in his father, who had to bear the brunt of his rebellion.

James felt harassed in both his family and his professional life. Besides having to contend with an increasingly difficult son, he was encountering more than his share of disappointments in the theater; his career was for the most part a succession of staggers and halts unless he took refuge on the road in his perennial vehicle. But his constant recourse to *Monte Cristo*, in addition to his weariness from playing the old role, left him a target for adverse publicity. The New York *Herald*, for instance, ran a full-page article headlined: Do Long Runs Weaken the Player's Brain? In the center of the pictorial layout accompanying the article was a photograph of James.

The older critics, familiar with his record, were sympathetic, the younger ones impatient toward him. "What's the matter with James O'Neill?" said a columnist in 1903. "With *The Manxman* consigned to the attic, [he] faces the approaching theatrical season with no plans. The spirit of that able and revengeful financier, Monte Cristo, still haunts him down through the corridors of time. . . . [His] career as a box-office favorite seems to have come to an abrupt halt. Liebler and Co. have tried various experiments with this star but invariably public clamor has compelled a return to *Monte Cristo*. . . . The only excitement aroused by his tour in *Honor of the Humble* last season was the conflagration which mercifully destroyed the scenery."

In spring 1904 James was happy to join other stars in a gala revival of a famous old work, *The Two Orphans*, as the crippled hero, Pierre, a role in which he had scored nearly thirty years earlier with the distinguished Union Square Stock Company. It was a warming bath of auld lang syne on both sides of the footlights, an occasion for pleasant tears among veteran theatergoers and members of the company. The production boasted a cast, besides Mr. O'Neill, of Kyrle Bellew, Margaret Illington, Grace George, E. M. Holland and the yesteryear emotional star, Clara

Morris, of whom Sarah Bernhardt said, "She doesn't act, she suffers, she dies." *Orphans* ran for months and toured the following season. James, free for a time from his professional worries, was heartened further by his notices, especially some words from the *Dramatic Mirror:* "James O'Neill's Pierre was the truest and finest thing in the cast. [He] possesses one of the richest and most sympathetic of voices, and he uses it beautifully."

After *Orphans*, James turned for the first time to vaudeville. Once scorned by "the legitimate" as vulgar and tawdry, vaudeville had mushroomed all over the country, acquired respectability with prosperity, and now was paying high salaries for famous names in dramatic sketches. Following the lead of other stars, James announced that he would tour the two-a-day in a scene from *Virginius*, an early nineteenth-century tragedy, and made his vaudeville debut in New York at Proctor's 23rd Street. Shortly afterward, his reception having been less than cordial, he revised his plans.

"Yes," he said, "I am going back to the old piece, and why shouldn't I? The managers and public want me in it, and when you come right down to [it], where is there a better melodrama for love or money? Things have got so now that all there is in acting is money. If animated by a love for art, a man wants to produce a legitimate play, it takes a small fortune . . . and after all this risk and trouble, you are likely to make a failure. *Monte Cristo* is a play that appeals to all classes, from the boys in the gallery to the swells in the boxes."

Over a period of several decades the play constituted a bonanza for James O'Neill; he once estimated that he had earned over eight hundred thousand dollars from the Dumas work. Yet a large part of that wealth proved as worthless to him as the millions he handled on stage as the Count of Monte Cristo. Driven by his old fear of poverty, he constantly tried to augment his money through outside investments; almost invariably they were ill-advised.

"Your dear daddy's queer investments," George C. Tyler later wrote to Eugene "were a continual source of worry to both Will Connor and myself. When we protested, he pooh-poohed. But there was a pathetically humorous side to it all. He was nearly always 'done' by an Irishman! Such a lover of his own people was he that any plausible swindler had simply to possess an Irish name in order to get his ear, and if he happened to have an O' in front of it, all the king's men couldn't hold the dear fellow back. . . . I am awfully sorry to hear that his estate wasn't larger."

Eugene himself once said: "There was no [one] business in which he dropped a fortune. . . . The truth is, he did lose a fortune, and a big one, during his whole career, but *Monte Cristo* enabled him to afford the losses. He was an easy mark for anyone with a spare gold mine, zinc mine, coal mine, silver mine, pieces of real estate, etc. — and he rarely guessed right. But he never went into anything so heavily it could ruin him."

James's accumulation of real estate, nearly all of it in New London, was a particular source of aggravation to Ella and the boys. What he invested in mining stocks he could minimize, if not conceal from the others; real estate was too tangible to hide. The family was irked primarily because, whenever they complained of his being tightfisted, he used the defense that his money was tied up in property. "Land is land," he would say, "and it's safer than the stocks and bonds of Wall Street swindlers." Fancying himself a shrewd businessman, he resented their gibes about his being a dupe of his favorite bar companion, Thomas F. Dorsey, attorney, realtor, toper, and the town character. Dorsey, the O'Neill boys used to say, could hardly wait each year for the arrival of summer and their father so that he could unload another broken-down tenement, another piece of land no one else would touch.

Moon-faced, round-bellied, Tom Dorsey was a Falstaff to the sports around town, a terrible example to the sedate, and to his family a casual husband and father — his half-dozen or so children managed to grow up without too much paternal attention. Younger-looking than his years (until age and a full beard gave him a patriarchal façade), he resembled nothing so much as a mischievous boy who had swallowed a beer keg. Stories about him were always in circulation, but no one told them with more relish than the subject himself: The management of the Mohican Hotel, after being informed by Dorsey that the Chinese ambassador was going to stop over during a tour of New England, spent hundreds of dollars for a public banquet and for a streamer across State Street, welcoming the Chinese; the ambassador's tour skipped New London. . . . Dorsey invited a priest to be his guest on the observation train on Boat Day, then told off the father when he appeared with a number of priests. . . . Dorsey somehow succeeded in having a navy destroyer shifted upriver, miles from its designated berth. . . . Dorsey in a disguised voice telephoned his wife: "Madame, are you married to a fat scoundrel named Dorsey? I regret to inform you that he just dropped dead on State Street." To which her weary voice returned, "You stop that nonsense, Tom Dorsey, and come on home."

Though the O'Neill boys resented the real estate man, they could not help enjoying the clown. Eugene, who told everyone that Dorsey belonged in a book, finally used him as an off-stage figure in *Long Day's*

Journey; to have brought him on stage would have introduced too much comedy and thrown the play out of focus and character.

Dorsey once said of Eugene: "Always the gloomy one, always the tragedian, always thinkin'. My God, when he looked at you he seemed to be lookin' right through you, right into your soul. He never said much and then spoke softly when he did speak. Brilliant he was too, always readin' books. We're all Irish around here and knew the type. He was a real black Irishman." A black Irishman, he explained, was one who has turned against his Faith and spends the rest of his life in quest of something else to believe in, something that will give meaning to his life.

Of James O'Neill, the realtor said, "A softhearted man, always good for a touch. He was a great Irishman, a great Democrat [Dorsey was almost the only Irishman in town who voted Republican] and good Catholic."

The properties Mr. O'Neill acquired through his crony were rarely the bargains he imagined but, contrary to his wife's and sons' suspicions, neither did he generally lose on them. James had great faith in New London and its future, even though it had been stagnant since the decline of whaling in the mid-nineteenth century. The trouble was that the old families sat on their wealth, averse both to taking any business chances and to allowing any municipal improvements that would cost them money in new assessments. "I never could get the notion out of my head," a frequent visitor told a reporter, "that New London bore a likeness to a nice, prosperous old gentleman who wore silk underwear and took his morning bath regularly, but loved shabby old outer garments."

For decades it remained, save for a summertime quickening, somnolent. But one year a spirit of get-up-and-go, promising to substantiate James O'Neill's wildest optimism, swept the town, sparked primarily by a live-wire mayor named Bryan F. Mahan; he went into action when it appeared that the largest ocean liners and other shipping were going to be forced out of New York Harbor by inadequate pier facilities. Somehow Mahan persuaded the Connecticut legislature, normally economy-minded, to approve a million-dollar grant for new docks, and excited his towns-people by enlisting the support of no less than J. Pierpont Morgan. As the big-city press took notice, the New York *Herald* said that the new spirit in New London would carry it "to the front as one of America's greatest ports as surely as God made little green apples." Another paper thought that the town's facilities would rival the great docks of Liverpool.

The atmosphere of the old whaling town was electric with anticipation. While Jamie made sardonic remarks and Eugene looked on skeptically, practically everyone else, with their father in the van, was thinking big; half the town seemed to have gone into real estate and promotional schemes to sell to the other half. It was only coincidence that not long before this Edward S. Harkness, an heir to Standard Oil millions (and a prime target of Eugene's revolutionary talk), had established a magnificent estate in the adjoining village of Waterford, and Morton F. Plant, another multimillionaire, had built an even more splendid place on the Groton side of the Thames; but it all added to the smell of money in the air. Streets and sidewalks were newly paved, new parks established around town, over a hundred thousand dollars quickly raised in a campaign to found a girls' college, other money raised to bring in fresh industry, all on the basis that New London was to become another Liverpool.

Things settled back to normal when it developed that the ocean liners were going to remain in New York, yet James went on buying and selling through Dorsey. The boom brought him one windfall: the city, long annoyed about one of his ramshackle properties on the edge of a fine residential section, paid his price of twelve thousand dollars, about three times the rightful sum, and promptly razed what everyone called an "eyesore." James used to boast of the transaction whenever the family criticized his dealings with Dorsey.

But one year, worn down by Ella's aversion to their cottage and the town itself, he told friends that he was placing most of his property on the market and would settle elsewhere. "Mrs. O'Neill's health," said the *Telegraph*, "is not of the best in this climate, which is the principal reason for making the change. [Mr. O'Neill] will always have a soft spot in his heart for New London, he says, and will return frequently to visit his old friends." Several months later, having won Ella over by convincing her she would be even more discontented elsewhere, he was able to announce that the family would remain. At least in New London Ella had her cousins nearby. The Brennans, a chatty outgoing group, were always glad to call and do little services for her; the Sheridans, a reserved and close-mouthed clan, provided a peaceful haven whenever she chose to visit them.

One way or another Ella managed to get through the long empty summers, but the summer of 1905 was particularly hard on her — twenty-seven nights in a row of fog and foghorn. How she felt about it can be gathered from *Long Day's Journey*, as the mother, loquacious from morphine, rambles on familiarly to the servant girl: "It wasn't the fog I minded, Cathleen. I really love fog. It hides you from the world and the world from you. . . . No one can find you or touch you any more. . . . It's the foghorn I hate. It won't let you alone. It keeps reminding you, and warning you, and calling you back."

Confronted with one son talking revolution, another interested in little but liquor and women — all this on top of his old worry about Ella — James O'Neill was hard pressed to retain his natural zest for living; yet somehow he repeatedly bounced back. As the summer of 1906 approached he was in a cheerful frame of mind. Eugene, ending his four years at Betts, had passed the entrance examinations for Princeton, leading the father to hope that college would cure him of his half-baked radical ideas; James moreover had found a new script he liked, *The Voice of the Mighty*, dealing with Salome and John the Baptist, which he was going to perform next season; finally, he was looking forward to his second trip abroad, including a visit to Ireland. He was making the trip not only to spare Ella a summer in New London but to give himself a holiday after touring all winter in "positively the farewell season" of *Monte Cristo*.

From Ireland he wrote his new author, James Slevin, that in London he had seen a revival of Wilde's *Salome*: "He tells his story in most picturesque language, delicate figures, and subtle conceptions, but very little action. You, on the other hand, have presented your play in a series of strong dramatic actions and incidents, painted your pictures with a broader brush and with a more virile hand. His pleases the student — yours will please the people. . . .

"I have been down to the old home and found every familiar place the same, but strange faces greet me on every side. I sat for hours on the old porch last night, thinking of the dear ones departed. . . .

"Ireland is the most peculiar place in the world. Prolific in its benefits to all other countries, it never seems to benefit itself. There is not a nation that cannot boast of some great man, soldier, statesman or poet, originally from this quaint little place. And here it is, as quiet and unassuming as though it had never been the mother of half of the great men of the world.

"*As a sacrificing mother*
Every self-ambition shuns,
So hast thou, my selfless nation,
Lived and labored for thy sons.

"*Oh, thou hero-bearing country*
Write upon the page of fame
Boldly in thy emerald letters
Erin, thy eternal name.

"Now, my boy, all I can say to you is work, work, work. I'll give your play such a production as will surprise the public and managers alike."

This summer, the same one during which Richard Miller of *Ah, Wilderness!* takes some hesitant steps toward manhood, the O'Neill boys were on their own — Eugene for the first time — and they made full use of their opportunity to enjoy the pleasures of New London free of their parents' inhibiting presence. Eugene joined his brother as a familiar face at the Crocker House bar and others around town, including the one in the Winthrop Hotel, down by the railroad station, where sports and traveling salesmen found women out for a good time; the Winthrop bar would later serve as the model for the one in *Ah, Wilderness!* in which Richard meets a prostitute for the first time and retreats with his virtue intact. O'Neill's own experiences at the same age were less innocent; under Jamie's guidance he became well acquainted with Bradley Street, where the brothels elbowed one another and even flanked police headquarters on both sides. It was this summer that Eugene — with the Betts years behind him and Princeton in the offing — began to run wild, his personality to develop a darker, fiercer edge. Not that several months' freedom changed him; it simply sharpened his appetite for doing as he pleased, spurring the forces of revolt rising within.

7

❈

Princeton Undergraduate

"PRINCETON was all play and no work," O'Neill said afterward, "so much so that the Dean decided I had, by enormous application, crowded four years' play into one, and he graduated me as a Master Player at the end of that year."

Allowing for humorous hyperbole, it is true that he got little if anything from his brush with higher education. He entered Princeton in September 1906 prepared to find it lacking, and of course Princeton did not disappoint him; the same thing would have happened had he gone to Yale, Harvard or any other college. Ripe with rebellion against anyone and any institution set in authority over him, he was scarcely in a frame of mind to conform, to adapt to college.

"It was not until I had to shift, mentally as well as physically, for myself, that my awakenings came," he said in 1920. "I was studying Shakespeare in classes, and this study made me afraid of him. I've only recently explored Shakespeare with profit and pleasure untold. . . . Why can't our education respond logically to our needs? If it did, we'd grab for these things and hold on to them."

Shakespeare, as he implied, first encountered at college? O'Neill afraid of him? He was more than slightly exaggerating. Why, Shakespeare had been a member of the O'Neill family so long as Eugene could remember — his father, instead of singing in the bath, used to hold forth as Othello, Caesar, Romeo. Indeed, Eugene himself was fond of quoting not only Byron, Baudelaire and Swinburne but the Master. As for his "awakening" after Princeton, it was precisely because he was already launched on his own quest for answers that he found the curriculum stale, flat and unprofitable. Loti and Daudet seemed hopelessly quaint after Shaw, Ibsen and Wilde; algebra, physics, spherical trigonometry, all required courses — how could they help satisfy his great need to find some meaning in life?

"I am perhaps excusing myself," he said in the same 1920 interview, "for the way I loafed and fooled and got as much fun and as little work as I could out of my one year at Princeton, but I think that I felt there, instinctively, that we were not in touch with life or on the trail of the real things."

He and Princeton were simply a mismatch; he entered the school one of the hungriest minds and best-read members of his class, and one of the least qualified to fit in. He was scarcely college material. The hazing, the prescribed black dress for freshmen, from black garters to black "dinks" or "beanies"; the football crowds, the excitement in the air when "the Team" went up against Yale and Harvard, the school cheers and songs that everyone learned, the "rushes" as freshmen stormed their way over sophomore bodies into the gym — all the cherished rites and observances that gave others the feeling that they "belonged" were the very things that put him off. At the same time Eugene yearned to be part of something larger than himself; he both felt superior to and envied those who belonged, he wanted friends and did not want them, he wanted most of all the strength to stand alone.

In several plays O'Neill was to indicate his feelings about those who bask in campus life. Of Sam Evans in *Strange Interlude* he said that although he has been out of school several years "he still wears the latest in collegiate clothes and as he looks younger than he is, he is always mistaken for an undergraduate and likes to be. It keeps him placed in life for himself." This is virtually a love pat compared with his treatment of T. Stedman Harder in *A Moon for the Misbegotten:* "No matter how long he lives, his four undergraduate years will always be for him the most significant in his life, and the moment of his highest achievement the time he was tapped for an exclusive Senior Society at the Ivy university to which his father had given millions. A not unpleasant man, affable, good-looking in an ordinary way, beginning to take on fat, he is simply immature, naturally lethargic, a bit stupid."

Eugene's attitude is also reflected in one of his earliest one-acters, *Abortion*, which takes place at a college reminiscent of Princeton and concerns a disastrous romance between a star athlete and a poor girl. Significantly, the latter's brother is tubercular and named Joe Murray; O'Neill would later write a play set in a TB sanatorium, *The Straw*, in which the hero, obviously one of the author's self-portraits, is named Stephen Murray. In *Abortion* Joe Murray confronts the athlete, a youth of monied background: "I've always hated all your kind. Yuh come here to school and yuh think yuh c'n do as yuh please with us town people. Yuh treat us like servants, an' what are *you*, I'd like to know? A lot of lazy no-good dudes spongin' on your old men." Although himself among those with well-to-do fathers, O'Neill emotionally identified with the underprivileged, with the outsider.

Since he said little in class, avoided extracurricular activity, and always left it to the other person to make overtures of friendship, he went largely unnoticed at Princeton. In after years most of his schoolmates could hardly remember him and a good many were even surprised to learn that he had been in the class. But the few who did come to know him never forgot him; he was different, one of a kind. On his side, Eugene found the others too ready to conform, too eager to fit in; he was determined to declare his individuality in every possible way. Where most students decorated their rooms with pillows in the school colors, tennis racquets crossed on the wall, pennants and posters to the eternal glory that was Princeton, he had his own ideas of decor. His quarters were on the top floor of University Hall, a sprawling four-story building of early Victorian vintage (since razed) at Nassau Street and University Place.

"You could have knocked my eyes off with a stick," a country-bred youth from the West recalls, "the first time I went to Gene's room. He had a fish net up on the wall, with souvenirs hanging from it, almost all of them theatrical: actresses' slippers, stockings, brassieres, playbills, posters, pictures of chorus girls in tights, and I remember a hand of cards, a royal flush. But what got me was that among all this stuff he had hung up several condoms — they looked like they'd been used. Very gruesome."

Princeton in 1906 was in a transitional stage. Woodrow Wilson on taking over the college presidency several years earlier had, in his phrase, found that "the side-shows [sports and social affairs] were swallowing up the circus [studies]." He set out to change the emphasis. Under his regime the scholastic life shortly picked up momentum and, a year before O'Neill's enrollment, gained fresh impetus from his bringing in fifty young instructors to launch the preceptorial system. "Fifty stiffs to make us wise," the irreverent called them. The old policy had featured lectures to large assemblies of passive ears; under the new system, a handful of students met regularly for an exchange of minds with their preceptor.

Since the social- and sports-minded were largely against Wilson, young O'Neill was for Wilson. He quickly developed an antipathy, however, to one of the eminent men of the campus, Dr. Henry van Dyke, ordained minister, educator, author and lecturer of inspirational outlook, a daintily built man who went about the country delivering creamy expositions of homogenized Christianity, talks with such titles as "The Contagion of Virtue." Eugene later told a friend: "I hold van Dyke in grudging memory because his sermons were so irritatingly stupid that they prevented me from sleeping [in chapel]."

Actually, he had another, even stronger motive for disliking the little professor. As one who hoped to make his own mark in poetry, Eugene resented the other man's literary success; he could leaf through scarcely a magazine — *Atlantic Monthly, Century, Harper's, Scribner's* — without finding the prolific Princetonian represented by a poem or story or article. And the low opinion he held of van Dyke's talent only intensified his sense of grievance. Moreover, van Dyke had a son among the undergraduates who was a star contributor to the *Nassau Literary Magazine*. One of the latter's compositions was a fairy tale in which, according to the *Daily Princetonian*, the "good prince gets the princess and the bad prince nothing, of course, but the old theme is treated with a delicacy and spontaneity which make it new."

Eugene felt that if the van Dykes represented in academic life a standard to strive for, academic life was not for him. He had been at Princeton only a short time when he realized that he did not want to remain four years; but neither did he care to clear out immediately or have to leave at mid-term. For all his boredom in class, resentment about compulsory attendance at chapel, disdain for college life in general, it was preferable for a time to any foreseeable alternative. He attended a minimum of classes, enough to keep from being dropped, spent a good deal of time in his room reading, and early qualified as a "Trenton bird" — one of the fast souls who, unsatisfied with a stein or two and close harmonizing at "the Nass," frequented the bars of nearby Trenton for less restrained drinking. But where most "Trenton birds" confined themselves to beer and whiskey, he developed a taste for absinthe drips. "He used to wander off," classmate D. C. Benton recalls, "into the most fantastic and exotic excursions of the mind that could be induced by wormwood and alcohol." Another student, who roomed opposite him at University Hall, said that "on a number of occasions he came home or was carried home in a condition of extreme and sometimes crazy intoxication, yelling and making all sorts of noise. But beyond checking to make sure he was being looked after, I left him to his colleagues." One time his bar cronies, instead of bringing him home, carried him to the cemetery and left him on one of the historic graves, Aaron Burr's.

Although he got little from Princeton itself, the year was not all "fun and fooling," for he found his own teachers outside the classroom, chiefly through Tucker's bookshop. One book that left on him, in his words, an "indelible impression" was Oscar Wilde's study of fastidious evil, *The Picture of Dorian Gray*. At that disturbing age when man is hardest driven by his goat's hoof and hunger, Eugene came across the book at a particularly impressionable time; increasingly fascinated by the seamy side of life and working toward a jaundiced view of the human animal —

all this on top of his early romanticism — he felt some identification with the decadent hero of Wilde's miasmic tale. Not with his epicene personality but with his steadfast journey into corruption, his deadening of his guilt feelings through greater and greater offense against his better self.

Trying to lessen the contrast between Dorian Gray's luxurious surroundings and his own prosaic quarters, he burned incense in his room and shaded the bare light bulbs with red crepe paper. In place of Dorian's descent to the lowest opium dives on the London water front, he drank absinthe (but told another student he was eager to "try" opium); patronized dollar whorehouses in New York's "Hell's Kitchen," where most of the customers were rough-looking characters in turtleneck sweaters, and visited homosexual bars in Greenwich Village to study the patrons. "He told us about the 'queers,' " a classmate once said, "but we took most of this as just part of his vivid imagination."

Somewhat like American tourists abroad who talk of seeing the "real" Paris, the "real" London, the "real" Rome, when thinking of the most disreputable parts of town, Eugene felt that he was experiencing "real" life in the Village and Hell's Kitchen. But *Dorian Gray* was to him more than a model for letting go. In the midst of its elegant attitudinizing and perfumed writing he came across thoughts as provocative as Bernard Shaw's but probing more deeply into the human condition: "Conscience and cowardice are really the same things. Conscience is the trade-name of the firm. That is all. . . . The terror of society, which is the basis of morals, the terror of God, which is the secret of religion — these are the two things that govern us. . . . Nothing can cure the soul but the senses, just as nothing can cure the senses but the soul. . . . When we blame ourselves we feel that no one else has the right to blame us. It is the confession, not the priest, that gives us absolution. . . . Each man lived his own life, and paid his own price for living it. The only pity was one had to pay so often for a single fault. In her dealings with man Destiny never closed her accounts. . . . Children begin by loving their parents; as they grow older they judge them; sometimes they forgive them."

When Princeton recessed for Christmas, Eugene and his mother traveled to San Francisco for a family reunion that found the father in subdued spirits. He had been forced to schedule more "farewell" engagements of *Monte Cristo*, the new play about John the Baptist having proven a failure. In addition James was saddened by the havoc wrought earlier this year by the great earthquake and fire. "Not an old landmark left," he lamented to a reporter, after touring the devastated area. "What a flood of recollections swept through my mind as I drove through the locality that the player people once favored! There are no buildings now where once stood my usual haunts. . . . Thirty years ago, when I walked along Kearny or Bush Street, I received friendly greetings every moment. Today not a single 'Hello, Jim' saluted me." (Years later Eugene told a girl in Greenwich Village that he had undergone the earthquake, that he had been thrown from bed and in fact had narrowly escaped death when the walls of his hotel collapsed. He gave such a graphic account of the Inferno-like scenes as the city burned, as though the scenes were again transpiring before his eyes, that the girl swallowed his story. O'Neill was persuasive not only because he was imaginative but because he had a visualizing mind.)

Despite Eugene's professed scorn for the theater, there were scattered indications that it interested him. John O. Hewitt of Mr. O'Neill's troupe, who first met him during the San Francisco visit, later recalled that "he seemed to enjoy playing around with the props backstage — the 'thunder sheet,' a large piece of tin with a rope attached, and some coconuts used for imitating the sound of a horse. We used to drum them on a slab of marble covered with a chamois cloth." Hewitt found him polite but taciturn, a well-dressed youth in a loose raglan outer coat favored by collegians.

At mid-term Eugene, squeezing by for a second semester, passed four of his seven courses — English, Latin and French handily, spherical trigonometry by the narrowest of margins. His French instructor, recalling that he had passed him, later said, "I can't just decide whether this is a reflection or not on me as a teacher." Once safely beyond the crucial mid-term point, Eugene became increasingly lax about his studies. More and more evenings were spent in Trenton, where he had found a girl with whom he could stay overnight; his weekends in New York were more frequent and stretched out longer. Yet, in the midst of his dissipations, he maintained a heavy schedule of reading and was constantly in trouble with the college library because of overdue books.

Gradually, without his making any particular effort to do so, he acquired a few friends, classmates who relished him as a "character." Stimulated, occasionally shocked, they were uncertain what to make of him, finding him more than one O'Neill: in general he was quiet, self-absorbed and moody, but after a few drinks could be entertaining as he expressed himself with humorous cynicism. He obviously was worldlier than the rest of them, yet also left the impression of acting more sophisticated than he really was.

"He was very interesting," Ralph Horton says, "but only if you knew him well, only if he bothered to open up." Richard Weeks, another who saw a good deal of him, recalled, "You couldn't always tell whether he was serious or joking, since he hardly ever cracked a smile. One time somebody made a remark about two girls known as 'Slats' and 'Slivers,' and to our surprise Gene — he was usually cynical about women — began defending them: 'Harpies going around defaming those poor girls,' and so forth." More often, according to Warren Hastings, he was apt to come out with something like, "There's no such thing as a virgin after the age of twelve." The other youths heard a good deal about Jamie, what a hell-raiser he was, all the women he had, and got an idea Eugene was trying to emulate his brother.

Hastings once asked him why he always talked about "the manure piles of life when the world also contains rosebushes." Because, Eugene said, both are facts of life but everybody dwells on the roses and pretends the manure doesn't exist. His conversation was laced with profanity ("Goddam it, I'm supposed to turn in a physics paper! . . . Jesus Christ, I could stand a drink!"), but it flowed through his talk as part of his intensity, without being offensive. He was forever quoting Swinburne, Shakespeare, and Byron, and was particularly fond of a passage from *Childe Harold's Pilgrimage* which he used to deliver in a mock-serious tone, at the same time leaving an impression that he meant it:

> *I have not loved the world, nor the world me;*
> *I have not flatter'd its rank breath, nor bow'd*
> *To its idolatries a patient knee, —*
> *Nor coin'd my cheek to smiles, — nor cried aloud*
> *In worship of an echo; in the crowd*
> *They could not deem me one of such; I stood*
> *Among them, but not of them; in a shroud*
> *Of thoughts which were not their thoughts. . . .*

In one of his last plays, *A Touch of the Poet*, O'Neill would use the passage as a leitmotif to help characterize the swaggering, self-deluded Irish protagonist, a man who has come down in the world. He likes to declaim the verse as he admires himself in a mirror.

Eugene's friends — they included not only Weeks, Hastings and Horton, but Raymond Terry, Al Zimmermann, Harold Bates and football player Tom Welch — looked on him as a "wild Irishman." For all his usual reserve, he could be explosively articulate when liquored up. His thick black hair tumbling over his forehead, heavy eyebrows adding exclamation marks to his flashing eyes, arms waving freely, his face flushed, he would hold forth — atop a chair or table — about everything.

Chiefly against everything. His family would have been startled by his torrent of words, the theatricality of his performance. "He would glare at you as though angry," Weeks recalls, "but this was just a mannerism, a reflection of his strong feelings, and didn't mean anything personal."

Almost invariably he got around to attacking religion and, in a scene reminiscent of the street-corner atheists of the day, would declare as he gazed upward, hands clenched by his side, chest thrust forward for the thunderbolt from on high: "If there is a God, let Him strike me dead!" He once told Weeks, however, that he was not an atheist but an agnostic. What kept him from being an atheist was the feeling that there *had* to be Something, Someone, some Purpose behind this life. The human mind, he added, could not comprehend or accept a meaningless infinity without beginning and without end.

Ordinarily his friends could handle him when he turned obstreperous from drink, but he was almost too much for them the night in his room he went berserk from absinthe. With him at the time was one Louis Holladay, not a student but a friend of Hastings's roommate, to whom Eugene had taken a liking. As Holladay told about it afterward, Eugene, eyes blazing, suddenly grabbed a chair, smashed it against a wall, and threw it out the window. Wrenching a leg off another chair, he smashed the washbasin, a water pitcher, other objects, and yanking open the drawers of his dresser was throwing everything on the floor when a revolver fell out. Scooping it up, he pointed the gun at Holladay and pulled the trigger several times, but nothing happened — the gun was empty or had jammed. Holladay dashed out to get help and returned on the run with Hastings, Weeks and another student. They found the place a shambles and O'Neill, wild-eyed, still on a rampage. It took all four of the other students to subdue him and tie him up with bed sheets. Then he passed out.

A gentler side of him was evident occasionally. James S. Dennis, who for a while ate at the same table in Commons as O'Neill, recalls that their group included an epileptic who had a number of seizures at mealtime. "The Negro waiter, a fine person assigned to our room, understood how to cope with these attacks," Dennis said, "because his wife was an epileptic. The usual scenario was S—— on the floor, efficiently administered to by the waiter, with O'Neill on the floor alongside of them, feebly trying to comfort S——. When the attack was over, O'Neill would be back at the table reading. He was almost always reading when I saw him."

In the spring of 1907 O'Neill saw his first Ibsen performance, *Hedda Gabler* with Nazimova. Though it was not until six years later that he

[121]

decided to write for the stage, a submerged part of him was already looking in that direction, evidently, for he saw the play ten times. Only an apprentice, an acolyte who has had the call, would have been so fascinated. The performance, he once said, "discovered an entire new world of the drama for me. It gave me my first conception of a modern theater where truth might live."

Despite his response to the performance, some of his reading was to him equally or perhaps more important. On a visit to his favorite book-shop he found Tucker enthusiastic about a book he had just published, one he regarded as "the greatest work of political philosophy and ethics ever written" — Max Stirner's *The Ego and His Own,* subtitled "The Case of the Individual Against Authority." With Germanic thoroughness Stirner took on the State, the Press, Parents, Family Life, Morality, Education, Liberalism, Socialism, Communism, Christianity, all religions, in fact, all schools of thought, and demolished just about everything in sight and ever known to civilization in favor of individualism inviolate, anarchism in its ultimate form.

"What's good," wrote Stirner, "what's bad? Why, I myself am my concern, and I am neither good nor bad. Neither has meaning for me. . . . *Everything sacred is a tie, a fetter.* . . . I decide whether it is the *right thing* in me; there is no right *outside* me. If it is right for me, it is right. And if for the whole world something were not right, but it were right for me, that is, I wanted it, then I would ask nothing about the whole world. So every one does who knows how to value *himself,* every one in that degree that he is an egotist; for might goes before right, and that — with perfect right. . . . All things," he summed up, "are nothing to me."

Eugene was suitably impressed by this "veritable breviary of destruction," this "striking and dangerous book," as James Gibbons Huneker called it. Yet it came to seem heavy-handed by comparison with another book he found at Tucker's, one of apocalyptic scorn, exaltation and prophecy, shot through with lyric feeling. It was Nietzsche's *Thus Spake Zarathustra,* and it broke over him like roman candles and pinwheels that, instead of flaring out, remained flaming. In 1928, a full two decades after he had first read it, he was asked if he had a literary idol. "The answer to that," he said, "is in one word — Nietzsche."

Like Stirner, Nietzsche attacked all phases of the established order, as well as man's charting of heaven and hell; but where Stirner was a professor wielding a bludgeon, the other was a dancer with a rapier. His book, rich in original thought, parable, psychological insight, and poetic imagery, meant many things to O'Neill. It spoke not only to the youth of eighteen but to the person he wanted to become, not only to the Catholic apostate with a grievance against God but to the homeless soul in search of a new faith; it both eased his feelings of unworthiness, of guilt, and offered support for his struggling sense of superiority. *Zarathustra*, in short, answered to practically all his moods and deepest feelings:

"Flee into thy solitude! Thou has lived too closely to the small and the pitiable." — "But thou, profound one, thou sufferest too profoundly even from small wounds." — "God is dead: of his pity for man hath God died." — "There is no devil and no hell. Thy soul will be dead even sooner than thy body: Fear, therefore, nothing any more!" — "One must still have chaos in one, to give birth to a dancing star." — "And often we attack and make ourselves enemies, to conceal that we are vulnerable." — "Slow is the experience of all deep fountains; long have they to wait until they know *what* hath fallen into their depths." — ". . . it is the same with man as with the tree. The more he seeketh to rise unto the height and light, the more vigorously do his roots struggle earthward, downward, into the dark and deep — into the evil." — "But the worst enemy thou canst meet, wilt thou thyself always be; thou waylayest thyself in caverns and forests. Thou lonesome one, thou goest the way to thyself!"

Eugene found Jamie in its pages, after he had begun to view him in a tragic light: "I have known noble ones who lost their highest hopes. . . . Then lived they shamelessly in temporary pleasures, and beyond the day had hardly an aim. . . . Then broke the wings of their spirit; and now it creepeth about, and defileth where it gnaweth."

Zarathustra even had something to say of Princeton, of all the Princetons of the world: "To all those belauded sages of the academic chairs, wisdom was sleep without dreams. . . . Blessed are those drowsy ones: for they shall soon nod to sleep."

As the pious find comfort and guidance in the Bible, O'Neill used to turn to *Zarathustra*. In 1927 he told critic Benjamin de Casseres that it "has influenced me more than any book I've ever read. I ran into it when I was eighteen and I've always possessed a copy since then and every year I reread it and am never disappointed, which is more than I can say of almost any other book. (That is, never disappointed in it as a work of art. Spots of its teaching I no longer concede.)"

Obviously something in the book, something basic, struck a deep chord in O'Neill. Why, looking beyond its manifest qualities, did it have such a fascination for him, what lay behind his feeling of kinship with the author? Some comments by Walter Kaufmann, the Nietzschean authority, throw light on the question. Kaufmann regards *Zarathustra* as a "major work of literature" but also finds that Nietzsche's "mature thought is clouded and shrouded by an excess of adolescent emotion. Nevertheless, despite the all-too-human self-pity and occasional bathos, the book is full of fascinating ideas; and probably it owes its unique success with the broad mass of readers not least to its worst qualities. . . . what we find again and again in *Zarathustra* are the typical emotions with which a boy tries to compensate himself.

". . . the most important single clue to *Zarathustra* is that it is the work of an utterly lonely man."

Eugene's time at Princeton was drawing to a close. He went through the motions of attending a few classes, taking a modicum of interest only in his English course under preceptor John Duncan Spaeth. Spaeth, recognizing his love of books and his background of literary knowledge, centered his attention on him whenever he chose to turn up, but Eugene's main interest lay in his outside pursuits. Practically every time his friends dropped by his room, they found him curled up in the window seat or slumped in a chair, his legs wound around the chair's legs, scowling concentratedly over a book, a cigarette perpetually dangling from his mouth; he was devouring among other authors Dostoevski, Gorki and Tolstoi, and between reading new books repeatedly dipped into *Zarathustra*. Occasionally the other youths found him writing and, though they never had a chance to read his efforts, surmised that he was working on a poem; besides quoting constantly from the poets, he often threw off humorous doggerel of his own invention.

More and more he followed his own schedule: days full of reading, nights of drink. He spent so little time outdoors that, normally well tanned, he was paler than he had been in years and became concerned about a pinkish tinge in his cheeks, fearing that it might portend tuberculosis. However, he made no effort to cut down on his smoking and dissipating.

In later years various stories arose, some inspired by O'Neill himself, as to the reason for his early departure from Princeton. He told one interviewer that he went too far with "general hell-raising." George Jean Nathan, the critic, who became a friend of his, launched the story that he was expelled for throwing a beer bottle through a window of Woodrow Wilson's residence; perhaps O'Neill, making a good yarn of it, actually told this to Nathan, or perhaps the latter made it up. The Wilson anecdote first appeared in *The Intimate Notebooks of George Jean Nathan,* a book containing profiles of O'Neill and several other writers. To a friend who had criticized the sketches, O'Neill wrote: "I think you are taking them too seriously. I think all those portraits are so obviously written in a vein of kidding exaggeration that they can't be considered as if they were meant to be accurate, sensitively-understanding portraits of whole men. . . . At any rate, mine amused me because I recognized so much of George's amusing biases in it."

Whether or not Eugene was the source of Nathan's story, he later made repeated attempts to quash it. "I *liked* Woodrow Wilson," he insisted in 1948. "I wouldn't have done a thing like that if I had been swimming around in a lake of vodka." And another time: "He's the last politician I ever have had any respect for. It was the division super-intendent of the Pennsylvania Railroad — that's whose window I threw the bottle through."

It all began one night late in April when Eugene and several other "Trenton birds," lingering too long over their drinks to catch the last trolley for Princeton, had to take the train to Princeton Junction and walk the rest of the way. To relieve the monotony of their three-mile hike along the railroad tracks, they threw stones at the glass insulators of the power lines overhead and found a new diversion when a dog began yelping. "Men," Eugene said, "there's a dog barking at us and I don't like it." After tossing stones at the dog, on a porch, and breaking a window, the youths closed in and were shoving around the porch furniture when a man rushed out, the local stationmaster, yelling and swearing; they took to their heels.

After a hearing before Dean Fine several days later, the malefactors were suspended for two weeks, from April 25 to May 8. In June, already debarred from several examinations for cutting too many classes, Eugene ignored the rest and was dropped for "poor scholastic standing."

Years later when leading universities wanted to give him an honorary degree, O'Neill accepted only once, from Yale, as a favor to an old friend, but thereafter declined such offers. To a correspondent in 1933 who said that Dartmouth was ready to honor him, he replied: "I'm no good at these public functions. This one honorary Yale Litt. D. I have will have to last me a lifetime . . . although if Princeton ever offered me one (which, of course, will never be) a morbid sense of humor might lead me to go through with that one!"

8

Father and Son

JAMES O'NEILL now had two problem sons on his hands. "God deliver me," he used to say, "from my children!" Whenever he began comparing his hard childhood with their privileged start in life, trying to prod them toward making something of themselves, they greeted him with bored faces, with stock answers and flippancies; just as he had a stock response to them, said more and more mechanically as the years piled up: "Ingratitude, the vilest weed that grows." The same charges and countercharges were bandied back and forth so often among them that the exchanges were almost like ritual. If the father complained of Jamie's acting, the latter said he never wanted to be an actor but had been forced into it; this would bring the father's rejoinder that he had to do something, he couldn't just drink and whore his life away. If the father told Jamie his face was too Irish for him to be gibing at the Irish, the response was unvarying: "Not when I wash it!" If the boys complained about the father being tightfisted, they could expect the answer that his money was tied up in real estate. If the father assailed them for turning away from Catholicism, they wanted to know what was the use of Mama being so pious, when all her faith had failed to save her. If the father criticized their drinking, they countered that they had inherited their thirst, which always brought his defense that drink was "a good man's weakness," that moreover *he* could "hold it" and had never missed a performance because of liquor.

All three used to fall back on the same apologetic excuse when one of them had thrust too cruelly and instantly felt ashamed of himself: "It was the liquor talking." Similarly, whenever Ella, under the influence of morphine, rambled on with wounding words, they told one another, "It's the poison in her talking."

James never allowed himself to brood for long, if he could help it, over family matters; brooding solved nothing, never relieved matters any, he felt, but during the summer of 1907 he had plenty to occupy his mind. Besides trying to decide what could be done with Eugene, he was busy preparing to open a repertory season in New York. He had long been in the habit of saying, "I object to Broadway, it is not Broadway that objects to me." His family, however, and his friends George Tyler and Will Connor knew better; "the Governor" resented and felt hurt that men less talented and less experienced were bigger names on Broadway.

Already in his sixties and aware that he was too old for *Monte Cristo* — at least in the early scenes as the innocent sailor — James was making a final major effort to establish himself as more than a one-part actor; his hopes were centered on *Virginius*, a venerable war horse that had served other actors well. The story of an ancient Roman who slays his own daughter to save her from the fate worse than death, the Sheridan Knowles play had been hailed in the early nineteenth century as the finest tragedy since Shakespeare — even Hazlitt was enthusiastic. Performed full blare by such trumpets as Macready in England and Forrest in America, it had thrilled generations of theatergoers and wrung from them a sea of tears over the virginal heroine's fate. James, who had played it on and off for years on the road, was now about to give it the full treatment for Broadway, along with *Julius Caesar;* the latter was chosen for reasons of economy, as he could use for both productions the same togas and pseudo-marble columns.

Eugene, with time on his hands, was around the Lyric Theater a good deal, sardonically eying the rehearsals. "Have you ever," he once inquired rhetorically, "seen a production of *Julius Caesar?* Did the Roman mob ever suggest to you anything more Roman than a gum-chewing Coney Island Mardi Gras or, in the case of a special all-star revival, a gathering of familiar-faced modern actors parading uncomfortably in togas?" Jamie, who took his own jaundiced view of the proceedings, went about murmuring in a stage whisper, "Sandals, scandals, sandals, scandals," while Mr. O'Neill worked at kneading his players into passable facsimiles of Roman patricians.

Word of his forthcoming engagement stirred some of his old admirers to reminiscence. "Much good material was sent to the storeroom," said W. E. Sage in the Cleveland *Leader* on August 23, 1907, "when Mr. O'Neill elected to play *Monte Cristo* for so many years. He was, and is, an actor of unusual powers and he would have been a far greater one if he had enlarged his endeavors. When I was a lad and used to haunt the old Academy of Music, he was then in his early manhood, and I have seldom seen a more personable actor: his eyes were bright, his hair curly, his manner graceful, his smile ingratiating. . . .

"Now he is wealthy and he is going to begin all over again. He couldn't have hit upon a better medium than *Virginius*. It is a pompous old play in places and its rolling phrases will fit nicely in his mouth. He will make them resound and clang. But it has its big human side, and there's where Mr. O'Neill will shine even more. He's an Irishman, which is only another way of saying that he has a deep capacity for sympathy. He has lived a half century or more in the world and so knows its sorrows, either directly or, more happily, through others. . . . If *Monte Cristo* hasn't spoiled him, he should give us scenes there that will put tears in his eyes and in ours."

Opening night James, touched by the warm response of an audience full of nostalgic old-timers, made a curtain speech between acts: "Though for the last thirty years I have occupied a somewhat conspicuous position on the stage, I have seldom visited New York. I am sure I don't know why. I am no worse than other actors." He smiled as he said it, as though only joking, and went on. "Tonight's greeting encourages me to say that I intend to be back among you every year of the few years that are still left to me, playing something of this sort, and when I depart for that Bourne from which no traveller returns I trust you may be able to say of me: 'Ah, well, he could do something other than dear old *Monte Cristo.*' "

One critic took up the gambit: "Worse than other actors? Mr. O'Neill has forgotten more about acting than some of our Broadway favorites will ever know. Play other parts than *Monte Cristo*? Hasn't the sorrow always been that he wouldn't play other parts. Only let them be parts that are of lasting interest, that can appeal to modern audiences, if Mr. O'Neill would make his visits to Broadway productive of more than curiosity to see and kindness to applaud a veteran of the Old Guard."

Although James himself won favorable word from practically all the reviewers, his vehicle was roundly panned: "Yesterday fighting an unequal fight with Today. . . . Its construction is almost child-like, its theatric devices worn out and long ago discarded. . . . Virginia is a virtuous idiot; Virginius a comfortable middle-class Englishman interesting himself in politics." The settings were found tasteless, the supporting cast, especially several gum-chewing "supers," criticized as far from Roman. At a later performance Jamie was singled out for censure: "James O'Neill, Jr., played Lucius, and ran all the way from Rome to the battlefield without turning a hair in his smoothly plastered locks, parted in the middle — which may or may not have been the style 450 B.C."

Once again, with *Virginius* and *Caesar* drawing poorly, James had to dust off Edmond Dantès. "It was the same old play acted in the same old way," commented the New York *Herald* on September 8. " 'The world is mine' tableau seemed as popular as ever and caught the house in much the same way as formerly. The audience no doubt considered Mr. O'Neill quite as good as ever."

Hanging around the Lyceum, Eugene increasingly sought out the press agent his father had hired this fall, James Findlater Byth, a cheery bantam with a homemade sort of face, a sense of humor that was generally directed against himself, and an impressive capacity for drink. There was something vulnerable and disarming about him, an abiding immaturity, that his drinking and constant talk of drink served only to emphasize. He suggested a fallen cherub, a youngster who had jumped into middle age without ever growing up.

It was fortunate for O'Neill, generally so wary of people, that he developed a real fondness for his father's new employee; if "the luck of the Irish" is more than a myth, it was at work when the two became friends. Byth would be at hand a few years later when Eugene attempted suicide in a flophouse on the New York water front; Byth was the one who saved him. O'Neill later would make several attempts to bring him alive on the printed page, not only from gratitude and affection but from sorrow over his wasted life and violent end — Byth was to succeed, where Eugene had failed, in killing himself at the water-front dive known as "Jimmy the Priest's."

No shadows darkened their relationship, however, as they became acquainted. Eugene, a good listener, enjoyed the press agent's low-pressure flow of gab, the casually dropped stories about his colorful past. In time Eugene heard about the fine Byth estate, including the "old manor house, the farms, the game park," that covered the greater part of a county in Scotland — "all heavily mortgaged," though, the other confessed; about Jimmy as an undergraduate at Edinburgh University, as a journalist in Scotland and London, as a Reuters correspondent in the Boer War, about his decline in family favor as he developed into the black sheep of the Byths. And eventually Eugene, when the other was deep in his cups one day, heard about the domestic tragedy that had launched him on liquor. It happened, Jimmy said, during the war in Africa; returning home to Cape Town from the front, unexpected, he found his wife in bed with one of his best friends. "In *flagrante delicto*," he murmured, "in *flagrante delicto*."

Though skeptical about certain parts of Byth's autobiography, particularly his story of a rich aunt of ninety who was going to leave him all her money, O'Neill accepted that he came of good family in Scotland, that he had had an eventful journalistic career, Boer War and all. As for the story about catching his wife in the act with his friend, maybe yes, maybe no; if it did happen, Eugene figured, Byth was simply using it to justify, chiefly to himself, his chronic thirst.

The only thing wrong with Eugene's amiable suspicions was that they failed to go far enough. There was in his friend's background no eminent family and fine country place in Scotland, no Edinburgh University or career as a wartime Reuters correspondent. Jimmy Byth — whom O'Neill eventually was to immortalize as "Jimmy Tomorrow" in *The Iceman Cometh* — was a fraud, an innocent, harmless one, yet still a fraud. On his death certificate he was listed as an "actor" (the Actors Fund of America paid for his funeral), but whether or not he ever appeared on the stage, he gave a performance much of his life.

James Findlater Bythe (he eventually dropped the "*e*") was born not in Scotland but, in 1866, in a hamlet named Church Town near the toe of Cornwall, only some fifty miles from the birthplace of another important figure in O'Neill's life — Sarah Sandy. He was not a scion of landed gentry but the son of an upholsterer grubbing out a lean livelihood in a district populated largely by miners. Efforts to learn something of his upbringing and education have been fruitless, but apparently there was good blood in his family background, for Jimmy was of innate fastidiousness and polite manners, which he often exaggerated for humorous effect. He had a good mind, he was well read. By the early 1890s he was in the United States and working around the theater in various capacities — advance agent for touring attractions, booking representative for a Chicago circuit, partner in a short-lived theatrical agency.

His knowing talk as a former war correspondent came not from firsthand experience in Africa but from doing publicity for a theatrical extravaganza, "The Great Boer War Spectacle, with General Piet Cronje, 'The Lion of South Africa,' and 1,000 Boer and British Heroes of the Transvaal . . . This Sensational Reproduction of Thrilling South African Battle Scenes Is the Most Wonderful, Inspiring and Realistic Spectacle Produced since the Days of Ancient Rome," et cetera, et cetera. First presented at the St. Louis World's Fair in 1904, the spectacle was repeated a year later at New York's oceanside playground, Brighton Beach. During his prolonged association with the show Byth soaked up some of the wartime lore and later enjoyed holding forth on his "experiences" in the African wilds. As he reminisced about Generals Cronje and Viljoen, about Captain Lewis and the flight of De Wet, all names and incidents featured in the exhibit, O'Neill drank it all in. Eventually he would draw on the other's "memories" in depicting two Boer War veterans in *The Iceman Cometh*, even toward naming them—"General Piet Wetjoen" and "Captain Cecil Lewis."

Eugene was not the only one Byth charmed. When Mr. O'Neill opened in Chicago, a man from the *Record Herald* dropped around to McVicker's Theater to interview him but became so interested in "J. Findlater-Byth," as he billed himself in the program, that the reporter ended by virtually costarring Byth in a long newspaper write-up. "When I said that I wanted to know why Mr. O'Neill played the Count of Monte Cristo," Richard H. Little wrote, "and intimated that I would like a complete answer, Mr. J. Findlater-Byth in spite of his proud Scotch lineage looked as if he wanted to embrace me. Instead he suggested that we go somewhere and have a bite. I speak the language of J. Findlater-Byth and understood that by a bite he meant in his mother tongue 'a wee drappie.' "

After the drink, Byth turned the interview into a round-robin discussion by bringing in the company's general manager and the general representative, then suggested that "all hands be piped forward to splice the main brace. The main brace was duly spliced." The conversation centered on Byth when the manager said he "had joined the Boer War when it wasn't looking, as a war correspondent, and had tarried to the bitter end. 'And you are a loyal subject of the King,' the manager said chidingly.

" 'But I was not fighting, old chap,' said the general press representative. 'I was a war correspondent for Reuters. I was not a pro-Boer merely because duty put me among them, don't you understand?' . . ."

Mr. O'Neill being still on stage, the party loitered near the wings and began talking about the trancelike stage he fell into while playing his perennial role. From the conversation quoted by reporter Little, one can get some idea of the mental strain it cost James to repeat, almost as an automaton, the lines he had said thousands of times. "We won't have to grab the Governor," Byth commented, "and shake him and make him take notice when he comes off stage in *Virginius* like we would if he were playing *Monte Cristo*. He loses himself completely in *Monte Cristo*."

The manager corroborated Byth's observation: "When he is Edmond Dantès on the stage, he is Edmond Dantès in the wings until we shake him and bring him back to himself. I always make it a point to be back of stage myself or have some one else here ready to seize him when he comes off in *Monte Cristo* and take him to his dressing room. Otherwise he would blunder around here for I don't know how long before he got himself out of the part. . . ."

After the performance the reporter found Mr. O'Neill in his dressing room, seated on a large trunk marked "Theater," looking thoughtful. "I am as much a prisoner of the Château d'If as Edmond Dantès ever was," he finally said. "The other day I saw in a Sunday illustrated paper a picture of a California redwood tree with the various events of the world's history pictured around in the order they had occurred since the tree began growing. When it was a little shoot, just appearing above the ground, Christ was born in Bethlehem. And so pictured out at various heights of the tree are drawings symbolic of the great episodes of the world. And, while these things were happening, away out in the California forests this redwood tree was growing.

"Do you know, I feel like that redwood tree. Twenty-five years, the time I have been playing *Monte Cristo*, is not long, and yet when I think back over that period I feel older than the California redwood. In that time I have seen great actors spring from obscurity to fame, flourish and die. [Richard Mansfield, who had died just a few months earlier, was probably uppermost in his thoughts.] I have seen careers built up and torn down. Children have been born and grown into men and women. Little towns where I once played one-night stands, or passed by entirely, have become flourishing cities. Inventions never thought of when I began playing Edmond Dantès have revolutionized everything.

"And all this time I have been climbing up on a rock, waving a knife, and announcing that the world was mine.

"Do you wonder I want to escape from it all? I want them to remember me as Virginius, but they won't. I suppose I will be Edmond Dantès throughout the play and down to the final curtain." A long silence, after he had finished, fell on the dressing room.

James O'Neill often found more understanding and sympathy among strangers, people like Richard Little who came around to interview him, than in his own family. Ella, while she would always love her husband, could never quite forgive him for engulfing her in a way of life alien to her. Jamie — his hostility was unwavering, though expressed generally in the guise of good-natured banter. Eugene was becoming, if anything, worse. He ran down the father, personally and professionally; complained to friends of his being miserly, and hit on ingenious ways of harassing him. He once marked a passage of Massinger's *A New Way to Pay Old Debts* and left it, open to the marked page, where he knew his father would find it:

> LOVELL: Are you not moved with the sad imprecations
> And curses of whole families, made wretched
> By your sinister practices?

SIR GILES: Yes, as rocks are
When foamy billows split themselves against
Their flinty ribs; or as the moon is moved
When wolves with hunger pined, howl at her brightness.

Eventually Eugene would have a change of heart. "My father's death," he wrote a friend in 1920, "leaves a big hole in my life. He and I had become great pals in the last two years." At a still later time, he said: "My father and I hadn't got along so well. We had had a running battle for a good many years, and I know there were times when he'd just about given me up. Not that I can blame him. If anything, he was too patient with me. What I wonder now is why he didn't kick me out. I gave him every chance to."

His looking back at his father was almost always from a position of affection and respect, of fond humor. The striking exception is, of course, James Tyrone's portrait in *Long Day's Journey*; but even here, though the play spells out the other family members' gravamen against him and, to a large degree, seems to justify their complaints, the play ultimately, on balance, arouses sympathy for him. One explanation for the harsh lineaments in the portrait is that the author son was depicting his father as he saw him, through overly critical eyes, at the time of the play – in 1912, when the two were at odds. Another answer, perhaps, is that O'Neill was demonstrating that he could take the most searching view possible of his father and yet show him as a worthy, likable person. But finally, in the last analysis, James's portrait should be judged not by itself but in context with the author's intent in the play as a whole: he was digging at the dark roots in the family's history, concentrating on elements that showed why and where their lives had gone so fatally wrong.

In any case, save for *Long Day's Journey*, O'Neill's other retrospective accounts of his father were totally favorable. Where he had once derided the "Irish peasant" in him, he came to value his peasant strength. Where he had long been wont to complain of his miserliness, he later gave a different picture; recalling a time when he was on a dollar-a-day allowance – this was after he was grown up – O'Neill added, "More than I should do in the same circumstances." Again, to Brooks Atkinson, he confessed himself an "A-One snob, where it came to cars and boats, which must have speed, line and class or 'we are not amused.' This snootiness dates back to early boyhood days. My father, the Count of Monte Cristo, always got me the classiest rowboats to be had, and we sported the first Packard car in our section of Connecticut way back in the duster-goggles era."

Where he had once ran down his father's acting, he came to use him as a measuring rod to disparage latterday players. "You can say what you want to about the theater back in my old man's time," he told George Jean Nathan in 1933, "you can laugh at all those tin-pot plays and all that, but, by God, you've got to admit that the old man and all the rest of those old boys were actors!"

Time and again he indicated that whatever was beneficial in his heritage derived, in his view, from James. "My nerves are lousy, it is true," he once said, "but otherwise I have my old man's constitution."

It is impossible to fathom his changed attitude toward his father, his about-face after their "running battle for a good many years," unless one realizes that essentially it was a sham battle — more precisely, a substitute battle — without his being aware of it. It was not until late in life that O'Neill consciously faced what in the depths of his being he had always known, that his standing quarrel was with his mother. He long believed that his feelings toward her were basically those of love and anguished pity, but, as his writings would prove, other feelings were also at work. When he enthusiastically joined in his brother's war of attrition against the father, his fervor, without his knowing it, was largely born of frustration, from being unable to move against his primary target — a guilt-ridden drug addict who crumpled at the first unkind word or, even worse, used a line of defense that stirred up all his own guilt feelings. The darkness and bitterness in O'Neill demanded a worthy opponent; his father, who had broad shoulders, was made to order for the role.

Of course there was more than this in their relationship. It's a rare son without grievances against his father, and Eugene harbored his full share — some legitimate, some inflated, some that were by and large unjust. But beyond this, beyond the normal conflict between the male generations, he needed, as a means of easing his burden of guilt feelings, to think the worst of his father. If James had lingered in barrooms while his young wife languished in lonely hotel rooms, if it was more his desire than her own that she had remained aloof from his troupe, suffering in isolation, but most of all if the doctor he called in to attend her in childbirth was nothing but a cheap "quack" — if all this were so, no wonder she had fallen victim to morphine. She was not to blame. Neither, certainly, was he for being born. It was James's fault, the fault of that "quack" doctor. Eugene hugged all this to himself, yet it brought him little relief. Unlike his brother, his feeling of triumph whenever he scored off the father was short-lived.

The central clue to understanding his relations not only with his father but with his mother and brother as well is that he, unconsciously, was forever on the defensive with all three. Behind his thoughts was always the ghost of a thought that in the depths of their souls they regretted his existence. Had he never been born, the wife and mother would have escaped her "curse," they all would have escaped what that "curse" had done to their lives.

In the fall of 1907 Eugene, his mind full of Nietzsche, Tucker and Shaw, of lines from Byron, Swinburne, the Rossettis, entered the business world by way of a company in which his father owned stock. James, knowing it was hopeless to try to make an actor of the boy or anything else in the field — he was so critical of the theater — found him a secretarial job with Henry L. Brittain's New York–Chicago Supply Co. on lower Broadway, in the Wall Street area of high finance. Though the company dealt in a number of products, Eugene later said only that it "sold ten-cent jewelry, giving an alleged phonograph with one record as a premium to children and seminary girls who disposed of the shabby baubles." It was characteristic of him that he should fasten on the one item, "shabby baubles"; it probably summed up what he thought of his business career, if not all business life.

He took his office duties less than seriously, despite James Findlater Byth's announcement to the press that the actor's younger son had made a "successful debut in the manufacturing business." The job interested him only to the extent that the salary of twenty-five dollars a week financed his drinking and other pursuits. He spent more time in reading, daydreaming, and mulling over his efforts at verse than in attending to the firm's correspondence; one day, in line with his practice of transcribing other men's poetry to improve his own, he copied Dowson's "Impenitentia Ultima" on a Brittain letterhead promoting Kodagraph Home Motion Picture Machines and Films.

Always reticent about his old dream of becoming a poet, O'Neill would later characterize this period in his life as "just drifting," without ambition, with no thought of writing. To all appearances he did seem without purpose. He liked to talk of his favorite authors, trying to instill in others his enthusiasms — Schopenhauer was among the latest — but otherwise seemed interested only in enjoying himself. He was at the time at his most active sexually, both in New London, where he was having an affair with a married woman, and in New York. Constantly on the town so far as his limited funds allowed, he explored Greenwich Village and Hell's Kitchen, frequented the wide-open Tenderloin district, and often dropped into Jack's, a celebrated restaurant at 43rd and Sixth Avenue that was open around the clock, seven days a week.

Located across the street from the Hippodrome, where herds of elephants roamed through the spectacles and battalions of chorus girls disappeared into a tank of water, Jack's put on its own kind of show; it was a gathering spot for actresses and Tammany Hall politicians, newspapermen, sporting heroes and gamblers already a legend in their time, ladies too smartly turned out to be quite respectable and college boys gaping at the celebrities. Various worlds mingled there comfortably under the alert eye of paunchy John Dunston, who used to say in a voice richly Irish, "I give 'em a squar-r-re deal." And he did: his place served some of the best plain food in the city, as well as top-quality liquor, at decent prices. (Strong men wept when Jack's, disdaining the shoddy expedients imposed by the Prohibition era, closed in the 1920s; to listen to old-time literati reminisce about it, it was another Mermaid Tavern.)

While Eugene was fond of Jack's, his favorite hangout was further south on Sixth Avenue, an old yellow building at 30th Street, just a stone's throw from Tucker's bookshop. It was the Haymarket, in the heart of the Tenderloin, an area of saloons, brothels, dance halls, opium dens and gambling dives that originally was known as "Satan's Circus." Built just after the Civil War as a variety theater, the Haymarket was converted in the 1870s into a dance hall and soon became one of the most notorious establishments in the entire infamous area. Listen to an early moralist fulminating on the subject:

"The dives of New York are the hot-beds of its crime. Under the brilliant glare of gas-jets and the seductive strains of music, vice germinates, grows, buds and yields its bitter fruit. The 'dance of death' begins with the Haymarket, grows feeble in Billy McGlory's or the Black-and-Tan, and ends in the river or at the potter's field. A pure girl who visits the Haymarket, if such a one ever does, attracted by the gay scenes and the fascination of the waltz, may feel sure of her own power to keep from going lower in the scale of sensuality; but as surely as a displaced stone goes tumbling down a hillside, she rushes onward to the black fate which awaits her. . . .

"On the outside it is not a particularly ornate building; in fact, by daylight the structure is rather repulsive. At night it shines with the brilliancy of a Broadway theater and becomes animate with the licentious life of the avenue. The easily swinging doors creak half the night with the entrance or exit of depraved women and their masculine escorts."

This horrendous account was written in 1888, the year of O'Neill's birth, but the place had not changed essentially by the time he joined its habitués, as witness one of his early poems, "The Haymarket":

The music blares into a rag-time tune —
The dancers whirl around the polished floor;
Each powdered face a set expression wore
Of dull satiety, and wan smiles swoon
On rouged lips at sallies opportune
Of maudlin youth whose sodden spirits soar
On drunken wings; while through the opening door
A chilly blast sweeps like the breath of doom.

In sleek dress suit an old man sits and leers
With vulture mouth and blood-shot, beady eyes
At the young girl beside him. Drunken tears
Fall down her painted face, and choking sighs
Shake her, as into his familiar ears
She sobs her sad, sad history — and lies!

Eugene was generally accompanied in his Saturday night rounds by Edward Keefe, a dark, sleek-haired youth from New London, who was in New York studying art. Their excursions on the town fell into a pattern. After dinner at Jack's or at Mouquin's, a place favored by artists Robert Henri, John Sloan, George Luks and others for its honest French food and homey atmosphere, the two often had a few beers at the German Village, opposite the Metropolitan Opera House, which was heavily patronized by college students. From there they would wander over to Sixth Avenue, the heart of the Tenderloin, to mingle with a crowd largely made up of streetwalkers, drunks, hustlers for gambling houses and brothels, and sports seeking a good time. Since neither Eugene nor Keefe ever had much money, their pleasure chiefly consisted of looking on; sometimes they dropped into Little Cairo, one of the livelier dance halls, but almost invariably they wound up their night at the Haymarket.

Keefe shared a studio apartment in the Lincoln Arcade building at 66th and Broadway with a blond young giant in his mid-twenties, prematurely balding, named George Bellows, the same who would become a noted exponent of the "Ash Can School" of painting. Though outgoing and friendly, Bellows rarely joined the other two in their nighttime prowlings. Born in Columbus, Ohio, where he grew up "surrounded by Methodists and Republicans," he was a former college athlete who had remained a disciple of clean living; an American Original, an American Innocent, he did not smoke, drink, or chase after women, but without being priggish about it. To him none of this was pleasurable, yet he had a great capacity for enjoying himself. An exuberant overgrown child with a child's appreciative eye for everything, together with an artist's perception, he was in love with the city and found beauty where few dreamed of looking — in, for instance, the drab surroundings of Sharkey's boxing club. Though Eugene was genuinely fond of the artist, he used to rib him about his Y.M.C.A. mode of living, especially after he learned that Bellows intended to remain a virgin until marriage.

In one respect O'Neill was like Bellows, for he too perceived beauty among the dregs, in what is commonly viewed as ugly; but otherwise the two men were opposites. Where the painter was content to be a spectator, the aspiring poet felt driven to take part; he was receptive to all pleasures and experiences. Influenced by his favorite authors to set his own standards and become a law unto himself, he seemed intent on establishing his position beyond the limits of conventional morality. "Gene," Keefe says, "wanted to try everything, wanted to experiment with everything — and I mean everything. He seemed hungry for experience. He once told me of reading about an interesting drug, hashish, that gave you remarkable sensations of time and space. He was eager to try it, he said, because it was not habit-forming. I finally managed to get a prescription from a doctor friend in New London, but for some reason we never followed through. Maybe he feared it was habit-forming."

Had O'Neill consciously set about preparing himself to become a playwright, he could scarcely have done better than to follow his present way of living. At Jack's, at the Haymarket, at various way stations in the night world of New York, he was encountering a wide variety of people who revealed their basic selves under the influence of liquor and in their pursuit of pleasure. In addition he was, as Keefe put it, "always reading, reading, reading." Finally, as his father's son, he had free access to most of the offerings around Broadway and, despite his constant running down of the theater, took advantage of his opportunity to see nearly all the good things that came along.

In his view the good things were not the home-grown products that played to packed houses but the serious importations that pleased only the few. What audience tastes of the day were like can be gathered from something Booth Tarkington once said about *The Man from Home*, a smash hit of the 1908–1909 season he had coauthored. A story of American tourists abroad, it was intended to satirize those who ran down Europe's historic splendors in favor of the sights back home. "So when we built up the Hoosier in our play," Tarkington recalled, "we gave him a lot of this kind of jingo patter. We thought our audiences would be amused *with* us and *at* him, and yet like him as we did. Instead, they cheered all his boastings. . . . They burst with loud patriotic applause when he said, 'I wouldn't trade our State Insane Asylum for the worst ruined ruin in Europe.' The popular success of the play might be called accidental."

While shows like *Polly of the Circus, Paid in Full* and *Man from Home* dominated the stage, the adult-minded could occasionally find plays to their taste — if they were quick to catch the short-lived engagements. In the 1907–1908 season, for example, Arnold Daly presented repertory that included Yeats's *Kathleen ni Houlihan* and *The Hour Glass,* and followed this with a revival of Shaw's *Candida* for thirty performances; the Irish Players, headed by Dudley Digges and J. M. Kerrigan, gave Lady Gregory's *The Rising of the Moon* twenty-four showings, while von Hoffmannsthal's *Electra,* starring Mrs. Patrick Campbell, was put on nine times.

Forever trying to convert others to his way of thinking, to prod them awake, Eugene took Keefe to see *Rosmersholm,* with Mrs. Fiske and George Arliss, and introduced him to Tucker's bookshop, where Ed dutifully bought both *Thus Spake Zarathustra* and Stirner's paean to the Ego. When Eugene was not talking up Nietzsche, he was likely to hold forth on the greatness of Ibsen. "The populace thinks of Ibsen as very dreadful and deep," he once said. "He's deep, all right, and sometimes dreadful, like life itself, but he's also intensely human and understandable. I needed no professor to tell me that Ibsen as dramatist knew whereof he spoke."

Despite his serious nature, there was a side of O'Neill that delighted in the antics of low comedians, in the blare and high spirits of musical shows. He was particularly fond of music, not so much of Schubert, Chopin and other composers he had first heard in his mother's dreamy sessions at the piano but love songs, novelty numbers, the foot-tapping tunes of the day. After he turned seaman, the old chanteys became one of his lifelong delights; and he would also be a great fan of New Orleans jazz and "the blues," of Irving Berlin, Bessie Smith and "Fats" Waller. Like everything else he felt deeply about, music entered into his playwriting; from his early sea plays on through his last works, he would repeatedly use song to help establish mood, atmosphere, period feeling.

As his taste in music suggests, he had a broad streak of sentimentality, but the softer elements of his nature were rarely in evidence to those around him. During this period of knocking around New York he gave every sign, for all the difference in their personalities, of becoming another Jamie, an aimless, hard-living soul who would always have to fall back on a wealthy father. The O'Neill who eventually would shake up the American theater and help bring it of age was well submerged in the youth who made the rounds with Keefe and others, among them Ray Terry, who also had dropped out of Princeton after one year, and Louis Holladay, whom Eugene had met through friends at college.

"Who knows," he said in 1920, looking back on his earlier self, "just what is going on inside of him?" Another time he told Barrett H. Clark: ". . . when my memory brings back this picture or episode or that one, I simply cannot recognize that person in myself nor understand him, nor his acts as mine."

He could have been thinking of his running amok at Princeton, the time he and Holladay were drinking absinthe, or of the time he turned violent without provocation in Jack's restaurant. Ray Terry, who was at the bar when it happened, recalls the incident: "It was a hot afternoon in midsummer and Gene came in. I asked him if he'd have a drink, but without a word he leaned forward — he had long arms — and hit the bartender on the jaw. A whistle blew and the flying wedge went into action — did you know the waiters at Jack's were the first to use the flying wedge to give someone the bum's rush? Anyway, Gene was well pummeled and tossed outside, straight into a hansom cab. I couldn't understand the fellow, why he did things like that. I asked the bartender but he didn't know. There'd been no argument between them, any kind of trouble before.

"A week or so later I met Gene and he had the worst pair of black eyes I've ever seen, almost down to his cheeks. He always had circles under his eyes, and looked as though he didn't get enough sleep. He wasn't in good shape when I knew him. He was hollow-chested, his hands were shaky — from drinking, I used to think, but I understand he had a bad tremor late in life.

"I never really felt close to him, he always seemed to be brooding, till drink brought him out of it. He liked the rough seamy places — 'seeing life,' he called it. Some of the places he took me to, they'd give you knockout drops and roll you. When he had money he seemed eager to get rid of it; I remember our once having lobster and champagne at three in the morning at Jack's."

A few times Eugene took him to Greenwich Village to call on Louis Holladay and his sister Paula, known as "Polly." They generally wound up the evening, Terry recalls, "sitting on the floor and passing around a bottle." For Eugene and the Holladays, who came from the Midwest, it was the start of a lasting friendship. Like him they were indifferent to conventional standards and hostile to the established order, something that was to be expected of their unorthodox background. Their father, according to friends of the family, was a college professor who was shot to death in a St. Louis bordello; their mother Adele, it was common knowledge, got along on the bounty of her lovers. Polly, who had more character and drive than her brother, supported herself through a succession of restaurants that eventually would make her a well-known figure in Greenwich Village. Tall and large-boned, she had a heavy jaw that kept her from being physically attractive, yet there was something appealing about her, a quality of shyness, of emotional depth; her eyes were alive with intelligence and she had a good brow. Women found Louis Holladay uncommonly good-looking; he was large and blond and had a sensual face. For years he made sporadic efforts to become a writer but existed chiefly on a scattering of make-do jobs, the generosity of his girl friends, handouts from his mother and from Polly. Eugene, ill at ease with most people, felt comfortable around Louis and Polly; like him, they were outsiders, rebels who looked down on the obedient herd.

Eugene's job with the Brittain company lasted only a year or so. He later said it ended because the firm had failed, but he was telescoping events; Brittain, who suffered reverses and moved to smaller quarters in 1908 — when Eugene's alleged services ended — did not go bankrupt until three years later. But even had the business prospered, it is doubtful that young O'Neill would have remained there much longer; he had become increasingly restive, despite his light duties, at having to waste his days in an office. Since his sole ambition was to experience "life" and write poetry, his relations with his father, who was at a loss what to do with him, grew more and more strained. To avoid the arguments that generally broke out when they were together, Eugene began to stay with friends — at Keefe and Bellows's studio, with Louis and Polly, sometimes with a new friend named Frank Best, a young advertising man whom he had met through the Holladays.

The elder O'Neills, now living in a suite in the Lucerne Hotel, at 79th Street and Amsterdam Avenue, had few visitors other than two of Ella's cousins from New London, Agnes and Lillian Brennan, who had settled in the city. The sisters shared a small flat in the upper reaches of Manhattan, where Agnes, around thirty, gave piano lessons. Lillian, ten years older, made ladies' hats. Both, though opposite in personality, were great talkers. Agnes, plump and goodhearted, was hard of hearing and talked incessantly to divert attention from her handicap. Lillian, however, had much to say because she had definite views on everything and felt it her duty to tell others what they should do and how they should live.

Once Eugene outgrew his youthful impatience with Agnes for being so garrulous, he came to like her. But he always shied clear of Lillian, who for years warned Mr. O'Neill against the sort of books his sons were reading, urging him to do something about it, and told him that he was not bringing up the boys properly, that he could blame only himself that they were not turning out better. Lil was her mother's daughter; when Eugene's first collection of plays was published (at his father's expense), Mrs. Josephine Brennan dipped into the volume and quickly disposed of it in the furnace. "Someone ought to tell Eugene," she declared, "to get out of the gutter!"

Sometimes when Agnes visited the O'Neills she brought along a young friend, Sadie Koenig, who hoped to become a concert pianist. Despite Ella's general reluctance to meet people, she welcomed the young girl; the latter aroused in her bittersweet memories of convent school, of her own dream of becoming a professional musician. If James happened to be in town, he would greet the callers with a friendly tap on the shoulder and, "Come on in, girls." On several occasions Sadie was mystified by Mrs. O'Neill's manner; she appeared vague, detached, could hardly speak intelligibly. On one such occasion James told the visitors not to concern themselves with her "as she'd had a glass too many." Ella, who had seemed lost in herself, came out of her abstraction and told her husband, "You've had too much yourself."

"I don't think they really wanted visitors," Miss Koenig once said. "Agnes, yes, I suppose, but not me — they were simply being kind." Occasionally Eugene was at the apartment when the pair dropped by and he too gave Sadie something to think about, not only because he smelled of alcohol each time but because he was rude to his mother. The girl was distressed by their arguing back and forth, each accusing the other of taking "too much."

It was a disheartening period for James O'Neill; on top of his concern about Eugene being at loose ends, his career seemed to be running out. In the fall of 1908 he opened in *Abbé Bonaparte,* a sentimental drama that was roundly panned. "Crude, melodramatic, and so talky as to be positively boring," said a critic in St. Louis. Another, in Toledo, was even more lethal: "Better a thousand years of *Monte Cristo* than an evening of *Bonaparte.*" James's frame of mind was unmistakable in his words to a reporter in Indianapolis: "There is many a star who ought to be shoveling coal and many a staress who ought to be over a wash tub. I don't know where the good young actors are coming from. Too many of the younger players are too lazy to study. [Jamie in *Bonaparte* inspired the comment, 'Heredity appears to have failed in his case.'] They want the salary without working for it."

After a few weeks of disastrous houses James closed the play, told friends that the box office always suffered during a Presidential election campaign, and took part in some Democratic rallies in New London for

William Jennings Bryan, who was making his third bid for the Presidency. James had admired the silver-tongued Bryan for his grass-roots liberalism and his oratory ever since his "Cross of Gold" speech had stampeded the national convention in 1896. But the old actor's choice of candidates was no more fortunate than his taste in scripts.

Eugene felt the impact of his father's mood. Reduced to a dollar-a-day allowance, he complained to friends about his father being miserly and worked himself up to a fine state of aggrieved feelings. After reaching a boiling point, he told Ed Keefe, "I'll get even with the old bastard!" Somehow he managed to assemble the funds to hire a flaming redhead from a Tenderloin brothel ("She looked more like a whore," he later said, "than twenty-five whores") and to reserve box seats for a Florenz Ziegfeld musical starring Anna Held, the producer's wife. O'Neill and his companion could hardly have been seated more conspicuously at the show, called *Miss Innocence;* he knew his father would be upset and angry when word got back to him.

Finally tiring of this sterile feuding that brought him little satisfaction, of hanging around the Tenderloin, he thought of an old farm his father owned in Zion, New Jersey. Keefe and Bellows, who wanted to paint some landscapes, readily fell in with his plans. On a snowy day in January 1909 the three young men arrived in Zion and set about trying to make themselves comfortable in the run-down old place, where no one had lived for years. Shutting off the rest of the house, they settled in two rooms and matched coins to determine who should share the one bed. Bellows, who lost, slept on a mattress on the floor. "Bellows and Keefe and I did our own cooking and everything," O'Neill once said, "and damned near froze to death. They painted and I wrote a series of sonnets, bad imitations of Dante Gabriel Rossetti." According to Bellows, the talk among them was "either very high or very low."

After they had been in Zion awhile Mr. O'Neill, impressed by their Spartan spirit, sent them several bottles of whiskey and a box of cigars. Louis Holladay paid them a visit but, finding the life too rough for him, stayed only a weekend. The three remained at the farm a whole month and during that time became friendly with Edgar Durling, son of the local postmaster.

"I used to think," Durling once said of Bellows, "he painted the crookedest trees I ever saw. But that was a painter's license, I suppose, just like a poet's." He recalled also that O'Neill "used to laugh about being thrown out of every hotel down around Trenton [a reference apparently to his year at Princeton]. I asked him once, 'Gene, what do you do anyhow?' And he answered, 'Oh, I try a little writing — but I wouldn't tell anybody.' "

9

Marriage and Flight

IN the late 1950s Mrs. Kathleen Pitt-Smith, who was O'Neill's first wife, briefly, and the mother of his first child, sat in her apartment on Long Island and dipped gingerly into the past. Throughout the interview she referred to her former husband as "Mr. O'Neill," in an impersonal tone suggesting that he was someone she had once known but slightly, formally.

"I can't remember how we met," said Mrs. Pitt-Smith, "it's so long ago. . . . We were in a group . . . not that Mr. O'Neill belonged to the group. It wasn't connected with anything, any organization, it was just a group. . . . Frank Best? The name sounds vaguely familiar, but I can't place him . . . I met George Bellows, I believe — Mr. O'Neill took me to his studio once.

"Mr. O'Neill was so different from everyone I'd ever known. He seemed very romantic to a girl of my upbringing. Unlike other young men I knew, he got along without working, he had a small allowance from his father. The usual young man sent you flowers, a box of candy, took you to the theater, but mostly we talked and walked, generally in the park along Riverside Drive. . . . He was always immaculately groomed, in spite of being unconventional; he led a bohemian sort of life. . . . The books he read were 'way over my head. . . . He talked a great deal about his brother, about his sense of humor and being up on everything — no, I never met him. It was obvious he admired his brother very much.

"When I knew Mr. O'Neill he was writing some poetry but he never gave me any idea he hoped to be a writer. It wasn't unusual for a young man to write poems to his girl, telling her how much he loved her, praising her charms, that sort of thing. . . . I was shocked, no, astounded is the word, when I began hearing about him years later as a playwright. I was the most surprised person on earth when he started becoming famous.

"I'll tell you the first thing that made me feel he was a playwright — *Ah, Wilderness!* It showed he was versatile, that he could write plays like anyone else. But why did he write that one about his family [*Long Day's Journey Into Night*], how could he do it? I don't believe in washing your dirty linen in public. How could he write that about his mother? And his father, he wasn't that way, so far as I knew.

"I can understand how his mother became a drug addict — she had it hard! An actor's wife does. . . . No, I never met her, she was sick during the time I knew Mr. O'Neill. I had the impression his father married her out of a convent — she was going to become a nun or was studying at a convent school, I can't remember which. It was the general impression around that she was very religious."

Though Mrs. Pitt-Smith seemed to her visitor to be holding her memories at arm's length, determined to regard them impersonally, the past seemed to reach out occasionally and engulf her. At one point, carried away by her thoughts, by the tide of reminiscence, she let drop that she had been "deeply in love" with O'Neill. In answer to questions, sometimes volunteering remarks, she denied various things that had been published about her relationship with Eugene and his parents. "It isn't true that his father ever ran him down to me. He never told me, 'Why do you want to be married to him? He's a drunken good-for-nothing bum.' There was never any conversation between us like that."

Shortly after he and Kathleen were married, O'Neill began his record of far-flung travel, first to Honduras, then to Buenos Aires. Their child was about a year old when Eugene phoned one day "out of the blue" and came around to see him for the first time; this was also the last time husband and wife ever met, though years later he became friendly with his son and, in addition to other financial help, paid for his education. "No," Mrs. Pitt-Smith said, "we never saw each other again. Why should we? We were two people ignoring one another's existence."

O'Neill for his part, in later years, laconically termed their romance "a mistake." Another time, thinking of his three marriages and several affairs, he said of Kathleen, "The woman I gave the most trouble to has given me the least."

They met in the spring of 1909, when both were twenty. Eugene couldn't help responding to her striking attractiveness, to a faint wistful quality he sensed in her personality. Tall, brown-haired, large grayish-blue eyes set well apart, good chin and stately neck — looks that spelled breeding — Kathleen Jenkins was the daughter of a well-born high-spirited mother and a father of good background but with a weakness for liquor. Charles E. Jenkins had seemed a suitable match when Katie Camblos married him; born in Brooklyn of pre-Revolutionary stock, he was a prominent member of the Larchmont (N.Y.) Yacht Club and working as an appraiser of objets d'art for Tiffany's, the jewelry house. At the time of his marriage, in 1887, he was living at the Barrett House in Longacre Square — the same hotel where Eugene Gladstone O'Neill was to be born the following year.

As for Katie Camblos, she had grown up in the plushy milieu of the Gramercy Park area, surrounded by maids and family coachman, as a daughter of Henry S. Camblos, a member of the New York Stock Exchange and the Union League Club. At sixteen she fell in love with a medical student five years older who returned her affection, but her conservative high-minded father, who carried himself with military erectness into advanced old age, dismissed the youth as "too fast." Katie was thirty when she decided to marry Charles Jenkins, a year older than herself.

Not long after the birth of Kathleen, their only child, the parents moved to Chicago, fortified with introductions to Mrs. Potter Palmer and other society leaders. Jenkins's drinking, however, as well as dwindling funds, quashed any of the family's social aspirations. During the ten years they lived in Chicago there were times the family had insufficient food; Katie, who had had her own personal maid while still a young girl, was reduced to doing her own housework and scrubbing the floors. "But she never complained," her daughter recalled. "She used to say life is too short and precious to waste time on regrets. Mother was quite a person."

Only after the Jenkinses had returned east did Katie's family learn that she was unhappily wed, that her husband was a hopeless alcoholic; she endured his drinking and shiftless ways several more years before leaving him to establish a home for herself and her daughter. They were living in the Clearmont, an apartment house on West 113th Street, when Kathleen and Eugene met. One of her girl friends was being courted by Frank Best. The two couples began to make a foursome.

For both Kathleen and Eugene their relationship spelled a new experience. If he was different from the other young men of her acquaintance, she was the first "nice" girl he had ever known more than casually. At Betts he had shied away from the daughters of good families; while going to Princeton, he had sought easy conquests, if not ready to settle for commercialized sex. Chorus girls and actresses were in a special category; however respectable their upbringing, they were part of show business with its instant camaraderie, its ready mingling of the sexes. "Nice" girls were something else again. He professed to find them uninteresting, and while his attitude was sincere, it is also true that he felt at a loss around them; neither his brother's tutelage nor his own personality had equipped him for pleasant small talk. Kathleen was as new to him, for all his seeming worldliness, as he to her.

During the months of their romance she saw nothing of his dark side; though he would have a sociable drink when the two couples were out for an evening, he never in her company drank to excess. Aroused by her evident interest in him, Eugene ended by imagining himself in love for the first time. He wrote poems praising her beauty and pledging eternal devotion, he read to her the sensual, sweetly sad lyrics of Swinburne and Dowson, while she reacted to the attentions of the intense, darkly handsome youth by falling deeply in love. It was an intoxicating state of being, the two drifting pleasurably under the spell.

Though Mrs. Jenkins shortly gathered that her daughter took more than a passing interest in Eugene, his family was unaware of the relationship until months later. The O'Neills were busy with their own pursuits. Jamie, who had floundered for years as a member of his father's troupe, seemed to have found himself at last; happily free of costume and swordplay, he was touring to cordial notices in a breezy comedy hit, *The Travelling Salesman*. As for Mr. O'Neill, he occupied himself with a succession of activities. Performing an excerpt from *Virginius*, he appeared in the annual tour of the all-star Lambs' Gambol. Elected head of the Green Room Club, he drew praise from the *Dramatic News* on June 12: "New life will be put into this organization because Mr. O'Neill is an aggressive campaigner, and he never permits anything to slumber." To recoup from his disappointing winter James, for the first time since his start in the theater, took on a summer engagement, appearing in *Virginius* at the Delmar Garden, an amusement park in St. Louis. "The audience made up in enthusiasm," said one critic, "what it lacked in size. His artistry unmarred by the unusuality of his surroundings, Mr. O'Neill gave an excellent performance. The shrill cries of merry-makers on the scenic railway at times contrasted strangely with the Roman atmosphere and olden heroism of *Virginius*."

The elder O'Neills and Jamie came and went at the Lucerne, paying scant attention to Eugene, who was becoming concerned about his romance with Kathleen. Though touched by her ardor, indeed flattered, he also was surprised and uneasy that he could arouse such feeling. At the bottom of his reaction was the child whose mother, acting like a stranger, had often shut him out, whose father had left him in a boarding school; at the core of his being he felt incapable of inspiring love, unworthy to be loved. Much as he hungered for affection, a strain in his nature would always urge him to pull back once he had met love with love.

This pattern of feeling, of response and counterresponse, was at work in his relations with Kathleen, though below conscious thought; in the foreground of his concern were other matters. He had no means of supporting a wife, even had he loved her, but it was becoming increasingly evident to him that they were incompatible. His interests were not hers; they spoke a different language. Whenever he talked of Nietzsche and Ibsen, of Schopenhauer and Dostoevski, she was politely interested, but that was it — politely interested. They could never build a satisfactory life together. He would have to do something, find some way of ending the romance; in his quandary he could think only of turning to his father.

Like his son, James O'Neill shows to poor advantage in the entire Kathleen Jenkins matter. Upset and apprehensive, he immediately thought of his troubles with Nettie Walsh in the Chicago courts, and was ready to suspect the worst; he believed that the girl had been influenced by Eugene's having a well-to-do father. Both he and Ella (she wanted to know as little as possible about the new situation) felt that the development was inevitable in the sort of life the boy had led in recent years, but when James tried to play the moralistic father, Eugene reminded him of Nettie Walsh.

The best solution, James decided, was to put a great distance between the two young people, and when he told his son what he had in mind, Eugene was jubilant — a chance for the kind of adventure he had always dreamed about! Arrangements would be made for him to join a mining engineer named Fred C. Stevens who in a few weeks was to leave his home in Portland, Oregon, to prospect for gold in Spanish Honduras. Stevens, due to sail from San Francisco, was being subsidized by a New York mining-stock company, Pryor & Donovan, in which James had invested some of his wife's money.

With that problem settled, Mr. O'Neill turned his attention — none too happily — toward learning his role in a new Liebler production. Scheduled to open on Broadway in late September, *The White Sister* was an emotional tale about a nun and her onetime fiancé, a soldier whom she had thought slain in Africa; Viola Allen was to star in the production, with James playing a secondary role, as a priest, for the first time since he had achieved stardom more than a quarter of a century earlier. As the play entered rehearsal he told friends that he had accepted the role only out of friendship for George Tyler.

His son meanwhile, preparing himself for the tropics, was assembling the proper gear and reading all the books on Central America he could find, as well as tales by Jack London and Joseph Conrad. Feeling reprieved from an untenable situation, Eugene, with mingled emotions of relief and bad conscience, informed Kathleen of the forthcoming expedition. Kathleen, too in love to be suspicious, had no idea that he was going away because of her or that he had even discussed her with his father; it was clear that she expected him to marry her. Though Eugene would have preferred to let matters between them drift, he finally, unable to let her down, yielded to her desire, the two agreeing that the marriage should for the time be kept secret. On October 2, 1909, Kathleen and O'Neill were pronounced one, "till death us do part," at the Trinity Protestant Episcopal Church in Hoboken, New Jersey, just across the river from New York City.

This period of O'Neill's life, as well as his father's affair with Nettie Walsh, was evidently in his mind when he wrote *Abortion*, his short play about a college hero's ill-fated affair with a poor girl (named "Nellie"). The college boy tells his father he can't explain, even to himself, how he happened to become involved with the girl, then adds: "Be frank, Dad! Judging from several anecdotes which your friend Professor Simmons has let slip about your four years here, you were no St. Anthony. . . . I have played the scoundrel all the way through. I realize that now. Why couldn't I have felt this way before, at the start? But at that time the whole thing seemed just a pleasant game we were playing; its serious aspects appeared remote, unreal."

If the fate of the girl in the play — she dies from an abortion — represents unconscious wish-fulfillment on the author's part, he made commensurate atonement by killing off his counterpart; the college boy commits suicide. Action and consequences, O'Neill's plays would always follow a moral pattern; for all his efforts to recast himself in a Nietzschean mold, to take up a position beyond good and evil, he could never escape the influence of his ethical upbringing, of his Catholic-bred conscience.

Since Ella preferred to bid her son good-by in private and Jamie was again on the road in *Travelling Salesman*, Mr. O'Neill and newly wed Kathleen, flushed with emotion and looking her prettiest, were the only ones at Grand Central Station to see Eugene leave on the first leg of his long journey. This was the first time Kathleen met her father-in-law. "He was gracious and very pleasant to me," she once recalled with a wry smile, "but if he'd known we were married, I'm sure he wouldn't have been so pleasant."

On October 16, the day Eugene reached twenty-one and man's estate, he was sailing off the western coast of Mexico, his mind full of Conrad, Jack London, and of what lay ahead; he also could not help thinking of Kathleen and the marital mess he had left behind. He had written her reassuring letters from the train, during the long ride across the continent, but her image began to fade as the banana boat, steaming southeast, lengthened the distance between them. By the time he debarked at Amapala, excited by his first glimpses of the lush, steamy life of Honduras, the events of his recent past, like something rather dreamed than experienced, seemed shadowy and unreal; his new life engulfed him.

Stevens the engineer, a Columbia University graduate who preferred the vigorous life to desk work, had brought along his wife Ann, a pleasant-looking brunette; both were in their early thirties. Whatever reservations Eugene initially had about her presence on the venture, he quickly learned to admire her as a "woman in a thousand." Honduras was a familiar story to Stevens, for he had spent the previous winter there; but his wife also took to it like a veteran, proving her mettle in the nearly hundred-mile journey on muleback from Amapala to the capital city of Tegucigalpa, almost all of it through mountainous terrain. Eugene himself became "terribly sore" from the rugged three-day climb — Tegucigalpa is over three thousand feet above sea level — and was several days getting over his stiffness.

From the outset he found the reality of Honduras both more and less than what he had imagined from his reading. Always sensitive to his environment, he soaked up the sights, sounds, smells — the smells were inescapable — of his tropical milieu. The poverty appalled him. "The native villages," he wrote home, "are the most squalid and dirty it has ever been my misfortune to see. Pigs, dogs, chickens and children all live in the same room and the sanitary conditions of the huts are beyond belief." Other aspects of the country, though, delighted his romantic soul: bands tootling away in the plazas during long soft evenings; crowds in colorful dress strolling about; the *mañana* attitude, so unlike the fast pace of New York; men strutting around "with a six-shooter and a belt full of cartridges on their hip — just like a three-cent Western melodrama."

Eugene lost little time in "growing a mustache in order to look absolutely as shiftless and dirty as the best of them." He wore a bandolier tossed over his right shoulder, had a machete dangling from his belt, and with an air self-consciously casual carried a .30-30 Winchester rifle (all he ever bagged was a lizard). Thus loaded down with the standard equipment and soon deeply tanned, he came to seem as acclimated as any old-timer. His feelings were something else again; for all his sense of excitement at being in Honduras, he was sometimes prey, he wrote his parents, to "spells of dejection and the blues." But then, after assuring them that such feelings were brief, he told them not to worry as "the devil takes care of his own."

He liked both Stevenses; the engineer was quiet, hard-working, his wife uncomplaining and pleasant under the hardships, and their steadfast personalities helped pull him out of his depressions. (Judging by the first play he wrote, *A Wife for a Life*, a brief thing about a young miner in love with his older partner's wife, the future playwright had some romantic thoughts about Ann Stevens.) His favorable opinion of the couple did not, however, prevent his starting to feel aggrieved. After weeks of sweating through the rigors of jungle life, of itching all over from flies, fleas, ticks, gnats and mosquitoes, of forcing down "rotten food, vilely cooked," he complained in a letter home: "I don't know if I am getting any salary or not as Stevens has said nothing about it. It would sure be some shock to find out I was enduring all this for love."

Things were not going well with the prospecting party. At first they had made camp along the upper Rio Seale, a swift narrow river branching off the Rio Guayambre, but the alluvial pickings proved lighter than Stevens's findings the previous year on the lower Seale, so they moved back to his original camp site. Days of washing sand and other sediment in the lower Seale also failed, however, to raise hopes of early wealth; Stevens on weighing the results from six pans found he had seventy-five cents' worth of gold. "The river has lots of gold, hundreds of pounds," he wrote his sister back in Portland, "but won't give it up without a lot of work."

After the mayor of Donli told them that "the early Spaniards took most of the gold from the sands," the prospectors set out in search of ore deposits, hacking a path with machetes through the jungle forever encircling them, almost impenetrable. The bottomless black nights spent on bivouac made a lasting impression on O'Neill; he would have more than imagination to draw upon for *The Emperor Jones*, the story of a fugitive Negro ruler lost in the jungle, in the grip of hallucinations and rising panic. "The forest is a wall of darkness dividing the world," O'Neill wrote in *Jones*. "Only when the eye becomes accustomed to the gloom can the outlines of separate trunks of the nearest trees be made out, enormous pillars of deeper blackness. A somber monotone of wind lost in the leaves moans in the air. Yet this sound serves but to intensify the impression of the forest's relentless immobility. . . ."

O'Neill's exploitation in *Emperor Jones* of his stay in Honduras affords a glimpse of the various beings that can inhabit one man's body, of the parallel yet separate existences of a writer and his everyday self. No one reading Eugene's complaining letters ("fleas that infest the native huts and eat you alive at night . . . an acute bilious attack caused by the rotten food") could have imagined that one day he would distill his experience for a drama of poetic fantasy and nightmarish beauty. Which one was closer to the essential O'Neill: the scornful youth who wrote his parents that "the natives are the lowest, laziest, most ignorant bunch of brainless bipeds that ever polluted a land," or the empathizing artist who stripped Brutus Jones of his veneer of civilization to reveal the primitive soul, fearful and superstitious, that lurks in us all? The O'Neill, for that matter, who ran out on Kathleen, or the one who in his writings displayed such great compassion for the victimized of life?

On top of other things bothering the young gold-hunter, practically all his mail from the States aroused, for one or another reason, unhappy thoughts. Jamie's postcards as he toured with *Travelling Salesman* and a letter from a bartender friend served chiefly to remind him of the amenities of life back home. And Kathleen's letters brought to the fore things he would have preferred to forget. After a while he stopped answering her; he had more pressing concerns to think about.

Discouraged by their efforts around the lower Rio Seale, the mining party decided to investigate a native's tip about "lots of gold" in the Rio Guineo not far away. Hiring a mahogany dugout, Stevens and Eugene with several helpers followed the Seale into the Guayambre, turned off again into the broad Rio Patuca and poled along for four days until reaching the Guineo. They were able to travel only a few miles further, not only because the Guineo flowed so swiftly but because fallen trees made it hazardous. After grounding the dugout, the party tried to push ahead on foot. "This we soon found to be impossible," Eugene wrote his parents, "as the tropical jungle was so dense that cutting a trail would take months." They returned to their camp on the Seale.

Shortly after arriving in Honduras he had sounded optimistic in his correspondence: "Taking it all in all I like the country and the people and think there is every chance in the world for making good." He advised "Papa" that there was a great deal of mining land, worth holding for the future, that could be bought "for a song." But Christmas Day, as he wrote to his parents, found him in the depths: ". . . after having been in all the different zones of this country I give it as my fixed belief that God got his inspiration for Hell after creating Honduras. Until some just Fate grows weary of watching the gropings in the dark of these human maggots [the natives] and exterminates them; until the Universe shakes

James O'Neill, Jr., second from left, in scenes from The Travelling Salesman

these human lice from its sides, Honduras has no future, no hope of being anything but what it is at present — a Siberia of the tropics. As long as the yearly revolutions keep up foreign capital and foreigners will steer clear of the whole outfit. Even granting that the revolutions cease it will take an awful lot to get an American (who has not previously slept in a cow-shed and eaten out of a trough) to live here for any amount of time. . . .

"Since Nov. 11th when we left Tegucigalpa we have had absolutely no butter, bread but three or four times and milk about the same number. Nothing but beans — and lots of times we cannot even get them — *fried*, rice, *fried*, salt dried meat, *fried* (much tougher than leather) with sometimes an egg or two thrown in. But eggs are very scarce. All the natives have chickens but they are too lazy to look for the eggs. We always get 'tortillas' — a heavy soggy imitation of a pancake made of corn, enough to poison the stomach of an ostrich. There is the limit of your bill-of-fare — breakfast, dinner, supper — day after day — week after week. Everything they cook is steeped in grease — alike unhealthy and unsatisfying. You get terribly hungry and force down a lot of this food and the result is your stomach gets in bad condition. No fresh meat. Game is scarce and difficult to bag where we are now. The flies are fierce and *I have never been free from bites one day since I arrived in this country*."

After a detailed horrendous description of the various types of flying, crawling, burrowing insect life, and of their depredations on human flesh, he ended: "Cannot tell how much I miss you both. I never realized how much home and Father and Mother meant until I got so far away from them. Lots of love to you both. Your loving son Eugene.

"P.S. Menu for Christmas dinner/Beans/Tortillas/One egg/Tea made of lemon leaves."

The letter so revels in complaint and self-pity that, considered by itself, it seems almost laughable; considering that it was written to his parents, one of them a timid apprehensive mother, it seems unforgivably thoughtless. It seems so, that is, unless one bears in mind that it was written by a young man riddled with guilt feelings and indoctrinated with the Catholic tenet of doing penance for one's sins. Beneath his complaints about the natives, the food, the insects, the state of his health, he unconsciously is telling his mother: if you are suffering, so am I; if your life is a burden, so is mine. There was in him, certainly, a great deal of self-pity, yet more than self-pity was involved. From the depths of his being he felt impelled to look on the dark side of things, to take the bleakest possible view of his circumstances, to, in short, punish himself. He was unworthy, he did not deserve to enjoy life.

"Out of thy poisons," said Nietzsche, "brewedst thou balsam for thyself. . . . Of all that is written, I love only what a person hath written with his blood. Write with blood, and thou wilt find that blood is spirit. . . . Creating — that is the great salvation from suffering, and life's alleviation. But for the creator to appear, suffering itself is needed, and much transformation."

Nietzsche had in mind someone like Eugene O'Neill. Not only self-destructive forces were at work in him but counterforces toward self-realization, a sublimating drive that would enable him to find relief through the written word. "I kept writing," he once said, "because I had such a love of it. I was highly introspective, intensely nervous and self-conscious. . . . When I was writing, I was alive." Another time, to a discouraged young author: "Keep on writing, no matter what! That's the most important thing. As long as you have a job on hand that absorbs all your mental energy, you haven't much worry to spare over other things. It serves as a suit of armor."

He was speaking from the heart: writing was to become the most important thing in his life. Wives, children, friends, even the financial independence and world-wide fame his efforts brought him — none of this meant as much to him as the act itself, the therapeutic act of writing. His outpouring of plays once he began writing attests to the tremendous psychic drive behind his work, to the great tension and force generated in him by his heritage in conjunction with the circumstances of his life. In O'Neill, as in all creative persons, there was a need to establish unity out of chaos, to wring meaning and beauty from the sprawling confusion of his days; but beyond this, writing served him as a safety valve, as an outlet for the aggression, self-hatred and guilt encased within him. Writing not only gave him a reason for being but enabled him to go on living.

Eugene had intended to remain in Honduras until June, the start of the rainy season, when *colentura* (malarial fever) became prevalent and most foreigners left the country; but a malarial mosquito with a poor sense of timing changed his plans, for he came down with the fever well ahead of the endemic season. Weak from chills, sweating and high temperatures, he said good-by to the Stevenses and, accompanied by an Indian guide, took off on muleback for the ten-day trek back to Tegucigalpa. On his arrival he found the only hotel solidly booked because of a fiesta the following day. The American consul gave him shelter and called a doctor, who kept him in bed for three weeks. The nights being cold, from the city's high altitude, the consul supplemented the blankets on a shivering O'Neill with some old American flags. "I looked," he later cracked, "just like George M. Cohan."

Although glad to leave Honduras behind, he found the long trip, in view of the situation awaiting him at home, not long enough. In angry letters from his father, in anxious ones from Kathleen, he had learned that the two families now knew of the marriage and that she was expecting a child. With his bent for self-dramatization, it must have seemed appropriate to O'Neill that his homecoming should coincide with a period of rising global tension. In the spring of 1910 people all over the world were looking skyward with mounting interest and anxiety as Halley's Comet loomed ever larger and brighter to the naked eye. Popularly regarded since ancient days as a portent of impending wars and the death of kings, of great famines and climactic victories – it was noted around the time both of Caesar's death and of Christ's resurrection – the comet was expected to put on its most brilliant show in mid-May, when the earth was to pass through its long glowing tail. The ignorant and superstitious took this to mean that the world was in danger, if not coming to an end. The stock market dipped; farmers instead of tilling the field took to cyclone cellars; people removed lightning rods from their homes; coal miners in Colorado remained underground, after their working shifts, for better protection, while others in Pennsylvania refused to enter the mines, preferring to die in the open. (Kathleen and O'Neill's child, a boy, who would be born when the celestial display was at its zenith, grew up prone, like his father, to self-dramatization; he always felt that Halley's Comet had a malign influence on the course of his life.)

With Kathleen on his mind, Eugene had his own cause for apprehension as he landed back in New York, ill-prepared by the drowsy pace of Honduras for the traffic and crowds, the busy tempo of the city. After fortifying himself with some drinks he arrived at the Lucerne and, to his great relief, found the apartment empty; but his mood changed swiftly. In the midst of unpacking, the sight of the machete he had brought back triggered a violent reaction. Seized by uncontrollable fury, like the time he had gone berserk at Princeton, he began hacking at things in the apartment, chiefly venting his rage on the legs of the furniture – possibly from some impulse toward castration. When his mother returned she found a scene of wreckage, with Eugene asleep on the floor, overcome by liquor and exhaustion.

But another day, his head in her lap as she tried to console him, he wept to think that he was already married and an expectant father. He felt that his life was ruined before it had really begun, and kept repeating, as though this summed up everything, that he was "only twenty-one." Ella never knew what to expect from him, whether childlike he would turn to her and James for comfort or present the face of a dark brooding stranger impossible to reach. Perhaps she understood him better than she admitted to herself. The one completely mystified by the boy was James. "My father," Eugene once said, "was worried about me. He didn't know how to handle me . . . he only wanted me to settle down and make a living. He often used to think I was just crazy."

James's solution for possible trouble from the Jenkinses was, as previously, to place a distance between the two young people. Touring at the time with *The White Sister,* he arranged to have his son join him in a "made" position (this was O'Neill's first formal connection with the theater, his first salaried job) as assistant company manager. "A courtesy title," he later said. "I had to sit at the gallery door and see that the local ticket taker didn't let in any of his friends. We would soon get acquainted and everything would be all right."

The White Sister was everything he despised in the theater — sentimental, contrived, wallowing in grease-paint emotionalism — and it was further guilty, in his eyes, of romanticizing the Catholic Church. Based on a novel by F. Marion Crawford, it opened with organ music and the chiming of church bells. Some idea of the play may be gathered from the following passages:

"If I broke my vow and went to him, all the world would point at him: the man who married a renegade nun. Our names would be linked together, not proudly as they ought to be, but in shame! No! God hath parted us: let no man put us together. . . .

"I am only a woman who has loved a man very, very dearly! And he must not know what torment it is. He must never know the truth. Promise you will never tell him! Promise! Promise! (organ music swells)."

Eugene resented the play not only in itself but for relegating his father to a subordinate role. Shortly after the latter's death, Eugene lamented to George Tyler that his father had "suffered as a retribution in his old age [for squandering his talent on *Monte Cristo*] the humiliation of supporting such actor-yokels" as Viola Allen and Pauline Frederick. In the last years of his life James himself, to his family and such intimates as Tyler and Will Connor, spoke with regret and bitterness of his career; but while he was still in the theater his true feelings were generally well masked. A few months before Eugene joined *White Sister* his father's associates threw a small party celebrating his "sixtieth" birthday (actually, his sixty-third). In acknowledging a newspaper's congratulations, James wrote: "Life in 60 Middle Row has the same charms we knew at fifteen when we first sat in the gallery. . . . Must say that all my years on the stage form one grand poem of happiness to myself. I love life fully as well as ever, and my friends a whole lot better."

However, a faintly forlorn note can be heard behind his remarks at the celebration. Thinking evidently of his early years of high promise, he said that his "one ambition was to reappear as Iago before retiring from the stage." Some forty years after the event he was clutching at the memory that he had once alternated with the great Booth himself in the leading roles of *Othello*.

Eugene's ordeal by F. Marion Crawford lasted only from mid-March in St. Louis till the tour folded in Portland, Maine, at the end of April, but it was long enough for him to become restless; as usual, he sought refuge in reading. Of everything he read at the time Conrad's *The Nigger of the Narcissus* made the deepest impression, one passage in particular standing out from the page: "The true peace of God begins at any spot a thousand miles from the nearest land; and when He sends there the messengers of His might it is not in terrible wrath against crime, presumption and folly, but paternally, to chasten simple hearts — ignorant hearts that know nothing of life, and beat undisturbed by envy or greed." The words lingered with him — "the true peace of God . . . a thousand miles from the nearest land. . . ."

When *The White Sister* settled for two weeks in Boston, prior to its closing in Portland, he spent his days haunting Mystic Wharf, hungrily eying the ships arriving and departing, especially those outward bound. He repeatedly visited the pier where a Norwegian barque, the *Charles Racine*, was starting to unload before taking on a cargo of lumber destined for Buenos Aires. Ever since childhood, his early summers in New London, he had felt drawn to the tall sail-winged ships, like so many great mothers to the sea gulls; he could remember when schooners and barques, brigs and yawls were an everyday sight on the Thames, but their day was practically over. The *Charles Racine*, for all its steel bulk and efficient grace, was almost a ghost, something from bygone times resisting time's count-down. The old square-rigger was still on Eugene's mind as the tour ended, as father and son returned to New York wondering what lay in store from Mrs. Jenkins and her daughter.

The Birth of a Boy/ Reveals Marriage/ of "Gene" O'Neill// Young Man, In Honduras,/ Doesn't Know He Is Dad// May Not Hear News For Weeks/ Working At Mine To Win/ Fortune For Family — thus ran a headline in the New York *World* on May 7, 1910. In a story that came chiefly from Mrs. Jenkins, the newspaper reported that Kathleen had had a ten-and-half-pound child the day before, that she and the son of James O'Neill were childhood sweethearts and had been wed the previous July in Hoboken. They had gone about it quietly, the article said, because of Mr. O'Neill's objections to the marriage, based on the difference in religion between the two families. "My daughter told me,"

Mrs. Jenkins was quoted as saying, "that she had begged Eugene to be married by a priest, but he declined. But the child is to be baptized in the Catholic faith, as Kathleen feels it would be a sin not to do so. . . . He will be named Eugene Gladstone O'Neill 2d.

"It was at the request of Mr. James O'Neill that my daughter's marriage was kept a secret. Mrs. O'Neill had been ill all winter and the announcement of her son's marriage, it was feared, would have grave consequences to her. She was only told recently. She seemed pleased when she learned of the baby's birth."

Rather than "pleased," Ella was greatly upset by the notoriety. A reporter who tried to obtain the elder O'Neills' comments was told at the Lucerne that "they had gone out of town for a week." Apparently Mrs. Jenkins had given the *World* an exclusive story on the "romantic marriage" in hopes that a newspaper splash would force the O'Neills to accept Kathleen. But if this was her stratagem, it more than failed in her purpose; it backfired, leaving her daughter and herself open to a humiliating aftermath.

Gene O'Neill Home,/ But Not with Wife, said a headline in the *World* on May 11. Under a two-column photograph of Kathleen, the story said that she had been unaware of her husband's return to the city, thinking that he was in Honduras "working to make a fortune for her and their infant son." Instead, the article added, he had been living for the past week at a Times Square rooming house at 123 West 47th Street, had dined with his father at the Green Room Club, and been seen in recent days around Broadway. "When Mrs. Jenkins was told yesterday that her son-in-law was here," the *World* reported, "she at first refused to believe it. She was so shocked she could say nothing for several minutes. Then, with tears of mortification filling her eyes, she exclaimed:

" 'It seems impossible that "Gene" is in town and has remained away from his wife and their baby. There must be some mistake, but if there is not, Eugene's attitude is inexcusable. He knows how we all feel toward him and that he could have come to this house to live any time since his marriage to my daughter. There would have been no "mother-in-law" about it, either, and he knew that. I felt toward him as if he were my own son. If he is living in New York without coming to see his wife and baby, I am pretty certain who is responsible for his behavior.

" 'No, I will not say who that person is.' "

James's plan of strategy was defensive — to avoid contact with the Jenkinses if possible, say nothing to the press, and await further developments. There were none, after the follow-up story in the *World*. Neither Kathleen nor her proud, high-spirited mother was a second Nettie Walsh. The O'Neills won the war of nerves by default.

10

Home to the Sea

A MONTH after the news broke about his being a husband and father, Eugene was on the *Charles Racine* bound for Buenos Aires. "It happened quite naturally — that voyage — as a consequence of what was really inside of me — what I really wanted, I suppose. I struck up one day by the wharf in Boston with a bunch of sailors, mostly Norwegians and Swedes. I wanted to ship with somebody and they took me that afternoon to the captain. Signed up, and the next thing we were off."

The only thing wrong with his account, given years afterward, is that it runs contrary to the facts. The facts are that he was never a member of the *Racine* crew nor did his presence on the ship come about so casually and easily as he pictured. In an off-hand way he romanticized the episode.

Following the newspaper notoriety, Eugene was eager to get away, and his months in Honduras, despite the insects, malaria, and other hardships, had sharpened his wanderlust. Talking things over with his father, he defined his stand: he was temperamentally incapable of holding down any kind of regular job, working in the theater was to him equally unattractive; he wanted to travel, see something of the world, try to find himself (he later said that he envisioned himself as a Conradian figure, a kind of "super-tramp"). From hanging around Mystic Wharf and becoming friendly with sailors off the *Charles Racine*, he had learned that while it was unauthorized to carry passengers, it unofficially from time to time accommodated men who were not exactly passengers and yet not members of the crew, either. Eugene felt certain that the captain would be willing for a sum to take him along; he wanted to make that voyage to Buenos Aires, he wanted those weeks on the Norwegian windjammer.

If James had any reservations, he soon, partly from lacking ideas of his own, fell in line with his son's desire. A long trip at sea, besides being healthful for the boy, would take him away from the Tenderloin and other unsavory places, not to mention the situation with Kathleen and her infant. The routine and discipline of life aboard ship (the boy needed disciplining, God knows!) certainly couldn't do him any harm. And Buenos Aires — it might be good for him to be on his own for a time, far from home, might help him to mature. The more James thought of the prospect, the better he liked it; he agreed, if suitable arrangements could be made, to stake him to the voyage.

Both father and son were impressed, in a trip to Boston in late May, on meeting Captain Gustav Waage. As well they might be: nearly six feet tall, broad shoulders, eyes of calm authority, a vigorous air despite silvery gray hair and mustache, the captain had all the signs of a born leader, the assured look of a man who knew his job and knew that he knew it. He was highly regarded, Eugene later learned, in shipping circles all over the world for record voyages and the A-1 condition of his cargoes. His word carried weight with his employers, the Sigval Bergesen line of Stavanger, Norway; when Bergesen thought of adding a steam ship to his fleet, back in the 1890s, Captain Waage persuaded him to build, instead, a sailing vessel. "I will sail," he said, "as long as the winds blow." He had gone to sea when fourteen years old and been master of the *Racine* since it came into being in 1892; until his death in the late 1920s he looked down on steam ships as "things that boil themselves across the sea."

James knew his son would be in good hands, and an agreement was reached: seventy-five dollars for the fare, with Eugene to lend a hand in the less hazardous duties; he wanted to share in the work. Though Captain Waage was never enthusiastic about carrying these semipassengers — unless adaptable, they could be a burden — he welcomed the passage money, no small sum to him, as additional revenue for his company. Able-bodied seamen on the *Racine* were paid fifty-four kroner a month, about $13.50 in American currency, while ordinary seamen drew thirty kroner.

After Eugene was set for the voyage, a friend decided to join him and paid seventy-five dollars for his fare, but the latter's identity is unknown; efforts to learn who he was came to little. In a letter dated June 7, 1910, Captain Waage wrote his employer that "the passengers are two boys whom I have been asked to take care of, and it is understood that they are going to work on the voyage." But this is all, the lone descriptive reference to O'Neill and his companion in the extant papers of the *Racine*.

Questioning of scores of people who had known O'Neill in his earlier years ended in meager findings — two or three persons with vague recollections of having heard that he and Louis Holladay once shipped out together. Also, two crew members of the 1910 voyage, Osmund Christophersen and Rolf Skjørestad, were unable years later to recall the friend's name or much about him, though "Holladay" sounded familiar to Christophersen. They retained sharper memories of O'Neill because, unlike his companion, he took a great interest in life aboard the old steel barque. Skjørestad and a man in Buenos Aires named Fred Hettman, who briefly met Eugene's friend, recall him as blond and pleasant-faced – a description that fits Louis – so it may have been he; but there is no apparent way of ever verifying this, for Holladay died in Greenwich Village in 1918.

A few days before the *Charles Racine's* scheduled sailing the voyage was in danger of ending before it began. Fire broke out May 28 on Mystic Wharf only a ship's length away from the *Racine*, destroying the sheds of a lumber company and five railroad cars full of spruce and hard pine; flames shot as high as a hundred feet in one of Boston's most spectacular blazes in years, and the *Racine* was saved from catching fire only by the quick action of fireboats in wetting it down with streams of water. "South Channel was lighted by the reflection of the flames," the Boston *Globe* said on May 28, "and it looked like a lake of molten metal." Superstitious and mystical as O'Neill was, he probably took the fire as Fate's handiwork, as some kind of portent from Destiny. On May 30 Captain Waage wrote Bergesen: "When I came on deck and saw the fire I thought the days of the *Charles Racine* were numbered. A weak breeze was in our favor, otherwise it would have been bad for us as the whole wharf was full of planks and boards. . . . The damage [to the pier] amounts to several hundred thousand dollars, but it will not prevent us from continuing the loading."

With more than a million feet of lumber stowed below deck and the rest of the load secured on deck and hatches, the voyage got off on June 6 to a faltering start. Towed away from the pier by a bustling little tug, the ship had to anchor for two days in Boston Roads because of headwinds and dense fog before it could head out to sea. Since there has been a great deal of romancing in print about this voyage – the impression is often given that O'Neill was immediately plunged into the sardine-like existence of the fo'c'sle, handed a moldy hardtack and cup of bilge water for his first meal, and sent clambering aloft to the topmost rigging – let it be noted here that he and his friend received special treatment. The fresh information in this account is based not only on the hitherto untapped reminiscences of Christophersen and Skjørestad but on those of Captain Severin Waage, son of the 1910 master. Though the latter was not on the 1910 voyage, he sailed for years on the *Racine* both before and after

O'Neill and drew generously on his memories in giving a detailed picture of life aboard the windjammer.

Eugene and his friend, instead of being squeezed in the fo'c'sle, had their own quarters, a small cabin portside and aft generally used as sick bay; also, they took mess with the captain and two mates, though this was no special boon, as officers and hands shared more or less equally in the same fare. Instead of working the regular twelve-hour shift that got under way at six in the morning, the two young Americans usually began around eight and could knock off whenever they chose; but they generally put in a good day's work, especially Eugene. And instead of their having to take turns standing watch at night — Captain Waage would not entrust the duty to green hands — their nights were free. It was an ideal arrangement for Eugene; free to work or not, with plenty of leisure in a voyage lasting for weeks, he was both participant and spectator, part of the ship's life and able to stand apart from it and observe. Hungry to learn, totally receptive, he crammed a year's experience into the one voyage.

In addition to the captain and mates, O'Neill and his friend, the *Racine* carried a crew of nineteen. It was rumored among the ship's complement that the two young men had been leading fast lives ashore and had gone to sea at their families' instigation to straighten themselves out. The crew found Eugene taciturn and self-effacing, rather melancholy-looking, as though nursing an old sorrow. Yet actually he had never before known such joy, so great a sense of self-fulfillment. "I can remember in my sailor days," he once said, "what a thrill of release it gave me to feel the great ocean ground-swell start to heave the ship under me. It meant freedom then — an end of an old episode and the birth of another — for life then was merely a series of episodes flickering across my mind."

In shipping out he was doing more than running away from Kathleen and all that home represented, the aimlessness and maddening frustration of his days; he was running *toward* something. He hoped to find out who he was and what he was, he hoped to develop in response to his new life a new self giving more scope to his essential being. So far back as he could remember he had dreamed of such a voyage; now that he was on his way, it filled him with what can best be called religious ecstasy, a sense of being in mystical communion with the secret heart of things. "The true peace of God," Conrad said, "begins at any spot a thousand miles from the nearest land." Amen, O'Neill could say; the lapsed Catholic who could never go home again found peace for a time between Boston and Buenos Aires.

To his mortification he was seasick at the start, but by remaining in the open rather than clinging to his bunk, he recovered in several days and began to take pleasure in the incessant rolling and tossing. His spirits expanded as the *Racine* headed southward, carrying him ever further away; and as the nights grew warmer, he enjoyed lying on deck, under stars that seemed from the rocking of the barque to stream rhythmically back and forth across the sky.

He made repeated attempts to capture in poetry what the voyage meant to him, but poetry, for all his striving, was never his forte; his ear was faulty, his images hackneyed, his choice of words uninspired. All too often his verse was imitative, his pieces about the sea, for example, tending to recall Kipling and Masefield. One of his efforts, entitled "Free," reflects not only his happiness at the time but memories of Kathleen and his nights in the Tenderloin:

> *Weary am I of the tumult, sick of the staring crowd,*
> *Pining for wild sea places, where the soul may think aloud. . . .*
>
> *I have had my dance with Folly, nor do I shirk the blame;*
> *I have sipped the so-called Wine of Life and paid the price of*
> *   shame. . . .*
>
> *Then it's ho! for the plunging deck of a bark, the hoarse song of the*
> *   crew,*
> *With never a thought of those we left or what we are going to do;*
>
> *Nor heed the old ship's burning, but break the shackles of care*
> *And at last be free, on the open sea, with the trade wind in our hair.*

The poem, he once said, was "actually written on a deep-sea barque in the days of Real Romance." He did better, however, by the *Charles Racine* and all it symbolized to him when a dozen years later he wrote a speech of lyrical keening for Paddy, a nostalgic old Irish seaman, in *The Hairy Ape:*

"Oh, to be scudding south again wid the power of the Trade Wind driving her on steady through the nights and the days! Full sail on her! Nights and days! Nights when the foam of the wake would be flaming wid fire, when the sky'd be blazing and winking wid stars. Or the full of the moon maybe. Then you'd see her driving through the gray night, her sails stretching aloft all silver and white, not a sound on the deck, the lot of us dreaming dreams, till you'd believe 'twas no real ship at all you was on but a ghost ship like the *Flying Dutchman*. . . . And there was the days, too. A warm sun on the clean decks. Sun warming the blood of you, and wind over the miles of shiny green ocean like strong drink to your lungs. . . . 'Twas them days a ship was part of the sea, and a man was part of a ship, and the sea joined all together and made it one."

O'Neill was not yet finished with distilling his memories of the *Charles Racine*. Some thirty years afterward he made a final attempt to pay it fitting tribute in *Long Day's Journey*, as Edmund tells his father about the transcendent high points of his life:

"I lay on the bowsprit, facing astern, with the water foaming into spume under me, the masts with every sail white in the moonlight, towering high above me. I became drunk with the beauty and singing rhythm of it, and for a moment I lost myself — actually lost my life. I was set free! I dissolved in the sea, became white sails and flying spray, became beauty and rhythm, became moonlight and the ship and the high dim-starred sky! I belonged, without past or future, within peace and unity and a wild joy, within something greater than my own life, or the life of Man, to Life itself!"

Obviously O'Neill is telling of a time he had been swept out of himself by simultaneously experiencing two directly opposed emotional states: he had felt alive at a keyed-up pitch of intensity and had reveled in an intoxicating sense of oblivion, of psychic annihilation. The answer as to which state was dominant can be found in something he told a girl in New London not long after his last turn at sea. The girl, named Olive Evans, had asked whether he had ever in his life been really happy; after telling her of the radiant hours he had spent on the bowsprit of the *Charles Racine*, feeling himself one with the ship, like something disembodied and absorbed by the sea, he added, "And at such times I was in love with death."

He said that in 1912, when he was struggling to find himself, tormented by self-doubt, despairing of ever coming to terms with life. He gave the same answer more fully in 1940, after financial success and world-wide fame, after three Pulitzer Prizes, after a Nobel Prize, when he wrote: "It was a great mistake, my being born a man, I would have been much more successful as a sea gull or a fish. . . . I will always be a stranger who never feels at home . . . who must always be a little in love with death!"

Early in the voyage Captain Waage, feeling it might be detrimental to the ship's discipline, advised Eugene against fraternizing with the crew; but he was talking to the wrong person. Eugene was eager, behind his reserved exterior, to make friends with the seamen. The first evening of good weather, when they had collected on the main hatch and were lounging by the rail, he turned up with a box of corncob pipes and gave one to everybody (he probably got the idea from reading of old Single-ton and others in the Conrad novel with their eternal pipes). After such an overture the crew began to warm toward him, especially as he continued to go out of his way to be friendly. Whenever he finished a book — he had brought along a small library — he gave it to the crew; and he constantly sought them out as they sat around talking and reminiscing. He listened with an intent face that spurred them to ransack their memories and spin out their tales at length.

He came to know them well. There was Gustav Gustafsson, a Finn and the strongest of the crew, who, in O'Neill's words, "was constantly boasting that he had been in jail in every seaport in the world of any importance. He said the worst one was in India . . . [He] was always saying when ashore, 'I know an old boiler down the docks we can crawl into.' " (Words that "the Hairy Ape" would use in kidding an elegant churchgoing lady on Fifth Avenue: "Hello, Kiddo. Got anyting on for tonight? I know an old boiler down to de docks we kin crawl into.")

And there was first mate Gabrielsen, a tall, bony stooped-over man who had been engaged for twenty years and sending money all that time to his fiancée. And three Negroes from Jamaica, one of them with a name that delighted Eugene — Lancelot Silver Garth — who kept to them-selves when off duty. And sailmaker Hansen, in his sixties, who had signed off in Antwerp with two years' pay, spent some and been robbed of the rest in a few days, then rushed back to his old berth on the *Racine*, not only broke but fleeced of most of his clothes; he cut up an old sweater to make himself a pair of socks. And Eugene heard of the two Finnish brothers, recent crew members, who during a stopover in port were drunk and fighting aboard ship when one pulled a knife on the other; the latter ran away, never to return, leaving his brother to mourn and weep openly, "Axel is gone, but he left a pair of shoes for me."

Eugene, soaking it all up, heard tales of hazardous and ill-starred voyages, of shipwrecks, narrow escapes from death, and shipmates long dead whose grave was the sea. Tales of goodhearted whores who would feed you when you were broke, and of others hand in hand with the "land sharks," men more dangerous than the sea sharks who would kill you for your last dollar. Tales of the greedy boarding masters, such as Tommy Moore of Buenos Aires (his name figures in one of O'Neill's sea tales), with whom both seamen and ship captains had to contend; in return for sheltering a penniless sailor for a few days and finding him a berth, the boarding masters would exact months of advance pay from the man and a commission from his skipper — "blood money" the men of the sea called it. One boarding master, paid so much per head for supplying part of a crew, slipped a dead man among the drunks carried on board.

Tales of monotony, loneliness, hardship, tales of Buenos Aires as among the roughest, wildest of all seaports. To give O'Neill an idea of what he might expect when they landed, one crewman told him of a madam who distributed business cards on which she had written: "Come up to my house, plenty fun, pretty girls, plenty dance, three men killed last night."

The crew members extended themselves in swapping yarns before Eugene not only because of his look of hungry interest — they listened to one another largely from boredom, to pass time, they had heard the stories before — but because of something in his attitude that warmed them. They sensed that he more than liked them, more than sympathized with them; they sensed that he — this was unique in their experience — respected them.

They were not mistaken. So far as O'Neill was concerned, Conrad could have had the *Racine* men in mind when he wrote of the *Narcissus* crew: "They had been strong, as those are strong who know neither doubts nor hopes. . . . Men hard to manage, but easy to inspire; voiceless men — but men enough to scorn in their hearts the sentimental voices that had bewailed the hardness of their fate. It was a fate unique and their own; the capacity to bear it appeared to them the privilege of the chosen!"

While undoubtedly Conrad influenced O'Neill's attitude, the basic feeling was still his own — he felt a kinship with seamen. "They were," he said in after years of the *Racine* crew, "fine fellows. I've never forgotten them, nor, I hope, they me. Indeed, I look on a sailor man as my particular brother." He said a great deal in the few words: the child at St. Aloysius and De La Salle who had felt isolated and unloved, the adolescent who at Betts had rebelled and assumed a sophistication beyond his years, the hard-drinking wild Irishman who had both looked down on and envied the well-adjusted at Princeton, the youth who had sought "real life" in the Tenderloin and Greenwich Village — the O'Neill, that is, who had always been plagued by a sense of not "belonging" felt on the *Charles Racine* that he had come home, that at last he belonged. The inarticulate seamen who bore more and felt more than they could ever express, who were their naked selves, too vital or plain or lacking in wit and guile to wear a mask — these were his brothers. He belonged, just as he had always suspected, among the rootless and disinherited.

"I liked [seamen] better than I did men of my own kind," he once said. "They were sincere, loyal, generous . . . I've seen them give their own clothes to stowaways.

"I hated a life ruled by the conventions and traditions of society.

Sailors' lives, too, were ruled by conventions and traditions; but they were of a sort I liked and that had a meaning which appealed to me . . . discipline on a sailing vessel was not a thing that was imposed on the crew by superior authority. It was essentially voluntary. The motive behind it was loyalty to the ship!"

Though Eugene in after years would refer to the Norwegian barque as an "old hooker," he knew better; he was talking from affectionate familiarity. The *Charles Racine*, admired in shipping circles for fast voyages, was in top condition (Captain Waage saw to that) and classified "100 A1," the highest of ratings, by Lloyd's of London. But life on the vessel was no luxury cruise for semipassengers, especially for one so willing as Eugene to join in the work; the work, he soon found, was unending. Dressed in khaki trousers, light-colored shirt and tennis shoes, he pitched in with the others in hauling sheets and braces, chipping rust, painting, shining brass, sanding the teakwood masts — work generally carried on to the accompaniment of sea chanteys.

The men, according to Rolf Skjørestad, used to sing a particular chantey during a particular job. "We had songs for all types of work — hoisting anchor, belaying, setting sail, securing sails, pumping, and even for scrubbing the deck. Some of the things we sang were 'Rolling Home,' 'Blow the Man Down,' 'Whiskey Johnny,' 'Homeward Bound,' 'Sally Brown,' 'Rio Grande' and 'I Will Pay Paddy Doyle for His Boots.' They made the work seem easier." Eugene joined in the singing, too, happily, even if his dark concentrated face rarely betrayed his feelings. It took him a while to learn the lyrics; though the songs were sung more or less in English, the words often sounded foreign in the fog of Norwegian, Finnish, Swedish and German accents. But it added flavor to the singing — "Whiskey Johnny" seemed more authentic as "Viskee Yonny." O'Neill would later use the old ballads not only in his short sea plays but in *Mourning Becomes Electra*, *The Iceman Cometh* and other long works.

After the fried beans and greasy tortillas of Honduras, the food on the *Racine* seemed quite tasty, though at a later time O'Neill said jokingly that he had been served "something called coffee, and something called tea." According to Osmund Christophersen, the mess was considerably better than that on most sailing vessels, but as the weeks lengthened and the supply of fresh rations ran low, everyone grew tired of fish balls, fish cakes, tinned meat and salt pork. Fresh bread only twice a week, hardtack the rest of the time. Supper was usually *lapskaus* (meat stew from leftovers) or *plukkfish* (creamed leftovers of fish). Eugene soon realized that Lancelot (Landy) Garth, the cook, would never win prizes for his art.

Whereas the "Old Man" and his mates were solely interested in making the best time possible, everyone else welcomed days when, the winds subsiding, the ship slowed down enough to allow fishing, a chance for fresh food. To Captain Waage's regret there were quite a few days of good fishing. In catching bonitos the men used a stout line, an iron hook, and as bait a white or red rag; for "springers" and sharks a man with a harpoon was lowered near the water, while three or four others stood ready at the rail — Eugene usually among them — to hoist the big ones aboard. Occasionally flying fish would be on the menu, without their having to be caught; at night the flying fish — streaks of silver drawn by the lanterns — could be heard flopping on deck, a sound that sent the men racing to find them before they wriggled overboard. The race was generally won, however, by the two cats on board, honored members of the ship's complement.

Between Boston and Buenos Aires the *Racine* ran a full gamut of weather. Favored in the beginning by the winds, breezing along under full sail at twelve knots, the barque made such good time — it reached 8 degrees north latitude in sixteen days — that the skipper was hoping for a record voyage. But then, his luck running out, the ship encountered some of the worst weather he had ever known; for the first time in all the many times he had sailed to Argentina, the southeasterly trade winds failed him and he was forced to tack. Further south, as the ship was tossed around by a hurricane — one of several it encountered — some of the lumber secured on deck was torn loose from its chains and wiring, hurled about to the danger of the men, and finally washed overboard as the ship heeled and mighty waves pounded the deck.

"During the worst hurricane," Christophersen recalls, "O'Neill and his friend were out on deck for a little while and watched the raging of the storm. Though O'Neill's melancholy eyes seemed more melancholy than usual and both men were a bit pale, they appeared to accept the whole thing calmly. When I asked O'Neill the next day what he thought of the weather, he said, 'Very interesting, but I could have wished for a little less of it.' O'Neill was well liked on board. We thought him an interesting strange bird we all loved to talk to."

The voyage finally turned out to be among the slowest in the ship's history; bedeviled by headwinds, storms, and fickle trade winds, the barque took all of fifty-seven days to cover the fifty-nine hundred nautical miles to Buenos Aires. Its following trip of fifty-seven hundred miles to Bridgewater, Nova Scotia, lasted forty days, while the return sailing to Buenos Aires took only thirty-seven. The voyage was made to order for Eugene. Lasting nearly two months and out of sight of land the entire time, it made him familiar with the monotony and the loneliness of the seaman's lot; it gave him in the course of one sailing a complete education in the many faces of the sea, in the fullness of its fury and thundering splendor.

Priding himself on the experience, O'Neill used to say that a man had never really been to sea unless he had sailed on a windjammer. Christophersen, who worked on ships for twenty years and rose to be a first mate, felt less nostalgic about the life. "When for months on end you saw no one but your shipmates," he said, referring to the three years he spent on the *Racine,* "you got mighty sick of them. I have seen grown men start fighting over who could tie the best knot. Every insult was settled by a fist fight, and the weaker man had to watch his tongue. By the time we got to Buenos Aires that trip, everybody — O'Neill, too, I'm sure — could hardly wait to get ashore."

On August 4 Captain Waage wrote in the weather log of the voyage: "Fifty-seven days at sea. At 5:30 P.M. anchored in the roads of Buenos Aires. All's well. God be praised."

11

Depths of Buenos Aires

THE hidden autobiography dispersed in O'Neill's work often betrays its presence by sounding recurrent themes. It is touch-and-go for a time in *Strange Interlude* whether Nina Leeds will "dive for the gutter just to get the security that comes from knowing she's touched bottom and there's no farther to go!" In *Mourning Becomes Electra* Orin Mannon says, ". . . you get so deep at the bottom of hell there is no lower you can sink and you rest there in peace!" In *The Iceman Cometh* a full raft-load of characters, shipwrecked in life, have taken refuge in Harry Hope's joint, a place one of them calls "the No Chance Saloon, Bed-rock Bar, the End of the Line Café, the Bottom of the Sea Rathskeller! Don't you notice the beautiful calm in the atmosphere? That's because it's the last harbor. No one here has to worry about where they're going next, because there is no farther they can go. It's a great comfort to them."

O'Neill was drawing on his own history, a period that began in Buenos Aires, when he wrote in this vein of Nina, Orin, the lost souls in Harry Hope's saloon. O'Neill started for the bottom under the illusion that he was simply living life to the fullest; instead, as one riddled with guilt feelings and unknowingly bent on punishing himself, he was responding to one of the strongest drives in his unconscious. The peace he sometimes found in the depths came from more than knowing he could sink no farther; it came also from the flagellant satisfaction of doing penance for his sins. At the same time, as a riven soul at war with himself, he was, somewhat like Dorian Gray, committing greater and greater offense against his better nature in order to deaden all scruples and feelings of shame. "I landed in Buenos Aires a gentleman, so-called," he once said, "and wound up a bum on the docks in fact."

He began his stay in Argentina with sixty dollars (140 pesos), two suitcases of clothes and a few books, an eagerness to explore his new environment, and the sobering thought that he must soon find work. From the *Charles Racine* he and his friend went to the old Continental Hotel on Avenida 25 de Mayo, but only Eugene checked in — four pesos ($1.70) a day for room and board. The hotel, once first class, was now largely patronized by farmers and other plain folk from the pampas, and since it generally was filled or near capacity, preferred its guests to double up. While registering Eugene fell into conversation with one of the guests, Frederick Hettman, and finding him *simpatico*, took up his suggestion that they share quarters. Several years older than Eugene, with a friendly open face and an outgoing personality, Hettman was from California, a recent graduate of Stanford University who was working as a surveyor in the Province of Cordoba.

"Gene and I got off to a good start," he recalls, "when I asked whether he was related to the James O'Neill who had been playing the Count of Monte Cristo forever. When he said it was his father, I just stood there with my mouth open, finally recovering enough to say, 'Let's go in to lunch.' "

A man of great vitality, Hettman, who has had an adventurous career in mining, engineering and other outdoor pursuits, remained actively working until his late seventies. His memory of things forty and fifty years ago is uncommonly sharp, but he retains only vague recollections of O'Neill's companion — he was not impressed by him. Uncertain today why the other newcomer failed to check into the Continental, Hettman recalls only that he spoke of trying to find work in an amusement park — Argentina in 1910 was celebrating its centenary with a mammoth exposition — and that they met several more times; it is his impression that O'Neill's friend shortly returned to the States.

Although Buenos Aires was a boom town, a mecca for Englishmen and Europeans who found things difficult at home, well-paid employment was virtually nonexistent, Eugene soon learned, for those without special qualifications and training. A few days after his arrival he went to work at the Singer Sewing Machine plant for five pesos (about two dollars) a day. When he applied for a job, the Singer man asked him if he knew how many models the company made. "Fifty?" Eugene guessed. "Fifty!" echoed the other man with a pained face. "Five hundred and fifty! You'll have to learn how to take each one apart and put it together again." But his words were wasted. Eugene had always regarded machinery with suspicion, and felt that machinery reciprocated his attitude. Finally he was handed a sledge hammer and put to work breaking up old sewing machines that had been accepted for trade-in allowances. Several weeks later he quit, after telling Hettman, "I'm not going to be a hewer of wood and drawer of water."

If desirable jobs were scarce for someone like O'Neill, opportunities for pleasure — any sort of pleasure so long as one had the money to pay for it — were unlimited, especially around the water front; and the Continental was only a few blocks from the area, from the sailors' cafés, elbowing one another, and the cheap whorehouses. "For the single man," according to a local saying at the time, "there is nothing to do at night but go to bed or go to hell." Eugene was too restless and too eager to meet life for an early bedtime.

One Saturday night, after dinner at the hotel, Fred turned in to sleep while Eugene headed for the bars. He returned the following morning without his hat and coat, with his shirt bloodied and his trousers looking as though he had been sitting in a mud puddle. In one hand he had a sack of peanuts, in the other several bananas, from which he was having breakfast. "I went to the bar on the next block," he told Hettman, "where the Pollock girls serve those big schooners of beer and got into an argument with some Germans at the next table, then a big Dutchman threw me out in the street. The next couple of bars seemed full of drunken Turks. The last place, near the Retiro railroad station, had a happy gathering — mostly sailors, and I knew a couple of them. Eventually I got mixed up in a brawl, lost my coat, had my shirt torn. . . . I can't remember the rest that happened."

Hettman, who preferred quieter diversions, took his new friend to the vaudeville shows at the Casino, the horse races among the lush surroundings of Palermo, and introduced him to a better class of drinking spots. One Sunday, as they strolled around the grounds of the Centennial Exposition, Eugene seemed particularly interested in the livestock exhibit; after eying a blue-ribbon specimen, he improvised:

> *If it weren't for the bull and his long red rod,*
> *We wouldn't have any beef, by God!*

When Eugene had his way, they made for the bars on Avenida Alem and Paseo Colon, near the docks, generally ending at one known as the "Sailor's Opera" that was always ringing with song, argument, the clink of glasses and a babble of languages — English, French, Italian, Spanish, German, all the Scandinavian tongues. Among its attractions was an all-girl ensemble of violinists on a raised platform who conscientiously sawed away but whose efforts were inaudible — their violins were stringless. The music was actually provided by an all-male group, seated behind

[173]

them, or at other times by a piano-thumping soloist. In lieu of musical talent some of the girls, to justify their salaries, appeared before their admiring public without any underclothes beneath their short dresses.

"It sure was a madhouse," O'Neill once said. "Pickled sailors, sure-thing race track touts, soused boiled-white-shirt déclassé Englishmen, underlings in the Diplomatic Service, boys darting around tables leaving pink and yellow cards directing one to red-plush paradises, and entangled in the racket was the melody of some ancient turkey-trot banged out by a sober pianist. . . . But somehow a regular program was in progress. Every one present was expected to contribute something. If your voice cracked, your head usually did, too. Some old sailor might get up and unroll a yarn, another might do a dance, or there would be a heated discussion between, say, Yankee and British sailors as to the respective prowess of their ships. And, if nothing else promised, 'a bit of a harmless fight' usually could be depended upon as the inevitable star feature to round out the evening's entertainment."

While Hettman could enjoy looking on at the rowdy joints, he was baffled by his roommate; as the son of James O'Neill, he must have had a privileged upbringing, yet he seemed primarily interested in exploring the dregs, in getting into scraps and being knocked around. Occasionally at the Sailor's Opera the two sat at a corner table, farthest from the center of uproar, to talk themselves out, and Fred once asked him what he wanted to do with his life, whether he had any particular ambition. The answer came as a surprise: he hoped to become a poet, to write things that would live. As he said this he took from his wallet a wrinkled paper which he slowly unfolded, a page from a magazine with one of his poems. The verse, after describing a prostitute under a street lamp slipping money into the bosom of her dress, went on to compare her favorably with women who sell themselves in loveless marriage for financial security. (Efforts to track down this early poem have been unsuccessful.)

Some fifty years later Hettman still recalled the care and pride with which Eugene opened the paper, the seriousness of his expression as he spoke of his dream. But this was the only time he ever indicated any literary interests or ambition; he seemed far more interested in enjoying the life around him than in self-expression. The recent past was also on his mind, however, for he told Fred about running out on a girl whom he had gotten pregnant. "I believe Gene was sorry for what he had done, because he told me the same story two or three times and seemed sad about it all — it was like a confession he wanted to get off his chest."

After two months at sea O'Neill was in prime shape when he landed in Buenos Aires, but his health inevitably deteriorated under his present mode of living. "Gene didn't eat much," Hettman recalls. "He was more interested in drinking. When he was short of money he tried to get through the day with just beer, but if he were in funds or someone was treating, his favorite was a big glass of gin with just a drop of vermouth and soda — that had a bigger kick than anything else."

When the Californian first noticed that his roommate had a tremor of the hands, he assumed it was "hang-over shakes," then came to realize that there was something peculiar about it — it seemed unrelated to his drinking, for the trembling came and went. His hands generally shook when he raised a glass to drink or held a newspaper, but were under perfect control when he rested his arms on something as he wrote.

So early as his boarding school days O'Neill was troubled on and off by a hand tremor, but it is uncertain whether this came from tension and "nerves" or whether it represented the intermittent start of a condition that eventually would become the crowning disaster of his life. In the early 1940s, when he was at the peak of his talent — shortly after completing his two masterworks, *The Iceman Cometh* and *A Long Day's Journey Into Night* — the trembling grew progressively worse and finally forced him to stop writing. Had his mental powers also been affected, his situation would have been only pathetic; what raised it to tragedy was that his mind, fertile as ever, was teeming with ideas for the most ambitious work of his career, a nine-play cycle, but his hands refused to obey him. O'Neill believed he had inherited a predisposition for the affliction from his mother, since she had a slight tremor of the hands and shoulders; but he also felt that his early dissipations, the long beating he had given himself, had aggravated the condition. "He died," his widow once recalled, "when he could no longer work. He died spiritually. And it was just a matter of dragging a poor, diseased body along for a few more years until it too died."

Hanging around the Sailor's Opera and other cafés, Eugene became friendly with a young American working in Buenos Aires who shared his zest for life in the raw, and they sometimes made the rounds together. Years later this bar acquaintance, after stipulating that he was not to be named in print, reminisced frankly about O'Neill and the night life of the Argentine capital. For convenience's sake, in referring to him here, the fictitious name of "Barnes" is employed.

"The business of prostitution was chiefly carried on," Barnes said, "in parlor houses which were supervised by the police, taxed by the municipality, and medically checked on by the Department of Public Hygiene once a week. If the girls were O.K., their books were stamped 'Sana.' Generally a French or Polish madam was in charge, and had a string of ten to fifteen girls imported from Europe. You almost never ran across an Argentine girl in one of the places. The category of the house, the prices it charged, depended on the section of the city it was in, and also of course on the quality of the girls, their age, looks, et cetera. The section around Junin Street, just off Corrientes, was considered first class. A bright red light always hung in the entrance hall — this was law — so it couldn't be mistaken for anything else. When you first entered, the girls who were unoccupied would form a circle around you and open their bathrobes to show what they had.

"One night four or five of us wandered into a place on Junin Street, and it must have been an awfully busy night — not even the madam or cook was in sight. The place had a revolving round table on which the girls sometimes posed as living statues, in the nude, of course, while another pushed the wheel around. Since no one was there to entertain us, we took turns in taking a ride, striking all kinds of poses. But when Gene's turn came, he gave the floor a good wetting — said he didn't know where the toilet was. He was about finished when the madam came out, took one look and blew her whistle — all the madams carried them. The cops came a-running and threw us all out, and we were lucky to get off so easily. Gene had been drinking, of course, but what made him do things like that?"

During Eugene's first weeks he became friendly with a girl named Maria, one of the few native-born prostitutes, who was of better than average intelligence and eager to improve her English. Eugene introduced her to Barnes as his "mistress," explaining that after the first time or so she began sleeping with him for nothing. But this relationship did not last long. One day Barnes happened to meet her and got an angry reaction when he mentioned O'Neill; Maria said she would have nothing more to do with him, finally telling Barnes that the last time they had slept together O'Neill said something during their love-making that left her feeling "humiliated."

Bars and brothels formed only part of the pleasure scene; in the rough water-front district of Barracas, a suburb, were some of the most popular attractions, theaters so-called but actually ramshackle structures that showed pornographic movies made in France and Spain. The main hall of these places was generally lined on both sides with cubbyholes, rooms just large enough for a bed. Between screenings, Barnes recalled, prostitutes "went through the audience offering themselves — two pesos a quick tumble in one of the smelly cribs — like peanut and popcorn butchers working their way through the grandstand at a ball game."

"Those moving pictures in Barracas were mighty rough stuff," O'Neill once told an interviewer. "Nothin' was left to the imagination. Every form of perversity was enacted, and, of course, sailors flocked to them." Apparently feeling that this sounded like a slur, he hastened to add, "But, save for the usual exceptions, they were not vicious men. They were in the main honest, good-natured, unheroically courageous men trying to pass the time pleasantly."

In 1914 he would draw on his memories of those water-front nights in writing the first of his notable sea tales, *Bound East for Cardiff*. Two shipmates are reminiscing in the play: "D'yuh remember the times we've had in Buenos Aires? The moving pictures in Barracas? Some class to them, d'yuh remember? . . . I do that; and so does the piany player. He'll not be forgettin' the black eye I gave him in a hurry. . . . [Remember] the days we used to sit on the park benches along the Paseo Colon with the vigilantes lookin' hard at us? And the songs at the Sailor's Opera where the guy played ragtime – d'yuh remember them? . . . I always liked Argentina – all except that booze, *caña*. How drunk we used to git on that, remember?"

Eugene remained at the Continental Hotel only several weeks, though he continued to see Fred Hettman regularly; even four pesos a day for room and board were too much for the state of his finances and the extent of his thirst. Fortunately the *Charles Racine* was still in port, unloading its cargo of lumber; with Captain Waage's permission, Eugene had many of his meals on board and slept in his old cabin whenever he could find his way back to the ship at night. In answer to Osmund Christophersen's query about his friend, he said that he had taken a job with "the dirty movies." It was obvious to the crew that O'Neill was leading a rough life ashore; the last time Rolf Skjørestad saw him he looked "as though he'd been sleeping in his clothes."

He was at the pier, looking more somber than ever, when the barque sailed away in ballast on September 26 for Bridgewater, Nova Scotia. Left homeless by its departure, he settled in a sailors' boarding house on Calle Mexico and sought means to keep alive. "I wasn't doing much choosing," he once said, "I was grabbing whatever came along." One of the things he grabbed at was helping load a German square-rigger, the *Timandra*, even though "that old bucko of a first mate was too tough, the kind that would drop a marlin spike on your skull from a yardarm." He found the work as unpleasant as the mate: "Those South American Germans – they used to send the folks home souvenirs and Christmas presents which included stuffed beasts, ore, anything in the world, provided, as it seemed to me, that it would break your back." He would later vent his grievance against the German ship, referring to it under the thinly disguised name of

The Charles Racine, *on which O'Neill sailed from Boston to Buenos Aires. He always regarded the two-month voyage as one of the high points of his life*

S.S. Ikala, *the real-life model for the* S.S. Glencairn *in O'Neill's cycle of sea plays*

This photograph, made in the early 1920s
shows 252 Fulton Street, New York City
a year or two after it had housed "Jimmy
the Priest's"

Chris Christopherson, the real-life
model for the character of the same
name in Anna Christie,
photographed in 1910

Amindra, through one of his characters in *The Long Voyage Home:* "I know dat damn ship — worst ship dat sail to sea. Rotten grub and dey make you work all time — and the Captain and Mate wus Bluenose devils."

After the *Timandra* stint he managed to obtain work with the local branch of a United States electrical supplies firm by posing as a drafts-man. The office manager quickly saw through his pretense, however, and after remarking in a tolerant tone, "Well, well, so you're a draftsman," assigned him to tracing plans. The job, well within his limited capabilities, was his easiest in Argentina, yet he quit after a few weeks; it was too boring, too confining, for one of his temperament.

Trying to give his landlady on Calle Mexico the impression that he was still employed, he used to leave early each morning and remain away all day. When she became suspicious because of his mounting bill and was ready to toss him out, he got in touch with Hettman, who came and went in his surveying work. Fred, about to leave again for Cordoba, gave the woman 140 pesos to cover two months' room and board for his friend. That problem settled for a while, Eugene felt free to idle around the docks and while away his nights in the bars and other sailor haunts. From all outward signs he was just another of the drifters around the Paseo Colon and the Plaza de Mayo. "I wanted to be a two-fisted Jack London he-man sailor," he later said, "to knock 'em cold and eat 'em alive." Writing, he implied, was among the farthest things from his mind.

But all this time, until he recognized his true course and turned toward the stage, he was quietly steering by the light of Swinburne and the Rossettis, Dowson and Baudelaire; he was consciously absorbing the life around him with poetry in mind. Behind his dissipations in the Tender-loin and Hell's Kitchen, his touching bottom in Buenos Aires, was a drive, among other drives, to see life whole, unflinchingly, to experience everything, the highest and the lowest, and then to project the essence of himself into enduring verse. These years, as he wrestled with poetry, the barometer of his dreams must have given wild readings, both up and downward. Regardless of the shortcomings of his poems, they often contain revealing glimpses of the inner man; one of them, "Submarine," though written a few years after Buenos Aires, suggests the rebellious young Irish-American who made himself at home in the underlife of the water front:

> *My soul is a submarine.*
> *My aspirations are torpedoes.*
> *I will hide unseen*
> *Beneath the surface of life*
> *Watching for ships,*

Dull, heavy-laden merchant ships,
Rust-eaten, grimy galeons [sic] of commerce
Wallowing with obese assurance,
Too sluggish to fear or wonder,
Mocked by the laughter of waves
And the spit of disdainful spray.

I will destroy them
Because the sea is beautiful.

That is why I lurk
Menacingly
In green depths.

His first plays of merit were sea plays, concerned with the crew of a tramp freighter he called the S.S. *Glencairn*. Most of the characters in the *Glencairn* tales are composite portraits, modeled on various men with whom O'Neill had shipped or whom he had known while "on the beach" in Buenos Aires and other places; in a few instances, however, the playwright drew heavily on his memories of a particular individual. "Smitty the Duke," for one, is largely based on a young Englishman of evident breeding, impeccable manners, and bottomless thirst Eugene met at the Sailor's Opera; they roomed together for a time.

Blond, in his mid-twenties, he was, O'Neill once said, "extraordinarily handsome, almost too beautiful, very like Oscar Wilde's description of Dorian Gray. Even his name was flowery." His history, in O'Neill's account, was as colorful as his appearance. The "younger son of a traditionally noble British family, he had been through the English public schools, had acquired a university accent, and finally down in London, became one of its lordly young men. Then suddenly he messed up his life — pretty conspicuously. Though he didn't have to leave England, he couldn't face life there, couldn't bear the thought of daily reminders of what he'd lost — a lady — and decided to try South America. When [he] left a café, most of its liquor went along with him."

Apparently Eugene swallowed his story whole, yet it seems a shade too perfect, like something lifted intact from the sentimental fiction of the day: all the advantages of birth and wealth, every assurance of an enviable future; then a scandal, a stained reputation, the adored one lost forever; self-exile in Buenos Aires among the pimps, crimps, bullies and prostitutes of the water front, endless nights of drinking in a vain effort to Forget. It's all there, all the ingredients of hackneyed fiction. Perhaps the young man's history was everything he claimed, or perhaps he was a member of

James Findlater Byth's romanticizing tribe. In either case, it was almost inevitable that the sentimental mist that sometimes adulterates the fresh salt air in the *Glencairn* plays should thicken around Smitty the Duke, the fictional counterpart of Eugene's déclassé roommate.

Another young Englishman O'Neill met in a café was of a different breed, Charles Ashleigh by name, poet, journalist, adventurer, radical, one who had early dedicated himself to helping reshape the world in a Socialist image. He later, after Buenos Aires, wandered up into the States and became active in the Industrial Workers of the World, commonly known as "the Wobblies," a militant group greatly feared by the vested interests; in 1918 he was among a host of I.W.W. members tried in Chicago for subversion and antiwar activities – a famous trial that drew international attention. John Reed, the noted journalist and war correspondent, described him at the time as "fastidious, sophisticated, with the expression of a well-bred Puck."

Ashleigh, who was working as a free-lance reporter for the Buenos Aires *Herald* when he and Eugene became acquainted, later wrote of their brief friendship: "It was too warm for the theater, and I was tired of the noisy and over-decorated cafés of the Calle Florida or the Avenida de Mayo. So I wandered down to dockland, the untidy streets which stretch the length of the miles of docks. Passing a seaman's café, I thought that here might be the means of killing a half-hour. The place was full of men and tobacco smoke. Tables were thumped, and voices raised. The syllables of a dozen languages clashed. . . .

"There was no vacant table, so I picked one where but a single customer was sitting – a rather morose, dark young American. I ordered a glass of beer, and listened to the music supplied by the mulatto pianist, pounding out popular tunes. Now and then some husky stoker or deck hand would rise, walk lumberingly and self-consciously to the pianist's platform, and full-throatedly bellow out some sea song, or perhaps some mournful sentimental ditty of inordinate length.

"I ordered another schooner of beer and gazed glumly about. My companion also appeared to be subdued, and looked with black-browed boredom on the scene. I took him to be second or third mate of an American vessel, or perhaps a ship's young engineer. Half an hour passed; neither of us had said a word. Then my mood exploded into speech: 'Good Lord, I'm sick of this. I haven't talked with a soul all day.' My companion straightened up, and looked at me with faint awakening interest. 'Nor have I. Have another drink?'

"So I had another drink, and within minutes we were well launched, discussing sailing ships and steamships, Conrad and Keats, the mountains and ports of South America, politics and the theater. I especially remember Keats, because at that time O'Neill was writing poetry, which appeared then to be his main interest. I also was trying to write verse; and I remember how we each produced manuscripts from our pockets, exchanged them across the sloppy table, read, discussed, criticized. We sat up all night, talking, talking, talking, with the ardor and exuberance of youth. We ranged the world, conversationally, and I don't know how many schooners we consumed during the debauch of talk. And then at dawn we parted, agreeing to meet the next day. And after that there were many nights of savory talk and of long inquisitive wanderings around Buenos Aires, together with this young vagabond, sailor, poet, who was later to be acknowledged as America's foremost playwright."

Another time, thinking of those nights, Ashleigh said that he would always remember his "crazy meeting with Gene in a water-front tingel-tangel joint in Buenos Aires. I would never have forgotten him had he never even written a line. B.A. wasn't much of a 'cultural' town and meeting him was like finding water in the desert. Nothing happened with us except talk, young guys' talk, full of fog and fireworks and faith in beauty and effort."

There is a little mystery attached to this period of O'Neill's life that has escaped previous notice. According to what he later said, he made a round trip between Buenos Aires and Durban, South Africa, "tending mules in a cattle steamer" — he once identified the vessel as British — but was not allowed to land in Durban since he did not have at least a hundred dollars, as required by local law. This is practically all he ever said on record about a two-way voyage which would have lasted nearly two months.

In an attempt to learn something about the voyage, a list of all British freighters making the round trip between Buenos Aires and Durban during the time of O'Neill's stay in Argentina was sent to the General Register and Record Office of Shipping and Seamen in Britain; the ships' articles of all these sailings were checked by the Register but O'Neill's name was not found among any of the crews. Though this may be discounted as negative evidence — perhaps he shipped under an assumed name or on a non-British vessel — the Register uncovered testimony of a positive nature indicating that he never made the voyage: when O'Neill was signed on by the British freighter that carried him home from Argentina, he stated that this was his "first" ship, in other words, his first berth as a working seaman.

It seems, after such findings, that the African trip was fictitious, that O'Neill wanted to inflate his record as a seaman; but there is a complicating factor, added by Fred Hettman. Several weeks before Eugene's credit expired at the boarding house on Calle Mexico, Fred returned to town and dropped by to see him, only to be informed by the landlady that he had sailed for Africa. The thought now arises that possibly Eugene, hard up for drinking money, persuaded the woman to return part of his rent payment, money advanced by Fred, and after directing her to tell Hettman he had left for Africa, cleared out early. In sum, the weight of evidence indicates that he never made the voyage to Durban, yet uncertainty remains.

His final months in Argentina were a period of almost unrelieved destitution. In hopes of improving his lot, he wandered down the coast to La Plata and applied for work at the Swift packing house, impulsively telling the foreman — an impulse he promptly came to regret — that he wanted to "start at the bottom." Taking him at his word, the man assigned him to sorting out raw hides, a job he detested even more than his back-straining work on the *Timandra*. He was on the verge of quitting when fire broke out, destroying the warehouse. "I didn't do it," he once said, "but it was a good idea."

Nearly forty years later, talking to Hamilton Basso of the *New Yorker* magazine, he made it sound as though he had suffered through the job only yesterday. "The stench was unforgettable," Basso wrote. "O'Neill still shudders when he recalls how the smell got into his clothes, his mouth, his eyes, his ears, his nose, and his hair."

Out of work again, often hungry, Eugene suffered fresh misfortune in a recurrence of the malarial fever he had contracted in Honduras; it required his last ounce of endurance to keep going those final weeks in Buenos Aires. Some idea of his desperate state may be gained from what he told Basso: "I was then twenty-two years old and a real-down-and-outer — sleeping on park benches, hanging around waterfront dives, and absolutely alone. I knew a fellow who used to work on a railroad down there and who had given up his job. One day, he suggested that we hold up one of those places where foreign money is exchanged. Well, I have to admit that I gave the matter serious consideration. I finally decided not to do it, but since you aren't given to taking a very moral view of things when you are sleeping on park benches and haven't a dime to your name, I decided what I did because I felt that we were almost certain to be caught. A few nights later, the fellow who had propositioned me stuck the place up with somebody he'd got to take my place, and he *was* caught."

The S.S. *Ikala*, on which Eugene sailed home, was the model for his fictional S.S. *Glencairn*. In his writings it became a "rusty lime-juicer," an atmospheric backdrop for Smitty the Duke's humiliation at the hands of his shipmates, for Yank's painful death one fog-shrouded night en route to Cardiff, for bumboat women and drunken brawling at a time of full moon in the Caribbees. In life the vessel was just another tramp freighter, a "three-island" type, like so many ships at the time in the British merchant fleet, with nothing in its appearance, personality or history to set it apart from the others. Built in 1901, the 2800-ton freighter had originally led a wandering existence as the *Planet Neptune* until a change of ownership in 1909 brought it the prosaic name of *Ikala*. Whatever his reason, O'Neill was long reticent about the true-life counterpart of his S.S. *Glencairn*, identifying it only as the British freighter on which he had returned from Buenos Aires. He told one persistent reporter that he had forgotten its name. When in 1932 he finally did identify it, the name, whether O'Neill or the interviewer was at fault, appeared in print erroneously as the *Ikalis*, a sister ship of the *Ikala*.

In March 1911 the *Ikala*, undermanned as it prepared to leave for New York, took on a few "wandering Willies" and "scenery bums" — transient hands who would join a ship just to get from one place to another. On March 20, the day before its departure, it added "E. G. O'Neill" of 201 West 79th Street (the Lucerne Hotel), New York; in signing on he stated that this was his "first" ship. As a novice anxious to make the trip, he began his career for the nominal pay of one shilling a month but still had to do his full share of the work — scrubbing deck, chipping rust, painting. On the *Charles Racine* he had experienced the poetry of life at sea, had been part of the collaboration of wind and sail and ocean; on the *Ikala*, jammed into an odorous fo'c'sle, routed out for duty at all hours and in all sorts of weather, he became familiar with the dull labor, the monotonous prose of a seaman's existence.

"This sailor life ain't much to cry about leavin'," says the dying Yank in *Bound East for Cardiff*, "just one ship after another, hard work, small pay, and bum grub; and when we git into port, just a drunk endin' up in a fight, and all your money gone . . . Never meetin' no nice people; never gittin' outa sailor-town, hardly, in any port; travellin' all over the world and never seein' none of it; without no one to care whether you're alive or dead. (With a bitter smile) There ain't much in all that that'd make yuh sorry to lose it. . . . I was just thinkin' it ain't as bad as people think — dyin'. I ain't never took much stock in the truck them sky-pilots preach. I ain't never had religion; but I know whatever it is what comes after it can't be no worser'n this."

O'Neill made almost nothing of the master of his fictional ship; the latter appears but briefly as a colorless figure in only one of the three plays set aboard the *Glencairn*. Captain Robert Carruthers of the *Ikala* was, however, a distinct personality, a small man with a neat Van Dyke beard whose size and dapper appearance belied his stature as a disciplinarian. Descended from a long line of Solway Firth masters, himself a man who had gone to sea at fourteen, he seemed quite tall when dressing down a sailor or coldly admonishing one of his mates; otherwise, the sole indication of his character was the measured control, the determination, with which he puffed on his pipe. Since he ran such a tight ship, the crew was constantly changing; the freighter left Buenos Aires with only an assistant cook in the galley.

Decades later Eugene still remembered the mess on the *Ikala*, especially the "preserved" potatoes. "Preserved how, for God's sake! I never found out." He subsisted chiefly on marmalade and hardtack, yet thrived. "Starve? No, never felt better in my life, weighed a hundred and sixty-five." After sleeping on the benches of the Paseo de Julio and the Plaza de Mayo and scrounging for something edible to keep him alive, even the *Ikala* was an improvement.

Of the deck gang of fifteen, chiefly English, Swedish, Russian and Danish, O'Neill long remembered one man in particular, though he erroneously recalled him as "Norwegian" — there were no Norwegians aboard. "The great sorrow and mistake of his life, he used to grumble, was that as a boy he had left the small paternal farm to run away to sea. He had been at sea twenty years, and had never gone home once in that time.

"He was a bred-in-the-bone child of the sea if there ever was one. With his feet on the plunging deck he was planted like a natural growth in what was 'good clean earth' to him. If ever a man was in perfect harmony with his environment, a real part of it, this Norwegian was.

"Yet he cursed the sea and the life it had led him — affectionately. He loved to hold forth on what a fool he had been to leave the farm. There was the life for you, he used to tell the grumblers all in the fo'c'scle. A man on his own farm was his own boss. He didn't have to eat rotten grub, and battle bedbugs, and risk his life in storms on a rotten old 'limejuice' tramp. He didn't have to wait for the end of a long voyage for a pay day and a good drunk.

"No, sir, a man on his own farm could get drunk every Saturday night and stay drunk all day Sunday if he wanted to! (At this point the fo'c'scle to a man became converted to agriculture.) Then, too, a man could get married and have kids.

"Finally the Norwegian having got rid of his farm inhibitions for the time being would grin resignedly, and take up his self-appointed burden of making a rope mat for some 'gel' in Barracas he had promised it to the next trip down."

En route to New York the *Ikala* stopped for several days at Port of Spain to pick up 250 tons of bunker coal as ballast and a consignment of 555 bags of Trinidad coconuts. O'Neill once said that an incident during the layover "remotely suggested" the idea for one of his sea tales, *The Moon of the Caribbees*. This was all he ever said about it, but certain circumstances suggest the likely nature of his inspiration; because of the shallowness of the harbor at Port of Spain, the ship had to anchor a half-mile from the jetties, and consequently the crew's only means for getting liquor was to have someone smuggle it aboard. In *Moon of the Caribbees*, which opens peacefully as the *Glencairn* is anchored off an island in the West Indies, bumboat women smuggle some rum aboard under their loads of fruit. The quiet tropical night shortly erupts into an enthusiastic brawl among the seamen — the ban on liquor was designed to prevent this sort of thing — while the bumboat women clamor on the side lines to be paid for their rum and some hasty love-making.

Though Eugene was on the *Ikala* less than a month, he soaked up impressions and stored away images that eventually would materialize not only in the four *Glencairn* plays but in several of his long works. When he arrived back in New York on the night of April 15, he had been away from the States nearly a year. Shivering from the cold and nervous about his reception, about all the questions that would be asked, he left the freighter the following day, Easter Sunday, to rejoin his family.

12

Jimmy the Priest's

THE reunion was scarcely a success on either side. James and Ella found their younger son as restless, as unsettled as formerly, while he found it strange, really disconcerting, that after all he had been through, things at home had remained virtually unchanged. It was as though time had stopped for the others. He felt that he had undergone a lifetime of experience since boarding the *Charles Racine*, yet here was his father still playing in *The White Sister* — it was about to end its career with a week at the Manhattan Opera House — and all more or less the same with his mother and Jamie. Primarily, though, he was unhappy about himself. He had shipped out in search of something — maturity, a better understanding of himself, a sense of purpose in life — and had returned as directionless as ever, feeling, if anything, even more isolated, more of a stranger in the family.

During his absence Ella had had an upsetting experience. Strolling with a friend near Riverside Drive, she had paused to admire a husky infant being wheeled by an attractive young woman, but immediately afterward was thrown into a state of agitation; as they moved on, her companion informed her that the child was her grandson, the woman pushing him her daughter-in-law. The elder O'Neills, as well as Eugene, were uncertain how to resolve the situation with Kathleen, but one day on impulse he phoned his wife that he wanted to drop by and see her.

Their own reunion was polite, uncomfortable and fruitless, the last time husband and wife ever met. At one point Eugene asked to see his child, who was asleep in the next room. "He was a beautiful baby," Mrs. Pitt-Smith said years later. "I know all mothers believe that, but I've seen plenty of babies and he really was unusual. His face was all rosy and flushed, the way a baby is when he's been sleeping, and he behaved beautifully when I picked him up. He didn't burst out crying or anything like that, the way most babies will if you suddenly break in on their sleep and hand them to a stranger. He seemed to take to Mr. O'Neill, which pleased me very much. After a while he fell asleep again, in Mr. O'Neill's arms, and I put him back in bed.

"All evening I kept expecting Mr. O'Neill to say why he'd called, why he'd come to see me, but he never did. . . . No, I can't remember what we talked about — it happened too long ago."

The routine at home, after Buenos Aires and the sea, soon palled on Eugene; even the Haymarket seemed dull by comparison with the Sailor's Opera and the dives of Barracas. Edgy and more than ever critical of his parents, he spent as little time around them as possible. He drank whenever in funds, hung around with Jamie, who was "at liberty" after two seasons of *The Travelling Salesman*, and increasingly haunted the dockside area of lower Manhattan; he felt more at home there than anywhere else, among the seamen, dollar whores and other hard-bitten drifters.

At 252 Fulton Street, opposite Washington Market and only a few doors from the river-front sprawl of West Street, was an old red-brick building, four and one-half stories, that was destined to play an important role in O'Neill's life and in his writings. No name was on the saloon at 252, which Eugene began to patronize, only a window sketch of a large beer glass and under it in faded yellow letters, "SCHOONER — 5¢," to relieve the bare frontage of plate glass and swinging doors. The interior, which smelled of beer, cigar smoke and, faintly, of unwashed bodies, was similarly plain: an old mahogany bar at the left, an uncovered free-lunch spread at the right, sawdust on the floor, in the rear a few round tables with chairs grouped near a large pot-bellied stove. In lieu of a regular back room, a curtain could be drawn to separate the table area from the rest of the saloon.

The place was known as "Jimmy the Priest's" after the distinctive individual who ran it, a withdrawn man, something of an enigma in the neighborhood; few if any knew his surname or scarcely anything else about him. His full name was James J. Condon; around fifty years old when O'Neill became one of his habitués, Condon had had bars on nearby West Street before taking over the Fulton Street Spot in 1908.

His customers used to argue among themselves about the origin of his nickname, some contending that he had studied for the priesthood but that "something happened"; others, that he had two or three brothers in the church, while still others thought he got the name from his rather clerical appearance. O'Neill sided with the last group in sketching him as "Johnny the Priest" in *Anna Christie:* "With his pale, thin, clean-shaven face, mild blue eyes and white hair, a cassock would seem more suited to him than the apron he wears. Neither his voice nor his general manner dispels this illusion which has made him a personage of the water front. They are soft and bland, but beneath all his mildness one senses the man behind the mask — cynical, callous, hard as nails."

In the reminiscences of two men who for years worked for a ships' chandler next door to Jimmy the Priest's, there emerges a fuller portrait of the faintly mysterious barkeep. "Jimmy," said Mario Alessi, "feared nothing. In most bars if a customer turned nasty, the bartender would first try to calm him down, but not Jimmy. The moment he smelled trouble, he'd grab the man, no matter how big he was — Jimmy was tall but thin — and give him the bum's rush through the swinging doors. He did it so fast he bowled over the toughest characters. There were two steps at the entrance, high stone ones, and sometimes the man would stumble and land flat in the street, yet Jimmy never looked over the doors to see if he was hurt or anything. He'd just return behind the bar, looking as cool as ever — he was a real poker face. I never heard him raise his voice, but you could tell when he had his Irish up."

Condon, nevertheless, had a softer side. Alessi, as well as several other youths who had gone to work on Fulton Street at an early age, found him an easy touch for carfare home, and another employee of the ships' chandler, John Callan, recalls that he was generous to seamen down on their luck. He gave shelter to more than a few in his flophouse above the saloon, according to Callan, and, unlike the regular boarding masters, never squeezed them for "blood money" when they had landed a berth. To both Alessi and Callan he was something of a Jekyll-Hyde mixture of offhand kindness and cynical toughness. Though his impassive blue eyes missed little, he never interfered when one of his regulars followed a drunken transient out of his place with the obvious intent of "rolling him."

Whether Eugene first heard of the saloon through shipmates on the *Ikala* or happened on it by himself, its primary attraction was cheap drinks — five-cent whiskey of passable quality, a sixteen-ounce schooner of beer for a nickel, where most places charged the same for a ten- or twelve-ounce stein. Also, it remained open later than other bars in the area, till well after midnight, and no one bothered you if you fell asleep with your head on a table. It wasn't long before Eugene, instead of returning to his parents' apartment at the Lucerne, moved into the flophouse over the saloon; he paid three dollars a month for one of its cells.

"Jimmy the Priest's," he once said, "certainly was a hell hole. It was awful. One couldn't go any lower. Gorky's Night's Lodging was an ice cream parlor by comparison. The house was almost coming down and the principal housewreckers were vermin." But he was dramatizing. Far from ever collapsing, the building, around a hundred years old when Eugene lived there, was afterward occupied for nearly a half-century by a ships' chandler, Williams & Wells, which loaded its floors with heavy maritime supplies and equipment. In use to the end, the structure finally was razed in 1966 to make way for the forthcoming skyscraper of the World Trade Center.

If Eugene found the place "coming down," it probably was because he so often saw it wavery and insubstantial through an alcoholic haze; most likely, too, he was misled as to the condition of the building itself by the makeshift flophouse on the second and third floors. In "Tomorrow," the only one of his short stories ever published, a first-person narrative largely set in the bar and flophouse of "Tommy the Priest's," he told of sharing a double room that had twin beds, a kerosene lamp, and a window overlooking the rear yard. Actually, the accommodations at Jimmy's were simpler and cruder than he described, for there were no "doubles" and rooms offering the luxury of a view. Instead, the place had rows of windowless cells down the length of each floor, on both sides and separated by an aisle; the cells, just large enough for a cot and a chair, had wire mesh topping the partitions and flimsy doors which could be locked. These minimal precautions were designed to discourage the men from rifling one another's pockets and from mixing it up in drunken brawls. Their mattresses were of straw, the cheapest kind, an economy dictated not only by the low rent but by the fact that the men not infrequently befouled themselves in bed — after which the mattresses were thrown out. On each of the floors were a sink, a toilet, a small stove, and suspended from the ceiling a kerosene lighting fixture. None of the cells had its own lamp; the place otherwise would have burned down a hundred times over from its careless, hard-drinking lodgers.

O'Neill's widow, reminiscing about the life they had had together — travels in Europe and the Far East, a château in France, fine homes on the Atlantic seaboard and in California — once recalled that all this had apparently meant less to him than his down-and-out period around the water front. He was fondest of dwelling on the time that he "drank too much and inferior liquor, and wore his body and soul out, without proper food or even a bed at night. . . .

"The strange part of it is that Gene's pride seemed to be in *those* years. I said to him once, half-jokingly, 'I have dragged you about Europe, I have worked like anything to show you all the beautiful spots and I have never heard you once say you liked this or that or the other.' 'Well,' he said, 'I liked them but they weren't very exciting.'"

The seven dollars a week Eugene was getting from his father would have sufficed at Jimmy the Priest's had he lived on an even keel, but he always seemed anxious to get rid of the money; it went fast in prolonged binges, in drinks for fellow lodgers, in a quarter to this one, a half-dollar to another. After several days of this careless spending and lending he was, until his next allowance, reduced to beer, an occasional five-cent whiskey, and the free-lunch spread. At noon every day the spread featured a large pot of soup, not too bad until flecked with flies and other insects. The majority of Condon's customers, stand-up drinkers who were in and out of the bar quickly, ignored the lunch, but his lodgers and other hangers-on depended on it; even when they were out of beer money, he allowed them a bowl or two of soup and other food. Condon, for all his reserve, gave his regulars a feeling of last-ditch security.

They were, according to O'Neill, a "hard lot, at first glance. Every type — sailors on shore leave or stranded; longshoremen, waterfront riffraff, gangsters, down and outers, drifters from the ends of the earth. . . . They were sincere, loyal and generous. In some queer way they carried on. I learned at Jimmy the Priest's not to sit in judgment on people."

The Fulton Street spot would serve not only as the model for the bar in *Anna Christie* but among the models for the one in *The Iceman Cometh*. Since prostitutes figure in both plays, this has given rise to the impression that they used to frequent Jimmy the Priest's; actually no women of any kind were to be found there, for Condon's place, which had no family entrance and separate back room, was strictly stag. But there were other saloons in the vicinity where streetwalkers hung out, where the future playwright became acquainted with the Anna Christies, Coras, and fat old Marthys he was to write about. The women found a ready supply of customers among the farmers and workhands of Washington Market and the sailors and roustabouts who thronged the area.

The area boiled with life not only from the Market, as wagonloads of food poured in and dribbled out, but from the dockings and sailings of the Fall River, Providence, and New Bedford lines, from the river-front commerce of West Street, from the ferry lines disgorging and swallowing up commuters, from the regular rise and fall of activity around the *Evening Globe* plant on adjacent Dey Street, as newsboys and delivery men streamed out with the editions, while printers and other pressmen descended in thirsty shoals on the saloons.

Often when he tired of his lively surroundings Eugene would wander down to the Battery to sun himself on a bench and take in the calming view — liners, freighters, tugs and ferries moving around in the harbor,

sea gulls circling overhead and winging by; and sometimes he was ener-
getic enough to work on a poem. A few months after he had settled at
Jimmy the Priest's the New London *Telegraph* ran some verse that was
signed "Contributed." From its content, as well as the fact that he was
visiting New London at the time, there is reason for thinking that "Shut
In" was written by O'Neill:

> *I know how the beast of the desert feels*
> *As the steel bars shut him in,*
> *I know how he fights a superior force*
> *With never a chance to win,*
> *How he paces across his narrow cage*
> *As he drags his life in fruitless rage —*
> *For I, too, am shut in. . . .*
>
> *Bound by a chain of circumstance*
> *To a life that knows no peace;*
> *Fettered more closely than bird or beast,*
> *By duties that never cease;*
> *Closely the bars of my cage are set,*
> *Strong to withstand my wild regret —*
> *And no hope of release.*

James O'Neill felt almost as unsettled this summer as his younger son;
now that *The White Sister* had closed he was worried about the upcom-
ing season. Although he told friends that Liebler's was going to costar
him with Viola Allen in a new work on Broadway, he made plans for a
vaudeville engagement in scenes from a Tennyson play and informed the
press that it would be "one of the most elaborate productions in this line
ever seen." Tyler and Will Connor, both of whom admired and loved
"the Governor," had difficulty reassuring him that his career had not
ended. They found it still harder to arouse him from depressed thoughts
about his sons. One holed up in God knows what sort of place down by
the docks, and why, what was the sense of it? There must be something
wrong with the boy's mind! As for the other one, his precious namesake,
no use going on about him, it was too old a story. Tyler and Connor
always knew "the Governor" had talked himself out when he eventually
would say, "God deliver me from my children!"

Though Eugene found the primitive accommodations of Jimmy's
flophouse endurable the first several months, he felt differently in July;
July began in a blaze of heat, the hottest spell in many years. The cells at

Condon's were like ovens with the doors closed, and even when the heat wave ended, the place remained airless and stifling, its usual smell of urine and stale flesh more sour than ever. After days of getting his best sleep in the rear of the saloon, his head on a table, Eugene decided to ship out again, but he had had his fill of freighters from his few weeks on the *Ikala*. On July 22 he sailed as an ordinary seaman on a luxury liner, the S.S. *New York* of the American Line, bound for Southampton.

To its passengers the *New York*, with its rakish lines, covered promenade deck and other conveniences, represented the height of seagoing luxuriousness. To its crew it was something else again, packed as they were into quarters that belied the size of the ship and given a mess that featured salt beef, salt pork, dried fish and canned meat. Eugene, with memories of the *Charles Racine*, found his new berth an "ugly, tedious job, and no place for a man who wanted to call his soul his own. . . . There was about as much 'sea glamor' in working aboard a passenger steamship as there would have been in working in a summer hotel. I washed enough deck area to cover a good-sized town."

Yet he did not mind the work so much as he resented the passengers, especially the women, promenading in fine clean clothes, chatting and laughing, while he was on his knees scrubbing the deck. It is unlikely that anyone noticed him, yet he felt patronized, an object of distaste. He would later project his resentment onto "Yank," the burly stoker of *The Hairy Ape*, whose great self-pride starts to crumble after the society heiress calls him a "filthy beast."

Yank, in spite of his forbidding exterior, was an O'Neill protagonist close to O'Neill's heart, meaning more to him than appears in the play. As an apprehensive soul who admired the strong and fearless, Eugene looked with awe on the swaggering "black gang," the firemen and coal passers of the stokehold. He had observed their clannishness ashore but it was not until he sailed on the American liner that he fully realized the hostility between them and other seamen. They looked down on the deck hands as weaklings, while the latter professed to find the black gang almost subhuman.

The stokers often complained of the harshness of their lot, but actually they gloried in it; it enabled them to prove their toughness. A contemporary newspaper account leaves nothing to the imagination as to what they had to endure: "An inferno, all smoke and heat and fire and nakedness, is the stokehold of an ocean liner. As you enter it, picking your way over the burning ashes, the hot blast from the furnace mouths smites you in the face; it scorches your eyes and sears your lungs with every gasping breath you draw. . . . Life seems impossible in such an atmosphere.

"And yet the inferno hums with life and strenuous, almost savage, industry. Opposite the huge boilers, quivering with suppressed power, like so many chained giants, are the figures of men as if carved in ebony, glistening with the sweat that streams from every pore. They are working furiously, with muscles swelling and knotting as if they would burst through [the] skin. . . . Gathering up a shovelful of coal, each man propels them with a quick forward thrust of the body into the white hot heart of the furnace and with a dextrous turn of the wrist spreads them evenly over the fire. Then, quick as the eye can follow, another shovelful succeeds and another. . . .

The *New York*, which normally took a week for the trip to England, developed mechanical trouble and arrived a day late at Southampton. After landing most of its passengers and making its regular short run to Cherbourg to deposit the rest, it returned to Southampton to enter drydock for repairs and general overhauling. Eugene had the unexpected opportunity of soaking up the atmosphere of a British port. Among the apparent results of his layover is the background of *The Long Voyage Home,* one of the *Glencairn* cycle, which, though set in a bar on the London water front, is probably based on a dive he had known in Southampton — "a squalid dingy room dimly lighted by kerosene lamps." The English types who infest the pub (O'Neill the Irishman must have enjoyed sketching them) are similarly unprepossessing: "A slovenly barmaid with a stupid face sodden with drink. . . . A round-shouldered young fellow . . . his face is pasty, his mouth weak, his eyes shifting and cruel. . . . Fat Joe, the proprietor, a gross bulk of a man with an enormous stomach. His face is red and bloated, his little piggish eyes being almost concealed by rolls of fat."

Another work reflecting his brief stay in England is an early full-length play that, never staged or published, is virtually unknown. *The Personal Equation* tells of a rebellious young American ("I'm a college boy if that one year I wasted in college makes me one") who becomes active in anarchists' circles and ends a martyr to the cause, shot during a seamen's uprising in Liverpool. In mid-August 1911, labor strife erupted throughout England but nowhere with such violence as in Liverpool, close to Ireland and heavily populated by the Irish. By comparison with Liverpool, Southampton was relatively quiet, yet the crews of the many ships in port were not immune to the general excitement, the nation-wide mood of labor protest. The stokers and deck hands buried for the time their traditional feud in the age-old antagonism of the have-nots toward the haves, as they pledged their support for the dock laborers and transport workers in their threat of a general strike. The strike did materialize, paralyzing the country and arousing fears of imminent anarchy; all railroads stopped running, all ships were frozen in port, and food supplies ran low in the cities. It was, at the time, the worst scare from labor in Britain's history. What would afterward be known as the Great General Strike of 1911 lasted only a few days, however, after which conditions returned more or less to normal.

Before long the black gangs and the deck hands resumed their old postures of, in O'Neill's words, "healthy contempt" for one another. But during the period of fraternizing he made friends with a muscle-plated stoker named Driscoll, off the S.S. *Philadelphia*, a sister ship of the *New York*; the friendship got off to a good start with hero worship on one side, on the other, bellowing good-humor and rough affection.

Though Driscoll was born in Ireland, O'Neill later described him as a "Liverpool Irishman," a misstatement born probably of O'Neill's dramatizing cast of mind, his feeling for what was artistically right. "Years ago," he said, "some Irish families settled in Liverpool. Most of them followed the sea, and they were a hard lot. To sailors all over the world a 'Liverpool Irishman' is the synonym for a tough customer." Since Driscoll was plenty tough, his birthplace, so far as O'Neill was concerned, had to be Liverpool.

Five feet seven, in his early thirties, built rather like an upended anchor, with massive arms and shoulders overarching a sturdy body, he was, O'Neill said, a "giant of a man, and absurdly strong. He thought a whole lot of himself, was a determined individualist. He was very proud of his strength, his capacity for grueling work. It seemed to give him mental poise to be able to dominate the stokehold, to do more work than any of his mates."

His image recurs over and over in O'Neill's writings, sometimes under his nickname of "Yank" — he was a naturalized American — but more often under his real name. He appears as "Driscoll" in all four *Glencairn* pieces, with a double-sketch of him as "Yank" in two of the same playlets. O'Neill used him again as the model for "Lyons," a stoker, in the short story "Tomorrow," and borrowed something of his personality for "Mat Burke," the heroine's suitor in *Anna Christie*. But all these depictions pale beside his portrait as the ill-fated hero of *The Hairy Ape*. His personal impact is felt instantly as the play opens: "He seems broader, fiercer, more truculent, more powerful, more sure of himself than the rest [of the stokers]. They respect his superior strength — the grudging respect of fear." O'Neill's somber view of Driscoll as projected in *The Hairy Ape* was a kind of afterthought, inspired by the dramatic circumstances of the stoker's death; but during their short friendship Eugene took him at face value — a vital two-fisted male who was on top of life.

When the *Philadelphia* sailed from Southampton on August 19, with Driscoll again lording it in the hold, Eugene was one of the deck crew. This time he bore the rating of able-bodied seaman, at $27.50 a month, an advance of $2.50 over his pay as an ordinary seaman on the *New York*. To win the rating he had had to demonstrate that he was familiar with ship's nomenclature, could tie all the standard knots and, in his words, "box the compass and do several other things which the ordinary seaman cannot." The promotion meant a great deal to him; to the end of his life he preserved the yellow slip of paper, his discharge from the *Philadelphia*, certifying that "E. G. O'Neill" was an able-bodied seaman. "The last one I shipped on," he once said, a shade of regret in his voice.

Another memento he would always cherish, a heavy black pull-on jersey sweater with American Line embroidered in white across the chest, was part of the uniform the crew had to wear at the start and end of the sailings, a bit of dressing-up for the passengers' benefit. He would wear the sweater on and off for years, holding on to it, symbol of days when he was "free," long after it had become riddled with holes. Some twenty years after he had quit the sea his wife Carlotta Monterey, chancing on the tattered garment, had it darned without his knowledge and presented him with what seemed a practically new sweater; at first he was unable to say anything, he was so moved.

As an "A.B." on the *Philadelphia* his duties were much the same as on the other liner — swabbing deck, shifting baggage and mail — but in addition they included an occasional two-hour watch in the crow's-nest. This was his favorite turn of duty. Once, while standing dawn watch, he was caught up in the same sort of mystical exaltation he had known on the sail-winged *Charles Racine*. In *Long Day's Journey*, he describes the moment: "A calm sea, that time. Only a lazy ground swell and a slow drowsy roll of the ship. . . . Dreaming, not keeping lookout, feeling alone, and above, and apart, watching the dawn creep like a painted dream over the sky and sea which slept together. Then the moment of ecstatic freedom came. The peace, the end of the quest, the last harbor, the joy of belonging to a fulfillment beyond men's lousy, pitiful, greedy fears and hopes and dreams!"

Eugene received $14.84 when he signed off the *Philadelphia* on August 26 — pay covering his service on the two vessels — and his friend Driscoll, whose monthly pay was $40, drew $25.77 for his round trip on the liner. Some of their money went for drinks at Jimmy the Priest's, but Eugene refrained from sinking into one of his "booze busts." Whether his father had left word for him at the saloon or he felt an urge to see his family, he shortly quit the city.

In New London he had a reunion with Ed Keefe, who had switched from art studies in New York to the practice of architecture in his home town (both "Bread and Butter" and *The Great God Brown* were partly inspired by his history), and renewed an old friendship with two of the McGinley boys, Art and Tom (the family in *Ah, Wilderness!* is modeled to some extent on the easygoing McGinley clan, including the mother). Eugene also saw something of Judge Frederick P. Latimer, editor of the *Morning Telegraph,* a perceptive and kindly man who was to be the first to encourage the literary ambitions of James O'Neill's prodigal son. One of Latimer's pet features in the *Telegraph* was the "Laconics" column, a catchall for topical comment, humor, and poetry, the latter generally by well-known poets. The September 1 column, however, included some verse from an anonymous contributor, entitled "Shut In," that began:

> *I know how the beast of the desert feels*
> *As the steel bars shut him in . . .*

A day later the *Day* ran a story, headlined O'Neill Is Fond of Odd Voyages, that probably was written by Art McGinley, one of the reporters. Intermingling fact and fancy, the article states that Eugene "has poked his way into the majority of the countries of the world. . . . He acted in the capacity of assistant manager with [*The White Sister*] but found it much less fascinating than hobnobbing with Arabs, Chileans, Turks and others of the weird gentry. The wanderlust is on him again and in a few weeks Mr. O'Neill will be off on a tramp freighter which is to cover many thousand miles before coming back again to the land of the Stars and Stripes. . . . Although reared in an atmosphere of plenty and refinement, from which life as a member of a steamer crew is a far cry, [he] enjoys the odd experience and finds the men of the crew easy to get along with.

"He has never felt the call of the footlights, as has his older brother, James, although the younger Mr. O'Neill is said to have inherited much of his father's splendid dramatic talent; but some day after circumscribing the globe several times, he may settle down to a stage career."

If he had been eying the theater, his father probably would have discouraged him; James was taking a dim view of the stage in general, his own career in particular. Despite his earlier talk of costarring with Viola Allen in a new work on Broadway, of heading a sumptuous Tennyson production in vaudeville, he had had to fall back yet again on "that God-damned play." The impresarios of the two-a-day wanted him only if he would appear in a tabloid version of *Monte Cristo.* Though forced to take up their offer, he was determined to omit the famous line that had come to sound increasingly ironic in his own ears: "The wor-rld is mi-n-ne!"

While friends knew how frustrated he felt, the public got a different picture. The *Telegraph* reported on September 19 that he had accepted an "unusually flattering offer" to tour in the Dumas condensation throughout the winter and spring in this country, and that the booking company planned to "send him to Europe for a special engagement of seven weeks next summer. Mr. O'Neill's domestic and foreign tours will occupy nearly a year, and he will realize very handsomely from the contract. Mrs. O'Neill will accompany him."

Busy preparing to open his tour in Waterbury, James had scant patience with his son's vague plans of going to sea again. Where was the future in all this, when was he going to cut out this romantic nonsense and settle down? Though Ella agreed with her husband, she had little to say. She always felt on the defensive with Eugene, a feeling he reciprocated. In *Long Day's Journey* Edmund reproaches his mother, "I've been away a lot, and I've never noticed it broke your heart!" The mother: "(Sadly) You might have guessed, dear, that after I knew you knew — about me — I had to be glad whenever you were where you couldn't see me."

After telling friends that he was shortly sailing on a freighter around the world, Eugene returned to New York in mid-September, to Jimmy the Priest's. Perhaps he did intend to ship out again but, as events turned out, his seafaring days were over. It was, considering the briny flavor of so much of his writings, a surprisingly short period of his life. *Ile, Thirst, Fog, Where the Cross Is Made,* the *Glencairn* cycle — the majority of his one-acters that found production were sea tales. Of his full-length works, *Anna Christie, The Hairy Ape* and *Gold* come instantly to mind, but there are others; scenes aboard ship figure also in *The Fountain* and *Marco Millions, Strange Interlude* and *Mourning Becomes Electra,* while the waves can be heard lapping in the backgrounds of *Beyond the Horizon, Diff'rent* and *Long Day's Journey.* Further, the only time of his professional career he ever dramatized another man's work he chose Coleridge's ballad of the haunted mariner.

Clearly, O'Neill himself was haunted by the sea, as both his writings and his personal history attest. Aside from his career as a seaman, he was to live a large part of his adult life — in Provincetown, Bermuda, Sea Island, Georgia, and Marblehead — at the water's edge. The question is, what lay behind his obsessive feeling for the sea? One answer is that O'Neill the romanticist was more than ordinarily responsive to the sea's eternal fascination for the poet and the adventurer in us all. The chief answer is probably to be found, though, in *Monte Cristo*. Among the most striking images projected by the play is that of its hero reborn, so to speak, in the ocean. After years of death-in-life as a prisoner, Dantès is thrown into the water a supposed corpse and emerges with a new identity as the heir to the Monte Cristo fortune. The image must have made a deep impression on Eugene. From time immemorial man has instinctively regarded the sea as a source of life, as among other things a kind of universal mother; the sea calls to our inmost being, reminding us (if "reminds" is the right word for something beyond conscious thought) of the comfort and security of the womb, of the tide-like flow of blood in the mother's all-sheltering, all-nourishing body; the sea calls to the earliest, earliest ancestor behind our being, to the unicellular organism that drifted with the tides, that once had its home in the sea. There is, in short, something of atavistic validity, of emotional and poetic truth, behind the fanciful scene in *Monte Cristo* — Dantès's rebirth in the watery depths.

As one who felt wronged by life, Eugene O'Neill identified himself, unconsciously, with Edmond Dantès, an innocent young sailor grievously mistreated by fate; but to emulate Dantès's transformation into the Count of Monte Cristo, he would have to "die" and be "born" again. Significantly, he used to say that the ideal way to end one's life was to swim out until one grew tired and finally went under. That O'Neill had a strong death-wish is obvious from even a cursory examination of his life and his work; but in favoring death by drowning he, with the image of Edmond Dantès-Monte Cristo rooted in his soul, expressed not so much a death-wish as a wish to be reborn and start all over again as someone else.

Thomas Mann has another thought on the question of the sea's fascination: ". . . the eyes that rest on the wide ocean and are soothed by the sight of its waves rolling on forever, mystically, relentlessly, are those that are already wearied by looking too deeply into the solemn perplexities of life." At Jimmy the Priest's, Eugene tried to escape the "solemn perplexities" through drinking. Shipping out again would have meant just another *Ikala* or one of the big liners that would have had him scrubbing deck from one shore to the next; he preferred taking refuge in James J. Condon's "Bottom of the Sea Rathskeller." Occasionally he worked as a stevedore, helping load mail on the ships, but most of the time he drank, till his money ran out, dreamed of being a great poet some day, and spent shapeless days and nights listening to the hopes, regrets, and drunken maunderings of his fellow outcasts.

In later years he would give the impression that he sank completely into the underlife of Condon's bar and the water front, yet he was not entirely isolated from the outside world. Once a week he called at the

Liebler office for his allowance; his father, touring in vaudeville, had made the arrangement so that he could keep in touch through Tyler and Connor with his impossible son. Though Eugene used to grumble about the weekly calls — why couldn't the money be sent? — the visits regularly pulled him, if only briefly, out of his inertia and drift, kept him from feeling entirely alienated from his family, unwanted, disowned.

But more crucial to his survival was his poetry; besides giving him something to cling to, the hope that he might one day be a poet worthy of the name, his writings served as an escape valve for some of his inner turmoil: "I know how the beast of the desert feels/As the steel bars," etc. Also, he found a measure of relief in reading things that voiced his unhappy state. Several months after his return to Fulton Street the "Laconics" column of the New London *Telegraph* ran a poem entitled "Not Understood" that, circumstantial evidence suggests, was sent in by Eugene. Though the author was listed as "Unknown," it was written by Thomas Bracken, an Irishman who emigrated to New Zealand in the mid-19th century:

> *Not understood. We move along asunder;*
> *Our paths grow wider as the seasons creep*
> *Along the years; we marvel and we wonder,*
> *Why life is life, and then we fall asleep —*
> *Not understood. . . .*

> *Not understood. Poor souls with stunted vision*
> *Oft measure giants by the narrow gauge.*
> *The poisoned shafts of falsehood and derision*
> *Are oft impelled against those who mold the age —*
> *Not understood.*

O'Neill's fellow lodgers were a mixed lot, seamen, longshoremen, workmen at Washington Market, printers from the *Globe*, a grab bag of others, including a broken-down telegrapher known as "the Lunger," who was prone to spells of violent coughing. "The Lunger" when drunk took pride in being able to spit blood but became agitated if someone mentioned "consumption"; all he had, he used to insist, was "bloody bronchitis." Since he daily consumed more than a quart of the five-cent whiskey, his coughing before long was permanently stilled. Other lodgers were of a hardier breed, "Shorty," for instance. After the snows came,

Shorty, a dock worker, used to walk barefooted around the block to demonstrate his toughness. One night several fellow drinkers set out with him to prove that they were equally rugged but shortly tore back to the saloon, roaring their discomfort, to bake their feet around the stove.

Chris Christopherson was one Eugene would never forget. A thickly built man in his early forties, sandy-haired, with pale blue eyes and a straggly mustache, he projected, despite his weather-beaten exterior, a kind of innocence. "He had followed the sea so long," O'Neill once said, "that he got sick at the thought of it . . . he spent his time getting drunk and cursing the sea. 'Dat ole davil,' he called it. Finally he got a job as captain of a coal barge."

During long nights in the saloon, Eugene heard much of his history: descended from a line of sailors and born in Tönsberg, on the southern coast of Norway, he had shipped out at fourteen on a windjammer owned by a relative and had become a ship's mate when only twenty-two; his earliest known ancestors on both sides of the family had perished at sea, Ola Olsen Smidsrud in 1719, Jan Sørensen in 1744. In one breath he would curse the fate that had sent him roaming the world — in Buenos Aires he had contracted a recurrent case of malaria — when he most wanted to remain at home with his family; but in the next breath, thinking of his comedown to a barge, he used to boast that he was a real sailor, he had served on the old sailing ships.

Under his real name, still inveighing against "dat ole davil" and cast in his true-life role as a veteran seaman reduced to bargeman, Chris Christopherson is a central figure in *Anna Christie;* in other respects O'Neill took liberties with his portrait. The play presents him as a widower, good-natured but feckless, whose only child has been forced by circumstance and his neglect into prostitution. The real Chris, more responsible than O'Neill pictured him, had a wife and six children in Tönsberg and used to return home every third year for prolonged periods, once remaining for over two years; he often lamented to his family that if he remained in Norway he could not earn enough to support them properly. All his children, unlike Anna Christie, had a proper upbringing and grew into respected members of the community.

"His end in real life," as O'Neill told it, "was just one of many of the tragedies that punctuate the history of Jimmy the Priest's. Everybody got very drunk at Jimmy's one Christmas Eve, and Chris was very much in the party. . . . [He] tottered away about 2 o'clock in the morning for his barge. The next morning he was found frozen on a cake of ice between the piles and the dock. In trying to board the barge he stumbled on the plank and fell over."

Here again O'Neill tampered with fact, either from being misinformed or consciously from a sense of drama. Chris fell overboard not at Christmas time but on a warm night in fall, on October 15, 1917. Eight days later a harbor police launch found his body floating in broad daylight near the Statue of Liberty; he was wearing black pants, a gray sport shirt, a gray coat sweater, and had on his person forty-eight cents and a pocketknife. Identified by an uncle, with whom he had lived in Brooklyn, he was buried in Evergreen Cemetery. Only a few years later O'Neill would win a Pulitzer Prize for the play in which Chris wanders about muttering, "Dat ole davil!"

On one of Eugene's weekly calls at the Liebler office he met an old friend who beamed with happiness at seeing him — Jimmy Byth, his father's onetime press agent. He had aged visibly in the few years since he charmed the Chicago newspaperman with his whimsical talk of the Boer War and his fondness for a "wee drappie." Not time but drink had taken its toll. His last regular employment had been with Paine's fireworks display at Coney Island several years earlier. After a number of bad breaks, he said (Eugene rightly suspected that he had drunk himself out of a succession of jobs), he now was getting along on an occasional day's typing for Liebler's and other theatrical agencies. But he was not discouraged, oh, no, not at all, he assured Eugene; he was going to take a new grip on himself "tomorrow." He was confident everything would be all right "tomorrow"!

"I looked searchingly at his face," O'Neill has written, "the squat nose, the wistful eyes, the fleshy cheeks hanging down like dewlaps on either side of his weak mouth with its pale, thick lips. The usual marks of dissipation were there but none of the scars of intense suffering. The whole effect was characterless, unfinished; as if some sculptor at the last moment had suddenly lost interest in his clay model of a face and abandoned his work. . . . Forgetful of the last kick, his eyes had always looked up at life again with the same appealing, timid uncertainty, pleading for a caress, fearful of a blow. And life had never failed to deal him the expected kick. . . . Spurned, Jimmy had always returned, affectionate, uncomprehending, wagging his tail ingratiatingly, so to speak. The longed-for caress would come, he was sure of it, if not today, then tomorrow. Ah, tomorrow!"

This portrait appears in the short story "Tomorrow," written in 1916; Byth figures again, though sketchily, in a one-act work written three years later, "Exorcism"; O'Neill would draw him once more, this time definitively, in his 1939 giant of a play, *The Iceman Cometh*, as one of the lost souls in Harry Hope's dive. In both the short story and the long play he is known as "Jimmy Tomorrow."

After the chance meeting in Liebler's office, Byth settled at 252 Fulton, taking over a cubicle next to Eugene's. In spite of his gentle manner and precise speech, the crew at Condon's quickly accepted him, not only as Gene's friend but for himself; he was a sympathetic listener to their tales of misfortune and bucked them up by his unwavering belief that their luck was going to change. If they also respected him, it was less for his colorful past, his career as a Boer War correspondent, than for his capacity to match them drink for drink.

Byth in no time felt perfectly at home. Somehow, in a cell scarcely large enough for cot and chair, he found space for his broken type-writer — he was going to have it fixed "tomorrow" — and his collection of books. After earning several dollars from one of his occasional stints of typing, he would return to Condon's looking alcoholically pleased with himself and carrying "books of impossible poetry and incredible prose, written by unknown authors and published by firms one had never heard of . . . books with titles like *A Commentary on the Bulls of Pope Leo XIII*, or *God and the Darwinian Theory*, or *Sunflowers and Other Verses*." Sometimes Eugene would turn on him for wasting good money on the unreadable junk, money that would have bought a drink or two, some rich Italian cheese and fresh bread. But he could not remain angry long; Jimmy was so anxious to please, so eager to be liked, and moreover he had a disarming explanation of why he bought these particular books — they were orphans, the sort no one really wanted.

Life on Fulton Street always perked up whenever Driscoll blew in with a shipmate or two, fresh off one of the American Line vessels, all primed to get drunk and roaring an invitation to Eugene, Jimmy Byth, and others to join him. It meant several days of drink, songs, drink, arguments, drink, yarning about the sea, and occasional attempts by Driscoll to stir up a fight. Not that he was angry at anyone; he just wanted to test his strength against another's, just wanted "to have a bit av fun wid 'im." Eugene once, with the Dutch courage of drink, accepted his challenge but was told to be a "good bye" or he would get a spanking.

Less than two years later, O'Neill would abandon this chaotic existence in which he seemed practically indistinguishable from the other hard-living souls around the water front and settle down to writing plays. A great jump for him to make, yet not so great as it may appear; he was never the complete drifter he would afterward make himself out to have been. Aside from his efforts at poetry, more was at work in him than he himself realized: a submerged part of him had long had its sights fixed on the stage. When he turned playwright it was not an overnight transformation but a matter of an underground drive finally surfacing. "Now that I look back on it," he said in 1923, "I realize that I couldn't have done better for myself if I had deliberately charted out my life."

There were scattered indications that for all his constant running down of the theater, it fascinated him. While going to Princeton, to recall one instance, he had been so impressed by *Hedda Gabler* that he had seen it ten times. Again, while holed up at Jimmy the Priest's and supposedly concerned only with getting enough to drink, he kept an eye on what was happening around Broadway. In late 1911, when Liebler & Co. brought over the Abbey Players from Dublin for their first American tour, Eugene saw every one of their productions — Synge, Yeats, Lady Gregory, T. C. Murray — during their six weeks at the Maxine Elliott Theater.

The Abbey engagement gave him and Byth something new to talk about, especially the tumultuous opening of Synge's *The Playboy of the Western World*. Half the city in fact was talking about it, the riot that broke out at the theater — the actors pelted with eggs, stink bombs, and rotten vegetables; members of the audience fighting one another; a number of people arrested — all because the author had depicted his countrymen as enamored of violence. Eugene was scornful not only of the humorless Irish whose sensibilities had been outraged by the comedy but of the critics who failed to realize that the Dubliners were pioneers of a new style of acting, honest, true, without the familiar tricks.

"My early experience with the theater through my father," he once said, "really made me revolt against it. As a boy I saw so much of the old, ranting, artificial, romantic stage stuff that I always had a sort of contempt for the theater. It was seeing the Irish players for the first time that gave me a glimpse of my opportunity . . . I thought then and I still think that they demonstrated the possibilities of naturalistic acting better than any other company." Like a good Irishman he added, "In my opinion the Moscow Art Players could not hold a candle to the original Abbey Theater company."

Though *Playboy* attracted most attention in the 1911 engagement, it was another work by John Millington Synge that most impressed O'Neill. In fact *Anna Christie*, while inspired by the author's acquaintance with Chris Christopherson, also owes something to Synge's haunting *Riders to the Sea*. An actress from Ireland, Eileen Curran, who attended a rehearsal of *Anna Christie*, was constantly reminded of *Riders*. After the rehearsal she went over to O'Neill and said, "You've written about the conflict between a man and the sea just as Synge wrote of the conflict between an old woman and the sea." Then she quoted old Maurya's famous line near the end of the play: "They're all gone now, and there isn't anything more the sea can do to me . . ." O'Neill gave her a stony, sidelong look and finally said, "It would take someone who was Irish to feel that."

Another play that made a lasting impression on him was T. C. Murray's *Birthright*, which tells of a stern old farmer whose two sons are totally unlike one another. Hugh, the older one, is fond of poetry and more sensitive than his brother Shane, who is a young edition of the father — harsh and hard-working. Apparently *Birthright* influenced O'Neill in the writing of both *Beyond the Horizon*, a story of two dissimilar brothers on a farm, one of whom has a touch of the poet, and *Desire Under the Elms*, which concerns an old farmer who prides himself on being hard.

When Eileen Curran discussed the Abbey Players with O'Neill, he wondered why Murray had not written a third act to the play, and Eileen said, "Because he couldn't sustain it." To O'Neill's comment that the play lacked a love story, she replied, "Oh, Irishmen back away from love," but then added, "There is a love story in it — the love between the boy [Hugh] and the mother, the mother and the boy, the most deadly kind of love." O'Neill's face darkened as Eileen went on, "She's a terrible woman for all her sweetness and being gentle, she's so partial to her favorite, waiting up nights for him, giving him the best of everything, and the other boy has to take the leftovers."

As Eugene was adding to his theatrical education through the Dublin troupe, the past caught up with him: he got word that Kathleen wanted a divorce. She was not seeking alimony or even support for the child; all she wanted from him was evidence of adultery, the only basis for divorce in New York State. Glad to escape so lightly from the consequences of their romance, Eugene assented readily. After he and his father's attorney had conferred with a friend of the Jenkinses, a lawyer named James C. Warren, certain arrangements were made.

On the night of December 29 O'Neill met Warren and several other men at an uptown restaurant, where they all had some drinks, the party afterward stopping at other places for more liquor. All this was to make it seem a sociable time on the town among friends, instead of what it was, a prearranged evening, a farce, in deference to the divorce laws. The group finally ended at a brothel in the Times Square area, at 140 West 45th Street, where O'Neill went upstairs with one of the girls. Warren would afterward testify in court that he "saw this Eugene O'Neill and this woman in bed together; O'Neill at the time was undressed." The woman also, he said, was "undressed."

For all his familiarity with whores and whorehouses, the episode affected Eugene more than he had anticipated. It seemed to him that he had been made the butt of an obscene joke, that he had been used as a pawn in society's shabby hypocritical business; he felt humiliated, degraded. In after years he would speak well of Kathleen, but at the time he felt bitter toward her. That she had behaved so well throughout their relationship, especially now in regard to alimony and the child's support, only spurred his guilt feelings and his resentment.

The start of the New Year found him looking in both directions, at his past and his apparent future. Though he had undergone many periods of black depression in his twenty-three years, this was the worst. It was not the result merely of one night's experience in a brothel; that night and all it symbolized had simply intensified a feeling of defeat that had long been growing in him, beneath his carousing with Driscoll, Byth and others. He could not hole up at Jimmy the Priest's forever. In his eyes there was only one thing that could justify his existence, to become a great poet, and he despaired of ever achieving it. Jimmy Byth and his constant talk of "tomorrow" — wasn't he himself guilty of pipe-dreaming? He had failed not only himself, he seemed a curse in others' lives. It had begun with his very beginning, with what his birth had inflicted on his mother and the whole family. And now Kathleen and her mother, and the child they were rearing. He could see nothing ahead for himself except further misery — for others, also, if they got too close to him.

In 1922 O'Neill drew one of his more revealing self-portraits as Michael Cape, a playwright, in *Welded*. Cape is "thirty-five [O'Neill was then thirty-three], tall and dark. His unusual face is a harrowed battlefield of supersensitiveness, the features at war with one another — the forehead of a thinker, the eyes of a dreamer, the nose and mouth of a sensualist. One feels a powerful imagination tinged with somber sadness — a driving force which can be sympathetic and cruel at the same time. There is something tortured about him — a passionate tension, a self-protecting, arrogant defiance of life and his own weakness, a deep need for love as a faith in which to relax."

After a quarrel with his wife that leaves him despairing and bitter, Cape ends his evening with a streetwalker. In his distraught state he has some sort of wild notion that he can use her to kill all his feelings of love, all his better instincts. The prostitute is bewildered by his incoherent talk, a hysterical outpouring of scorn for himself, for life in general, and his now sympathetic, now hostile attitude toward her:

"Yes, I have a home, come to think of it — from now on Hell is my home! . . . You're my salvation! You have the power — and the right — to murder love! You can satisfy hate! . . . Thoughts keep alive. Only facts kill — deeds! Then hate will let me alone. Love will be dead. I'll be as ugly as the world. . . . O love of mine, let down your hair and I will make my shroud of it. . . . Do you know what you are? You're a symbol. You're all the tortures man inflicts on woman — and you're the revenge of woman! You're love revenging itself upon itself! You're the suicide of love — of my love — of all love since the world began! . . . There's no freedom — while I live. (Struck by a sudden thought) Then, why — ? An end of loathing — no wounds, no memories — sleep!"

The scene between Cape and the prostitute exemplifies the shrill, over-wrought tone of *Welded*, among O'Neill's poorest works; the play is of interest primarily for the light it throws on its author's capacity for whipping himself into the darkest and bleakest of moods. Michael Cape's harping on "kill" and "shroud" and "suicide" and "death" seems — even for one of his nature — excessive within the context of the play. His tirade becomes more understandable and significant when one knows that the play's author was once in such despair that he attempted suicide; Cape's outburst in short gives some idea of Eugene's frame of mind in the early days of 1912 as he arrived at that desperate decision.

His attempts to drink himself out of his mood were unsuccessful; as the effects of liquor wore off, his feelings of self-pity, self-hatred and hope-lessness returned in force. ("No, I'm not drunk," Cape says. "I thought of that — but it's evasion. And I must be conscious — fully conscious . . .") Eugene could see only one solution. His first idea was to kill himself by jumping into the harbor, off the Battery, but he was deterred by thought of the icy waters. Instead, at a time that it was possible to obtain morphine without a doctor's prescription, he knew it would be easy to get Veronal tablets. He stopped at several pharmacies around Fulton Street, buying a supply in each place; he wanted to be sure he had enough veronal to do the job properly. Back in his cell at Jimmy the Priest's, completely sober, he swallowed all the tablets and stretched out.

13

❀

Return to Life

JIMMY BYTH, ineffectual "Jimmy Tomorrow," who could do so little to save himself, was the one who saved him. For days he had watched O'Neill with mounting unease — the latter's mood was unmistakable — but since Byth's efforts to be of some cheer were rebuffed, he could only watch quietly from the corner to which he had been relegated and tell himself that Eugene would feel better "tomorrow." Nevertheless, despite his penchant for finding a bright side of things where none existed, he felt increasingly worried the day his friend was late in turning out; there was no chance he might be sleeping off a hangover, as his drinking had tapered down to almost nothing. After calls and knocks at his cell failed to draw a response, Byth pushed his way in and found him in a coma.

For the next several hours the lodgers spelled one another in pairs to keep Eugene on his feet and walking to wear off the effects of the Veronal. Every so often in their trips around the block — the sharp January air also had a beneficial effect — the rescue party, with O'Neill a dead weight between them, ducked into Condon's bar to toss down a warming shot. Byth meanwhile got in touch with Liebler's office, most likely with Tyler or Connor, and obtained money for medical attention. As Eugene began showing signs of recovery, his friends began celebrating.

In 1919 O'Neill wrote a one-act play about his suicide attempt that he later in effect disowned, not because "Exorcism" was so bad but because it was too nakedly autobiographical. After seeing it in performance, he collected all the scripts and destroyed them. Although the play itself has vanished, its general content can be pieced together from its press notices and the reminiscences of cast members Jasper Deeter, who played the would-be suicide, and Alan MacAteer, who played a roommate named

"Jimmy." Deeter's chief recollection is that the protagonist's wife was in the process of getting a divorce and that he felt bitter toward both her and the prostitute with whom he had gone to bed in order to provide evidence of adultery. MacAteer, who says that his role was similar to "Jimmy Tomorrow" in *The Iceman Cometh*, recalls that O'Neill seemed more than normally worried about the play during rehearsal.

The reviews of "Exorcism" were mixed. Alexander Woollcott of the *New York Times*, the only critic who was enthusiastic, gave the fullest account of the story: "[It] exhibits a young man of a substantial and correct family who is so full of contempt for it that he has walked out head high and fallen into the gutter. He is down to the dregs of existence when the play begins, equally revolted by the character of his life and by the prospect of a surrendering, prodigal-son return. He is so plagued by the questioning devils within him that even a fresh start on a farm out West has no appeal to him. So he swallows poison, placidly says, 'That's over,' and curls up on his miserable bed. [The "poison," interestingly enough, was morphine.]

"Twenty-four hours elapse and you find him stretched out under the delighted ministrations of two drunken friends, who are bibulously pleased with themselves for having yanked him back from the brink of the grave. You see him slowly reviving, only to find the ugly, inescapable world still closing in around him. . . . The suicide comes back to find everything wearisomely the same — everything except himself. Slowly he realizes that when a fellow tries hard to kill himself and seems to fail, the effect is quite as though he had succeeded. The person revived is a new person, the life ahead is life in a new world."

O'Neill's action in writing and then tearing up the too autobiographical "Exorcism" testifies to a duality in his nature. One of the most withdrawn of individuals, he was at the same time subject to a force of virtually equal strength to bare himself, to tell all, from a need to explain and justify himself. This need, this drive, was at the bottom of his turning playwright; properly speaking, he did not choose to become a playwright but was driven to it.

In after years he could not keep from telling friends of his suicide attempt, but then, true to his duality, would proceed to make it sound like farce — after the confession, an attempt to wipe out the confession by joking about it. According to what he told Agnes Boulton, the lodgers celebrated his return to life with such enthusiasm that they ended up falling-down drunk. Finally Byth and several others took him in a taxi to Bellevue, but the situation was misjudged at the hospital and his companions were led off to the alcoholics' ward. "I was still in a sort of daze,"

Miss Boulton reports him as saying, "when I heard the interne telling me he'd take care of them. . . . They'd all been taken away protesting incoherently, of course. 'Tough job you had!' the interne said politely. The taxi man was grinning; he evidently thought I'd had a tough job too. I got into the taxi and drove back to Jimmy the Priest's and managed to get potted to the gills. We all thought it was the biggest joke in the whole damn world. . . .''

Another account similarly farcical, though of different detail, is given by George Jean Nathan. Adding his own waggish embellishments, he reports that when O'Neill's fellow lodgers were unable to arouse him with "nudges, pokes and peremptory kicks, an ambulance was quickly summoned and our friend was carried off at a gallop to Bellevue. With the brothers grouped solicitously about his cot, two internes worked over him for an hour before he again gave signs of life. Three hours later, the dose of Veronal not having been so large as he believed, O'Neill was back in the world once more and, with a whoop of joy, the brothers put on their hats and moved mysteriously toward the door. 'We'll be back soon,' they observed significantly — and were gone. Four hours later, they reappeared, all beautifully and magnificently drunk. It developed that they had rushed to O'Neill's father and had got fifty dollars from him to pay the hospital fee for his son's resuscitation. 'You dirty bums!' groaned O'Neill, with what vocal strength he could muster. 'How much you got left?' Thirty-two dollars, they reluctantly informed him. 'All right, divide!' he insisted. And with his sixteen dollars safe in hand, he rolled over, grinned satisfiedly, and went happily and peacefully to sleep."

O'Neill did more than make light of this crisis in his life; he went so far as to revise fact. He led Nathan and others to believe that shortly before his suicide attempt his good friend Byth had killed himself. "Beith's [sic] suicide," Nathan reported, "together with certain personal emotional misfortunes in an encounter with Cupid [an apparent reference to Kathleen] weighed upon O'Neill's mind."

Although the short story "Tomorrow" gives no indication that its author ever tried to kill himself, it lends illusory weight to the Nathan account that Byth's death was a factor in O'Neill's own attempt. The story, told in the first person, ends with "Jimmy Tomorrow" leaping from an upper window at Tommy the Priest's; in other words, it gives the impression that the narrator, O'Neill, was living at the flophouse at the time of his friend's death. Actually it was more than a year after Eugene had quit Fulton Street that Byth made his fatal leap. Found unconscious in the rear yard of Condon's place on June 6, 1913, with both legs broken and a fractured skull, he was removed to the downtown branch of New York

An extract from the manuscript of O'Neill's short story "Tomorrow," written in 1916,
illustrating the smallness of his handwriting from the start of his career

Hospital, where he never regained consciousness. He was buried at the expense of the Actors Fund of America in Evergreen Cemetery, Brooklyn, the final resting place a few years later of Chris Christopherson.

O'Neill's motive in linking his attempt with Byth's death? He probably wanted both to play down Kathleen's unwitting role in his suicidal mood (in his references to her he always tended to minimize their relationship) and to play up the importance to him of James Findlater Byth. In trying to immortalize Byth in "Tomorrow," "Exorcism" and *The Iceman Cometh*, O'Neill was acknowledging a debt he could never really discharge. In 1930 he said of "Tomorrow": "As a personal record of a section of my life and the memory of a dear personal friend whose tragic end is there explained, I hold it in high affection. As writing, it leaves a lot to be desired."

The most reliable index of Eugene's frame of mind after his suicide attempt is not to be found in the humorous accounts he gave Miss Boulton and Nathan but in "Exorcism." Like its protagonist, he felt that he had exorcised his "devils"; at last he was free to leave Condon's place and make his peace with his family.

It was only by chance, according to what he always said later, that he joined his father's vaudeville tour in *Monte Cristo*. Though the details varied somewhat practically each time he ran through the story, it remained substantially as follows: while living at Jimmy the Priest's he found five dollars in the street, went to a gambling house and was lucky enough to run the stake up to five hundred dollars — in one version, a thousand — whereupon he threw a drinking party for his buddies and lapped up so much himself that he finally passed out. He awoke, without any idea of how he had gotten there, on a train bound for New Orleans. "After I'd had a quart and a half of bourbon," he told Tom Prideaux of *Life* magazine in 1946, "I could walk straight and talk rationally, but my brain was nuts. If anybody suggested that I climb up the Woolworth Building, I'd be tickled to death to do it." He probably landed on the train, he added, because someone had mentioned to him while drunk that New Orleans was a nice place to visit. By coincidence, his standard story went on, he arrived in the southern city when his father happened to be playing there. Since the latter refused to give him the return fare to New York, offering him, instead, a role in the show, he had no choice but to join the tour.

The tour eventually became a farcical high point of O'Neill's reminiscences, with his making it sound like a blur of endless drinking, on-stage shenanigans, and scenes from a contemporary *Rake's Progress*. He told Russel Crouse, for instance, that he and his brother stayed in whorehouses rather than in hotels and one time arrived at the railroad station at the last minute, with red kimonos showing beneath their outer coats. According to another tale, he and Jamie were once so drunk on stage that after kneeling before their father, as the Count of Monte Cristo, they had to be helped to their feet before they could stagger off. Indulging his sense of the ridiculous, he went so far as to tell one credulous lady that he and Jamie, togged out with straw hat and cane, did an entr'acte of song and dance in the Dumas condensation.

"The least said about those acting days," he wrote a friend in 1938, "the better. The alcoholic content was as high as the acting was low. They graduated me from the Orpheum Circuit with degree of Lousy Cum Laude. If the tour had lasted a month longer I would also have won my D.T. The one remorseful thought . . . is that I didn't warn audiences in advance about my performance so they could all get drunk, too. It must have been a terrible thing to witness sober." And from a 1931 letter: "I am proud to say that I preserved my honor by never drawing a sober breath until the tour terminated. My brother and I had one grand time of it and I look back on it as one of the merriest periods of my life."

In all these jovial recollections the one important thing he never mentioned was that his brief vaudeville career followed hard on the heels of his suicide attempt; had he mentioned it, his friends would rightly have suspected that he was glossing over a painful chapter of his history. Carlotta Monterey once complained of the "silly and hoodlumish legends" that had developed about his earlier years and urged her husband to put some truth in them. "Nonsense," he replied, "what do I care what they say — the further from the truth they have it, the more privacy I have! It's like a mask!" Apparently Miss Monterey never guessed that he himself was the source of some of the legends.

His joining the tour, contrary to his standard story, was scarcely a matter of chance. In mid-January, James O'Neill was performing in Memphis, Tennessee, when he got word about Eugene — probably from Tyler or Connor — together with reassurance that the boy was out of danger. Members of the company noted that Mr. O'Neill was in an agitated state, as a rumor spread that his younger son had had "some kind of misfortune." Several days later they heard that he had sent his son money to join him, in response to a telegram that began: "To eat or not to eat, that is the question." O'Neill later denied sending such a wire but since he had his own story to promote, his denial is not surprising. The paraphrase of Shakespeare sounds like him, having the bantering tone he would assume to cover his discomfiture in approaching his father. In New Orleans, right after Memphis, a subdued family closed ranks as

Eugene was reunited with his parents and brother. He remained under wraps for days, unseen by the rest of the troupe until the next stop, Ogden, Utah. The company had the impression, one of them recalls, that "something was going on among the O'Neills, something was being hushed up" in regard to the younger son.

Jamie was alone in the family in accepting the significance of Eugene's desperate act, the only one with some idea of the emotional state that had driven him to it. Ella wanted to hear as little as possible about it, while James, for his peace of mind, tried to minimize it as a result of drunkenness, committed when the boy was not responsible for his actions. Eugene refused, however, to go along with his evasion. "I was stone cold sober," Edmund insists to the father in *Long Day's Journey*. "That was the trouble. I'd stopped to think too long."

James O'Neill felt hard pressed on all sides. Shortly after the tour had begun, two firms in which he had invested a total of nearly forty thousand dollars went bankrupt (one was the Henry L. Brittain company, Eugene's onetime employer), stirring up all his old fear of poverty. And the tour itself was not going well. In Waterbury, his opening stand, audiences had refused to accept the condensation as the "real" *Monte Cristo* because he had left out its best-known line; after that, he went back to claiming the world as his own, though to little avail.

Like other stars of "the legitimate" appearing in vaudeville, James had to pay his company from his own salary; he told the press it was "well up in the four figures," but it actually was $1250. In line with the usual practice, he assembled a troupe as cheaply as possible and, as often happened, ran into criticism about the caliber of his support. It was small comfort to him that practically all the reviewers had favorable words for his own portrayal, that some were even indulgent about his lopsided vehicle — a four-act play that lasted three hours cut to a running time of forty minutes. What weighed heaviest on him was that audiences failed to respond with anything like enthusiasm.

"That cut-down version was wonderful," Eugene once said. "Characters came on that didn't seem to belong there and did things that made no sense and said things that sounded insane. The Old Man had been playing Cristo so long he had almost forgotten it, so he ad-libbed and improvised and never gave anybody a cue. You knew when your turn came when he stopped talking."

While this may be somewhat exaggerated, it could not have been too far off the mark. One critic, expressing the same view more tactfully, thought the condensation would be "very interesting to those acquainted with the story." A second, after finding that James "has lost none of that splendid style, that magnetic ability, that wonderful and dignified personality," added that "the play has glided beyond the comprehension of vaudeville audiences, which look more for buck and wing dancing, the sensational, the comic and the ragtime." Still another reviewer was caustic about the production: "A couple of stage hands wave a sheet; the light man turns on the green flood; somebody behind the scenes beats a tin pan. That is a storm at sea."

To an actor who once had hoped to succeed Edwin Booth, it was a humiliating comedown. James found himself jammed into a bill that included John and Mae Burke ("will set you to laughing in spite of yourself"); Hawthorne & Burt ("other funny people who defy a sober face"); Belle Adair ("one of the most artistic and dainty girl acts of the season"), and Golden's Russian Troubadours ("they sing well, play the balalaika, and dance cleverly, but how much Russian there is in the troupe can be left to the individual judgment").

In Cincinnati, where he had grown up and faced his first audience at the National nearly a half-century earlier, he made the rounds of his old neighborhood. A newspaperman who called on him afterward found him in an autumnal mood: " 'Ho, hum,' said James O'Neill, laying his hat slowly on the dressing room table of his room at B. F. Keith's Theater. 'Ho, hum.'

"Why 'ho, hum'?

" 'I was just thinking,' he said, 'just thinking whether it all pays. . . . I suppose when a man gets to my age that he begins looking backward. You see, I am somewhat over sixty. I am not so inclined to look backward in other places. But when I stand before the old National, I am carried to the beginning . . . my life passes in review. I suppose I stood down there an hour. I was wondering where, had I not gone on the stage, I would be now; whether I would have been more, or less, successful; whether I would be here at all; whether I would be more or less happy. You can't help such thoughts, you know, at this time of life.' "

Cincinnati, Chicago, Memphis, New Orleans, twice a day, "The worrld is mi-n-ne!"

On the long train ride from New Orleans to Utah, the O'Neill family sequestered themselves in one car while the rest of the troupe was deployed in another, but occasionally James dropped by to see how his players were faring. During one visit he fell to reminiscing about his early days in the theater, that period, golden in his thoughts, when he had appeared opposite Booth and Forrest, Neilson and Cushman. All the great ones were gone, he said, all that had made the theater a real theater had practically vanished, with scarcely anyone left able to play the classics.

Carried away by nostalgia, he was almost keening. He ended by launching into his favorite passage from *Othello*, the Moor's defense of his marriage to gentle Desdemona: "Most potent, grave, and reverend signiors . . ." His listeners were stirred. The Old Man had given the speech with all the music and meticulous diction of his famous cello-like voice, as though he had been performing to a vast audience. Perhaps in his own mind he had. Forty years earlier the great Booth had said that Jimmy O'Neill's Othello was better than his own; the aging James O'Neill clung to that memory.

In Ogden, where his younger son was to make his debut, James introduced him to reporters who called backstage before the opening performance. When one of them said, "He's a handsome chap, takes after his father," the latter demurred: "Oh, no, he's better-looking than I ever was." His compliment, partly calculated to arouse in his son some feeling of pride and self-confidence, failed to have the desired effect. Though Eugene's roles were of the smallest — a courier who silently hands a note to the Count of Monte Cristo, a jailer with but two words to say — the thought of appearing before an audience had him almost paralyzed with stage-fright. He complained to fellow actor Charles Webster of feeling foolish in his jailer's outfit — chiefly, a voluminous black cape and a fierce-looking mustache attached by wire to his nose. He couldn't help worrying that if he sneezed ("these theaters are awfully dusty, you know"), the mustache might fly off.

His first appearance in the prison scene may charitably be described as inauspicious. As he and Webster, a fellow jailer, bent over the body of the Abbé Feria, Eugene said in a quavering voice, "Is he . . . ?" Infected with the other's nervousness, Webster replied in a brisk, blasé tone, "Yes, he's dead," and the audience roared. As the noise subsided, the two jailers could overhear Mr. O'Neill in the wings, "What happened, what did they do, why's the audience laughing?" After the pair had made a hasty exit at the other side of the stage, they hid in the flies and looked down on Mr. O'Neill prowling about and muttering to himself, "Where are those boys? I'll kill them."

His anger was short-lived, an expression more of nervousness over Eugene's debut than of real indignation. It was an awkward time for father and son; having reached a truce, they were trying to fumble their way toward some kind of understanding. In spite of Eugene's stories later that he had raised hell during the tour, he was for the most part on his best behavior. After his crisis at Jimmy the Priest's, he felt purged of his darkness and in a mood to start afresh; if his "devils" had not been exorcised, they had been stilled for a time.

Charles Webster, the only one of the troupe around Eugene's age, found him "quiet, polite, friendly in a reserved sort of way." Webster's memories of the tour, of the way the two brothers behaved, are in striking contrast to the picture O'Neill always gave. "If he gave the impression later on," Webster said, "that the two of them pulled off all kinds of funny things on stage, well, he was just making up a good story. It's true that Jamie practically always smelled of alcohol when he went on, but he was never staggering, not during a performance; it was impossible for the audience to tell he'd been drinking. As for Eugene, he took a drink or two after a performance, but never before. It seemed to me he was pretty respectful toward his father. So was Jamie, more or less, but I can't say he made any real effort to turn in a good performance."

Jamie displayed so little aptitude for his assignments that some of the company thought that he was new to *Monte Cristo* and costume drama in general. The final duel scene in the forest, which was supposed to end the show on a note of excitement, lost much of its effectiveness because of him. "Imagine an actor," his father used to complain, "who can't even fence!"

Had Jamie wanted to, he could have had a creditable career in the theater, for he possessed the necessary qualifications. But he knew that he could never equal — still less, surpass — his father, so why bestir himself? In *The Travelling Salesman* he had displayed a flair for contemporary farce that won him uniformly good notices; back in his father's company, he slumped into his old indifference and enlivened things for himself by indulging in practical jokes. Charlie Webster, nineteen, new in the profession and eager to make good, was one of his targets; not that Jamie had anything against the young actor, he simply wanted to have some fun. In Webster's chief role — all members of the small troupe had to "double" and even "triple" — one of his speeches included the line, "I thought it my duty to repress calumny." For days Jamie, attempting to trip him up, whispered in his ear as he was about to go on, "I thought it my duty to repress *calomel*." The day finally came when Webster said "calomel" and, though the audience failed to notice it, Jamie was satisfied; of such triumphs was his life comprised.

He liked to give the impression that nothing touched him, that he looked on life as a joke, but his brother's suicide attempt affected him more than he let on. The sole indication was in his drinking; moderate during the early weeks of the tour, it became heavier when Eugene turned up. Despite his usual air of hail-fellow-well-met, he was at bottom a loner. As he drank he became increasingly standoffish — except toward his brother — wrapping himself around in hauteur, his face reddish, his eyes glazed.

From the outset the tour had been an ordeal to Ella. With James confined to the theater all hours by the two-a-day schedule, she constantly faced the alternative of being lonely at the hotel or of enduring the hectic atmosphere backstage. Generally, in spite of her distaste for the flashy world of vaudeville, she accompanied James to the theater, where she would immure herself in his dressing room and try to ignore the brassy music and the sounds of merrymaking drifting in from the stage. Ella managed for a while to maintain her balance, but after the news about Eugene, followed by his appearance, her good intentions began to crumble. His presence reminded her of the course his life had taken in recent years, of things in general she preferred to forget. She increasingly took refuge in the euphoria induced by, as she called it, her "medicine," but which her family called "that damn poison."

Members of the company saw little of Mrs. O'Neill, only occasional glimpses as she slipped in and out of her husband's dressing room; some felt that she was preternaturally shy, others that she was of uncertain health. Starting in Ogden she gave them fresh cause to wonder. Whether Eugene's joining the act had aroused her or some other factor was working on her drug-disoriented mind, Ella turned up in the wings one day, silent and wraithlike, then started to edge out. Mr. O'Neill, on stage at the time with Webster, let out a low gasp as he caught sight of his wife. Frozen in his tracks, he was about to signal for the curtain to be dropped when, at the last moment, a stagehand stopped her. Though James afterward told his actors to be on the alert whenever his wife ventured near the stage, she almost drifted on at several other performances. For the rest of the tour James, while on stage, found himself constantly darting an anxious glance into the wings.

Ogden, Salt Lake City, Denver . . .

After Denver, a layoff week, and James welcomed it as a respite from pressure that was starting to tell on him; where he had previously been courteous and affable with his troupe, he was now showing signs of irritability. Ella's behavior on top of Eugene's suicide attempt on top of unresponsive audiences — it all was becoming too much for him. At sixty-five he at last was starting to feel his age. The plain physical demands of putting on a show twice a day, amid the hurly-burly of vaudeville, was more tiring than he had anticipated. "I find that vaudeville people," he told a reporter, "are so much busier than any other class of actors that they don't have time for anything but work. . . . Since I've been in vaudeville, I've scarcely done anything but live in the theater. It has had my nose against the grindstone."

With no prospect of the pressure diminishing, he finally came to a decision. On February 14 *Variety* reported that James was shortly terminating his Orpheum Circuit tour, though he had contracted for about eighteen more weeks. "The production and star have been favorably received," it said, "but Mr. O'Neill's support brought adverse comment all along the line and the voluntary cancellation has followed."

Despite the article in *Variety*, James was less disheartened by criticism of his company than by the tepid response of audiences to his own portrayal. "I wonder," he said in a parting shot at vaudeville, "just how long the public will tolerate and endure the fearful dances which seem to pervade our every amusement. There is nothing graceful, nothing refining, nothing inspiring about these wriggles and trots and hugs — indeed, they do away with every semblance of art and poetry and leave one flat against the stark materialities. But the people seem to demand them — and in the final analysis the people get what they want."

After a week's stand in St. Paul, where the tour ended, the family returned to New York in early March, all four O'Neills still together. But this was not the way Eugene later told it. As part of his picture of having a drunken merry time in vaudeville and driving his father to distraction, he always said that he quit while the company was still playing in the West. Just before his departure, according to one of his accounts, his father told him, "Sir, I am not satisfied with your performance," to which Eugene replied, "Sir, I am not satisfied with your play."

That O'Neill should make up such tales is not surprising. He had to ridicule his association with the tour; it helped relieve his feeling that he had made a fool of himself in public from Ogden to St. Paul. Also, joking about it served as a smoke screen, beclouding the fact that his acting fling had followed hard on his suicide attempt.

During the family's few weeks in New York, before leaving for New London, Eugene often visited 252 Fulton, drawn not only by his feeling for his good friend Byth but for the place itself. If this was where he had almost gone under forever, this was also where he began to climb out of the depths. In later years he never tired of reminiscing of this period and often told his wife Agnes Boulton that he "must" write a play about Jimmy the Priest's.

"Oh, God, those old days!" he said. "Nobody'd believe it, nobody'd understand it. . . ."

14

The Cub Reporter

Fʀᴏᴍ *A Long Day's Journey Into Night*, set in the summer of 1912, one might assume that after the vaudeville tour Ella O'Neill entered a sanatorium. As the play begins father and sons are happy to have the mother home again, over "the habit," and they are hoping that this time her cure will be lasting. Whether Ella actually went to a sanatorium in early 1912 or her playwright son made this up is uncertain, but the important thing today is the use he made of such a development. Ella's drug addiction was the central torturing fact in their lives. What better way for O'Neill to dramatize this than by opening the play with the mother cured, her family cautiously cheerful, and proceeding to show their deepening despair as she once again retreats into the phantom-world of morphine? There is of course more than this in *Long Day's Journey*, but the mother's addiction, its effect on the others, is what provides the line of continuity tying everything together. Surely it was not by chance that O'Neill gave the mother, rummaging in the attic of the past, the final word in the play: "Then in the spring something happened . . . yes, I remember. I fell in love with James Tyrone and was so happy for a time."

How many times Ella underwent a cure, where and in which years, remains one of the family's well-kept secrets. If she did enter a sanatorium this spring her stay was short; by mid-April, only a month or so after the vaudeville tour, the family was installed in the cottage on Pequot Avenue, with James telling friends they would remain through the summer if his "wife's health permits." The chances are that Ella, rather than submit to the prolonged agony of yet another cure, cut down on morphine as best she could before they returned to the Pequot colony.

James always felt better when he could get back to New London. Basically a "simple, unpretentious man," as his son once said, he enjoyed puttering around the grounds of his place, yarning with Captain Keeney at his fish store on the dock, looking after his various properties, and spending long afternoons at the comfortable Crocker House bar. But this spring and summer several things, all the more welcome after his discouraging winter, helped spur him into good spirits.

To start with, he sold one of his pieces of real estate at a tidy profit. Next, to the relief of all the O'Neills, especially Eugene, Kathleen filed for divorce and, true to her word, sought no alimony or support for her child. (No one could guess from *Long Day's Journey* that Edmund/Eugene had ever been married, still less that he was a father.) The uncontested action was heard June 10 in Supreme Court in White Plains, New York, where Kathleen had established residence, and an interlocutory decree was awarded a month later. James and Ella, who had never accepted her as their daughter-in-law or Eugene O'Neill 2d as their grandson, promptly put both out of mind; Eugene, though he generally pretended otherwise, found them rooted in his conscience.

Topping off these agreeable developments, James, still smarting from his reception in vaudeville, was approached to star in a film of *Monte Cristo*. Like other notables of the stage he had long looked down on "the flickers," but the once-despised medium had begun to acquire respectability. In signing with the newly organized Famous Players Film Company, headed by Adolph Zukor and Daniel Frohman, James was making his debut under the best auspices; the company's first release was to be the French-made *Queen Elizabeth*, with Sarah Bernhardt. "We hope," Frohman announced, "to have all the famous stars of the American stage before the moving picture camera soon. At present we are directing our efforts to make the *Monte Cristo* production a notable one."

Despite publicity that it would be filmed at great expense in Bermuda and would have in its supporting cast such well-known actors as Edmund Breese and Frederick de Belleville, the actual circumstances of its production were less impressive. At a cost of slightly over thirteen thousand dollars it was made in ten days at locations in and around New York, with James the only name player in a cast that included his elder son.

Heartened by the chance to record for posterity his famous impersonation, he returned to New London enthusiastic about the movies. "He seemed to forget that he was on State Street," one of the *Telegraph* staff reported on August 13, "and as he recounted the way in which the scenes were laid, his voice shook with emotion and his mobile face took on the varied characteristics of his part. . . . Mr. O'Neill was offered $10,000 outright for his interest in the film, but he preferred to retain his royalty."

A few months later James, whose contract gave him twenty percent of the profits, felt less buoyant about the movies when a three-reel *Monte Cristo* made by William Fox preceded his five-reel version to the screen. While James filed suit against the rival company for infringing on his rights to the Dumas story, Famous Players canceled plans for a gala Broadway opening of its own film. Though it is not true, as some movie historians report, that Famous Players shelved the film permanently — it was quite widely shown, starting in late 1913 — it was never the money-maker James had hoped. According to records of the production recently discovered, he eventually made close to four thousand dollars in royalties, besides receiving a court-awarded share of the rival movie's profits.

No problems loomed, however, as he finished enacting Edmond Dantès for celluloid and settled down with his family for their first summer together in several years. He felt more or less content with the way things were going, and for a change had little cause to worry about his younger son. Though he looked with a more indulgent than sanguine eye on Eugene's dabblings in verse, he was glad to find him seriously intent on something other than drinking; most of all, he was relieved that the boy seemed over his great restlessness, whatever it was that had driven him to sea and landed him in that Godforsaken hole down by the docks.

Resuming his usual life in New London, Eugene took long swims in the Thames, off Scott's wharf, where as a youngster he had dreamed away hours among the anchors, sails and old windlasses; in late July the *Day* reported that he swam the river on a diagonal course, a distance of over a mile, in "good time." Loaded down with books, he made regular trips between home and the massive pile of granite at the head of State Street, the public library. He knocked around town with Art and Tom McGinley, Ed Keefe, "Hutch" Collins and "Ice" Casey, especially when they were paying their respects to the Crocker House bar or McGarry and Neagle's, a favorite oasis of the Irish.

There were also many evenings at one of his old hangouts, the Second Story Club, actually Dr. Joe Ganey's office and living quarters, which long was regarded as the center of bohemianism in New London. Their "bohemianism" consisted chiefly of playing cards, drinking Doc Ganey's beer, adding to their sexual lore from choice passages in his medical books, and of knowing their way around notorious Bradley Street. Ganey, who later married, settled down and became a respected figure of the community, originally affronted proper New Londoners by having a mistress with whom he lived openly, a beauty named Kate, with black hair, natural high coloring, and a superb figure. Most of the habitués of the Club used to dream of succeeding him as her protector; it was not uncommon to see Kate and Doc, flanked by a half-dozen of the town's young bachelors, having dinner at the Crocker House. By 1912 she had been gone for several years — after quitting New London she turned showgirl in a Lillian Russell musical — but Kate remained a choice topic of conversation around the Club, not only as a beauty but as a "regular fellow." She once, in male disguise, accompanied the boys to a cockfight.

Located years later on Long Island, Kate had sparse recollections of O'Neill: "I only saw him a dozen or so times, can't say I got to know him. He never really seemed there with us. I remember one time, must've been 1908 or '09, when we were at Doc's cottage on the Niantic River, right where it joins the Sound. Gene was sitting on the railing and looking at the river, the boats going by, as if he was miles away — that was typical of him. He'd answer yes or no, as few words as possible, if you asked him something, but he'd never volunteer to talk. Not that he was unpleasant or unfriendly, just always seemed to have something on his mind."

For all his habitual reticence he could be quite voluble about things that interested him, though it generally took some drinks to get him started. He liked to tell of Buenos Aires and life at sea, expressing himself in the steamy vernacular of the fo'c'sle and salting his accounts with phrases he had picked up — "Gawd blimey!" was one of his favorites. But outside of his reminiscences he gave no indication of what he had been through in the past several years; he seemed the same Gene O'Neill who had first shipped out.

Eugene, though, felt a great difference in himself. He found that, without conscious effort, story ideas, scraps of plot and dramatic situations — peopled largely by seamen, prostitutes, other battered souls — were welling up and crowding his thoughts. He continued to work on poems but also began to record his story ideas, expanding some into detailed outlines. By fall he had a bureau-drawerful of pages covered with his minuscule handwriting. A girl who read some of the things concluded in after years that he had written all this down with the theater in mind, that he turned playwright in 1912. A number of other New Londoners came to the same conclusion, basing it on something he said more than once this year: "Some day James O'Neill will best be known as the father of Eugene O'Neill." The boast stuck in the minds of all who heard it because they found it so preposterous.

O'Neill himself always gave the following year as the start of his playwriting; he told interviewers that an extended period of ill-health in 1913 led him to take stock and decide what to make of his life, that it was then he determined to bend his efforts toward the stage. Indeed, he used to say that he never thought seriously of writing until he settled on playwriting. Constantly making light of his verse, he for instance told one interviewer: "Everybody does that [writes poetry] when he is young." From the best available evidence, however, it appears that he had poetry in mind when he boasted that his own fame would eventually outstrip his father's. The notes and outlines that piled up in his drawer? He presumably intended to develop them as short stories, with the hope that his earnings from prose would subsidize the time he gave to poetry. In the next few years he would complete a number of short stories but after selling only one would abandon the form. If O'Neill turned playwright in 1912, as one or two of his chroniclers maintain, it certainly was an unconscionably long time before he came up with his first work for the theater, *A Wife for a Life*, a brief one-acter, written in late summer of 1913.

Eager to gain some writing experience under editorial guidance, Eugene had his father speak for him about a job with the *Telegraph*, New London's morning paper. When James broached the matter to Judge Frederick P. Latimer, the editor in chief, and business manager Charlie Thompson, they pointed out, as everyone knew, that the paper was chronically hard up. What, they wanted to know, could they use for money in paying the boy? After James agreed to reimburse them for his son's salary, Eugene went to work in mid-August for the *Telegraph* for ten dollars a week, unaware that his father was subsidizing his formal start as a writer. His day began between four and six in the afternoon, depending on his assignments, and often lasted till two or three in the morning. Since the trolley cars stopped running at midnight, he bought a bicycle and became a familiar sight in the elm-lined streets as he pedaled to and from work, six days a week, all but Saturdays.

Like most cub reporters, he was so anxious to make an impression that he overwrote. Less forgivably, on some of his first assignments he became so absorbed in the human story, the drama, behind the events that, until the error of his ways was made clear to him, he was negligent in getting the essential facts. Of the five "W's" sacred to journalism — Who, What, Where, When, Why — the only one that really interested him was Why.

Malcolm Mollan, the city editor, once laced into him about one of his articles, but first disarmed him by saying, "The smell of the rooms is made convincing; the amount of blood on the floor is precisely measured; you have drawn a nice picture of the squalor and stupidity and degradation of that household." Then came the crusher: "But would you mind finding out the name of the gentleman who carved the lady and whether the dame is his wife or daughter or who? And phone the hospital for a hint as to whether she is dead or discharged or what? Then put the facts into a hundred and fifty words — and send this literary batik to the picture framers."

Mollan was not alone in thinking him ill-suited to the job; the average newspaperman around town felt dubious about a reporter who wrote poetry and always seemed lost in himself. Art McGinley, a seventeen-dollar-a-week reporter on the rival newspaper, the *Day*, used to rib him that he would cover a fire by writing an "Ode to Death." After he had become famous, word flourished among his former associates that his brief career had marked a new low in the history of journalism, and Eugene himself helped the legend along by cheerfully agreeing that he had been a "bum reporter." It all became a matter of record in 1931 when Robert A. Woodworth wrote an article for the Providence (R.I.) *Journal*, entitled "The World's Worst Reporter," in which he portrayed O'Neill brooding Buddha-like over a typewriter in the *Telegraph* office without ever striking a key: "Night after night for a week or more it was the same story. Smoke and dream, smoke and dream!

" 'Hey, Mal! When is that guy going to get busy and do some work?' one of us asked the city editor. 'He sits in there and smokes, but he never turns in any copy. If he'd do something some of the rest of us wouldn't have to run our legs off, or, if he'd get another job somewhere, we'd get somebody else who would work.' "

The article goes on at length in this vein, describing the scene so vividly that one can practically see the rest of the staff glowering "night after night" at the cub reporter, thoughtful yet sterile. The most interesting thing about the article, however, is not what Mr. Woodworth put in but what he left out: at a time that he reportedly was working for the *Telegraph*, "running his legs off" because of O'Neill, he actually was on the other newspaper, the *Day*.

While it is true that Eugene scarcely made an impressive record in journalism, the legend of his hopeless showing is inflated beyond fact. On several occasions he returned drunk from his assignments, and the last time this happened Mollan threatened to fire him. "Hell, you can't do that," Charlie Thompson told the editor in confidence, "his father is paying his salary." In general, though, despite a few lapses, Eugene was conscientious about his job and grateful to it for giving him a "wonderful insight into small town life." Mary L. Raub, the "girl Friday" of the office, recalls that the atmosphere was "very informal, but they were serious about their work — there were deadlines to meet — and they took pride in covering a story better than the *Day*."

Eugene's few months on the *Telegraph* were among the most pleasant he had known, for he not only liked the work but found his colleagues interesting; the others on the news staff, besides Latimer and Mollan, were Joseph H. Smith and Charlotte Molyneux Holloway. While each was a distinct individual, the most colorful one in a way was Miss Holloway, short, plump, in her mid-forties; she had a face so graphically Irish that one could almost pick out the various counties, from Mayo to Cork and Kerry. As much public figure and speaker as newspaperwoman, she was tireless in promoting Irish causes. James O'Neill, who had a theory that Shakespeare was Irish, thought well, exceedingly well of her. Eugene's favorites on the paper were Charlie Thompson, humorous, easygoing, and Judge Latimer, particularly Latimer. "He's the first one," O'Neill once said, "who really thought I had something to say, and believed I could say it."

O'Neill paid him more lasting tribute in *Ah, Wilderness!* In certain surface aspects the editor father in *Wilderness* was modeled on postmaster John McGinley, once a newspaperman, who presided amiably over a menage of one girl and seven boys, including Art and Tom, among Eugene's close friends. The portrait also contains a lineament or two of James O'Neill; but essentially Nat Miller of the play was based on Latimer. Like Miller, Latimer was an editor of independence, a devoted family man, and a well-read person who carried his learning lightly – in sum, an understanding soul who would be more amused than alarmed by a firebrand seventeen-year-old son such as Richard Miller, who constantly sounds off for Revolution, the Guillotine, and Emma Goldman.

A onetime lawyer who had never really cared for the law and a former justice of the peace who had felt miserable whenever he sent someone to jail, Latimer found his proper niche when an uncle took over the *Telegraph* in 1910 and placed him in charge. He was a fine editor and columnist – his writings reflected his hospitable mind and generous character – but at the same time was too honest and idealistic for his own good. He spoke his mind without regard for the consequences. His father-in-law, a power in local Republican circles, had him all set for a judgeship until he came out with an editorial criticizing some Republican bigwigs.

Since he himself steered by his own lights, he was better able than a Mollan or a Woodworth to assay the cub reporter's potentiality. "The four things about him that impressed me at once," he said in 1925, "were his modesty, his native gentlemanliness, his wonderful eyes, and his literary style. It was evident that this was no ordinary boy, and I watched what he thought, wrote and did with extreme interest."

Eugene would "grieve like a stricken collie," according to Latimer, "if you so much as looked an unkind thought at him," yet he also courted criticism and argument with his unorthodox views. "When we sailed with him on the river or talked with him of moonlit nights or in the shadows of a smelly back room," Latimer said, "he used often to make us choke with wrath at the queer wildness of his ideas. . . . I thought he was the most stubborn and irreconcilable social rebel I had ever met." Between cub and editor it was a case of Shaw, Tucker and Nietzsche versus Thomas Jefferson and Abraham Lincoln.

For the next several years, until Eugene quit New London, he had Latimer read most of his writings; Latimer got to know him well. "There was something in Eugene at that time," he once said, "an innate nobility which inspires and drives a man against whatever hindrance to be himself, however Heaven or Hell conspires to rob him of that birthright. From flashes in the quality of the stuff he gave the paper, and the poems and play manuscripts he showed me, I was so struck that I told his father Eugene did not have merely talent, but a very high order of genius.

"I thought it astonishing how keen was his wit, what a complete iconoclast he was, how richly he sympathized with the victims of man-made distress, how his imagination was running high as the festering skies above Ye Ancient Mariner; his descriptions strong and his spirit hot to produce something worth while for the sake of its own value and in utter scorn of its commercial value or conventional fame. . . .

"If he could only be in one of two places in a town — the church or the jail — I know where I would find him!"

It was no sinecure Eugene had on the *Telegraph*: he covered barroom fights and marriages, accidents and fires, political rallies and water-front events, besides contributing verse to the "Laconics" column; he rewrote items that came in the mail, wrote heads for his own stories, and read proof on advertisements. Unlike the *Day*, a more conventional daily, the *Telegraph* encouraged its reporters to get color and humor, some individuality, into their writings, and Eugene was glad to oblige. A survey of the newspaper during the time of his employment discloses a number of articles that bear in one way or another his signature: a quotation from Byron; a reference to the town's Monte Cristo Garage, which his father had financed; a jocular description of the various kinds of drunkenness ("There is the peaceful, smiling, cordial 'bun'; there is the wobbly 'slant' and there is the swaggering, chip-on-the-shoulder, stop-me-if-you-can brand"). Sometimes, as in a story about a ship with an adventurous past, the young reporter gave vent to his poetic strain: "The men who manned the ship in those days are either dead or scattered to whatever wild parts of the world that the 'Red Gods' have called them. . . ."

Another story presumably written by Eugene, concerning a schooner driven onto the rocks off Fishers Island, is noteworthy for a repeated Freudianism. After first giving the correct name of the vessel, the *Maggie Ellen*, the article refers to it as the *Mary Ellen* (Mrs. O'Neill's given name). A few years later O'Neill was to write a one-act play about a demented sea captain whose hopes are centered on a ship that will never return — a ship, long since foundered, called the *Mary Allen*.

In the Presidential election this fall Eugene, voting for the first time, would cast his ballot for Debs, the Socialist. On the *Telegraph* meanwhile, enjoying a latitude he would have known on few other papers, he covered Socialist events with partisan feeling: "I. Polsky, a native of this country, spoke for more than two hours on the Parade [a gathering spot at the foot of State Street] Saturday evening to a crowd of several hundred. He told of the failure of the Republican Party, of the Democratic Party in the southern states, where it is in power, and of the candidate of the Progressive Party, while he was President, to improve the condition of the working classes or prevent the growth of unemployment. He showed that only the radical changes which Socialism advocates will be of any effect. . . ."

It was in his verse for the "Laconics" column, however, that he had most leeway to express himself; many of his contributions were humorous and satirical, take-offs from Kipling, Robert Burns, and James Whitcomb Riley. The following, published on September 2, is characteristic of a number poking fun at the major presidential candidates:

> *Our Teddy opens wide his mouth,*
> *N'runs around n'yells all day,*
> *N'calls some people naughty names,*
> *N'says things that he shouldn't say.*
> *N'when he's nothing else to do*
> *He swells up like he'd like to bust,*
> *N'pounds on something with his fist*
> *N'tells us 'bout some wicked trust.*
> *I always wondered why that was —*
> *I guess it's cause*
> *Taft never does.*

In his rhymes he made light of local issues that everyone else took seriously, was facetious about the hardships of being a newspaperman, and in more serious vein sniped at the vested interests, including Standard Oil, U.S. Steel, and the meat-packing houses of Swift, Armour, and

Cudahy. Years later he wrote a friend who wanted to republish his verse from the *Telegraph:* "It would be a shame to waste good type on such nonsense. If those small-town jingles of my well-misspent youth were amusingly bad, I would have no objection, for their republication might hand someone a laugh, at least. But they're not. They are merely very dull stuff."

At the time, however, he thought well of them and took issue with Latimer's belief that his forte was prose, that he would end not as a poet but as a novelist. After some hesitation about baring himself in print, he began contributing poems of a personal nature, such as "Nocturne," which appeared on September 13:

> *The sunset gun booms out in hollow roar*
> *Night breathes upon the waters of the bay*
> *The river lies, a symphony in gray,*
> *Melting in shadow on the further shore.*
>
> *A sullen coal barge tugs its anchor chain*
> *A shadow sinister, with one faint light*
> *Flickering wanly in the dim twilight,*
> *It lies upon the harbor like a stain.*
>
> *Silence. Then through the stillness rings*
> *The fretful echo of a sea-gull's scream,*
> *As if one cries who sees within a dream*
> *Deep rooted sorrow in the heart of things.*
>
> *The cry that Sorrow knows and would complain*
> *And impotently struggle to express —*
> *Some secret shame, some hidden bitterness. . . .*

Nearly twenty-four when he started working for the *Telegraph,* Eugene had never been seriously interested in any of the New London girls. Under Jamie's tutelage he had early become acquainted with the brothels of Bradley Street, and there had been an affair with a married woman somewhat older, but he had had little contact with properly reared girls of his own age — Kathleen had been the lone exception. His reputation around town was none too good, not only because of his drinking, his going to sea, his being divorced, but because of his brother's poor name; townspeople, especially those with nubile daughters, tended to lump them together. One evening he was sitting with a girl on the porch of her home when her father came along and ordered him away.

"It was a sort of wishing out loud," the playwright said when asked whether *Ah, Wilderness!* was autobiographical. "That's the way I would have *liked* my boyhood to have been."

Eugene's feeling of rebirth after his suicide attempt left him hungry, probably unconsciously, to capture some of the youth he had missed; in his behavior this year he often seemed more like the callow hero of his nostalgic comedy than one familiar with the dregs of life. Infatuated with a young dancer who was summering on Pequot Avenue, he used to slip notes under her door addressed "To the Beautiful Unknown." He wrote poems to a girl named Mabel in which he referred to her as "Queen Mab." But both girls paled to him when he fell in love with Maibelle Scott, whom he would later portray as Richard Miller's breathless sweetheart. *Wilderness* affords glimpses of O'Neill not only in 1906 but in 1912.

Maibelle, eighteen, was among the prettiest girls in town — large blue eyes, the freshest of complexions, all soft curves. She was rather shy and blushed easily, yet had a mind and will of her own, qualities inherited, most likely, from her paternal grandfather, Captain Thomas A. Scott, the bearded lord of Scott's dock, who once had loomed giantlike to a dreamy youngster. Maibelle displayed some of her grandfather's spirit in becoming Eugene's girl, considering his equivocal reputation around town.

The O'Neills and the Scotts, living a block apart on Pequot Avenue, had been acquainted for years but without being close; James was friendly, however, with old Scott's two sons, "Young Captain Tom," head of the wrecking concern — the old mariner had died in 1907 — and Maibelle's father, John Scott, who ran a grocery on the wharf. As old-timers of the neighborhood, the Scotts were aware of something "peculiar" about Mrs. O'Neill and had heard rumors that she was an alcoholic or a drug addict; practically the only times they ever saw her was when she went out for a ride or when the family was walking to and from meals at a nearby boardinghouse. Out of regard for her popular husband, however, people generally refrained from speculating aloud about her.

In the summer of 1912 Maibelle's recently wed sister Arlene and her husband Byron Fones moved into one of Mr. O'Neill's properties, the Pink House, next door to the Monte Cristo cottage. Eugene, lounging around the porch at home, began to keep a lookout for the young beauty, only yesterday a chubby schoolgirl, who regularly called on Arlene. One day Arlene was walking along Pequot Avenue when Eugene rode up on his bicycle, dismounted, and joined her; after a fumbling gambit, something about the weather, he blurted out, "I'd like to meet your sister. Of course I know her . . ." Arlene, several years younger than Eugene but feeling matronly in the face of his shyness, informed him he would be sure to meet her if he attended Bessie Young's wedding a few nights later; Bessie's mother ran the boardinghouse where the O'Neills took their meals.

Though the evening of the wedding was warm, Eugene, eager to make an impression, borrowed one of his father's opera capes and had it draped carelessly over his arm as he approached Maibelle, bowed, and said under his breath, "At last we meet!" She was both amused and flattered. They had little chance to talk as he was not only a guest but a reporter covering the affair and had to leave early. At eleven that night, to her parents' annoyance, the telephone rang; it was Eugene asking for a date.

"A very pretty wedding took place last evening . . ." his account began in the *Telegraph* on September 25. "The bride wore a charming gown of crepe meteor over white satin trimmed with silk lace and carried a shower bouquet of Killarney roses. The bridesmaid was Miss Jennie Payne, who wore white lace over pink satin and carried a bouquet of pink roses. . . . Miss Angenetta Appledorn was the pianist and played both the Mendelssohn wedding march and the one from *Lohengrin.*" After disposing of the principals, he gave Maibelle top billing: "The young ladies who served were: Miss Maibelle Scott, Miss Mildred Culver, Miss Jennie Strictland, Mrs. Byron Fones . . ."

In *Ah, Wilderness!* fifteen-year-old Muriel McComber's father is scandalized to find letters Richard Miller has written her containing choice passages from Swinburne ("That I could drink thy veins as wine, and eat/Thy breasts like honey . . ."). After forbidding her to have anything further to do with him, McComber tells Nat Miller that his son is "dissolute, blasphemous" and accuses the boy of "deliberately attempting to corrupt" his daughter's morals. His attitude is only a slight exaggeration of how Maibelle's parents felt about Eugene.

Several days after the wedding he took her to a matinee of *The Bohemian Girl* at the Lyceum; it was their first and last date in public. As soon as he had left, after bringing her home, Mrs. Scott told her daughter she would "shoot him" if he ever came to the house again. But where young Miller's father defends him, James and Ella sided with the Scotts. The latter were, however, somewhat irked by one of James's remarks: "Oh, Eugene falls in love with every pretty face he sees." Ella, under the misapprehension that a girl who phoned was Maibelle, told her: "You'd better stay away from him. He isn't a good influence for you or any other girl." Talking from the other side of her mouth, though, she told

Mrs. Young, the boardinghouse keeper, "I don't want him marrying a grocer's daughter."

But the romance flourished in spite of, or perhaps spurred by, parental opposition. The two young people met regularly at the Pink House until Arlene's husband, taking a dim view of Eugene, ended the convenient arrangement. Judge Latimer, who told Maibelle that Eugene was of uncommon promise, had them to dinner several times. They used to run into one another "by accident" at the library. Most often they met at a prearranged spot on Montauk Avenue, a street paralleling Pequot Avenue, and would wander toward Ocean Beach, the public resort at the far end of the Pequot area; and if the weather was bad they generally got together in the home of Maibelle's best friend, Mildred ("Mid") Culver, until time for the latter's mother to return from her job as a schoolteacher. Mildred, who found it all very exciting, carried messages between them and in other ways helped further the romance. O'Neill would have her in mind when he drew the good-natured daughter, Mildred ("Mid") Miller, in *Wilderness*.

Though Eugene and Maibelle managed to meet regularly, they exchanged letters once and even twice a day. He wrote her not so much love letters as a running account of his thoughts, suggestions about books for her to read, commentary on those he was reading, quotations from his favorite poems, and sometimes included his latest rhymes. He seemed intent above everything else on educating her, on awakening her to the solemn depths and harsh realities of life. "I have to get that book by Nietzsche," she told Mildred. "Eugene wants me to read it." There was little about himself or his outlook that he withheld from Maibelle; he told her about Buenos Aires, Jimmy the Priest's, and his suicide attempt; he occasonally referred to Kathleen, always with respect, and once said of their relationship, "It was a mistake, it should never have happened." His frequent criticism of the Catholic Church, of all organized religion, was interspersed with praise for Socialism and anarchism. He often talked of the joy of being at sea, and more than once told her: "The perfect way to die is to swim out under a full moon and finally go under."

Years later Maibelle, an attractive matron living on Long Island, told a visitor: "He was so different from anyone I'd ever met, I was fascinated. He was well read, he'd traveled, he was full of ideas, he knew so much about almost everything — I got a great deal from knowing him. A very sensitive and gentle person. He was always a gentleman around me, never drunk or anything like that, and I couldn't understand why people talked against him, including his own parents. I felt that he was very much misunderstood. He really felt that he would be famous some day, more famous than his father, and that all the people who'd talked against him would finally recognize that he was different.

"One time we went to a party up near Norwich, and I was surprised at how quiet he was — he seemed ill at ease — but around me he was perfectly relaxed and always had a great deal to say. He could be so enthusiastic about many things, books he was reading, life at sea, certain poets, yet at the same time there was a sad streak in him, a what's-the-use sort of attitude. When I met my husband, I realized the feeling was different. I knew then that I had never loved Eugene but had only been fascinated."

The young reporter lost no time getting down on paper his feelings about Maibelle; from "Only You," published in the *Telegraph* on September 27:

> *We walk down the crowded city street*
> *Lingeringly, side by side*
> *You throb with the city's ceaseless beat*
> *While I in a dream abide.*

> *For how can its harsh triumphant din*
> *Make me shudder or rejoice?*
> *When the only sound in the dream I'm in*
> *Is the music of your voice. . . .*

In contrast to his frame of mind, the atmosphere at home was dispirited, not only because his parents were upset over his interest in Maibelle but because James's career had struck a new low. The season was already under way and he still had had no offers worth considering — the first time he had found himself in such a situation since his apprenticeship nearly a half-century earlier. The uncertain future of his *Monte Cristo* film also weighed on him as he talked "poor mouth" to his family, a refrain that would echo throughout *Long Day's Journey*. Outside the home, though, he as always appeared self-assured.

O'Neill Gets Many Offers, read a headline in the *Day* on September 21, the account stating that he "has made no plans for this season, theatrically, and may not play. Recently a manager came here, wishing to secure Mr. O'Neill for the leading part in *The Angelus*, which has been produced abroad with much success. Charles and Daniel Frohman have also made a proposition to Mr. O'Neill, but he has accepted no offer."

Months later, after he had landed in a Broadway success, he told a reporter: "I spent the summer at my home in New London and got through the warm months without any trouble, but my first visit to New

York made me restless. I felt like an old war horse that had been put aside, and it was most uncomfortable. For since I first went into stock in minor parts in 1868, the stage has been my home. I had too much leisure. I didn't know what to do with myself. I tired of reading and would spend hours pacing up and down. This made my wife nervous. . . ."

Before September ended, James had a furnace installed, the first heating system to supplement the fireplaces since the family moved into the house in the 1880s. They were staying on late this year, the longest period the four of them had ever been cooped up together under the same roof. Ella's only consolation was that the lighthouse at the end of Pequot Avenue had discontinued its siren the previous year, one that the harassed community used to refer to as lighthouse keeper Charlie Field's "dying cow." But although it was no longer in use by 1912, the time of *Long Day's Journey*, O'Neill used the foghorn in the play with a motif effect, both as a touch of mournful atmosphere and a recurrent subject of conversation among the Tyrones.

In October, after the *Telegraph* (presumably with Mr. O'Neill's permission) had raised Eugene's salary to twelve dollars, he began talking to Maibelle of marriage, but she felt that they should defer any such plan until he was better established financially. It was also in October that he developed a stubborn cold, together with a racking cough, and began losing weight, a loss he could ill afford. Several weeks later, after being drenched in a rainstorm while cycling to work, he started suffering at night from chills and fever. Eager to continue with his job and seeing Maibelle, he told himself it probably was only a recurrence of the malarial fever he had contracted in Honduras. Ella alternated between making light of his condition and fussing anxiously over him; hostile to all doctors, she became agitated whenever James suggested the boy should see Dr. Harold Heyer, the family physician.

Finally too ill to continue working, he quit the *Telegraph* in November and underwent an examination; the tentative diagnosis was "pleurisy." Ella reacted to his illness by leaning more heavily on morphine and ended by requiring medical attention herself. A young nurse who was sent to the house by Dr. Heyer to look after her found a scene that could have been lifted intact from *Long Day's Journey*. Mabel Reynolds, the nurse, once recalled her own long night at 325 Pequot Avenue:

"It was between four and five in the afternoon when I got there. I could hear loud voices inside, like an argument going on. I rang the bell, I finally had to knock, and somebody called, 'Come in.' They were sitting — the father and two boys — in the dining room at a round table. There were glasses on it, and there was a bottle. One of them waved me up, 'Go on upstairs.' She was in bed and looked terrible, she looked — this is a horrible expression but it will give you the idea — she looked like a witch, with her white hair and large dark eyes. She was rocking back and forth, wringing her hands. 'My son, my son,' she kept repeating, and tears were running down her face.

"And all the time this awful shouting was going on downstairs. They all must've been pretty much under the weather. I couldn't hear what they were saying but the boys were shouting at the father. All of them, though, were making their share of noise. I knew right away this was something I didn't want to go through more than once. It was really pretty rough. 'My son, my son,' she went on — I guess I heard it a hundred times — and once or twice she mentioned something about a baby son who'd died. I didn't know whether she meant Eugene when she said 'My son, my son,' or if she meant the one who'd died. Once she got up and started to pace the floor, back and forth, back and forth. She said she was in pain. I had quite a time getting her back in bed.

"I never knew the boys but I'd heard a lot about the older one. Everybody knew he was a problem, always in some kind of scrape. I used to see the mother being driven around New London. The only time I ever got a close look at her, before all this happened, she was on Main Street near the Starr drug store. I remember looking closely at her because she was the mother of this character around town — she seemed very gentle, a real lady. It seemed strange that she would be the mother of someone like that, but that night she certainly wasn't ladylike.

"She quieted down after a while, but it was hours and hours. I gave her an alcohol rub, to make her comfortable, and noticed hypodermic marks on her arm — no, I hadn't heard that she was a drug addict. If the night had been any worse, I don't know what it could have been like — the quarreling and shouting going on till three in the morning or so. No one was around when I left in the morning. I don't know where they were, they never came upstairs. When I left there I was quite disturbed, and I remember taking a long walk before going back to the hospital — I was still in training then. . . . No, I never went back."

Eugene's illness was worse than pleurisy, it was one of the most feared of all diseases, tuberculosis. Long among the foremost causes of death all over the world, it was known not only as "the White Plague" and "the Great Killer" but on both sides of the Atlantic — because so many Irish fell victim to it in the hovels of their country and in the tenements of America — as "the Irish disease." At first Ella O'Neill refused to accept the doctor's findings, stubbornly insisting that her son's illness was only a "bad cold." In a day when it was commonly thought that heredity played a role in the disease and that the Irish were predisposed to it, she had a special reason for regarding tuberculosis with dread: her beloved father had succumbed to it.

After Dr. Heyer's diagnosis a nurse named Olive Evans was engaged to stay at the house and look after Eugene. Eugene himself had chosen her as they had friends in common and he thought she would be more indulgent than a stranger; but Olive, though good-natured and sympathetic, was dedicated to her profession and firm about his obeying the doctor's instructions. While her memories of her stay with the O'Neills — she was there for about a month — sound nothing like the nightmarish experience of the other nurse, she found it other than a normal household. Unaware of Ella's addiction, she was puzzled on sometimes hearing her downstairs rocking and weeping. "It was a whimpering sound, like a kitten," she recalls. "I once said to Eugene, 'Shouldn't I go downstairs and see about your mother?' He told me not to; he was very insistent about it, and said I was never to go unless invited. I never was."

Patient and nurse got along well on the whole. She found him full of contradictions, so much so that her own feelings about him were contradictory: "He was charming and the longer I knew him, the better I liked him, but he could also be sarcastic and sharp. . . . He was shy, really quite shy. . . . He liked to shock me. I thought he was strange, a bit peculiar, and always felt he was like he was because they'd never had a real home and family life. . . . He was hard to handle, not for me, but the doctors. You couldn't order Gene to do anything because he'd get stubborn. You had to coax him; 'Please, Gene, this is going to help you, it's for your own benefit, please take it.' And he would. . . . I thought he was much younger than I was, but later learned we were the same age. Not that he was childish, because he wasn't, but there was something about him. . . . He was like a naughty child when he couldn't get what he wanted. I had the feeling he wanted sympathy, that he was dying for affection and understanding. . . . When he was in the dumps, he didn't want to eat, and at first I used to try and coax him, but after a while I stopped trying. I felt he wanted to torment someone else, make them suffer, too."

One day Olive happened on some of his writings in a bureau drawer ("just notes and rough drafts"), and after promising to keep the pages in order was allowed to read them. One of the outlines was about an old barge captain who hated the sea; years later, after she had seen *Anna Christie*, Olive assumed that he was already working on plays when she took care of him. Some of the things she read struck her as shocking, and she told him so. "Oh, no," Eugene replied, "you're too naïve. They aren't immoral, they're unmoral," and he once described himself to her in similar terms.

He continued to write ocasionally for the "Laconics" column, verse that generally expressed his restlessness at being marooned at home. One of the poems, published on November 19, was entitled "The Call":

> *I have eaten my share of "stock fish"*
> *On a steel Norwegian bark;*
> *With hands gripped hard to the royal yard*
> *I have swung through the rain and the dark.*
> *I have hauled upon the braces*
> *And bawled the chantey song,*
> *And the clutch of the wheel had a friendly feel,*
> *And the Trade Wind's kiss was strong. . . .*
>
> *For it's grand to lie on the hatches*
> *In the glowing tropic night*
> *When the sky is clear and the stars seem near*
> *And the wake is a trail of light,*
> *And the old hulk rolls so softly*
> *On the swell of the southern sea*
> *And the engines croon in a drowsy tune*
> *And the world is mystery!*
> *So it's back to the sea, my brother,*
> *Back again to the sea. . . .*

Although he wanted sympathy, he sometimes went out of his way, mingling fiction with fact, to present himself in an unfavorable light. Reminiscing about Buenos Aires, he told Olive that "girls fourteen and fifteen years old used to wait for the ships to come in, especially American ships. All you needed for them to sleep with you was a bag of candy — they loved American candy. One of them picked me up shortly after I arrived and lived with me the whole time I was there. She was an orphan and homeless."

Olive thought him vain because he was constantly studying himself in the bureau mirror and finally asked whether he would like the bureau moved to where he could see himself while in bed. "After I did it," she recalls, "I told him, 'Now you can see your madonna eyes,' and he looked shy and pleased. He had heavenly eyes, the most beautiful I've ever seen. So did Mrs. O'Neill — large, dark, dreamy eyes." But apparently more than narcissism was behind his preoccupation with his own image. A few years later a friend, George Cram Cook, making the same assumption that Olive Evans had, told him, "You're the most conceited man I've ever known, you're always looking at yourself." O'Neill denied it in words the other never forgot: "No, I just want to be sure I'm here."

Most of the time he was ambulatory, but whenever his temperature edged upward he remained in bed. Toward the end of November Dr. Heyer had him aspirated by Dr. Daniel Sullivan, a surgeon, to draw off fluid from his thoracic cavity. The nurse was moved to sympathetic tears by his stoicism; his only reaction as the tubing pierced his flesh was to clap his hands over his face and let out a grunt. "I thought to myself," Olive says, "he must have some real stuff in him to take it like that."

With Eugene and Ella the only family members regularly at home, it was a quiet household; James was in New York most of the week, trying to land a worthwhile role and attending to his suit against the makers of the rival *Monte Cristo* film, and Jamie was absent the entire time Olive stayed at the house. It was her impression that he was in one of the Keeley Institutes for alcoholics. Though Eugene always spoke warmly of his brother, the nurse felt relieved by his absence, for she had heard around town that he had a foul tongue.

Olive was off duty several hours every afternoon and almost always had notes to transmit between her patient and Maibelle, either directly or through Mildred Culver. One day, the only time the nurse was ever in the downstairs rooms, she was summoned to the telephone. It was Mildred calling, and the nurse answered noncommittally — yes, no, that's right, and so forth. Mrs. O'Neill afterward called her into the living room: "I don't want you carrying messages from Maibelle Scott." When Olive protested that it was Mildred on the phone, Ella broke in: "I know what's been happening. There are many reasons why we don't want this affair to go on, and religion is the principal reason."

Despite his illness, Eugene managed to see Maibelle a few times. After Dr. Heyer had agreed with his suggestion that carriage rides would be good for him, he had Olive obtain his father's permission to hire a hack whenever he liked. The first time they went riding he had the driver stop after several blocks and told the nurse he would pick her up later — he was going to meet Maibelle. He returned indignant from one ride because Maibelle had been wearing a veil tied in back and refused to take it off so he could kiss her. Olive thought he was deeply in love ("he once cried because they couldn't get married") but also couldn't help suspecting at times that he was "in love with love."

There was a side of him that enjoyed his illness; reduced to a feeling of dependency and brought into closer contact with his mother than in years, he reacted by becoming childlike — it was in his voice when he spoke to her, in his general attitude. Ella, afraid of being infected, rarely visited his room but would make nourishing drinks, generally eggnogs, and bring them halfway upstairs. Though he welcomed her solicitude, he used to complain to Olive about the concoctions; Ella, who had never developed any facility for running a household, was at a loss in preparing even the simplest foods. While his manner toward his mother was affectionate, his attitude toward his father was distinctly hostile. He often referred to him as "the Irish peasant," and Ella would protest weakly, "Oh, please, Geney, don't call Papa that." He would scarcely lift his head to say hello when his father looked in to see how he was feeling. Once, coming upstairs, James stumbled and fell on the small landing at the turn, and Olive rushed out to help him up, inquiring whether he was all right. He kissed her lightly and said, "Thank you, my dear, for caring if I was hurt."

Every Friday, as the time approached for his return from New York, Ella was constantly at the front windows for the first sight of him driving up in a hack; he would half-run up the walk with his arms outstretched as she rushed toward him. When Olive mentioned this to a friend, the other sniffed, "Once an actor, always an actor," but the nurse felt it was no make-believe. "He was gentle with her and devoted — they gave every sign of being very much in love." Olive found him unfailingly courteous and pleasant, and used to resent it when Eugene would call down to Ella, "Where's the Irish peasant this morning? Has he gone to Mass yet?"

After months of relative harmony between son and father, their relations had become strained when Eugene began courting Maibelle; and now his illness had led to a new source of contention — the question of a sanatorium. James, who had spent thousands for Ella's care in private sanatoria, felt that they charged exorbitantly for their services without really helping any; he wanted Eugene to enter the state-run institution in Shelton, Connecticut. Eugene was against the place as largely handling charity cases. Some of the most bitter moments in *Long Day's Journey Into Night* center on this issue as Edmund attacks his father as miserly and without pride. In self-defense Tyrone launches into an account of his bleak childhood, of the factors leading to his life-long fear of poverty, and ends: "(With grim humor) It was in those days I learned to be a miser. A dollar was worth so much then."

In the son's outburst and the father's reply one can see defined O'Neill's central problem with *Long Day's Journey*: he was writing at once an indictment and a defense of his family. The need to justify himself drove him to picture his parents and brother in all their frailties and offenses, but at the same time he was saying that he had at last made his peace with them; he was projecting both his original view of the family, as he remembered it, and his deeper insight, his more compassionate attitude afterward. Through *Long Day's Journey* he was pronouncing absolution on the "four haunted Tyrones" for what they had done to one another; yet the play, though written to exorcise his ghosts, bears witness that they would forever haunt him.

O'Neill took liberties with the past in *Long Day's Journey*, for he was giving not a literal account of things as they were but a distillation of the family's history. The son's ruling concern with truth was matched by the artist's concern with selective emphasis, with maximum impact. He telescoped events, he altered chronology, he invented circumstance, he suppressed fact, he modified this, he touched up that, all in the name of artistic truth.

While some of his revisions of fact are relatively unimportant, others are of major significance within the context of the play, especially in regard to the question of James O'Neill's miserliness. The play gives the impression, for example, that Eugene was treated by a "cheap old quack"; yet Dr. Heyer (called "Hardy" in the play) was a reputable physician, and Dr. Sullivan, whom he brought into the case, one of the town's leading surgeons. On this score, in short, the play is unfair to James. But then, redressing the balance, it leads us to believe that he yielded about the "state farm" and that Eugene never went there, whereas he actually did. However, James' choice of the institution seems less outrageous than the play maintains when one knows that Ed Keefe's older brother was then, in 1912, at Shelton; the Keefe family, besides owning property, had a thriving grocery store. Probably James first thought of the Shelton place because one of the Keefes was a patient there.

Long Day's Journey is misleading, too, about another aspect of the Shelton matter, for it says through Edmund that everyone would be scandalized if he, the son of famous, well-to-do James Tyrone, should enter the charity institution. The fact is, everyone did know that Eugene was going to Shelton — the news was reported in both local papers — yet this apparently made so little impression that Maibelle Scott, Olive Evans, Mildred Culver and others close to him at the time had in later years forgotten about it. Evidently few of the townspeople knew anything about the institution, and there is reason to believe that Eugene himself was not fully prepared for what he would find in Shelton.

Shortly before he was to leave for the sanatorium he returned hours late from one of his carriage rides and so drunk that, while Ella wept, the driver and another man had to help him upstairs. Olive was both concerned that he should jeopardize his health and worried about herself; she remembered his telling her of his return from Honduras, the time he was intoxicated and chopped up the furniture. The nurse locked herself in her room and left the house the following morning. Several days later, after a telephone call from Mrs. O'Neill, she returned. "He was quiet and sullen when I went back," she recalls. "He was never exactly a happy soul but toward the end he was in a darker mood."

On December 9 the *Telegraph* ran a story that James O'Neill would appear on Broadway for Liebler & Co. in *The Deliverer* (later retitled *Joseph and His Brethren*), a "wonderfully scenic" production with a cast of "more than two hundred." James was to play the dual roles of Jacob the patriarch and Pharaoh. That same day the newspaper reported, under the head, Goes to Shelton Today: "Eugene O'Neill of the *Telegraph* staff, who has been seriously ill with pleurisy . . . will leave today for Shelton, where he will take what is called the 'rest cure' for several weeks. The acute attack of pleurisy . . . was a heavy strain on his lungs and, while neither is affected, it was deemed wise by his physicians to give them the benefit of out-door living and sleeping. . . ."

15

Birth of a Playwright

THE morning was cold and dull, heavy with the threat of impending snow. Olive accompanied Eugene to New Haven, where he was to meet his father for the last leg of the trip. "He was frightened," she recalls, "and said very little. I tried making conversation to get his mind off things but finally had to give it up. He just stared out the window most of the time, though I don't imagine he saw what he was looking at. It was snowing when we got off, and three or four coffins were just being transferred from another train to ours. I'll never forget the expression on his face. He was upset but trying to hide it, and made some kind of grim joke that that was what was waiting for him at the sanatorium."

Son and father, arriving by hack, found the state farm a depressing scene, worse than Eugene had expected. Opened only two years earlier, the Fairfield County State Tuberculosis Sanatorium in Shelton consisted of three weather-beaten structures, a farmhouse and two shacks, that had been converted for infirmary purposes without being converted very far. With time it would develop into a large up-to-date institution (the name was later changed to the Laurel Heights Sanatorium) but in 1912 its appearance on a near-bare wind-swept hill was enough to dishearten even the healthy. When inmates of the state's poorhouses contracted tuberculosis, they were sent there for free care, while others of any means paid four dollars a week. Its turnover in patients was high, most of them being terminal cases. December showed the place in the bleakest light.

Dr. Edward J. Lynch, who in a few years would become superintendent of the sanatorium, received the O'Neills. He later recalled the son as tall, well-dressed, monosyllabic, and the father, dignified in a Homburg hat, as "solicitous and anxious." The doctor saw little more of Eugene than he did of Mr. O'Neill, for Eugene, admitted on December 9, had himself discharged on the eleventh. He remained just long enough to get a thorough examination and learn that his chances for recovery were "good if he had adequate rest, food and treatment."

James was feeling guilty and on the defensive when Eugene joined the family in New York. There is no need to imagine the scene that took place between them; it is all spelled out in *Long Day's Journey*, though the play occurs before Edmund leaves for a sanatorium. In fact some of the exchanges between Edmund and Tyrone have more point if one revises the chronology. Tyrone's apologetic reply that the doctors had told him that the state institution was a "good bargain" must have been James O'Neill's line of defense afterward, not before, just as it was afterward that Eugene, once he had been there, was so outraged at the thought of the "state farm."

Following the experience at Shelton, James, eager to make amends, sent his son to two specialists with national reputations, Dr. Livingston Farrand and Dr. James Alexander Miller. On December 17 the latter wrote about Eugene to Dr. David R. Lyman of the Gaylord Farm Sanatorium in Wallingford, Connecticut: "He is in excellent general condition and is, I believe, a very favorable case. He has almost no cough or expectoration and no fever and is only a few pounds below normal weight. . . . Will you be good enough to write me immediately whether you will be able to take him?"

In *Long Day's Journey* Tyrone, after yielding about the state farm, tells his son that the specialist had also recommended a sanatorium that was subsidized by some wealthy industrialists, one that charged a mere seven dollars weekly and yet was rated among the finest TB institutions in the country. It was Gaylord Farm he was talking about, a nonprofit institution endowed through the efforts of the pioneering Anti-Tuberculosis Association of New Haven County, and the charge, as Tyrone said, was only seven dollars a week. Eugene was admitted there on Christmas Eve. He and his father were supposed to arrive in the afternoon — James had hired a car in New York — but were delayed by the car's breaking down several times and a snowstorm of blizzard proportions that raged all day. When they finally reached their destination, cold, worn-out, hungry, they found the place half-empty; part of the staff and a good many patients, those advanced in recovery, were away for family reunions and holiday feasting.

The timing of his arrival did not pass unnoticed. "I thought to myself," a nurse recalls, "that anyone coming to a sanatorium on Christmas Eve didn't have a home of his own." In after years O'Neill would always minimize the date of his admission, but his words tended to evoke the image of a child at boarding school, all the more lonely around the holidays: "To an actor's son, whose father had been on tour nearly every winter, Christmas meant less than nothing. As a boy I never disbelieved in Santa Claus. I had hardly heard there was one — not that I lacked my share of gifts, but that we never had much chance for a winter home and so Christmas was just a holiday without the usual associations."

The admitting physician found him, except for being seven pounds under his normal weight of 153, in good general condition. He told the doctor he might have contracted the disease while "visiting dives and tenement houses as a reporter." More likely, though, he believed what he later told a friend, that he got a "dose of those germs" from the "lungers" at Jimmy the Priest's.

Gaylord was a distinct improvement over the Shelton place: a half-dozen or so trim-looking buildings, several hundred acres of rolling farm and woodland, located on the brow of a hill overlooking the distant Blue Hill Mountains. It had, considering its function, a reassuring atmosphere, due largely to Dr. David R. Lyman, the superintendent, a fine-looking man in his mid-thirties, quiet, dignified, with an air of easy authority. Since Lyman himself had had TB, there was personal commitment in his war on "the Great Killer." Gaylord reflected both his kindly character and in lesser degree the determined nature of Mrs. Florence R. Burgess, plump-faced head of nursing, who gave the impression of being queen — to Lyman's kingship — of all she surveyed. Founded in 1904, the sanatorium began with one doctor (Lyman), one nurse (Mrs. Burgess), six patients, and a bank balance of $92.20; eight years later it accommodated around a hundred patients and was recognized as one of the best-run TB sanatoria in the East. The spirit Dr. Lyman gave it was such that many former patients regarded themselves, to use their own term, as "alumni," the institution itself as their "alma mater."

Life at Gaylord was totally organized. On admittance patients were housed in the infirmary for close surveillance and care, and allowed out of bed for meals — at first for one, then two, and so forth — in accordance with their condition. The high point of the week, full of tension, came on Saturday morning as everyone lined up at the telltale scales: if a patient had gained, fine, but if he had lost . . . The length of the infirmary stay depended upon one's progress. From there patients went to a cottage or a "shack" where they slept on an open porch even in the coldest weather; cold fresh air was at the time considered beneficial for the tubercular. Paralleling the infirmary routine, patients were allowed to walk to meals as their health improved, initially once a day, then twice, and so forth.

Before long Eugene was transferred to Hart Shack and going to the main building for all his meals. "Thanks to a constitution from my father that I had done my damndest to wreck," he once said, "I only contracted a very slight incipient case. The devil is certainly partial to the damned-fool, is my explanation."

Once he felt secure about his prospects for recovery, he was not unhappy in his new life. His reaction to Gaylord was somewhat similar in fact to the way he had felt about Betts Academy, and on the same basis: his surroundings were more or less peaceful; he was well looked after, as though by an all-attentive mother; he was, finally, away from his family and the family tensions. But, as at Betts, no one could have guessed how he felt from his air of detachment and characteristic somber expression. A few years after he had left there he wrote Dr. Lyman: "In the measure that I love my work, and am proud to have been able to do the little I have, so much the more deep is my gratitude to you and to Gaylord Farm for saving me for it. . . . and [the] recollections of my stay there are among the most pleasant of my memories."

At the outset he established his closest relations not with other patients but with several nurses, particularly Mary A. Clark, in charge of the infirmary, and Katherine Murray, both of whom were warmhearted persons, well-read, especially in poetry, and devoutly Catholic. Their feelings toward him were mixed; they were at once fond of him and unhappy about his views, particularly his antagonism toward the Church. He impressed them as having little family feeling. According to one of his stories, he and his brother were at the pier, waving good-by, when their parents sailed one year for Europe; the hawser was pulled in, the anchor hauled up, yet the ship lingered. He finally, as he recounted it, tired of the delay and said to his brother, "Oh, to hell with it, let's go!"

Clare O'Rourke, fresh out of the nuns' hands in Ireland, was another nurse with whom he became friendly. "My first sight of him," she recalls, "was his bouncing into the treatment room one morning, resentful because the doctor had called him down about something or other. My, how he hated rules and regulations! — like the one that you couldn't go on exercise [take a walk] if you had a temperature." Encountering her one day as she was telling her beads, he said, "You'll get over that Irish superstition when you've been in America a while." Clare, who felt that he was rejecting not just the Church but everything, found him unpredictable: "It seemed to me he was looking for a sympathetic ear. He could be gentle and sensitive, but there was also a rough sadistic streak in him." Even his appearance struck her as a case of extremes. "When he was feeling good, he was really quite handsome — there was something boyish about him. But if he was out of sorts, his whole face changed, everything sagged, especially his mouth; it had a cruel and sardonic look. I was fascinated by his mouth, it was so expressive."

One of his early full-length plays, *The Straw,* is based on his stay at

Gaylord. Dr. Lyman is depicted under the name of Dr. Stanton, a "handsome man of forty-five or so with a grave, care-lined, studious face lightened by a kindly, humorous smile. His gray eyes, saddened by the suffering they have witnessed, have the sympathetic quality of real understanding." In Miss Gilpin the playwright gave his impression of Mary Clark: a "slight, middle-aged woman with black hair, and a strong, intelligent face, its expression of resolute efficiency softened and made kindly by her warm, sympathetic gray eyes."

The hero, Stephen Murray, is a small-town newspaperman with literary ambitions, in other words, one of the many self-portraits in O'Neill's plays: a "tall, slender, rather unusual-looking fellow with a pale face, sunken under high cheek bones, lined about the eyes and mouth, jaded and worn for one still so young. His intelligent, large hazel eyes have a tired, dispirited expression in repose, but can quicken instantly with a concealment mechanism of mocking, careless humor whenever his inner privacy is threatened. He gives off the impression of being somehow dissatisfied with himself but not yet embittered enough by it to take it out on others."

Eugene was writing regularly to Maibelle, who was in Florida with her parents for the winter, and for a time to Olive Evans. "When he first went in I heard from him practically every day for a month or so," Olive says. "Not that there was anything between us — he was just lonesome, I suppose." His letters to both girls often contained poems, and he also showered his new friends at Gaylord with his rhymes. In a tribute to Miss Clark he referred to her as "kindest of bosses that e'er bossed . . . angel of old pneumo-thorax." Katherine, who thought him irresponsible in regard to women, inspired a mock-serious love poem of which the following lines are characteristic: "Why not reform my life? Thru and thru,/ Scour and cleanse my soul of the mire,/ A regular Christian thing to do." For Miss O'Rourke he came up with a parody of the *Rubáiyát*: "Oh, Clare, could you and I with fate conspire/ To call this damn thermometer a liar/ Would we not shatter it to bits/ And then remold it to our heart's desire."

Most of his verse, however, was of a serious nature. One day he dropped by to see Katherine but a patient had just died and she was too upset for conversation; several hours later he handed her a poem, "To T.B.":

> *The Song and the singing are over*
> *I am done*
> *Dead are the love and the lover*
> *You have won.*
> *The laughter of life and the gladness*

The travail of life and the sadness
The wisdom of life and the madness
All are one. . . .

Every few Sundays the monotony of his days was broken by a visit from James, brief reunions between a son who said little and a father who, in the face of the other's reserve, was guardedly cheerful. After some worrisome months James was in good spirits, heartened both by Eugene's steady improvement and an upturn in his own fortunes. *Joseph and His Brethren,* a colorful melange of sex and biblical spectacle (the sort of thing Cecil B. de Mille would one day splash across the screen) was drawing crowds to the Century Theater. Mr. O'Neill, along with costars Brandon Tynan as Joseph and Pauline Frederick as Potiphar's wife, was basking in favorable press notices. From Jamie, who played a small part as one of the brothers, Eugene had a less flattering critique: "The only decent actor in the whole damn company is the camel in the second act."

In general O'Neill was so quiet around the other patients that in after years most of them could remember almost nothing about him except his reticence. In the relative privacy, however, of Hart Shack — it housed only six patients — he was constantly quoting Shakespeare, not just a few lines but long passages from memory. Hilmer Rosene, a fellow lodger, recalls that "he gave the lines with some feeling, but without hamming it up. I had the idea he was doing it for his own enjoyment, not to impress anyone or entertain us." O'Neill once cautioned Rosene, only fourteen, one of the youngest at Gaylord, that it was dangerous to sleep with the moon shining on one's face; the moon, he said, could pull it out of shape. He looked so serious as he said this that it was not till later that the boy realized he was spoofing.

Eugene's health improved so much that less than two months after entering Gaylord he was, in line with a general practice, given a few days' leave. Instead of visiting his family in New York, he spent the time in New London and told everyone that he had been discharged as completely over his "pleurisy." On February 21 the *Telegraph* said that he looked "the picture of health. . . . Mr. O'Neill has gained nearly twenty pounds and is feeling fit as a fiddle. He will remain here for several days renewing old friendships and receiving the congratulations of many friends on the successful outcome of his convalescence." On the twenty-fourth the paper, after he had left town, reported that he "will spend the remainder of the winter in Jacksonville, Fla. Many New Londoners find the land of Ponce de Leon a congenial winter home and there is at present a

*O'Neill,
bottom left*

*Dr. David R. Lyman, superintendent
of Gaylord Farm Sanatorium, and
Mrs. Florence R. Burgess, head of
nurses, both at the left*

O'Neill and Clare O'Rourke

Mary A. Clark and Katherine Murray

Catherine Anna ("Kitty") MacKay, the real-life model for Eileen Carmody, the heroine of The Straw

considerable colony from this city there." On March 19 the *Telegraph* said: "Postal cards from Eugene O'Neill, who is in Jacksonville, Fla., report that he is getting on splendidly and will return north in April."

Unless the postcards were nonexistent, with Judge Latimer in on the hoax, Eugene must have sent them to someone in Florida (Maibelle later said she was not the one) who in turn mailed them at Jacksonville. From New London he had gone directly back to Gaylord and the open porch at Hart Shack, where snowflakes would drift in on his pile of blankets.

No matter how much he sometimes chafed at his confinement, at rules and restrictions, he came to realize that his illness was the best thing that could have happened to him. "It was at Gaylord," he says, "that my mind got the chance to establish itself, to digest and valuate the impressions of many past years in which one experience had crowded on another with never a second's reflection. At Gaylord I really *thought about* my life for the first time, about past and future. Undoubtedly the inactivity forced upon me by the life at a san forced me to mental activity, especially as I had always been high-strung and nervous temperamentally."

It was at Gaylord that Eugene O'Neill decided to write for the theater, or, more precisely, that he finally became aware of a decision he had unconsciously made long before. At last he knew himself and had an identity to create that answered to his deepest needs; he was going to be a playwright. Despite his inner excitement, he set about preparing himself methodically, thoroughly. Determined to so saturate himself in the drama that it would become second nature for him to think in dialogue, in terms of entrances and exits, he began reading plays as fast as the postman could deliver them, the writings chiefly of foreign dramatists — Synge, Yeats, Lady Gregory, Brieux, Hauptmann. The cleaning maid for Hart Shack used to complain, "That man and his books — they're all over the place!" Where he had once read Ibsen for his advanced views, he now turned to him for lessons in dramaturgy. Yet he was even more impressed by another giant from the North, one who aroused his most fervent admiration — August Strindberg, the self-tortured Viking from Sweden. Strindberg, joining Nietzsche, became the second god in his literary pantheon.

A quarter-century later in his Nobel Prize acceptance speech O'Neill hailed him as "that greatest genius of all modern dramatists. . . . It was reading his plays . . . that, above all else, first gave me the vision of what modern drama could be, and first inspired me with the urge to write for the theater myself. If there is anything of lasting worth in my work, it is due to that original impulse from him, which has continued as my inspiration down all the years since then."

No doubt he exaggerated in crediting the Swedish master with turning him toward the stage — volumes of Strindberg were not lying around at Gaylord — but there is no question of the other man's impact on him. The day he wrote his Nobel Prize speech, in 1936, he told a friend, Sophus Keith Winther: "I wish immortality were a fact, for then some day I would meet Strindberg." When Winther demurred, "That would scarcely be enough to justify immortality," he was surprised to get a quick vigorous reply. O'Neill, generally low-voiced and so slow of speech that he seemed to lose his way among his thoughts, came back instantly with, "It would be enough for me!"

To O'Neill, Strindberg was not only a daring innovator who had gone beyond Ibsen in broadening the dimensions of the drama but a kindred spirit, a man who expressed his own somber view of life. As he read *The Dream Play* and *The Link, The Dance of Death* and *The Father*, it was like reading pages from his own family history. Wife to husband: "What have I to forgive? Dearest, you forgive *me!* We have been torturing each other." Mother to son: "You are always asking all sorts of questions, and in that way you spoil the better part of your life . . . Don't quarrel with God! Don't go around feeling that life has wronged you."

When Eugene was around thirteen he overheard his mother confiding to someone that she had been against having her last child, that it had been her husband's desire that they should have another one. Strindberg, who as a child had felt unwanted and unloved, has the Captain in *The Father* tell his wife: "My mother did not want me to come into the world because my birth would give her pain." The Poet of *The Dream Play*, like Eugene settling into the depths in Buenos Aires and at Jimmy the Priest's, wallows in the mire in order to coarsen his skin ("Then he cannot feel the stings of the wasps").

Where most people find in Strindberg's writings a nightmarish distortion of man's time on earth, O'Neill found an account of relentless truth. Above all it was Strindberg's desolate picture of family relations, particularly between husbands and wives, that struck in O'Neill the deepest chord. In *The Link* the Baron says to the Baroness: "There is room in me for both love and hatred, and while I love you one minute, I hate you the next." Again, an exchange in the same work between the Pastor and the Judge: "Well, that is love. . . . What then is hatred? . . . It is the lining of the coat."

Like his precursor, O'Neill saw those bound by the closest of ties as both victims and torturers of one another. In play after play he would sound the Strindbergian theme of love-hate, of the war between the sexes: in "Bread and Butter" and *Before Breakfast*, in *Beyond the Horizon* and *Welded*, in *Mourning Becomes Electra*, in *Dynamo*, in *More*

Stately Mansions — and this is but a partial list. Perhaps the most important thing he took from Strindberg was the courage to explore in his writings the darkest corners of his own character.

Shortly after Eugene's return from New London the sanatorium admitted a patient, Catherine Anna MacKay, twenty-three, from Waterbury, who had been there once before. She would later serve as the model for Eileen Carmody, the luckless heroine of *The Straw* who falls in love with Stephen Murray. The play's description of Eileen is in fact virtually a photographic likeness of Kitty MacKay: "Her wavy mass of dark hair is parted in the middle and combed low on her forehead. . . . The oval of her face is spoiled by a long, rather heavy, Irish jaw contrasting with the delicacy of her other features. Her eyes are large and blue, confident in their compelling candor and sweetness; her lips, full and red, droop at the corners into an expression of wistful sadness."

Kitty/Eileen had cause to be sad; the eldest in a family of ten children, she had been boxed in by life with no chance of escape. The death of her mother, from tuberculosis, had forced her to quit a secretarial job to take on the more onerous work of keeping house and looking after the family; and her father, a singularly unattractive man, hard, tightfisted, given to self-pity, only made things worse for Kitty. When she fell ill, he regarded it not so much a misfortune for her as an imposition on himself — he would have to hire a housekeeper to replace her. First admitted to Gaylord in 1911, Kitty had left after six months not because she was fully recovered but because she was worried about conditions at home and the youngsters. Though Gaylord always had a long waiting list, such was the personal impression she had made originally that Dr. Lyman gave her top priority as soon as he had word she considered returning.

Lyman discouraged romances between the patients, finding that "the healthy heart" interferes with "the cure of the sick lung." Eventually he would stress his view in a printed card, handed to all patients on their arrival, that bore the legend: Scatter Your Attention: Do Not Concentrate. Without mentioning her by name, Lyman once said that the girl on whom the heroine of *The Straw* was modeled was "one of the unfortunate cases" that prompted him to issue the warning.

In Kitty, brighter and more sensitive than most of the other women patients, with a yearning for the finer things of life, O'Neill found the sympathetic ear he had been seeking. Whenever they were together her face, generally pensive, took on animation, now smiling, now serious, in harmony with his moods. As he talked of books, the theater, and life at sea, she felt in touch with a larger, more colorful world than she had ever known. She ended by falling in love with him. As for O'Neill, without his deepest feelings being involved, he was stirred by the hungry interest, the generous emotions that shone through her shyness.

At the same time Kitty was a little afraid of him; his views were so unconventional, and the books he championed were, by all the standards of her upbringing, immoral. After learning that at home she had belonged to an amateur dramatic group, he lent her a volume of Brieux. Kitty was shocked and fascinated to read of mercenary parents who force their children into loveless marriages, of sexual conflict between husbands and wives, of prostitutes more admirable than pious churchgoers and, still worse, of an innocent wife and a syphilitic husband. Immediately after reading the book she told Mrs. Emma Wolodarsky, a fellow patient in Cottage 4: "I shouldn't have read it, I'll have to go to Confession."

Irked presumably by something Maibelle had written him, Eugene showed her photograph to Kitty and said he was through with her; Kitty, he added, could be his new girl and he would let her know if his feelings cooled. When Kitty complained to her friend Emma of his heartlessness, the latter, a sympathetic soul but more worldly, said that O'Neill's frankness was to his credit, that most men would have fed her a romantic though dishonest "line."

Cottage 4 became a center of interest to Eugene, not only because of Kitty MacKay but because of Katherine Murray, now housed there as a patient. This was not unusual at Gaylord: nearly all its nurses had begun as patients and after their recovery had joined the staff; in some instances a nurse's health deteriorated, forcing her to revert to her original status as one of the patients. Health, illness and death were not far apart at Gaylord Farm, and O'Neill, with a mild case, was in the privileged position of being both participant and observer.

He got along fairly well with everyone on the staff save with Mrs. Burgess, in spite of her efforts initially to be friendly with the son of James O'Neill. On one of his first Sundays at the farm she mentioned something to him about going to Mass. "You should have seen the look he gave me," she later said. He offended her another time by declining her invitation to tea, after which the firm-chinned matron kept a critical eye on his friendship with the two girls in Cottage 4. One day Kitty wept to Eugene: "She accused me of doing things — carrying on with you." He was furious. "Why didn't she call me in, if I was breaking the rules? I'm going right in there and tell her where to get off!" Kitty and Miss Murray had great difficulty dissuading him from having it out with Mrs. Burgess.

O'Neill was the lone bright spot in the life of the girl from Waterbury. Much as Kitty loved her family, she used to dread her father's Sunday visits, generally with several of the youngest MacKays in tow; instead of trying to be of some comfort to her, he constantly harped on his financial problems. O'Neill once overheard him telling her that the children needed shoes and he himself needed a suit and he didn't know where he was going to get the money for it all. Whenever Eugene ventured to criticize her father, she was so pained that he had to desist. It all came back to him — Kitty and her mean-spirited father, her feelings about an ex-reporter with literary ambitions, the daily routine at Gaylord — when he set out to write *The Straw; The Straw*, after *Long Day's Journey*, is most true to an actual period of his life.

In the play Murray, encouraged by Eileen Carmody, writes some short stories that launch him on a promising career. Just before his discharge from the sanatorium — his had been a mild case — she confesses her love; but Murray, too self-centered to give of himself, can only feel sorry for her. Months later, concerned at not hearing from her, he visits the sanatorium and is shocked to find her dying; without his love she had lost the will to live. After a nurse urges him to give Eileen some final days of happiness by telling her he loves her, he realizes that he truly does, that he will be lost without her.

O'Neill's feelings for Kitty, unlike those of his fictional counterpart, never grew into love, though he would later protest, when a friend found Murray's sudden passion unconvincing, that he himself had had such an experience. As for Kitty MacKay, whatever the depth of her affection, the relationship between her and Eugene was less intense than the one in the play; in life there were no desperate disclosures, no last-minute transformations — only a shy, friendly parting. Kitty died not at Gaylord shortly after her one-sided romance with O'Neill, as the play might lead one to imagine, but at home two years later, in 1915, surrounded by her father, four sisters and five brothers.

As the weather turned warm with the coming of spring Eugene sat by the hour on the steps of Hart Shack reading, working on poems, or simply gazing with an abstracted look at the distant Blue Hill Mountains. Sometimes he transcribed another's poetry, once copying down Christina Rossetti's noted threnody: "When I am dead, my dearest,/ Sing no sad songs for me;/ Plant thou no roses at my head,/ Nor shady cypress trees . . ." Despite the melancholy pleasure that part of him derived from his situation, he became increasingly restless as his health returned; often at night, when everyone was supposed to be in bed, he would slip off with a fellow patient or two to the saloons of Wallingford. Since he was to be discharged soon, he was unconcerned that he might be detected in such escapades.

On May 24, 1913, exactly five months after his arrival, Dr. Lyman recorded in his dossier that Case No. 1059 was in "A-1 shape, no symptoms, no fatigue, breathing much easier and stronger, looks and feels perfectly well." Eugene immediately relayed the good news to his father, who in turn wrote to Lyman for confirmation: "My son — Eugene — writes me that he was examined on Saturday [May 24], and is declared absolutely free from contagion; — that is, he is so thoroughly cured that no one — not even his ailing mother can become infected with tuberculosis by living in the same house and eating at the same table with him — I ask you if this is true. I do not wish to jeopardize my wife's health, and our plans for the summer will depend on your reply. . . ."

Dr. Lyman replied on May 30 that Eugene's case "has always been one that we could call 'closed tuberculosis,' where there is no sputum with bacilli and in consequence no danger of contagion. . . . I do not believe your son is absolutely cured or that any case is in less than three or four years' time. I do feel that his case is thoroughly under control, the lungs being, as far as I can see, clear; and that in his present condition he would not be a menace to any one."

While saying good-by to Miss Murray, O'Neill expressed the wish that he could in some way repay her many kindnesses. "The best thing you could do for me," she said, "would be to go back to your Faith." His face clouded but he remained silent, as she added, "I'll always pray for you." Katherine would have felt better could she have known his response to a poem she later sent him — Francis Thompson's *The Hound of Heaven*. He read it so often he could reel it off from memory, all one hundred and eighty-three lines.

Eugene had told Kitty he was going to kiss her good-by no matter who was around, even "Her Highness" — his usual way of referring to Mrs. Burgess. Kitty's face was aglow when she told Emma Wolodarsky that he not only kissed her but had said she would find herself some day in one of his plays.

Loaded down with books, he left Gaylord on June 3 and remained overnight in New Haven to celebrate, starting with drinks at the Hofbrau Haus. Clare O'Rourke, who had left the sanatorium at the same time, bound for a nursing post in New Haven, met him for lunch the following day and found him dissipated-looking but contrite. "I have to get to New London sober," he said, "or I'll shock the Old Man." Suddenly grinning, he told her of his parents' dismay at his appearance when he returned from Buenos Aires. His clothes were shabby, he needed a shave, he looked, he cheerfully recalled, "like a bum."

16

Prolific Novice

THIS summer was Eugene's happiest yet in New London; he and
Maibelle, resuming their romance, met almost daily for long walks
during which, despite his taciturnity around most people, he was never at
a loss for words. Their conversation was generally about things they were
reading — under his guidance she was digging into Strindberg, Nietzsche,
Wilde, Verlaine — but he was also starting to express himself like a
writer in whom ideas were incubating. "There's a story in every one of
those houses," he used to say, as they wandered around the outskirts
of the Pequot colony, and another thing he often told her was, "Everybody wears a mask," implying that he intended to portray people as
they truly were.

His relations with his father had taken a peaceful turn, fostered by a
new forbearance on Eugene's part; apparently what he had seen of
Kitty's father and the impression he had gained of his fellow patients'
lives had led him to a more favorable view of his own lot. Shortly after
his return home James — acting on Dr. Lyman's advice that the boy
should have plenty of sunshine and fresh air — bought him a used power
launch, an eighteen-foot Atlantic dory, for two hundred dollars (his
entire five and one-half months at Gaylord had cost only $167.35), and he
spent many hours on the river, stretched out naked in the bottom of the
boat. Passengers on the Block Island steamer used to complain about him,
for his dory sometimes drifted within view of the steamer, but he continued his sun-bathing on the river.

The first thing he wrote for the stage, after being home several months,
represented an attempt to make some money. He would later dismiss it as
"nothing . . . dashed off in one night," but he was sufficiently excited at
the time to tell his friends about it. Under the heading, Eugene O'Neill/
Writes Sketch/ For Vaudeville, the *Telegraph* on August 20, 1913,

reported that he had "received the copyright for the act from Washington. He expects to market it this fall. Mr. O'Neill has considerable literary talent, which was evidenced when he was a member of the *Telegraph* staff. He heretofore has confined himself to poetry and has written much worthy verse; this is his first venture into theater writing."

Inspired evidently by his stay in Honduras, *A Wife for a Life* tells of two gold prospectors in the Arizona desert — one middle-aged, long estranged from his wife, misogynistic; the other young, idealistic, in love with a woman who, though unhappily wed, has remained true to her marital vows. The dialogue is hopelessly stiff and sentimental; Jack, the young one, is describing his beloved to his friend: "In the corrupt environment of a mining camp she seemed like a lily growing in a field of rank weeds. I longed to take her away from all that atmosphere of sordid sin and suffering; away from her beast of a husband[Jack knows of him only from the wife] who was steadily ruining that beautiful young life and driving her to desperation. . . ." The denouement reveals, needless to say, that the one's wife is the other's great love. The older man, who had vowed to kill his rival, muses aloud: "So I have found him after all these years and I cannot even hate him. What tricks Fate plays with us. . . . Greater love hath no man than this, that he giveth his wife for his friend." Curtain. For all its feebleness, this very first work sounds what would be a predominant note in O'Neill's writings: "What tricks Fate plays with us."

In preparing himself to be a playwright Eugene not only devoured all sorts of plays — Hauptmann and Clyde Fitch, Wedekind and William Vaughn Moody — but observed the life around him with a sharpened interest. The previous summer his father had added to his holdings a small farm near the swampy bottom of Niles Hill Road, thereby acquiring a new tenant, John ("Dirty") Dolan, pig farmer and unregenerate individualist. O'Neill took both a writer's and a fellow Irishman's delight in Dirty Dolan, cunning, suspicious, fond of whiskey, and endowed, as *Long Day's Journey* puts it, with a "terrible tongue." He was a squarish tree-trunk of a man, bandy-legged, with arms like massive branches; ruddy-faced from the sun and all his drinking, he had soft blue eyes and a habitual grin that gave him a deceptive genial look. His farm might have been lifted intact from the Irish countryside: chickens, ducks and baby pigs wandering through the house, freshly laid eggs in corners of the rooms, an old piece of harness tossed aside. Often one would see Dolan half-asleep, in drunken contentment, on his hay mower as his spavined mare trudged up and down the field. Once, when he had to enter the hospital but refused to bathe, a friend proceeded to wash his dirt-encrusted feet as Dolan howled, "You're taking my toes off!" James O'Neill constantly grumbled about his new tenant and the difficulty of prying the rent out of him (twenty dollars monthly), but, like his sons, relished this prime specimen of Irish peasantry.

Adjoining the farm was the outer reaches of the domain of Edward Crowninshield Hammond. Slightly over six feet tall, broad-shouldered, pink-faced from privileged living, he looked like an American version of a British country squire — exactly the sort a good Irishman like Dolan would hate on sight. A running quarrel erupted between them this summer, with both threatening to go to law, when Hammond discovered a break in his fence that allowed the Dolan pigs to use a pond which in wintertime supplied the Hammond household with ice. O'Neill would exploit the feud in *Long Day's Journey* and *A Moon for the Misbegotten*, and, taking a partisan view, would picture the farmer as making a fool of the propertied gentleman. Still later, in one of the little ironies of time, the Hammond estate would become a community enterprise — the Eugene O'Neill Memorial Theater.

O'Neill took liberties in portraying the two men. Called Shaughnessy in *Long Day's Journey* and Hogan (presumably because he kept hogs) in *Moon for the Misbegotten*, Dolan was, for all his raffishness, a faithful Catholic; but O'Neill, giving vent to his own bias, depicted him in *Moon* as loudly and humorously anti-Catholic. In other respects, the farmer's personality as projected in both plays is quite faithful to the original. As for his opponent, called Harker in *Long Day's Journey* and T. Stedman Harder in the other play, he is essentially Hammond but given some of the background history of Edward S. Harkness, who had a magnificent estate next to Hammond's. Where the latter was worth a million or so, Harkness was worth around two hundred million; his father had been one of the partners of John D. Rockefeller, Sr., in establishing the Standard Oil empire. Though Harkness and Hammond looked somewhat alike, both being large tweedy men with glowing faces, their temperaments were different: the multimillionaire was quiet, shy, yet public-spirited; Hammond, who had a vigorous manner, was snobbish and short-tempered. But to Eugene O'Neill, a disciple of Tucker and Emma Goldman, the two men were as one. "Eugene," in Maibelle Scott's words, "resented anybody who had a lot of money."

In a comic high point of *Moon for the Misbegotten* Harder makes the mistake of confronting the farmer, thus giving the latter the opportunity to put on a display of outraged innocence; the scene ends with Harder fleeing from Hogan's torrent of abuse. The fictional counterparts of Dolan and Hammond never appear in *Long Day's Journey;* at the start of the play Edmund, repeatedly choking up with laughter, tells his parents about the showdown between the two men, an episode that provides a bright touch of background before the shadows start to thicken around the self-tormented Tyrones.

To foster the claustrophobic atmosphere of *Long Day's Journey* and lend weight to Mary Tyrone's complaint of feeling isolated from the life beyond their walls, O'Neill depicted the family as having a housekeeper-cook and a maid; in life, since Ella had difficulty finding adequate domestic help and was at a loss in running a household, the O'Neills generally went out for their meals. In the summer of 1913 they began patronizing the Rippins' boardinghouse on Pequot Avenue, the Packard, only a few blocks from the Monte Cristo cottage. Mr. and Mrs. James Rippin had come to the States from rural England, near Wales, in the 1880s and settled with their seven children in New London in the early 1900s. The father, a short, taciturn man with a walrus mustache, worked as a gardener, was interested in trotting horses, and disapproved of free-and-easy American ways; he believed in raising children with a firm English hand. Taller than her husband, pleasant-looking with a young face, Helen Maude Rippin was, without being domineering, the center of strength at 416 Pequot Avenue; quietly able, hard-working, she baked bread, cut her own steaks and roasts from beef she bought in large slabs, made some of her daughters' clothes, and handled family matters with calm good sense. Her tact sometimes took a playful turn. Once, when several of her daughters were edging toward a row, she had them put on Hallowe'en masks — this was after they were grown up — and told them to go ahead with the controversy; what had threatened to become heated broke up in laughter.

All the O'Neills took quickly to Mrs. Rippin. James used to visit the kitchen after a meal, bow, and compliment her on the food — he was particularly fond of her roast beef and Yorkshire pudding. His sole complaint about her, he used to joke, was that she was English. Sometimes, to her husband's annoyance, he would deliver a passage from Shakespeare with all the air of being on stage, whereupon she would rise to the occasion by ad-libbing a suitable response. Though Mr. Rippin, like his wife, was fond of literature, he also was possessive and found this byplay quite undignified, if not downright silly.

Two of the Rippin girls, Emily and Grace — the latter known to everyone as "Doll" — lived with their parents, while a third, Jessica, worked as a dietitian in the Philadelphia school system and often spent weekends at home. Emily, who helped her mother with the boarders, was short, well-curved, and outgoing; her cheery, slightly impish talk made the mother laugh against her will. Her parents used to refer to her, with a shade of disapproval, as their "American daughter." Doll, a receptionist for a dentist, and Jessica were more reserved but also had a sense of fun. All three girls would come to know Eugene well.

Seeking as much privacy as possible, the O'Neills ate at the far end of the dining room and always came late, generally after the other guests had finished. The conversation at their table was usually confined to low-voiced exchanges between the two boys, with Emily getting the impression they were often being humorous at their father's expense, but he seemed oblivious of their remarks. The boys used to eat quickly and leave before their parents were through. Mrs. O'Neill, who warmed to Emily's blithe personality, would give her a shy smile and a few friendly words, but on several occasions acted peculiarly.

"She acted," Emily says, "as though she didn't know me, just kept staring at her plate the whole time. One time she pushed away her plate so hard — I didn't see it — the food spilled over on the table, even on the floor. But Mr. O'Neill just went on calmly eating — he was a slow eater — as if nothing was wrong. The boys weren't with them any of these times. A week or so later she'd return looking pale and Mrs. Rogers [a Brennan cousin] was usually with her. Sometimes Mr. O'Neill came with just the boys and took back a basket of food for her. 'She isn't well,' he used to say."

Ella, who always regretted not having a daughter, used to borrow Emily to go riding with her and once in a while had the girl visit her at home. During the next several years Emily would hear a good deal about the O'Neills' private life, both past and current, as Ella was constantly looking back. The trouble the family had had from Eugene bulked large in her reminiscences. "She seemed to feel," Emily recalls "that he didn't have proper respect for women. According to her, Mr. O'Neill said he'd see Eugene in the gutter before he'd support him if he married one of the New London girls. They weren't worried about Eugene but for the girl's sake. Mrs. O'Neill also told me she'd gone through two fortunes [presumably the inheritances from both her mother and her brother, about whom practically nothing is known], and that was why Mr. O'Neill didn't give her an allowance. He felt that she didn't know how to handle money, that if she had any she'd give it to the boys and they would never work."

At summer's end Eugene was installed at the Rippins' for the winter, though ordinarily the family took in a few lodgers, besides accommodating boarders, only in the summertime. When James broached the matter shortly before leaving to tour in *Joseph and His Brethren*, Mr.

Rippin, after some reluctance, consented on condition that the boy would adjust himself to the household routine and impose no added burden on the family. James paid twelve dollars weekly for his room and board, and used to enclose another dollar for his personal use. Even had Eugene dared to jeopardize his return to full health by drinking, he lacked the funds.

At first his living at the Packard was a strain on both sides, partly because his hands trembled. Since the tremor, an on-an-off thing, was generally worse at the start of a day, Mrs. Rippin tactfully suggested that he might like to sleep late and breakfast alone — an arrangement that helped ease the situation. Mornings found him abstracted-looking, more than normally laconic. He used to take up a post by a window over-looking the river while listening to his favorite records on the Victrola, particularly "The Songs of Araby," which he would play over and over until Emily, with a running line of humorous complaint, bustled him into having breakfast. Immediately afterward he would retire to his room and settle down to writing.

From the start he tried, in their term, to "wise up" the Rippin girls; he lent them an unexpurgated *Decameron*, expatiated on the virtues of Socialism, and constantly ran down all phases of the established order. His proselytizing efforts fell on unreceptive ears. Emily was not interested in such matters, though she enjoyed parts of the *Decameron*, while Doll and Jessica had their own convictions. He went out of his way to shock them, often casting himself in an unfavorable light; he left Kathleen, according to one of his stories, after learning that she was pregnant. (When Olive Evans had asked whether he missed his son, he rejected the thought, referring to the child as "just an accident of nature." In *The Straw* Murray distresses Eileen by telling her that he doesn't care for children: "I don't get them. They're something I can't seem to get acquainted with.") As part of his educational campaign — and to give the impression of being a rakehell — he talked frankly of his love life, telling them about sleeping with a girl late one night in the passageway of a train and, in the high mark of his amorous career, having sex twenty-one times in a single week.

Jessica read some of his playwriting efforts and found them "morbid and sordid," but was particularly critical of his views on marriage. "He once told me he wanted to live on a barge, with his quarters at one end and his wife's at the other, because he didn't want her hovering around him all the time. I couldn't take his romance with Maibelle Scott seriously after that; and there were always poems to read and criticize, things he was writing her." Jessica felt that there was something vaguely literary about the affair, that if he were truly in love he wouldn't have had someone else read poems intended for his beloved.

Around Mrs. Rippin he was always on his best behavior, spending hours with her in the kitchen, generally when she was sewing and had her mind free for talk. In his regard for her there was something of the feeling with which he had once looked up to Sarah Sandy. "Now, Eugene, you mustn't get discouraged," Mrs. Rippin used to say, "you'll make out all right, just wait and see." She did not read any of his plays — he apparently never wanted her to — but knew from her daughters what they were like and once asked why he didn't write things that ended happily. "Because," he said, "they don't exist. Life doesn't give us happy endings."

Shortly before moving in with the family he wrote his second play, a one-acter entitled *The Cough*, later renamed *The Web*, which concerns a tubercular streetwalker, a pimp, and a kindhearted burglar. While the plotting is simple and the dialogue crude, the work is not without points of interest; its battered heroine, the first of many prostitutes he would write about, foreshadows *Anna Christie*. "Yuh don't know the game I'm up against," she tells the burglar. "I've tried that job thing. I've looked fur decent work and I've starved at it . . . there was always someone who'd drag me back. . . . They — all the good people — they got me where I am and they're goin' to keep me there. . . ."

Though *The Web* is blatantly melodramatic — the pimp shoots the burglar and frames things to make it seem that the girl had killed him — the young author was already straining to touch a point higher than melodrama: "(Rose seems in a trance. . . . She seems to be aware of something in the room which none of the others can see — perhaps the personification of the ironic life force that has crushed her. . . . Suddenly she stretches both arms above her head and cries bitterly, mournfully, out of the depths of her desolation) 'Gawd! Gawd! Why d'yuh hate me so?' "

Eugene's life at the Rippins' fell into a productive routine: he would write all morning, take a long swim, write in the afternoon before meeting Maibelle, and he often worked till late at night. In addition to his playwriting he was, in an attempt to make some money, dashing off scenarios for the movies; he told the girls that he would not give his best to the screen. Undiscouraged that the scripts constantly returned, he would tear them up and whip off others. Chronically broke, he borrowed from the girls for stamps and cigarettes, promising to repay them after he had become successful. "There was no doubt in his mind," Doll says, "that he'd be famous some day, more famous than his father." One morning, before leaving for work, she found the following note from him, together with a manuscript: "You will bring me good luck '*por cierto*' if you mail this for me. Please put a stamp on the envelope inside the outer envelope in case of rejection. Then seal and mail. Caesar and his fortunes are inside, so be careful! Thanking you again and a-gain, pledging my oath that you are as good as you are adorable, and assuring you I am the fond slave of your every whim."

It seems significant that he always wrote for the screen on a typewriter but for the theater by hand. Behind the dual practice were most likely his different attitudes toward the two mediums: for the movies he was writing off the top of his head, concocting stories simply for money, whereas he was trying to get something of himself into his plays. His handwriting was distinctive — even, flowing, and minuscule. With time it would so dwindle in size that persons transcribing his manuscripts would have to use a magnifying glass. O'Neill gave more than one explanation for his script. He sometimes said that he found it easier to cope with his hand tremor by writing small; other times, that he fell into the practice when a sailor and found paper scarce on the ships (but he was not writing plays at the time or, so far as is known, anything else of length). He also once told a friend that he began his day with a dozen pencils sharpened as fine as possible because this helped him to pierce through to his unconscious and, further, that he wrote small so that he would not be tempted to keep rereading what he had written, thus slowing himself down.

Presumably the tremor did have some effect on his script, for as the one grew worse with the years the other tended to diminish; but none of his explanations is entirely satisfactory, since his handwriting was small from the start of his literary career. Perhaps the answer is to be found in the diagram in which he outlined his feelings toward his parents and Sarah Sandy; the writing in the diagram, more like rippling lines than words, is almost indecipherable even under a magnifier. He apparently wanted to assure that no one could read the document should it happen to fall into another's hands. Similarly, in writing his plays he essentially was communing with himself; part of him shrank from divulging himself to the public.

While the Rippin girls were privately skeptical about his literary prospects, Eugene found encouragement in a new member of the family; James Rippin, Jr., one of the three sons, had married a girl named Jane Deeter, a social worker in Philadelphia, and brought her home on a visit during their honeymoon. A person of culture and superior ability — in a few years she was to become national director of the Girl Scouts — the bride came from a theater-minded family (her brother, Jasper Deeter, would be among the leading actors of the Provincetown Players, the first group to stage O'Neill's work). One evening she persuaded Eugene to read some of his plays.

"It went on for hours, till about four in the morning," Jim Rippin once said. "Jane was terribly impressed and told him, 'They're wonderful, something ought to be done about them.' Ordinarily he mumbled, you could hardly understand him [Jessica thought that he always spoke "as though he had a cigarette in his mouth"], but that night he talked clearly — he wanted you to hear every word. He added comments to help us visualize the action; if a man went to a barn to hang himself, he [Eugene] made the motions of putting the noose around his neck. It was more than a reading, he acted everything out.

"His hands trembled terribly, especially that night, and he was nervous and restless, always moving around. He'd sit on the table or squirm around on the sofa or sit on the arm of a chair, then move on and sit somewhere else." The bridegroom soon became annoyed at the young writer. "After that night I could hardly have Jane to myself — he was always hanging around her."

Though Eugene had his own room at the Rippins', he followed the open-air practice at Gaylord and slept most nights on the back porch, facing the river; with the waves lapping nearby, he could imagine himself aboard ship, especially when the fog closed down to a chorus of foghorn and ships' whistles. As the weather turned cold, small rugs were hung to cut the sharpness of the wind and he encased himself in heavy clothing — woolen pajamas, stocking cap, the "American Lines" sweater. Sometimes he had a sleeping companion, the family's black-and-white cat Friday; in a letter to the Rippins he later recalled "that winter with you when Friday used to climb my porch on zero nights and crawl into bed with me, leaving the rat he had killed thoughtfully on the floor for me to step on in case Nature called me to get up."

It was a rugged regimen he followed, for he also, in the belief that it helped his recovery, went swimming once or twice a week throughout the winter. A doctor who called at the house one day to treat Emily for tonsillitis was startled to see a young man in a bathing suit rush down the hallway and disappear out the back door. From a rear window the doctor saw Eugene, barefooted, race up and down the snow-covered beach, plunge into the water, and a few minutes later come dashing back. But he thrived on it all; after years of disordered existence he reveled in the Rippins' quiet domesticity. "I've never worked harder or with pleasanter surroundings," he wrote Jessica in 1919, "than I did those *cold* months in the Packard. Your family gave me the most real touch of home life I had had up to then — quite a happy new experience for an actor's son! I've never forgotten to be grateful to all of you for it — above all, to your mother."

The rest of the family, particularly her husband, felt that Mrs. Rippin spoiled Eugene, but she maintained that she simply felt sorry for him. While this may have been partially true, she was genuinely fond of the boy and could not help responding to the great interest he took in her and all her activities. As Christmas approached she secretly worked on kimonos as gifts for Emily and Doll whenever they were out of the house, and Eugene, keeping lookout, would warn her when one of them was approaching.

Christmas morning the Rippins gave him a matching set of necktie, socks and handkerchief, and invited him to take part in their festivities, for which the entire clan was gathering. He thanked them but politely declined and left for home, the empty Monte Cristo cottage. That afternoon persons taking walks on Pequot Avenue to work up an appetite for their holiday dinners were amazed, the *Telegraph* reported the following day, "to see a young man swimming with apparent delight in the icy waters . . . near the local plant of the T. C. Scott Co." It was Eugene; he probably both felt sorry for himself and took a fierce Nietzschean pleasure in imagining himself a heroic figure above the well-fed herd.

On his return that night he presented Mrs. Rippin and each of the three girls with a large box of chocolate candy and told them that he had sold one of his film scenarios for fifty dollars; this was the first that they had heard about it. Outside of his own words, everything suggests that he made up the story to prevent the Rippins from feeling sorry for him; in all likelihood, unless he wired his father for money to buy the gifts, he borrowed it from Judge Latimer or some other friend.

From time to time he had visits from his father and brother, separately. Whatever pleasure he may have derived from seeing his father was diminished by the latter's admiring talk of Brandon Tynan, his fellow star in *Joseph and His Brethren*; jealous of the friendship that had developed between them, Eugene suspected, not without cause, that Tynan was the kind of son his father would like to have had. Dublin-born and now in his early thirties, Tynan was a devout Catholic, a supporter of Irish causes, an advocate of clean living and clean theater (he once rejected the role of the amoral groom in Strindberg's *Miss Julie*), an ambitious hard-working chap who respected his elders — practically everything, in short, that the O'Neill boys were not.

James O'Neill's feeling for his costar (he could see his early self in the dedicated young actor) was reciprocated. "I loved him," Brandon Tynan once said, "everybody in the company did. He was the same with everybody, from stagehands and bit players to Pauline Frederick and the other leads. He told me about the time he was in *The Passion Play* and gave up drinking, cigars, everything, out of respect for his role. Well, I was the same way — I didn't take a drink or smoke the entire time I was in *Joseph*. I was proud to be in that show, and enjoyed getting to know 'the Governor.' We used to go to Mass together every Sunday, even on the road.

"I couldn't understand why Jim wasn't more like him. He once told me, when he was liquored up, 'I had a fifty-thousand-dollar education and all I'm worth is twenty-five dollars a week.' He used to help his father dress — that was part of his job — but I never saw them together outside the theater."

While *Joseph and His Brethren* was playing in Hartford, Eugene with Art and Tom McGinley motored there to see it. In the grill of the Hotel Hueblein they found Mr. O'Neill and Jamie having their pre-theater meal — the father at one end of the room, his namesake at the other. James had long been inured to his son's personal behavior but was losing all patience with his professional transgressions. As the tour lengthened and Jamie became increasingly bored, his conduct on stage became correspondingly lax. At a performance in Madison, Wisconsin, the balcony was crowded with University of Wisconsin students feeling jubilant over a football victory that day; in one scene, when Mr. O'Neill as the patriarch Jacob had his wife Rachel by the arm, a student yelled, "Ten yards for holding!" Jamie laughed louder than any of the college boys.

Gareth Hughes, who played brother Benjamin in the biblical spectacle, recalled another incident: "One of the saddest things I ever saw happened during the Chicago engagement. Jim went on a bender — it wasn't the first time — and for a few nights I had to double in his part. He finally returned one evening, still in bad shape, and botched the job of putting on his make-up but somehow got out on stage before anyone stopped him. We were all worried about what would happen when 'the Governor' saw him. Well, when he was carried on in his high litter, he caught sight of Jim in the crowd — bleary-eyed, grotesquely made up, unsteady on his feet — yet he managed to give his beautiful closing speech (I can hear him now, his voice was so melodious). The crowd of supers lifted the palm fronds as they chorused, 'He raiseth the poor from the dust — from the depth he raiseth the lowly, O Lord of Hosts — Blessed is the man who trusteth in Thee.' Then the curtain fell.

" 'The Governor' was helped down from the litter and he advanced toward Jim, his fine old face full of sorrow and anger as he cried, 'You goddam louse!' "

Years of dissipation had taken their toll of Jamie's looks; his "habitual

Left to right, Gareth Hughes, Charles Ashleigh, James O'Neill, Jr., and Malcolm Morley on the town one night in Chicago. Excepting Ashleigh, who had met Eugene O'Neill in Buenos Aires in 1910, the others were in Joseph and His Brethren.

expression of cynicism," in Eugene's words, gave "his countenance a Mephistophelian cast." Though the brothers were rarely demonstrative toward one another — both tended in their relations to adopt a bantering manner — they somehow gave an impression of deep feeling between them. During one of Jamie's visits to Eugene, the two were asked whether Ella had ever been on the stage. "That's what I thought," said Mrs. Rippin, on getting a negative reply. "I was sure your mother had always been a lady." Whereupon Jamie came back with, "Wait till I tell Pauline Frederick what you said!"

Jamie had spread the story around New London that he was in love with "Polly" Frederick, among the most beautiful women on the stage, and that she returned his feeling. Unfortunately, according to him, she refused to marry him unless he gave up drinking — a stipulation he found impossible to meet. The story would develop into one of the few romantic legends attached to the name of James O'Neill, Jr.; yet it seems to have been without any basis other than that he apparently nursed a secret affection for the actress. Several persons associated with *Joseph and His Brethren* — not only Brandon Tynan and Gareth Hughes but Malcolm Morley, another actor, and John Cronin of the backstage crew — later scoffed at the thought that she had ever been in love with Jamie. Tynan: "I never heard a word about it, and you know what a hotbed of gossip the theater is. If there had been anything between them, I'm sure I would have known." Hughes: "No, the Pauline Frederick story is just that — a story." Morley: "I heard nothing about his attachment to Pauline. I am certain there was nothing there." And Cronin: "Polly was very democratic, well liked by the company. She had just left a wealthy husband to return to the stage. I never heard of anything between her and Jimmy, and doubt there's anything to it."

Yet Eugene himself believed the story, for he not only helped to circulate it at the time but in later years. Also, he apparently had it in mind when he wrote in *Ah, Wilderness!* of the bittersweet romance between Lily, an old maid, and the bachelor uncle, likable, feckless, who repeatedly drinks himself out of a job; for years Lily has refused to marry him unless he reforms. Uncle Sid, viewed through a haze of nostalgia and drawn with humor, bears a marked resemblance to self-destructive Jamie O'Neill.

At the end of January the Rippins welcomed an old friend, Clayton Hamilton, playwright, critic, lecturer, whom they had first met when he visited New London on a writing assignment for Richard Mansfield. A large teddy bear of a man, prematurely white-haired, "Ham," as the family called him, laughed easily, was given to practical jokes and comic hyperbole, but under his clowning took the theater seriously. With him on the midwinter visit was his recent bride, quiet, dignified, the opposite of her ebullient husband.

Reacting to Hamilton with mixed feelings, Eugene was at once eager to talk with him about playwriting, afraid of being patronized, and jealous of his warm relations with the family, particularly with Mrs. Rippin. Eugene kept his distance. On his side Hamilton, who was friendly with James O'Neill, was curious about this laconic, somberly handsome young man, so unlike his genial actor father. "I looked the lad over," he has written. "He had large and dreamy eyes, a slender, somewhat frail and yet athletic body ["Ham" was impressed by his midwinter swims], a habit of silence, and an evident disease of shyness." Echoing her husband, Mrs. Hamilton once said of their first meeting at the breakfast table that O'Neill "seemed an unobtrusive young man who did not wish his silences interrupted."

During the couple's stay of nearly a month Eugene finally unbent sufficiently to divulge that he was working on plays and to ask Hamilton's advice. The latter, having heard that he had been a sailor, sensibly pointed out that there already were poets and novelists of the sea — Conrad, Kipling, Masefield, Jack London — but no such playwrights. Here, so far as the theater was concerned, was virgin territory, a fertile opportunity for one of Eugene's experience. The advice was, however, unnecessary. Though Hamilton would afterward believe that he had given him the idea of writing about the sea, Eugene had already completed *Thirst* and possibly *Fog* or *Warnings* before the Hamiltons' visit.

The first thing that strikes one about these playlets is that all three are concerned with shipwrecks, which immediately raises the thought that the author exploited the subject because disaster at sea is so dramatic. But from a psychological view, the most obvious aspect is that ships may be taken as a mother symbol. Both *Fog* and *Thirst* deal with survivors after a liner has foundered, while *Warnings* ends with a sinking. The latter work, which concerns a ship's wireless operator on the verge of deafness, is chiefly noteworthy for its honest account of the protagonist's grubby home life.

Set adrift in *Fog* are a businessman, a peasant woman with a child, and a poet. The latter has "big dark eyes and a black mustache and black hair pushed back from his high forehead." Reminding one of the author's suicide attempt at Jimmy the Priest's, the poet says to the businessman, "Did you ever become so sick of disappointment and weary of life in general that death appeared to you the only way out?" He had wanted to go down with the ship but in saving the mother and child had been forced to save himself. Largely a running debate between the two men, *Fog* has the poet, an obvious mouthpiece for O'Neill, speaking in behalf of suffering humanity, while the businessman, smug, materialistic, selfish, represents the average run of men. The play, though more or less naturalistic, ends on a note of the supernatural: a vessel that has been searching for survivors of the shipwreck locates the lifeboat through the "weird" crying of a child — the peasant woman's son, who has been dead for hours before the rescue party arrives on the scene. Exactly what O'Neill meant by this mystical touch is uncertain, but he seems to suggest some kind of affinity between the dead child and the poet.

In *Thirst* three survivors — a dancer, a gentleman, and a mulatto seaman who for the most part remains ominously silent — face death from thirst and exposure to the elements; the action takes place on a raft with sharks lurking nearby. Overhead the sun glares like a "great angry eye of God." Though overly melodramatic, too contrived in its touches of ironic pathos, the play has flashes of genuine feeling, of effective writing, and occasionally expresses the essential O'Neill. Gentleman: "I would like to have seen [the captain's] soul." Dancer: "You would have found it no better and no worse than the souls of other men. If he was guilty [of the shipwreck through negligence] he has paid with his life." Gentleman: "No. He has avoided payment by taking his life. The dead do not pay."

O'Neill would later amplify on this thought in *Mourning Becomes Electra*, his retelling of the old Greek legend of the House of Atreus, with Agamemnon, Electra, and the others depicted as Americans of the Civil War period. At the end Lavinia (Electra) pronounces judgment on herself: "I'm not going the way Mother and Orin went [through suicide]. That's escaping punishment. And there's no one left to punish me. I'm the last Mannon. I've got to punish myself! Living alone here with the dead is a worse act of justice than death or prison!"

As *Thirst* and *Electra* suggest, O'Neill, despite his apostasy, would forever be haunted by the Catholic doctrine of doing penance for one's sins; though the two plays were written more than fifteen years apart, the viewpoint is the same. Indeed a number of such parallels can be found in his work; his early writings, for all their shortcomings and crudities, adumbrate views that were to find fuller, more urgent expression in his mature dramas. O'Neill was nearly twenty-five when he turned playwright; his insight would deepen with time, he would become more assured and skilled in his art, but there would be little if any essential change in the man himself, in his basic outlook on life.

James O'Neill, who had grown up in the theater of Forrest, Cushman and Booth, was almost as bewildered by his son the playwright as by his son the water-front drifter. "He did believe in me, in a way," Eugene once said, "but . . . he thought I was crazy. He didn't see why I should write the kind of plays I did, and he pointed out, quite properly, that there was no market for them; but he must have thought there was something there — something he did not like or maybe quite understand. He believed I might some day amount to something — if I lived."

While unable to appreciate his son's writings, Mr. O'Neill felt relieved that at last he was trying to make something of himself and consented to finance the publication of a volume of his plays. On March 31, 1914, he wrote a check for three hundred dollars as the initial payment to Richard G. Badger, head of the Gorham Press of Boston, with an additional hundred and fifty to be paid on receipt of the proofs; Badger had recently issued the work of such established playwrights as Augustus Thomas and Rachel Crothers, but at the same time, as a pioneer of the "vanity press," was not averse to dealing with unknown authors who could pay their own way into print. The contract with Eugene G. O'Neill, providing that he was to receive twenty-five percent of the gross receipts, stated that the book would be "handsomely printed on heavy wove paper and bound in antique boards; also that the first edition will consist of one thousand copies."

In addition to the three sea plays and *The Web*, the story of the prostitute and the burglar, the volume was to include a fifth work, *Recklessness*, a conventional thriller about a young wife, her lover, and her conscienceless older husband. Written in a period of six to seven months, the plays testify less to the author's potential talent than to his productivity and his preoccupation with violent death; they contain a total of ten deaths from shooting, stabbing, drowning, automobile accidents, and exposure on the high seas, not to mention the deaths of the untold hundreds who perish in the various shipwrecks. Lurid, sentimental, contrived, the early works are all this, yet they are noteworthy on at least one count: by dealing with such unheard-of things in the American theater as cannibalism (*Thirst*), as radical-minded poets (*Fog*), as prostitutes ground down by poverty (*The Web*), they demonstrated that the playwright was determined to go his own way, heedless of Broadway standards. All five plays, despite their melodramatic nature, contain at least a thought, a line, some approach to the subject matter indicating that the author had gone to school under such men as Shaw, Ibsen and Brieux, that he enters the theater as a rebel. A few years later he was to describe the plays in the *Thirst* volume as the "first five Stations of the Cross in my plod up Parnassus."

[273]

His stay with the Rippins ended suddenly. On May 5, a few days after his return home, he wrote Jessica in Philadelphia that he had been busy "launching boats, manicuring the front lawn of the ancestral acres, pruning the first act of my four-act drama, walking to meals and back again, eating, sleeping, answering Father's voluminous correspondence (he takes a mean advantage of my knowing how to typewrite). . . . I had no idea I would have to leave 416 in such haste, but Father was lonely and had to solace himself with the comforting presence of his younger mistake, so I collected my Lares and Penates and blew. . . ."

The letter, his earliest extant one of length excepting two he wrote his parents from Honduras, rambles on for pages, affording revealing glimpses of Eugene Gladstone O'Neill in 1914: "I find my present solitude, though pleasant in the main, rather irksome at whiles, especially on days like this, when the rain monotonously and fretfully patters on the roof. God weeps and men curse, and all of life becomes a tragic folly and an idiotic pose. . . . Father is in New York and I am sitting here writing to you and freezing to death because I am too lazy and inert to light the furnace. . . . So you see my mood and the weather's mood chime perfectly. If I had not reserved the inestimable pleasure of unburdening myself to you on just such a day, life would be truly unbearable. . . . I would commit suicide if I could find a tree strong enough to hang myself on without getting wet to the skin. . . .

". . . there is *only one thing* to do on a day of Spring rain and that is — but why burden you with details? Suffice it to say that I cannot do it, being alone. . . . I ain't got no pashinut friends upon whose buzum I c'd lay my weary bean. . . . Do you wonder I am sad? I see youth flit by while I toil not neither do I spin in the vineyard of Love. . . .

"Meanwhile the low-browed ape which is the flesh of me clamors for requital, as once ten thousand years ago it ran gibbering through the prehistoric gloom and sprang from tree to tree in pursuit of its female. The mud inside of me churns and bubbles. I seethe with longings; desire has me by the throat, and I — I go for long rows or mow the lawn. . . . Alas it was not always thus. Rise up, ye ghosts of the past, and speak for me! O loves of old, cry aloud the tale of your delicious infamies! My soul is whitened with the scars of many old leprosies. And now — now, forsooth, I am Sir Galahad, the Virgin Knight, sans reproach, the devil fly away with me! To refuse sin to the unrepentant sinner — that is too cruel. Lord, hear my prayer! I would sin!

"What is sin? Tell me, sweet Jessica. I think it is the bad digestion of a man of sixty, a dream of sour grapes conceived in the brain of an old maid with a hare-lip. Sin and its punishment, virtue and its reward; piffle upon piffle until everything in the world is turned upside down and all that is delightful is dubbed 'Bad' and all that is disagreeable and ugly 'Good.' The immortal Gods deliver me from Good and Evil! . . . To be true to one's self and one's highest hopes — *that is Good!* . . .

"And, after all, what's the difference? 'We are such stuff as dreams are made on and our little life is rounded with a sleep.' I and my ideal, you and your ideal, all of us poor human midges with our fretful whining cry, our feeble droning wail of impotence — dreams and thin dust of illusions which will vanish when the dreamer vanishes. . . . And above and around us the ever-mocking laughter of those immortal and immoral Gods.

"Volplaning down from such lofty ether of Nietzsche-Schopenhauer philosophical discussion which ends nowhere and is as aimless as life is, and returning once more to New London, the acme of all that is prosaic, I would say that I have a bone to pick with you."

After complaining that she had referred to him in a recent letter as "very, very young," he added, "As if life were a question of years! Surely it is not a question of how long but of how much one has lived. . . . Experience is the only true test of one's age. How much of life have you made a part of yourself? Have you reached out for everything, tried for everything, hesitated before 'No, you must not,' realized *with joy* every new sensation, stripped things of their husk, and picked out your own Bad and Good with a clear eye and a robust, not a sickly conscience? If you have, then you have lived much more than ninety-nine hundredths of the grey beards, whatever your age may be, and your opinion of life in general is worth infinitely more than theirs! . . . I have lived much more than any three men in the town and you ought to know it. My ideas are hardly based on inexperience or a cloistered existence. . . .

"Keep on plodding? Sure I will. I don't care very much for your choice of a word to express the strivings of an impecunious young author to project the phantasmagoria of his own brain on paper, but this may be prejudice on my part. I always connect the word with Gray's 'The plowman homeward plods his weary way.' I'll keep on with my rainbow chasing, and who knows, I may in time find the fabled pot of gold. At any rate there is a joy in the battle itself well worth the attempt. . . .'"

The four-act drama mentioned in the letter was "Bread and Butter," both O'Neill's first long play and the start of what would be a sizable gallery of self-portraits (the poet in *Fog* was only a sketch). A Princeton graduate with "abnormally large dreamer's eyes" and an urge toward self-expression, John Brown, who lives in a small New England city, hopes to become not a writer but a painter. His father, a self-made businessman from farming stock, hopes that he will study for the law — a circumstance that recalls James O'Neill's original dream for his first-born.

Complicating young Brown's situation, he is in love with Maude Steele, the daughter of a prosperous shopkeeper, "a remarkably pretty girl of twenty with great blue eyes, golden brown hair and small delicate features." But after this favorable description, reminiscent of Maibelle Scott, the author added, "Her rather kittenish manner and the continual pout of her small red mouth indicate the spoiled child even before one hears the note of petulance in her soft, all-too-sweet voice." (Eugene's romance with Maibelle was ending during the period he wrote the play.)

In the belief that his son will eventually abandon serious art and settle for a profitable career as a commercial illustrator, Mr. Brown agrees to finance him to a year of art studies in New York. For his scenes of life among the artists, O'Neill drew on the period when he hung around with Ed Keefe and George Bellows at the Lincoln Arcade Building; indeed one of the characters, a blond good-natured giant from the West, is patently modeled on Bellows. Another phase of O'Neill's history, his friendship with Jimmy Byth, is suggested by a would-be playwright among the group of bohemians. "I'm always going to start that play — tomorrow," he says. "They ought to write on my tombstone: The deceased at last met one thing he couldn't put off till tomorrow."

After young Brown's father cuts off his allowance and he finds it impossible to pursue art while earning a living, he yields to a "great sickness and lassitude of soul, a desire to drink, to do anything to get out of [himself] and forget." A friend cautions him, "You're only ruining your health and accumulating a frame of mind where you think the world hates you."

Finally, unable to resist his love for Maude and her pleadings, he marries her and enters her father's business with the thought of painting during his leisure. Husband and wife, like characters out of Strindberg, grow to hate each other. After several years of marriage Maude is "still pretty but has faded, grown prim and hardened . . . and wears the air of one who has been cheated in the game of life and knows it; but will even up the scale by making those around her as wretched as possible." Though John's oldest brother has always loved Maude and wants her to get a divorce and marry him, she refuses to set her husband free. The play ends with his suicide. "John Brown's body," to quote from the song that evidently gave O'Neill the name of his protagonist, "lies a-moulderin' in the grave."

This earliest of his full-length works foreshadows other of his writings, particularly *Before Breakfast*, in which a scold drives her writer husband to suicide, *Beyond the Horizon,* in which a young romanticist, eager to travel and see the world, marries a commonplace girl and drags out a wretched existence, and *The Great God Brown,* in which an artist, a mystical figure, takes up architecture to support his family while proceeding to drink himself into an early grave. At one point the hero of *Great God Brown,* referring to his rival, sings derisively: "William Brown's soul lies mouldering in the crib but his body goes marching on!"

The most interesting thing about "Bread and Butter," however, is not that it prefigures several of O'Neill's other works but that it offers a prospectus of a large portion of his writings. Images and themes that would recur over and over are already dramatized here: the artist (poet, painter, writer, or simply dreamer and seeker of beauty) crucified by life; the artist at war not only with forces without but within; a vigorous progenitor who has children of softer natures — softer in both favorable and unfavorable senses — a story element that adumbrates the large issue of a changing America, from hardy self-reliance to overcivilized values; conflict between father and son; a scoffing brother who takes little seriously; rivalry and hostility between brothers; a devoted, understanding wife, as embodied in the hero's younger sister; men of business shown in a poor light; persons fond of drinking depicted sympathetically; liquor viewed as both a means of escape and, as James O'Neill used to say, a "good man's weakness"; the love-hate relations of the sexes; the "tomorrow" or "pipe-dream" motif. When one examines "Bread and Butter" together with O'Neill's first one-acters, one finds many, if not most of the strands that would weave in and out of the entire body of his writings; with an artist's instinct, he at the outset chose material and issues close to his heart, central to his concern.

Another thing worth noting about "Bread and Butter" is that whereas most contemporary plays were in three acts, this one ran to four. Since O'Neill first gained a reputation with his one-acters and early in his career wrote such intermediate-size plays as *The Emperor Jones* and *Diff'rent,* it is generally thought that his subsequent extra-long works represented a radical development and change in his writing; yet, as the four-act "Bread and Butter," suggests, he set his own course from the start, and from the start was impatient with the restrictions of standard dramaturgy. There was in fact, for all his instinctive sense of theater, a novelistic strain in his playwriting; he had a novelist's awareness of the rich confusion of life and was to make repeated attempts to approach the depth and complexity of the novelist's art. If he wrote briefly in his one-acters and unconventionally short in *Emperor Jones,* it was because his subject matter demanded it, but the novelist in the playwright, the man who was to write *Strange Interlude* and *The Iceman Cometh*, was always there. When he told Jessica that he was "pruning" his long play, his choice of verb was apt. Not only in his multiact mammoths but in nearly all his full-length works he wrote expansively, throwing in everything, getting it all off his chest, then proceeded to trim, cut and tighten.

Plays had poured out of him from the time he had gone to live with the Rippins; he had written four of the short pieces that would be in his *Thirst* volume, he had written his first full-length work, and ideas for plays continued to press him onward. "That's the year I thought I was God," he once said. "I'd finish them and rush down to the post office to ship them off to Washington to be copyrighted before somebody stole them."

After completing "Bread and Butter" he proceeded in the next several months to write three one-act plays that were utterly different from one another. *The Movie Man*, the least interesting, deals with two Americans in the midst of civil warfare in Mexico who are making a film based on the hostilities. O'Neill apparently got his idea from the newspapers; for several years they had been carrying page one dispatches almost daily about revolution and counterrevolution south of the border. As talk mounted in the press that Washington might send troops to protect American investments in that country — talk that was followed by the landing of Marines at Veracruz — Eugene was fired to write a poem protesting the move. Turgid, shrill, taking pot-shots at militarism, chauvinism, the government, organized religion, and "the plutocrats who cause the woe," the poem, a lengthy one entitled "Fratricide," was published May 17, 1914, in the New York *Call*, a Socialist newspaper.

Abortion, another play he wrote this spring, is the one that draws on his year at Princeton and presumably his romance with Kathleen. Some of the dialogue is almost word for word with lines in his letter to Jessica: "We've retained a large portion of the original mud in our make-up. . . . It was the male beast who ran gibbering through the forest after its female thousands of years ago."

The first thing to be said about his third work, "Children of the Sea," is that it is in a way incredible; it is so markedly superior to *Abortion* and *The Movie Man* that it is difficult to believe that all three were written around the same time. O'Neill himself once said of the sea play: "Very important from my point of view. In it can be seen, or felt, the germ of the spirit, life-attitude, etc., of all my more important future work." "Children of the Sea," with but slight revisions and a new title, *Bound East for Cardiff*, would gain recognition as the first of his memorable S.S.

Glencairn cycle. Into it the author distilled some of his feelings about the hard lonely life of men who follow the sea. Its story is of the plainest: Yank, injured in a shipboard accident, lies dying in his bunk as the *Glencairn* wallows eastward on a fog-shrouded night. Between groans of pain he talks of the sailor's common lot, of the hereafter, while his shipmates, clumsy, inarticulate, try to comfort him. Death appears to Yank in the guise of "a pretty lady dressed in black." As his good friend Driscoll prays over him, the first time he has prayed in years, another shipmate says in an awed whisper, "Gawd blimey!" Curtain.

Told in crude, flavorsome sailor talk, the play was more truly poetic than any of O'Neill's poetry; more to the point, it reflected the spirit of brooding compassion, of tragic inevitability, that would distinguish his mature writings. Not only a great advance over any of his previous works, it was among the finest one-act plays yet written in America. Such an accomplishment so early in his career is impossible to explain (we can only murmur something about "the mysteries of creativity"), for O'Neill was still fumbling his way. It would be several more years before he wrote anything else so good as "Children of the Sea."

17

End of a Long Nightmare

WHEN Ella O'Neill told her husband she wanted to make a final attempt to overcome her "curse," he was against it; there had been too many times she had returned from a sanatorium resolved to keep a grip on herself, inspiring hope in the family that perhaps this time she was permanently cured, only to backslide and plunge them all, herself particularly, into new depths of despair. But Ella, who had something new in mind, was determined. In *Long Day's Journey* the mother says that years ago she discovered that her soul was no longer her own; but, she adds, she had never lost hope that some day the Virgin Mary would forgive her and help her to redeem herself. "I will hear myself scream with agony, and at the same time I will laugh because I will be so sure of myself."

The playwright was projecting future events when he had the mother rest her hopes on her religion. For her final struggle Ella went not to a sanatorium but to a convent as one facing a spiritual crisis; she apparently felt that undergoing a cure in its hallowed confines would be in the nature of a commitment to her faith, of a pact with God, that it would give her the strength thereafter to resist the terrible craving. It seems most likely that Ella's redemption was assured once she decided to enter a convent, that she already knew, unconsciously, that at last she was able to free herself; for so it came to pass. Her stay in the convent marked the end, after more than a quarter-century, of her suffering the torment of the damned.

From the little that Eugene told Agnes Boulton a few years later, she gathered the impression that his mother's cure took place in 1914 or 1915. It probably occurred in spring of 1914, judging by a flurry of items in the New London newspapers at the time. On March 26 the *Telegraph* reported that James O'Neill was taking a two-week vacation from *Joseph and His Brethren* because his wife, in New York, was "ill." For the next two months there were constant mentions in the local press touching on the state of her health and reporting day-to-day changes in James's plans: he has withdrawn from *Joseph* for the rest of the season because of her "serious sickness"; he will not, he will, he will not appear in the Lambs Club's annual Gambol; his wife "has been very sick, but is much improved"; he has opened the Monte Cristo cottage; he has left with his sons for Brooklyn, where his wife is "seriously ill." Finally, on May 28, the *Telegraph* reported that the O'Neill men had returned home, that Mrs. O'Neill "is greatly improved and will come here next week to spend the summer."

The previous fall James had taken an apartment in New York at the Prince George Hotel on East 28th Street, near Fifth Avenue, and this became, after the cottage on Pequot Avenue, the family's second base of operations. None of the news items said anything about Ella being at the hotel or in a hospital; the only clue to her whereabouts is the mention of the father and sons going to Brooklyn to be with her. Presumably the convent where she underwent her final struggle and achieved her great victory was located in Brooklyn.

Ella remained after her cure as retiring as ever. The only change in her routine was that she began attending church regularly, but that one change meant to her the difference, literally, between heaven and hell. For her husband and elder son, her recovery from the long nightmare was a source of unalloyed happiness; for her other son, despite the relief he felt for her sake, her deliverance was the ultimate twisting of the knife. If she could free herself after all these years, after the habit had its claws into her so deeply, why couldn't she have succeeded at the start, before she had bequeathed him a legacy of lifelong guilt feelings? Eugene O'Neill's sense of tragedy and tragic irony came not from immersing himself in the works of Nietzsche and the ancient Greeks, in the writings of Strindberg, but from his own life.

Part of his appeal for Maibelle Scott, she once indicated, lay in his "streak of sadness"; though she was his junior by a half-dozen years, it aroused her maternal feelings. By the spring of 1914, however, their romance had worn thin. "There was no unpleasantness or arguments," she once said, "and it wasn't because I was interested in someone else. We simply, well, drifted apart."

Perhaps the romance foundered because Maibelle refused to sleep with him, because both realized that their relationship had become static after developing as far as it would go. In one of his poems to her, sounding a familiar theme of his verse, he had said: "And yet 'tis better far to live one day/ Wholly; to realize one glorious sin/ And then to die, than to drag out our lives/ Through years of commonsense to dull decay. . . ."

While this might be dismissed as poetic attitudinizing, he had expressed similar sentiments in his long letter to Jessica, with whom he was trying to work up an affair: "I have told you how I long for someone in my amorous loneliness, someone who will combine in the same proportion in which I have them spirit and body; who will not be wholly of the earth earthly or of the spirit spiritually; who will have the courage of a healthy conscience; who will be a joyous animal frank in her approval of her flesh and proud, not ashamed of it, knowing that it is not in things themselves but in the eye that looks at them that guilt dwells; who will practice not deadening restraint but exultant freedom; in a word, one who will take the hour and live it fully, wholly, as if it were the last hour of her life, as if it were to be eternal. There you have it! I don't believe there is such a woman."

His line of emancipated thought failed to sway Jessica, who had inherited her mother's sense of proportion. Of two minds about him, she was both intrigued by his original views, his touch of the poet, and put off by a streak of hardness she found in him. "He had a mean-looking mouth," she says, "he could be sarcastic and cutting. Clayton Hamilton had the wrong idea about him — he thought Eugene hadn't been around girls much and was so pleased that he got to know us Rippin girls. He seemed to think that Eugene was still growing up when he'd already passed most of that stage long before. His quietness misled people."

As his feeling for Maibelle waned, he felt increasingly attracted to a tall brunette he saw around town, well-built, strikingly pretty, dressed with more individuality than the other girls; one of her outfits featured a red tam-o'-shanter and extra-long tartan scarf. "I have been tracking you for months," Eugene said, when he finally met Beatrice Ashe. Not quite eighteen, though her assured air made her seem a bit older, Bee was the only child of a devoted father — he was superintendent of the local trolley-car system — and of a mother slightly dubious about her independent character. She had a pleasant soprano voice, sang at social affairs and in church, had dreams of a professional career, and among her wide circle of friends was generally at the center of activity.

New London was too small for her to be unaware of Eugene's equivocal reputation; shortly after he began courting her, in fact, she received an anonymous letter that, without naming him, warned her to be more careful in choosing her friends. Beatrice, who liked to make up her own mind, decided that he was misunderstood, generally maligned; she found him "gentle, sensitive, poetic." Before long he was writing her poems with such titles as "From a Child to a Child" and "A Rondeau to Her

Nose." One evening at home Beatrice, while singing "Just a Little Love, a Little Kiss" to her own accompaniment, became aware of a presence in the room and turned around; Eugene, overcome by the sweet sentiments of the lyrics, was standing there with tears in his eyes. The next poem he wrote her was named after the song.

For all his quiet manner she soon learned that he was of a possessive and jealous nature. "He never liked it," Bee says, "when the phone rang. There were boys I'd been friendly with and wanted to keep as friends, but he often told me, 'You must bury your dead, you've got to bury your dead.' He even resented my girl friends. When we were alone together, he had plenty to say and was full of life — he never laughed out loud but used to grin with his eyes. The moment someone joined us, though, he'd become silent, morose-looking, and after they left was apt to make sarcastic remarks about them."

Both being fond of swimming and the sun, they began meeting regularly for all-day outings at the beach; Bee, who lived on West Street in the center of town, would go out on the trolley, while Eugene would get there in his motor launch. After anchoring just offshore he would swim in carefully with his face out of the water to keep his food, tied atop his head, from getting wet. After Bee saw the kind of sandwiches he brought — thick slabs of bread, hunks of meat without butter or seasoning — she started bringing enough lunch for them both. Since Eugene wanted to keep her to himself, their usual picnic spot was not within Ocean Beach proper, where they would meet other young people they knew, but an isolated strip opposite Alewife Cove, on the property of Edward Crowninshield Hammond. Though Hammond was the one who detested trespassers and had roving guards to drive them off, it was Harkness of the Standard Oil millions who aroused Eugene's special ire. Sitting on Hammond's land, he used to shake his fist in the direction of the imposing Harkness estate and inveigh against "the power of Mammon."

One of the poems he wrote this summer, "Upon Our Beach," begins:

> *There is a house on a distant hill —*
> *A cold lonely ugly house, a millionaire's house.*
> *The world would say this is his beach;*
> *   he has a stamped paper to prove it —*
> *We know better — and we have our hearts*
> *   to prove it. This is Our Beach.*

As in his relations with Maibelle, he tried to influence Bee's taste in literature, her way of thinking. Among the first books he lent her was *Thus Spake Zarathustra*, but she was more taken with Wilde's *Salome*, an edition with Beardsley's sinuous, unholy-looking illustrations; Eugene himself found the sketches "amusing," particularly the one of Salome holding the head of John the Baptist. In his efforts to teach her about "life," he held forth on Strindberg and Emma Goldman, Ibsen and Sudermann, besides telling her of the red-light houses of Buenos Aires. Beatrice had never met anyone so well-read as Eugene, so full of literary allusions. Thinking of Eilert Lövborg, in *Hedda Gabler*, he used to tell her as they made a date for the following day, "I'll be there with vine leaves in my hair!"

Though around home he spoke critically of the Irish, in reaction to his father's chauvinism, it was obvious to Bee that he was proud of being Irish, particularly an O'Neill, for he often alluded to his ancestry. He once told her the legend of "Red" O'Neill, who during a boat race cut off a hand and threw it up on shore; the winner of the race, the first to touch the beach, was to receive a large tract of land. Bee was not the only one who would receive a lesson in Irish history and myth; for years he was wont to tell friends, but with an air of mocking himself, about his being a descendant of the early kings of Ireland.

Like most fledgling authors Eugene, in spite of all he had heard from his father about the uncertainties of the theater, indulged in dreams of early success. He was so eager to get "Bread and Butter" to producer George Tyler as quickly as possible that he mailed it at the railroad station, where he ran into Clayton Hamilton.

"I innocently expected an immediate personal reading," he recalled to Hamilton years later, "and a reply within a week — possibly an acceptance. I asked you for information regarding the reading habits of managers, the chances of scripts from unknowns, etc. You handed me the desired data — with both feet! You slipped me the unvarnished truth and then sandpapered it! You wound up in words to this general effect: 'When you send off a play remember there is not one chance in a thousand it will ever be read; not one chance in a million of its ever being accepted — (and if accepted it will probably never be produced); but if it is accepted and produced, say to yourself it's a miracle which can never happen again.' I wandered off feeling a bit sick, and thinking that you were hardly a fit associate for budding aspirations. . . .

"But your advice stuck in my mind, and kept sticking there for many years, years in which managers kept proving to me how right you were. . . . Yes, of all the help you were in those years, I think that bit ranks brightest in my memory. It was a bitter dose to swallow that day but it sure proved a vital shock-absorbing tonic in the long run. It taught me to 'take it' — and God knows that's the first thing most apprentice playwrights need to learn if they are not to turn into chronic whiners against fate or quitters before their good break comes."

His hopes wavered like a seesaw this summer as he awaited word from Tyler and wondered whether Hamilton had exaggerated the odds against him; in the meantime, he began working on another full-length play. It can hardly be coincidence that "Bread and Butter," written as he and Maibelle were splitting up, ends in an embittered marriage and a suicide, with the wife painted in the bleakest of colors, while his new one, *Servitude*, written when he was in a state of euphoria over Beatrice, ends happily for all and, further, depicts the protagonist's wife as a paragon of all the domestic virtues.

A story with overtones of both Ibsen and Shaw, *Servitude* is partly concerned with what happens to a Nora after she has slammed the door; primarily, however, it deals with a novelist-playwright of advanced views who, though married, is pursued by the ladies. David Roylston is a "tall, slender, dark-haired man of thirty-five with large handsome features, a strong, ironical mouth half-hidden by a black mustache, and keenly intelligent dark eyes" — obviously, O'Neill did not bother to look very far for his model. In his writings Roylston advocates the "ideal of self-realization, of the duty of the individual to assert its [sic] supremacy and demand the freedom necessary for its development."

Trying to live up to his views, one of his fans, a beautiful woman with a rich husband, has walked out on her marriage to make her own living and attain a "higher plane" of happiness; after starting to doubt herself, she seeks out Roylston for reassurance. At first Mrs. Frazer finds him the mentor of her dreams, then comes to realize that he is thoroughly egocentric and selfish, a man who patronizes his noble, self-abnegating wife. The play might have been called *The Education of David Roylston;* after viewing himself through Mrs. Frazer's eyes, he vows that he will be a loving husband and father — he had been as a stranger to his two children — and that the rest of his marriage will be a "life-long honeymoon."

It is impossible to believe in his reformation or, for that matter, to find any distinction in the play itself; its only value lies in what it unwittingly tells us about O'Neill's attitude toward women. His portrait of Mrs. Roylston bears a significant resemblance to the wife in one of his last plays, *A Touch of the Poet*, and there is even a marked similarity between key speeches of the women in the two works, written nearly thirty years apart. Mrs. Roylston, who believes her husband is having an affair with Mrs. Frazer: "I have loved him, loved him, loved him with all my heart and soul. . . . If that has no power to hold him — then I have

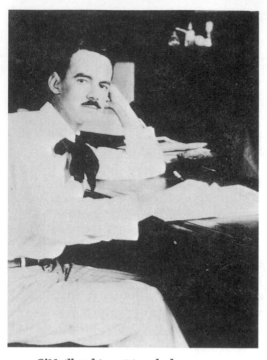

*O'Neill at his writing desk at
home in New London, circa 1914*

*Judge Frederick P. Latimer, the chief
model for the editor father in Ah, Wilderness! and the first person to believe
O'Neill was talented*

*Mrs. James Rippin and the cat Friday, which
often shared O'Neill's bed the winter of 1913–
1914, when the fledgling playwright stayed
with the Rippin family*

O'Neill and Beatrice Ashe in 1914

O'Neill, left, with friends in New London

O'Neill, right, with friends at Ocean Beach, New London. Edward Keefe is next to O'Neill, and Arthur McGinley fourth from the right.

lost him." Mrs. Frazer: "How unhappy you must have been!" Mrs. Roylston (scornfully): "Unhappy? . . . How little you know! I have been happy in serving him, happy in the knowledge that I have had my little part in helping him to success, happy to be able to shield and protect him. . . ."

Alice Roylston is young, attractive, well placed in life; Nora Melody of *Touch of the Poet* is dumpy, graying, only forty but looks much older from years of drudgery; yet the two women are sisters, born of the same feelings and fantasies in the author. Nora's husband, a onetime hero in the wars against Napoleon — the play is set in New England in the 1820s — looks down on her. Their only child resents the father's lordly airs and posturing but most of all his disdainful treatment of the mother. Normally the most gentle of souls, Nora is aroused when the girl says that if she had any pride she would walk out on the father. Nora: "I've pride in my love for him! I've loved him since the day I set eyes on him, and I'll love him till the day I die! (With a strange superior scorn) It's little you know of love. . . . It's when, if all the fires of hell was between you, you'd walk in them gladly to be with him, and sing with joy at your own burnin', if only his kiss was on your mouth! That's love, and I'm proud I've known the great sorrow and joy of it!"

Just as recurrent dreams are of more than ordinary significance, recurrent character types in a writer's work are particularly close to his interior life; from the portraits of Mrs. Roylston and Nora Melody, it appears that the author cherishes a fantasy of a devoted, all-sacrificing wife who asks nothing more than to serve her husband, that this is the sort of woman the author dreams of for his own. Such an interpretation, it should be said, is practically dictated by hindsight, for O'Neill's personal history would bear out what the two plays suggest.

While Eugene's deepest feelings tended one way, he talked — in all conscious sincerity — another. Sounding a good deal like his protagonist in *Servitude*, he constantly urged Beatrice Ashe not to be governed by her parents but to lead her own life, to be a free independent soul; her first and overriding duty, he said, was to be true to herself, to realize her potentiality. Actually, despite his words, there was in her a greater streak of independence than he bargained for — it both irked him and made her seem more desirable. Beatrice, who had a mature head on her young shoulders, felt that he would expect anyone he married to devote herself to him, content to place her own desires and needs after his. Their relationship was more spirited, on a higher level of intensity, than his romance with Maibelle Scott.

In midsummer he received a questionnaire from Gaylord Farm inquiring about the state of his health, what sort of work he was engaged in, his salary, and so forth; the data so compiled were used by Gaylord in its campaign for public support. Eugene replied that since his discharge he had worked at the "Art of Playwriting — also prostitution of the same by Photo-play composition," and added, in a burst of imagination, that his average weekly earnings were thirty dollars. Amplifying on his brief answers, he wrote at length to Dr. Lyman: ". . . to ask a struggling young playwright with the Art for Art's sake credo how much he earns per week in terms of contaminating gold, is nothing short of brutal. . . . Furthermore, to force him to confess that he basely befouls The Ideal by fabricating Photoplays is to put him to the blush in heartless fashion.

"But such is the damning fact — to such depths of degradation have the loud and ravenous howls of the well known wolf at times driven me. For while my adventures with High Art have been crowned with a sufficient amount of glory, I am bound to admit they have failed to be remunerative. Therefore, when I set down my earnings at thirty dollars a week, I am speaking in the main of the returns I have received from the Movies. It is hard to form an estimate because my fortunes have been nothing if not fluctuating.

"However, let me relieve your mind of the appalling idea that you have been misled into preserving the life of a mere Motion Picture scribe. . . . Five of my one-act plays are shortly to be published in book form, and two of them will, I think, eventually be produced by Holbrook Blinn at the Princess Theater, New York. Also, I am hard at work finishing a four-act play which, by God's grace, may see the footlights next season."

Through the letter, which leaned more heavily on fiction than on fact, O'Neill sought to impress a man he admired and felt deeply indebted to; he not only referred to his stay at Gaylord as his "second birth" but to Lyman as one who had "resurrected" him. The letter also represents, no doubt, wish fulfillment. The "glory" that had already crowned his playwriting was of course pure fantasy, and as for his earnings, there is no evidence that he had yet earned a penny from his film scenarios. Not surprisingly, he neglected to mention that his father was subsidizing the publication of his plays.

When *Thirst And Other One Act Plays* appeared in August, Eugene gave one of the first copies to Maibelle Scott. They met by appointment at Ocean Beach primarily for him to return, as she had requested, all her letters; since he never said anything about his own correspondence, she kept his, over two hundred letters, and finally burned them (this is the sort of thing that hastens biographers into old age) several years later when she was about to be married. Their meeting at the beach was the last time they ever met other than fleetingly by chance. "It was a sad occasion," she recalls, "we both felt it. But he was also elated over the book — he thought it meant he was really on his way."

In his copy for Maibelle he wrote: "In memory of all those sweet minutes and days and hours which have now gone glimmering thro' the dream of things that were!" He added to this a poem that concluded: "Give us, ah give us but Yesterday!" (O'Neill was always lavish in using exclamation marks, not only in his plays but in his correspondence and other writings — a literary mannerism he possibly derived, unconsciously, from the exclamatory dialogue of *Monte Cristo*.)

After struggling over an inscription for Beatrice's copy, he wrote: "All that I had I brought/ Little enough I know/ A poor rhyme roughly wrought/ A rose to match thy snow/ All that I had I brought." Dissatisfied with his effort, he apologized for its "inadequacy" and tried again on the opposite page: "Under the morning star/ We shall arise and know/ Who led our steps so far/ And set us dreaming so,/ And to life's chorus then/ Our lips shall cry Amen!"

His friends on the *Telegraph* gave the book a proper send-off with a story on August 20 headlined, Gene O'Neill's/ Book of One-act/ Plays Published. After summarizing the plots, the account added: "*The Web* and *Recklessness* are in the hands of Holbrook Blinn, the well-known actor. Mr. Blinn has been favorably impressed with both plays and they may soon be seen at the Princess Theater. . . . [O'Neill] has displayed considerable ability along literary lines."

His father's response was less encouraging. "My God!" he said, as he threw up his hands, "where did you get such thoughts?"

Despite his own reservations, James did his best around Broadway to promote his son's writings; with a mingled air of pride and anxious uncertainty he showed them to Tyler and Will Connor, to Brandon Tynan and Irvin S. Cobb, the humorist. Cobb, on returning one of the plays, commented, "No manager would want to put on a play like this. And even if he did, no audience would sit through it."

Tynan, eager to please "the Governor," was the one who forwarded two of the plays to actor-manager Holbrook Blinn. A year or so previously Blinn had opened a little jewel box of a theater, the Princess, for the exclusive presentation of one-act plays, fare of a more sophisticated nature than was generally to be found on Broadway; in his words, "satire, light comedy, pure horror, 'punch,' froth and tragedy — everything *bien raffiné* and quite different." Blinn's experiment would fail after several seasons but to the end Eugene kept hoping he would hear favorable word about *The Web* and *Recklessness*.

Considering George Tyler's long close relationship with James, one might expect him to have made some effort to be helpful — not to the extent of producing the immature efforts of his friend's son (besides "Bread and Butter," Eugene sent him *Servitude*), but to the extent of reading the work and offering advice; the most he did was to let the boy down gently. "It's funny now to look back," Tyler said in 1934, "and think of the bright way I behaved when James O'Neill used to bring me round the plays that his young son Gene had written and ask me to tell him what I thought of them. . . . I figured it was just run-of-mine paternal pride that made his father bring me these scripts of his. So I'd take them in and forget about them for a while — maybe read a little, but I wouldn't take oath I did that often . . . and then I'd give them back to his father with the customary polite remarks about how Gene undoubtedly showed signs of talent, and deserved encouragement, but needed more development and had better wait a while."

What actually happened was that Eugene's plays were set aside and forgotten almost as soon as they arrived. Two years later, after Liebler's had gone bankrupt, Eugene would get back both plays in their original wrappings, untouched, unread.

The book-buying public was no more interested in *Thirst* than the theatrical producers. O'Neill was to tell Mark Van Doren thirty years later that the book became "the A-1 collectors' item of all my stuff and has sold for as much as $150 a copy . . . the publisher at one time offered me all the remainder of the edition (and that was practically all the edition, for few copies were sold) at 30 cents a copy! With the usual financial acumen of an author, I scorned his offer as a waste of good money on my lousy drama!"

Except for a review in the Baltimore *Sun* and several articles in the New London press, which were of course puffs for a local son, *Thirst* received only one other notice, by Clayton Hamilton, but this did not appear until the book had been out nearly a year. Hamilton's review in the *Bookman* magazine in April 1915, almost in its entirety: "This writer's favorite mood is one of horror. He deals with grim and ghastly situations that would become intolerable if they were protracted beyond the limits of a single sudden act. He seems to be familiar with the sea; for three of these five plays deal with terrors that attend the tragedy of shipwreck. He shows a keen sense of the reactions of characters under stress of violent emotion; and his dialogue is almost brutal in its power. More than one of these plays should be available for such an institution as the Princess Theater in New York."

In later years O'Neill repeatedly acknowledged his debt of gratitude to

Hamilton for the *Thirst* review and the sobering, indeed chilling advice at the railroad station; but he neglected to mention that Hamilton also played some part in another phase of his apprenticeship. When "Ham" and his wife returned to New London this summer, taking a cottage near Ocean Beach, Eugene showed him some of his plays — the critic found in them "appreciable promise" — and asked his opinion of Professor George Pierce Baker's playwriting course at Harvard. Eugene wanted to study under him. Hamilton, who thought well of the plan, helped him to win his father's approval and suggested to Eugene that he communicate directly with Baker.

"All my life," Eugene wrote him on July 16, "I have been closely connected with the dramatic profession. My father is James O'Neill, the actor, of whom you may perhaps have heard; so, although I have never been on the stage myself . . . I can claim whatever knowledge there may be gained from a close association with members of the profession. . . .

"Although I have read all the modern plays I could lay my hands on, and many books on the subject of the Drama, I realize how inadequate such a haphazard, undirected mode of study must necessarily be. With my present training I might hope to become a mediocre journeyman playwright. It is just because I do not wish to be one, because I want to be an artist or nothing, that I am writing to you. . . .

"If varied experience be a help to the prospective dramatist I may justly claim that asset for I have worked my way around the world as a seaman on merchant vessels and held various positions in different foreign countries. . . ."

After word from Baker to submit a sampling of his work, Eugene wrote on July 29 that under separate cover he was sending two one-act plays recently completed (probably "Children of the Sea" and *Abortion*). "As for my standing at Princeton [his previous letter had mentioned his year there], I am hardly proud of it. I went there with the idea of getting through with the smallest possible amount of work, and I succeeded in paying so little attention to the laws regarding attendance, etc., that I was 'flunked out' at the end of the Freshman year for over-cutting.

"I do not think it would be fair to judge me by my Princeton record. I was eighteen then, but now I am fast approaching twenty-six, and the Princeton Freshman and I have very little in common. . . ."

While he was corresponding with the professor, momentous events were happening in the world. The newspapers reported that the centuries-old strife between Ireland and England had flared up again, with four dead in Dublin, "shot down by the King's own Scottish Borderers, following a street encounter in which the British soldiery fired into the mob." Washington was "keeping an eye" on Pancho Villa in Mexico. More seriously, trouble was coming to a head among the European powers; the Czar of Russia ordered a mobilization of four million men, and in Berlin the Kaiser said: "We shall, with God's help, so wield the sword that we shall restore it to its sheath again with honor."

The development of greatest interest to young O'Neill, however, was reported in the New London *Telegraph* on August 29; he had been "admitted to the class in higher English at Harvard University conducted by Professor Baker. This is a post-graduate course and specializes in playwriting." Before September ended, the family, as so often in the past, was widely scattered: Mr. O'Neill and Jamie were in Chicago, where *Joseph and His Brethren* had opened a lengthy engagement; Ella was at the Prince George Hotel in New York, and Eugene in Cambridge.

"I want," he had written Baker, "to be an artist or nothing."

18

Baker's Course

THOUGH born, reared and educated in New England (Providence, April 4, 1866; Harvard '87), with Yankee common sense and practicality bred into his bones, George Pierce Baker was so reckless as a youngster as to become stage-struck, and he never recovered. He was a missionary whose god was Shakespeare, whose religion was the theater. In the bastion of tradition that was Harvard, he was also a radical in spite of himself; a kind of scholastic Bourbonism would dog him most of his career, even after he had won recognition as the "father of modern American playwrights."

Rather portly, with a large head and thinning hair parted squarely in the middle, Baker wore pince-nez glasses that seemed an inseparable part of himself. When he looked directly at one, his head tilted back appraisingly, his eyes had a startling intensity. "[He] was a man," said novelist Thomas Wolfe, one of his students, "whose professional career had been made difficult by two circumstances: all the professors thought he looked like an actor and all the actors thought he looked like a professor."

Wolfe's summing-up is more epigrammatic than illuminating, yet there is a kernel of truth in his words. Baker seemed at home both in the classroom and amid the orderly chaos of backstage. What made him suspect in the higher echelon of Academe was not his appearance but his ties with Broadway, his interest in contemporary drama. The academicians felt that everything worth saying in the theater had already been said for all time by the Elizabethans and the ancient Greeks.

English 47, the course in playwriting that made Baker's reputation, was never exactly planned and nursed along; somewhat like Topsy, it just grew. At Radcliffe, the women's college known as the "Harvard Annex," where he also taught, he found the authorities more hospitable to change and innovation than his own superiors. One day in March 1903 he told his

Radcliffe class in contemporary drama that instead of submitting a thesis, they could turn in a play; and this, as all but one of the girls acted on his suggestion, was the beginning. Two years later, after contending with Harvard President Eliot's indifference and with outright opposition from the almost canonized Kittredge, he finally succeeded in winning approval for a similar project — practical instruction in the writing of plays. Finding quarters for the new course posed a problem until the day Eliot, visibly brightening, said: "There is Dane Hall, which no one can use because of the odor of chemicals." Dane Hall it was.

Among the ten in the historic first sessions of English 47 were two juniors — the rest were seniors and graduate students — named Van Wyck Brooks and Edward Brewster Sheldon; Sheldon was the one who brought the course early prominence. Acting on Baker's repeated advice to the class ("Get your material from what you see about you"), he hung around the poor sections of Boston sympathetically observing the Salvation Army's work among the derelicts; before the term ended he had written the first act of a drama entitled *Salvation Nell* in which Minnie Maddern Fiske would appear profitably on Broadway. A few years later his *Romance,* starring Doris Keane, was among the major hits of the decade. Eugene on arriving in Cambridge found himself surrounded by would-be Sheldons.

"We sat at a long oblong table," Everett Glass, one of his classmates recalls, "with Professor Baker at the head, looking like a successful and preoccupied corporation head who seldom smiled. We were his dozen for the season of 1914–15. Strangers to one another, somewhat isolated isotopes, but sharing a common dream. One other thing we had in common — a sense of elation at having been chosen from many applicants to sit at the feet of the Oracle. Each privately nourished hopes that the Miracle Man could help him also to become a successful playwright."

The class no longer met in malodorous Dane Hall but in a room of Massachusetts Hall, overlooking Harvard Square, that was sparsely furnished with chairs, the long table, and little else. The room was often cold, reminding some students that the college authorities were not overly interested in what went on there, but Baker made up for the official indifference by going about his job wholeheartedly.

Three works were required of the neophytes: a one-act play adapted from a short story Baker had approved, an original one-act composition, and an original full-length play. For all three the students wrote a scenario and, after a go-ahead signal from Baker, fleshed it out with dialogue. This was among the major things O'Neill learned from the course; he subsequently followed the same procedure in almost all his long plays — first the scenario, then the play itself. Baker, without divulging the author's identity, would read a script to the class — he had a fine resonant voice, reading with authority and feeling — next, call on the students for criticism, and would end with his own observations. As a true New Englander, committed to the gospel of self-reliance, he refrained from constructive advice. "He would tell us what was wrong with our work," a student once said, "but he would not tell us specifically how to fix it. That, he called collaboration, and he would not collaborate." It was his way of forcing his disciples to function to the limits of their ability.

To James O'Neill's son much of what he taught was "old stuff," for Baker's tastes tended to be conservative — his models were the well-made plays of Scribe, Pinero and Jones. Indeed, it was his opinion, as he told Eugene, that "Children of the Sea" was not a "play at all." Yet Eugene "respected his judgment" and was far from feeling that his Cambridge period was time wasted. "Yes," he once said, "I did get a great deal from Baker — personally. He encouraged me, made me feel it was worth while going ahead. My personal association with him meant the devil of a lot to me at that time. . . . I learned some things that were useful to me — particularly what not to do. Not to take ten lines, for instance, to say something that could be said in one line."

Although only one or two of O'Neill's classmates came to believe that he was of uncommon promise, they all felt the impact of his personality. "He stuck out of that class," John V. A. Weaver wrote in 1926, "like an oyster in a lunchroom stew. . . . We others listened with scared respect to the professorial admonitions, urgings and objurgations. Not so the fierce-browed, sardonic young man at whose left I sat. These theoretical vaporings were to him simply so much asafoetida. While we sat, open mouthed and earnest, he would writhe and squirm in his chair, scowling and muttering in a *mezzo-voce* fearful imprecations and protests. This was, to me, delightful, fascinating anarchy. To have such nerve as to pooh-pooh (that is a euphemism) this new gospel — and to get away with it — this O'Neill was a man indeed!

"Of him too, we were frightened. He kept so much to himself. He did not invite approach. For some weeks we left him alone. Then one day Dr. Baker read aloud a scenario by an aspirant. It was lugubrious, it was flamboyant, it was very, very earnest. Several of us gave timid suggestions. It came O'Neill's turn. He waited some moments. Finally he said, without a smile, 'Cut it to twenty minutes, give it a couple of tunes and it's sure-fire burley-cue.' . . . Falling into the academic stuffiness of our 'little group' it broke, once and for all, the ice. We howled with laughter.

Dr. Baker smiled. From that time until we all parted in June there was a new ease, a refreshing relaxation in the meetings."

A vivid picture, all this, in an article that has been much quoted, but other members of the class maintain that Weaver exaggerated. Said Everett Glass: "I was never aware of such sufferings on O'Neill's part. He was immediately conspicuous by his mop of black hair, his striking appearance, and his silence. Baker was not hospitable to humorous or satiric interruptions, nor was O'Neill inclined to exhibitionism. In fact he gave the impression in class of being unusually reserved and rather shy, though I'm sure that in view of the kind of life and experience he had already had, the rest of us for the most part seemed to him rather callow and our efforts trivial."

And Donald L. Breed: "He was restless a lot of time, he apparently had a low threshold of boredom, but he never behaved the way Weaver said. I had the feeling he just wasn't terribly interested in the classes. He was friendly, though rather uneasy and inarticulate at times. You got the impression that he trembled a little, and seemed trying to keep from stuttering. He rarely contributed to the discussion, but when he delivered himself of a remark, it was impressive. We felt that Gene had things to write about because he had lived — Greenwich Village, the sea, South America — while the rest of us had led sheltered lives."

That he was already a published playwright did not escape his fellow students' attention, for he often went about during the first weeks with a copy of *Thirst* under his arm. Trying to create the illusion of a public demand, he used to drop into bookstores to ask for his own book, and finally worked up enough courage to request several of his classmates to do the same. They were a mixed group that year, "Baker's Dozen," ranging from a millionaire to a Jewish immigrant youth from Czarist Latvia. Felton ("Pinky") Elkins, a foxy-looking though not unpleasant face, thinning orange-red hair plastered down, was the rich one, a polo-playing socialite from California who would never really enjoy his privileged lot because somehow he had contracted a lifelong desire to be a writer. There would be a number of books bearing his name, all subsidized by the author. *Truth, Tattle and Toyland*, published several years before he enrolled at Harvard, was a slender volume of epigrams aping Oscar Wilde: "Society is Toyland. . . . Toyland is an artificial garden next door to the truck-patch of humanity. . . . Sarcasm is a polite way of being rude. . . . Listening to scandal is a nerve-wracking pleasure, the only relaxation being to create one." And so forth. Despite the elegant, disenchanted tone of his writings, Pinky Elkins was an enthusiast, a hero-worshiper, and in O'Neill he found a new hero. After reading *Thirst* he urged everyone to buy it and repeatedly said: "Gene is going to be the greatest dramatist in America." Elkins became his closest friend in the class.

Johnny Weaver, who later gave the impression that O'Neill, Elkins and himself had been virtually inseparable, was a slight boyish chap of twenty-one, talkative, with an eager, anxious personality. A friend of his parents had financed him to a year with Baker and he was forever saying, "I'm not getting anywhere, I've got to make good, I'm not getting anywhere . . ." Most of the class found him rather trying. Several students thought O'Neill "foul-mouthed," but he was only amused when the word got back to him; he had gone out of his way, he said, to shock those he found overly genteel. Among them was a soft young man who blushed easily and in an effort to appear more virile raised a mustache. Another once said, in a self-profile: "I was convinced then — and still am — that the sex act, without love, is only masturbation. Scarcely an ecstasy to be sought by a clean or proud or intelligent person. I was too busy to sit around drinking. Early to bed, early to work. Not a puritan nor a prig but too occupied to spit tobacco and tell dirty stories behind the barn with local yokels or Harvard classmates. I had lots of friends at Harvard by that time. Tennis was our game. Not tarts."

One of the brightest students, if not for playwriting, was William L. Laurence, the son of Latvian immigrants, later the science editor of the *New York Times*. He said little in class but over a beer could be eloquent as he expounded his views as a philosophical anarchist; he and Eugene whiled away some evenings exchanging views on Nietzsche and Schopenhauer, Ibsen and Max Stirner.

Lingard Loud, another classmate, was married to a young actress named Marian Tanner who eventually would be written up by her nephew as the effervescent heroine of *Auntie Mame*. The marriage did not last very long; a few years later, without forewarning, Loud was to walk out on his life with high-spirited Miss Tanner. In a critical picture of O'Neill, he once said: "He had a fine forehead . . . and a heavy mustache to hide his depraved mouth. He was resentful against God, resentful against his family, resentful, resentful." However, Marian Tanner recalls that originally her ex-husband was "greatly impressed with O'Neill, with his imagination, his ability, his personality. O'Neill was the only one Lingard ever talked about." Marian herself, who had Eugene to dinner a few times, found him "a dramatic figure. I felt both an anger and sadness in him, but more of sadness; yet his personality was also shot through with a mordant kind of humor — maybe 'sardonic' is the better word. He was sardonically humorous on the subject of his father and all the years he had played in *Monte Cristo*."

However experienced and worldly Eugene appeared to his fellow students, his letters to Bee Ashe suggest a lovesick youth. Scattered in his correspondence are such phrases as: "Sweet alms of your charity . . . I will be worthy of you . . . I want to be a daddy to my own little girl . . . my guardian angel . . . the great longing and the great loneliness I have . . . May God smile on our love . . . only the foolish [those in love] see the fairies . . . letters of flame written over my page of life." He took considerable care in writing Bee, revising and polishing his letters until he felt satisfied; his father once came across some of the rough drafts and, sounding like Nat Miller in *Ah, Wilderness!*, exploded: "My God, if these were printed they'd burn up the newspaper!"

In response to Eugene's repeated pleas for a souvenir, something of her own, Bee sent him a pair of orange stockings that had been attached to her bathing suit. "They were old and faded," she says, "and still smelling of salt. When I came out of the water, they'd be full of sand and trailing after me like two mermaid tails. Eugene wrote me that he wrapped them around him every night when he went to bed." This is not the only indication that he was inclined toward fetishism. In 1927 he wrote his wife Agnes Boulton that he was in a sensual mood and felt like turning out the light and going to bed with her picture. But the most striking example can be found in his 1928 play, *Dynamo*, if one regards the protagonist, Reuben Light, as being in some measure autobiographical. After Reuben turns against his parents' religion he comes to worship a dynamo thrumming at its work: "It's so mysterious . . . like the old stone statues of gods people prayed to . . . that part on top is like a head . . . and below it is like a body . . . round like a woman's . . . as if it had breasts . . . a great, dark mother!"

Eugene often wrote Beatrice of not feeling well — she got the impression he feared a recurrence of tuberculosis — and used to complain of the "psalm-singing family," named Ebel, with whom he was living at 1105 Massachusetts Avenue; but inasmuch as he made no effort to find other quarters, he probably was more comfortable there than he sounded. His father gave him ten dollars a week for living expenses, while his room and board — Mrs. Ebel was a good cook and set out a generous table — cost only thirty dollars a month. The Ebels, from Hillsboro, Kansas, were of the Mennonite faith. Professor Bartley Ebel, on leave of absence from his school to take postgraduate studies at Harvard, occupied one of two ground-floor apartments at 1105 with his wife and two small sons; the other flat was shared by his brother August, studying art in Boston, and his wife's brother, Daniel Hiebert, a medical student at Boston University. Eugene, who had a room in the two bachelors' quarters, found himself, unavoidably, part of the Ebels' religious observances. "We came," Professor Ebel says, "from a community where it was a general practice to read a portion of Scripture each morning at the breakfast table and to offer a prayer before each meal. We continued that custom in Cambridge."

The family group found O'Neill polite, taciturn, somewhat remote. "I had the feeling," Hiebert recalls, "that we had to get reacquainted almost every morning." But occasionally when alone with his roommates a relatively garrulous mood came over him; besides talking of his past, he was fond of quoting poetry. One of his favorites was Swinburne's *The Garden of Proserpine*, especially the lines: "We thank with brief thanksgiving/ Whatever gods may be/ That no life lives for ever;/ That dead men rise up never;/ That even the weariest river/ Winds somewhere safe to sea." Another work he often quoted begins: "I fled Him, down the nights and down the days. . . ."

He once pointed out, August Ebel says, that his initials spelled EGO. "He was joking, I suppose, but it seemed to me that he had a pretty good opinion of himself. Among the plays put on in Boston that winter was one called *Common Clay*, which both Hiebert and myself found fascinating, but O'Neill pooh-poohed it; and I thought to myself, it's easy enough to criticize, I'd like to see him do better — well, I guess he did.

"He liked to talk, once he got started, of his earlier days and his love for the unfettered life. According to his own accounts, he was rather a slave to wine and women, and when he indulged in a binge the hangover lasted for days. He talked of trysts with women in restaurants where waiters did not intrude. I think he told us of his indulgences not only for the interest of talking about them but to 'educate' us. His ideas were certainly different. He said that if he had a child, he would not bind him with conventionalities but would give him the freedom to reach his own conclusions. He apparently felt about religion that it was implanted by parents, teachers and priests in the minds of children, and that later they couldn't shake it off."

The Ebels saw little of him on weekends, for he would take off on Saturday and not return until late the following night, generally looking pale and drawn; the first time this happened the family was worried, as he had said nothing beforehand about being absent. Where he spent the nights is unknown, but he probably spent some with Pinky Elkins, who was recently wed and had rented a house, complete with butler, in Boston's aristocratic Beacon Hill area. After the weekend of his twenty-sixth birthday, in mid-October, he returned home appearing more worn than usual and remained in bed several days, suffering from a chest cold and general run-down condition. "You know how it is," he said lamely to Professor Ebel, "when you are out with young people."

A few Saturday nights he dined with some of his classmates, according to Corwin Willson, at an "Armenian restaurant where Gene warned us not to look into the kitchen if we wanted to enjoy the food, which was delicious and cheap — all you could eat for 25 cents. Then to the Old Howard burlesque house, and after the show was over we'd go to the James Hotel to see how the burlesque gals picked up 'boy friends.' "

Johnny Weaver has left the most detailed picture of O'Neill's nights on the town, always in the company of Elkins and himself. Telling of the start of their friendship, he wrote: "We repaired to one of the Shamrock bars which in the past made Boston a thing of joy. We drank ale. We continued drinking ale until four in the morning, feet on the rail, one hand in the free lunch. It was just one of those nights. Ribald tales, anecdotes of experience, theorizing about the drama . . . a bull session de luxe.

"We piled finally into a decrepit hack. We fell into O'Neill's room sometime about five. I had just purchased that day a copy of *Spoon River Anthology*. When the dawn broke I was sitting on a trunk, Elkins sprawled across the bed, O'Neill reading in his powerful melancholy bass, poem after poem from that disturbing collection. . . .

"Elkins contributed vitally to these halcyon episodes. He was an amusing conversationalist and he was a generous host. There were numberless dinners at the Beacon Street mansion, where I, very callow and greatly impressed, and Gene, jocularly insolent in a dirty brown flannel shirt, feasted amid quiet elegance and flunkies. . . . Always, afterwards, we would go to some new show. Elkins would buy up a whole box, and once we were seated, tear up the rest of the tickets."

Interestingly, other classmates and the Ebels recall Eugene as always being conservatively dressed, never in anything such as "dirty flannel shirts." It is interesting also that Weaver, among the many hundreds drawn upon for their memories and impressions of O'Neill, is the only one who ever described his voice as a "powerful bass"; almost everyone else said that he tended to speak so low and indistinctly that one had to strain to make out what he was saying. And finally it is worth noting that he never mentioned Weaver in any of his letters to Beatrice Ashe; the only classmates he ever mentioned were Elkins, Loud and a married well-to-do chap from Cincinnati named Colin Ford. Thus, it appears from all available evidence, other than Weaver's own words, that he exaggerated the extent of his friendship with O'Neill, that his reminiscences are somewhat romanticized.

Since Eugene did most of his writing in bed and also liked to sprawl out while reading — a habit he had developed at Gaylord — the Ebels had the impression that their lodger more or less loafed away his days; actually he studied and worked hard this year. Trying to become an "artist," he read insatiably in the literature of the stage, ranging from contemporary to Elizabethan and classical drama. In addition to his required classroom work he teamed with Colin Ford in writing a full-length biblical drama, "Belshazzar," which he once described as "worse than an Artzybasheff novel." Nothing is known of the work, for it was among fifteen or so plays, written between 1913 and 1919, that he afterward, as he said, "destroyed." In reality some of these "destroyed" works are on file with the copyright division of the Library of Congress, while others exist in typescript copies, but the biblical play is not among them. "Belshazzar" marks the only time in his life he ever collaborated; in all probability Ford, who made but slight impression on his classmates and who never amounted to anything as a playwright, paid Eugene to work with him. Eugene once told Daniel Hiebert that several of his fellow students — Elkins and Ford were the only ones with money — paid him to revise and polish their scripts.

The first thing he turned in for the course was "Dear Doctor" a one-act farce adapted from a magazine story, which Baker thought a likely prospect for vaudeville. When Eugene looked into this possibility he found that the story had been "stolen from a successful vaudeville sketch!"

The Sniper, his original one-acter, was inspired by the mass slaughter in Europe as millions advanced, retreated and dug in. Classmate Bill Laurence recalls that he and Eugene, besides discussing Nietzsche, Schopenhauer, et al., talked occasionally of the war and that both of them, without being disturbed at the prospect, thought Germany would be victorious. As a good Irishman, Eugene at the outbreak of hostilities had rather welcomed the thought of England being defeated; by the time he wrote *The Sniper,* however, his feelings were colored by newspaper dispatches of "the Huns'" atrocities in Belgium. Yet his play was not so much anti-German as anti-war.

It opens in a bomb-wrecked farmhouse as an aged Belgian mourns over the body of his newly slain son. "It is," the village priest tries to console him, "the will of God." From the priest's "general mumble" of prayer over the dead youth there emerge such words as "Merciful . . . Infinite justice . . . Infinite love . . . Infinite pity . . . Praise Thy infinite goodness." The old farmer, bent on revenge, is finally dissuaded by the priest; but on learning that his wife also has died under enemy action, he shoots several of the "cursed Prussians" before being disarmed. As he faces the firing squad, he tells the grieving priest: "To hell with your prayers! . . . (Spitting on the floor, fiercely) That for your God, who allows such things to happen!"

The German officer, shrugging off personal responsibility, says, "It is the law." The priest's reply, as the curtain falls, is unadulterated O'Neill: "Alas, the laws of men!"

Baker, according to Eugene, found *The Sniper* "worthy" but "not timely." Later, in the annual competition of the Harvard Dramatic Club, with Baker one of the judges, the works of three Radcliffe girls were chosen for production, while *The Sniper* was among several given "honorable mention." The Harvard *Crimson* ran a full report on the contest, but a story in the New London *Telegraph* had an additional comment that probably came from Eugene: "By an unofficial announcement of one of the judges, it was made known that Mr. O'Neill's play was not chosen for representation by reason of its theme, which deals with the war, this topic being avoided."

Despite Baker's tempered enthusiasm, Eugene was encouraged by the strong impression the play made on Pinky Elkins, his wife, and the latter's sister, Josephine Oliver, who was visiting them. In a letter to Bee Ashe that was partly designed, it seems, to make her jealous, O'Neill described the sister as "clever" and wearing "a million dollars in clothes and furs. The fair Josephine said the play made her cry — now you know why I found her clever." He added that she was a friend of Klaw and Erlanger, the Broadway producers, and had promised to call on them personally with the script. After dining with the Elkinses he paraded before the mirror at home, stroking his mustache, and thinking, "Perhaps they weren't kidding me. Perhaps I will be famous some day."

Shortly before Thanksgiving, a holiday that would give him a week in New London, he wrote Doll Rippin for help in finding a room — the elder Rippins being in Florida, the Packard was closed. "As my bank roll still retains its former state of perpetual leanness, the tax must not be more than ten dollars. If my bed and scroff can be arranged for less, why all the better! Every dollar saved means a new book for my library, and I need the books.

"I am overpowered with all kinds of work but, false modesty aside, I am more than holding my own, and have every reason to feel satisfied with the way things are going. Am taking up French and German again to acquire a real reading knowledge of the two languages. For I am anxious to read the good foreign plays which are not translated. [With the aid of a German dictionary he also read *Thus Spake Zarathustra* in the original.]

"Have been over to Radcliffe, the women's college run in connection with Harvard, the past two evenings working with the dear girls at the production of a four-act play written by one of them. . . . The sweet young things have their own theater, you know, which is more than the male section of Harvard can boast of."

In mid-November both New London papers ran stories about his studying with Baker and mentioned his *Thirst* volume; with less than truth they reported that the plays were attracting "wide attention" and that notable Broadway figures had predicted for him a "brilliant future." He must have been particularly pleased by the last words of the *Day* article on November 18: "Once started, the reader will not pause until he has finished the last lines of the last play. In all there lies the weird fascination spell which Edgar Allan Poe exercised upon his readers." O'Neill had a special feeling for Poe; he not only respected him as one of the authentic geniuses of American literature but felt a personal identification with the haunted author.

The Thanksgiving visit passed too quickly for him, he afterward wrote Bee, and he was already impatient for the next holiday. In a letter to Doll on December 10 he said: "Sure am sorry your Mother will not be back for Christmas. It would be more like coming home for me than any real 'home-coming' I have ever had before. However, this is purely a selfish reason, and I'm very glad for her sake she is far away from this lamentable New England — God's curse upon it!

"Harvard and Cambridge are commencing to bore me to tears — but then everything does nowadays, more or less — except one or two things!

"Be advised by my lot — which I know you will not — and never fall in love. It's too damned painful when one is away. Without a certain person near me, I am the shadow of a shade, the thin gray wraith of a dream!" He ended by suggesting a "family party in your old homestead sometime during the vacation. I'll promise to bring my own lunch! Is it a good idea?" He signed himself "Brother Eugene."

In early December, while he was looking forward to two whole weeks with Beatrice at Christmas time, his father's employers were forced into bankruptcy. Among the most successful theatrical firms since the late 1890s, Liebler & Co. had overextended itself in a season that was proving disastrous both on Broadway and the road. Though *Joseph and His Brethren* was in no immediate danger of folding, economy was imperative; the cast of over a hundred was reduced, expenses trimmed, all possible precautions taken for weathering the storm. "Out of love and loyalty to you," Brandon Tynan wired Tyler on December 7, "every member of the company doubled and trebled and went on even as extra people. If there is anything we can do, please let us know."

James O'Neill felt the strain. At a performance in Dubuque, Iowa, he made a slip of the tongue that went unnoticed save among his fellow actors. As Pharaoh he was supposed to say, "Joseph, thou shalt be over my whole house," but instead said, "over my whore house."

Ella had joined her husband during the long Chicago engagement and was still with him in the West. Leslie Austin, one of the actors, would always remember the time she came out of her shell long enough to console him. As the troupe was leaving Kansas City, he received a telegram from his brother informing him that their mother had just died, but urging him to remain with the company. While Austin sat in the train, undecided what to do, Mrs. O'Neill joined him and spoke comfortingly to him for a long time; on leaving she kissed him on the cheek. Mr. O'Neill afterward took her place at his side and told the young actor, who had decided to remain with the tour, that he was doing the right thing. James said that he had found himself in the same unhappy situation long ago; while performing on the West Coast he had received news of his mother's death, but "for the sake of the company and the theater" had remained at his post.

In the midst of James's concern over the Liebler bankruptcy he derived some consolation from his son's apparent progress in Cambridge and sent him for Christmas a large enough check for an outfit of clothing. Eugene bought a suit, overcoat, hat, pair of shoes and ended feeling, as he wrote Bee, "like a bridegroom." The phrase was not idly chosen; he often addressed her in his letters as "Dear wife," trying to persuade her to consent to their engagement.

Although he never told her about his great aversion to trains — his lifelong hangover from the years of touring with his parents — he constantly urged her to be at the station for his homecomings. "If you care to," he once wrote, "please — please do!" Beatrice never liked to meet trains or see someone off but, she says, "gave in to him on this because it seemed to mean so much to him." When he descended from the train at Christmas time, he had an uncertain grin as he waited for her to comment on the smart figure he cut in his new wardrobe.

His Christmas gift to Beatrice was a bloodstone scarab bracelet; what he would like to have given her was beyond his means. "There were two things," she recalls, "he used to talk about getting me some day — a black silk bathing suit and an ankle-length sable coat. For himself he wanted a player-piano. 'We're going to have one,' he often said, 'after we're married.' " He finally received one nearly twenty years later as a birthday gift from his wife, Carlotta Monterey, and told everyone it came out of a New Orleans bordello. It was one of his most cherished possessions; he would play it by the hour, pumping away at "Bedelia," "Alexander's Ragtime Band," "Waiting for the Robert E. Lee," and other vintage numbers.

In response to Eugene's desire for a "family party," the Rippin girls reopened the Packard one evening and found enough provisions to whip up an impromptu dinner. The party ended around the piano, Beatrice singing to Emily's accompaniment "A Little Gray Home in the West" and other songs, while Eugene, feeling mellow from some drinks, beamed at his girl. Heedless of the cold, the two took long walks, holding hands and talking incessantly. Nearly fifty years later a woman whose life had been weighed down by family cares recalled with envy in her voice a picture of them at the time: "I was walking across Williams Park when they came along. Bee was wearing a red plaid outfit, she looked radiant, the snow coming down and everything, and he was drinking her in with his eyes — they looked so happy, so much in love."

Eugene himself took a less roseate view of their situation. Once, while retrieving some books from the Monte Cristo cottage, he had Bee remain on the porch. "You wait right here," he told her. "All the busybodies in the neighborhood — after we leave they'll be up here to see whether two sets of footprints went in the house, and if they did, they'd think the worst!" He always felt himself under the suspicious eye of the town.

Every year or so Baker had a theatrical notable address a joint session of his Harvard and Radcliffe classes, and this time brought in Augustus Thomas; among Broadway's leading playwrights for several decades — *Alabama* and *Arizona*, *The Witching Hour* and *As a Man Thinks* — Thomas was a knowing craftsman who could concoct an effective blend of surface realism, local color and theatrical hokum. The students for the most part were, in Everett Glass's words, "duly impressed by his visit — a real live successful playwright in momentary captivity." A well-fed man in his late fifties, Thomas said that his usual approach was to write with a particular star in mind and, to illustrate, asked the students for some names. "The choice," Glass recalls, "finally boiled down to Margaret Anglin. Writing a play for her started off as a job in tailoring. A good tailor must of course know something of the lady's anatomy, what sort of thing looks best on her, so Mr. Thomas proceeded to enlighten us: 'Miss Anglin is no longer an ingénue, she is broad in the beam, she limps slightly, she is a dramatic actress. She could be a mother, an aunt, a deserted wife. . . .' After getting the lady's attributes clearly defined and blessing her with motherhood, we began to invent a suitable story. . . . It was a lively, entertaining session."

Eugene felt otherwise; to him the visiting celebrity, an old friend of his father's, typified everything that was shoddy and dishonest in the American theater. Long afterward, talking of his year in Cambridge, he took a passing swipe at the playwright: "I was one of the hardest-working students of the lot. But it's true that once someone started charting an Augustus Thomas play on the blackboard to show how it was built. I got up and left the room."

His full-length work for the course, first entitled "The Second Engineer," later "The Personal Equation," gave him a great deal of trouble. "I know all the pangs of childbirth," he wrote Bee, and added that he was "in a frenzy" about how to end it. The play is more autobiographical than it seems; while it is easy to recognize the author in his protagonist, a young radical who had "wasted" a year in college, it requires some probing to find any resemblance to James O'Neill in the hero's self-effacing father, a ship's second engineer. Yet the play reflects, as though in a distorting mirror, the relationship between the playwright son and the old actor; or, more precisely, it embodies some of the author's unconscious feelings and dream-fantasies about his father.

The most interesting character in "Personal Equation" is not the rebellious youth, who parrots the ideas of Tucker, Emma Goldman and the like, but the youth's widowed father. Though colorless on the surface, he is a man of deep feeling, mystically attached to his engines, as a compensatory fetish for his painful shyness in human relations, and almost cringingly devoted to his adventurous son. But the latter regards him with contempt, chiefly because of the father's near-servile loyalty to his employers; this offers a parallel with the way O'Neill felt about his father's love for the old-time theater and his decades of playing *Monte Cristo*. Adding an explicit footnote to the resemblance, the play refers to the engineer's thirty years of service with the shipping company; Mr. O'Neill appeared in the Dumas work on and off from 1883 to 1912 — a period of thirty years. Again, the hero's grievance that his father should be not a second but a first engineer expresses O'Neill's feeling that James should have been another Edwin Booth, a star of the first magnitude.

While the son-father relationship is its true concern, the play expends most of its narrative on the hero's association with some anarchists, including a young Russian girl, a sort of young Emma Goldman, with whom he is in love. Drawing on the author's experience with the American Line, particularly his stay in England during the Great General

Strike of 1911, the story tells of the anarchists' efforts to stir up seamen and dock workers on both sides of the Atlantic. The hero is delegated to sabotage the engines of a ship, the very one on which, by unfortunate chance, his father serves. The scheme fails when the latter, firing on panicky impulse, shoots his son in the head. Though the boy survives, his mind is destroyed, and for the rest of his life he will be as helpless as an infant; the father and the Russian girl join forces to take care of him.

As a work of theater, a blueprint for performance, "The Personal Equation" is practically worthless; the story is too obviously contrived, the dialogue wooden, and none of the characters, save the engineer, has any real individuality. Yet the play merits study as a subjective document containing, both consciously and unconsciously, autobiographical elements. Besides embodying the author's ambivalent feelings toward his father, the play suggests that in his relations with women the author desires not so much a wife as a mother-figure, someone capable and strong.

In a letter to Beatrice Ashe, Eugene likened himself to an unhappy child who wanted to run to his mother for comfort; but after a reply in which she alluded to this, he protested with some heat that he was not seeking "mother-love" but wanted her as his wife. Trying to explain as much to herself as to a visitor why she never became Mrs. Eugene O'Neill, Beatrice once said: "He was always talking about having his head on my breast — that's why, I suppose, I never married him. I felt that he wanted someone to baby him, that he needed to belong to somebody. But I also felt that he would have wanted to possess me, that he wouldn't have let me belong to myself. When I met the man I later married [her husband, a Navy career man, rose to be a vice admiral], one of the first things he said was that he wanted to be the father of my children. Eugene would never have said anything like that."

A newcomer joined Baker's class during the second semester, Malcolm Morley, a young English actor fresh out of *Joseph and His Brethren*, who had once met Eugene through Jamie. In Cambridge the two young men renewed their acquaintanceship. "I remember," Morley says, "Gene calling at my room once, all agog, one of the few times he ever showed much animation. He had discovered a saloon in Boston where they served a wonderful brew of English brown ale, and I had to drop everything and go over the river with him for a pint or so."

Comparing the two brothers, he said: "Gene always spoke of things as though they were tragedies, then laughed them off; Jamie regarded everything as comedy. I can see Jamie now as I think back: he had a dead-pan face except that his eyes, bright, if rather glazed, always seemed to be appreciating his own stories. When he came to the point of one of them, the corners of his lips would twitch and I knew this was where I was supposed to laugh, not that I needed prompting — he knew how to tell a story. On stage we nearly always stood together and he used to favor me with a running line of comment, *sotto voce*, always original and generally ribald. I learned a lot from him about the American theater, especially the actresses, and he once entertained a group of us young actors by debunking our heroes of the stage."

Occasionally Jamie displayed a more serious side. "He must," Morley said, "have been a great reader once. He seemed to know practically all the de Maupassant stories and used to tell them over and over. I remember his telling 'A Piece of String' almost verbatim, from beginning to end. Wilde's 'Ballad of Reading Gaol' and 'The Harlot's House' were other favorites of his, and still another thing — this should surprise you — was Rann Kennedy's play, *The Terrible Meek*, which he loved to enact; it's about the Crucifixion and has a surprise ending. I must say that in these readings he used far more expression than ever appeared in his acting in *Joseph*." Summing up, he said with British understatement, "I always found Jamie good company, although I did not share all his interests."

At Eugene's suggestion Morley paid the Gorham Press to publish a volume of his own one-act plays, with no better luck than that of the author of *Thirst;* the two young playwrights often commiserated with one another on the Broadway managers' lack of judgment and on the tastes of the book-buying public.

As classes ended, Eugene was one of four students invited to return for the advanced course. "He showed by the end of the year," Baker once said, "that he already knew how to write well in the one-act form, but he could not as yet manage the longer forms. I was very eager that he should return. . . . O'Neill, when with me, worked steadily and with increasing effectiveness. He seemed absorbedly interested in what he was trying to do."

With his father worried over the Liebler bankruptcy and talking "poor mouth" in his letters, Eugene was uncertain whether he would be able to return in the fall; but it was clear to Morley that he thought well of the Harvard professor. Summing up his view, O'Neill once said that only those who had studied with Baker "back in the dark age when the American theater was still, for playwrights, the closed shop, star system, amusement racket, can know what a profound influence [he] exerted toward the encouragement and birth of modern American drama. It is difficult in these days [the mid-1930s] . . . to realize that in that benighted period a play of any imagination, originality or integrity by an

American was almost automatically barred from a hearing in our theater. . . .

"The most vital thing for us, as possible future artists and creators, to learn at that time (Good God! For any one to learn anywhere at any time) was to believe in our work and to keep on believing. And to hope. He helped us to hope."

19

The Film Writer

O'NEILL's efforts as a movie scenarist are little known. His chroniclers heretofore have either totally overlooked this aspect of his early career or unduly minimized it; a typical account ventures to say, for example: "It is conceivable that O'Neill did try his hand at a photoplay or two." Actually, he made repeated attempts for several years, both before and after his course with Baker, to sell something to the movies. According to what he told the Rippin girls, he once complained to his father about being chronically broke, only to get the reply, "If you want money, write for it." To the young playwright, who scorned compromise in his chosen field, the mushrooming film industry seemed his likeliest prospect for quick money.

"If you have ideas – if you can THINK," said the advertisement of a writers' school that appeared repeatedly in the press, "we will show you the secrets of the fascinating new profession. Positively no experience or literary excellence necessary. . . . The demand for photoplays is practically unlimited. The big film manufacturers are moving heaven and earth in their attempts to get enough plots to supply the ever increasing demand. They are offering $100, and more, for single scenarios or written ideas. . . . WE ARE SELLING PHOTOPLAYS WRITTEN BY PEOPLE WHO NEVER BEFORE WROTE A LINE FOR PUBLICATION."

Though Eugene was inclined to dismiss such advertisements as bait for the untalented, he found their extravagant promise echoed in the news columns. "Film makers are suffering," said a syndicated columnist in the New London *Telegraph*, "from too much prosperity – of a sort. They can't get enough plays. They have exhausted the scrapbooks and grab bags. Now they are paying real money for scenarios. . . . If a writer appeared at the door of a movie studio two years ago with a plot under his arm the office boy was apt to bite him. Today he hears a succession of thumps inside when he sends in his name. The magnates are jumping over their desks on the way to meet him. Still they can't get enough plays."

Eugene began to write for the screen around the same time that he turned playwright; his scenarios were for the most part comedies (the Rippin girls thought they "weren't at all funny") and tales of adventure. It will be recalled that in one of his letters to Dr. Lyman he referred to his "prostitution of the Art of Playwriting by Photo-play composition." Despite his self-mocking tone, he reportedly once went so far, though it is hard to believe, as to contemplate appearing in a movie — with the view, presumably, of learning something about the new entertainment medium. According to a story in the *Telegraph* on August 7, 1914, he was to play Uncas in a film of *The Last of the Mohicans* to be made locally by Guy Hedlund, a former New Londoner who had become a movie actor and director. Hedlund and Eugene were old acquaintances; as boys around the Pequot they had compared notes on the writing of poetry. Nothing ever came, however, of the "Leatherstocking" project.

On his return from Harvard, Eugene told friends that Edwin Holt, a vaudeville headliner intent on a movie career, had commissioned him to write scenarios. The *Day* reported on July 16, 1915, that his first script had been "accepted and will soon be produced." From a story in the same paper on August 11 his debut as a scenarist seemed imminent: "The Eastern Film Co. of Providence, which has engaged Edwin Holt as one of its leading actors and Eugene Gladstone O'Neill of this city as a writer of scenarios, has purchased the *Morning Star*, a New Bedford whaling bark. The bark will be used to stage a number of moving picture scenes and actors will do all kinds of stirring deeds from the decks while she is anchored in the lower harbor [of New London]." But nothing came of this, either. If feats of derring-do were ever filmed on the old *Morning Star*, they were not based on a script by Eugene Gladstone O'Neill. That settled it; abandoning his dream of easy money from the movies, he realized that he would have to get along as best he could as a playwright.

The local press carried quite a few stories this year about the youngest of the O'Neills; though they generally identified him as the son of James O'Neill, he was now a minor celebrity in his own right, thanks to the generosity of Judge Latimer, Art McGinley and other newspaper friends in boosting his stock. In later years he would flee from publicity, gaining a reputation of being the least accessible of celebrities; but as a tyro eager for recognition, anxious to establish an identity outside the long shadow of the Count of Monte Cristo, he kept his friends posted on any news-worthy developments in his green career.

On June 12 Clayton Hamilton's magazine review of *Thirst* was reprinted in the *Telegraph*. "You can't imagine what it meant, coming from you," Eugene later wrote him. "It held out a hope at a very hopeless time. It *did* send me to the hatters. It made me believe I was arriving with a bang; and at that period I very much needed someone whose authority I respected to admit I was getting somewhere."

Several weeks after the *Thirst* article his morale received another boost when one of his poems, inspired by his romance with Beatrice, was the leading item in Franklin P. Adams's "The Conning Tower" in the New York *Tribune;* a good many writers who became famous first reached print in Adams's hospitable column. The following is characteristic of "Speaking, to the Shade of Dante, of Beatrices," published on July 5:

> *Lo, even I am Beatrice!*
> *That line keeps singing in my bean.*
> *I feel the same ecstatic bliss*
> *As did the fluent Florentine*
> *Who heard the well-known hell-flame hiss.*
>
> *Dante, your damozel was tall*
> *And lean and sad — I've seen her face*
> *On many a best-parlor wall —*
> *I don't think she was such an ace.*
> *She doesn't class with mine at all. . . .*

The *Telegraph* commented, in reprinting the poem the following day: "Mr. O'Neill's verse and plays have attracted much attention of late and the critics have many times predicted a brilliant future for the disciple of the muses and the protégé of the pen."

Paying his own kind of tribute, Jamie began addressing him as "Mr. Shakespeare." He would pop his head in the doorway while Eugene was writing and ask, "Which bottle [act] are you on now?" In his voice was a mingling of affection, derision, and something like respect; his feelings toward "the Kid" were hopelessly ambivalent, shot through with contradictions. Though the brothers rarely set out together for uptown, they used to break into knowing grins when they met at a bar and, inseparable for the rest of the evening, would finally make their way home together. Eugene warned Bee against having anything to do with his brother, giving her the impression that he himself was wary of Jamie, yet also left no doubt that he felt deeply about him. "Most of all," she says, "I think Eugene was sorry for him."

Beatrice was ill most of the summer, confined to her home with rheumatic fever. Left to his own devices, Eugene dropped in often at Clayton Hamilton's cottage near Ocean Beach, read tirelessly in the literature of the stage, and saw a good deal of his cronies from Doc Ganey's Second Story Club, particularly Charles ("Hutch") Collins. The only boy in a family of girls, Hutch was pampered by his mother and sisters but came under constant fire from his stern, exacting father. Like Eugene, Hutch had turned away from Catholicism at an early age. An all-round athlete and a reckless football player — it was always a question whether he would emerge from a game an early casualty or the star — he was less sure of himself than he appeared. Under Eugene's influence he developed a liking for poetry, especially Baudelaire, Oscar Wilde, and *The Rubáiyát,* and it was rumored that he too was writing verse. Eager for self-improvement, he became meticulous in his speech — his friends derided him as affected — yet used to slop around town in a well-soiled sweat shirt. Indignant when the shirt was missing once, he said it had taken him "a long time to get it that dirty!" There was in him something lastingly young; the author would have in mind not only himself but Hutch when he drew young Richard Miller in *Ah, Wilderness!*

In several years, when O'Neill had become the leading writer of the Provincetown Players in Greenwich Village, Hutch Collins would join the group and develop into one of its most dependable actors. But his was a pathetically short life, for he died in the influenza epidemic that swept the country in the winter of 1918–1919. "I cannot tell you," Eugene wrote a friend, "with what a shock of stunned surprise and overwhelming sadness I read the news. The idea of death coupled with Hutch seems like an unwarranted extra turn of the screw of tragedy . . . for he possessed, above all other men in my experience, such a pronounced delight in living. That eternal boy in him which exulted in his own bodily prowess and was so full of admiration for the muscular deeds of others was one of his greatest charms. Those who have known him only in the city — not his natural element — will hardly have seen this side of him. But to me he was always the Hutch of New London, an athlete brimming over with animal strength; always in a bathing suit in summer, whooping, diving, swimming, rowing, canoeing, sailing; in winter plowing through a blizzard in flannel pants and T shirt, bare headed, for the pure satisfaction of his defiant health. He belonged in the open spaces where sunlight is drunk. . . . In New London days we were thrown into the closest intimacy by the very narrowness of our environment. The things which interested us, which we found beautiful, had no part in the life of that small town. . . . And we were linked as twin disreputables in the village gossip. The same obloquy descended on both our heads."

Eugene's days this summer of 1915 were largely spent at the beach, his evenings in saloons favored by the Irish. Over in Ireland the old conflict between the advocates of Home Rule and the Crown was once more simmering and would boil up the following year in the Easter Rising, a bloody affair that Yeats was to lament as "a terrible beauty." In the bars of New London young O'Neill inveighed against the English with a fervor and an eloquence that won him new respect in certain quarters; his friends at Princeton, who had looked on him as a "wild Irishman," would have recognized this O'Neill. To Art McGinley it was an old story — he never knew anyone "more proud than Gene of being Irish."

Occasionally the Baker alumnus heard from Colin Ford, his erstwhile collaborator, and Pinky Elkins. Ford, whose father had a thriving insurance business in Cincinnati, wrote of his plans for starting a theatrical weekly and wanted Eugene on the staff. Elkins, seeking advice and criticism from one he expected to become "the greatest playwright in America," sent along his latest work. "If your play is meant for melodrama," Eugene wrote back, "it's there. If you mean it for tragedy, it's not. From the scenario I don't 'get' any of the characters as characters. They're simply types — types I have met before in the theater. Then it seems to me your whole theme and the method of developing it are somewhat sentimental and trite. Perhaps this is because there has been so much in the newspapers lately about prison reform, inequality of sentence, and the rest of the subject matter of your play. . . .

"My advice is: Keep the main idea — the injustice of Justice. It's big. It's fundamental. Too much can't be said about the farcicality of man-made laws. Can the sentiment. Write impartially and make your facts, your characters, drive home the point. Galsworthy's *Justice* is a model of what I mean.

"Of course I'm criticizing it all from the standpoint of tragedy. . . ."

Brave words, and revealing: when James O'Neill's son turned playwright, few Americans had ever tried writing tragedy for the theater; no one had yet achieved it. But tragedy was the only thing he was interested in writing, only tragedy could embody his view of life. "I see life," he said in 1923, "as a gorgeously-ironical, beautifully-indifferent, splendidly-suffering bit of chaos, the tragedy of which gives Man a tremendous significance, while without his losing fight with fate he would be a tepid, silly animal. I say 'losing fight' only symbolically, for the brave individual always wins. Fate can never conquer his — or her — spirit."

His letter to Elkins was not only about tragedy, melodrama, and the injustice of Justice but about the good time he had had on Boat Day, the yearly event that flooded the town with partisans of Yale and Harvard:

"The last college cheer is silenced, and the last stewed student has hied hence with his hangover." At Pinky's suggestion he had gotten in touch with Nina Jones, a girl from California who was summering in the New London area; the daughter of a railroad magnate, Nina had come east to study playwriting under Clayton Hamilton. "I like her very much," Eugene said. "On short acquaintance she seems to be all kinds of a regular person. It's a delightful treat to meet a girl whose bean is not simply a rendezvous for hair, and who is trying to do something worthwhile. Most of the God-bless-'ems in this locality have a large To Let sign painted on their more-or-less lofty brows."

As a protégée of Hamilton, Nina saw quite a bit of O'Neill and developed a romantic interest in him that he, figuring to make Beatrice jealous, did nothing to discourage. On July 16 the *Day* reported that he and Miss Jones "are to collaborate in a dramatization of a recent popular novel. The story is laid in the reign of Louis XIII." Like his other publicized projects, however, the collaboration never materialized; the chief result of his friendship with Nina was to introduce an element of strain in his relations with Beatrice.

Now that Ella O'Neill had conquered her addiction, the family had an occasional house guest. Malcolm Morley, en route from Boston to New York, spent several days on Pequot Avenue and found Mrs. O'Neill "a gracious lady who never said much. She generally left us boys to entertain ourselves. One afternoon, since I was fond of the water, they took me swimming. While Gene and I went in, Jamie sat on the beach making sometimes caustic, sometimes encouraging remarks. I had recently swum a mile across a bay on Long Island and was eager to show off my prowess. My ego was wounded when Gene, using a crawl stroke, left me well behind. He was a magnificent swimmer."

The visit passed without incident, relations in the family appearing to the guest quite usual and amiable. When he left for New York by steamer, Mr. O'Neill, who was also making the trip, invited him to share his cabin. "Before turning in for the night," Morley recalls, "we had a long talk — mostly about Eugene. The Old Man, as the boys called him, was sympathetic about Eugene's ambitions but kept stressing the fact that his plays were not commercial. 'Why,' he exclaimed, 'couldn't Gene write winners like *Monte Cristo* and *The Musketeers?*' "

Nearly seventy and wondering whether he had played his final role, James was going to New York in hopes of receiving an acceptable offer. He had been shaken badly by the bankruptcy of Liebler's, a firm he had worked for, with few outside engagements, since *The Musketeers* at the turn of the century. His old friend Tyler, one of his most loyal fans, had always come up with something for him, but now that the producer was trying to salvage his own career, the old actor felt adrift. Yet practically no one outside his family, save Tyler and Will Connor, was aware of his inner state. Around the Crocker House bar, at clambakes and picnics of the Thames Club and the Elks, he impressed everyone as the best of company, pleasantly self-assured, seemingly without a care. Few men were better liked. Approached this summer to run for the office of mayor, he declined with characteristic finesse: "Every politician seeking office aspires to the Presidency of the United States. If I were to enter politics, I should want to make that my goal and I can't be President because I was born in Ireland, God bless it!"

His son was to display an almost obsessional interest in masks, using them in a number of plays — *The Hairy Ape, The Ancient Mariner, The Great God Brown* — and writing articles about their possible value for the contemporary theater. From his own words, his interest seemed to derive from a feeling for the old Greek tragedies with their masked protagonists, but there was a more immediate source: he had grown up in a family that showed certain faces among themselves and different ones to the outside world. Beneath his brother's cheery "What ho!" and air of finding everything a joke, there was, O'Neill came to realize, a self-destructive and despairing soul. His father, so far back as he could remember, had always masked personal sorrow and professional worry under a hearty exterior. And there was his mother, whom outsiders thought of as a reserved, dignified gentlewoman; but after her death her son would tell a friend that her life as a semi-recluse had reminded him of "the Mummy" in *The Spook Sonata*, who lives in a cupboard, one of the most pitiable and appalling of all Strindberg's characters. Eugene O'Neill did not have to look to Aeschylus and Sophocles for tragic models, masked or unmasked; he found them, both naked to the soul and masked, in his own family.

"I hold more and more surely to the conviction," he wrote in the early 1930s, "that the use of masks will be discovered eventually to be the freest solution of the modern dramatist's problem as to how — with the greatest possible dramatic clarity and economy of means — he can express those profound hidden conflicts of the mind which the probings of psychology continue to disclose to us. . . . For what, at bottom, is the new psychological insight into human cause and effect but a study in masks, an exercise in unmasking? . . .

"Why not give all future classical revivals entirely in masks? *Hamlet* for example. Masks would liberate this play from its present confining status as exclusively a 'star vehicle.' . . . But I anticipate the actors' objection to masks: that they would extinguish their personalities and deprive them of their greatest asset in conveying emotion by facial expression. I claim, however, that masks would give them the opportunity for a totally new kind of acting, that they would learn many undeveloped possibilities of their art if they appeared, even if only for a season or two, in masked roles . . . the mask *is* dramatic in itself, *is* a proven weapon of attack. At its best, it is more subtly, imaginatively, suggestively dramatic than any actor's face can ever be."

James O'Neill continued to tell his friends in New London that he was inundated with offers, a fiction that the newsmen, whether or not credulous, helped him to promote. The *Day* reported on July 16 that his services were sought for a new company to be headed by D. W. Griffith, director of the sensational new film, *The Birth of a Nation*. From another story: "Mr. O'Neill does not relish the idea of forsaking the legitimate for the movies, but may do so. Practically every actor and actress of renown is now doing some moving picture work and many of them are devoting themselves exclusively to it." Yet another account, about his being offered $1750 a week for several months of film work, said that he "is holding out for more money and will probably get it." When the summer ended, James was, to use a Broadway euphemism, still "at liberty."

Eugene meanwhile was all set to return to Harvard. On September 21 he wrote Daniel Hiebert for help in finding temporary lodgings until he could "look around Boston and find a place to settle in for the winter. I want to locate in Boston this year. Cambridge is too darn dead." He was due to arrive the following Monday, the twenty-seventh. Several days after his letter, however, on the twenty-fourth, the *Day* said that he had "accepted a position as drama critic for a new weekly to be published in Cincinnati. Mr. O'Neill will be New York critic for the publication. . . . Because of this position, Mr. O'Neill will not resume his studies in Professor Baker's class."

But the account was incomplete and misleading. "I wanted to [return]," Eugene wrote Baker in 1919. "It was none of my choice. I just didn't have the money, couldn't get it, and had to take a job as a New York dramatic critic on a new theatrical magazine which never got beyond the promotion stage, although I was religiously paid a small salary [twenty dollars a week, he once said] for doing nothing for three months or so. But please do not believe for an instant that my failure to report was caused by any doubt as to your helping me further. I was too well aware of the faults in my work to harbor any such erroneous ideas of my own self-sufficiency. . . . Oh, indeed I wanted to come back!"

If the letter can be relied on (it has the ring of truth), his father, obviously, was responsible for his sudden change of plans. While it is possible that James simply decided at the last minute that he could not afford to send him to Harvard again, it seems more likely that Eugene said something or did something that so angered his father that the latter withdrew his support. For the next several years their relationship would generally be strained, with the son often complaining to friends that his father was tightfisted. But probably more than a question of money was behind his grievance: most of us tend, though unconsciously, to equate money with love in the context of family relations. Thus Eugene in finding his father miserly was at bottom complaining that his father's affection for him was likewise measured and rationed.

At the end of September the family closed the cottage on Pequot Avenue and left for New York. The *Day*, reporting their departure, said on the twenty-eighth that James had "received a number of offers, but has as yet signed no contract. Moving picture concerns have besieged him with contracts, while managers have sought his services both for the legitimate and for vaudeville. . . . Mr. O'Neill says he feels the same energy and enthusiasm for his work that he did thirty years ago."

James and Ella settled down for the winter in their suite at the Prince George, with their sons quartered only several minutes away in the smaller, unpretentious Garden Hotel at 27th and Madison Avenue. Named after Madison Square Garden, across the street, the hotel had a raffish kind of warmth from its clientele – gamblers, grifters, Tammany Hall ward heelers, petty racketeers, as well as successive waves of persons involved in the goings-on at the Garden, circus people and six-day bicycle riders, sportsmen and boxing promoters, poultry fanciers and horse breeders. The O'Neill boys, running true to form, spent a good deal of time in the hotel taproom, which was among the liveliest in the neighborhood. Jamie, who liked to play the horses – only the need to conserve his limited funds for drinking restrained his betting – spent hours studying the racing sheets and exchanging tips with other gamblers.

Eugene drank it all in, the inside gossip, the good-natured arguments, the drunken boastings, and began making notes in *The Bartender's Guide*, a booklet given free to regular patrons which told how to mix various drinks, listed the year's sporting events, and contained blank pages wherein the philosophical drinker might record his thoughts and soul-searchings. When *The Iceman Cometh* was produced in 1946, the author said that Harry Hope's dive was based on "three places I actually lived in"; though he neglected to name them, he evidently referred to Jimmy the Priest's, a saloon in Greenwich Village known as the Hell Hole, and the Garden Hotel. In fact one of the characters in *Iceman*, Ed Mosher, is based on someone Eugene came to know in the hotel's taproom, an old-time circus man named Jack Croak, large, fat, with a jovial laugh. The Garden Hotel would provide O'Neill with more than elements of *The Iceman Cometh*. For one thing, *The Emperor Jones* was born of a story he heard from Croak, whose experiences included touring with a carnival in the Caribbees. For another, in writing *Hughie*, largely a monologue by a tin-horn gambler in a sleazy midtown hotel, he would draw on his memories of the kinds of people and kind of talk he had known at the Garden Hotel.

O'Neill was always fond of slang, he had a receptive ear for the way the unlettered express themselves, and from years of hanging around saloons had acquired an easy familiarity with the vernacular. As time went on and he established a pattern of isolated living, apart from crowds and city life, his slang became outmoded; yet it would serve him well in his writings, particularly in one or two of his last works. As several critics, including John Henry Raleigh, have noted, *Hughie*, written in the early 1940s but set in 1928, offers a rich sampling of yesteryear argot. "The authenticity, concreteness and ease," Raleigh said, "with which O'Neill handled Broadway-ese in *Hughie* made him finally one of the masters of the literary use of the American vernacular. Compared to *Hughie* or even *The Iceman Cometh*, the language of Runyon seems even more artificial and coy, that of Lardner formally conscious and stilted, that of [Sinclair] Lewis a suggestive notation rather than an authentic representation."

But in 1915, as Eugene listened to the gamblers, touts and other sports in the Garden barroom, he was only an unknown playwright, plagued with doubt as to whether he would ever amount to anything. Discouraged by Broadway's indifference to his writing, he realized that he would have to pin his hopes on the experimental, noncommercial theater. Among the first things he had done on arriving in New York was to submit his *Thirst* plays and *Bound East for Cardiff* to the Washington Square Players, a recently formed group that was drawing attention.

Though organized rather quickly, the Washington Square Players was a product of something that had long been stirring in Greenwich Village and other cultural pockets of the city — the general dissatisfaction of a good many young people with the Broadway theater, vague desires and urgings on their part toward self-expression. Around 1912 a group headed by Philip Moeller, who was undecided between a literary and a musical career, and Edward Goodman, a schoolteacher and free-lance journalist, began to meet on Sunday evenings at the Ethical Culture Society on

Central Park West to give readings of plays — Barrie, Maeterlinck, original works by themselves, nothing advanced or racy; and occasionally they gave a public performance. One year, however, they were so daring as to put on a bill of Strindberg and Schnitzler, after which the head of the Society tactfully told Moeller and Goodman: "I think you have outgrown us." The two men turned to writing and directing plays for the Socialist Press Club; also, together with some kindred souls that included a Bryn Mawr graduate named Theresa Helburn and a stage-struck patent attorney, Lawrence Langner, they began meeting at one another's home to read Ibsen, Chekhov and Shaw.

The growing ferment was centered, however, in Greenwich Village. At the Liberal Club in Macdougal Street, where the members discussed and argued Socialism, anarchism, free love, free verse, birth control, and votes for women, where the members danced the new dances and held one another closely, they also had a theatrical program; Floyd Dell, fresh from book-reviewing and newspaper work in Chicago, put on bills of one-act plays, mostly his own, for which he served not only as author but as stage designer, scene painter and actor. Ida Rauh, the restless, unfulfilled wife of *Masses* editor Max Eastman, took an active interest in the productions. Helen Westley, who had appeared inconspicuously on Broadway, found herself half of a broken marriage and, like Ida, needed an outlet for her energy. The Boni brothers, who ran a hospitable bookshop next door to the Liberal Club, encouraged the theatrical ambitions burgeoning around them. A professor-farmer-writer named George Cram Cook, whose lifelong regret was that he had been born not in ancient Greece but in Iowa, had tears in his eyes when he saw a production of *Lysistrata* ("its beauty, its coming from so far away in time, its revelation of man and woman as they were two thousand years ago — and are . . . struck something tremulous in me"). "Jig" Cook, as everyone called him, would play a central role in the little theater revolution in America.

With so many dreaming of a theater to which they might contribute something, it was only a question of time before a new dramatic group came into being. One day an art dealer on Washington Square South who had an unused large room in the rear of his shop told Albert Boni that it was available free of charge to those seeking to advance the stage. After Goodman, Langner, Ida Rauh, Lucy Huffaker and a few other friends had looked over the place, they sent out a prospectus concerning a group to be called the Washington Square Players and drew a response that exceeded their hopes; the art dealer on hearing of this immediately decided that he would have to charge rent. The young entrepreneurs, seeking better accommodations, found an empty stable on Macdougal Street, but again ran into trouble: the Fire Department inspectors came around, then the Building Department inspectors, then the Health Department inspectors, each with a set of requirements. The cost of alterations was prohibitive.

The scene shifts to the Boni bookshop. One evening as several of the group were lamenting their housing situation a classmate of Albert Boni's at Harvard dropped by, Robert Edmond Jones. Tall, thin, intense, with a beard, mustache and mop of reddish-brown hair in striking contrast to his pale face, Jones was a dedicated soul who had once gone hungry in Europe in order to study under Max Reinhardt. He would shortly win immediate renown with his first Broadway assignment, the set and costumes for Anatole France's *The Man Who Married a Dumb Wife,* but that night in the Village he was as yet unknown. Appealed to for advice, he told them that a theater was not essential, that they could put on a play anywhere, even here in the shop. Why not right now? His challenge was immediately picked up by his listeners, a group that included Boni, Phil Moeller, Helen Westley, Egmont Arens and Karl Karsten. Glancing over the bookshelves, Jones pulled down a volume of Dunsany, chose *The Glittering Gate* (only two speaking parts), and went to work. He tore off long pieces of wrapping paper and rolled them into spears eight feet long for Arens and Karsten, the tallest men present, as the pair of silent guards; next, he threw coats over the heads of two other participants — they represented boulders — and gave them candles to hold: the footlights. Helen Westley and several others constituted an enthusiastic audience. Afterward, relaxing around the fireplace of the snug bookshop, the band of friends congratulated themselves on the performance. A legend would grow with time that the impromptu production, bringing a vague stirring to a head, marked the birth of the Washington Square Players, but it simply spurred a group that was already on the move.

Several weeks later they found a home, the charming little Bandbox Theater on East 57th Street; a German composer-impresario who was almost broke from producing his own musical comedies was eager to unload the lease. After Eddie Goodman had been named director and Lawrence Langner the business manager, an announcement was sent out to potential subscribers: "The Washington Square Players have founded an organization for those who cannot find response to their demands for quality of play and production in the usual New York playhouse. . . . There will be no restrictions as to the type of play produced except that the writing must be sincere, truthful and effective." Phil Moeller was more blunt in talking to an interviewer: "The American theater has no place for the subtler nuances of drama. The whole system is wrong. The acting is mechanical, the production lifeless and the scenery damn — no, it is worse, it is positively mid-Victorian. The trouble is that the whole system is commercial. The American theater is aimed at nothing but the dollar."

On February 19, 1915, they opened with a bill of one-act plays by Goodman, Langner and Maeterlinck that won a generally favorable press: "If the Players can keep up their present pace they will make the Bandbox an institution . . . $2 drama for fifty cents . . . a big hit." The *Evening Post*, however, dissented: "The appeal is distinctly to the 'highbrow' of revolutionary tendencies. That it will ever win an audience outside of the spiritual frontiers of Greenwich Village is not probable."

The second program, including plays by Moeller and John Reed, the celebrated young war correspondent, was also well received. From then on the group was inundated with scripts, among them one day a volume entitled *Thirst And Other One Act Plays* and a manuscript bearing the poetic title of *Bound East for Cardiff*. Everything produced by the Players had to win the unanimous approval of their play-reading committee. Whether the O'Neill works found a champion or two on the committee is unknown; all he heard was that none of his offerings had been accepted.

He had given the best that was in him to his plays; he had tried making money through film scenarios. Nothing had worked. During the summer he had told Beatrice that unless she loved him, unless she would marry him, he would return to his old life of hard drinking and other excesses. Discouraged now over his writings and the state of his romance, he was tempted to let go, to take refuge in drink, as he had done in Buenos Aires and down at Jimmy the Priest's.

"Altogether too much damn nonsense," he said in 1926, "has been written since the beginning of time about the dissipation of artists. Why, there are fifty times more real drunkards among the Bohemians who only play at art, and probably more than that among the people who never think about art at all. The artist drinks, when he drinks at all, for relaxation, forgetfulness, excitement, for any purpose except his art. . . . You've got to have all your critical and creative faculties about you when you're working. I never try to write a line when I'm not strictly on the wagon. I don't think anything worth reading was ever written by anyone who was drunk or even half-drunk when he wrote it. This is not morality, it's plain physiology."

Physiology would be a ruling factor in his life in the ensuing months. In the two years since he had turned playwright he had written eleven one-act plays, a number of film scenarios, three full-length plays and collaborated on still another — a remarkable record of productivity. He would have little to show, only a one-act play and a few poems, for the next year or so. Full of self-doubt and at war with himself, he would be drinking too much to get on with his salvation, with writing.

20

❈

Greenwich Village

IF WRITERS, artists, and kindred spirits were first attracted to Greenwich Village by cheap rentals, they fell in love with the area for less practical reasons: so many of the old houses, bearing witness to an elegant past, had large rooms with noble fireplaces; lower Fifth Avenue, starting at Washington Square and the Arch, seemed like a boulevard in Paris; the little Italian restaurants, where good red wine was an inseparable part of the meal and non-Latins were introduced to the glories of garlic, added another cosmopolitan flavor; the rooftops, instead of shooting arrogantly upward, maintained a homey reassuring level; and unlike the dull checkerboard pattern of the rest of the city, the crazy little streets – they followed old cowpaths – were individualistic, eccentric, twisting and winding and ending up in forgotten cul-de-sacs where yesterday seemed to live on. Traffic might race and roar elsewhere but here it had to slow down to a civilized pace.

Seeking refuge, Eugene burrowed into rather than became part of Village life. It would always be so; even after his plays had become the chief drawing card of the Provincetown Players, a group at the heart of the Village scene, he would seem detached, a man going his solitary way. The Village he returned to in the fall of 1915 was different from the one he had visited some years earlier, chiefly to see Louis Holladay and his sister Polly. Though outwardly it looked more or less the same, its spirit was new: what would later be known as its golden age (the Golden Age is always, someone once observed, in the past) was well under way. The Liberal Club on Macdougal Street, where everyone tried to keep up with the latest in art, literature, social reform, politics, psychology and sexology, was flourishing as both a fountainhead and a symbol of the new influences. The irreverent *Masses*, with articles by John Reed, Max Eastman and Floyd Dell, cartoons by Art Young and Boardman Robinson, John Sloan and George Bellows, Eugene's old friend, was whacking away at the fat cats and panjandrums of the national scene in its attempt to undermine the forces of orthodoxy and reaction; the *Masses*, in Dell's words, stood for *Fun, Truth, Beauty, Realism, Peace, Feminism, and Revolution*. Already vanished from the scene was Mabel Dodge's salon at 23 Fifth Avenue where she had tossed together from various worlds the most articulate and controversial figures; but though the famous Evenings had ended when her restless soul plunged her into other pursuits, the revolution she helped launch was a continuing fact in Village life.

It was a time and a place marked at once by selfless striving, idealism in action, and a sharpening of ego against ego. There were some who would make their enduring marks in the arts and the educational field, there were those, most of them represented in the pages of the *Masses*, who were dreaming of and working toward a better world for everyone, and there were also frauds, opportunists and directionless souls who had been attracted by the gaiety and excitement bubbling here as nowhere else in the country. Yet this was no coming together of pure and impure entities: pretension and false edges could be found in the consecrated; even the untalented and frivolous, quickened by the prevailing spirit, had half-seen visions. It was young life heated up to an explosive degree, a historical moment that found young people both activists and heirs, both victims and beneficiaries, of all the protest movements that had begun to agitate a post-Victorian world. Their common bond, rather negative than positive, was rejection of all the values, mores and attitudes their parents represented; whatever was new was better.

Village girls bobbed their hair, discarded corsets and layers of clothing for simple loose-hanging gowns and, at a time when even streetwalkers hesitated to smoke in public, sat in restaurants being conscientiously nonchalant as they puffed away on cigarettes. All this was only a surface token of their new independence. The Revolution promised most to and demanded most from women; a reverse kind of Mrs. Grundy presided over their sex life: girls fighting their own scruples took lovers not so much from passion as from principle to prove their superiority to bourgeois morality. Couples whose romances had become serious yet who wanted to appear emancipated would slip off quietly and get married; their friends thought they were only having an affair.

At Webster Hall costume balls were forever being held, all-night affairs where Villagers discussed issues of the day even as they danced, began new romances, broke off old ones, and drank as long as the supply lasted. Originally put on to raise money for the always hard-pressed *Masses,* balls were also sponsored by the similarly insolvent Liberal Club under the name of "Pagan Routs." The Routs and other dances were advertised by posters of naked girls in sensual poses, bereted artists, green fauns and other exotic figures; before long, as more groups resorted to the fund-raising idea, the fancy-dress affairs became increasingly undressed, alcoholic and uproarious. Older residents of the Village, not merely the "old families" in their fine homes but the more recent Irish, German and Italian immigrants packed away in tenements, were appalled by the bohemian invasion. To them, as a sociologist said, "living among the Villagers was almost like living in a large-scale disorderly house."

So far as Eugene was involved, though, all this — the lectures and symposia at the Liberal Club, the costume balls, the party-going — could have been happening on another planet. The only group activity he had been interested in, the Washington Square Players, had rejected him. Drifting around the Village he renewed his friendship with Louis and Polly Holladay, who by now were well-known figures in the community, Polly especially. After running a succession of little eating places, Polly had become an institution through her restaurant on Macdougal Street, beneath the Liberal Club. The earnest talkers and thinkers, and some more interested in dancing to the phonograph, would dine at her place before wandering upstairs for an evening's diversion. Not only club members but half the Village flocked to Polly's; Art Young, Floyd Dell, Ida Rauh, Helen Westley, Orrick Johns, the one-legged poet, and his wife Peggy Baird, who was among the first to bob her hair; Theodore Dreiser, a young redhead named Sinclair Lewis, Beckie Edelson, who was front-page news when she went on a hunger strike after being jailed for inciting a labor protest — they all ate there. The food was plain, ample and cheap, the atmosphere both relaxed and stimulating.

Sometimes Hippolyte Havel, Polly's lover, cook and factotum, while shoveling out food, would denounce the diners as "bourgeois pigs!" Few took him seriously, and Polly herself made no attempt to restrain him, which was just as well, for no one could. A fiery, bespectacled little man with goatee, mustache and wild hair, Hippolyte looked like the generally held image of a bomb-throwing radical. He was in fact a living caricature whose appearance matched his personal history: after years behind bars in a half-dozen European countries as a political agitator, he made his way to America and before joining forces with Polly had written for various publications, including Emma Goldman's *Mother Earth*. "Havel," Dreiser said, "is one of those men who ought to be supported by the community. He is a valuable person for life, but can't take care of himself." O'Neill,

Harold DePolo

*Hippolyte Havel, the real-life model for
Hugo Kalmar in* The Iceman Cometh

taking his own view, would depict him, still muttering "bourgeois pigs," as Hugo Kalmar in *The Iceman Cometh*. When mellowed by liquor, Hippolyte was effusively affectionate. "Hello, little monkey face," he would welcome a friend. But a drink too many and his on-tap fury against life came pouring out in shrill complaint and invective. The relationship between Polly and him ran to extremes even for a community used to stormy love affairs. Unburdening herself to a friend, Polly complained that he refused to commit suicide. "He promised me over and over again," she said earnestly, "but he just won't keep his word."

Eugene, looking in only occasionally at Polly's, found things more peaceful at her brother's place, a bar and restaurant known as the "Sixty" after its address, 60 Washington Square South. Though Louis Holladay, large, blond, slow-speaking, had grown heavier since Eugene first met him at Princeton, he remained attractive to women. His face was full of contradictions: fine large brow, commanding nose, thick sensual lips that hinted at weakness and self-indulgence. One acquaintance, summing up his appearance, thought he suggested a "masculine Oscar Wilde." Few people got to know him. A writer named Hutchins Hapgood was impressed by his "passionate reserve." Once, when the writer started to hold back Hippolyte from choking Polly, Louis said in a tone of restrained disgust, "Don't you know they like it?" Hapgood afterward wrote: "This may have seemed cold, but there was something about Louis which suggested deep passion, so dangerous to himself that he had to cultivate an attitude of cynical aloofness."

The Sixty was his first real chance to establish himself financially; for years, while making sporadic attempts to be a writer, he had gotten along by one expedient or another, chiefly a scattering of inconsequential jobs or handouts from Polly and his mother Adele. A lively matron of comfortable build and few scruples. Adele herself had been supported by a succession of lovers; but her son's newly opened establishment was largely financed, according to rumor, by Louise Norton, who had become the love of his life. A well-bred girl from a family of means, Louise had felt like Alice in Wonderland on first arriving in the Village; she had been delighted to meet people who felt free to be rude and girls as fluent as stevedores in using the four-letter words.

There was no feeling of "family" about the Holladays; they seemed three individuals, each leading a separate life. Yet there was a strong attachment between brother and sister, particularly on her side — he was probably the only person she ever truly loved. Louis, who was a year or so younger than Polly, once told Eugene that she had seduced him in early youth. Between daughter and mother relations were frozen, with no affection on either side. Outshone in looks and personality by Adele, Polly used to complain that anyone who looked at her more than once would be stolen away by her mother. O'Neill in dealing in *Mourning Becomes Electra* with incestuous feelings between brother and sister, with rivalry and hostility between daughter and mother, would have more than classical drama and the case histories of Freud to draw on for models. All three Holladays would come to an unhappy end: Louis a suicide from an overdose of heroin, Adele from jumping into the Hudson from a steamer, while Polly was to spend the final fifteen or so years of her life in a mental institution on Ward's Island.

Besides taking up again with the Holladays, Eugene made several new friends whose lives would for years weave in and out of his own. Christine Ell, the cook at Louis's place, was one he would always cherish. She had emerged strong from what would have broken a lesser person. The illegitimate daughter of a Danish servant girl and a German army officer, she had come to America at an early age with her mother and stepfather, a laborer named Lockhoven, and before she was ten went to work in the silk mills of New Jersey. Daily except Sunday wagons would collect the factory children before dawn and return them after dark. One day a youngster noticed a bird building a nest in a nearby tree and summoned some co-workers to enjoy the sight; the next day all the windows were frosted so that no one could see out. Many of the girls looked forward to the time their flat bodies would have filled out enough for them to become prostitutes. Other factory jobs for Christine, jobs equally grueling as a domestic, a sordid home life — when she was fourteen her stepfather seduced her. Yet this sort of childhood, such a family background, could not quench her zest for living; if anything, they sharpened it.

She would figure prominently among the images in O'Neill's mind when he wrote of Anna Christie, of Cybel the Earth-Mother prostitute in *The Great God Brown*, of the huge farm girl in *A Moon for the Misbegotten*. There was about her something larger than life, and she quickened the life around her. What would have been simple promiscuity in someone else seemed in her a generous giving. Both before and after marrying Louis Ell, a tall handsome man with vague-looking eyes, she slept around widely; yet she loved her Louis. Unfortunately, he was inarticulate, somehow unfocused, unable to satisfy the romanticist at the heart of her being. In trying to console herself with lovers, Christine sought, in her words, to "realize the dream of my life . . . an utter sympathy with some man," but her feeling for Louis always interfered. Though she realized that she hurt her husband, she also knew that through her his life was "richer and more interesting to him."

[330]

Before landing in the Village she and Ell were reduced for a time to rattling a tambourine on behalf of the Salvation Army; now she entertained friends with mock-solemn renditions of the Army's songs, including one with the line, "I'm ha-a-a-p-py because I'm sa-a-a-v-v-e-d!" More often Christine, a born mimic, enlivened parties with her accurate and devastating portraits of notables in the Village. When she "did" Hippolyte, of whom she was fond, he almost seemed to materialize. Dreiser was another of her favorite subjects; drawing herself up and taking on a heavy Germanic look, she would finally say, her eyes snapping with disapproval, "Everything is crap!" It sounded just like him, captured the essence of his personality. A few years later Charlie Chaplin was to be among the admirers of her impromptu performing.

But Christine was more than a clown and a self-dramatizing romanticist; in her was also the factory child who had known years of misery and grown up feeling an outcast. One day she wandered into a lecture hall where a woman she had never heard of, Emma Goldman, was speaking. Christine was transfixed. The woman spoke with force and passion of child labor, of the evils of capitalism, of the hypocrisy of the moral code, especially in regard to women, of the need for working people to band together and fight against the forces that oppressed them. After the meeting Christine sought out the speaker and poured out her heart; Emma was sympathetic, understanding, encouraging. For the first time in her life Christine felt that it was not her fault that she was an outcast — it was society's fault. A new spirit, an unfamiliar feeling of self-respect, was born in her that day. Though too personal in her approach to life to become part of any doctrinaire movement, she felt among her own among the Socialists, anarchists, Wobblies and other rebels of the Village. O'Neill took to her from the start; once, in a moment of drunken Irish romanticism, he called her "the female Christ."

Her appearance, as striking as her personality, reflected her mixed parentage — the army officer and the servant woman. She had long hair, a glorious golden-red, a fine large body, good legs, and the narrow feet of an aristocrat. Her face was something else again: overripe cheeks, outsize mouth, a pudge of a nose and eyebrows so pale they were scarcely visible, giving her light blue eyes a naked look. All in all, the body of a goddess with the face of a peasant.

One night at the bar of the Sixty Eugene found himself next to several men talking about the Village and Villagers, about how few of them were native New Yorkers. After he ventured to say that he was of the city, born in Times Square, he was welcomed into the conversation, and thereby met Harold DePolo, a writer for the pulps, who used three or four pseudonyms to accommodate his prolific output. Harold was another original but, unlike Christine, he also worked at it. Quick-witted, fast-tempered, pleasure-loving, he did not allow his being married to interfere with his pursuit of other women. It was a toss-up which he enjoyed most — women, drinking, poker or fishing; he went at all of them with gusto. Of Latin and Irish parentage, dark, good-looking, short and trim — a hard 130 pounds, he would tell you — DePolo was born and grew up in New York City. When he was around ten, his father abandoned his wife and children — there was also a girl — leaving Harold the man of the family, one who grew up eager to take the initiative and who hated authority in others. Not infrequently involved in barroom quarrels, he would smash the head of a bottle and threaten his opponent, generally much larger than himself, with the jagged neck.

Eugene, who said so little and feared so much, was amused and fascinated by the dynamic pulp-writer. He also found him good for his morale: after reading the plays in *Thirst* Harold assured the author that he was "the greatest," the hope of the American theater. They quickly became friends.

Louis Holladay's Sixty lasted only several months, something he could blame on himself alone. More versed in the subtleties of Baudelaire and Verlaine and in the credo of the Wobblies than in the simplest facts of business life, he neglected to get a liquor license; his place was closed by the law. At his trial the judge brushed aside his defense that he had regarded the Sixty not as a regular commercial bar but as a club for his friends. Louis, who had always had a grievance against life, emerged from a few months in jail deeply bitter; it would not have been so bad had his offense been something reckless and daring, but to be imprisoned over a liquor license! The only thing in his life that sustained him was his romance with Louise Norton.

At the southeast corner of Sixth Avenue and Fourth Street was an old saloon which sported — if that is the word — a sign with a life-size painting of a swan. Once smartly golden, the sign was now faded and drab. In the dim back room of the tavern a glass case contained a large stuffed swan, dusty, moth-eaten, wilted-looking. The place was called the Golden Swan, but to its habitués it was known as the "Hell Hole." Such disparate artists as John Sloan of the "Ash Can School" and the elegant Charles Demuth have left their impressions of the gamy old barroom. To Mary Heaton Vorse, writing its epitaph years later, it had a "smoky quality about it. Something at once alive and deadly . . . sinister. It was as if the combined soul of New York flowed underground and this was one of its vents."

The Hell Hole became O'Neill's favorite haunt in the Village, the place where he did most of his drinking. Several people he met there would serve him as models for characters in *The Iceman Cometh*. The play's Harry Hope, who has never once ventured out of his saloon in twenty years, had his counterpart in Tom Wallace, owner of the Sixth Avenue spot, who kept to his rooms in the hotel he maintained upstairs. Aged, heavy-set, his vision failing, old Tom was an unseen presence whose cane could be heard rapping day and night on the upper floor to summon one of his bartenders, John Bull or Lefty Louie; he wanted more beer and whiskey for himself and the cronies always around him. But while few of his barroom patrons ever saw him, everyone knew he was proudly Irish — the evidence was all over his place. In the middle of the bar mirror was a large photograph of Dick Croker, onetime boss of Tammany Hall, above a massive "X" formed by two shillelaghs. On the walls were photos of noted boxers, all Irishmen, as well as chromos of nude women and yellowing prints of race horses. There was also, in Maxwell Bodenheim's words, an "instrument of brazen agonies that played tunes of the day when you dropped a nickel into it." O'Neill, who loved the old instrument, kept an ear open for music contending with the hubbub in the barroom.

The crowd was mixed: thugs, writers, artists, red-faced coachmen, sneak thieves, pimps, an honest gambler or two, and until the law cracked down in 1917 on streetwalkers in bars, some of the fallen sorority. Women were admitted at the unobtrusive "family entrance" on Fourth Street after a dubious eying by John Bull or Lefty Louie, especially by the latter; Louie felt that women "brought trouble and police." In the back room, to which women were confined, one of the male regulars was a neatly dressed little man with a limp, always alone; after being sufficiently stimulated by an unhurried, almost rhythmical downing of drink, he would stand and, using his cane like a violin bow, saw away until his arms tired. Someone found out that he was a remittance man, a member of a wealthy family who was paid to stay away. Things were relatively quiet in the back. It was in the barroom, in an all-male atmosphere smelling of beer, urine and tobacco smoke, that the real life of the place went on — hearty drinking, loud talk, songs, quarrels, fights.

The Hell Hole was the favorite hangout also of the last of the Hudson Dusters, a gang that had once terrorized not only honest folk but the police of all Greenwich Village and had sometimes extended their depredations as far south as the Battery. The surviving Dusters worked chiefly, when they did work, as truck drivers and stevedores on the west side water front, augmenting their incomes by highjacking others' truckloads and helping themselves to choice items from ship's cargo. Whenever elections were held they put in a good night's work for Tammany Hall, their main job being to dump ballot boxes in the river if Tammany was worried about the outcome.

In spite of the mixture in the saloon, writers and artists drinking elbow to elbow with thugs, there was a gulf between them — the Hudson Dusters and their friends on one side, the Villagers on the other, for the two groups never fraternized. Yet the toughs accepted Eugene. His polite manner with everyone, his familiarity with the sea and water-front life, his capacity for drink and ability to hold it, his being an O'Neill — all the Dusters were Irish — all served to give him special status. But perhaps most importantly, these hooligans and gangsters, like the seamen on the *Charles Racine*, sensed that he respected *them;* at the root of the friendship was O'Neill's regard for those outside the pale, for those strong and daring enough to go their free lawless way. The Dusters called him "the Kid." If a fight broke out, one of them was sure to yell, "Get the Kid out of the way!" When he turned up thinly clad one winter's day, a Duster asked what size overcoat he wore, what kind he liked; the gang member was ready to go out and "lift" one. Eugene thanked him but declined, explaining that he had an overcoat at home; he felt so complimented by the offer that he told about it for years.

The first time Maxwell Bodenheim met O'Neill the latter was coping with several angry Hudson Dusters about a drinking companion of his who had bilked them in a furniture deal. "He managed to smother their rage," Bodenheim recalled, "and induce them to forego their intended vengeance. He did this with a curious mixture of restrained profanity, mild contempt, and blunt camaraderie which showed that he shared the spirit of these roughnecks and yet failed to share it." Bodenheim, who would become notorious for his love life rather than respected for his writings, was fresh out of Chicago, a poet of promise. Many people were put off by his appearance: pale blue eyes, reddish-blond whiskers contrasting unpleasantly with his dead-white skin — he was generally unshaven — and a missing tooth in front which gave him an old-young look. Eugene, however, not only liked his poetry but found the man himself interesting and enjoyed talking with him.

One of Eugene's pet convictions, according to Bodenheim, was that "poetry lurks in all of the objects of life, from the most common to the most ethereal, except that in the most common ones it is buried with a desperate skill and is much more difficult to unearth." Another of his theses was born, it seems, of an odd juxtaposition — his friendship with the Hudson Dusters and his familiarity with Nietzsche's vision of Overmen or Supermen. He once told Bodenheim that "the underworld and the creative upper-world would have to unite before the earth could become a safe and unhampered place for intelligent people — an aristocracy of swift brawn and equally quick mind ruling over the more sluggish, hypocritical, and unimaginative men and women in all walks of life."

Occasionally he wandered down to Fulton Street, hoping to run into Chris Christopherson or another of his old cronies, especially Driscoll. On one of his visits he was stunned and shaken to learn that his stoker friend had committed suicide a few months previously. On August 12, 1915, while the S.S. *St. Louis* was in mid-ocean, bound east for Liverpool, Driscoll had hurled himself over the railing; by the time he was dragged into a lifeboat, he was dead. The ghosts that would haunt O'Neill's thoughts, and finally materialize in his writings, were starting to accumulate. Jimmy Byth, little Jimmy Tomorrow, a crumpled bloody heap in the backyard of Jimmy the Priest's. Kitty MacKay, dying of TB at home, surrounded by a household of youngsters. And now Driscoll, the last person one would expect to kill himself — Driscoll with his swaggering spirit, his joy in his own strength. What could have done it, what could have destroyed it, that great zest he had for living? The question long buzzed in O'Neill's mind before sinking below conscious thought; as time went on, it would occasionally surface to plague him, then sink again, until it returned one day well soaked in his unconscious, dripping with associations, ready to be developed into a play entitled *The Hairy Ape*.

Save for occasional verse — one of his poems was entitled "What Do You See, Wan One?" — Eugene wrote nothing this winter. He was leading a disordered existence, the most disordered since he had holed up at Jimmy the Priest's; he would drink for days at a stretch, until his body rebelled and he was violently sick. His failure to interest anyone in his plays, his friend Holladay's trouble with the law, still worse, Driscoll's suicide — it all weighed upon him. In this frame of mind, feeling oppressed by everything, he met Terry Carlin, who allowed nothing to bother him, who owned only the clothes on his back and gave the impression of being a serene and glorious bum. Terry was a prime specimen of the hard-drinking and spellbinding talkers whose images enliven the pages of Irish literature, men with wild dreams that constantly outrun even their agile tongues. Joyce would have recognized him, O'Casey would have found him familiar. But Carlin was also a good listener, a tactful extrapolator, and had the gift of making others feel eloquent, too; he got by on his charm and his wits, managing to survive without working.

In his time Carlin had made a long and questing journey: unionism, anarchism (particularly, anarchism), free love, the teachings of Nietzsche, periods of living in the slums with pickpockets, prostitutes and other derelicts under the most idealistic and radical of social experiments — his route had covered all this. He had ended in total disenchantment. Sixty-one when he and Eugene became friends, he was a burnt-out shell of his original self, yet even in wreckage remained impressive. He eventually would turn up as Larry Slade, "the old foolosopher," in *The Iceman Cometh*. The playwright, remaining faithful to his model, describes him as "tall, raw-boned, with coarse straight hair, worn long and raggedly cut. He has a gaunt Irish face with a big nose, high cheekbones, a lantern jaw with a week's stubble of beard, a mystic's meditative pale-blue eyes with a gleam of sharp sardonic humor in them . . . his clothes are dirty and much slept in . . . an expression of tired tolerance [gives] his face the quality of a pitying but weary old priest's."

Once, at a peyote party in Mabel Dodge's apartment, Carlin was the lone person to soar confidently above the nightmarish spirit that gripped the gathering. "He frightened me," Mabel said. There *was*, if you probed beneath his genial manner, something disturbing about Terry: he was so detached from everything, so indifferent to everything the world thinks worthwhile. He loved children, was agreeable with everyone, yet in any real sense was almost impossible to reach. O'Neill was probably the last person who ever got through to him, who saw and knew the essential man; to the crowd in the Hell Hole and wherever else he hung out, he was simply an enjoyable bar companion, he was "good old Terry."

The early life of Terence O'Carolan, who grew up in the slums of Chicago, was outwardly the same as that of countless other children of poverty-stricken immigrants; the difference lay in Terry himself — sensitive, imaginative, a born visionary. "[My mother] taught me," he once said, "that I did not belong in this world; she did not know how deeply she was right. When she crossed my arms over my childish breast at night and bade me be prepared, she gave me the motive of my life. She told me I would weep salt tears in this world, and they have run into my mouth."

His story, as told in a series of letters over a number of years to Hutchins Hapgood, is a revealing account of his life, of the various stages in his disillusioning journey. Brought to America from Ireland at an early age, Terry, one of a large brood, went to work in a factory when only eight years old. "Ah, that first job!" he wrote Hapgood. "I was a triumphant Archimedes who had found his fulcrum. I helped move the world, for twelve hours a day and for two dollars a week. . . . Though we were Catholics on the surface, we were pagans at bottom. I had fed my fill on the fairy tales of Ireland. They strengthened my natural quality as a dreamer, my tendency to care only for the welfare of the soul. . . . I am a remaining product of the slums, consciously desiring to be there. I know its few heights and many depths. There have I seen unsurpassed devotion and unbelievable atrocities, which I would not dare, even if I could, make known. The truth, how can we stand it, or stand for it. . . . One cannot help noticing that they who have a hopeless passion for truth are left largely alone — when nothing worse can be inflicted upon them."

Many years after Carlin and O'Neill met in the Hell Hole the latter would write in *The Iceman Cometh* a play dramatizing the same theme — man cannot endure the truth, above all the truth about himself. All the life-wrecked souls in Harry Hope's bar subsist on dreams that they will get a grip on themselves "tomorrow," that "tomorrow" they will start a new and finer kind of life. "To hell with the truth!" says Larry Slade. "As the history of the world proves, the truth has no bearing on anything. It's irrelevant and immaterial, as the lawyers say. The lie of a pipe dream is what gives life to the whole misbegotten mad lot of us, drunk or sober."

Terry grew up to be an expert tanner but, more interested in self-realization than in worldly success, would take only occasional jobs. While still in his prime he gave up work entirely when a leather company welshed on paying him for an important service. "I am driven to be a parasite," he said afterward, "for honest living there is none."

For a few years he lived with a promiscuous servant girl named Marie who had been on the verge of letting go entirely. His love for her was not primarily sexual but philosophical, spiritual; he developed her mind, revealed to her the beauties of poetry, art, literature — she was of good native intelligence — and gave her a faith, the anarchist faith, to sustain her. But there was a cool, too logical, almost inhuman element in his idealism. Once, when Marie and a girl friend were so tired of a hand-to-mouth existence that they thought of turning streetwalkers, he told them: "The kind of prostitution you contemplate is no worse than the kind often called marriage. . . . But it generally leads to frightful diseases which will waste your bodies. . . . Perhaps you will be better off so than in domestic drudgery . . . if forced to one or the other, I recommend prostitution. It may be worse for you but, as a protest, it is better for society, in the long run."

Under the influence of *Thus Spake Zarathustra* he began expressing himself with a Nietzschean accent: "How we do fasten our own fetters, from chains to corsets, and from gods to governments. Oh, how I wish I were a fine lean satirist! — with a great black-snake whip of sarcasm to scourge the respectable ones!"

Like so many idealists who at last give up, Terry Carlin at the outset had unconsciously willed himself to eventual disillusionment by setting his sights too high, by demanding too much from life. He was coming to the end of his rope. Both a slum-nurtured Thoreau living within himself and a Dostoevskian soul yearning mystically to merge with the lowest of the low, he had always been hopelessly split. The civil war within him could not go on forever; it finally was resolved not by some kind of victory or even a truce but by exhaustion. "[I have] been suffering from an old malady of mine," he wrote Hapgood, "which is accompanied by such mental depression that I could not answer the communication of even a lost soul. . . . I am more and more alone, more and more conscious of a growing something that is keeping me apart from all whom I can possibly avoid."

This was the man Eugene met in the Hell Hole, yet he was not exactly the same man: by this time, some eight or nine years after his cry of despair to Hapgood, he had come out of himself and turned into "good old Terry." He had found, as *The Iceman Cometh* tells it, the peace that comes from resting in the depths; he carried the "Bottom of the Sea Rathskeller" around with him. Accepting each day as it came along, he felt reasonably satisfied so long as he could get enough to drink, and somehow he generally managed to; he could drink from morning to night without showing any effect (he had a whimsical theory that his years as a tanner had toughened his insides) except that he became more expansive and mellow. "Cheer up, Gene," he used to say, "the worst is yet to come." The two were virtually inseparable — the gray old Irishman in hand-me-downs and the dark-faced young Irishman who also took refuge in the bottle.

Once, when Eugene was staying at Terry's room to dry out from a prolonged binge, he declared that he was never going to drink again. After he had said this several times, Carlin went out and rounded up a half-dozen of the seediest derelicts he could find and had them file through the room, one at a time, shaking their heads sorrowfully at O'Neill, who was in bed, as they made reproachful sounds. Though Eugene afterward considered the incident a good joke on himself, he was so unnerved by the parade of human wreckage that he immediately resumed drinking. One is left with the impression that Terry's feelings toward him were not unmixed with destructive impulses. For a few years Eugene had in various degrees been under the benevolent influence of a succession of older men — Judge Latimer, Doctor Lyman, Professor Baker — but Terry, the oldest and most experienced of the lot, was only a partner in despair, or rather someone who had gone beyond despair to accept, if not welcome, defeat.

The sole restraint on Eugene's drinking was lack of funds. Whether from stinginess, as his sons complained, or from a desire to prevent them from wrecking their health, James was doling out to each of them a dollar a day. In addition to Eugene's resentment over his allowance, he was jealous of James's continuing friendship, a father-son kind of relationship, with Brandon Tynan. Already one of the leading young actors on Broadway, Tynan had now blossomed out as a playwright and was about to star in his own play, a romantic Irish comedy entitled *The Melody of Youth*.

Still "at liberty" and chafing over a feeling of being relegated to the shelf, James O'Neill decided to force his way, with good intentions, into the Tynan production. After being told by coproducers George Tyler and James K. Hackett that the play had no suitable role for him, he wrote them a letter that was widely reported in the press: "I've been doing a little private investigating and I have discovered that there's a blind beggar in the second act of Tynan's play. I insist upon playing that part. I don't care how small it is. As one of the older generation of players I want to make a little offering to one of the most promising representatives of the younger generation."

In all probability James was conscious of only generous motives in his offer, yet he was too much the actor, too hungry for applause and the waves of love that can wash up from an audience, one of the headiest intoxicants known to man, to be entirely selfless; he moreover had always had a healthy respect for publicity. Both he and Tynan reaped the benefit of his *beau geste*. "A notable event," said the New York *Morning Telegraph* on February 17, 1916, "was the presence of the veteran James O'Neill in the minor part of a blind man being led by a dog. Even in the few passages allotted him the forcefulness of Mr. O'Neill's matured talent stood forth and he received a hearty welcome." And the New London *Day* on February 26: "Mr. O'Neill continued in this part four nights. It added prestige to the show, gave it considerable valuable advertising and helped launch it on what promises to be a successful run. Big houses are seeing this comedy, which is of the *Bunty Pulls the Strings* school and which has an appeal for the Irish people like *Bunty* had for the Scotch."

Envious of Tynan's success and contemptuous of his work, Eugene relieved his feelings in cracks to Jamie about the "Old Man's" grandstand play and the Broadway theater in general. But for all his abuse of Broadway, he missed few opportunities to see the worthwhile things. Stirred by a production of *The Weavers*, Hauptmann's pounding drama of *massemensch*, he saw it not once but a half-dozen times. While he may have thought he went so often simply as an apprentice studying a master, it is probable that *The Weavers* served him also as therapy: as one loaded with hostility and in need of a bloodletting, he must have found some relief from his own anger in Hauptmann's anger against the fat-bellied factory owners, in the weavers' looting and killing and all-out revolt. Indeed, he told Peggy Baird, who went with him several times, that no other production had ever moved him so deeply.

A tiny blonde with wise-looking eyes, Peggy, whose marriage to poet Orrick Johns was drifting to a close, was among the first girls in the Village with whom Eugene became friendly. She had displayed talent while studying under Robert Henri at the Art Students League but was more concerned with living — poker games, a sociable drink with friends, the reform movements of the day — than with realizing herself through the discipline of art. Unlike so many Villagers, who had to work at being emancipated, she was by nature a free independent soul who took everything in her stride and accepted people as they were. Eugene felt at ease with her. Though scarcely any of his friends ever met his mother — even Art McGinley and Ed Keefe never saw her when they visited the cottage on Pequot Avenue — he took Peggy to have tea with her once at the Prince George.

One of his passions was the six-day bicycle races at Madison Square Garden, and he introduced Peggy to the sport. Fortified by drinks from the bottle he had brought along, he would sit there for hours at a time, silent for the most part, eyes fixed on the cyclists. He never told Peggy why the spectacle so fascinated him; perhaps to him it symbolized life — people whirling around and around without ever getting anywhere. With the thoroughness that characterized his approach to anything that interested him, he became an authority on the sport and from memory could reel off the riders' records as though reading them. Peggy, who found the spectacle tiresome, finally struck a bargain with him: for each time she went to the bicycle races, he would take her to a dance at Webster Hall.

Gradually, through his friendship with Peggy, with Christine, with Harold and Helen DePolo and the Holladays, he began to take a limited interest in the life of the Village, but he had to be prodded into it. What a schoolmate at Betts had said of him still applied: "He sat along the sidelines of fun, enjoying it in a semi-absent way." When he was not hanging out at the Hell Hole, he was generally at Luke O'Connor's, at the junction of Sixth and Greenwich avenues with Eighth Street, a saloon known as the "Working Girls' Home" — why, nobody seemed to know. O'Connor's was noted as the place where a young Englishman named John Masefield, on first landing in America in the 1890s, had swept the floor and polished the beer spigots.

As the weather turned warm Eugene, eager to escape from the city but too restless for another summer in New London, visited the DePolos, who had rented a cottage at Culver Lake in New Jersey. With him was Beckie Edelson, dark and vital-looking, whose activities as a union leader had been widely publicized in the press. It was Harold's and Helen's feeling that Eugene was less impressed by her looks than by her militant spirit, the fact that she had undergone a thirty-day hunger strike while in jail; he referred to it more than once during his short visit. Though urged to prolong his stay, he remained only a week or so. "You can have your lakes," he told Harold. "I have to be near the sea."

From time to time his friends had talked about Provincetown. Polly had had a restaurant there several years ago, with Hippolyte and Christine as her cooks; Terry knew the place and liked it — he used the wild berries and fruits of the region to make fermented drinks of a jolting strength; more and more Villagers were swelling its summer colony. The year before, a group of them had presented some one-act plays in a fisherman's shack out on a pier. Everything Eugene heard about the place sounded attractive — Provincetown, at the very tip of Cape Cod, one could not get closer to the sea than in Provincetown. In the latter part of June he and Terry headed for the old fishing village. At the same time the stage-struck colonists were planning a more ambitious season for the shack on the wharf, where at high tide the waters of the bay washed under the makeshift theater.

21

Theater on a Wharf

"THE great hope of the future," said William Archer, "lies in the fertilization of the large by the little theater, of Broadway by Provincetown . . . in the region of Washington Square and Greenwich Village — or ultimately among the sand dunes of Cape Cod — we must look for the real birthplace of the New American Drama."

The beginning on the Cape could hardly have been more modest, less promising of anything substantial. One evening in the summer of 1915 a few couples were sitting around a driftwood fire, after a picnic supper, on the beach in Provincetown. Nearly all were writers — George Cram Cook and his wife Susan Glaspell, Hutchins Hapgood and his wife Neith Boyce, the Wilbur Daniel Steeles, Mary Heaton Vorse and her husband Joe O'Brien — and they fell to damning the theater, not only the bourgeois and backward Broadway theater but the new, quite advanced Washington Square Players. Their chief complaint against the latter was that in putting on so many foreign works they were affording insufficient opportunity for our own playwrights. If Jig Cook was vehement in leading the attack, the others knew why: the Players had rejected *Suppressed Desires,* a one-acter he and Susan had written to satirize the new Freudian gospel. "Those were the early years of psychoanalysis in the Village," Susan once said. "You could not go out to buy a bun without hearing of someone's complex." What was especially rankling to Jig was that the Players in rejecting the work had praised it; after calling it fresh, witty and amusing, they added that it was "too special" for even their audience.

As talk flowed around the dying fire Neith Boyce, normally reserved and cool-voiced, grew surprisingly animated; it came out that she too had written a play, a one-acter entitled *Constancy,* having some fun with the stormy, much-talked-about romance, now ended, between Mabel Dodge and John Reed, the magazine writer and war correspondent. Before the picnickers drifted home they had decided to put on their own plays just for the hell of it, to amuse themselves and their friends. Probably Jig Cook, alone among them, was already looking ahead; novelist, poet, critic, sculptor, farmer, college professor, most of all dreamer and mystic and lover of ancient Greece, he was constantly flailing about, trying to thresh something significant and beautiful from his life.

The writers turned actors began rehearsing; Robert Edmond Jones, summering in town as a guest of Mabel Dodge, was drafted to devise the production, and what would grow into the Provincetown Players was born at 10 P.M., July 15, 1915. At that hour the first lines of *Constancy* were bandied back and forth in the Hapgoods' bayside cottage. The "stage" was the first-floor verandah of the house, the harbor serving as the backdrop, with the audience seated in the adjoining room. Ever imaginative, Bobby Jones used a revolving scheme to introduce variety, but it was the audience rather than the stage that revolved; after *Constancy*, the spectators reversed their chairs and faced inward for *Suppressed Desires*. This, contrary to universal report, was not the première of *Suppressed Desires* — it was first given a few months earlier, on March 5, at the Liberal Club in Greenwich Village. However, it took several performances in Provincetown to begin spreading the word about Jig and Susan's "too special" comedy, after which it went on to become one of the most popular works in the repertory of little theaters all over the world.

Two days after the program at the Hapgoods', Neith wrote her father: "I do love being here — nothing happens — one day is like another — except that the sea and sky are never the same — but life is easy and sweet — There is a wonderful pleasantness about this little place to me and each summer I feel it more strongly — We like this house better than any we have had here — it has two porches over the water. . . . We have also a pleasant group of people about us. . . . You will be amused to hear that I made my first appearance on the stage Thursday night!! I have been stirring up the people here to write and act some short plays — We began the season with one of mine. Bobby J. staged it on our verandah — The colors were orange and yellow against the sea. . . . I have been highly complimented on my acting!!! . . . I wish I had more interesting things to tell you — but as I said, nothing happens here. . . ."

Contrary to her "nothing happens," a good deal began to happen after that night. The following morning Jig and several others descended on Mary Vorse and in the name of all the arts demanded for a theater a wharf she owned, one containing an old gray fishhouse and a small shack.

But Margaret uses it, Mary protested, referring to Wilbur Steele's wife, who had installed in the fishhouse her easel and other artist's equipment. Margaret was soon painting elsewhere. Boats, nets, oars and sails were cleared out within hours; the pioneers assessed themselves five dollars apiece toward the cost of alterations, and a curtain was hung, a green rep that Mary's mother had made years earlier for "theatricals" in the attic of their home in Amherst.

For the opening of the Wharf Theater, once again *Constancy* and *Suppressed Desires*, the audience, as they would for the rest of the season, brought their chairs from home. Lanterns with tin reflectors served as footlights, and further illumination was provided from both wings by persons holding lamps. As rain beat down, drumming on the roof, and the flickering lights threw wild shadows — there were open knotholes and wide cracks in the rude flooring — the breezy old fishhouse took on, in the words of one participant, "depth and mystery." A second bill that summer, Wilbur Steele's *Contemporaries* and Cook's *Change Your Style*, was also well received; everyone, especially Jig and others with a hand in the productions, felt pleased with the results.

Jig Cook would never write the great plays and poems he felt stirring within him; all his works fell hopelessly short of his aim. The essence of Jig is to be found not in his formal writings but in the hundreds of scraps of paper on which he carefully recorded his meditations and visions. Forever invoking images of early Greece, he loved to hold forth on the possibility of founding another Athens in America. "One man cannot produce drama," he wrote after the first season on the wharf. "True drama is born only of one feeling animating all the members of a clan — a spirit shared by all and expressed by the few for the all. If there is nothing to take the place of the common religious purpose and passion of the primitive group, out of which the Dionysian dance was born ["Dionysian" was among his favorite words], no new vital drama can arise in any people."

But the man from Davenport, Iowa, a descendant of pioneers, was more than hopelessly visionary. Gifted with his hands, an artisan who loved fine wood and well-made homey things, a farmer who could grow corn in the desert, he was also — like his enterprising forebears — a mover and shaker when the spirit was on him; and he was moved and shaken by the possibilities he envisioned in the Wharf Theater. He felt that here at last he had found his mission in life, an intuition time would verify. All winter long, while others of the group gave only passing thought to the playhouse, the large man with the strong handsome face and premature gray hair was dreaming great dreams; by spring, he was charged with plans for the second season, as well as the energy to pull everyone along in his wake.

Even before enough plays were down on paper, the band of amateurs announced a season of four programs of one-act plays and began scouring the town from harbor to sand dune for a subscription audience — $2.50 for a pair of tickets to each bill. After enrolling eighty-seven subscribers for a total of $217.50, they spent the money on installing electricity and some circus seats — planks resting on kegs and sawhorses — that could accommodate a hundred persons who would submit to being squeezed. For days there was much going and coming on the oyster-shell road that led to the wharf, while sounds of hammering and sawing could be heard at all hours. When Jig and his aides finished working on the stage, a space only ten feet by twelve, they had an ingenious setup of four movable sections that could provide a surprising variety of playing areas.

Among those helping to fix up the playhouse were E. J. ("Teddy") Ballantine, one of the group's few professional actors; Hutch Hapgood, Bror Nordfeldt the artist, and sculptor William Zorach, but the only one to approach Cook's ardor was John Reed, "Jack" to everyone, even on first meeting. Several years earlier, moved by the plight of the Paterson (New Jersey) silk strikers, he had produced a mammoth pageant in Madison Square Garden with the factory workers themselves as the performers, perhaps the most stirring event ever staged in the Garden. More recently, while covering the civil warfare in Mexico and riding with Pancho Villa's men, he had taken time to see an old miracle play, given annually on the feast of the *Santos Reyes* (the Magi). "It flashed upon me," he afterward wrote, "that this was the kind of thing which had preceded the Golden Age of the Theater in Europe — the flowering of the Renaissance."

Tall and broad-shouldered, with a boyish face, Jack Reed was a combination of poet and man of action; he generally was to be found where things were happening, and not infrequently he himself stirred up the excitement. After only a day or two at Harvard he had approached classmate Bob Hallowell with, "I hear that you draw. Why don't we do a book about Harvard? I'll do the text and you do the pictures." "But," said Hallowell, "we don't know anything about the place." "Hell," came the immediate reply, "we'll find out doing the thing!" This sounds bumptious, the sort of thing one expects from a strapping Westerner — he was from Portland, Oregon — yet Reed was so honest with himself and about himself, so eager for experience, almost any kind of experience, so impatient with the arrogant, so full of good will toward the unfortunate and the exploited, as to be wholly likable. Indeed, Sherwood Anderson said of him, "I have never met a man who awakened so much quick affection in me."

Reed was not alone when he turned up on the Cape this spring. With him was Louise Bryant, a high-spirited and vivid beauty — large violet eyes, the reddest of cheeks, soft black hair — who had a strain of theatricality and self-dramatization. One of her photographs shows her in a proud, wide-legged stance, provocatively dressed in snug riding breeches and a gamin's cap. After she visited Russia she would favor dress boots, embroidered jackets and fur shakos. Photographs have rarely done her justice, for much of her allure was in her high coloring and vital personality.

She was, Reed said, "the first person I ever loved without reservation." On meeting her the previous winter in Portland, he had written a friend: "I think I've found Her at last. She's wild, brave, and straight — and graceful and lovely to look at. In this spiritual vacuum, this unfertilized soil, she has grown (how, I can't imagine) into an artist. She is coming to New York to get a job — with me, I hope." Louise did not accompany him to New York — she was another's wife — but several months later walked out on her marriage to throw in her lot with Jack's. At first happy and excited about introducing her to all his friends in Province-town, he found added cause for breathless enthusiasm in the Wharf Theater.

Preparations moved ahead quickly for reopening the playhouse, too quickly some thought, for after a promising opening bill was all set the group began to worry about the program to follow. A new play of Steele's had been accepted, another by Louise, though few felt happy about either work (one woman, envious of Louise's looks and her having a lover such as Reed, complained to intimates: "Just because someone is sleeping with somebody is no reason we should do her play"). What was needed, the players felt, was a "strong" work to carry the second bill. It was at this juncture that O'Neill, likewise at a critical point in his life, and Terry Carlin walked down the gangplank of the *Dorothy Bradford*, making one of its daily summertime runs between Boston and Prov-incetown.

On one of their first days in town Carlin was ambling along narrow Commercial Street, the main artery, when he was accosted by an old friend, Susan Glaspell: "Terry, haven't you a play to read to us?" Terry said no — "I don't write, I just think, and sometimes talk" — then added that the young fellow who had arrived with him had "a whole trunk full of plays." (Eugene later told someone that he had his writings in a small wooden box bearing the legend *Magic Yeast*.) Susan, taken aback at the thought of a trunk crammed with manuscripts, collected herself sufficiently to say, "Well, tell Mr. O'Neill to come to our house tonight at eight, and bring some of his plays."

Eaten up with curiosity about the new theatrical group and yet wary of what these amateurs might be like, Eugene had settled with Carlin at the eastern edge of town, toward Truro; his strongest impulse always was to keep his distance. But at nine that night he turned up at the Cooks' with the script of *Bound East for Cardiff*. Too shy and nervous to read his work to a band of strangers, he paced around in another room while Frederick Burt — like Teddy Ballantine, a professional actor — read O'Neill's first tale of the crew of the *Glencairn*. "He was not left alone in the dining room," Susan later said, "when the reading had finished. Then we knew what we were for. We began in faith, and perhaps it is true that when you do that 'all these things shall be added unto you.' "

Before long Eugene and Terry moved to the center of activity, taking a onetime sailmaker's loft opposite Reed's cottage, while Hutch Hapgood on July 1 wrote Mabel Dodge: "There is a bunch here now — in addition to the usual Provincetonians there are Grace Potter, Demuth, Hartley (visiting Reed), Carb (Bobby Rogers comes soon), Stella and her baby, Hippolyte acting as cook for the Reed crowd. Jack's house is full of guests. Boyd is here helping him. Terry Carlin and O'Neill (son of James O'Neill) have taken Bayard's studio. The play fever is on. Jig and Susan, Neith and Mary O'Brien, Reed, Burt and O'Neill are the enthusiastic inner circle. . . . I am trying to compose a book on Religion, a social novel, a one-act play and an essay! Mostly preliminary brooding. . . ."

On July 13, just two days before the season was to begin with new works by Neith, Reed, and a revival of *Suppressed Desires,* a fire broke out. Myra Carr, who had been working on some costumes with cleaning fluid, hung them too near the stove; flames and smoke billowed from the wharf. To one as Irish and mystical as O'Neill, it must have seemed a malevolent fate was at work — the same fate that had threatened his voyage to Buenos Aires by nearly burning down the *Charles Racine* along with Mystic Wharf. Everyone came running toward the playhouse, Jig was everywhere, directing the fire-fighting efforts, and the blaze was brought under control before irreparable damage had been done. Since two walls were badly scorched, Jig, Ballantine and Nordfeldt stained the other two sides black to make the scorched and unscorched look alike; there was a rush job of carpentry, a new curtain was quickly made, and the theater opened on schedule to a full and cordial house. "Why, it's like the Irish Players!" someone breathed as the curtain fell.

Others were similarly impressed. "In utter primitiveness and simplicity," wrote one spectator, "the theater beats anything that even a Western mining camp in the freshness of a boom could boast . . . at first glance it seems like a joke . . . [the players] are doing big work with limited facilities, as the theater is nothing but a rough room with a curtain separating stage from audience."

The première of *Bound East*, O'Neill's baptism as a performed playwright, came on Friday evening, July 28. Several days previously he had written Beatrice Ashe that he was busy directing rehearsals of the production. To himself he assigned the smallest role, that of the second mate, with only one line: "Isn't this your watch on deck, Driscoll?" In addition to his fleeting appearance he stood by, directly behind the set, ready to prompt the actors; and throughout the performance, as they lounged around in the fo'c'sle of the *Glencairn* and dozed in their bunks as Olson and Scotty, Davis and Yank, the players could hear the fast, hoarse breathing of the author-prompter. It must have been for Eugene a memorable night, fearful and glorious.

"I may see it through memories too emotional," Susan Glaspell wrote in 1927, "but it seems to me I have never sat before a more moving performance than our *Bound East for Cardiff*, when Eugene O'Neill was produced for the first time on any stage. Jig was Yank. As he lay in his bunk dying, he talked of life as one who knew he must leave it.

"The sea has been good to Eugene O'Neill. It was there for his opening. There was a fog, just as the script demanded, fog bell in the harbor. The tide was in, and it washed under us and around, spraying through the holes in the floor, giving us the rhythm and the flavor of the sea while the big dying sailor talked to his friend Drisc of the life he had always wanted deep in the land, where you'd never see a ship or smell the sea.

"It is not merely figurative language to say the old wharf shook with applause."

In his July 25 letter to Beatrice, Eugene had urged her — unsuccessfully, it turned out — to join him, assuring her it would all be quite respectable, for she could "stay with Jack Reed and his wife who lived right across," with Mary Vorse, "or with a dozen other households with females presiding." The reference to Reed's "wife" was premature, for the two would not be married until several months later, but it was significant. Attracted to Louise against his will, Eugene wanted Beatrice around to spur their flagging romance and save him from falling in love with Reed's girl. There was no chance, he felt, of Louise reciprocating his interest, but even if there were, he liked and admired Reed too much to want to hurt him. In his feeling for Reed he was responding to the other

The Wharf Theater in Provincetown

O'Neill, left, in Bound East for Cardiff, *his baptism as a performed playwright in Provincetown in 1916*

man's openheartedness. Though Jack had led an adventurous life since Harvard, he not only respected O'Neill as a writer but boyishly envied his going to sea and knocking around the water front. It was developing into an impossible situation for Eugene; he felt boxed in by his warm relations with Reed and his growing desire for Reed's companion.

Considering all this in conjunction with his lack of aggressiveness, his basic feeling of unworthiness, it seems doubtful that he would have ventured a move toward Louise. But Louise on her side was attracted, too, especially after noticing that the intense young man seemed uneasy around her; though he made little attempt to approach her, to become friendly, he kept shooting covert glances in her direction. One day, taking the initiative, she lent him a book of poetry containing a note: "Dark eyes, what do you mean?" Following through on her provocative gambit, Louise at the first opportunity told him, in strictest confidence, that because of Reed's health — despite his rugged appearance he had been troubled since childhood by a recurrent kidney ailment — she and Jack were not lovers but lived together like sister and brother. Eugene's defenses were breached. Eager to believe, fighting the proddings of conscience, he swallowed the story. "When that girl touches me with the tip of her little finger," he told Terry, "it's like a flame."

He would later draw on this episode in his life for one of the central situations in *Strange Interlude* — Darrell's romance with Nina Leeds, the wife of his best friend. Nina in fact is somewhat reminiscent of Louise Bryant, with her need to be a center of adoration. "My three men!" says Nina in a key scene of the play, referring to her husband, her lover, and the timid family friend whose feeling for her is sentimental and platonic. "I feel their desires converge in me! . . . to form one complete beautiful male desire which I absorb . . . and am whole . . . they dissolve in me, their life is my life . . . I am pregnant with the three!"

The third program on the wharf was notable for a little gem from Susan Glaspell, *Trifles*, which, like *Suppressed Desires*, was to become a prime favorite of little theaters everywhere. In late August came the second O'Neill première, *Thirst*, with Louise as the Dancer, Cook as the Gentleman, and Eugene, heartened presumably by his developing romance with Louise, finding the courage to enact the mulatto seaman, a monosyllabic role, yet the largest part he would ever play. Tanned a dark mahogany by long hours on the beach, he played the West Indian without make-up in what seemed almost type casting, not only because of his coloring but because, it was generally felt, his somber face lent conviction to the menacing sailor.

"You knew more about him," Mary Vorse said in 1942, "when you saw him swim. He swam like a South Sea Islander. Yet this recluse who shunned people was afraid to be alone. The unfriendly universe pressed down on him in the dark and filled him with the forebodings of naked primitive man. . . . There was no such darkness as Gene's after a hangover. He would sit silent and suffering and in darkness. You could have taken the air he breathed and carved of it a statue of despair."

Mary's impression was based rather less on this summer than on all the years she knew him; despite several bouts of heavy drinking, chiefly to relieve his anxiety at being in such close contact with so many people, this was among his happiest periods. He had been acclaimed for the first time by a company of his peers; he was in the throes of falling in love more deeply than ever before; there was the bay at his doorstep; and certainly not least, he found himself charged with ambition and energy after floundering aimlessly for nearly a year.

The chief thing he wrote this summer was *Before Breakfast*, the story of a slattern whose virulent tongue drives her writer husband to suicide; actually a long monologue, the play was modeled evidently on Strindberg's *The Stronger*, a two-character work in which only one person speaks. It probably was inspired also by O'Neill's own past, by his relationship with Kathleen. At Gaylord and now in Provincetown he told friends, though it was untrue, that his former wife had laughed at his dreams of a literary career. He was reshaping her in his imagination so that he could use her in his work; he had to get even with her for making him feel so small, for her unwitting part in his suicide attempt at Jimmy the Priest's. *Before Breakfast* is not the only instance of his hostility to Kathleen Jenkins; surely it is more than chance that the dead wife of one son in *Desire Under the Elms* is named "Jen," and the slovenly servant girl of *Long Day's Journey* "Cathleen." Eugene O'Neill was an emotional hemophiliac; his wounds, his grievances, would never heal. This was a primary source of the anguished feeling and pounding power in his plays, as well as part of the lifelong price he had to pay for his talent.

Aside from its biographical aspects *Before Breakfast* is significant as an experiment when viewed in conjunction with several of his long works; the author wanted to determine whether he could sustain an audience's interest with a monologue. The experimental one-acter would later guide him in writing *The Emperor Jones* and *The Hairy Ape*, both of them largely one-character dramas, but the early work was undisguisedly a monologue. Alone on stage throughout *Before Breakfast*, the shrew abuses her husband in the next room, deriding his hopes of literary success. Toward the end his trembling hand is seen to reach out for a pot of hot water, and shortly afterward a moan is heard; the wife looks in and begins screaming — instead of shaving he has cut his throat. When the play was done later this year in the Village, the trembling hand was O'Neill's, in his final "appearance" on any stage.

Other things Eugene worked on this summer were a short story about a hapless little chap in a water-front flophouse who finally runs out of "tomorrows," and a full-length farce entitled "Now I Ask You." With the latter work he was hoping to make some money; he was so hard up that on the players' endowment list, where some of the participants were down for as little as two dollars, he was almost the only one listed as an "honorary member." In one respect "Now I Ask You" is a rough first draft, labored and thin, of the winning comedy he was to write years later in *Ah, Wilderness!* In place of a Richard Miller who upsets his elders by parroting Emma Goldman and reveling in Swinburne's fleshly lyrics, the 1916 play has a rich man's callow daughter who alarms him by taking up with arty poseurs and prattling on about free verse, free love and futuristic paintings. The author was expressing through "Now I Ask You" his scornful view of self-conscious bohemians he had met in the Village and on the Cape.

Provincetown, because of the war in Europe, was relatively crowded; artists, writers, sculptors and camp followers of the arts who otherwise would have been in Paris or Rome flocked to the Cape. It was in and out of Jack's place, in and out of Mary Vorse's, in and out of Jig and Susan's — centers of social life in the colony. Reed had invited friends for a week or two but so many stretched out their stays that he had to rent a room elsewhere for quiet where he could write; and he also needed a refuge from volatile, voluble Hippolyte Havel, serving as cook in the Reed household between excited discussions of politics. Dismissed by Hippolyte as a parlor Socialist, Jack retaliated by calling him a kitchen anarchist. "The trouble with Havel," someone said, "is that he never gives *you* a chance to talk."

Two of O'Neill's new acquaintances who aroused his interest were artists Charles Demuth and Marsden Hartley, close friends for all the difference in their personalities. A dapper individual with a neat mustache and polished manners, Demuth, the only child of a rich family, had grown up in uncertain health, solicitously and jealously watched over by a strong-willed mother. He had early gained a reputation among art collectors of sophisticated tastes for his watercolors of flowers and circus performers. They made up in charm, wit and elegance what they lacked in strength; even his acrobats, despite broad shoulders and sturdy bodies, seemed more chic than virile. In contrast to Demuth, Marsden Hartley, a heavy-faced man and a self-tortured soul, had come out of poverty and found both life and art a painful struggle. A gifted artist who never received his just acclaim during most of his career, he would wrestle with many styles until he found himself in painting Maine landscapes and other studies of a Cézanne-like solidity. He was, like his friend, a confirmed bachelor. O'Neill would have the two artists in mind, but chiefly Charles Demuth, when he drew Charles Marsden, the prim, mother-dominated writer in *Strange Interlude*, who is afraid of women, afraid of life.

Hartley, a house guest of Reed's, was greatly impressed by Terry Carlin; years later he wrote of this summer: ". . . how clearly I see Terry's granite profile against the ruffled sea as he sat hour on hour in the doorway of Gene's fish-house, ruminating over what indescribable pasts, stroking the surfaces of life with a prophet's tenderness, gnawed too persistently with hungers, rich in emotions, thoughts, and the wiser way of knowing things, earned at what terrible costs."

In spite of O'Neill's guarded attitude toward people, there were several he took to quickly, particularly John A. Francis, who ran a grocery and dealt in real estate. Half-Irish and half-Portuguese, he was highly regarded not only by the large Portuguese colony — nearly all the fishermen or their parents had come from the Azores — but by the old-line villagers, who tended to look down on these immigrants of an alien culture. A large round-faced man with calm eyes behind steel-rimmed glasses, Mr. Francis had about him a touch of homey saintliness. As a small boy he had delivered milk on cold mornings behind a slow horse. After he became an established businessman, he still kept cows, milking them himself, and, though no longer in prime health, still made the deliveries. When a friend urged him to sell his livestock and take life easier, he said only, "The children have to have their milk." Had he been more businesslike and cautious in extending credit for groceries and shelter — he was particularly indulgent toward writers and artists — he would have ended wealthy. Although he took many under his wing, he developed a special feeling for the tense young playwright who turned up this summer. Through Francis's generosity, O'Neill and Terry were able to move from make-do quarters to the sail-maker's roomy shack, and because of him they never had to go hungry.

Susan Glaspell, the soothing, stabilizing influence in Cook's life, was another Eugene liked. Also from Davenport, she suggested the nicest kind of Midwestern librarian or schoolteacher: intelligent brown eyes, light brown hair neatly parted in the middle that took on a reddish glint in the sun, a well-modulated voice with a low pleasant laugh. Jig had been in his second marriage, with a second child on the way, when he realized it was Susan he had always loved — chiefly because Susan, who under her quiet demeanor had considerable drive, decided she must have Jig to complete her life as a successful writer.

On Jig's side it was a matter of shifting the center of his deepest love from an unusual mother to a wife out of the ordinary. To understand George Cram Cook, one had to know Mrs. Ellen Cook, or "Ma-Mie," as he and almost everyone else called his mother, who was summering with him in Provincetown; Ma-Mie had brought him up believing he was remarkable, that he would prove a genius. Susan has written of her: "Brave; thin; pure; inviolate; brittle; timid; thwarted; unconquered." Ellen had been a lonely child, left motherless when under five, with books as her dearest friends. Early in her marriage she established a summer retreat for the family on the banks of the Mississippi, a log cabin with Grecian urns and volumes of Plato, Ruskin and Shakespeare. "The Cabin," in Susan's words, "knew Beethoven, the mysticism of India, old rites and beginnings of art. None of these things perhaps realized, yet there as a presence, as a thing that was in the world." The solid folk of Davenport in the 1880s and '90s thought Ed Cook, a successful attorney, had a "queer" wife.

When Jig was at Harvard and wrote his parents that he wanted to spend his following year in Greece, Ma-Mie replied: "But if you cannot go, you will find beauty and art everywhere — under your feet and over your head. I also have always longed for the art of the world, and wondered sometimes why I was held here, but that very fact has forced my spirit to find its own beauty. If only we could do without a kitchen, live as they did in Greece, mostly on fruits and nuts, cultivating trees and vines rather than corn and pork, life with us might regain and surpass the beauty of Greece."

O'Neill, who would come to know Ma-Mie well and hear from Jig a good deal of the family history, used her as one of his models for the hero's mother in *More Stately Mansions*. Like small birdlike Ellen Cook, Deborah Harford feels lost among the barbarians of nineteenth-century America and she too has a place — in her case, a summer-house in her garden — where she takes shelter from the everyday world. Another resemblance between the Harfords and the Cooks concerns Jig himself. For a time, following the collapse of his first marriage, he drifted perilously close to the thin line that divides the rational from the irrational and in fact sometimes wavered over the line. In *More Stately Mansions* Simon Harford, hopelessly torn between wife and mother, is on the verge of a nervous breakdown, while his mother, after flirting with self-willed madness, finally closes the door on reality. Yet Jig and Ma-Mie were not the primary inspirations for the play; that distinction belongs to the author's own history, to a small boy who used to fear for his mother's sanity and his own, and whose mother used to take refuge from the rest of the family in a gazebo on the front lawn. *More Stately Mansions* is based not so much on Jig's close relations with his mother as on the playwright son's ambivalent feelings toward his own mother.

Everybody was in Provincetown this year: Floyd Dell, the bright young critic from the Midwest, an old friend of Jig and Susan and now working as Max Eastman's aide on the *Masses;* poet Harry Kemp with his lovely red-haired wife Mary Pyne, who always seemed off in a world of her own; Kyra Markham, a young actress from Chicago who had had a traumatic romance with Dreiser; Ida Rauh and husband Eastman (the latter thought O'Neill "darkly handsome but somber and sallow as a down-and-outer brought to Jesus by the Salvation Army"); Mabel Dodge, who turned up eager to see the girl for whom Reed, her former lover, had fallen. From Provincetown, Mabel wrote a friend: "I have a daemon of energy that drives me on & on — why — I don't know. I feel fairly sick when I am not somehow trying to add a mite more to the consciousness already in the world."

Mabel was not the only one hounded by daemons, though some of the others would be less fortunate than she. Jack Reed, who had all the prospects of outstanding success but was fatally infected with idealism, would become a passionate advocate of the Bolshevik take-over in Russia, write a brilliantly graphic history of the event, *Ten Days That Shook the World*, drive himself to exhaustion as a spectator-participant in the Revolution, and die just before his thirty-third birthday. He would be buried with high honors within the Kremlin — a life full of achievement though tragically short. After his death, Louise Bryant was to marry William C. Bullitt, a diplomat and author of distinguished social background, become restive in a few years, turning to drink, and wind up a grotesque creature drifting about the Left Bank of Paris and embarrassing old friends. She died while in her early forties. And Jig Cook, coming to feel unappreciated by his associates, would spend his last embittered years in Greece, where he grew a patriarchal beard and mustache, dressed in native costume that made him appear more Grecian than the Greeks, became fluent in the language, drank too much of the strong resin-flavored wine as he expounded to admiring shepherds and farmers on the glory that had once been theirs, and made wild threats about killing himself. Jig, who had dreamed so high, was to die of a rare disease contracted from his pet dog.

But in 1916 in Provincetown the future looked bright to Jig and Louise and Jack. "It was a great summer," Susan said later. "We swam from the wharf as well as rehearsed there; we would lie on the beach and talk about plays — everyone writing, or acting, or producing. Life was all of a piece, work not separated from play, and we did together what none of us could have done alone."

For every one Eugene met and liked this summer, there were a dozen about whom he felt dubious, among them Harry Kemp — Kemp the tramp poet, a designation he gloried in. A tall Midwesterner with virile, homespun looks, attractive to women, he had ridden the rods, had had an affair with Upton Sinclair's wife that was written up on the front pages of the nation's press, and had once stowed away on a ship with the lordly notion that the British authorities should welcome his pilgrimage to the land of Byron, Shelley and Shakespeare. He was, in short, the compleat bohemian. On first landing in New York he had surveyed the scene from a window of his grubby hotel and, shaking his fist at the city, shouted, "I'll beat you yet, you whore!"

He was determined, as he freely admitted, to become "the greatest living poet in the world," and was constantly descending on people to announce excitedly that he had just written "the finest sonnet since Shakespeare." Late one night he began hammering on O'Neill and Terry's shack, "Gene, Gene, I want you to hear my new poem!" only to get the sleepy response, "Go to hell." This, probably, was the origin of the legend that whenever O'Neill was busy writing he hung a sign on his door bearing the same brusque directive — "Go to hell!" He did post a sign but it read: "May wild jackasses desecrate the grave of your grandmother if you disturb me."

His feelings about Kemp were quite mild, however, compared with the way he felt about Abbie Putnam, a spinster in charge of the local public library. Abbie, in addition to sharing the natives' suspicion of the bohemian contingent in Provincetown, was hard-of-hearing and had no patience with people who spoke so low that she was unable to make out what they were saying. Eugene, who had to steel himself to withstand her hostile glances whenever he visited the library, would get his revenge when he wrote *Desire Under the Elms*: he gave the name of Abbie Putnam to the adulterous farm wife who slays her own child.

From the beginning the troupe on the wharf attracted publicity. A Boston newspaperman named A. J. Philpott, vacationing in town, wrote a lengthy, farsighted article for the *Sunday Globe* on August 13, accompanied by photographs of Cook, O'Neill, Louise and Susan, as well as of the playhouse high on its pilings. "These players," Philpott said, "are revolutionists. They care little for stage traditions and in their work so far they have given absolutely no consideration to the great American theatrical bugaboo, 'the tired businessman,' who desires to be amused. . . . They are paying more attention to that thoughtful class of people whose numbers seem to be increasing in this country — the class that suffers a little in the mental and spiritual travail incident to the growing life of the times — the class that thinks less about profits and more about human aspirations, justice and equality of opportunity. . . .

"Idealists! Dreamers! Yes, they admit it . . . for they also realize that it is out of such idealism that the real things come. . . . They believe that the tendency of the age is toward such idealism [Mr. Philpott obviously spent a lot of time listening to Jig Cook], and that stage managers and producers must inevitably turn to it, and that from the crude productions of their little theater on the wharf — or similar theaters — will flow some of the big theatrical successes of the future."

In singling out key members of the group, the *Globe* man wrote: "Many people will remember James O'Neil [sic], who played *Monte Cristo*. He has a son — Eugene O'Neil — who knocked about the world in tramp steamers and doing all sorts of adventurous stunts, and saw life 'in the raw,' and thought much about it . . . he has written some little plays which have made a very deep impression."

Of Louise he said that she "looks like a society bud, but she isn't; for she worked five years on the *Portland Oregonian* as a writer of 'specials' — a work that gave her a lot of knowledge she could never get in a seminary."

Though Susan should have expected it, she was "appalled" the day Jig said, "When we go to New York for the winter, we will take our theater with us." Even the modest season on the wharf, with the costliest set only thirteen dollars, had been a continuous struggle, financially and every other way. As Jig outlined his plans, Susan was thinking "how it had been through the summer. Many had been interested, and some of them had worked hard, but after all the others worked when they wanted to. . . . There were people who would be animated when they were with him, and then the next day — 'But really, I haven't time for it,' . . . they would have to be captured anew, or let go, and some one else captured. . . . And I was afraid people would laugh at him, starting a theater in New York — new playwrights, amateur acting, somewhere in an old house or a stable. . . .'"

Cook was determined, though, and he was supported by Floyd Dell, by Reed ("Jack thinks we can make it go"), and of course by O'Neill, who was eager to have a showcase for his plays. Toward the end of the season Jig found a new ally in Edna Kenton, a newspaperwoman from Chicago and an old friend of his and Susan's. Edna had scarcely landed from the

Dorothy Bradford when he rushed her over to the playhouse, slid back the great rear door to "let in the sparkling sea," and began telling her about the summer. "You don't know Gene yet," he said. "You don't know his plays. But you will. All the world will know Gene's plays some day. Last summer this thing began. This year, on the night he first came to Provincetown and read us *Bound East for Cardiff*, we knew we had something to go on with. Some day this little theater will be famous; some day the little theater in New York will be famous — this fall the Provincetown Players go into New York with *Cardiff* on their first bill.

"We've got our group of playwrights and they've got to have their stage. Gene's plays aren't the plays of Broadway; he's got to have the sort of stage we're going to found in New York. He's writing. Susan's writing. Jack Reed and Floyd Dell and the Hapgoods are writing. I'm writing — you're going to write us a play." In this he was wrong, for Edna never wrote one; she instead became a leading figure behind the scene and the first historian of the group.

To raise money toward their invasion of New York, the players on September 1 and 2 put on a review bill of *Suppressed Desires*, *The Game*, a morality play by Louise with a stylized set by the Zorachs, and *Thirst* — this in place of *Bound East*, which would have entailed casting problems as some of the original actors had already left for home. "Eighty dollars," wrote Miss Kenton, "was the resultant sum toward founding a New York stage for the liberation of the American playwright."

At a meeting in the playhouse on Monday evening, September 4, the members got down to the business of organizing formally, electing officers, forming an executive committee, and so forth. Hutch Hapgood, even more visionary than Cook, if possible, added a discordant note at the outset by crying, "Organization is death!" but his objection was brushed aside. After they had voted to call themselves the Provincetown Players, Eugene suggested that the name should "celebrate not only people but things — the thing," and proposed that the full name should be The Provincetown Players: The Playwrights' Theater. Question . . . all in favor . . . the ayes have it . . . so ruled! Shying away from anything sounding so like Broadway as "director," they elected Cook "president" and delegated him, along with Reed, Eastman and Freddie Burt, to draw up a constitution.

"Be it resolved," Jack read the following night, "that it is the primary object of the Provincetown Players to encourage the writing of American plays of real artistic, literary and dramatic — as opposed to Broadway — merit. That such plays be considered without reference to their commercial value, since this theater is not to be run for pecuniary profit. . . ." It truly was to be a writers' theater. "The author," he went on, "shall produce the play without hindrance, according to his own ideas. The author, with the assistance of the President, must select his own cast, see to it that they are rehearsed, and generally direct his production."

Such was the sublime faith of these pioneers that they proposed to give a bill of new works every two weeks throughout a full season; yet they had but a handful of plays worth doing again, not to mention a treasury containing only eighty dollars. This sum was quadrupled when eight members contributed thirty dollars apiece, making a grand total of three hundred and twenty dollars "for leasing, equipping and floating a New York theater."

The morning Jig set out to find their new anchorage, he stood alone on the rear platform and called out to Susan as the train began moving, "Don't worry!" He also said something indistinguishable. As Susan raced after him, he cupped his hands around his mouth: "Write — another — play!"

His cry summed up the major problem. Throughout their existence the Players would be hungry for more *Cardiffs* and *Suppressed Desires*, but there was only one Glaspell, only one O'Neill.

22

Adventurers on Macdougal Street

EN route to New York, Eugene stopped off in New London for a few days to visit with his parents and tell them about his summer in Provincetown. He also took the opportunity to inform the Rippin girls that he had found a new love, a beauty named Louise Bryant – news that took on added interest when Louise herself turned up briefly. Her visit must have been upsetting to James and Ella, for she roamed the neighborhood barefoot, wearing some trousers Eugene had lent her, her long hair flowing free and unkempt. "After the way he'd raved about her," Jessica Rippin says, "I expected something special, but she was a mess, she looked like a Greenwich Village character who could stand a bath. . . ."

On returning to the city Eugene took a room at 38 Washington Square South, only a few doors from Jack and Louise's apartment, and finished writing "Tomorrow," the story about his good friend Byth and Jimmy the Priest's. Whatever his guilt feelings over his affair with Louise, they must have been intensified by Reed's generous efforts on his behalf; as one experienced in dealing with editors, Jack sent the story to his own magazine, the *Metropolitan*, where he was a prized contributor and the star correspondent.

"I've read O'Neill's story 'Tomorrow,'" managing editor Carl Hovey wrote Reed on October 11, "and agree with you that he can write. This thing is genuine and makes a real man live before you. . . . But my judgment is that it would not interest the majority of people who take things as they come. There is a lack of either plot or a situation with suspense enough to carry the reader beyond the first pages. . . . With all its fine sincerity and effectiveness, there is a kind of over-emphasis and sense of repetition which makes the story drag."

Jig meanwhile had found the group a new home – "139 Macdougal Street leased by the Provincetown Players!" he wrote Susan on September 19. "Hurray! Paid $50 first month's rent from Oct. 1st. So that much is settled!" Just south of Washington Square, 139 was an old brownstone three rooms deep, and the band of volunteers led by Cook, a grimy, determined-looking Jove, went to work tearing down partitions to make an auditorium of the first two rooms, with the third as the stage. Though more space was desperately needed for dressing rooms, office, and so forth, the rent covered only the parlor floor, with the cellar thrown in for storage of scenery. Fortunately a number of Players lived along the block, the Bror Nordfeldts at 135 – since Margaret Nordfeldt was secretary-treasurer, 135 became the office – the Lucian Carys at 133, the Neil Rebers at 137, Ira Remsen and Donald Corley at 131, and their apartments became the dressing rooms. All this first season the foot traffic on Macdougal Street would include – to the delight of neighborhood children – angels and ghosts, queens and fools, "Life" and "Death," as well as O'Neill's seamen and castaways, shuttling between apartments and playhouse.

The Players had organized themselves as a "theater club" to bypass fire and housing regulations that govern standard theaters, as well as to avoid the possibility of censorship, but they found that this did not grant them immunity from harassment, from the do's and don'ts of the authorities. The forerunner of what was to be a parade of official callers dropped by, a building inspector, with the disheartening ukase that the proscenium arch must have a steel girder. The rent had taken fifty dollars, the girder would cost two hundred, seventy dollars was left toward everything else – seats, lighting, stage, curtain, the works. Old friends of the Wharf Theater were hurriedly tapped for subscriptions to the first New York season, but this was only a temporary alleviative. To attract new patrons, a guaranteed audience that would finance the season, a circular was drawn up and sent to a selected list of one thousand names, offering ten bills of one-act plays for four dollars. Experienced hands in such matters warned the group not to expect a heavy response, but this time, happily, they were wrong. After a discouraging trickle, checks and money orders began to stream in; and best of all a visitor from the forward-looking New York Stage Society, a sympathetic lady, appeared one day at 139, asked some questions, and returned to her organization with a favorable report. The Society – forever after of sainted memory to the Players – decided to buy sixteen hundred dollars' worth of subscriptions for its members.

Determined to be a free, experimental theater, without regard for the Broadway pundits, the Players decided against inviting the critics to cover their work; and it was only after debating about and weighing each name that they even included four reviewers on their mailing list. All four, impressed apparently by the independence of this band of amateurs, sent in their checks. So many other people did likewise that before long the group, in pleasant danger of being oversubscribed, closed the rolls. Yet easing of the financial situation was no cure-all; problems and crises would remain the norm in the day-to-day existence of the theater. "Even knowing we did it," Susan Glaspell wrote in 1927, "I am disposed to say what we did that first year couldn't be done. . . . You have the police to reckon with in creating your own beauty in New York; you have small boys who kick tin cans down Macdougal Street while the curtain is up, people upstairs who put their garbage in front of the theater just as the audience is arriving, the phonograph next door. . . .

"When I arrived in New York . . . my first glimpse of Jig was standing amid shavings, lumber and bags of cement explaining the Provincetown Players to a policeman and an impersonal-looking person from the building department. 'Now here is Susan Glaspell,' he said, as if I had entered just for this. 'She is writing plays. And there is a young Irishman, O'Neill' — turning to the Irish policeman. We all went downstairs to have a drink and talk it over. Broadway. That wasn't what we wanted to do. In fact, we weren't doing this for money at all. . . . The person from the building department looked a little less impersonal as Jig talked to him of plays out of American life, quite as if this were one of the man's warm interests. The Irish policeman remained a friend to the last, more than once telling us what to do when we would have blundered.

"I have heard Jig explain the Provincetown Players to firemen, electricians, women tenement inspectors, garbage collectors, judges. Our Italian landlady, our real estate agent, our banker, were drawn into the adventure. . . ."

For all the alterations and greater expense, the new accommodations were little better than those on the wharf. Though the walls were a warm smoky gray and the proscenium arch cheery with blue, vermilion and gold, the seats were still bare planking, layered like circus seats, with a narrow strip of backing designed to give some support but which instead dug into one's shoulder blades; a capacity of one hundred and forty as compared with one hundred in Provincetown, and for a stage a playing area only ten and one-half by fourteen feet. The curtain, that veil to the mysteries, was of the cheapest cloth, almost transparent. Clearly, the audience would have to be forbearing.

In trying to satisfy one inspector, the Players aroused the official ire of another. They should have had permission before tearing down anything and installing a girder; everything would have to be restored to its original state — an ultimatum handed down only days before the scheduled opening. Not until the great day itself, Friday, November 3, were the Players sure of being allowed to raise the curtain and begin their new life. *Bound East for Cardiff*, the second work on the bill, again had Jig as the dying Yank, O'Neill as the brief-spoken Mate. No waves washed under and around the playhouse on Macdougal Street, no fog or smell of fresh salt air, but the audience was once more caught up and moved by the little saga of the *Glencairn* crew. A kind of snobbery sprang up around the play; those who had been in Provincetown told newcomers, "Oh, but you should have seen it by the sea, up on the Cape!"

Eugene Gladstone O'Neill, aged twenty-eight, had been launched auspiciously, if modestly, in the New York theatrical scene.

Although the four subscribing critics were not expected to attend in their professional capacity, Stephen Rathbun of the *Evening Sun* gave the Players their first review on November 13: "Oyez! Hear Ye! Make way there! New Players are come to town.

"Not that they're heralding their arrival with any such clash and clatter. Instead, they're here already, have been for a week, put on a new bill next Friday night, and will play all winter. No advance notice and billboards for them; instead, the world shall make a path to their door, 139 Macdougal Street.

"The world has made path enough already, so that instead of playing two nights a week as planned they're playing five. The first night they turned away ten limousines — just like that — and on the nights the Stage Society has taken they have to install a carriage caller — in Macdougal Street!"

After an account of the group's birth on Cape Cod, Rathbun found Louise's *The Game* "so amateurish that the less said about it the better." He commended Floyd Dell's *King Arthur's Socks* as "good fun" but reserved his chief praise for the O'Neill work. "The play," he summed up, "was real, subtly tense and avoided a dozen pitfalls that might have made it 'the regular thing.' "

In his private life Eugene had less cause to be happy about the way things were going. Though he was reluctant to face up to it, Louise wanted his love without losing Reed's, a precarious situation of her own making and true to her character; a side of her enjoyed taking risks and chancing disaster, a side that even welcomed ruin. She must have known from the start that O'Neill would not be content with a discreet, part-time affair but would want her entirely for himself. As for Reed, it seems almost incredible that he was unaware of what was going on; yet he was too much in love and too trusting to suspect that his girl, his beloved, could be unfaithful to him. Moreover, although the Players were alert to everything happening within their circle, Jack was so well liked that no one cared to disillusion him, particularly now that Louise was his wife. They had been married early this fall, in the midst of his rehearsing to play "Death" in her play, *The Game,* and his arranging to enter Johns Hopkins in Baltimore to have a troublesome kidney removed. Somehow Louise managed to counter O'Neill's complaints about her becoming Mrs. John Reed, but the situation left him prey to conflicting emotions, torn between hope that his rival might succumb from the surgery and self-recrimination that he should harbor such thoughts.

Around Macdougal Street, especially among the women, it was generally felt that the dark-haired beauty had weighed the two men and married the one she thought would be more famous, as well as the one who could do more for her own career. Louise did not mind others knowing that O'Neill was madly in love with her, but sought to give the impression that she was interested in him solely as a talented individual who needed straightening out. The daughter of an alcoholic father, one of the few in the group who never touched liquor, she was trying to get O'Neill to reform. While still in Provincetown she did succeed in persuading him to go on the wagon, but found it a continuous struggle to keep him there. "I hope," wrote Bobby Rogers, a friend of Reed's, "that Gene is still keeping straight in spite of the temptations of the big city, and that you have made a permanent cure of him."

Reed was in the Baltimore hospital for a month, starting in mid-November, and Louise wrote him almost daily, ending with such phrases as, "I love you with my whole heart . . . Goodnight, my dear, dear lover . . . Goodnight, my darling old husband." But during the period that she was writing him such endearments, she was at the peak of her affair with O'Neill; he moved in with her as soon as Reed had left for Johns Hopkins. Too clever to avoid references to O'Neill in her letters, what she said of him was generally patronizing: "The old faithfuls Nonny and Gene are taking me to dinner. I'll weep in the middle of it if they aren't careful. . . . Nonnie & Gene had dinner here. I'm so *tired* of their old faces and their old chatter."

"Nonnie" was Nani Bailey, a cousin of Margaret Steele's, who had provided the Players with a meeting place by opening a restaurant, dubbed the Samovar, around the corner on Fourth Street, next to the Hell Hole. At one of the first meetings John Francis of Provincetown was "unanimously elected an Honorary Active Member, as recognition of [his] sympathy and valuable services to the Provincetown Players from the beginning of their experiment." Most of the group's business was less pleasant, especially if it had to do with scripts. "Harry Kemp left with me the MS. of his *Prodigal Son*," Jig wrote Susan, visiting in Iowa. "It isn't good enough. Parrish took up my time for hours with his telepathy farce. It's no good. . . . We have hardly any good interesting plays and if we don't get them, we're going to peter out. You must write one. I wish I had time to write one."

While Reed was in Johns Hopkins, Louise herself required medical attention but was vague in writing him what was wrong with her. She complained of her "insides" being infected and said that Dr. Harry Lorber had advised her to enter a hospital, in the possibility that he might have to operate, but would do his best to forestall surgery. When Jack replied that he would return to New York, on a stretcher if necessary, to look after her, she wrote back immediately on December 12: "I'm just the same — a little better maybe. They have to wait and watch developments. There will be no operation. . . . Wednesday I'll look for you — be *sure* to let me know when you are coming. Surprise parties won't do for me — darling — not now. . . ."

Various things suggest that her "illness" was an abortion. In the spring Louise and Jack were to have their first falling-out, not over O'Neill but apparently over a onetime sex fling of Reed's to which she reacted so violently that her own guilt feelings must have been involved. Eager to get away, she left for Paris as a news correspondent; Jack, besides getting her the assignment, went into debt to finance the trip. Hardly was Louise aboard ship when she began to question her precipitous behavior. "Please believe me, Jack," she wrote, "I'm going to try like the devil to pull myself together over there and come back able to act like a reasonable human being. I know I'm probably all wrong about everything. I know the only reason I act so crazy is because it hurts so much, that I get quite insane, that's all. . . . If this thing ever happens again *don't don't* get despondent. Maybe I'll understand better when I get back."

In reply, after blaming himself for the quarrel, Jack told her of taking an old friend, ill and threatening suicide, to see Dr. Lorber, and of his using the opportunity to discuss their own personal affairs. "Sweetheart, I do hope you're going to get all over your awful feelings by the time you come back. I had a long talk with Lorber about you, which I'll tell you sometime. Think about you and me a good deal, will you? It is not worth keeping going if you love someone else better." But he carefully avoided any reference to O'Neill.

Shaken by the thought of losing him, Louise wrote back: "Now, honey, dearest, I am feeling *very calm* as I write this. Nothing matters so much as my love for you — I don't know what you have said to Lorber or he has said to you — I don't love any one *else*. I'm *dead sure* of that. I just love you."

The Villagers in times of trouble were always turning to Harry Lorber, a sympathetic young Jewish doctor from the lower East Side, who looked on them as bright but irresponsible children who needed protection from themselves. When Mabel Dodge had the peyote party in her apartment, the one in which Terry Carlin participated, a young girl turned wildly irrational, bringing the whole thing to a panicky end. "We must call Harry Lorber," Hutch Hapgood said. "He is discreet, he won't talk." Apparently Louise had felt the same way in turning to Harry, but perhaps more conclusive evidence as to her illness may be found in *Strange Interlude*. When Nina Leeds is undergoing a period of nerves and uncertain health, she has her husband believing that "some woman's sickness" is responsible; actually, without his knowledge, she has had an abortion.

Reed's discharge from Johns Hopkins in mid-December meant the end of Eugene's cozy living arrangement. "O'Neill isn't seeing Louise now," Jig on December 23 wrote Susan, still in Iowa, "and is nearing the snapping point of suspense and tension. Jack Reed seems pretty well. Saw him four or five days ago at the Harvard Club. . . . O'Neill's nervous tension is a thing that I feel instantly when I see him. I mean that I instantly catch it from him — feel it myself in myself. Sort of anxiety complex. He likes to be with me since he discovered that I feel what he feels. But it isn't good for me. . . ." Shortly before hearing from her husband Susan wrote Louise, "Jig is so busy that I have had almost no news. There are things I am so anxious to know — most of all about you and Jack. . . ."

Somehow, in spite of the scarcity of worthwhile scripts, in spite of vendettas among the Players ("Nord is poisonous," Jig told Susan), in spite of the chronic problem of maintaining the interest, if not enthusiasm, of unpaid actors, carpenters and stagehands, the life of the little theater went on. "There were those," Donald Corley said, "who came to the playhouse to escape discontent, to find refuge from isolation, and to bring, boldly or timidly, their offerings. . . . A stitch was apt to be taken in a dress or a scene or a tree — two minutes before curtain on opening night."

James O'Neill, prepared to find the whole enterprise hopelessly amateurish, saw *Bound East for Cardiff* and came away impressed, as well as pleased that everyone seemed to have high hopes for his son. "Yes, yes," he said, in answer to several of the Players, trying to conceal his feelings of pride, "I think the boy has something in him."

His interest now aroused by the activities on Macdougal Street, James attended rehearsals of his son's next production, *Before Breakfast,* to lend the weight of his many years' experience. Poor James! He was better intentioned than advised. As Helen Deutsch and Stella Hanau recount in *The Provincetown,* a flavorsome history of the theater: "Father and son disagreed on every point. O'Neill Senior tried to instill in Mary Pyne [who played the shrewish wife] some of the histrionic technique which the Players had no wish to revive, while O'Neill Junior stalked up and down, muttering his displeasure." Eugene later took exception to the account, calling it "exaggerated" and contending that his ⸱father made some suggestions "I didn't agree with, but also some I thought were fine." His version of what happened can be viewed, however, with some skepticism, since by that time his feeling toward his father had softened.

William Carlos Williams, who appeared in one or two things at the Provincetown, recalls that Mr. O'Neill also took part in the staging of *Fog,* from the *Thirst* volume. Williams, hanging around for rehearsals of another work, was "impressed there in the dark and empty theater by what was going on before me. The shouts of the fog-bounders was full of the tension which such a scene would invoke in the hands of a master. . . . But of equal interest was the presence of an older man, the author's father. We didn't know whether to laugh or keep a straight face when informed that he was famous for acting the part of *Monte Cristo,* but we had to acknowledge that the man had made a success of the role.

"During the rehearsal the father would often interrupt the course of the play and when he did the son would be closely attentive; God knows he had to be because the father made no bones about it but let himself be heard above the clatter that was supposed to be going on during the scene. . . . [O'Neill] would leave the theater still talking with his father."

Perhaps relations between the two were best summed up by Hutch Hapgood; he felt that "in O'Neill's eyes his father appeared with all imperfections on his head, yet there was something quite close between them."

Even though the Players had no press agent, they were garnering their share of publicity. Under the headline, No Mark of "Sacred Cod" on Provincetown Players, a reporter of the New York *Herald* gave on December 3, 1916, a tongue-in-cheek account of the new group: "Their programs are of an uncontrolled shade of yellow, and the booklets that contain their plays are bound in vitriol blue and Paris green. . . . The narrow auditorium has wooden benches, upon which junior members of the art and literary coteries of the 'Washington Square Back' section

*Louise Bryant in the Russian-style dress she favored after visiting
Russia at the time of the Bolshevik Revolution*

John Reed in 1919

Louise Bryant

drape themselves in bohemian attitudes carefully copied from illustrations of Greenwich Village stories which they read in magazines when they were back in Peoria, Ill., or Hackensack, N.J., before they came to the seething city. . . . Monday night is the real Greenwich Village night at the Provincetown Players' Theater . . . on other nights outsiders like the Stage Society's members come in evening suits and top hats and all that swank. . . ."

The "booklets" referred to in the article are the first, second and third series of *The Provincetown Plays*, paper-bound volumes published by Frank Shay, one of the Players and a former aide of the Boni brothers; he had taken over their bookshop when they moved on to more ambitious ventures. *Bound East for Cardiff* is in the first series, *Before Breakfast* in the third. At fifty cents apiece, the pamphlets found scarcely any buyers (today they are collectors' items), but they brought the Provincetowners their first substantial notice from the press.

"The plays," said N. P. Dawson in the *Globe*, "are almost uniformly interesting, at least to read. There is nothing amateur about their literary qualities. And far from being foreign scum, they are, of course, all strictly home-made. In fact, so far as this particular 'little theatre' group goes, the members seem not only to write their own plays but to applaud them as well. They are the Sinn Feiners ('ourselves') of the theatrical world."

In a thoughtful long report in the *Tribune* Heywood Broun said: "As we understand it, an experiment is something which turns cinders into gold dust or explodes with a fearful crash and odor. In this sense the Provincetown Players have established a most efficient experimental theater. Some of the explosions can be heard even when the plays are read miles away from Macdougal Street. There is only a little gold dust, but then there never is much gold dust." After hailing Susan Glaspell for *Trifles* and *Suppressed Desires*, he said of *Bound East*: "Here is a play which owes more to the creation of mood and atmosphere than to any fundamentally interesting idea or sudden twist of plot. . . . Eugene O'Neill has written several short plays about the sea . . . he strikes a rich vein, the old Kipling vein."

Since the Provincetowners could not afford to pay royalties, Eugene was no better off financially than before, especially now that he was drinking again. Forty-six dollars in arrears on rent, he left 38 Washington Square — the landlady kept a trunk of his clothes and books — and took refuge with friends between periods of staying at the Garden Hotel. For a few weeks he shared a room with Louis Holladay and Barney Gallant, a short chap with thick eyebrows, thick black hair, and a great hunger to be Somebody. On arriving from Russia he had worked all hours for a shopkeeper uncle in St. Louis, who had promised to send him to Harvard; when Barney realized that the prospect would never materialize he drifted to New York, to the Village.

"Our room," he recalls, "was so close to a stable that we could hear the horses neighing and smell the place. Even among the three of us we had a hell of a time getting up the rent of three dollars a week. It was a large cheerless room with an iron double bed, and the first ones home would take the bed, leaving a blanket and pillow on the floor for the latecomer. We used to search one another's pockets for a nickel or dime if we were broke — we lived mostly on the free lunch in saloons. One morning I went through Louis's pockets, nothing there, but in Gene's I found a quarter and headed for Cunningham and O'Keefe's at 14th and Fourth Avenue — they were famous for their spread. After getting a nickel beer, I helped myself to a heaping plate of lamb stew. The bartender was glaring at me as I finished, so I ordered another beer before I took a big hunk of cheese.

"On the way back I slipped my hand into a pocket, but the change was gone, and digging around I found a small hole. . . . I was feeling pretty low when I faced Gene and Louis. 'Got any money left?' Gene said, as though talking of quite a sum. When I told him no, he said, 'Spent it all!' After I explained what happened, he was silent a few moments, then asked what they had for lunch that day. 'Irish lamb stew,' I said. 'I love Irish lamb stew,' he said mournfully, while Holladay laughed."

Eugene often complained that his parents did not allow him to lead his own life, but so far as his roommates could see the only restraint on him was lack of funds. "He was in no sense a Village 'character,' " Barney says. "He had little contact with the intellectuals and bohemians unless they happened to belong to the Provincetown Players." Though generally sparing of words, sometimes remaining silent for hours, he occasionally opened up about life at sea, his experiences in Buenos Aires, and would talk late into the night. "I think," Gallant said, "he was already shaping his plays, he was like a painter trying to fix a scene in his mind. He would watch us closely, gauging the effect his stories were having on us — we were, you might say, the audience." Others in the Village received the same impression, that O'Neill reminisced not so much for the pleasure it gave him as from an artist's instinct for reworking the past; in short, his yarn-spinning was a preliminary phase in his playwriting.

The Provincetown Players had started well with their first two programs, thanks to *Cardiff* on one and *Suppressed Desires* on the other, but with the third bill, which included *Before Breakfast*, they entered a slump; the fourth, fifth and sixth programs were also mediocre. "We lacked 'strong' plays," Edna Kenton once said. "Not only that, but we were growing weary too soon — the production of three one-act plays every two weeks was too much to have been undertaken by any amateur group. . . . We were beginning to see what we might have seen sooner, that we were expecting too much of our playwrights when we counted on them not only to write under pressure but to cast and direct. . . . Those were the days of the first frayed nerves, the days of rigidly private rehearsals closed even to active members, the days whose nights were mostly spent in reconciliation with enemies. The great good plays — the native dramas for the waiting native stage — did not somehow get written."

While the Provincetowners themselves were starting to feel discouraged, they impressed outsiders as a more or less worthy part of a growing movement in New York. The Washington Square Players, after two seasons at the Bandbox, had moved to the larger Comedy Theater in the Broadway area; the Neighborhood Playhouse on the lower East Side was in its second year of works by such men as Shaw, Chekhov and Dunsany; and a group headed by actor Frank Conroy announced plans for a new intimate playhouse in Sheridan Square, to be called the Greenwich Village Theater. Some of the old-time Broadway managers, especially David Belasco of the clerical collar and the Great Man pose, resented all the attention being paid to these bands of amateurs and semiprofessionals.

DAVID BELASCO SEES A MENACE TO TRUE ART OF THE STAGE IN TOY PLAYHOUSES AND LITTLE REPERTORY THEATRES, ran the headline of a lengthy story on January 7, 1917, in the New York *Herald*. "Theaters and acting organizations devoted to false ideals are not new," the manager fumed, "but never until this season have they been so vicious, vulgar and degrading. . . . I know whereof I speak, because I have attended every one of these places devoted to the so-called 'new art,' whose clumsy and amateurish directors have decided to be 'different.' . . .

"They call it 'new art,' whatever they mean by that. In the first place, art could not be new. It is as old as life itself. . . . This so-called new art of the theater is but a flash in the pan of inexperience. It is the cubism of the theater — the wail of the incompetent and the degenerate. As cubism became the asylum of those pretenders in art who could not draw and had no conception of composition in painting, so 'new art of the theater' is the haven of those who lack experience and knowledge of the drama. . . ."

In the midst of piling sarcasm atop invective, the old maestro kept reversing himself: "Not, mind you, that these amateur dramatic organizations are to be taken at all seriously by the legitimate stage producer, or that there is any fear of their encroachment upon the legitimate theater. . . . My opposition to this cult has made for me many enemies among the younger and inexperienced writers of things pertaining to the drama and the theater, but I must take this stand more firmly than ever and endeavor to protect our drama, the stage and the legitimate theater of America from those who would make a freak of it."

Drawing himself up to his full sorrowing dignity (he was a short, portly man), he concluded, "O Art, Art, how many freakish things are committed in thy name!"

Almost to the end of the season on Macdougal Street every other bill included an O'Neill work, though only *Bound East for Cardiff* made much of an impression; to maintain his quota, Eugene had to dust off two of his fledgling efforts, *Fog* and *The Sniper*. He had nothing new to submit to the Players because he found it difficult to write in the city — too many distractions, too many bar friends inviting him to have a drink; also, his equivocal, tantalizing relationship with Louise left him in no mood for concentrated effort.

After Reed's return from Baltimore he and Louise became less active around the playhouse, as he was scheduled to go to China early in 1917, with her accompanying him. It was three years now since he had first made a name for himself with his accounts of the civil warfare in Mexico. Rudyard Kipling had said that they "made me see Mexico." Walter Lippmann, one of Jack's classmates at Harvard, had written him of the same dispatches: "You have perfect eyes, and your power of telling leaves nothing to be desired. . . . If all history had been reported as you are doing this, Lord! I say that with Jack Reed reporting begins." The logical field of operations for Reed was the European war, rather than China, but he resisted such an assignment, having been depressed and angered by what he had seen in two prolonged visits to the embattled Continent. "Do not be deceived," he wrote after his first visit, "by talk about democracy and liberty. This is not a crusade against militarism but a scramble for spoils." Increasingly worried about the pro-Allied propaganda that was starting to engulf and sway the American people, he kept telling friends and, to the great detriment of his career, insisting in his writings that "it is not our war."

The prospect of Louise leaving shortly for a distant part of the world kept Eugene in a state of frustration and tension. As events turned out, the Reeds never went to China, but this made no difference in their weakening ties with the playhouse; Jack had bought a house in Croton-on-Hudson and they spent little time around the Village. Trying to get over his love for Louise, Eugene made halfhearted efforts to become involved with other girls, among them a pretty blonde named Betty Collins. They first met in the back room of the Hell Hole, brought together by Harold DePolo, who was having an affair with her roommate, a poker-playing beauty from Cuba. Over rounds of drinks the foursome fell to talking of books, and O'Neill seemed surprised that Betty had never read *Thus Spake Zarathustra*. "Thou goest to women?" he quoted at one point. "Do not forget thy whip!"

"He wasn't joking," Miss Collins recalls, "at least he had a serious expression when he said it. I could have gone for him — my God, what eyes he had! — but he was in love with Louise Bryant, everybody knew it. I saw Gene a few times after that and he wanted me to go to bed with him. I wouldn't, though, I knew I would just be a convenience for him. Some time later I ran into him again and he said, 'Well, Betty, I'm no longer in love, what about it?' 'But now I am, Gene,' I told him, so I never did sleep with him. Wonder what it would have been like. . . . I'm a little sorry now [said with a shrug and a smile] I didn't."

Around the first of the year James O'Neill became too busy with his own career to take an active interest in his son's. Long resigned to the thought that his acting days were over, James, who was seventy, appeared to shed years as he began rehearsing for *The Wanderer*, based on the parable of the Prodigal Son. To the old actor, who had long been worried about a rebellious son who wandered off to sea and hung around the most unsavory places, the role of the Jewish patriarch Jesse must have seemed like type casting. The production was being masterminded by his old associate in San Francisco, David Belasco.

Installed in the large Manhattan Opera House, *The Wanderer* itself was big, it was vulgar, it was splendiferous, it had, in short, all the sure-fire elements for success. "Makes as wide an appeal as *Ben Hur*," said Stephen Rathbun in the *Evening Sun*. "A lavish production, a colossal pageant, it will please millions," said Alexander Woollcott in the *New York Times*. But it was the reviewer for *Life* magazine who spotted the chief rhinestone in the flashy display: "The spectacular second act makes up for all the scriptural theeing and thouing in the other two. The establishment of Madame Nadina was evidently located in the red-light district of Jerusalem, and gives one a new impression of just what went on in that great Jewish metropolis."

Happy at being in a success and winning praise from a new generation of critics, James O'Neill was as myopic about the shortcomings of the new biblical exhibit as he had once been about Salmi Morse's *The Passion*.

"I accepted the role instantly," he told a reporter for the *Sun*. "I would not have returned to the stage in any other kind of play, because when one has acted on the legitimate for fifty years as I have, with such great actors as Edwin Booth and Edwin Forrest, it is impossible to be resigned to the commonplaces of the modern style of play."

Now that it was behind him, he even had a good word for his perennial vehicle: "I venture to predict that if *Monte Cristo* had never been seen here and was produced tomorrow it would have a record-breaking run on Broadway. You cannot get away from the appeal of human nature in such plays as this any more than you can dodge the appeal in *The Wanderer*. These plays are eternally human, for they deal in love, heroism, filial devotion, the emotions, ideals and passions that go to make up our lives today. . . ."

Eugene of course took a dim view of the opus at the opera house; yet it probably was *The Wanderer*, as well as the earlier *Joseph and His Brethren*, that planted the idea in him of using the Scriptures in several of his works. But where the Broadway Talmudists exploited their source material with splash, sentimentality and sex, he would invest his borrowings with a sardonic flavor all his own. In *The Rope*, for instance, utilizing the theme of the Prodigal Son, he has Luke Bentley return from his wanderings not contrite but intent on robbing his father, a half-senile miser. Though the latter seems overjoyed at his reappearance, he keeps urging him to hang himself on a rope that has been dangling in the barn for years, awaiting the prodigal's return. Actually, in spite of all early indications, the embittered old leprechaun loves his son — at the hidden end of the rope is a bag of gold coins for him. A parallel can be found between this aspect of the play and the author's relations with his own father: after complaining to friends for years about James being a skinflint, Eugene would one day picture him as having been indulgent and generous.

Apparently *The Rope* was inspired not only by *The Wanderer* but by one of the most famous of all short stories, *A Christmas Carol*. Around the time that Mr. O'Neill was appearing in the show at the opera house he was also slated to play Scrooge in a talking picture condensation of the Dickens tale; a recording of dialogue was to accompany the twenty-minute film. While the production never materialized, because of technical and other problems, the playwright son evidently had the Dickens classic in mind when he wrote his one-acter: both Scrooge and old Abraham Bentley after initially appearing as heartless misers are shown in a sympathetic light.

Regardless of its models, though, *The Rope* is entirely O'Neill's; raw, bitter, an unvarnished account of some vengeful humans. In addition to

[375]

being his most powerful short work, it foreshadowed *Desire Under the Elms*. Both plays tell of harsh lives rooted in the stony land, of embattled families in which children are pitted against the father for ownership of the farm, as well as in conflict with one another; and, in both, the father, after overworking one wife into an early grave, marries another who proves unfaithful to him. Further, old Bentley, who constantly quotes the Bible in abusing his family, prefigures one of the playwright's most vital creations — Ephraim Cabot, the hickory-tough old farmer of *Desire* who likewise invokes the Scriptures in justifying himself. "God's hard," he says repeatedly, "an' lonesome!"

Save when his own plays were involved or major questions of policy arose, O'Neill took little interest in the running activities of the playhouse — the reading sessions when the scripts were winnowed, the recruitment and casting of actors, the productions of other playwrights. Ill at ease around most people and with no capacity for small talk, he allowed few Provincetowners to get close to him. By now he looked on Jig and Susan as old friends; he was fond of Harry Kemp's wife, Mary Pyne, a gentle, otherworldly soul who, cast against type, had played the harpy in *Before Breakfast*; he enjoyed drinking with Frank Shay, a voluble redhead who was constantly ransacking Irish history to support his thesis that the O'Shays were of a more distinguished ancestry than the O'Neills. But Eugene's relationship — or, rather, lack thereof — with William Carlos Williams was more characteristic; in all the times the playwright and the poet saw one another around the theater, they never exchanged a word.

Among those Eugene met this winter was Saxe Commins, a medical student with a feeling for literature whose play, *The Obituary*, was given on the Provincetowners' fourth bill. As a quiet bookish lad growing up in Rochester he had suffered from the reflected notoriety of being Emma Goldman's nephew, later finding a more compatible milieu among the rebels and advanced thinkers of the Village. He became interested in the Macdougal Street group through his sister Stella, a tall, handsome woman who was married to actor Teddy Ballantine. Forced by lack of funds to switch from medical to dental studies, Commins was to go on to develop a thriving practice in Rochester, but making money was never his primary goal in life. In a display of character and moral courage, he abandoned his profession to begin obscurely as an editor in the book-publishing field. It was to prove a fortunate move for both himself and his authors, as he would prove one of the finest of editors, serving O'Neill and, among others, William Faulkner with great taste and complete devotion. Since both he and O'Neill were exceedingly shy, they were slow in getting to know one another but gradually became the closest of friends. O'Neill in fact would trust Saxe Commins as no other, while to Saxe their friendship would be a major source of gratification in his life — and, ultimately, a cause of major unhappiness.

The Provincetowners were in a way a lucky group. On the Cape, just as they were starting to feel desperate about one of their bills, O'Neill walked down the gangplank of the Boston steamer with *Bound East for Cardiff* in his luggage; now, when they were floundering not only from a shortage of good scripts but from a lack of competent directors, Nina Moise appeared on the scene. A product of "mid-Victorian parents" and private schools in Connecticut, Nina, who had both acted in and directed stock companies, was a pleasant-looking young woman with capable shoulders. A friend, suggesting she get in touch with the Macdougal Street group, advised her, "For God's sake, don't tell them you want to act — they all want to get out there and act." After corresponding with Cook, she met him at the Samovar and, as Nina recalls, "he practically grabbed me when I told him I was a director. The next day I went over to the theater and began making suggestions. They didn't know anything about blocking, staging, any of the fundamentals; they were bumping into themselves and stepping on one another's toes. My God, the stage was only fourteen feet!"

Though her knowledge and experience were as yet limited, Miss Moise seemed to the Provincetowners very knowing. "Don't you think," she told an actor, "that if instead of crossing so, you crossed *so*, the effect would be better?" And to another: "If you start moving on that line, you will find, etc., etc." Both Susan Glaspell and Neith Boyce, who were in the theater that day, made the newcomer feel welcome by urging her to stage their next productions. Without their knowing it the Players had weathered the worst when Nina turned up in January. In the process of putting on good plays and bad they had developed some capable actors — Ida Rauh, who specialized in dramatic parts and would become known as "the Duse of Macdougal Street"; Mary Pyne, Justus Sheffield, a lawyer by day; Susan, who turned out to have a natural gift for the stage; Hutch Collins, Eugene's old friend from New London, who had settled in New York. And now they had a director who made them seem, if not quite professional, at least less amateurish. Shortly after Nina began to take over, several of the group's friendly rivals from the Washington Square Players, namely Phil Moeller and Lawrence Langner, attended a performance and asked in effect, "What's happened down here?"

The seventh bill, with Nina in complete charge, was known as the "war bill," for it consisted of *The Sniper*, the antiwar play Eugene had written at Harvard, and works by other authors expressing similar sentiments. If the Players failed to enhance their reputation with this program, they did manage to reverse the decline into which they had been settling, and with renewed spirit entered the home stretch of their first year in the city. Thinking ahead to next season and the eternal problem of finding enough one-acters worth staging, they began talking about the advisability of putting on full-length works. At a busy meeting February 21 in Ida Rauh's apartment, Nina was named chairman of the producing committee, Edna Kenton and Ida were elected to the executive committee, to fill the gaps left by Jack's and Louise's resignations, and Hutch Collins was admitted as an active member. Concluding the evening, Eugene outlined the first two acts and read the other two of "The Personal Equation" his long play for Baker's course. Since it was never produced by the Provincetowners, the response to his reading must have been negative.

Nina's first impression of O'Neill was unfavorable, chiefly because he made no effort to be friendly. "For a long time I disliked him," she recalls. "I couldn't understand how any girl could be attracted to him — he was so withdrawn and morose — but when Gene decided he wanted me to like him, I did. When he smiled, a strange thing happened; it was like the sun coming through the clouds. But the lower part of his face was weak, sensual, perhaps cruel. He had the eyes of a dreamer and the mouth of a sensualist. The lower part of his face said one thing and the upper part another. It's the eyes, though, I'll always remember — they went in deep, too deep, you could drown in them."

Tormented by the relationship with Louise — he had seen little of her since the Reeds took the house in Croton — Eugene spent most of his time around the Hell Hole, drinking and brooding; occasionally he wandered down to Jimmy the Priest's, always alone, as though on some kind of pilgrimage. Adding to his sense of frustration, he had in mind some well-formed ideas for plays, chiefly about the crew of the S.S. *Glencairn,* but was too edgy to lock himself in, away from all distractions, and develop them on paper. He kept telling Harold DePolo, among others, that he could not stop drinking and get down to work so long as he remained in the city. "Maybe," he would say longingly, "if I could get back to Provincetown. . . ."

From the time he first saw it O'Neill had felt at home in the little fishing village at the tip of the Cape, almost encircled by bay and open sea; but he was reluctant to return alone, particularly at such a bleak time as March, and repeatedly urged DePolo to go with him. Finally Harold, after making his peace with his wife — the DePolos had two small children — felt free to accompany his friend.

23

❀

Maturing Playwright

O'NEILL was about to take a considerable step forward in his writing, an advance not so much over *Bound East for Cardiff* as over all his other efforts. Where *Cardiff* had been an isolated phenomenon, a remarkable achievement for a novice, his new works would prove that the first of the *Glencairn* series was far from a fluke. While it is impossible to identify all the operative factors behind his developing skill, it is possible to isolate at least one major factor. Like so many before him, he found that a playwright has no better instruction than a performance, than seeing his scripts animated and defined on a stage; whether the performance is better or worse than his script deserves, whether the audience accepts or rejects it, the author can learn from production as from nothing else about his craft, his art, about the shape and quality of his particular talent.

Four of O'Neill's works had now been performed, and only one had stood up under the searching eye of production, yet all four had shown himself to himself, had given him something to mull over, consciously and unconsciously. While watching his plays materialize on the pathetically cramped stage at 139 Macdougal, even while drinking and drifting around the Village, now tormented, now exhilarated by his affair with Louise, he had been ripening as a playwright.

In Provincetown, where he and DePolo settled at the New Central Hotel, Eugene established a regimen of writing and, to recover from months of irregular living, cross-country walks. Despite the sharpness of March, the two went tramping for hours at a time, O'Neill silent for the most part, whether absorbed in the severe beauty of the scene — gray sky, leaden sea, dun-colored sand dunes — or lost in thought over some troublesome pages. Unlike the playwright, DePolo spent little time brooding over his work; a kind of writing machine, so prolific he had to use several pen names, he could quickly grind out love stories, animal stories, adventure yarns, whatever the market demanded. In the evenings Eugene would revise his day's output or read, while Harold, ever eager for some "action," would rustle up a poker game at the Atlantic House, the other and livelier hotel in town.

Some days after their arrival they found themselves costarring in a comedy of errors that began as melodrama. While having lunch on March 28 they were approached by a grim-faced officer who said they were under arrest, and when Harold asked, "What for?" the other replied, "You know what for!" Figuring that small-town morality was at the bottom of it, that poker games were forbidden, Harold tried to tell the man that his friend was innocent, that he never played cards. When the man brushed this aside and still refused to divulge the charges, DePolo and O'Neill demanded to see his warrant. "This is my warrant," said Constable Reuben O. Kelley, and flourished a pistol.

The word spread fast. Minutes later, as the pair were being marched to the lockup in the basement of the Town Hall, some of the crowd that seemed to have sprung up from nowhere called out, "Kill 'em, kill the German spies!" The bewildered writers, who at last had some idea of why they had been arrested, were booked on "vagrancy" charges and held incommunicado in separate cells as an investigation got under way. Provincetown, like the rest of America, was feeling the effect of the war in Europe; the fear of saboteurs and other undercover agents of the Kaiser, keeping pace with the rising war fever in the nation, had finally reached the remote fishing village.

During the first year or two of the war the prevailing mood in America had been neutralist, despite an underswell of pro-Allied sentiment inspired chiefly by the "rape" of little Belgium. President Wilson, even after the sinking of the *Lusitania,* declared that we were "too proud to fight"; and Tin Pan Alley, echoing his stand, churned out such numbers as "Our Hats Off to You, Mr. Wilson" and "I Didn't Raise My Boy to Be a Soldier." When he ran for re-election in 1916 his supporters came up with the slogan, "He kept us out of war," but the spirit of the times soon shifted; the word now was "Preparedness!" Early this year (1917) Germany announced it was embarking on "unrestricted" submarine warfare, Washington shortly broke off diplomatic relations, and the Broadway tunesmiths, ever alert to the popular drift, were now chanting, "For Your Country and My Country," "Liberty Bell, It's Time to Ring Again" and "America Needs You Like a Mother — Would You Turn Your Mother Down?" Even pacifists became jingoists, the sober-minded frightened and angry, as a growing number of munition plants were destroyed by fires and explosions of mysterious origin, as U-boats began sinking unarmed American merchant ships.

It was an inopportune time for two strangers to appear in Province-town, strategically located at the end of the Cape, especially after personnel at the U.S. radio station in adjacent North Truro were "an-noyed and rendered suspicious by the action of prowlers." Constable Kelley, on being notified of the trespassers, did not have far to look for suspects. Those two at the New Central — what were they doing here out of season, why were they always wandering around the dunes and in this kind of weather? They couldn't be up to any good; he had better act before they slipped away.

The arrest sent shock waves of rumor through the village: the two were armed, they had drawn guns on the constable, they not only had plans of Provincetown Harbor and the radio station but wireless equip-ment for communicating with the U-boats. Meanwhile, as the stories ballooned, the police sent word to Secret Service authorities in Boston, who immediately dispatched agent Fred Weyand to the scene. After a weary seven-hour trip during which his car suffered two punctured tires, Weyand arrived to grill the prisoners. It was not long before he was convinced of their innocence; Eugene, besides identifying himself as the son of James O'Neill, probably referred him to John Francis, whom everyone in town knew and respected. In court the following morning the charges were thrown out, the two set free.

One of the plays O'Neill wrote around this time, *In the Zone*, is set in the fall of 1915 and finds the crew of the *Glencairn* apprehensive and jumpy as the British freighter wallows into the "war zone," waters in which U-boats are known to be lurking. The men come to suspect Smitty the Duke, one of their shipmates, of being a German agent after he has been espied secreting a small black box under his mattress. Does it contain a bomb for blowing up the ship, the men wonder, or equipment for signaling to the enemy? They finally force a showdown, with the con-tents of the box exposed, that leaves Smitty humiliated and themselves shamefaced at having inadvertently pried into his past. Since Smitty, like O'Neill, was suspected of being a spy or saboteur, it is generally assumed that *In the Zone* was inspired by the playwright's brush with the con-stabulary; according to Harold DePolo, though, *Zone* was written before their arrest.

O'Neill probably got his basic idea from a lengthy story in the New London *Telegraph* when he was on its staff, a time when he was reading the paper with special care. Under a headline on September 19, 1912 (Box Mystery/ Alarms Many/ Until Solved), the story told of a small black box that had been left for safekeeping with a local Italian shopkeeper. The latter began to fear that the dreaded Black Hand gang might have something to do with it, especially after a stranger dropped by to demand the box, and he notified the police; but the box turned out to contain only some men's clothing, and the seemingly mysterious incident to have an innocent explanation.

Shaken at being in the limelight and made to feel like a pariah, it was with more than ordinary pleasure that O'Neill received a fat envelope in the mails several days after his arrest — his short story "Tomorrow," with a covering letter. "Your story is a fine document," Waldo Frank of the *Seven Arts* magazine wrote on March 30, 1917, "and I believe that we shall buy it provided you can correct what seemed to us a few minor imperfections. . . . When you have made the changes will you send the manuscript back to us so that we can ship you a check for $50."

This was the first decent sum O'Neill had ever earned from his writings, for Frank wrote again on April 2, after getting the revised script: "You have done mighty well with this story and we are taking it." [Years later its author told Mark Van Doren, "I thought it was pretty devastating stuff at the time, and so evidently did (the editors), although I doubt if they were as overwhelmed by its hideous beauty as I was."]

"In your last letter you mentioned some plays. I hope you will send them. We are anxious for plays, and we never like to stop with one contribution from a new author."

Founded a year before in the sublime (and naïve) hope that "artists and critics could dominate America," the *Seven Arts* had at its helm James Oppenheim and Waldo Frank, abetted by Van Wyck Brooks, Louis Untermeyer and Randolph Bourne. "It is our faith," said the magazine's initial call to arms, "that we are living in the first days of a renascent period, a time which means for America the coming of that national self-consciousness which is the beginning of greatness. . . . What we ask of the writer is simply self-expression without regard to current magazine standards."

Besides buying "Tomorrow" — it was in the June 1917 issue, the only O'Neill story ever published — the magazine paid another fifty dollars for *In the Zone*. "The play is recommended," Frank wrote him on May 17, "by its real color. You seem to be a true romanticist — although how you manage it in these latter days is beyond me. Most romantic writing today is conventional and dead. Yours is alive, though, and that's the wonder of it." Before the play could appear, however, the magazine folded, a casualty of its own integrity and America's entry into the war; while almost everyone else was marching to the drums of chauvinism, the

Seven Arts stood apart, a skeptic in the reviewing stand. Its days were numbered — it lasted only a year — after it published Bourne's iconoclastic "The War and the Intellectuals" and Jack Reed's "This Unpopular War," a piece that nearly landed the editors in jail.

In the midst of working on plays and being arrested Eugene had not forgotten Louise; hardly a day passed without his writing her — he had a mounted photograph of her in his hotel room — and without his hearing from her. What Louise wrote him can only be surmised, but one man's impression of his letters to her is available. Not long after Louise's marriage in the early 1920s to William C. Bullitt, she handed him a thick packet of letters to read, afterward feeding them into the fireplace.

"If the letters were sincere, and they sounded so," Mr. Bullitt once said, "O'Neill was certainly at one time violently in love with her. His letters to Louise were wails of despairing, unrequited love. Louise burned them — without sign of emotion — merely because she believed that the private emotions of individuals were not the concern of anyone else.

"So far as I know, Louise was never in love with O'Neill. She thought he had talent, felt sorry for him, and tried to help him. She described to me his frequent fits of drunkenness and his suicidal inclinations. On more than one occasion she helped literally to pick him out of the gutter."

Excepting *In the Zone*, which evidently was first, it is unknown in what order O'Neill wrote three other plays in this productive period, but there is no question as to his favorite. "That was my first real break with theatrical traditions," he once said of *The Moon of the Caribbees*, and another time called it "my pet play of all my one-acters." Virtually without story, it tells of a languorous night as the *Glencairn* lies anchored off an island in the West Indies, the plaintive sound of native chants drifting in from shore. Bumboat women come aboard with rum hidden under their loads of fruit, the men pair off with them for hasty lovemaking, a donnybrook erupts among the now drunken seamen, the women are ordered ashore by the first mate, peace settles again over the ship as Smitty the Duke, sitting on the side lines, muses over his past and the night's happenings.

Full of sensuous color, the most lyrical and evocative of his *Glencairn* cycle, *The Moon* is an engaging vignette, but O'Neill found in it more than it seems to contain. He valued it at the particular expense of *In the Zone*, which he came to downgrade, probably because it proved his most successful one-acter. "When *everybody* likes something," he once said, with his lifelong suspicion of popularity, "watch out!"

In 1919 he told Barrett H. Clark: "I consider *In the Zone* a conventional construction of the theater as it is . . . and *The Moon* an attempt to achieve a higher plane of bigger, finer values. . . . Smitty in the stuffy, grease-paint atmosphere of *In the Zone* is magnified into a hero who attracts our sentimental sympathy. In *The Moon*, posed against a background of that beauty, sad because it is eternal, which is one of the revealing moods of the sea's truth, his silhouetted gestures of self-pity are reduced to their proper insignificance. . . . Perhaps [when we meet] I can explain the nature of my feeling for the impelling, inscrutable forces behind life which it is my ambition to at least faintly shadow . . . in my plays."

Whether or not he overrated *The Moon — Bound East for Cardiff* was equally free of stock devices and conventional storytelling — he was now writing some of the finest one-acters yet written in America. *The Long Voyage Home*, the fourth and last of his *Glencairn* tales, was apparently inspired by the *Ikala* deck hand who used to lament humorously that instead of running away to sea he should have become a farmer at home. Called Olson in *Long Voyage*, he has just signed off the *Glencairn* with the intention of returning to Sweden to work on his parents' farm. But fate — the sort of fate O'Neill so often invoked in his writings — double-crosses him; at the end he is carried off, unconscious from knockout drops, to the *Amindra*, the "worst ship dat sail to sea."

Ile, O'Neill's final work this spring, was based on the true-life story of a couple still living at the time in Provincetown, Captain John Cook, among the last of the whaling men, and his wife Viola, who had returned from one of his voyages "queer in the head." Everything had gone wrong on that voyage, early in the century. After a year of poor whaling, Captain Cook's men had demanded that he head south for home; instead, determined to return with a "full" ship, he held to a northern course. In general Provincetowners believed that Viola Cook's spirit had been broken not so much by the isolation and bleak surroundings of the voyage as by her husband's cruelty to his men; it was said in fact that he had shot and killed one of the mutineers. In her later years Mrs. Cook used to frighten children, as she leaned out the window, by shaking her false teeth at them; when the moon was full the neighbors could hear her wailing hymns far into the night. And there was a story that she had taken to honing her kitchen knives as sharp as whaling knives, while her husband never went to sleep without shoving heavy furniture against his door.

Among the grimmest of O'Neill's playlets, *Ile* opens on a whaling voyage as the men are on the verge of mutiny and Captain Keeney's wife of losing her reason. Whether the playwright had yet read *Moby Dick*, a book he was later known to admire greatly, there is something of Captain

Ahab, but without his mythic quality and epic size, in Captain Keeney. "He just walks up and down like he didn't notice nobody," says one of the crew, while another calls him a "hard man — as hard a man as ever sailed the seas." It is Keeney's own words, however, that characterize him. "I don't give a damn 'bout the money," he tells his mate, "I've got to git the ile!" Like Ahab, he defies circumstance, he is determined to force his will on life.

For all its laconic power, *Ile* is most interesting today not in itself but as foreshadowing certain of the author's other writings. Captain Keeney bears a likeness to both the obsessed mariner in *Gold* and the granitic old farmer, who prides himself on being hard, in *Desire Under the Elms*. Mrs. Keeney affords glimpses of the naïve heroine in *Diff'rent* and the wretched young wife in *All God's Chillun Got Wings;* but there is yet another character she more closely resembles, Mary Tyrone of *A Long Day's Journey Into Night*, except that the latter escapes reality not through insanity but through morphine. In short, Mrs. Keeney is the earliest image of Ella O'Neill in her son's writings. Ella's unhappy awakening from her romantic dreams about James O'Neill and the theater can be heard behind Mrs. Keeney's words to her husband: "I guess I was dreaming about the old Vikings in the story books and I thought you were one of them. . . . I used to go down on the beach, especially when it was windy and the breakers were rolling in, and I'd dream of the fine free life you must be leading. (She gives a laugh which is half a sob) I used to love the sea then. But now — I don't ever want to see the sea again."

Eugene remained at the New Central Hotel only a few weeks, until quarters he had rented from John Francis were ready for him. Located on the harbor side of Commercial Street and popularly called after its landlord, who had his grocery on the ground floor, "Francis's Flats" was a four-story frame structure with a spare New England look; in time it would become gilded with stories about O'Neill (some of them true) and other writers and artists who had found shelter there. After moving in, Eugene, who never liked being alone for long — DePolo had returned to the city — wrote Terry Carlin to join him.

One of the books he read this spring was *Light on the Path*, on the recommendation of Terry, who was partial to the cloudy reaches of mysticism, particularly Eastern mysticism. Eugene was so impressed by the book — the author was listed simply as "M.C." — that he painted some of its precepts on the rafters in Francis's Flats; at the same time he revised the text slightly and, true to his dramatizing nature, added exclamation marks:

"Before the eyes can see, they must be incapable of tears!" — "Before the ear can hear, it must have lost its sensitiveness!" — "Before the voice can speak, it must have lost the power to wound!" — "Before the soul can fly, its wings must be washed in the blood of the heart!"

Whatever influence Terry Carlin had on his young friend's reading was unimportant alongside of the contribution he would make to his writings, particularly *The Iceman Cometh*. He not only served as the model for Larry Slade but unwittingly gave the playwright the idea for one of the main strands in that complex, multilevel masterpiece when he told him an inside story about the McNamara case. Eugene already knew the main facts of the case, for it was long front-page news: the dynamiting of the Los Angeles *Times* by anarchists in protest against its editorial policy, the early arrest and imprisonment of the McNamara brothers, the capture several years later of the third culprit, Matthew Schmitt. Schmitty was finally apprehended, Carlin told Eugene, through a Judas in the movement, the son of a leading anarchist woman, who informed on him to the authorities. In *The Iceman Cometh* O'Neill, converting the facts to his own use, would depict in Don Parritt a guilt-wracked soul who had informed on his own mother, a prominent anarchist.

Originally Eugene had intended to remain in Provincetown through the summer, but events in the world were forcing a change in his plans. On the night of April 2 President Wilson went before a tense, expectant gathering of both houses of Congress: ". . . we will not choose the path of submission . . . we have no quarrel with the German people . . . we desire no conquests, no dominion . . . we are now about to accept the gage of battle with this natural foe of liberty . . . the world must be made safe for democracy . . ." Within days of Wilson's address the country was being mobilized.

If one can believe a letter Eugene wrote Dr. Lyman, he tried to enlist in the Navy but was turned down "for minor defects which will not count in the draft, I understand." He added that he had claimed exemption as an "arrested tubercular case. . . . Will I have to have a certificate from you to prove this?

"I am not trying to dodge service but, from what I hear, conditions in the camps and at the front are the very worst possible for one susceptible to T.B. Is this so? . . . I want to serve my country but it seems silly to commit suicide for it."

It is possible that, appalled at the prospect of ending in the Army, he opted for what he saw as the lesser of two evils and did try to enter the Navy; but it seems more likely that he made up the story to win Lyman's support. Despite his assuring Lyman that he "wanted to serve," his feelings had not changed since "Fratricide," his diatribe against war, in the Socialist *Call*, or, for that matter, since his writing *The Sniper* at Harvard. His feelings had, if anything, been strengthened by his associations with the rebels of the Village, particularly with Reed, whom he greatly admired.

"I know what war means," Jack wrote in the *Masses*. "I have seen men die, and go mad, and lie in hospitals suffering hell; but there is a worse thing than that. War means an ugly mob-madness, crucifying the truth-tellers, choking the artists, side-tracking reforms, revolutions, and the working of social forces." Reed did more than speak his mind to a limited readership that shared his views; he spoke up in Washington at a Congressional hearing on the draft bill: "I am not a peace-at-any-price man, or a thorough pacifist, but I would not serve in this war. You can shoot me if you want. . . ."

Concerned over what the immediate future might bring, Eugene left Provincetown in late spring to join his family on Pequot Avenue. Draft registration day in the nation, June 5, began in New London with three blasts of the fire alarm whistle, followed, as Eugene noted with sardonic relish, by the ringing of every church bell in town ("With words of God instilling hate," he had said of the clergy in "Fratricide"). He registered at the Ockford Hose House but at the same time claimed exemption on the basis of his tubercular history.

Too restless to do any writing, depressed by the war fervor evident on all sides, he moped around at home, upsetting his father with his radical views. To James O'Neill, who had landed on these shores an ill-fed child and ended a national figure, any talk against America was anathema. Relations between the old actor and "the boy," as he would always think of his younger son, had for the past year or so been relatively amicable, ever since the latter had joined the Provincetown Players and shown signs of straightening himself out. James in fact, trying to get closer to him, had offered to get him a room at the Prince George, but Eugene declined; he was afraid, he told a friend, that if he became too dependent on his father, he would "never amount to anything." This summer, though, with James highly emotional about his adopted country and Eugene in his most intransigent mood, they were at odds again.

The possibility of being drafted was not the only thing weighing on him; there was always Louise. After her quarrel with Reed this spring, apparently over another woman, he had hoped she would turn to him; instead, she was going to Paris as a newspaper correspondent. As always when he wanted to escape from himself, he took refuge in liquor. One night after some drinks he told James that he was "the worst actor in the country," but immediately afterward had the grace to amend this: "No, you're only second — Corse Payton [a notoriously bad actor of the day] is first."

The following day Mr. O'Neill phoned Art McGinley to tell him about it, and added, "I think New London's starting to get on Eugene's nerves. Perhaps it would be better if he went back to Provincetown. What about your going with him?" Art was receptive to the idea, having recently quit his newspaper job to enjoy himself before being drafted. An easygoing chap with a dry sense of humor who took little if anything seriously, McGinley would eventually settle down and become sports editor of the Hartford *Times*.

The two young men were well liquored by the time they arrived in Provincetown, after a crossing on the *Dorothy Bradford* during which the captain had threatened to clap them in irons unless they stopped passing their bottle among the crew. Welcomed by Jig and Susan, Wilbur Steele and others, Eugene felt that he had come home, but Art was made to feel an outsider. "McGinley the Patriot" they began calling him, after he had defended Wilson's policies and this country's entry into the war. He was surprised at the respect shown his drinking companion by all these writers and artists, some of them well known, and began to view him in a different light. "There was a reading one night of one of Gene's plays," he recalls, "and the actress giving the reading kept interrupting herself to say, 'This is wonderful, this is great.'

"Most of what these people talked about, art, literature, the teachings of Freud, was over my head — it almost seemed to be in another language. When I mentioned this to Gene, he said, 'Don't be so impressed. They're pretending to know more than they do.'"

McGinley could remember his friend as a "collegiate fashion-plate," with no apparent ambition other than to emulate his fast-living brother. In Provincetown he found another O'Neill, one careless of dress — old pants, tennis shoes and, if the day was cool, the American Line sweater — who was dedicated to his work; still partial to liquor, but only at times.

"Gene," he says, "was a periodic drinker, and once started wouldn't stop — I guess he couldn't stop — until he really was sick. He was the most trying morning-after drinker I've ever known. He would gloom up and not say a word, or else talk of suicide, he was so disgusted with himself. But when he stopped drinking, he would work around the clock. I never knew anyone who had so much self-discipline.

"And integrity, too — he wouldn't prostitute himself. One of the New York producers wanted him to write a play about submarine warfare and offered him a healthy advance. Gene certainly could have used the money, but he turned him down. 'It's just cheap theater he wants,' Gene said, 'melodrama, some kind of claptrap.' "

While he was anything but affluent, his circumstances were slightly better than those of the year before. His rent at Francis's Flats was forty dollars for the entire season — paid for out of his *Seven Arts* money — and his father was sending him eight dollars weekly for meals at one of the hotels. Trying to conserve their funds for drinking, he and his roommates, McGinley and Carlin, made sporadic attempts at cooking in. One day they prepared a large pot of oatmeal, but it was still on the hotplate, almost petrified, when Art left weeks later. Another time they cooked some dead squid gathered from the beach, only to find them as tough and resilient as tennis balls.

It is uncertain what Eugene worked on this summer, but outside of his spurt of productivity in the spring, when he wrote the three *Glencairn* plays and *Ile*, he finished two more things this year: "The G.A.N.," a one-act farce, and "The Hairy Ape," a short story based on his stoker friend Driscoll. Though he later destroyed both works, some idea of the short story may be gained from what Carl Hovey, managing editor of the *Metropolitan*, wrote the author: "In some ways I admire 'The Hairy Ape' immensely — for its sincerity and vividness, its real quality. I wish we could make effective use of it in our magazine. Its length, however, is against it, and also the ending. To express this man's feelings and revolt, you use, I think, too many words. And the ending strikes me as not so good as the rest. To take your man through so much simply human feeling in order to have him join the I.W.W. as the outcome, seems unfinished, or not just the right turn."

O'Neill once said that the story contained merely "the germ idea" of the play he later wrote, but Hovey's comments, the fact that the original version already had that expressive title, *The Hairy Ape,* and the fact that in both the story and the play the protagonist has some contact with the I.W.W. all suggest that the two works were more than passingly related. From the denouement of the story — the protagonist's finding himself by joining the Wobblies — it appears that O'Neill was under the influence of Reed, Mary Vorse, and other pro-labor militants. This was, however, a passing phase. *The Hairy Ape,* the play, would be written entirely out of himself, out of his own heart; the play is based not only on Driscoll but on the younger son of Ella and James O'Neill, a man forever haunted by feelings of not "belonging."

A substantial change had come over the Provincetown Players in a year's time; they had traveled part of the route from idealistic youth to sobering maturity. Last summer they had been swept along by a feeling of excitement, a spirit of fun, as they worked together on the wharf, a feeling that had endured for a while as they carried their theater to New York. Their predominant mood this summer was one of recuperation and stocktaking. A number of people had dropped out along the way: Dell, Eastman, Nordfeldt — the latter, who was constantly feuding with Jig, by popular request. But more importantly, Jack and Louise, who had been at the shining center of the group, had turned to other things. Eugene missed them both, one nearly as much as the other.

Jack's name came up often this summer, for his friends were concerned over his career. Only a year ago he, still with the *Metropolitan*, was thriving; but his stand against the war, the deepening tone of radicalism in his writings for the *Masses* and the *Call*, had had their effect. Early this year the *Metropolitan* had reluctantly dropped him, and none of the other ranking publications would hire him unless he agreed to fall in line.

In August, Eugene got the unhappy word from Louise, newly returned from her newspaper stint in Paris: she and Jack were going to Russia. The news could hardly have come to him as a complete surprise. Throughout the summer there had been considerable talk among the Provincetowners about the great upheaval in Russia — the ousting of the Czar, the take-over by advocates of moderation, the struggle now going on between liberals and revolutionaries. Even to the apolitical writers and artists in Provincetown, normally indifferent to world affairs, it was apparent that something crucial was taking shape in the former realm of the Romanoffs.

With events in Russia moving to a showdown, Reed had become increasingly eager to cover what he felt was even more important than the European war. Seeking an assignment, he had besieged editors from New York to Washington, but without success; they all were afraid to touch him. Finally the *Masses* group, which all along had wanted him to represent them but had lacked the funds, raised the money through some friends. "Less than a year before," Granville Hicks has written, "Reed could have gone almost anywhere in the world for almost any paper in the country and been paid almost any sum he wanted to name; now he was going to Russia, to do the best reporting of his life, for the *Masses* and the *Call*, with the *Seven Arts* thrown in for kudos." Louise, ironically, had no such trouble as Reed's, for on the basis of her Paris dispatches a press syndicate was ready to send her across. Any lingering dream Eugene might have had after she went to France died with this latest development. His case was hopeless; whatever he could offer her paled in comparison with the color and adventure, the opportunity to make a name for herself, she would find at Reed's side in Russia.

Brooding over his foundered romance, he listened with but half an ear when Cook, enthusiastic over *Ile* and the new *Glencairn* tales, talked about casting them. Between sessions of writing and going on periodic benders, Eugene spent a good deal of time around the beach; he would swim out so far, lost to sight, that his friends would worry, or else would sit on the shore for hours at a time, gazing out to sea. Around this time he began harboring vague notions and images for a new long play, but with an artist's instinct allowed the story to shape itself. "The idea usually begins in a small way," he once said when asked about the inception of his plays. "I may have it sort of hanging around in my mind for a long time before it grows into anything definite enough to work on. . . . I never try to force an idea. I think about it, off and on. If nothing seems to come of it, I put it away and forget it. But apparently my subconscious mind keeps working on it, for all of a sudden, some day, it comes back to my conscious as a pretty well-formed scheme."

There was a mentally retarded youngster in Provincetown who used to seek out O'Neill when he was on the beach. Unlike most people, who more or less ignored the boy — there were even a few who liked to tease him — Eugene was always patient and gentle with him. One day the youngster, who generally sat alongside of his friend without a word, apparently taking comfort from merely being close to him, began asking questions.

"What's beyond the ocean?"

"Europe."

"What's beyond Europe?"

"The horizon."

Long pause. "Yes, but what's beyond the horizon?"

When O'Neill returned to New York in the fall, aware from time to time of a play taking form in his mind, he found that the phrase had remained with him, echoing to his inner ear. "Beyond the horizon . . ."

24

Girl in the Hell Hole

Earlier this year O'Neill, merely seeking criticism, had sent three of his fo'c'sle plays, *Ile*, *Long Voyage Home* and *Moon of the Caribbees*, to H. L. Mencken of the *Smart Set;* he felt that they were not the sort of thing the magazine could use. Instead, Mencken wrote back that he liked the plays and was forwarding them to drama critic George Jean Nathan, his coeditor. "I received a letter from Nathan also," O'Neill once said, "and to my surprise the three plays were published in *The Smart Set!*" The magazine, because of Nathan's great interest in the theater, was the only one in the country to include plays regularly. Giving O'Neill his most important recognition to date, as he himself felt, *Long Voyage Home* appeared in the October 1917 issue, around the time that he returned to the city; *Ile* and *Moon* were to appear the following year. He received seventy-five dollars for each play. Decades later a scholar, after surveying the magazine during the Mencken-Nathan regime, 1914–1923, concluded that of its one hundred and ten plays the three by O'Neill were the "most distinguished."

James and Ella were properly impressed by their son's new recognition, though they disapproved of the magazine itself. Sophisticated, irreverent, often gleefully destructive as Mencken and Nathan tore into their pet antipathies, the *Smart Set* loomed more importantly on the literary scene than its limited circulation, about 50,000, would suggest. It stressed, in the coeditors' words, a viewpoint of "enlightened skepticism" and aimed not for wide popularity but for the approval of "the civilized minority."

Chronically hampered by a small budget — its usual rate of payment was only one cent a word for fiction and articles — the magazine provided a haven for writers just getting started, for those with something a little "different" to say, and for established authors whose more daring efforts could find no other market. When Somerset Maugham, whose tales normally brought from fifteen hundred to twenty-five hundred dollars, found the more proper monthlies afraid of his *Miss Thompson* (its dramatization as *Rain* would make Broadway history) he sold it to *Smart Set* for two hundred dollars, the highest price the magazine had ever paid a writer. But its most important function, besides being a rostrum for its two editors' drolleries and fulminations, was as an outlet for those serving their apprenticeship, O'Neill for one, F. Scott Fitzgerald for another. After decorating his walls with one hundred and twenty-two rejection slips, Fitzgerald, trying to get together some money to marry his Zelda, made thirty dollars on a story in *Smart Set*, his debut in public print.

Things in general were looking up for O'Neill; in addition to *Long Voyage Home* appearing in a leading magazine, he had found another showcase for his work. The Washington Square Players, who had once rejected him, were going to present *In the Zone* on their opening bill and also were considering *Moon of the Caribbees* for later presentation. If he seems an ingrate for not giving the plays to his own group, he was only following Susan Glaspell's lead; the previous season, when the Province-towners were so hard up for scripts, her *Trifles*, the finest one-acter she would ever write, was produced not by the theater she and Jig had helped to found but by the Goodman-Langner-Moeller group. The latter, unlike the Provincetowners, paid royalties.

O'Neill was better off all around in his new association. The Washington Square Players had a regular theater, they had more experienced actors, they were equipped to give him a more professional production than his own group. Also, they could do more to foster his reputation since, again unlike the Provincetowners, they courted the press. When their new season opened on October 31, *In the Zone* was welcomed by the critics as the best of the offerings. Louis Sherwin of the *Globe:* "I don't know where this young man got his knowledge of the speech of seafaring men, but this is the second play he has written about them with remarkable power and penetration." An anonymous reviewer on the *Times:* ". . . of a very high order, both as a thriller and as a document in human character and emotion." And Burns Mantle of the *Mail* went so far as to call the author a "genius."

An O'Neill work again dominated the bill when the Provincetowners began their season on November 2; as one Broadway columnist expressed it, *The Long Voyage Home* and *In the Zone* "are the talked-of things these days." With the critical kudos came the first personal publicity. Who Is Eugene O'Neill? said a headline in the *Times* on November 4, answering its own query with an outline of his history. After mentioning

[393]

his fondness for Provincetown, it added, "There he lives in what was once a shed from which the boats went out. At high tide the waves come almost to his door, and it is to their sound that he writes his plays of the sea." The Boston *Transcript* in a survey of the latest presentations, both on Broadway and off, gave top billing to the Village playwright with a lengthy discussion of his two new productions. "Clearly," the article on November 8 summed up, "here is an unusual talent for the observation of life and the manipulation of theatric effect."

Eugene was heartened of course by all the attention and praise, but it also underscored to him his financial position; here he was being heralded as among the most promising talents in the theater, yet he was still dependent upon his father. In one breath he told friends he was determined to become self-supporting, independent of his family, and in the next complained of his father being tightfisted (it was around this time that he, whether or not consciously, was conceiving *The Rope*, his prodigal-son play). Drifting around the Village he felt at loose ends, not only because he had written himself out for the time being but because his life was barren of love. A year ago he had been in the midst of his half-joyous, half-painful affair with Louise, and now she was in Russia with her husband and he was alone.

As he nursed his wounds — "probed" is probably the more accurate word, for there was in him a need to keep his wounds fresh and aching — he hungered for a woman's companionship, understanding, and affection. The first one he turned to was Nina Moise, now the full-time director, at fifteen dollars weekly, for the Provincetown Players. When they first met he had been too wrapped up in Louise to pay attention to any other woman, but in his present mood he was favorably inclined toward someone like Nina, pleasant-natured, dependable; moreover, he was grateful for her high opinion of his work, for her capable staging of his scripts.

Miss Moise once, wondering aloud as to what she had meant to O'Neill, expressed the belief that their friendship had meant more to her; yet it appears that he, though their relations never developed into a romance, derived from her some comfort and warmth. Nina, who had had a sheltered upbringing, was both fascinated and shocked by his unconventional views, his seeming callousness. Once, while telling her of his past, he casually mentioned that before sailing for Honduras he had got married. "I have a son," he added, "somewhere in this world." "Somewhere in this world!" she gasped. "Don't you know where, don't you ever see him?" "Oh, my God, Nina, don't be sentimental. No, I've never seen him." Aside from the slight exaggeration, for he had seen the child once, he was denying more to himself than to Nina feelings of responsibility and guilt that later events would substantiate.

In his softer moments he evidently saw himself as another Marchbanks, the young Shavian hero, also named Eugene. One night he told Nina that he was appealing to her in the words of the poet to Candida; Nina, who was unfamiliar with the play, later found that Marchbanks declares, when Candida asks what he has to offer her: "My weakness! my desolation! my heart's need!" Another time, when some Provincetowners were dining together, O'Neill caught Nina's hand as she passed near and pulled her toward him. "Nina, I think you'd better marry me." "Sure, when, tomorrow?"

Recalling the incident, she says, "That's when our friendship took a personal turn. He didn't seem to be joking — at the moment. I think he was just a very lonely man who needed somebody."

Of all the plays he had ever read, the one he would most like to have written, he once said, was *The Dance of Death*, which is among Strindberg's most powerful works, a lacerating study of marriage in which the couple try to destroy one another. Of his own plays he favored *Moon of the Caribbees* by far, and was greatly annoyed that the Washington Square Players were still undecided whether or not to produce it. "No one else in the world," he boasted to Nina, "could have written that one."

Unlike most of the authors she staged, O'Neill rarely attended rehearsals, and he generally avoided his first nights. After *The Sniper* was put on, Nina had asked him what he thought of the performance. "I didn't see it," he said, "an opening is no place for a nervous writer." Indeed, he told her, "When I've written a play, I'm through with it." Though his words are not to be taken literally, they contain a basic truth about his attitude toward his work: the writing came first and last in his regard, the writing was the only thing that really mattered. He once got into a prolonged discussion, an argument really, with Peggy Baird when he said that he wrote for himself alone, that after he had written something he was not concerned with its fate, except for financial reasons, and that he was not interested in what critics or audiences might think of it. Peggy countered that while such an attitude might be true of poets, real poets worthy of the name, playwrights, of all writers, were dependent upon others — actors, director, audience — to bring their work to life. Back and forth the discussion raged, with O'Neill standing his ground; the only important thing to him was the writing.

In all likelihood his stand was largely based on two distinctly separate things. He rarely was satisfied with the way his scripts shaped up in performance, something that was true of him not only when his work was staged under handicaps on Macdougal Street but later when done with outstanding actors and the fullest resources of Broadway. "Few people realize," he said toward the end of his career, "the shock a playwright gets when he sees his work acted. . . . I am not saying that some of the actors and actresses who interpreted my plays did not add something to them. But, after all, even an owl thinks her owlets are the most beautiful babies in the world and that's the way an author feels about his stage children."

For another thing — and this was far more important than his dissatisfaction with his productions — the writing of his plays counted heavily with O'Neill because of the confessional necessity at the root of his creative drive. Essentially he did write for himself. Had he not found through writing an outlet for his frustrations, his fantasies, his aggressions, for in short his quarrel with life, he might well have destroyed himself, either quickly through decisive action, as he had once attempted to do at Jimmy the Priest's, or the slow way through drink, as his brother would do eventually. He told Nina that he was "through" with a play once he had written it because he was less concerned with what would happen to it than with giving body and life to a new idea that possessed him, a condition that was practically constant. "I have ideas for ten years of steady work in my notebooks," he said in 1924, after he had written twenty-six one-acters and nearly twenty longer plays, not to mention an unknown quantity of poems and short stories. His internal pressure must have been tremendous.

Between periods of writing he usually fell to drinking; in fact Nina had the impression that he was "generally under the influence" whenever she saw him. "He was never reeling drunk, you understand, but it was a pretty regular thing with him." Once, while gulping down some whiskey, he made a face and shuddered. Nina asked why, since he seemed to find it so distasteful, he ever touched the stuff. O'Neill smiled, not happily. "Didn't you know? All real drinkers hate the taste — it's the effect they're after."

At the Provincetown things were always in a state of flux, people dropping out, new faces joining the group, but some would remain for years, to the unhappy end. Among the most faithful and active would be James Light, tall, lean, sandy-haired — an interviewer once described him as a "sad-eyed, dreamy young man with a faint mustache, heavy eyebrows and a futuristic expression." Gifted, versatile, undecided whether to become an artist, an architect or to pursue a literary career, Jimmy had studied at Carnegie Tech and Ohio State prior to winning a scholarship to

Columbia University. He arrived in town too late, however, to enroll in the fall term of 1917 and was casting about for something to do when a professor suggested that he get in touch with the group in Macdougal Street. Taking him literally, Light moved into quarters above the playhouse at 139, gave Jig a hand with the carpentry, and made his debut in Susan's *Close the Book* on the opening bill.

In addition to becoming a central figure in the Players, he recruited another member, Charles Ellis, a former classmate of his at Ohio State, who was now studying at the Art Students League. After a chance encounter in the streets, Ellis became Light's roommate and started with the group by painting scenery. He was to emerge, after several minor roles, as a talented young actor in the part of Luke, the prodigal son in *The Rope*.

For the second bill on Macdougal Street, O'Neill again contributed the strongest work, *Ile*, with his old friend Hutch Collins, one of the Provincetowners' most dependable actors, as the stern whaling man. While Floyd Dell's *The Angel Intrudes* was being cast for the third program, a slender assured girl gave a sensitive reading as the heroine — her voice, Max Eastman thought, was "as thrilling as a violin" — and won the assignment. The girl was Edna St. Vincent Millay, whose first volume of verse, *Renascence*, had been published earlier in the year; doubtful that poetry would prove a means of livelihood, she hoped to earn her way as an actress. In spite of her coppery gold hair, her small even features, and her grayish-green eyes, the impression she generally made was less than vivid — there was a touch of reserve about her, a subdued quality. Yet in moments of animation or whenever on stage she could appear not only beautiful but radiant, iridescent. "Vincent," as friends called her, was to give some of the group's most enchanting portrayals, especially in light comedy.

Joining her later this season would be her sister Norma, a luscious blonde, with a flair for acting. Gradually the group was building a nucleus of interesting, at times exciting, players, but one never knew from one bill to the next how things would shape up. "Some of the very worst acting on any stage," Edna Kenton said, "has been on the stage of [the Provincetowners] — and some of the best." On a more temperate note, Alfred Kreymborg recalls: "Anyone fired with an unquenchable desire to become a thespian, and even anyone who had no such ambition, was commandeered to try a small part. . . . Zorach, who cavorted like an elephant and could never memorize his lines in rotation, was converted into a 'heavy,' and Louis Ell, the omnipresent stage-hand, carpenter and electrician, into a frolicsome comedian [the latter, Christine's husband,

George Cram ("Jig") Cook, head
of the Provincetown Players

Susan Glaspell

M. Eleanor Fitzgerald, the well-loved
"Fitzi" of the Provincetown Players

James Light

A painting by Charles Ellis showing, left to right, James Light, Charles ("Hutch") Collins, Christine Ell, "Jig" Cook, and O'Neill

was added to the payroll this fall]. . . . The leading woman of the company, especially when the script called for a tragedienne, was Ida Rauh. . . . Floyd Dell acted quite as well on the stage as off [he probably was inspired by the rapturous love affair he was having with Edna Millay], while Harry Kemp ranted like Bottom, the weaver, and tramped about as if life indeed lay underfoot [an allusion to Harry's book, *Tramping on Life*]."

When Kreymborg referred to persons being "commandeered" he most likely was thinking of Cook's *The Athenian Women*, the group's first full-length production, which strained the resources of the Provincetowners to the limit; in three acts and six scenes, it called for a cast of over thirty players, as well as settings to represent the architectural glories of historic Athens — all this on a stage ten and one-half by fourteen feet! Into his play, given as the fifth bill of the 1917–1918 season, Jig had poured not only some of his most enthusiastic visions of ancient Greece but his most solemn thoughts on the advisability of a Socialist society, the terrible costs of war, and the rewards of peace. Based on Aristophanes' *Lysistrata*, which had once reduced Jig to tears, *The Athenian Women* was his protest against the war raging in Europe; unfortunately, it was more earnest than eloquent. One spectator later recalled, according to Deutsch and Hanau's *The Provincetown*, "that the stage was inordinately crowded, that the building was cold, that the actors, in their cheese-cloth robes, with difficulty cloaked their shivers in Periclean dignity."

Opinion varied widely among the Players about Cook, ranging from those who thought him cloudy-minded, if not fatuous, and overbearing, to such champions as Michael Gold, who said, "Jig Cook's sublime, gallant, crazy theatrical faith is one tradition I hope will never end." Of their first meeting Gold has written: "I had a play. It was a very naïve one-act play — they produced it later. I walked in, and there, bent over a table in the clubroom, was a strange and impressive person. He just sat there, staring into the candle flame, which was the only light in the place, and twisting a lock of hair on his forehead [Jig always twisted that lock when he was thinking hard].

"I sat down. Minutes passed and he didn't say a word. Then he began talking like a character in a Dostoevski novel. I had never heard such talk before. He talked as though he had known me for years. He glanced through the play and I told him what I was trying to do. I was an assistant truck driver for the Adams Express Company, but he made me feel like a god! He told *me* what I was trying to do. It was what he did for everyone, great, small, dumb or literate."

O'Neill's feelings toward him were mixed; their relations over the years would fluctuate. O'Neill respected his dedication and idealism, his high view of what theater should be, and he was grateful for Jig's faith in him; but he also would become impatient with his strain of impracticality, his vague yearnings and hopelessly fanciful ideas. On his side Cook was both ready to do his utmost for the playwright and, though he tried to suppress the feeling, not a little envious of him. Poor Jig, not a good writer, not a good actor, not a good director, yet a genius of sorts, the one who lit the flame in the Provincetown Players and did the most to keep it burning.

At the end of their first season in Macdougal Street the Players, after a vain attempt by Cook to find better accommodations elsewhere, had expanded to the second floor. While their facilities were still inadequate, they now had an office, dressing rooms, and a meeting place, as well as their own restaurant. The restaurant was under the comfortable, if not quite fastidious, auspices of Christine Ell; though only dinners were supposed to be served, she took good care of her friends. "In the afternoons," said Edna Kenton, "Christine would bring in pots of tea, several packages of biscuits, salt and sweet, a jar of jam or a wedge of cheese, and then sit down again to the peeling of potatoes or the stringing of beans for dinner while she talked with us on aesthetics or free will vs. determinism or the latest upset in our always creaking machinery of 'organization.' "

Where Jig worked at it consciously, Christine, following her natural bent without thinking of it, helped imbue the Players with a "family" spirit, a feeling that they were more than a group putting on plays. "We were a real commune," Jimmy Light said many years later, with a tone of yearning for times past. "We lived at the Provincetown. I don't mean we really did — we all had our separate places — but the Provincetown was our spiritual home, our headquarters, our club. There was always something going on, and we had opening night parties, real saturnalias in the classical sense, where we would burlesque and satirize what we'd been doing in the theater. It was a way of working off steam; things got pretty tense, you know, backstage, and this was our outlet. One time Edna Millay and Ida Rauh were in different plays on the same bill, and several of us approached Edna on the q.t. and suggested that she burlesque Ida's character, then we did the same with Ida. I can still see Edna sitting at a table that night making up, putting on a heavy mouth to give herself a sexy look."

To start the parties Jig, with a lordly air, would dip the first cupful from a bowl of punch, actually a large granite pot from the kitchen. If anyone charged him, as the evening wore on, with getting drunk, he had a stock reply: "It's for the good of the Provincetown Players. I am always ready to sacrifice myself for a cause." One night Norma Millay, after several trips to the punch bowl, swung Harry Kemp, no light stripling, over her shoulder and danced across the floor. There was far more conversation, however, than horseplay at the parties; in all corners were earnest, impassioned talkers. "This is really a Russian atmosphere," said a friend of Hutch Hapgood's, as he looked over one gathering, "this is the atmosphere of Dostoevski, there is a tumultuous inner life here, externally expressed."

There *was*, as the man noted, a Dostoevskian tone at 139 Macdougal, but it was not confined to the Provincetowners. Throughout the Village there was a mood of febrile animation, of anxiety, a sense of things coming to an end, as an America at war cracked down on Socialists, pacifists, Wobblies, all dissenting voices to the existing order, even on suffragists; dozens of the latter, including society women, were clapped behind bars and treated like common criminals after they had picketed the White House. When Arturo Giovannitti, the I.W.W. poet, was jailed, Jig told Susan, "They say they'll arrest everyone who tries to help the arrested. People are afraid to offer bail for fear of being taken themselves." What most depressed the Villagers, however, was the government's moves against the *Masses;* besides suppressing the magazine, the authorities indicted Eastman, Dell, Reed in absentia — he was still in Russia — and several others on charges of obstructing recruiting and enlistment, and of conspiring to promote insubordination and mutiny among the armed forces. The parties at the Provincetown were not merely an outlet for tensions engendered backstage, as Jimmy Light said, but a means of forgetting for an evening apprehensions over a worrisome present and a more threatening future.

The weather intensified the bleakness of the times; it turned cold, bitterly cold, record-setting cold — 6 below, 10 below, 13 below — and the snows seemed heavier than ever. Making it all worse, there was a coal shortage because of the war, leading the authorities to impose "heatless Mondays." People worked in offices and shops wearing overcoats, schools shut down, the theaters were threatened with closure. "White nights," O'Neill would mutter as he plowed through the snowdrifts, bound for the Hell Hole, Luke O'Connor's or, after the bars had closed, "Romany Marie's," a small upstairs restaurant on Washington Place; it was run by Marie Marchand, a cheery Rumanian Jewess who was fond of large earrings and gypsylike dress. Sometimes Eugene was joined by his brother, though the latter took a jaundiced view of the Village and "the Kid's" association with the Provincetowners. Jamie felt that instead of wasting time on a bunch of amateurs and half-baked bohemians Eugene should hang around the Astor bar getting to know the theatrical crowd, that he should aim for Broadway.

The next girl Eugene became interested in, after Nina Moise, seemed typical of the Village — unconventional, idealistic, determined to lead her own life. At nineteen Dorothy Day had already been through a good deal when she and the playwright met. From a solidly Republican and Episcopalian family background, she had turned Socialist at college, worked as a reporter for the *Call*, been Floyd Dell's assistant on the *Masses*, picketed the White House with other suffragettes and been thrown into jail. A tall rangy girl with a fine strong face and seemingly inexhaustible energy, Dorothy had a driving walk, as though life were too short for all she wanted to experience. She sat in the saloons for hours, matching the men drink for drink, and knew ribald choruses of "Frankie and Johnny" her companions had never heard of.

But Dorothy was not the complete bohemian and rebel she appeared. Often while returning home at dawn from a dance at Webster Hall or from the taverns, she would drop in to early Mass at St. Joseph's on Sixth Avenue. Malcolm Cowley was with her once when she suddenly headed into a Village church as Vespers were being held, and at one point he noticed tears rolling down her face. Decades later, after she had become nationally known as founder and head of the controversial Catholic Worker movement, a Profile of her in the *New Yorker* would begin: "Many people think that Dorothy Day is a saint and that she will someday be canonized."

Without ever appearing with the Provincetowners ("I read for a part once but was too nervous"), Dorothy was close to the group as a friend of Mike Gold, who wanted her to marry him. Though a radical in politics — he became a leading Communist writer — Gold was quite conventional in his personal feelings and resented the warm friendship that sprang up between her and O'Neill. However, according to Dorothy, it was not so much romance as companionship the young playwright wanted. "He couldn't bear to be alone. Only an hour after I'd left him to go to work — I was on the *Liberator* magazine then — he'd be calling me from the Hell Hole or some other bar to come back." They were together constantly, riding all night on the Sixth Avenue "El," driving around the water front with Hudson Dusters, and once he took her down to Jimmy the Priest's, but they were in and out of the place quickly. "You shouldn't be in here," the bartender told her, since the place was for men only.

Sometimes Mike Gold or Maxwell Bodenheim joined them in their all-night bar sessions and drifting around. "One of the fine things about Gene," Dorothy says, "is that he took people seriously. He took Max seriously — as a poet, I mean. He took Terry Carlin seriously. He took Hippolyte seriously, and almost no one else did. After Hippolyte'd had a few drinks he would get up in the center of the room and whirl around, while the rest of us laughed. But not Gene. 'This man's been in every prison in Europe,' he used to say. 'He's suffered for what he believes in.' Gene was very responsive to people who had suffered."

He urged her to read Strindberg and Baudelaire — Dorothy felt that he was not simply recommending two of his favorite authors but was trying to influence her thinking — and often quoted Baudelaire's thought about taking "the downward path to salvation." In the Hell Hole one night he recited all of *The Hound of Heaven*, and it seemed to Dorothy, possibly because she found the words peculiarly true of him, that he gave special emphasis to: ". . . my heart is as a broken fount, Wherein tear-drippings stagnate." Shortly after this introduction to the poem she began dropping into St. Joseph's when Mass was being celebrated.

Dorothy, who hoped to become a writer herself, looked up to O'Neill as a genius — she rated the *Glencairn* tales with Conrad — and thought him "glamorous" in a somber way, but without being physically attracted to him. It was her impression that he "couldn't really love anybody. I felt that he would devour you because he was devoured by his talent, his all-consuming urge to write." Eugene, for his part, seemed content that their relationship should remain more comradely than romantic; though he suggested a few times, rather offhandedly, that she sleep with him, he never became resentful at being turned down.

One evening he was sitting alone in the Hell Hole when a girl entered, lit a cigarette, and settled herself with an air of patient waiting. Of her first encounter with Eugene O'Neill, Agnes Boulton says in *Part of a Long Story:* "Then I noticed that a man was staring at me. . . . He was dark and was wearing a seaman's sweater under his jacket. There was some-thing startling in his gaze, something at the same time both sad and cruel. . . . His somber expression gave me the feeling that he had once known me somewhere. There was a poignant and expressive silence in the back room. I began to get uneasy. . . ." Several months later when Eugene returned to Provincetown, Agnes was with him, not long after-ward becoming his wife.

The eldest of four girls, Agnes came from a family of advanced views and artistic interests. Her father, Edward W. Boulton, was a painter, an amiable, retiring soul who had been among Thomas Eakins's protégés (he helped Eakins make the death mask of Walt Whitman); he eventually would serve as one of O'Neill's models for the professor father in *Strange*

Interlude. Her mother, among the first emancipated women, smoked long before it was the daring thing for Village girls to do. Twenty-four when she and the playwright met, Agnes had been born in London while her parents were visiting there and had grown up in Philadelphia and various parts of New Jersey and New York. Slender, pretty, with brown hair and grayish-blue eyes, she had drawn O'Neill's attention because he found a resemblance between her and Louise Bryant. But where Louise was charged with nervous energy, carried herself proudly and dressed vividly, Agnes was quiet, softly feminine, and favored subtle colors. Nina Moise was to find her "like a violet," while to Jimmy Light she would seem a figure out of Rossetti: "You know, the Blessed Damozel leaning down from heaven. I don't think she looked at all like Louise."

The strained silence between the two strangers in the Hell Hole was broken the moment Christine Ell blew in, at once embracing and kissing Agnes, who had been waiting for her, and firing at O'Neill a running line of endearments and questions. As the three settled together and Christine began ordering drinks, Agnes noticed that the dark young man's clothes were rumpled, as though he had been sleeping in them.

The three shortly became a foursome when Jamie appeared. Jamie was, to use one of his terms, "polluted" and moved carefully to keep from falling. To Agnes his face seemed "so ordinary in some ways, so unlike his brother's, that it gave [her] a queer shock that first time. . . . He was wearing a suit of loud black and white checks, a bowler, and a topcoat was over one arm. His collar was rather tight against his reddish neck, there was a small carnation in his buttonhole, and his tie was carefully tied." His first words, just as his brother and Christine expected, were "What ho!" then, "I got lost in the subway, looking for a big blonde with a bad breath!" He leered all the while but, Agnes thought, it was a "kindly leer, with some sort of a Punch and Judy show behind it; yes, his smile was like the smile of Punch, with the lips pressed together and some secret behind it that he wasn't telling anybody. . . ."

He flirted outrageously with both girls, first with Christine, praising her eyes, her hair, her bosom, her teeth — he said they looked strong enough to tear a man to pieces. Focusing next on Agnes, he called her "beautiful as a wild Irish rose" and lamented that his brother had met her first, that he never stood a chance with women when "the Kid" was around. At the height of his comic keening he removed the now wilted carnation from his buttonhole and handed it to Agnes, though she had a feeling that he never really saw her. Eugene said little, at times smiling at his brother's clowning, but for the most part seemed to resent Jamie's flattery of this new girl, as well as her air of enjoying it all.

When the party broke up, Jamie turned down Macdougal Street with

Christine, roaring like a lion in order, as he said, to scare off her husband (one of his favorite routines was going to a zoo and annoying the lions by outroaring them); the other two silently headed across Washington Square to the Hotel Brevoort, where Agnes was staying. She was concerned that he should be so lightly dressed on such a cold night, particularly when he lingered at the hotel entrance, holding her with an outburst of words. Much that he said was lost on her, she was so taken aback by his sudden verbosity, but she would never forget his final words, as his eyes searched hers: "I want to spend every night of my life from now on with *you*. I mean this. *Every night of my life*."

Lying in bed, her mind buzzing from the night's happenings, it seemed to Agnes that Gene O'Neill was "the strangest man" she had ever met; but while his image dominated her thoughts, a number of other things were also on her mind. She had come to the city for the winter to make some money, not only to support herself and her two-year-old daughter — her husband was dead — but to help her family. She had left them all behind on a dairy farm she owned in Connecticut, one that rarely paid its own way, to concentrate on magazine writing and possibly get some kind of job. Since the age of seventeen or so, Agnes had been selling short stories to the "pulps" and better magazines, and now had worked her way up to making as much as one hundred and fifty dollars on a novelette; it was still insufficient, however, to meet her needs. Christine, whom she had met through Harry Kemp — Kemp was an old friend of the Boulton family — had once told her of an easy factory job that she could combine with writing; Agnes had meant to ask her about this, but then she had met an intense, dark-faced young man and his amusing brother . . . it was a long time before she fell asleep.

What did she think of Gene, Christine asked when Agnes phoned the next day, then burbled on about a party that was to be held several nights later at the Provincetown; she must be sure to join them. The room was crowded, smoky from cigarettes, but the one person Agnes wanted to see was missing; she moved around uncertainly, getting her first glimpses of people she would come to know well — Jig and Susan, Ida Rauh, Nina Moise, Hutch Collins, Jimmy Light. There was much talk of acting, scripts and rehearsals, all of it more or less boring to Agnes, for she had never been interested in the theater. Eugene finally appeared, his eyes sweeping slowly over the crowd, yet it seemed to her that he was primarily conscious of something going on inside himself. Though she was standing next to Christine, he ignored her as he nodded toward Christine, awakening in Agnes an excited response; she felt that some crucial issue had been joined, that the two of them were locked in some kind of invisible struggle.

Determined that he should acknowledge her presence, she walked over to him, "Hello, remember me?" He smiled politely, at last made a polite rejoinder, and a moment or so later vanished into the next room. Although it was in semidarkness, she could make out that he was taking a long gulp from a bottle. When he reappeared, it was to startle everyone. Standing on a chair to reach a large clock over the mantel he declaimed: "Turn back the universe,/ And give me yesterday./ Turn back . . ." Carefully opening the glass face, he made a reverse circle with the hour hand, while the place buzzed with comment and muffled laughter. The next thing Agnes knew, as a great depression swept over her, he was seated on the floor at Nina Moise's feet. He took her hand and for a moment held it against his forehead, as Nina gazed down at him with maternal tenderness.

He was not only ignoring Agnes, he was going out of his way to upset her. The day after they met he had dropped by Christine's, hoping to learn something about this new girl. Sensing what was on his mind, Christine gave him a glowing account of Agnes, then spoiled everything by bringing out an old newspaper story about her, from the *Evening World:* "No money in milk cows says woman dairy farmer who's made a brave fight. . . . Down in New York to help the poor farmers win a milk strike — young widow has supported herself, a baby, and a herd of cows by her pen. . . ."

Eugene felt betrayed. She had seemed to him "alone and virginal"; instead, she was a widow, a mother, and not only that but a female farmer! He had intended to pass up the party but reconsidered after some drinks that night; this Boulton girl — she meant nothing to him, and he would let her know it. "Then I deliberately and drunkenly turned back the hands of the clock and sang that goddam song because I saw you and wanted to hurt you. Everyone thought I was thinking of Louise. I wasn't — I was acting a part. I knew they'd whisper about it — some kindly soul would be sure to tell you that I was suffering because of Louise."

Against his efforts to forget Agnes, he came to realize that had she meant nothing to him, he would not have made a spectacle of himself that night. And it was obvious that she was attracted to him; whenever they happened to meet, which was not infrequently, since the Village was a small place and they had friends in common, he found her eying him affectionately. Before long they were going about together, with Dorothy Day often making it a threesome. His feelings wavered between them, for he felt drawn both by Dorothy's generous approach to life, her vitality and courage, and by Agnes's softer charm. "I was in love with his work," Dorothy says, "while Agnes was in love with him. She had a great sweetness, she was willing to submerge herself and wait on a man she loved, take care of him, do everything."

One evening as rain turned to snow Eugene, thinking apparently of the bloody Easter Rising in Dublin, pointed out to Agnes a triangular building in Sheridan Square where "the Revolution" would come to America. He would be up there with his comrades, a machine gun at each window, and until their ammunition ran out and they were slain at their post they would shoot down the agents of reaction besieging them. This spot, this building in Greenwich Village, he said, would forever after be sacred to lovers of freedom.

Moved by the passion of his words, Agnes thought him more poet and Irish rebel than playwright; but sometimes the dark spirit in him turned against Agnes herself. One night they were in someone's cold dingy flat, together with Hutch Collins and Scotty Stuart, a wood carver and one of the habitués of the Hell Hole, who often performed with the Province-towners. For some reason Stuart had taken a dislike to Agnes, though O'Neill seemed unaware of it; he was in a glum mood which alcohol did nothing to lighten. Once, while Agnes was sitting on a bed in the next room and watching Hutch prepare some coffee, Eugene loomed in the doorway, yanked her to her feet and pushed her ahead of him. He spent most of the evening discussing poetry with Scotty and at one point quoted from Richard Middleton, an Englishman virtually forgotten today but long one of Eugene's favorites. The poem: "I am only a dream that sings/ In a strange, large place,/ And beats with impotent wings/ Against God's face. . . ."

After Hutch and Stuart finally left, O'Neill summoned Agnes in a commanding voice to join him in bed. Both were fully clothed, the place was so cold, and fell asleep without sexual overtures on his part; he later confessed, however, that he had planned to take her there and then, with hate rather than love, to kill any feelings he had for her. Awaking first the next morning, Agnes lingered in the adjoining room until Eugene appeared. After a stiff belt of whiskey he "began talking and I stood there listening to him, amazed and shocked and yet somehow untouched. He began a tirade against me, couched in language that he had learned at sea and in the dives of the waterfront, and I listened for a while and then opened the door and went out."

Later that day, after weeping and repeatedly telling herself that she would not stand for such abuse, she found a large envelope for her at the front desk of the Brevoort. No letter but a copy of the Middleton verse and a manuscript of the author's favorite *Glencairn* work. Her resentment vanished as she read the play; it seemed to her rather poetry than theater. Immediately afterward she hurried to the Hell Hole; she knew he would be there. "Gene! I just finished *The Moon of the Caribbees.* Oh, Gene. . . ."

Then it all came out: his year-and-a-half of torment over Louise; his determination to prevent such a thing ever happening to him again; his depression over the milk farmer story, when he had thought her free of children, family, any relationships; his instant jealousy on seeing her with Hutch, his desire to hurt her. "Again I've gone down into my private inferno. For all your sweet ways I am not sure of you. . . . I want it to be not you and me but *us* . . . in an aloneness broken by nothing. Not even by children of our own. I don't understand children, they make me uneasy, and I don't know how to act with them. . . . And this must be my life — *our* life — from now on. I will build my house not on sand but on a rock."

It was impossible for him to write in the city. He planned to return to Provincetown before long. Would she go with him? Her answer was yes. He looked down at her shoes, wet from the walk through Washington Square; she was shivering, but not from the cold. "Haven't you got any other shoes? Those look as if they had danced all night in all the sordid places of the world. . . . The snow is very deep at Provincetown. Often it lies in the streets for weeks."

To conserve her funds, Agnes moved from the Brevoort to a small apartment on Waverly Place. Among her first visitors was Mary Pyne, gentle, soft-voiced, mystical, in striking contrast to her self-dramatizing stallion of a husband, Harry Kemp. She was concerned over Agnes's romance with Eugene and reports that she intended to accompany him to Provincetown; Mary felt that Agnes had never seen the real O'Neill since he was generally under the influence of liquor whenever she was with him. And there was Louise. "She will come back from Russia and want him back. She is much more clever than you, and they were very much in love. That is, if torture is love. I sometimes think Gene enjoys being tortured. What you will give him is something else, but he may want to go back to the pleasure of being tortured."

On January 16, 1918, Eugene wrote John Francis inquiring whether there was a vacancy in a row of new studios he had built, something suitable for himself and "one other person." He expected to arrive within two weeks. Francis replied two days later that he could have any of the studios to the end of the year for seventy-five dollars and after giving a few other details added, "The harbor is full of ice, it is a pretty sight, but hard on the fishermen."

O'Neill was delaying his departure for Provincetown to have a reunion with his old friend Louis Holladay. After his jail term for violating the liquor laws, Louis had led a disordered existence until he went to Oregon, at Louise Norton's urging, to straighten himself out by managing an apple orchard owned by her family. After being there a year, he was due back in town, and all his friends were primed to celebrate; everyone expected that he and Miss Norton would shortly be married.

Holladay returned on January 22, tanned, vital-looking, in high spirits, but some uncertainty exists as to what happened that day, for Agnes gives one account, Louise another. According to the latter, she had written him while he was still in Oregon that she had fallen in love with another man (it was Edgard Varèse, the avant-garde composer, whom she later married), and that she never saw Louis when he returned. According to Agnes, the two had a fateful reunion in the Hell Hole during which Louise broke the news of her new romance, then vanished, at which point Louis, who had smilingly refused all offers of a drink, began drinking.

There is in fact confusion in the entire picture subsequently given of that night, of the events leading up to the nightmarish climax — Holladay's death from an overdose of heroin. Agnes's recollection is that Dorothy Day told her Louis obtained the heroin through "some shifty character" in the Hell Hole; Dorothy herself says he got it from a waiter in a restaurant on Prince Street, where they all had dinner; Christine heard that Terry Carlin helped Louis get the drug, while Robert A. Parker, a writer, who was in the middle of things that night, denies that Terry had any hand in the matter, but declines to name the person he thinks responsible. He added, however, that not only Louis but Charles Demuth and he himself took some of the heroin.

Whatever the facts about the earlier part of the evening, however Louis obtained the narcotic, a group that included Holladay, O'Neill, Dorothy, Demuth and Parker — Agnes had already returned home — ended at Romany Marie's at 133 Washington Place; there was a fire going in the fireplace, a comfortable atmosphere in the little restaurant. As they relaxed and drank coffee, Louis, briefly showing a small bottle, placed some white powder on the back of his hand, near the thumb, and sniffed. "Heroin," he said, in answer to a question. Immediately angry, O'Neill told his friend he was being foolish and reckless, then hurried out into the night. Not long afterward Holladay slumped over on Dorothy's shoulder, heavy and motionless, and someone exclaimed in a half-whisper, "He's dead!" Within seconds the only ones in the place were Dorothy, Romany Marie, and the dead man.

Dawn had already broken when Dorothy, after telling Marie she would be back, headed for Waverly Place to get O'Neill. He refused to return to the restaurant, rolling away from her and burying his head in the pillow, but Agnes went with her. Back at Marie's place, Dorothy took the bottle from Louis's pocket and later, though a policeman was already posted, managed to slip it to Bodenheim when he turned up. Polly shortly appeared, grim-faced, and told the coroner, as was true, that her brother had a history of heart trouble; the death certificate attributed his end to "chronic endocarditis."

Hutch Hapgood was having breakfast that morning at the Brevoort when Demuth "came in looking like a crazy man. He literally seemed a being in hell. I never saw such a look of complete horror on any human being's face." Hutch later learned from Christine what had happened, after she had calmed down from a flood of hysterical tears; but a "feeling of death," as one of the group expressed it, lingered around the Provincetown for days.

In the immediate aftermath of his friend's death Eugene sat in the Hell Hole trying to drink himself senseless, wrapped in a gloom that plainly announced he wanted no one to approach him, then went uptown and stayed for a while at the Garden Hotel with Jamie. He came and went at Agnes's apartment, still drinking; though he had subsided into a quiet, almost gentle mood, he was unable to pull himself together and prepare to leave town. Finally one day he turned up all packed, helped Agnes with her suitcase, and they took a taxi to the Fall River Line pier, less than a block from Jimmy the Priest's. Whether being in the area of his onetime hangout reminded him of his own suicide attempt or whether his thoughts were already in Provincetown, he was not only running away from something, he was running toward something; he was eager to settle down again to writing. "Writing," he once said, "is my vacation from living."

25

Second Marriage

AFTER the steamer to Fall River, a stop-and-start milk train that took hours to crawl to the end of the Cape. They arrived tired, yet O'Neill's dark eyes were glowing — Agnes had never seen him look so happy — as John Francis ushered them into the studio on Conwell Street. A few hours later, after they had slept, he cried out, "God! My God — how wonderful to be here!" She would become familiar with the cry, "that shout of mingled triumph and relief," for she was to hear it every time he finished a play.

The studio, just one good-sized room, contained an inside balcony at the head of a stairway. Before long Eugene was established on the bed on the balcony, a writing board across his knees, and generally was too self-absorbed to be aware of Agnes's activities below. Agnes, after tidying up the place, plugged away at short stories, as the days commenced to pass with dreamlike smoothness. Eugene's only regret was that the studio, being on a back street, had no view of the bay, and he spoke of their moving to Francis's Flats when the weather turned warm. In the afternoons they generally took the long walk to their landlord's grocery. Fresh snow fell on the already whitened streets; not only were there icebergs in the bay, as Francis had written, but they loomed on the shore line only feet from Commercial Street; an Arctic-like atmosphere of inviolate stillness and purity enveloped the village.

At first the two felt happily isolated, forgotten by the world, until the world began to reach them through the mails. *In the Zone* was wanted for vaudeville. After seeing the Washington Square Players' production, Albert Lewis, who ran a booking agency with Max Gordon, had sold Martin Beck on taking *Zone* for the Orpheum circuit. Ordinarily Lewis & Gordon paid royalties of fifty dollars a week for a one-act play but after prolonged negotiations, complicated by the fact that the Players were to share equally with the author, the agency raised its offer to seventy dollars. Heartened by the windfall, Eugene told Agnes that they ought to get married; but uncertain how to go about it, they kept putting it off.

The idyllic tenor of their days could scarcely have ended more dramatically: a letter from Louise. She was back from Russia after traversing "three thousand miles of frozen steppes" to throw in her lot with O'Neill's; on page after page she declared her love, with a slighting reference or two to the girl with whom he had become involved. The entire letter smacked of self-confidence; she must see him at once. Eugene assured Agnes she was the one he now loved, but after all Louise *had* crossed "three thousand miles of frozen steppes" to see him; in all fairness to her, he should go to New York to tell her how he felt about Agnes, and to have a formal parting. In his desire to see Louise again he possibly was responding most of all to his dramatic instinct, to his feeling for clear-cut episodes and denouements; the dramatist in him must have reveled in the situation. Agnes, however, thinking of Mary Pyne's warning, saw him "beginning to suffer already before my eyes. . . . I could see him remembering all the dark passionate travail of their love. . . ."

Originally silent when he had told her about Jack and Louise living together like brother and sister, Agnes now ridiculed such a possibility; but he clung to his belief, primarily, no doubt, because it had eased his conscience in sleeping with the wife of a friend. In the midst of their discussion another letter from Louise arrived, special delivery, strengthening his view that he should go down to see her, while Agnes expressed fears that once in the city he might start drinking again.

That night he spent hours over a reply to Louise in which he reviewed the frustrating course of their romance and ended by suggesting that since he was busy writing, she come to see him. It was inconvenient, she wrote back, for her to make the trip and, besides, she wanted to see him alone. More letters followed, sometimes two a day, and O'Neill began looking haggard and distraught. She now wrote that while in Russia she had told Reed she loved them both but that Eugene needed her more and she wanted to live with him; from selfless love Jack, according to her, had released her to his rival.

The new disclosure intensified O'Neill's self-torment. Uncertain what to say, he procrastinated until the day Agnes hit upon a compromise that struck him as fair to both sides, one that would force Louise to prove her sincerity. He wrote her that Agnes would not consent to his going to New York but was amenable to their meeting at a halfway point, Fall River (this meant that he would lose only a day or so from his writing, and that he would not be tempted to resume drinking); Agnes would

Agnes Boulton O'Neill, the playwright's second wife

wait in Provincetown for his decision after he and Louise had talked things over.

Louise's reply was quick and vehement. She was involved in affairs of great moment, far too busy to waste time on a trek to Fall River; Agnes was beneath her notice, and as for Gene, he was not the person she had once imagined. Some time later Agnes heard that Louise spread stories around the Village that she had rebuffed O'Neill on her return from Russia, that he had lurked around her doorstep for days, drunken and despairing.

So far as is known the two never met again; she faded from his life, except to haunt the writing of several of his plays, around the same time that she began to loom in the public's consciousness. Shortly becoming a national figure through her efforts to win support for the Bolsheviks, Louise spoke at public rallies, wrote a series of articles that were syndicated in the press (and later compiled into a book, *Six Red Months in Russia*), and attacked America's policy toward the Revolution in her appearances before Congressional committee hearings. Generally dressed in dramatic Russian fashion, she established herself as a symbol of the emancipated and daring New Woman.

Life in Provincetown resumed its peaceful course for Eugene and Agnes. One day their next-door neighbor, a soft-spoken artist named Lytton Buehler, called on them. His appearance at their door was so well timed that they realized he must be familiar with their daily routine, that the walls between the studios were so thin he must overhear much of their conversation. Buehler, it turned out, wanted to meet them so that he could introduce them to a friend of his, Mrs. Alice Woods Ullman, a small attractive woman; and she wanted to meet them, it developed, to help pave the way toward their getting married.

At Mrs. Ullman's suggestion, they decided to have the rites performed at the home of a local minister, the Reverend William J. Johnson (a civil ceremony, which O'Neill would have preferred, was not possible in Provincetown). But first they would have to confer with John D. Adams, the druggist, who had something to do with marriage licenses. After getting their approval, Alice asked Mr. Adams to call on them, to spare them the embarrassment of an interview in his store; unfortunately, she neglected to tell the young couple of their impending visitor.

It was one of the first fine days of spring — a hot sun, the bluest of skies, the birds busy at their nest-building. After luxuriating in the sensuous warmth of the day, Eugene closed the door, stripped, and pulled Agnes over onto the couch. He was fast asleep, Agnes half-dozing, when a knock sounded; feeling too lazy and comfortable to respond, she assumed the caller would turn away. Instead, Mr. Adams, figuring that he had not been heard, opened the door, stepped inside, and in a booming voice announced, "I've come to see about you getting that marriage license, Mr. O'Neill!" While Agnes cowered among the bed sheets, O'Neill sprang up, completely naked, the two men confronting one another in a deafening silence. "Ah," Mr. Adams finally said, retreating toward the door, "I'm afraid I've come too early. But Mrs. Ullman said you would be through with work by two o'clock. Suppose we make it at half-past four?"

The wedding took place on April 12, 1918, with the certificate noting that it was a "second marriage for both parties." While Eugene appeared calm, even somewhat amused during the preliminaries, Agnes became increasingly nervous. Before the ceremony they had considered it a mere formality; but later, as they walked home, Agnes felt that it had made a "difference — that we had come into a new estate. I felt it in the proud way Gene held my arm. We were awed and deeply happy."

O'Neill was both more and less than "awed" by the proceedings; he was left prey to a welter of emotions. Two days later he wrote Nina Moise that he was married "in the best parlor of a parsonage by the most delightful, feeble-minded, Godhelpus, mincing Methodist minister that ever prayed through his nose. I don't mean to sneer, really. The worthy divine is an utterly lovable old idiot, and the ceremony gained a strange unique simplicity from his sweet, childlike sincerity. I caught myself wishing I could believe in the same gentle God he seemed so sure of. This sounds like sentimentality but it isn't. It's hard to describe — the wedding of two serious children he made out of it; but it was startlingly impressive."

In his first days in the studio O'Neill wrote *The Rope*, forwarded it to Jig, and increasingly possessed by ideas and images for a new long play, took up the greater challenge of *Beyond the Horizon*; he had the title before the nature and story of the eventual work had crystallized in his mind. Initially he had thought of writing a play with a "multitude of scenes that would have appalled any producer. I wished to show a series of progressive episodes, illustrating — and, I hoped, illuminating — the life story of a true Royal Tramp at his sordid but satisfying, and therefore mysterious, pursuit of a drab rainbow. . . ."

His next words (he wrote all this to a friend in 1920) convey his impatience with the limitations of the stage and indicate that he already was thinking in terms of theatrical marathons — an ambition that was to find expression in *Strange Interlude*, nine acts; *Mourning Becomes Electra*, a trilogy in thirteen acts, and *The Iceman Cometh*, twice as long as the standard play. "I dreamed," O'Neill went on, "of wedding the theme for a novel to the play form in a way that would still leave the play master of the house. I still dream of it; and when audiences develop four-hour attention power and are able to visualize a whole set from one or two suggestive details, then!"

While O'Neill's concept of the Royal Tramp was "seeking to evolve into some fixed outline" in his mind, the basic story idea for *Beyond the Horizon* came to him in an "unexplainable flash." He recalled the deck hand on the *Ikala* who used to grumble amiably that instead of going to sea he should have remained on the parental farm – the same seaman whose image had inspired *The Long Voyage Home*.

"What," O'Neill wondered, as he later said, "if he had stayed on the farm, with his instincts? What would have happened? But I realize at once he never would have stayed, not even if he had saddled himself with his wife and kids. It amused him to pretend he craved the farm. He was too harmonious a creation of the God of Things as They Are. As well expect a seagull to remain in a barnyard – for ethical reasons.

"And from that point I started to think of a more intellectual, civilized type – a weaker type from the standpoint of the above mentioned God – a man who would have my Norwegian's inborn craving for the sea's unrest, only in him it would be conscious, too conscious, intellectually diluted into a vague, intangible, romantic wanderlust. His powers of resistance, both moral and physical, would also probably be correspondingly watered. He would throw away his instinctive dream and accept the thralldom of the farm for – why almost any nice little poetical craving – the romance of sex, say.

"And so Robert Mayo was born, and developed from that beginning, and Ruth and the others, and finally the complete play."

Another apparent source, even though O'Neill was not conscious of it, was T. C. Murray's *Birthright*. Like the latter work, *Beyond the Horizon* is a story of two contrasted brothers on a farm, but in this case they are devoted to one another. Andrew Mayo is his father's son, a born farmer who loves working the earth; Robert, several years younger, is poetic, imaginative, hungry to roam the world in search of the Beauty that lies "beyond the horizon." At the same time he is secretly in love with Ruth Atkins, whom everyone expects will marry Andrew. All set to ship out on a sailing vessel, Robert impulsively divulges his love and learns that he is the one she cares for. Renouncing his dreams and wanderlust, he settles down to married life with Ruth, while Andrew, to escape being a daily witness to their happiness, replaces his brother on the ship.

Three years later we find the couple in a miserable state. He is ill, a failure at running the farm, their small daughter being his only consolation, and Ruth, realizing that she should have married his brother, has come to despise her dreamy, ineffectual husband. The once-thriving farm is now a desolate scene. A visit from Andrew only sharpens their unhappiness, for Robert finds that his brother, instead of deriving from his travels some quickening of mind and spirit, has become coarsened, materialistic; he has turned into a moneygrubbing speculator. And Ruth, who had nursed romantic illusions, learns that he no longer loves her. When Andrew returns after a few more years, Robert is dying from tuberculosis, Ruth prematurely aged, and their child dead. At the end Robert crawls to a high point on the farm for a view of the rising sun and with his last breath welcomes his death: "It's a free beginning — the start of my voyage! . . . beyond the horizon!"

Flesh-and-blood people, not stereotypes, in a story increasingly grim — here was something new in the American drama, a gasp, a shout of anguished life to awaken the soft and somnolent audience, a clarion call that would hearten less daring playwrights. "I could curse God from the bottom of my soul," cries the despairing hero, "if there was a God!" Here was an author determined to speak his mind and guts without regard for the shibboleths of Broadway. James O'Neill's son had already signaled his intent in his one-act plays. In *Beyond the Horizon* he committed the deed: he introduced the American theater to life, the sad realities of everyday life, and began changing that theater into one more genuine, more vital, more sensitive to the human condition.

Beyond the Horizon contains various elements, more or less transformed, from O'Neill's history. Its central situation, first of all, is similar to the one in which the author, John Reed and Louise Bryant found themselves: two men well disposed toward one another, almost like brothers, in love with the same girl, who favors now one, now the other. The author's experience with tuberculosis is a second element. Again, the hero's father (named James, by the way), a vigorous farmer, suggests James O'Neill's peasant feeling for land. In yet another parallel, Mr. Mayo's anger toward Andrew for quitting the farm recalls Mr. O'Neill's unhappiness that Jamie at bottom rejects the theater. *Horizon*, finally, is autobiographical in its portrait of Robert Mayo, a weak, talentless O'Neill, a dreamer haunted by images of faraway places but without the playwright's drive, his great need to express himself, to communicate his austere view of life.

"We should feel exalted," O'Neill once said, "to think that there is something — some vital, unquenchable flame in man which makes him triumph over his miseries — over life itself. Dying, he is still victorious."

[418]

And another time: "The point is that life in itself is nothing. It is the *dream* that keeps us fighting, willing, living! Achievement, in the narrow sense of possession, is a stale finale. The dreams that can be completely realized are not worth dreaming. . . . A man wills his own defeat when he pursues the unattainable. But his *struggle* is his success! . . . Such a figure is necessarily tragic. But to me he is not depressing, he is exhilarating!"

O'Neill, in other words, was swimming against the tide; as a champion of tragedy, he was a traditionalist, despite his sympathy with advanced trends in the theater and his own urge toward experimentation. Unlike Ibsen, Shaw and other architects of the modern drama, men who rejected the standards and attitudes of the past, together with the classical models, the young American was looking both forward and back. He hoped to develop a "tragic expression in terms of transfigured modern symbols and values . . . which may to some degree bring home to members of a modern audience their ennobling identity with the tragic figures on the stage."

For all his achievement in *Beyond the Horizon* — at last an American tragedy, viable and persuasive — the play had distinct shortcomings and flaws. If it loomed so impressively, it was partly because the level of the native drama had always been so low. *Horizon* was, for one thing, rather verbose, a fault the author would acknowledge a few years later when he cut the script for a revival. For another, its language, though sufficient for his purpose and clearly superior to what was to be heard in the Broadway playhouses, lacked the grace and power that might have invested the story with some of the stature of classical tragedy. This is judging O'Neill by the highest standards, of course, but he called for it by aiming high.

"Rhythm" was a favorite word of O'Neill's; he constantly talked of the rhythm of life, of rhythms of beauty, of aiming for rhythm in his plays. In *Beyond the Horizon*, disregarding the conventions of the tight, well-made play, he imposed a rhythmic pattern on his story by dividing all three acts into two scenes, with an alternate change of setting each time. "One scene," he said, "is out of doors, showing the horizon, suggesting the man's desire and dreams. The other is indoors, the horizon gone, suggesting what has come between him and his dreams. In that way, I tried to get rhythm, the alternation of longing and loss . . . rhythm is a powerful factor in making anything expressive. People do not know how sensitive they are to rhythm. You can actually produce and control emotions by that means alone."

Some reviewers would later pounce on his pattern as a weakness, a sign of his inexperience, but at least one, Kenneth Macgowan, would praise him for the very same thing: "Instead of tying the story down to the dour inside of a small farmhouse . . . he has added to each [act] a short scene out in the open. One more example of the new imaginative freedom of our writers in dealing with stage mechanism and structure."

As a story *Horizon* seems for the most part to develop more or less naturally, like life itself, from the character of its people, but as one might expect of an author who felt at a loss with children, the play falters whenever the Mayos' small daughter appears; she is only a puppet, a whimpering cry, whose scenes with her doting father run to mawkishness. When one asks why O'Neill gave the couple a child, one has detected the story's main weakness, its chief instance of contrivance. For the type of play the author had in mind, he needed something to bind husband and wife together. Had there been no child, Robert Mayo on discovering his marriage a mistake could have walked out on Ruth to pursue his lifelong dream. The playwright, using such a development, could still have written a tragedy (what the dreamer might learn "beyond the horizon" about himself or about life could prove even more devastating than wasting away on a mean farm — at least Mayo died with his dream intact); but it would have been tragedy of another kind. As a disciple of Strindberg, O'Neill was intent on depicting love as a trap and marriage as a prison, especially for the male.

It seems significant that he had yet to meet Agnes Boulton and contemplate marrying again when he thought of writing about a Royal Tramp — a man, obviously, without restrictive family ties — wandering over the world in quest of some vague but shining goal; and that the play he actually wrote, after he had taken a wife, was about an ill-starred and suffocating marriage. It all suggests that regardless of what sense of fulfillment he felt as a husband, an unconscious part of him yearned to be free.

At the same time it is too narrow a view to regard *Beyond the Horizon* as simply O'Neill's variations on a theme by Strindberg; the play also dramatizes the unhappy fate of two men who were false to their essential natures. If Robert betrayed himself in abandoning his dream, Andrew sinned equally, if not more greatly, in deserting the farm, in tearing up his roots. He was already set in his rightful place in life; Antaeus-like, he could be strong and flourish only so long as he remained in contact with the earth. Through Andrew's story O'Neill was passing judgment on an America that seemed to him to have lost its way, betraying its brave past and defiling its national soul in its pursuit of success, in its emphasis on material things. He would later set out to explore and dramatize the same theme on a gigantic scale, in a nine-play cycle entitled *A Tale of Possessors Self-Dispossessed* and covering a hundred and fifty years of American life, something he intended as his masterwork and his ultimate statement; but ill-health was to prevent him from carrying out the project.

As he was finishing *Beyond the Horizon* ("working like the devil on it — six and seven hours a day"), he felt under pressure from various sources to visit New York. John D. Williams, a Broadway producer who had been introduced to his plays on Macdougal Street by George Jean Nathan, was eager to meet the author and have first crack at his new long play. The Greenwich Village Theater in Sheridan Square, which was going to present *Ile* in mid-April, wanted him to attend the final rehearsals; also, the Provincetowners had scheduled *The Rope* for their closing bill in late April and they too wanted his advice and guidance.

"I am very glad to hear from Susan," he wrote Nina Moise on April 9, "that you are going to direct *The Rope*. . . . You know my work and understand the spirit underlying it as few people do. Therefore I have complete confidence in your direction. I know you will let me know of any cuts which may appear advisable. You know I'm no stickler when it comes to cuts when I can *see* them. . . ."

His following words, according to Nina, refer to a time he went out of his way to upset her, an episode involving another girl. "What use," he said, "for Mr. Hyde to discuss Dr. Jekyll . . . or vice-versa? I might as well try to account for the leopard's spots as for my own. The moreorless [sic] Good God put them there — probably, as in the leopard's case, for camouflage so that I may dream on my branch — unhunted!

"One part of me fiddles betimes while Rome burneth and while the other part perishes in the flames — a martyr giving birth to the soul of an idea. One part of me is the author of my life-play tearing his hair in a piteous frenzy as he watches his 'worser' half play the lead and distorting the theme by many strange grimaces. Believe me, from line to line, the poor wretch can never tell whether the play is farce or tragedy — so perverse a spirit is his star.

"Enough! This all reads like Jabberwocky but it's the best I can do. . . . There's the germ of the truth in it somewhere, I feel."

In spite of his "complete confidence" in Nina, he disapproved of her editing of *Rope*. "Have just finished looking over the script," he wrote on April 14, "with the cuts marked on it. Some of them, as you will see, I have reinstated. It isn't in character for old Bentley to cut the sequence of his biblical quotations. He learned and repeats them by heart. Also it spoils the rhythm. I don't agree with you about the exposition. It's dramatic exposition if I ever wrote any, and characterized, I flatter myself. . . . If the thing is acted naturally all the exposition will come right out of the characters themselves. *Make them act!* Don't let them recite the lines. Of course it will drag if they do that.

"I've made quite a few cuts myself, as you will see. Tried to quicken the scene at the end and think I've succeeded. . . . I really — (between us) — don't think such cutting would be necessary in A 1 acting production where the actors could hold the attention by the vividness of their characterization — but — oh, well — you know.

"Your personal objection to the prospective branding of father does credit to your gentle soul, Nina; but isn't it exactly what a drunken Luke would immediately think of, feeling the grudge he does — and with his sweet mother's influence squirming in his heredity?

"On the level, Nina, I haven't time to rewrite even if I thought it required it. I am up to the ears in work getting the long play in shape for Williams. . . . I think you've misunderstood what I was driving at. . . .

"P.S. Go easy on the script, for Gawd's sake! I haven't had time to browbeat my wife into doing my typing yet."

John D. Williams read *Beyond the Horizon*, liked what he read, sent the author a five-hundred-dollar advance and placed the work under option. "I had been trying," he later said, "to get Conrad to do a play for me. His stories of the sea are so marvellous, but he simply cannot write a play. I wanted something with a feeling of the sea, without the sea scenes. . . . In *Beyond the Horizon* the farm is played against the sea, and is against the adventuring spirit of the latter. It is the most honest tragedy I have ever seen. . . . It is utterly devoid of 'stage English,' and is the only play by an American author I have ever seen which is."

It was an excited and happy playwright who arrived in town, confident that at last he was on his way; his jubilation was premature, however, for the play would not reach the stage for nearly two more years. After checking in at the Garden Hotel the O'Neills were caught up in a round of activity: seeing old friends and receiving congratulations on their recent marriage, rehearsals of *The Rope*, a meeting with Williams, a reunion between Eugene and his father's old friend, George Tyler, who wanted to read *Horizon*. But Agnes was not to meet her new in-laws until fall; James, with Ella accompanying him, was on tour in *The Wanderer*.

Both O'Neill and Williams, a handsome, well-mannered bachelor in his late thirties, favorably impressed one another at their first meeting. "I had heard," Williams afterward said, "that [O'Neill] had spent some time on the ocean, and that was just what I wanted. . . . I thanked goodness that he was not a laboratory-made playwright." Though Williams liked to maintain, jokingly, that college graduates had an unfortunate effect on the theater both as playwrights and playgoers, he himself was a Harvard man, well-read, interested in the arts, representative, in short, of a new breed starting to appear among the Belascos and other old-line showmen of Broadway. Though not above sponsoring strictly commercial pieces, he had gained a worthy reputation by producing such literate plays as Galsworthy's *Justice*, in which John Barrymore had emerged as an outstanding young actor, and Somerset Maugham's *Our Betters.* O'Neill initially thought himself fortunate in his first Broadway producer; he would come to find him erratic, undependable, a man with a serious drinking problem.

With *Horizon* under option, *In the Zone* in vaudeville, and the Greenwich Village Theater, which paid royalties, staging *Ile*, Eugene had cause to be contented with himself. Feeling prosperous, he bought a gray gabardine suit and a gray hat, though Agnes never cared for him in a hat; she thought it made his face look small. As much to please her husband as herself, for he was critical of her appearance, especially when they were meeting people, Agnes bought a new outfit also — navy blue silk suit, blue shoes, gloves and handbag — and hoped she looked as well as Gene.

When *The Rope* opened on April 26, only one reviewer covered it, Heywood Broun of the *Tribune;* the other critics, annoyed that the Provincetowners still failed to provide free press tickets, were boycotting their productions. Broun found that the play "tells an enthralling story in a highly proficient way" and singled out Charles Ellis, in the role of the son, as "distinctly good." Several weeks later *The Rope* attracted considerably more attention from the press when produced by the Washington Square Players. "It has strength in such degree," said the Brooklyn *Eagle*, "as to be almost brutal." The playwright was even more pleased by subsequent praise from *Theater Magazine:* "His copy reads as well as it acts and that is saying much. There is real literary worth in Mr. O'Neill's output."

Things had gone more or less smoothly in the first several weeks of the visit, with Eugene declining all offers of a drink. It was not in his nature, however, to be at peace with himself for long unless he was writing. In reaction probably to his good spirits earlier, he turned silent and glum as he and Agnes, with Jamie set to accompany them, prepared to return to the Cape. The day they were to leave, Agnes came back to the hotel after doing some errands and as she approached their room could hear Eugene talking. "I recognized the tone of that voice, and knew what it meant. . . . There was a silence inside — and I heard the gurgling of liquor being poured from a bottle. . . ."

Five times Agnes went to Grand Central to change their train reservations for a following day, then gave up, deciding to get the tickets whenever they departed. While Eugene's associates on Macdougal Street thought him safely back in Provincetown, he was holed up at the Garden, drinking and reminiscing with Jamie, as Agnes sat helplessly by, wondering what she could do to relieve the situation. Over the years husband and wife were to have many discussions about his drinking. He was worried, he once told her, about his periodic binges, not so much because of his hangovers, prolonged and painful as they were, as because of what liquor can do to the brain. Where the normal consistency of the brain, as he described it, is like the raw white of an egg, it becomes hardened from too much alcohol, like the cooked white of an egg. "I will never, or never have written anything good when I am drinking," he said, "or even when the miasma of drink is left."

Unlike so many people, O'Neill never became boisterous and loud when he drank; neither did he stagger or show the other usual signs of inebriation. After the first few drinks, though he moved slower, he seemed to gain in vitality, talking and smiling more freely. After downing too many, however, his humor became increasingly sardonic, sharp-edged, until he sank into a despairing mood. "He never," Agnes has written, "seemed to be what is called *drunk*," but during their years together there would be "some sudden and rather dreadful outbursts of violence, and others of bitter nastiness and malevolence . . . [when] he appeared more like a madman than anything else."

Shortly before they were supposed to leave town he had written Mr. Francis asking him to move their belongings from the studio to his former apartment in the Flats, which had a commanding view of the bay. He assured Agnes that he was eager to return to Provincetown and settle down again to writing — an idea had come to him, he said, for a new long play — yet he went on drinking with Jamie. At times he dug mindlessly into the *Saturday Evening Post*, an old routine of his for spacing out the drinks during a prolonged binge and for getting through the torment of a hangover; he generally had a pile of old copies for such occasions and would begin reading wherever he happened to open the magazine, even in the middle of a story. The *Post*, he told Agnes, was his "narcotic."

Though loath to let the Provincetowners know that he was still in town, he got in touch with several of his favorite barroom friends. One was Jack Croak, rotund, jovial, formerly employed in carnival shows, who had an endless fund of stories about the strange fauna and colorful mores of circus life. Another of Eugene's visitors was Joe Smith, a quiet good-natured Negro gambler he had met in the Hell Hole. Once the owner of a gambling house, until the dice and cards ran against him, Joe was an authority on the Negro community of Greenwich Village, an aspect of the New York scene that was dwindling as black Harlem developed. O'Neill, who felt that he heard about "real" life from Smith and Croak, would use them both as models for characters in *The Iceman Cometh* — gambler Joe Mott and Ed Mosher, a onetime circus man.

Finally tiring of his stale alcoholic existence at the Garden, he had Agnes make the necessary arrangements and, his brother with them, they departed from Grand Central. The other Pullman passengers were at first amused, then irritated as the night wore on, by Jamie's periodic announcement that he was "looking for a big blonde with a bad breath." During several nerve-racking hours in Boston, Eugene inveighed against the railroads for not providing better connections, Jamie disappeared, and Agnes went looking for him in nearby saloons and restaurants. They got together just before train time, but now they were four, for Jamie had acquired a mangy, dispirited-looking dog. As O'Neill and Agnes boarded the train, his brother and the conductor got into an argument over the dog. The train was well out of Boston when Jamie reappeared to announce, beamingly, that "Bowser" was in the baggage car and that "the boys from Brooklyn are coming over the bridge!" — a favorite expression of the two brothers for delirium tremens.

It was days before Eugene could taper off completely from drinking. "Life's a tragedy — hurrah!" he would say in a scornful tone that suggested he both meant it and was mocking himself. He and Jamie sat around by the hour, a bottle handy, talking of the past and philosophizing about life, or rather Eugene philosophized while his brother jeered.

"I will tear down the curtain of Eternity that God has hung in the sky! Vomit all my poison up — on the bread and on the wine!"

"Swallow your poison instead, Kid!" Jamie retorted. "The curtain of Eternity has been there a long time and I don't think that you're the one to tear it down. I tried it once — it shattered to pieces like broken glass in my hands."

Sometimes the conversation became ribald. "Life," said O'Neill, "is a farce played by a baboon who feels in his invertebrate bones a vision that, being an ape, he cannot understand. He scratches his fleas absently, with melancholy eyes, and then hangs upside down on the nearest branch and plays with his testicles."

"My trouble," his brother returned, "is that there is nobody who wants to play with *mine!*"

When Eugene expressed determination to "find the answer," Jamie took up the thought. "You'll *invent* the answer, Kid — you'll never find it. You think the answer's in that goddamn play of yours? . . . There ain't no horizon in the first place — it's an illusion that happens in your eyeball. . . . Where'd the beyond-the-horizon idea come from? *Think back, Kid!* I heard it every week when Mama used to drag me to Mass. *'Be a good little boy! Be nice to everybody!'* — that's what it all boiled down to, didn't it? So your Robert gets kicked around and never goes to them thar far-distant places, but it's all there waitin' for him — beyond the horizon! 'There'll be pie in the sky by and by' — for your Robert — when he's dead! . . .

" 'Life's a tragedy — hurrah!' That's what you're always saying, ain't it? But you're wrong — life's no tragedy if you got GOLD. Filthy lucre, the spondulics, the old ace in the hole, the stuff that glitters! I've seen through all the glittering that ever went on, and the only real glitter is the glitter of gold. *Women?* — I've got them doped out! *Fame* — what has it done for Papa? *Education* — what's it done for me? Mama gives me twenty-five cents every morning after breakfast for spending money!"

His words started a new train of thought in Eugene. "Gold? You're right — I'd like to have a pile of money — rich like Rockefeller! . . . I would like to be possessed of an inexhaustible sum of money!"

After a lengthy silence during which he appeared to brood with gloomy relish over some idea, he went on to give a picture that Agnes found rather chilling — that of a strange community in which he was in supreme and complete command. This was not, apparently, a spur-of-the-moment conception born of alcohol but rather a recurrent daydream that he cherished; a few years later, when completely sober, he drew for Agnes virtually the same picture.

"There is a place," Agnes has written, "an estate, as it were, of great extent (and this must be entirely in *my* mind, for I am sure if he described it at all, he described it as being of great beauty but I see . . . this estate as being dark, with somber trees). It contained within it everything necessary for his happiness and his comfort, and it was enclosed all around with a great fence, through which no one could enter; and the gates were barred and guarded. But the thing which even now I don't quite understand [Agnes wrote this account forty years later] was that within this province and outside of it too, as though he possessed or dominated the world, he was the wielder of immense and unlimited power: over ideas; over things; over people and their ways of life, not only of his own life but of all those with whom he came in contact. . . . And all this was a thing of *this* world; a domain on *this* earth. . . . I don't remember any specific mention of human beings to whom he was related in this place — a woman, or women, lovers or friends — although

*Mrs. Fifine Clark with Shane,
O'Neill and Agnes's first child*

*O'Neill, Agnes, right, Margery Boulton (Agnes's sister), and Saxe Commins on
the beach in Provincetown, circa 1920*

there were people there, all of whom must have been in an unusual relationship to him, for over them . . . this power of his was complete."

O'Neill also talked sketchily of his private utopia to Kenneth Macgowan, who became one of his closest friends. It was Macgowan's chief recollection afterward that the place was located in a remote frozen land, somewhat like Siberia, and that the high walls surrounding it were topped by broken glass, to keep out everyone O'Neill did not like.

A large estate . . . gloomy . . . an icy locale . . . O'Neill always in complete control of the situation, with life-and-death power over the people of his community, and rich as Croesus . . . Agnes's and Macgowan's memories afford significant clues as to the origin of his wish-fantasy; though it may seem curious that O'Neill, who disliked cold weather, should place his dream-domain in a Siberia-like region, this circumstance is particularly revealing. Let us go back many years to an unhappy child at boarding school, a large estate beside the Hudson, much of the school year covered with snow and swept by bitter winds, where black-garbed nuns taught their small charges about an unseen yet all-powerful God. This, apparently, was one source of O'Neill's daydream. The other, no doubt, was Edmond Dantès, in his triumphant emergence as the Count of Monte Cristo, endlessly wealthy, superbly sure of himself as he manipulates the destinies of those around him, allowing this one to live, deciding that that one must die.

A fantasy such as O'Neill's would be conceived only by someone who felt so insecure, so unequal to the demands of the everyday world, that he yearned for a life he could dominate. Given O'Neill's heritage and other circumstances, it was probably inevitable that he should turn dramatist, playing God to and ordering the lives of his Robert Mayos, Lavinia Mannons and Theodore Hickmans.

While glad to have his brother with him in Provincetown (Agnes felt that Jamie was the only male with whom her husband was "completely at ease *all the time* — without self-consciousness"), Eugene began to be irked by the lack of privacy. One morning Jamie emerged from behind the partition where he slept to exclaim cheerily, "What ho, kids! For a newly married couple you rattle the bedsprings not at all! I can hear every time you turn over in bed, but that's all!"

Sex was constantly on his mind; he had long been obsessed with an idea that because of his fast living from a relatively early age he would become impotent at forty — and he would be forty at the end of the summer. One evening he recalled the time that he had devised some kind of water contraption outside his hotel window so that the two girls with him and Eugene would think it was raining and remain all night. Concerned over the impending change in, if not end of, his love life, he speculated on the sexual practices of lesbians, homosexuals and other deviates; Jamie in his time had encountered all sorts.

"Last night, ah yesternight," he quoted from the Dowson poem, "between her lips and mine there fell thy shadow, Cynara . . ." He was thinking of actress Pauline Fredericks, whom he often talked about as the great love of his life. "No, Mr. Jimmy," he recalled her saying, "it's liquor or me. Not both, never!" — then he added, "And, what ho, it was liquor!"

Eugene, after eying his brother reflectively: "Pauline is just an image that you fool around with in your sentimental moments. You convince yourself that if she'd married you, you wouldn't be hanging on to Mama, letting her secretly hand you out a quarter a day!"

"Mama — there's never been another like *her*, my little kid brother! She takes that bath every morning, all that sweet-smelling stuff in it — what for? The old man! The old bastard doesn't appreciate her even now. Sometimes I go into the bathroom and dip my hands into the water before it's all run out — umm!" His face was aglow with the thought.

Increasingly annoyed by their cramped living arrangement and its effect on his work, Eugene vented his feelings on Agnes. She had been getting letters from her family, chiefly concerning problems with the farm, that left her depressed. "Why," demanded O'Neill, "don't they leave you alone? . . . You know what our agreement was — as well as I do!"

Before their marriage he had made it clear that it was to be, in Agnes's words, "*he and I*, in a world of our own . . . to be alone with me — that was what he wanted. . . . As for having any children of our own, I'm sure we never thought of it. A strange attitude, perhaps, for people getting married, but then Gene was an unusual person, and so perhaps, at that time, was I. . . ."

It was obvious that he was only slightly interested in her family; both they and his own parents, he said, were to be kept at a distance, though of course he and Agnes would see them from time to time. As for Barbara, Agnes's young daughter, he took it for granted that she was content to remain with her grandparents. While Agnes more or less went along with his view, the child was sometimes on her mind; she wrote a sonnet about Barbara and sent it off to let the girl know that her mother was thinking of her.

Perhaps, as Agnes said, both she and O'Neill "never thought" of having children, yet it appears that such a possibility troubled her, if only unconsciously. During the first months of their marriage she wrote a short story about a woman whose husband suspects her of having a lover — she has been acting secretively — and beats her; actually, she has become pregnant from her husband, who dislikes children, and is worried about breaking the news to him.

The O'Neills' housing situation was solved, as so many of their problems were to be, by John Francis; large, Buddha-like, with expressionless eyes that took in more than they apparently registered, he ventured to say one day to Agnes that it must be difficult for Mr. O'Neill to write — the three of them in one small flat. Why not take the adjoining apartment as well? He would let them have it at a special price, since they would be occupying the entire floor. Almost as soon as Jamie's personal effects were moved into the other flat, Eugene, his mood brightening, was hard at work. Sometimes the slightest thing was enough to set his creative mind functioning; during Joe Smith's visit at the Garden he had mentioned something about a Negro gangster known as "Dreamy," a name that struck a responsive chord in O'Neill's imagination. At first he thought of writing a short story of a psychological nature, but his bent for the dramatic prevailed as his ideas coalesced into a one-acter about a young Negro, running from the law, who risks capture, if not worse, to see his dying grandmother.

The Dreamy Kid, less commendable for its quality than for its attitude, is one of the first American plays to treat Negroes not as comical or melodramatic stereotypes but as human beings, a mixture of good and bad, of strength and weakness. In another aspect of his pioneering approach, O'Neill originally thought of having a white prostitute as the Dreamy Kid's girl friend; but since this would have added a distracting element to the story, he changed her to a Negress. A few years later he was to shock the conventional and infuriate the bigoted with *All God's Chillun Got Wings*, the story of a white girl married to a Negro.

Susan and Jig, eager to have an O'Neill work on the opening bill in the fall, were at first enthusiastic about *Dreamy Kid*, then came to view it more soberly and hoped that he would write another, stronger play. While casting around for ideas he became interested in a story Agnes was writing about a retired sea captain but which was giving her trouble. After advising her how she might develop it, he fell to thinking of how he himself would handle it and ended by writing an entirely different story. *Where the Cross Is Made*, a one-acter, concerns buried treasure, the ghosts of murdered seamen, and a deranged old mariner who awaits the return of his ship, refusing to acknowledge that it had sunk long ago. It can hardly be mere chance that the name of the ship embodying all his hopes, the *Mary Allen* — it is named after his dead wife — is so similar to the given name of the playwright's mother. The author, indulging in private symbolism, apparently had in mind the tragic situation in his own family: all the years the O'Neill men had hoped that their wife and mother would return to them from the depths.

If this interpretation seems forced, consider what O'Neill did several years later when he elaborated the one-acter into a full-length play entitled *Gold*. In *Gold* Captain Bartlett wants his wife to christen his new ship with her name, but she refuses after discovering that the treasure he expects to bring back is stained with murder. Since O'Neill makes an issue in *Gold* about the naming of the ship, he called the wife not Mary Allen but Sarah Allen, the latter becoming the name of Bartlett's vessel; had he not made the change, the former Mary Ellen Quinlan might have guessed what was on her son's mind. Yet the new name is itself significant when one recalls the nursemaid who had been like a second mother to him.

Summer 1918 in Provincetown: a restless, unsettled time with an undercurrent of apprehensiveness, for the war is not only raging in Europe but has crept close to the shores of America. German submarines were detected lurking off Cape Cod and in other coastal waters. To prepare the public for what might happen, newspapers ran a sketch, based on "best official sources," showing New York City under aerial bombardment, with ships ablaze and sinking in the harbor. In Provincetown sailors thronged the streets and prostitutes arrived in droves as the old fishing village became a base for units of the Atlantic fleet. In early June the port of Provincetown, for the first time in its history, was closed by the Navy Department as a "precautionary measure." A few weeks later, after a tug and string of barges were shelled by a U-boat off Orleans, Eugene sent his parents a reassuring letter that the Cape was in no special danger.

Viewing the great conflict in terms of the individual, he wrote a one-acter, a minor thing entitled *Shell-Shock*, about an army officer who wrongly attributes a selfish motive to his heroism when under enemy fire in No Man's Land. The playwright's feelings against the war would be expressed more effectively in *Strange Interlude*, a peacetime story. While the two works are totally unlike one another, the one-acter contains story elements that suggest Sam Evans's hero-worshiping of the dead Gordon Shaw in *Strange Interlude*.

The war weighed also upon Jig Cook, but he was primarily concerned with its effect on the Provincetown Players. At the end of the recent theatrical season both the Washington Square Players and Frank Conroy's troupe at the Greenwich Village Theater had gone out of existence, largely because of problems aggravated by wartime conditions; and it was a question whether or not the Macdougal Street playhouse would be able to resume in the fall. Some of its leading figures were now in uniform; Nina Moise, unsure about the group's future, had gone to work in California for the Red Cross; but even more seriously, a new crackdown by the building authorities had raised doubts that the Provincetowners could remain at 139. Compounding the uncertainty, Jig was starting to blow hot and cold in his capacity as the driving force behind the group. "I have spells," he told Susan, "of hating this whole business of trying to get money and a place for the Provincetown Players."

After his morning's stint of writing, O'Neill generally visited the Cooks, not only to talk over the Players' prospects for fall but to spend time with Susan, whom he found stimulating. Though Agnes knew that he was not romantically interested in the older woman, she could not help feeling jealous. She envied Susan's quiet self-assurance, her wide range of interests, her ability to hold her own conversationally with everyone. When Agnes finally confessed her feelings, Eugene was amazed; but while he felt free to make prolonged calls on the Cooks, he resented it whenever Agnes left him for an hour. One day she was having lunch with Helen and Harold DePolo — they had taken a cottage in Provincetown for the summer — when O'Neill turned up and forcibly propelled her toward home. "Gene," DePolo says, "was the most possessive and jealous man who ever lived."

Given O'Neill's temperament, it was inevitable, regardless of how devoted Agnes might be, that incidents would scar their marriage. Like Strindberg, if to a lesser degree, he prepared an inferno for himself by his suspicions about and demands on his wife; he had a compulsive need at times to descend into a private hell of his own making. "Gene," Agnes later wrote, "was very impressed by Strindberg's anguished personal life as it was shown in his novels (*The Son of a Servant* and others, all autobiographical); particularly of his tortured relationship with the women who always seemed to be taking advantage of him. . . . These novels Gene kept by him for many years, reading them even more frequently than the plays. I don't know — but I imagine he had the same feeling of identification with the great tortured Swede up to the time of his own death."

Nevertheless, except when the undercurrents of mistrust and hostility in O'Neill would erupt, he generally had a sense of completion, of leading a richer life with Agnes. "After nearly a year's experience with double harness," he wrote Jessica Rippin in 1919, "I can state in all honest sincerity that my former existence by my lonesome was not living at all . . . I am very happy and as much in love as on the first day . . . My wife, your Mother will be tickled to hear, was born in London of English-

American parents. (Damn those English! They always have taken possession of Ireland!) She is a writer like myself, only her speciality is short stories. So we're interested in exactly the same things and have small excuse for flinging the plates about. . . . Agnes is very pretty. As I have other opinions less prejudiced than my own might be to back me up in this matter, I give you the above statement as a fact."

Despite their living in the center of things at Francis's Flats and being in regular contact with a number of persons — not only the Cooks, the DePolos, the Wilbur Steeles and Mary Vorse, but Christine, who had opened a restaurant for the summer, Terry Carlin and some others — Eugene generally gave the impression of being detached from his surroundings, from almost everyone. To Agnes's embarrassment, he would, if bored by the conversation around him, immerse himself in the handiest book or magazine; his friends, however, seemed to accept this as part of his nature without being offended. Among those he met for the first time this summer was Hazel Hawthorne, sixteen, pretty, sparkling with revolt against the dullness of life at home in a small Massachusetts town. Hazel, who was looking after the children of some vacationers, wrote a poem that appeared in the July issue of the *Liberator* magazine, a successor to the *Masses,* and was flattered that the O'Neills and the Cooks took an interest in her. But she felt crushed when her employer, herself a would-be writer and envious of the attention paid the girl, told her that at a party at the O'Neills' some of the group had made fun of her verse.

"Gene," Hazel says, "must have realized that I'd heard something about it — I guess I was acting distantly toward him — because he came to me on the beach one day and said that he liked the poem, 'all but the last four lines.' He talked to me as one professional to another, which was certainly kind of him. I knew that the last four lines were insincere, tacked on for literary effect, and felt that he was right in not liking them.

"I was invited to tea occasionally, and Gene would go in and out of the room, restless, often appearing in a state of tension; yet on the shore and in the water he was relaxed, especially in the water, where he swam with suppleness. I found Agnes most attractive, slender — lean, rather, as if not well nourished. She had a long scarlet cape that set off her tan beautifully, and they seemed to me the most romantic couple around that summer. My impression of that group in 1918 is of some wit and some talent but that the only extraordinary element was in the center — and the center was O'Neill; also, he was the only real worker in the group, Demuth and Zorach excepted."

There was a new book that impressed them all, James Joyce's the *Dubliners,* but no one was more excited about it than the O'Neills —

Agnes because of her own short-story writing, Eugene because of its rich Irishness, its projection of so many aspects of the Irish mind and temperament through a gallery of individuals unsparingly drawn. Yet his enthusiasm for the *Dubliners* was, if anything, exceeded by his feeling for the other Joyce book he hastened to read, *A Portrait of the Artist as a Young Man.* On page after page of Joyce's account of his childhood and youth, in the persona of Stephen Dedalus, he found a record of his own beginnings. Like O'Neill, Joyce had been a lonely child at a Catholic boarding school, had felt isolated in his own family ("He felt that he was hardly of the one blood with them"), and had found his own teachers outside the classroom ("All the leisure which his school life left him was passed in the company of subversive writers whose gibes and violence of speech set up a ferment in his brain before they passed out of it into his crude writings").

At least one similarity between the autobiographical novelist and himself must have seemed remarkably coincidental to O'Neill, for the Irishman too had been haunted by the Count of Monte Cristo: "The figure of that dark avenger stood forth in his mind for whatever he had heard or divined in childhood of the strange and terrible. At night he built up on the parlor table an image of the wonderful island cave out of transfers and paper flowers and colored tissue paper." But the other parallels were more significant. Joyce, also, had rejected his religion, to his mother's deep distress, and he again, like O'Neill, found it impossible to shed his early indoctrination. "It is a curious thing," one of Dedalus/Joyce's friends says to him, "how your mind is supersaturated with the religion in which you say you disbelieve." And finally Joyce, as O'Neill was to do later, had dedicated himself single-heartedly to the pursuit of truth and art: "This race and this country and this life produced me. . . . I shall express myself as I am. . . . [The soul] has a slow and dark birth, more mysterious than the birth of the body. When the soul of a man is born in this country there are nets flung at it to hold it back from flight. . . . I shall try to fly by those nets. . . . To live, to err, to fall, to triumph, to recreate life out of life!"

Although O'Neill never acknowledged a debt to Joyce, as he did to Nietzsche and Strindberg, it seems likely that the other man had some effect on him, if only to sharpen his own zest for the quirks, the humanness, the stubborn individuality of the Irish. (Joyce when asked for his opinion of O'Neill's plays declined to commit himself, saying only that the playwright was, as Richard Ellmann recounts it, "thoroughly Irish.")

Jamie in Provincetown was not quite the jaunty sport of the New York bars. Though still amusing company, he was, for him, relatively subdued; both his past and his future seemed to weigh on him. Occasionally, when he had had too much to drink, one caught glimpses of his growing jealousy of his brother; he used to say that if he had not been "pushed" onto the stage at an early age but had been allowed to write, he too would have been a success.

His favorite companion, after Harold DePolo, was Christine, with whom he was carrying on what would be among his last affairs. Since he made a great show of gallantry around her, paying her the most extravagant compliments, everyone thought his interest in her was only talk, an Irishman's enjoyment of his own blarney; beneath his clowning, however, he had some real feeling for the large redheaded girl with the strong body, smudged face and outgoing heart. One day someone dropped by her restaurant between mealtimes and found the two making love on one of the tables. Many years later O'Neill, apparently with this affair in mind but taking considerable liberty with fact, would write in *A Moon for the Misbegotten* about his brother's sad final days and his abortive romance with a huge warmhearted farm girl who pretends to be sluttish.

Sometimes Eugene and Agnes, to escape for a few hours from their friends and the congested life along narrow Commercial Street, would trudge the several miles to "the Outside," the further side of the Cape, with its view of the open sea, a long shore line of foaming surf, and mile upon mile of sand dunes, silent, sun-washed, forever changing shape, if imperceptibly, from the play of the winds. Invariably the two would end up at the same place, an old Coast Guard station overlooking Peaked Hill Bars. The authorities had abandoned it a few years earlier as unsafe because of the encroaching sea; but then the sea began to retreat from the sand cliffs and the old station. For a season or two Sam Lewisohn, a New York financier, who had bought the place from the government, and Mabel Dodge, who had refurnished it for him, took turns using the station as a summer retreat; now vacant again, unused for some time, it had an air of peaceful desolation.

"This is the house you and I should have," Eugene said on one of their visits, as he looked around at the great sweep of beach and sky and sea. "We would live here like sea gulls, two sea gulls coming home at night to our home!"

As the summer passed, he swam and loafed on the beach, awaited word from Williams about some action on *Beyond the Horizon* (the latter hoped to sign John and Lionel Barrymore for the roles of the Mayo brothers), and continued to write. He had hardly finished one play when ideas for another possessed him. "Let the dead past," he often said to Agnes, "bury its dead," yet he himself, as so many of his plays indicate, was continually haunted by the past. He found himself thinking of old Chris, forever cursing the sea, and Kitty MacKay, smiling apologetically whenever she coughed; before the summer ended he had begun writing scenarios for plays about them both. When he ran into trouble with *Chris Christopherson* (in its final version it would reach Broadway as *Anna Christie*), he would turn to *The Straw*, a work based on Kitty and others at Gaylord Farm. While the O'Neills lingered on in Provincetown, expecting to hear from Williams any day, Jig Cook left for the city, all set for a showdown with the building authorities.

26

Moving Day on Macdougal Street

THE confusion, the idealism, the energy, the devotion, the seesawing of hope and depression that marked Jig Cook's leadership of the Provincetown Players are well illustrated in some letters he wrote Susan, still on the Cape, as he bustled about the Village on behalf of his beloved theater. Following are some extracts from the correspondence.

September 10, 1918, from 139 Macdougal Street: "Here I am for the first time with a place to write — and now Christine seems to have taken away the ink. I am on the stage writing on the table that used to be upstairs. . . . Christine and her mother only just got out of here today. . . . They are awfully messy and dirty — table covered with remnants of their meals, other remnants left in a frying pan. . . . If things do come together in an organization of what is left of us I am going to give Christine a prohibition talk. . . . I spent the morning moving furniture, scenery, etc. into some sort of classification. Louis Ell made an awful hodge-podge mess of all the stuff that had to be stored here. . . . The disorganization and mess in the minds of Louis and Christine reflects itself in the visible dirty disorder they leave as their hall-mark.

"I'm going to get into old clothes tomorrow and move things into shipshape. . . . Had a wonderful talk with [Jack Reed] about Russia. He gave dozens of amazing facts (which I had partly divined) about the relations of the Entente powers to the Bolsheviki. . . ." Jig ended with the hope that Tammany Hall "pull" might enable the Players to remain at 139.

September 20: "Yesterday morning the Inspectors — Tenement House and Building Depts. — settled it that we can't stay here. I showed them the plan for 133 [Macdougal], and they said that was all right. . . . I find I'm rather glad. It revives my interest to fit up a new and bigger place. I can swing it all right. . . . Plenty of people are interested in going on.

The Millay girls are in on it — I have a play of Edna Millay's. . . . You see our losses will be made up by accretions from the wrecks of Wash. Sq. & Greenwich Village Players. . . . Hope you'll have time to do a new play. Will you ask Gene to send me his two new ones. I wouldn't be surprised if we could get enough men to do [*The Moon of the Caribbees,* as yet unproduced] at 133.

"Tell Gene to pass the word to his friends to send in contributions to the Playhouse Fund. Would his father do anything? . . . Have dozens of letters to write, and *am writing them.* Also am reading plays."

September 22: "Have had no answers to letters asking for contributions. These letters went mostly to people with money but not deeply interested in us. We will have to come closer into people without money but who are interested. . . . It's lonesome here — the work is lonesome. If there were only *one* person to work and play with in the theater!"

October 24, from 133: "It's awful the way things have kept me from writing. I've had no place. Both 139 and 133 are in chaos. The carpenters are building the new office partition around this desk where I sit. The plumbers are changing toilets around; the electrician and tinsmith are in and out every minute. . . . We work — Neil Reber, Louis Ell and I, assisted by Hutch Collins and Jimmy Light occasionally — until ten o'clock every night. I'm up again at 7:30 to open up for the early morning workmen. . . . Ida [Rauh] and Teddy Ballantine are starting the plays — the rehearsals. . . .

"Oh dear, Little Bear, this is a mess of a life. Some of it is fun, though. It's good to see the place begin to take form. The stage floor is up and the frame-work of the proscenium arch. We are spending lots of money. The plumber alone gets $350. The electrician gets $240. Those are the biggest bills."

Earlier this year, before the Players learned that they might have to vacate 139, they set out to raise money for substantially improving the place or for establishing themselves in better quarters. Through contributions of five and ten dollars the drive managed to accumulate around seventeen hundred dollars, then stuck at that figure; hundreds more were needed for the move to 133 and for remodeling the place. At virtually the last hour Albert C. Barnes, the "Argyrol king," who had advanced tastes both as an art collector and a theatergoer, came to the rescue with a thousand-dollar check. The group was also fortunate in having the same landlady as before: Mrs. Jennie Belardi, a plumpish Italian woman in her early forties who enjoyed food, opera and the theater and looked with a sympathetic eye on the vagaries of the artistically inclined — she herself had once hoped to be an actress. From the group's first days on Macdougal Street she was not only their landlady but friend, advisor, candid critic and among their most faithful boosters. With her indulgence, the Players went about the job of tearing 133 apart and putting it back together in the semblance of a theater.

A four-story building of pre-Victorian vintage, 133 had been in turn a residence, a storehouse, a stable, and a bottling works. As Jig and his cohorts took over, alterations were made downstairs and up: storeroom, workshop and dressing rooms in the basement; theater on the ground floor; a combination of restaurant and clubroom upstairs, with Christine again installed to dispense the meals. A marked advance over their previous home, the new playhouse had a stage twelve by twenty-six feet, little wider than the old one but nearly twice as deep; a raked floor to afford everyone a good view, and a seating capacity of two hundred. Some critics would still complain, however, of "penitential benches." The walls were a deep orange, the seats black, the ceiling indigo, and at last the Players had a curtain that, as Edna Kenton said, "worked smoothly and did not excite the audience to cheers by its eccentric hitchings along the rods." Finally, left over from the time when the place had housed a stable, there was a hitching ring on one wall, around which Donald Corley painted the legend: Here Pegasus Was Hitched.

In Provincetown Eugene had more than the Players' new home to think about. The September issue of *Current Opinion* magazine, boosting his spirits, ran a condensation of *In the Zone* and took the occasion to praise the author: "No more striking talent has been revealed in recent years in the American theater than that of Eugene O'Neill. . . . His work, as critics of no less distinction than George Jean Nathan and Clayton Hamilton have so eloquently pointed out, has an authenticity and a vigor quite unparalleled by any of our advertised journeymen playwrights of the Broadway school. [His] first sustained effort, a full-length play, is to be presented in New York this season."

Days passed, however, then weeks, without word from the producer. Williams, as O'Neill would learn, was preoccupied not with *Beyond the Horizon* but with a revival of Wilde's *An Ideal Husband* and immediately afterward with a comedy from the French of Sacha Guitry. Eugene had been telling his friends that the Barrymore brothers were going to be in *Horizon,* until one day Susan Glaspell called his attention to a theatrical news item: John Barrymore had been signed for Tolstoi's *Redemption,* opening in October. O'Neill tried to console himself that the play would find only a limited audience, that Barrymore would soon be available for the part of Robert Mayo; instead, the Tolstoi work was to run for months.

The uncertain status of *Horizon* was only one in a series of disappoint-ments and worries. As countless Americans fell victim to an influenza epidemic of world-wide proportions, Eugene was alarmed to hear from Jamie that "Mama" was among the afflicted. Her case turned out to be a light one, but a great many other people were less fortunate; as the death toll mounted, schools, business establishments and public gathering places, including theaters, staggered along or shut down entirely. The vaudeville tour of *In the Zone*, among the minor casualties, was suspended for six weeks. Topping off this unwelcome development, Eugene had new word about his mother that was far more serious: one of her breasts was cancerous and would have to be removed, an operation that was shortly performed by a Dr. John Aspell at St. Vincent's Hospital in New York.

When peace, after four bloody years, finally came to Europe in early November, Eugene was too drained emotionally by personal and profes-sional concerns to respond adequately to the end of the carnage. Adding to his low spirits, he had an urgent letter from Jig that *Where the Cross Is Made*, scheduled for the Players' opening bill in late November, posed special problems; his help was needed in the production. Reluctantly, for he had wanted to remain on the Cape until word that *Horizon* was about to enter rehearsal, he and Agnes returned to the city.

His associates were so glad to see him, surrounding him like an affec-tionate family, that Agnes thought he had shaken off his depression; instead, beneath his evident pleasure at being fussed over, he was primed to erupt. There was a party at the new theater welcoming him back and, despite his intention to pass up all liquor — he was going to introduce Agnes to his parents the following day — he changed his mind and had a few highballs. Apparently still in a genial mood as some of the group adjourned to an Italian place for dinner, he began downing straight shots. Agnes, while keeping an eye on him from the opposite end of the table, fell into animated conversation with Teddy Ballantine, probably the last person with whom she should have been engrossed; Teddy, starting to gain a Broadway name as a character actor, was in *Redemption* with Barrymore. After catching sardonic glances from her husband, Agnes went over to him and whispered that they ought to leave. In response, he "got to his feet, gave me a push that sent me backward, leaned toward me, swinging as hard as possible with the back of his hand, and hit me across the face. Then he laughed, his mouth distorted with an ironic grin. . . ."

In the ensuing confusion Ballantine's wife Stella, after telling off O'Neill, scooped up Agnes and hustled her away. Dawn was already breaking when O'Neill, exhausted and penitent, returned to the Village hotel where he and Agnes were staying. They were supposed to call at the Prince George that morning but Eugene, in no condition to face his parents and nervous about Agnes's first meeting with them, had her phone that he had fallen ill during the trip from Provincetown; they would be around that night.

As they stood outside the door of James and Ella's suite, Eugene hesitated a few moments before he knocked. Agnes had a good idea from photographs Eugene had shown her of what his father looked like, but he had no pictures of his mother. "She's lovely," Agnes thought, as she and Ella embraced, simultaneously appraising one another, and James, after a friendly query, kissed his daughter-in-law on the brow. While James was mixing drinks in the bathroom, Ella said to her son that he looked well, then added, "And isn't it wonderful about your play! Your father is so pleased — he may not show it, but he is so pleased!"

Eugene had told Agnes little about his mother — only that she was convent-educated, devout, had been lonely as a young wife touring with her husband, and had a great aversion to theatrical life. It was some time before Agnes learned that Ella had been a drug addict for most of her married life and that her addiction had begun with Eugene's birth.

Sixty-one when she and Agnes met, Ella, soft-voiced, pale-skinned, white hair carefully groomed, expensively dressed in quiet taste, gave the impression of one who had always led a sheltered, privileged life. After a flurry of anxiety over her breast operation, she had regained the air of serenity that had marked her since her great victory over morphine. The suite at the Prince George, despite some theatrical memorabilia, chiefly reflected her personality: vases of flowers, a sewing basket, silver dishes, a coffee percolator, a picture of a nun tenderly contemplating the crucifix cradled in her hands.

In the midst of a conversation with Agnes about her daughter, Ella said, "I always wanted a little girl so much, and then I had three boys." When Agnes looked surprised, her mother-in-law added sadly, "One died when he was a year old — my own fault. He might not have died if I hadn't left him; we had a good nurse, a very good nurse, and James wanted me to go with him on tour. He can't seem to manage without me. I think Eugene is going to be the same about you."

Finally, after the elder O'Neills had begun glancing nervously toward the door, Jamie arrived. "What ho! The prodigal returns . . ." It was obvious from his fixed smile and careful movements that he was tight. While Eugene grinned in welcome, Ella and James eyed their elder son with an old sorrow at once resigned and stern. When Ella reproved him for being intoxicated, especially after he had promised to remain sober this evening, James snorted angrily, "Haven't I told you that his promises amount to nothing?" The evening dwindled into quiet huddles between the brothers, between the two women, as James grimly buried himself in a newspaper.

John D. Williams, who had already shown himself uncommunicative, now proved elusive as well. After several vain attempts to see the producer and find out what, if anything, was happening with *Horizon*, O'Neill was caught up in the activities at 133 Macdougal. The staging of *Where the Cross Is Made* became, according to Edna Kenton, "one prolonged argument." Eugene, with Jig backing him, insisted that the play be done as he had written it, ghosts and all, while Ida Rauh led some dissidents who maintained that the audience would laugh at the apparitions. "The forms of Silas Horne, Cates and Jimmy Kanaka," as given in the stage directions of *Where the Cross*, "rise noiselessly into the room from the stairs. . . . Water drips from their soaked and rotten clothes. Their hair is matted, intertwined with slimy strands of sea-weed. Their eyes, as they glide silently into the room, stare frightfully wide at nothing. Their flesh in the green light has the suggestion of decomposition. Their bodies sway limply, nervelessly, rhythmically as if to the pulse of long swells of the deep sea."

Ida, who was both directing the production and playing the daughter of the deranged sea captain, pointed out that the first row of spectators was only four feet from the stage. Under such circumstances, she argued, it was impossible to create any illusion of the supernatural, and at the dress rehearsal urged O'Neill to eliminate the ghosts.

"No," he said. "They're rotten, but they won't be so bad tomorrow night. . . . This play presumes that everybody is mad but the girl, that everybody sees the ghosts but the girl. . . . I want to see whether it's possible to make an audience go mad, too. Perhaps the first rows will snicker, perhaps they won't — we'll see."

While embroiled in controversy with half the Players, Eugene was making friends with the new secretary, M. Eleanor Fitzgerald, "Fitzi" to everyone. Because of other commitments, she began working for the Provincetowners only part-time but from the start gave them the full measure of her generous spirit and seasoned ability. Born on a farm in northern Wisconsin, she had grown up accustomed to hard work, always applying herself wholeheartedly to whatever the job at hand. If Jig Cook was the torchbearer leading the Players, she proved a sort of Earth Mother whose strong shoulders would long support them over the rough stretches — would support them, indeed, until the unavoidable end. Eugene took to her instantly. Along with Sarah Sandy, Mrs. Rippin, Christine and one or two others, she became a leading figure in his pantheon of indomitable womanhood.

In her time Fitzi, both a rebel and a committed spirit, had trained as a nurse with a view of going to Africa as a missionary, had booked lecturers for a Chautauqua circuit, and finally had found her proper milieu in the radical movement. She became secretary to Emma Goldman, worked for the latter's *Mother Earth* magazine, was involved in various projects with Alexander Berkman, the great love of her life, and was still associated with him and Emma when she joined the group on Macdougal Street.

The first time O'Neill saw the tall handsome woman with reddish-gold hair, she was, almost simultaneously, answering the phone, stuffing circulars into envelopes, presiding at the box office, and giving directions to workmen in the reconversion of 133; through it all she maintained an air of steadfast calm. Unlike so many others at the playhouse, Fitzi had no urge toward artistic self-expression but instead was content to serve those who were gifted. Even before she said anything, Eugene sensed that she was on his side in the row over *Where the Cross*.

The opening of the new playhouse on November 24 received scant attention from the press, but Heywood Broun, loyal as ever, was on hand to welcome the new O'Neill play. The following day he said in the *Tribune* that it was "among the best things which the Players have done . . . exceedingly thrilling," and praised Hutch Collins as the deranged old mariner and Ida Rauh as his daughter. Despite Broun's enthusiasm, the play is wordy and contrived, among O'Neill's weaker sea tales; perhaps he deserved credit for bringing ghosts on stage for serious dramatic purpose, but this can also be discounted as not so daring as regressive, a throwback to his father's lurid theater. Originally he thought the play "one of my best" (he practically always thought his latest work his "best"), but later was to write George Jean Nathan: ". . . where did you get the idea that I really valued *Where the Cross Is Made?* It was great fun to write, theatrically very thrilling, an amusing experiment in treating the audience as insane — that is all it means or ever meant to me."

The O'Neills had decided to spend the winter in West Point Pleasant, a seashore resort in New Jersey, where Agnes owned a house. Before they moved in, however, there were complications, all because Agnes and her parents had failed to keep one another posted on their plans. She thought that they would remain on the farm in Connecticut; instead, assuming that the young couple was going to winter in Provincetown or New York, they had taken over the Old House, as the family called it. Eugene was ignorant of all this, but Agnes was frantic when she learned of the houseful in New Jersey — not only her parents, three younger sisters and small daughter but her maternal grandmother plus a dog and three cats. While O'Neill was busy with rehearsals of *Where the Cross Is Made,* letters flew back and forth between Agnes and her mother. At last the situation was resolved: the Boultons rented a small place in West Point Pleasant and decided that since Eugene wanted quiet and solitude so that he could write in peace, they would not even call on him and Agnes; he could remain unaware that his in-laws were living nearby.

O'Neill was in an edgy mood as he and Agnes settled down at the Old House. Hoping daily for word from Williams, he would grow tense whenever the postman was due, afterward subsiding into gloom. He made sporadic attempts to resume working on *Chris Christopherson* and *The Straw* but found it difficult to concentrate, partly because he soon would have to return to the city for rehearsals of *The Moon of the Caribbees,* scheduled to open late in December. In addition, he was worried about the vaudeville engagement of *In the Zone;* though it had been booked for forty weeks, the public, now that the war was over, had tired of wartime stories and his agents, Lewis & Gordon, were pessimistic about the chances of *Zone* continuing much longer. It seemed to Eugene that his cares were unending, for in the midst of everything else he heard from Jamie in early December that "Papa" had been struck by an automobile while crossing Fifth Avenue, near the Prince George. His injuries were not serious — he was recuperating at the hotel — but it all added to his son's anxious frame of mind.

Eugene returned alone to the city, Agnes remaining behind to attend to daily chores, and immediately was involved not only in rehearsals of his *Glencairn* vignette but in a running debate over general policy. After the Players' opening bill they had been attacked by a theatrical weekly for their independent attitude toward the press. Should they continue to go their own way, remaining an experimental theater, the argument went, or should they pay more attention to outside, professional judgment? The Washington Square Players were no more; the troupe at the Greenwich Village Theater had folded; the Provincetown was now the city's foremost little theater. Could they continue as "free" as they had begun, concerned with no one's view except their own? It finally was decided not to send tickets to the press — they couldn't afford to give away a block of tickets for each opening — but to take care of critics who requested seats. The Players also agreed to seek publicity, for they realized, belatedly, that from the start individual members of the group had sought public notice for themselves. To the distress of Jig and certain others, the adventurous amateur spirit that had once marked the group was weakening.

Even though *Moon of the Caribbees* had some of Eugene's favorites among the Players — Hutch Collins as Driscoll, Charlie Ellis as Smitty the Duke, Scotty Stuart as the Donkeyman — he was not happy with the way it was shaping up in rehearsal. In the pre-opening confusion the "island" that provided part of the background for the S.S. *Glencairn* — four feet of beaverboard painted green — was shifted to the back yard of 133 and forgotten. When retrieved the following day, the set was sodden from being rained on. A new island was, in Edna Kenton's words, "painted, tried out, given a few despairing last strokes and set a few feet behind the *Glencairn* just in time and no more for the rising curtain."

The critics were not impressed by the author's own favorite among all his one-acters. One reviewer called it "just an interlude of a drama, with prelude and afterlude left to the imagination of the spectators," while another dismissed it as a "rather pointless tale about an uninteresting young man." Shortly afterward O'Neill wrote Nina Moise that the Provincetowners, especially himself, missed her direction, and said of *The Moon* that "what with a small stage, a large cast — (which was never very large at rehearsals — as you can guess) and the difficult set, well — just use your imagination."

Busy with chores at the Old House, Agnes had intended to remain in New Jersey but changed her mind after a wire from her husband on December 20: "Will not leave until you come." She found him in the back room of the Hell Hole, surrounded by Jamie, Harold DePolo and other friends, reciting *The Hound of Heaven:*

> *Yea, faileth now even dream*
> *The dreamer, and the lute the lutanist. . . .*

From somewhere he had acquired a white dog of uncertain parentage which he regarded with alcoholic affection, and after his brother had made his usual spiel about "the boys from Brooklyn coming over the bridge," he decided to call his new pet "Brooklyn Boy." Relieved that his wife had joined him, Eugene lingered over his drinks, but Agnes was worried that they would miss the "Owl" at midnight, the last train home until morning. When she finally managed to extricate him from the Hell Hole, Jamie and Brooklyn Boy were with them; Eugene was determined to take the dog back to New Jersey, though Agnes protested that the train had no accommodations for animals. En route to the Garden Hotel to drop off Jamie, the taxi had to stop for a traffic light, and the next thing Agnes knew, her husband had bolted with the dog. Early next morning Agnes, back home, was aroused from sleep by male voices somewhere in the house. She finally traced them to the kitchen, where Eugene was having drinks with a truck driver who had given him and the dog a lift from town.

During his stay in the city Eugene had told his father about the abandoned Coast Guard station in Provincetown and of his great desire to own it. It was an ideal place for him to live during the summer, an inspiring place; he should be able to do his finest writing there. He was so emotional and persuasive on the subject that James, who at first thought it just another of his son's crazy romantic notions, was won over; the price, only a thousand dollars, covered the station with all its furnishings and several adjoining smaller structures.

On December 24 Eugene wrote Mr. Francis, the agent for Sam Lewisohn, that his father had "absolutely assured" him that he would buy the place for him and that a check for five hundred dollars as the initial payment would be forthcoming shortly. After wishing Francis and his family "the merriest of all Christmases," he said, "I haven't forgotten the money I still owe you but [*In the Zone*] has been skipping weeks with devilish regularity and my long play hasn't started rehearsals yet. But better times are coming and when they arrive I will send you a check the first thing."

Despite his prospective ownership of Peaked Hill Bars, as the station itself was called, the approach of the holidays threw him as always into a depression. Though he had told Agnes that he was not going to let Christmas affect him this time, the atmosphere in the Old House was dispirited; on New Year's Eve he immersed himself in the *Saturday Evening Post* and a bottle.

Apparently the holidays spurred memories of Gaylord Farm, where he had arrived one Christmas Eve, for the early days of 1919 found him moving ahead with *The Straw*, his story of an ill-fated romance in a sanatorium for the tubercular. "We had breakfast," Agnes has written of his daily routine, "waited for the mail, and then Gene went into the west bedroom and in that abstraction that signalled the approach of work, sharpened pencils, neatly piled up paper, put a glass of water on the table next to the bed, and, with my father's drawing board propped against his knees and a pillow behind him, looked absently at the sheet of white paper on which (in his tiny handwriting) there would soon come to life one of those *others* who shared the days with us in the Old House." Lunchtime passed in virtual silence, for he was "still absorbed in the work which he had been doing for three or four hours and to which he would shortly return."

In calling the protagonist of *The Straw* Stephen Murray, O'Neill apparently borrowed from both literature and life — Stephen after young Dedalus in Joyce's novel, the surname after Katherine Murray, one of O'Neill's favorite nurses at Gaylord, and a patient there named Murray, an easygoing chap whom O'Neill had liked. Stephen Murray is in short the playwright's portrait of himself as a young man; just as Dedalus/ Joyce commits himself to literature before *A Portrait* ends, O'Neill had committed himself to the theater before he left Gaylord.

Taking courage presumably from Joyce's candor about himself in the book, O'Neill drew a by and large unflattering self-likeness in *The Straw*. Stephen Murray is too egocentric to be really sympathetic; he has difficulty relating to other people. After telling Eileen Carmody that both his parents are dead, he adds: "A family wouldn't have changed things. From what I've seen that blood-thicker-than-water dope is all wrong." Had Murray been less self-absorbed, he would early have sensed how Eileen felt about him and later would have known that her hopeless passion for him was at the bottom of her failing health.

A work of uneven quality, *The Straw* is better as character portraiture than as story. Although Murray's belated realization that he loves Eileen is scarcely convincing, he himself is more or less persuasively depicted. And still better are the portraits of Eileen, her father, her cowardly fiancé, and the ham-handed Mrs. Brennan, who succeeds Eileen in looking after the Carmody family. All four are both individualized and fairly representative of familiar types in Irish letters: the long-suffering and quietly heroic daughter or wife or mother; the loutish husband or father, only a step or so removed from his bog-trotting forebears; the cautious young man set on rising in the world, and the self-righteous nag (Mrs. Brennan) who darkens the lives of those around her. In writing *The Straw* O'Neill probably was influenced not only by *Portrait of the Artist* but by Joyce's other book, for Eileen and the other three would look perfectly at home in the *Dubliners*.

One morning in New Jersey, Eugene, who had grown deeply attached to Brooklyn Boy, appeared before Agnes with an ashen face, unable to tell her what he had just seen from a window; when Agnes looked, she saw the dog's body sprawled on the front lawn, his throat slit from ear to ear. They never found out who was responsible but apparently the deed was an expression of the hostility that had greeted them from their first days in West Point Pleasant. Agnes finally realized that some of their neighbors, people she had known for years, resented that she and her husband, a withdrawn-looking stranger, had taken over the large farm- house while the rest of her family was crammed into a smaller place.

Agnes would subsequently profess to find some humor in the situation — the precautions and stratagems she had to employ to prevent Eugene from learning that her family resided nearby. Her father, a gentle soul who had never earned much from his painting, had taken a job at ten dollars a week in the local hardware store, chiefly to earn rent money. Agnes dropped by the store so often, ostensibly to make various little purchases, that her husband began to suspect she was romantically interested in someone working there. When he finally chanced to learn of his in-laws' proximity, he was upset, but feeling awkward and on the defensive, deferred meeting them.

At the end of January he was shocked and saddened to hear from his brother that Hutch Collins had died after a brief siege of influenza and pneumonia. "The idea of death coupled with Hutch," he wrote Susan on the twenty-ninth, "seems like an unwarranted extra turn of the screw of tragedy . . . for he possessed, above all other men in my experience, such a pronounced delight in living. . . . In New London days we were thrown into the closest intimacy by the very narrowness of our environment. . . . You can imagine, then, my sense of deep personal loss, of abiding sorrow. . . ."

In the same letter he asked Susan to relay his apologies to Jig for a testy note he had written him a few days earlier: "My only excuse is that my own troubles have left me groggy and ill-tempered. I can get nothing definite from Williams and it looks as if the long play would not go on this year — the most astoundedly prosperous in theatrical history! . . . Also *In the Zone* ceased two months ago. . . . Many other things are all balled up. 'Winter of my discontent' is right! To get away from all this muddle and be free to work, I have signed a contract with the American Play Co. to take charge of all my plays, business end."

The company was headed by Elizabeth Marbury, among the first career women, who had launched herself in the 1890s as the American representative of various British and Continental playwrights. A person of culture and fastidious tastes, though built on rude beer-barrel proportions, Miss Marbury was at home in society and artistic circles on both sides of the Atlantic, maintaining offices in London and Paris as well as in New York. She was to play a fateful role in O'Neill's life in the mid-1920s by reintroducing him to an actress, Carlotta Monterey, who had appeared in one of his Broadway productions; Miss Monterey would become his third wife, the one to whom he was married longest, to whom he was married when he died.

O'Neill became a client of the American Play Co., not through Miss Marbury, however, but through one of her partners, Richard J. Madden, a gentleman in a hyperthyroid business where gentlemen are rare, an agent of taste and integrity who handled only those writers he respected. After seeing a number of O'Neill productions, he sought out the author one night, after a performance of *Moon of the Caribbees,* to say how much he liked his work. The two men adjourned upstairs to Christine's restaurant, where they talked for hours. At the end O'Neill asked Madden to become his agent and they shook hands in agreement.

"It was refreshing," Madden afterward told his wife, "to find someone in the theater who's so intelligent." Like a number of others who became good friends of Eugene's — Saxe Commins, Kenneth Macgowan, Robert Edmond Jones, Russel Crouse, press agent Robert Sisk — Madden felt that there was something vulnerable about him and developed toward him a protective feeling. Stark Young the critic, though never one of the playwright's intimates, had the same kind of response; he once wrote in his diary, after a few hours with O'Neill: "A handsome face on which for the moment there was a certain shade of brutality, which seemed to change immediately into a kind of delicate and fierce withdrawal — or shall I say a proud shadow? — and also a kind of covered entreaty . . . as was usual in his case I felt vaguely an emotion of pity and defense. Though there was nothing particularly to defend him against, I wanted to defend him, to take his part."

Shortly after Eugene's gloomy account to Susan of the state of his affairs, his prospects brightened somewhat. John Williams, as quick in picking up scripts as he was slow in producing them, was enthusiastic about *The Straw* and ready to place it under option. Also, a thriving young firm headed by Albert Boni and Horace Liveright decided to publish in the spring a collection of O'Neill's one-acters and gave him an advance of one hundred and twenty-five dollars against royalties of ten percent. Entitled *The Moon of the Caribbees and Six Other Plays of the Sea,* the volume was to include, in addition to the four *Glencairn* tales, *Ile, The Rope,* and *Where the Cross Is Made.*

Albert Boni, after he and his brother turned over their bookshop to Frank Shay, had gone to work for an advertising firm, where he became acquainted with Liveright, a dynamic young man eager to be outstanding. Financed by a rich father-in-law, Horace had plunged into several enterprises with the hope of becoming independently wealthy, but each time had failed. Boni & Liveright began its existence in 1917 with $12,500 put up by Liveright's in-laws — this was the last time, they said, that they would stake him — and Boni's idea for a publishing house that, in addition to offering new books of quality, would feature a "Modern Library" of the classics at popular prices. Though the Modern Library flourished, the two partners proved incompatible; after a few years of wrangling they

[449]

tossed a coin to decide who would buy out the other, and Boni lost, at which point the firm became Horace Liveright, Inc.

In the 1920s Liveright was to shake up the publishing world with his legal battles against the censors and his championing of such new voices as Hemingway and Sherwood Anderson, e. e. cummings and T. S. Eliot, Ezra Pound and Robinson Jeffers. Where practically all other publishers were deferential to book reviewers and literary editors, Horace put them on the defensive; the first time Harry Hansen entered his office, Liveright opened fire: "What are you doing for Dreiser? I've got Dreiser and O'Neill, the two greatest American authors, and what have you editors done for me? Nothing!"

O'Neill's pleasure over his forthcoming Boni & Liveright publication was offset by his concern over *Horizon*. On February 3 he wrote John Francis that the production was being held up by the unavailability of the Barrymore brothers. "So it is in this damned theatrical business . . . delay after delay, everyone trying to do you, and you get small satisfaction out of them when you raise a kick. It's very discouraging, the watchful waiting." But in a letter the following day to Jessica Rippin, he put a better face on his circumstances: "I look about the same, act about the same, and am hardly at all as 'famous' as you are flattering enough to make out. All I can hand myself is that I have worked like the devil for the past three years with but few let-ups for celebrations, and I am glad to be able to say that this hard labor is at last showing some results and winning for me a bit of recognition. . . . I'll wind up the autobiography by adding that, though toned down, I'm still unreformed and strive to continue so."

Eugene told both Jessica and Mr. Francis that he had sold *The Straw*, but the deal, after a tentative agreement, never materialized; since Williams refused to commit himself as to when he would produce the work, Eugene decided that he had better look elsewhere. It was a trying time for both husband and wife; whereas he had professional disappointments, she had private worries. After feeling strange for some days Agnes went to a doctor and learned, as she had begun to suspect, that she was pregnant. "Now," the doctor said, "you can go home and tell your husband the good news."

His immediate response was to question the diagnosis, then he fell silent. "I could not tell," Agnes later said, "what he was thinking about. I was miserable imagining what he *might* be thinking about. He was withdrawn, deep in himself, not hostile, not even perturbed, so far as I could see. But there was no contact between us. . . ." Later that day he was aroused from his abstraction when one of the cats that had been left behind by the Boultons gave signs of giving birth, as had been expected, and indicated that she wanted someone to stand by. At first Eugene was annoyed at having to, in Agnes's words, "hold her paw" during the event, but moved at the sight of her delivery he ended by singing some of his favorite chanteys. The songs, he claimed, helped ease her labor pains.

He worked chiefly this winter and spring on *Chris Christopherson*, which was giving him considerable trouble. From the outset Chris is more or less as he will appear in *Anna Christie* — good-natured, feckless, forever cursing "dat ole davil," the sea — but his daughter and her suitor are pallid by comparison with their eventual metamorphoses. Where the 1919 play presented Anna as a proper young woman who had been reared in England, the play bearing her name would depict her with vitality and color, even a touch of poetry, as a prostitute with a feeling for the sea. Again, where the early work portrayed her suitor as a ship's officer, a young American who dislikes responsibility (he has a distant, albeit colorless resemblance to O'Neill), *Anna Christie* would bring on a swaggering stoker, Irish from stem to stern (his Irishness is overdone, however, almost to a point of caricature), who bears a likeness to the author's old friend, Driscoll.

The chief virtue of *Chris* is its flavorsome life-size portrait of the title character, but it contains someone else worth noting. Among the patrons of Johnny the Priest's bar is a traveling salesman who, says Johnny, is "the kind ought to leave red eye alone. Always ends up his drunk here. Knows no one'll know him here 'cept me and he ain't 'shamed to go the limit. Well, he's a good spender as long as he's got it." Though seen too briefly to be interesting in himself, he affords a glimpse of the creative workings of O'Neill's mind; he is a preliminary sketch for one of the playwright's most powerful creations, Hickey, the proselytizing salesman of *The Iceman Cometh*, who always tends "to go the limit" and who ends spreading despair and the smell of death among the lost souls in Harry Hope's saloon.

Accompanied by Agnes, O'Neill visited town from time to time to keep abreast of affairs at the Provincetown and confer with Dick Madden about various matters, in particular how to bring some pressure to bear on Williams. The visits frequently ended with Eugene hitting the bottle. On March 19 Agnes wrote Helen and Harold DePolo to thank them "for putting us up. . . . Very quiet here — nothing but the rain to listen to. . . . At present [Gene] is Saturday Evening Posting."

Occasionally they stayed in Polly Holladay's quarters above her restaurant, the Greenwich Village Inn at Sheridan Square. One night, annoyed by the smell of some dying gladioli, Eugene was about to toss them out when he discovered a wad of money, chiefly dollar bills, in the vase; Polly was in the habit, it seems, of stashing the day's receipts in various places around the apartment. Going to the window, he dropped the dripping bills one by one to passers-by in the early dawn. "They looked at last," he said in a pleased voice to Agnes, "at the sky!"

At the Provincetown the season was ending inconclusively, with the Players neither advancing their reputation nor, save financially, losing ground; they wound up the year with a deficit. After *Where the Cross* and *Moon of the Caribbees*, given on the first two bills, there were no further O'Neill premières. A full-length drama by Susan Glaspell, *Bernice*, was well received, but a short work by Jack Reed satirizing the Versailles peace conference, *The Peace That Passeth Understanding*, was generally frowned on as being in poor taste; Wilson, Lloyd George and Clemenceau were shown in a clownish light, and at one point the smaller European nations, symbolized by dummies, were tossed out a window.

"The Little Theater movement," said an article in the *Nation* on May 3, 1919, "is now in its second and perhaps its most difficult stage. The novelty of purpose and appeal is gone. The instigators of a little theater are no longer pioneers in a trackless and alluring forest. Many paths have been cut and trod during the last eight or nine years. . . . It is not so much the work of exploration as of settling in the new land that confronts the promoters of the little theater today."

On May 1 Eugene wrote George Jean Nathan that he was sending copies of his Boni & Liveright volume to both him and Mencken in appreciation of their "encouragement and constructive criticism," reported that *Chris Christopherson* was finished, and expressed the hope that when he visited town in several weeks' time they would finally meet. There is reason to believe that they did get together then, but confusion exists as to other circumstances. Where Nathan later placed the scene at the offices of the *Smart Set*, O'Neill said, "I can't for the life of me recall much about my first meeting with Nathan. It was with John D. Williams at some restaurant, I believe, and I was three-fourths 'blotto.' I remember thinking how much he looked like an old friend of mine [Harold De-Polo] who wrote animal stories at that era for Street and Smith."

Wherever they met, the two men were favorably impressed with one another. Nathan thought the playwright an "extremely shy fellow, but one who nevertheless appeared to have a vast confidence in himself . . . a deep-running personality — the most ambitious mind I have encountered among American dramatists." On his side O'Neill found the critic "warm and friendly and human where I half-expected an aloof and caustic intelligence completely enveloping and hiding the living being. *Half*-expected — for his letters to me had given me an inkling."

The meeting marked the start of a lifelong friendship. Though the two were opposites in almost every respect, it might be said of Nathan, as was said of O'Neill, that he was a "man with a mask" — or, more accurately, a man of various masks. A dandy, an iconoclast, a gourmet and self-professed hedonist, a superior intellect acutely aware of his own superiority, an American Original who cultivated his originality, Nathan reveled in paradox. He was, in the words of one of his biographers, "not so much an imp of the perverse as an imp of the inverse." Of German-French parentage and born to wealth in the unlikely setting of Fort Wayne, Indiana, he read *Faust* when he was only twelve ("understanding everything in it save that which was important") and by fifteen had read all of Shakespeare, as well as, at his father's orders, some of the bawdier Restoration comedies.

One chapter in his first book on the theater was called "The Unimportance of Being Earnest." He himself sounded at times like a latter-day Wilde ("What interests me in life . . . is the surface of life: life's music and color, its charm and ease, its humor and loveliness. . . . Nonsense is the privilege of the aristocracy. The worries of the world are for the common people"). Despite this elegant tone, however, no other American critic ever fought so tirelessly or forcefully for standards of quality in the theater, for writers who set their own course. He became the leading champion in America not only of O'Neill, who scarcely celebrated "life's music and color," but of O'Casey, the impassioned chronicler of the rude and brawling Dublin tenements.

O'Neill's appearance in the American theater clicked, Nathan said in 1923, "with all the precision and critical timeliness of the entrance of the United States Marines in a piece of popular whang-doodle. Just as this drama seemed about to be laid low by unremitting stereotyped dullness and preposterous affectation, he jumped upon the scene with a bundle of life and fancy under his arm, hurled it onto the stage, and there let it break open with its hundred smashing hues to confound the drab and desolate boards. Instantly — or so it seemed — the stage began to breathe again . . . today the pre-eminence of O'Neill is taken for granted even by such bizarre aesthetes as in the years before had placed in turn upon the same pedestal Augustus Thomas, Charles Klein, Eugene Walter and Edward Sheldon. [Nathan was foremost in deflating the reputations of the Sheldons, Walters, et al.]

"In even the poorer of O'Neill's plays — and he has written poor plays as well as brilliant — one feels a trace of power and bravery. He may on occasion work weakly, but he never works cheaply. Always there is perceptible an effort at something original and distinguished."

Professor Baker was another to whom Eugene sent the Boni &

Liveright volume, together with a letter on May 9 in which he reviewed the state of his affairs. After telling of his frustration over *Beyond the Horizon,* he said that he was awaiting the verdicts of Arthur Hopkins and David Belasco on *Chris,* and called *The Straw* "the best of them in my opinion, but on account of its subject matter, I anticipate a long period of waiting. . . . I wish you could read these three plays. They would interest you I feel sure, because they are sincere and because they demand a freshness of treatment and a widened scope for the playwright's subject material."

The volume of plays, he said, was a "small token of my remembrance of all I owe to my year under your guidance. . . . I realize I must have seemed woefully lacking in gratitude because, seemingly, I have never had the decency to write — and I know the interest you take in the work of your former students. But I'm really not as bad as that. In all honesty, I have waited more out of small-boy ambition than anything else. I was confident that the night would come when I could approach you with that digesting-canary grin, and pointing to the fiery writing on the wall of some New York theater, chortle triumphantly: 'Look, Teacher! See what I have done!' "

His growing reputation was bringing him new correspondents, among them Barrett H. Clark, an author and critic, who wanted biographical data. "I'm glad," O'Neill afterward wrote, "the stuff I sent you will fill the bill. I was rather afraid it looked as if I were making a Jack London hero of myself — whereas . . . I cannot recall one heroic passage in those experiences!"

Clark used the information in his review of the *Moon of the Caribbees* volume in the New York *Sun* on May 18. After terming it "the most significant [collection of one-act plays] that has been published in this country," he said that the author "makes you feel, even in his feeblest work, that he understands the secret springs in the men and women he sets before you. . . . The atmosphere with which his best plays are saturated is not factitious. . . . A cheap set such as was used in his play *Ile* was all that was necessary in the way of material equipment. To this day I feel the presence of mountains of ice outside that forecastle. O'Neill used his imagination where Belasco would have collaborated with the ice company. . . .

"I have been privileged to see the MS. of *Beyond the Horizon.* . . . While I am not at liberty to describe it, I may say that the author is well able to handle a striking theme and living characters in a long play. I see no reason why O'Neill should fail to be recognized as our leading dramatist . . . he has now only to develop, to widen his vision of men and women and do his best, unhampered by the material success that is sure to come to him."

The critics were uniformly enthusiastic about the collection of sea plays. Heywood Broun in the *Tribune:* "Our belief that Eugene O'Neill has a very unusual talent for the theater has been confirmed by reading his plays." The *Review of Reviews:* "He may well be termed the Joseph Conrad among playwrights." The *Nation:* ". . . places him definitely among the handful of American dramatists whose future is of genuine importance to our theater."

Eugene and Agnes were in a euphoric mood as they headed for Provincetown in late May, cheered not only by the book's reception but by thoughts of their destination, their new home — the old Coast Guard station, solitary as a ship, overlooking the sea.

27

✵

Launched on Broadway

"A more bleak or dangerous stretch of coast," says *The Life-Savers of Cape Cod*, "can hardly be found in the United States than at [Peaked Hill Bars]. The coast near the station rightly bears the name 'Ocean Graveyard.' Sunken rips stretch far out under the sea at this place, ever ready to grasp the keels of ships that sail down upon them, and many appalling disasters have taken place there."

But in summertime, as the ocean rolls in rhythmically under a great arch of sky and sea gulls drift overhead and sandpipers skitter along the beach, nothing could be more serene, nothing more soothing. "I feel a true kinship and harmony," O'Neill said, "with life out there. Sand and sun and sea and wind — you merge into them, and become as meaningless and as full of meaning as they are. There is always the monotone of surf on the bar — a background for silence — and you *know* that you are alone. . . . You can walk or swim along the beach for miles, and meet only the dunes — Sphinxes muffled in their yellow robes with paws deep in the sea."

Harry Kemp, who spent many summers in a shack among the dunes, has also left his impression of the scene: "The sunrises are enormous, spraying the east with unimagined colors . . . when there are clouds, they march like cities moving, in whatever direction the wind blows. Out in the ocean a strange life goes on. Porpoises roll and sport. Herds of fish drive this way and that. . . . Whales are often seen. . . . In the back, in the heart of the dune-country, there is a petrified forest buried. Bone-white sand-carved bits of wood and what were once greening branches work up through the sand. . . ."

O'Neill would never be happier than he was this summer. Everything about his new home — the house itself, its location where land and water met in unending if imperceptible change — was perfectly attuned to his temperament and tastes. The nearest habitation was the new Coast Guard station a half-mile away, built a few years earlier when it appeared that "only a trifling further encroachment of the sea is needed to undermine the bank and tumble [the old station] into the grasp of shore breakers." But after years of nibbling away and during storms tearing away at the land, the sea, turning benevolent, began adding to the shore line; it was as though the waves were intent on preserving a suitable home for a playwright of the sea, a chronicler of souls shipwrecked in life and adrift without compass.

Built inside and out of weathered wood to withstand the onslaught of the elements, the station nestled in a craterlike site nearly encircled by the ever-shifting dunes; sand would drift high against the walls, chiefly on the eastern and northern sides, so that one could walk up slopes onto the roof, but the wind kept hollowing out the bank toward the west. Before he and Agnes could move in, Eugene spent days, sometimes aided by one or two of the local Portuguese, digging away sand that half-buried the structure; new windowpanes had to be installed to replace those that were rendered opaque from one year to the next by the whirling sand. The O'Neills' first child would call the place "the house where the wind blows."

Moving in became a kind of treasure hunt with the treasures in clear view and lying all about; the new owners explored their home in a daze of happiness, for everything was, in Agnes's words, "beautiful and unusual and useful." Mabel Dodge in refurnishing the place had indulged her taste for the artistic but without violating the functional character, the honest homemade nature of the station. The predominant colors were blue and white, especially white — white ceilings and walls with so many coats of paint they were luminous, gleaming even in the dark, and nearly all the furniture was white. The floors were a deep Chinese blue, and here again there had been repeated coatings of paint, ending in a strangely vivid blue that suggested the essence of the sea. For further color: curtains, cushions and other accessories predominantly blue and yellow, as well as large platters and bowls of Italian earthenware. The over-all effect was one of luxurious simplicity.

It was the essential character of the house itself, however, that meant most to O'Neill. In describing the place to an interviewer he dwelled not on Mabel's improvements but on the original utilitarian features of the old lifesaving station: "The stairs are like companionways of a ship. There are lockers everywhere. . . . The big boat room, now our living room, still has steel fixtures in the ceiling from which one of the boats was slung. [This was the room where bodies of the drowned were once laid out.] The look-out station on the roof is the same as when the Coast Guards spent their eternal two-hour vigils there."

O'Neill too was to spend countless solitary hours on the roof, absorbed in the ever-changing view, feeling himself at one with "sand and sun and sea and wind." His study on the second floor, reached by a companion-way and facing seaward, was rather like an echo chamber, for the sound of the surf was ever-present and seemed louder here than on the beach; his windows, unlike those in the rest of the house, were curtainless to afford an unobstructed view of the ocean. He did most of his writing on an outsize bunk generously supplied with cushions, but he also had a large plain desk that the nearby Coast Guardsmen had made for him from the woodwork of a salvaged ship.

In his daily routine, work merged with recreation and recreation with work, one stimulating the other. He would write all morning, swim before lunch, nap afterward, then work several more hours revising what he had written earlier that day, after which he often went swimming again. He was without fear in the water. Jerry Farnsworth, an artist, recalls walking along the beach one day after a "nor'easter" when there was a "terrific surf, with grass torn up and thick with sea-weed — nobody else would dream of going in — but Gene was right in the middle of it, like a creature of the sea. He was doing a back-stroke, bringing his arms directly overhead and back, which would sink his head, then making a full semi-circle downward that gave him tremendous push."

For the past year or so he had become increasingly intent on being physically fit. First in New Jersey, now at Peaked Hill, he would pummel away at a punching bag until his arms tired; he took long walks along the beach as much for the workout as for the pleasure of exploration, but next to swimming his favorite hours were spent in a kayak. "Gene once made one of those trips," Harry Kemp said, "about five miles offshore. He finally came up alongside a fishing schooner to ask if there was a spare codfish aboard. The skipper took one look at him . . . then he roared, 'You git back to shore quick as you can, you crazy loon!' But Gene seemed to regard the kayak as being safe as an ocean liner. Often he'd paddle clear around [the tip of] the Cape and into Provincetown harbor."

From Provincetown proper to Peaked Hill was about three miles but it seemed more like thirty as one slipped and slogged one's way across the dunes (Kemp once likened it to "walking in deep snow without snow shoes"). The landscape was so desolate and wild as soon as one left Snail Road, which led into the dunes, that the old station had an air of being at a vast distance from civilization. To obtain groceries and other supplies Eugene and Agnes would walk to the village about once a week and, heavily laden, ride back in the wagon of a local drayman; their mail they got through the Coast Guardsmen at the nearby station, who made daily trips to town in their own horse-and-wagon. Evenings at Peaked Hill were largely spent in reading by the large fireplace in the living room, built extra deep to accommodate large pieces of driftwood, after which the O'Neills would fall asleep to the sound of the surf.

Terry Carlin spent part of the summer with them, though neither he nor Agnes really cared for one another. To Agnes the old fellow, with his irresponsible ways and constant drinking, constituted an unhealthy influence on her husband, while Terry, who looked on women as a troublesome element in a man's life, felt that the easy relationship between him and his young friend had been diminished by the latter's marriage. "Jig said yesterday," Hutch Hapgood wrote his wife, "that the 'atmosphere' of the O'Neills is much better and sweeter than when Terry was with them — & I find them very good together."

O'Neill concentrated this summer on revising *Chris Christopherson*, which Williams, who had first call on the playwright's output, had turned down, Arthur Hopkins had never bothered to read, and George Tyler had placed under option. Now that so many authoritative voices were praising the chronicler of the S.S. *Glencairn*, Tyler realized that he had been somewhat hasty a few years earlier in dismissing the literary ambitions of his old friend's difficult son. Though he had some reservations about *Chris*, particularly its ending, he intended to produce it in the fall.

"Have been busy," Eugene wrote him on June 8, 1919, "getting settled in my new place up here . . . but now I'm all fixed to 'stay put' and expect to start work on the change in *Chris* at once. I've got it all mapped out in my head, and it shouldn't take long." He was, however, unduly optimistic, for the task of revisions ate up most of his summer, he and Tyler meanwhile carrying on a heavy correspondence about his problems with the script.

"I feel sure," he wrote on June 13, "you will find that the revisions I have made fill the bill and strengthen the ending greatly." Weeks later the producer replied: "I wish you would have another try at that last scene. . . . The trouble with the darned play is it's so wonderfully good for five scenes that it is almost absolutely necessary to become positively great in the last scene. . . . Please don't think me hyper-critical. My twenty-five years of experience should be worth something, shouldn't it?"

"It is a darned hard scene to write, that last one," O'Neill immediately answered on July 20, "darned hard to carry on what has gone before to *the* one inevitable conclusion without becoming artificially theatrical and falsifying characters that have been built up with so much care in the scenes preceding. . . . I'll promise to think hard . . . and preserve an

*O'Neill, Agnes, and
Shane, circa 1921*

*O'Neill on the roof of the
Peaked Hill Bars Station*

The Station in the late 1920s

The Station after a storm in 1931, as it was slipping into the sea

open mind to any hint for improvement which the God of playwrights may deign to whisper. . . . At present I feel confidence in the scene as it is. This is a delightful sensation for an author — to be cherished with care for it seldom lives long." True to his apprehension, he wrote nine days later: "After careful consideration and rereading I have come to the conclusion that you are right and that the last scene can be much improved by an extensive revision. . . ."

The conflict in *Chris*, as in *Anna Christie*, arises both from the old bargeman's efforts to influence his daughter against marrying a man who follows the sea and from her internal struggle as to whether she should accept her suitor. In one version of the early work the author had Chris attempting suicide; in another, planning to kill Anna's prospective husband. But O'Neill would never devise a denouement that entirely satisfied him, not even after he had drastically rewritten the story and achieved a hit with *Anna Christie;* he would in fact come to undervalue the play, chiefly because most critics, contrary to his intention, found its ending more or less optimistic.

From time to time the past reached out to O'Neill from the day's mail or the daily newspaper. Late in the summer he received a questionnaire from Gaylord Farm in regard to the state of his health, his work, and other circumstances. "The return in money," he wrote Dr. Lyman on September 2, "my plays have so far brought in is, I can say without boasting, but a poor indication of their artistic success and recognition. In the measure that I love my work . . . so much the more deep is my gratitude to you and to Gaylord Farm for saving me for it."

It was with mixed emotions, however, that he sometimes thought of Louise and Reed. There was no chance of his forgetting them, even had he tried, for the two were often in the news. Earlier this year Jack had been acclaimed for *Ten Days That Shook the World*, a graphic history of the Russian Revolution; but both he and Louise had been denounced in the press when they testified before a Senate committee investigating Bolshevik propaganda in America. Though Reed had outwitted his inquisitors at the hearing, the press coverage tended to make him look at once foolish and sinister; one editorial, in fact, bore the headline, "One Man Who Needs the Rope."

His friends knew a different John Reed. During a brief visit to the Cape this summer, the last time Susan and Jig ever saw him, he unburdened himself: "I wish I could stay here. Maybe it will surprise you, but what I really want is to write poetry." When they urged him to follow his heart, he shook his head, looking troubled, and said that he had "promised too many people."

While Reed and Louise became increasingly radical and activist-minded, O'Neill was growing more and more skeptical about social reform. "Time was," he said in 1922, "when I was an active Socialist, and, after that, a philosophical anarchist. But today I can't feel that anything like that matters. . . . It seems to me that man is much the same creature, with the same primal emotions and ambitions and motives, the same powers and the same weaknesses, as in the time when the Aryan race started toward Europe from the slopes of the Himalayas. He has become better acquainted with those powers and weaknesses and he is learning ever so slowly how to control them." It was as much Nietzsche as O'Neill talking, as his following words indicate: "The birth-cry of the higher men is almost audible, but they will not come by tinkering with externals or by legislative or social fiat. They will come at the command of the imagination and the will."

At summer's end Eugene rented a small cottage in Provincetown, called Happy Home, where he and Agnes were to spend the winter and where their first child would be born. Through a doctor's miscalculation, the baby was expected in late September, but did not actually arrive until weeks·later. In his letter to Dr. Lyman the playwright had expressed measured hope that rehearsals of both *Chris* and *Horizon* were "to start any day now," but here again his expectations were premature. Tyler, among Broadway's most active managers, became busy with three productions that were to open within a month's time ("I have been almost off my nut from overwork," he wrote Eugene), while Williams also was occupied with other projects.

After O'Neill and Williams failed to reach an agreement about *The Straw*, the playwright centered his hopes on a thriving new organization, the Theater Guild, headed by Lawrence Langner, Philip Moeller, actress Helen Westley and several others from the defunct Washington Square Players. Launched early this year at the Garrick Theater with Benavente's *Bonds of Interest*, which failed, the Guild had only $19.50 in its treasury when it opened St. John Ervine's *John Ferguson*. This one was fortunate enough not only to please both critics and public but to arrive as the actors of the city, organized by Actors' Equity, went on strike, closing nearly every theater in town for months. *John Ferguson*, with a non-Equity cast, was exempt from the walkout and played to packed houses in a longer engagement than it otherwise would have had. The new firm was on its way to score the most impressive producing record in the history of the American theater, yet nearly a decade would pass before the Langner-Moeller-Westley group sponsored a work by the country's leading playwright.

"The Theater Guild," O'Neill wrote George Jean Nathan, "have seen [*The Straw*] and rejected it. They said it was most excellent but not the kind of play for their public. Since *John Ferguson* inoculated them with the virus of popular success — quite contrary to their expectations — I'm afraid they've become woefully worried about the supposed tastes of 'their public.' . . . And the latest I hear is that James K. Hackett is to star for them in *Silas Lapham*. My God! The trouble seems to be that you can't eliminate the weakness of the old Washington Square Players by merely changing the name."

Following his disappointment over the Guild, Eugene told Madden to submit *The Straw* to Tyler and on September 29 wrote the latter: *I earnestly request you to read this play!* It is far and away the best and truest thing I have done, ten times more dramatic and heart-searching than *Chris!* Even if you are busy, I'm so confident in this play that I'll guarantee you won't regret the time spent in reading it."

Nearly a month later, after no word from Tyler, Eugene wrote again, voicing the hope that he would shortly read *The Straw*, inquiring about the status of *Chris*, and adding that the "heir to this branch of the clan" was expected at any time. On October 25 the manager replied that he was deferring production of *Chris* until he had "no other company in rehearsal and nothing to distract my mind from the work. I'm crazy about the play and I want it to make history. . . . The situation theatrically at present is terrible — that is, it is so congested. Plays which are ready to go out of New York cannot leave because they have no place to go to. . . . Laurette Taylor starts rehearsal next week and there isn't a theater in the United States to put her in when she is ready! Of course, one may open up for a star of this magnitude but it's by no means sure."

Eugene received the news in a "spirit which, if it rises not to Job, at least sinks not to Jeremiah. Even though you are the manager, I can't see my way clear to reviling you with the customary curses. I'll admit I'd like to. When the first blizzard finds me in flannel underwear panning out the corners of an empty coal bin and dreaming of sun-drenched coral islands, I probably will anyway."

He had two new plays already "mapped out" (one was *Gold*, the amplification of *Where the Cross Is Made*, the other probably "Exorcism," the one-acter based on his suicide attempt at Jimmy the Priest's), but had deferred working on them, he told Tyler, for fear of being summoned any day to New York for rehearsals. Now that *Chris* was apparently off until after the Christmas holidays and Williams still had no definite plans for *Horizon*, he saw "clear water ahead" and was going to settle down again to writing. He ended by once more urging the manager to read *The Straw* as soon as possible.

Besides worrying over the fate of his scripts, Eugene became increasingly anxious about Agnes's seemingly overdue delivery. She was under the care of Dr. Daniel H. Hiebert, the playwright's onetime roommate in Cambridge, who had settled in Provincetown this year to begin practicing medicine. In the early hours of October 30 the O'Neills' first child was born, a ten-and-a-half-pound boy with black hair. As Eugene afterward leaned over his wife's bed to kiss her, he whispered, "I knew we'd forgotten something. A crib for him!" The child was named Shane Rudraighe O'Neill, after one of Ireland's most celebrated warrior-kings, popularly known as "Shane the Proud."

Eugene, who began calling him "Shane the Loud," wrote Tyler on November 1 that his voice "already carries further than the Old Man's," and in a letter four days later to Tyler's press agent, John Peter Toohey, he said, "If you've got a mob scene rehearsing, I'd like to place him. His Grandpa's voice!"

O'Neill was hoping, he told Toohey, that when Tyler finally got around to reading *The Straw* he would be "sufficiently impressed to take the chance. I honestly believe that the American managers are lagging behind their public. . . . I think that there is now a numerous and growing audience, in the big cities anyway, who really demand something more than just a couple of hours' amusement, and that . . . any manager can afford to produce plays that would have been impossible before we got into the war. How about *The Jest, Redemption* and *John Ferguson?* I don't believe that any of these three would have stood a burglar's chance three years ago. The psychology of the average audience member has changed a lot . . . and is changing."

Trying to influence Tyler through his press agent, he went on: "I take it that the principal objection to *The Straw* on popular grounds would be the T.B. element; but I believe that the idea of tuberculosis is now too familiar to the people at large to be fraught with the old ignorant horror. The Great White Plague is more of a household companion than most people realize. . . .

"I honestly believe my play would have a good fighting chance because it is at bottom a message of the significance of human hope — even the most hopeless hope. . . . For we know deep down in our souls that, logically, each one of our lives is a hopeless hope — that failure to realize our dreams is the inexorable fate allotted to us. Yet we know that without hope there is no life, and so we go on pursuing our dream to the last gasp, convinced in spite of our reason that there must be some spiritual meaning behind our hope which in some 'greener land' will prove it was all justified." The letter to Toohey is but one among countless indications that despite O'Neill's apostasy, he could nev∘r root out the religious element in his nature.

Tyler at last read *The Straw,* found it "wonderful," but neglected to mention whether he was going to produce it. "Your note," the author immediately replied on November 9, "has put me into that torturing state popularly known as 'up in the air.'" A few days later, after reassuring word from the manager, he wrote again: "A million rousing cheers! I'll tell you frankly why I'm so anxious to get your signature to a contract. It isn't that your word with me isn't worth more than a thousand legal bonds — God forbid! It's just that I need the advance money quite urgently."

His financial circumstances, despite his growing reputation and favorable prospects, had deteriorated since last winter, when he and Agnes had lived in her house in New Jersey; now there were three of them and various new expenses, including rent, doctor's fees, and the hire of a housekeeper-nurse, Mrs. Fifine Clark, living with them. Mrs. Clark was to become an integral part of the household, practically a second mother to Shane, just as Sarah Sandy had once been to the infant Eugene, and would remain with the family until the marriage broke up in the late 1920s.

A comfortably built woman in her mid-fifties with olive skin and dark hair streaked with gray, Mrs. Clark had more iron in her make-up than her soft voice and motherly appearance suggested. So far as is known, Shane Rudraighe O'Neill was the first child she had ever taken care of; she loved him to the point of adoration, becoming increasingly possessive about him, and had it been possible would gladly have supplanted Agnes in his life. Her past was checkered. Born in France, she was a midinette in Paris when she met and married Clark, a ship's captain from Province-town. Though eyed with suspicion by the local women when she arrived on the Cape around 1890, Fifine became active in the Ladies Aid Society of one of the churches; not that she was particularly religious but rather that she was determined to become part of the community.

After her husband died she kept house for a Mr. Berry, a Province-towner with a practical sense of humor; the sign on his shop said "Junk" most of the year, but in summer, when the village bulged with vaca-tioners, he would reverse the sign to display the legend "Antiques." For a year or so Mrs. Clark ran a boardinghouse for sailors, and while her place itself was unprepossessing ("It looked," one of her friends recalls, "like a pack rat's nest"), she had retained a Frenchwoman's flair for cooking. Since both O'Neill and Agnes were lean, while Fifine was plump, their friends used to joke that she starved the couple and stuffed herself.

At the end of November, leaving Agnes and the baby in Mrs. Clark's care, Eugene headed for New York to visit his parents and try to expedite production of his scripts. The train was only past Truro when he began writing Agnes that he missed her: "I already feel that pang of a great emptiness which always gnaws way down at the roots of my soul as soon as I become sickeningly aware of the vacant spot by my side where you should be. I love you so, My Own! You must believe that and also that I need you, your help and sympathy and love, as I have never before needed you. You said you thought my need had grown less, but that is mistaken nonsense. (Nonsense!) It has grown day by day, hour by hour, as you crept into my inner life, my finer soul, until now that part of me is your creation, the soul of me. You are the wife of all of me but mother of the best of me. So ignore my bad moods and my irresponsible tongue. They are the leopard's spots; and, after all, a leopard isn't such a bum creation, taking him all in all. . . ." (It will be recalled that once before, in writing to Nina Moise, he had referred to his "leopard's spots.") Apparently Agnes had expressed doubts about his feelings toward their child, for he ended. "Kiss Shane for me. I *do* love him 'in my fashion.' "

For the past year, ever since he was struck by a car, James O'Neill had been in uncertain health and after long seeming younger than his age now looked his seventy-three years. Aware that his time was running out and eager to improve his financial position for Ella's sake, he had devoted much of his summer in New London to buying and selling real estate. Among the properties he disposed of was the Monte Cristo cottage and two adjacent houses, all of it sold for thirty-one thousand dollars. Also, to help his wife avoid part of the inheritance tax, he transferred some of his holdings to her, using his old friend Dorsey as an intermediary party in the transactions. But whatever his private fears about himself, the old actor — to reassure Ella — talked confidently of plans for building "in the near future" on some of his land.

Before leaving town he was interviewed by a reporter for the *Day* and took the occasion to boast about his son's *Beyond the Horizon* and *Chris Christopherson* being slated for Broadway production. The two plays, the newspaper said on September 6, have been read by "some of the most famous authors" in the country and found "wonderful." Mr. O'Neill, the article added, was looking forward to a reunion in New York with his younger son.

"The Old Governor and Mama . . . both appear extremely glad to see me," Eugene wrote Agnes, "especially after the detective work at the greeting failed to discover my breath guilty. They are full of thous. questions concerning the baby and are crazy to see him." Much of his letter was a half-humorous lament over the growing "dryness" of the city, the result of antiliquor legislation recently enacted by New York State, a prelude to the imminent imposition of the Volstead Act. "Papa," he said, "had only *one-quarter of one bottle* left of the treasure when I arrived — and that is now gone, need I add? *And he is at a loss where to get more!* Honestly! He still loves Wilson but hates his native land — U.S. — and swears to beat it hence with all his gold to some country where gentlemen may still be ungentlemanly. . . . There's nothing at all for me here now that [Prohibition] is in force. Of course, it did make me happy to see Paw 'n Maw again, and I suspect I'll spend most of my time right under their wing. So don't worry about me! I'm a good, good boy!"

His first day in town he went shopping with Ella at Lord & Taylor's ("Mama knows everyone there"), and bought a tweed suit for sixty-five dollars, an overcoat for eighty-five dollars, and some incidental clothing. He had, if not quite a streak of the dandy, a love of fine clothes, inherited probably from Ella; and now that he was becoming a playwright of note, he felt he should dress the part when in town and making professional calls. "I decided," he told Agnes, "that pure sport clothes were a luxury one couldn't afford before laying the foundation of a regular, bread-and-butter costume. After *Chris* brings home the bacon will be time enough for me to exhibit my strange fancies. Not that the present clothes are the absolute usual. They have too much class for that."

He remained in the city for about a week, just long enough to learn that neither Tyler nor Williams could give him a firm commitment and that things were, as usual, confused and hectic on Macdougal Street. Jimmy Light and Ida Rauh were now running the playhouse in place of Jig, who had yielded the reins for a year. The job of leading and inspiriting the Players had drained his energy, and he wanted time to regain his drive. Behind his taking the sabbatical was also a burgeoning envy of O'Neill and his forthcoming uptown productions; along with getting a good rest, Jig, hoping to make his own mark as a writer, intended to concentrate on a play or two.

With or without Cook at the helm, the Provincetowners had difficulty finding scripts of merit. *The Dreamy Kid*, which had been considered inadequate for the opening bill last season, helped launch the new one on October 31 and proved the strongest item on the program. It was notable, if for nothing else, for employing an all-Negro cast. Several years earlier there had been a pioneering production in a midtown theater, "Colored Players in Plays by Ridgely Torrence," but, outside of Negro stock companies, the almost universal practice was to cast white actors in black-face for Negro parts. While Torrence, a white man, deserves credit for good intentions and for being a forerunner of sorts, he sentimentalized and idealized his colored Granny Maumees and Madison Sparrows beyond credibility, as compared with the author of *The Dreamy Kid*, who handled his characters with realism and clear-eyed sympathy. As an astute critic would later point out, "Dreamy was a killer because he was hunted, not just hunted because he was a killer." *The Dreamy Kid* can be regarded as O'Neill's apprentice work for *The Emperor Jones* and *All God's Chillun Got Wings*, as well as for his portrait of the Negro gambler in *The Iceman Cometh*.

On one of his evenings in town Eugene dropped around to the Hell Hole and was happy to find so many of "the old bunch" present — Hudson Dusters and the like. His pleasure at being accepted as one of the group is evident in the account he wrote Agnes: "There was no whiskey in the house and Joe Smith told me they couldn't get it more than two days a week now — and then it had to be stolen by some of the gang out of a storehouse. . . . All hands were drinking sherry and I joined this comparatively harmless and cheap debauch right willingly. . . . Some 'hard' ladies of the oldest profession, who seemed to know me, were in the back room along with a drunk. . . . He had a huge roll of money and was blowing the house. I suspected he was being 'framed' for a 'frisk' and kept my eyes to myself. . . .

"It was quite an 'old time' night down there — minus drunkenness — and I thoroughly enjoyed it. No Villager came to spoil the atmosphere, thanks be!, and the Hell Hole was itself again." After telling Agnes that without her he felt "empty and hollow," he added that he would return in a few days "and be your other — and first born! — baby again!"

The final weeks of 1919 were hard on O'Neill as he marked time, hoping from one day to the next for news that would summon him back to New York. Tyler, however, beyond deciding on character actor Emmett Corrigan for the title role of *Chris*, had again become involved with two or three other productions simultaneously. As for Williams, he was preoccupied with a melodrama by Elmer Rice, *For the Defense*, starring Richard Bennett and due on Broadway in mid-December; but he talked vaguely of doing *Horizon* as his next offering, with Bennett in the part of Robert Mayo. "I'm still," the playwright wrote Barrett Clark on December 13, "at the nerve-wracking job of waiting for a production of my two sold long plays. No suitable theaters to be had, say both Tyler and Williams. It's a great season!"

Just as the year was running out he learned from the newspapers about the end of Jimmy the Priest's; it ended in a Bowery-style *Götterdämmerung*, with men dying in their chairs in the back room and up in the flophouse from poisonous booze. The word around Fulton Street was that Condon (the press accounts referred to his saloon not as "Jimmy the Priest's" but as "Jimmy's Place") had been dealing with a responsible bootlegger until the day several thugs dropped by and told him he was to buy his supply from their boss "or else." Two days after Christmas one of Condon's lodgers was found dead at a table in the rear and a second man in his bed upstairs, while two others, violently ill, were removed to Bellevue Hospital, where they proved beyond medical care. A fifth man, not a lodger, known as "Honey Mike" McGowan, who had been drinking with the others, died in agony at home. When autopsies on the brains of all five found ethyl and the deadly methyl (wood) alcohol present in substantial quantities, Condon and his bartender were arrested and held without bail on homicide charges.

The *Tribune*, after one of its men had visited 252 Fulton, reported on December 29: "A narrow hallway, lighted by a gas jet, gives ingress to the rickety stairway leading to the upper two floors which are given over to lodgers, who for the most part are employed along the waterfront. The white-washed walls are bearded with cobwebs and crowded with beds. The bar was locked yesterday, but the lodging house, in the enforced absence of the proprietor, was being conducted by a one-eyed man clad in overalls and a cap. 'Everybody that's left is on their feet,' he volunteered by way of explaining that none of the other lodgers had been afflicted."

The case against Condon and his bartender had at first seemed airtight, but it fell apart under investigation. The victims, it turned out, had also had drinks in another saloon before being stricken and, further, the liquor taken as evidence from 252 (though, oddly enough, not until a day or so after the deaths) was found free of noxious ingredients. The charges against the two men were dismissed, but Condon, who had been so well known around the water front, was ruined; he immediately afterward vanished into obscurity.

Thinking of his stoker friend Driscoll, of old Chris and little Jimmy Byth, Eugene was saddened by the passing of the Fulton Street spot. Months later he told an interviewer that after the enactment of the Prohibition act he most regretted that "the hangout of many of my old pals, Jimmy the Priest's, has gone the way of many good things, nevermore to be seen."

He had little time, however, in the early days of 1920 to brood over the past, for matters began coming to a head in regard to both *Horizon* and *Chris;* by January 5 he was back in New York. "My firebrand letter to John D.," he wrote Agnes, "produced immediate results — a messenger boy to the [Prince George] this morning with a reply. He is stirred to the heart, it seems, and rather sore. . . . He also phoned Madden saying 'O'Neill didn't know how much he (W) had done for the play.' He's a great joker, surely, is Mr. Williams. Madden and I are to see him tomorrow and get down to brass tacks. We have agreed that he must 'show us' or give up the play."

His letter contained news of all three of his plays. Tyler initially had tried to get film actor William Farnum for the title role of *Chris*, then settled for Emmett Corrigan, but it now appeared that the role might be filled by Godfrey Tearle; the latter, in spite of being in a quick failure on Broadway, had scored a personal triumph. "All the managers," Eugene said, "are after him. Tearle told me he had read at least fifty American plays sent to him by Belasco, etc., but none was artistic enough to make it worth his while staying in this country. He had his passage booked back to England — then read *Chris* and decided to stick around a while."

The word about *The Straw* involved Tyler's latest star, nineteen-year-old Helen Hayes, who was to open in a new play in Boston in the spring. The producer, Eugene said, was thinking of putting on a single matinee of *The Straw* to "see if she can play the part. Tyler claims she is going to prove *the* great emotional actress of the future." Ending on a personal note, he wrote that his father had "been pretty sick and looks bad but is getting better."

About a week later, on January 14, he was moved on reading a tribute to his father in the *Morning Telegraph:* "That noble veteran of the stage, James O'Neill, is suffering from a serious ailment. . . . Several millions of the American public, of two generations, will hope and pray for Mr. O'Neill's speedy and complete recovery. He has been one of the American stage's most brilliant actors, and he is endeared to the public for his memorable performance of *Monte Cristo*." But the article was unduly alarmist, for that same day Eugene wrote Agnes that his father was "on his feet again" and had felt well enough a previous evening to stay up late with Tyler and Will Connor. The two men, according to Eugene, were already well "boiled" when they arrived, becoming more so after James brought out a jug of whiskey, and "had a brawl over whether *Ile* or *The Rope* was the best one-act play ever written. . . . Tyler and I 'went to the mat' on what was or was not the matter with the American theater. They never left till one A.M. It was quite fun. The old man didn't drink but the excitement cheered him up. . . . Tyler, in spite of his 'bun,' was astonished to find I could be talkative."

Williams was another who learned that O'Neill, for all his usual reticence, could speak up. After a heated exchange during which the playwright threatened to take back his play unless it went into production without further delay, the two men settled on a compromise that called for *Horizon* to open in the first week of February with a series of four matinees, after which it would be given at night on a split-week basis with *For the Defense*. Also, the playwright was to get better terms under a new contract — royalties of five, seven and one-half, and ten percent, instead of his former three, five and six.

Although disappointed over the projected schedule, O'Neill had been waiting nearly two years for a production and felt that under the circumstances — the season was booming, theaters were scarce — Williams's offer was the best he could hope for. In planning to open with matinees Williams was following a practice that had developed in recent years for introducing works of merit but of uncertain box-office strength; if the plays proved popular in "special matinees," they were booked for a regular run. Williams, however, concealing his doubts about *Horizon*, led Eugene to think that he was opening with matinees because they would enable him to assemble the best cast possible for the crucial first performances. Besides having Richard Bennett of *Defense* for Robert Mayo, he was borrowing from another production Helen MacKellar to play Ruth and Edward Arnold the older brother.

Apparently Eugene was unaware that Richard Bennett, a man with great ambition and drive, as well as his full share of actor's ego, had also been urging Williams to place *Horizon* in production; Bennett's share in the proceedings was less, though, than he would afterward claim. Months before the play entered rehearsals he told an interviewer he was "going to do the O'Neill piece, no matter how long I have to wait." He also wrote a friend, Pinky Elkins (the same Elkins who was Eugene's classmate at Harvard), that he had "started to blue pencil [*Horizon*] . . . and God knows it needs some blue pencilling . . . it seems terribly stretched out. . . . But having done so much with a rotten subject, such as I have been getting, I myself think that with the acquiescence of the author, a great play can be made out of *Beyond the Horizon*." Later, after the play had been acclaimed, he told Elkins that "very few beside Williams believed in it and even he got cold feet — I had to do it all, cast it, cut it, and produce it."

Eugene's first days in town were largely devoted to tightening the play. "I labored until 2 A.M. on the cuts," he wrote Agnes on January 14. "Finished up the first two acts. A great many cuts made by W. are all right but some are very silly and I will not stand for them. [These, presumably, were the cuts made by Bennett.] He leaves that up to me, however." The following day he spent the entire afternoon on the script with both Williams and Bennett, then worked all night at the latter's home, going over the play line by line, with the actor reading them aloud. Bennett had brought out a bottle of absinthe and the two men sipped frappés as they worked.

"If we hadn't had it," Eugene told Agnes, "we couldn't have kept awake. Do you know what time the work was finished? 7:30 A.M.! . . . When I came home I was too tired to get to sleep . . . and in addition my brain was full of subtle fireworks from the queer poison of absinthe. I sat down and wrote a prose poem. . . . When I wrote it the whole world was shot through with White Logic and I seemed to see through the whole game. Looking over it now, I think it's fine and nutty."

After long hoping for and dreaming of this day, he was all keyed up. He felt both as though "a mine were about to go off" inside him and as though he "could work 24 hours a day without eating." In addition to the job of shortening *Horizon*, he was conferring with Frederick Stanhope, who was to direct *Chris*, and found it difficult "to keep both the plays separate in my mind and think clearly about each of them." Dr. Aspell, who had performed the breast surgery on Ella and now was attending Mr. O'Neill, gave Eugene a "quick once-over" at the hotel and warned him: "You'll snap if you don't take care. Let down! Don't worry! Forget your work and rest!" In telling Agnes about it, Eugene added, "Good advice, maybe, but how the hell can I keep it at this stage of the game?"

Practically everywhere he went — at Williams's office, at Tyler's, at Bennett's home, in his sessions with Stanhope — there were drinks, and to avoid seeming a "prig," he would take a few. Also, Christine had invited him to a "farewell John Barleycorn party" at the playhouse, but he told Agnes not to "worry about my making a fool of myself. I'm a wise guy — when I know it's necessary."

A refrain of loneliness and of longing for Agnes runs through his letters ("I wish I could board that Fall River boat tonight. . . . I'll be home to you as soon as God will let me. I can't stand being away much longer. . . . I'd like to lay my tired buzzing old head on its own old place"); but thinking of how it would be if she and the baby were with him in a hotel room, he said nothing about her coming to the city. Agnes finally asked point-blank whether she could join him in February; Mrs. Clark, she said, would be glad to accompany her and look after Shane. "I wish you were here, My Own," he wrote back, "but you will be later on."

From Christine's affair, which proved a "fizzle," he went on to the Hell Hole, consumed a quantity of "red ink," and ended by spending the night in a room upstairs. He afterward felt so rotten that he omitted writing his usual daily letter to Agnes. Alarmed when a day passed without hearing from him, especially now that he had resumed drinking, and aggrieved that he had said nothing further about her joining him, she poured out her feelings on January 21. After expressing the view that he was justified in having the absinthe at Bennett's place, Agnes upbraided him for attending Christine's party, reminding him that he had said he no longer enjoyed the parties at the Provincetown and felt that most of the crowd, envious of his forthcoming Broadway debut, would like to push him down "into the dirt." At a time like this, she went on, when he should have all his wits about him and be in good shape for the rehearsals of *Horizon*, drinking was the last thing he should be doing. It was hard on her, she concluded, to be so far away when the "big event," something they had awaited for so long, was about to happen.

His reply was quick and heated: "These sort of letters are not the kind that do any good . . . especially as I have been home here without leaving the [Prince George] ever since Monday doing a severe penance for my crimson-ink sins of Sat. night and Sunday. I assure you my sojourn in the Village — with the exception of about 2 hours at the P.P., was entirely spent at the Hell Hole where no one is trying to 'drag me down.' The night I slept there Lefty, Leo, Chuck and I camped in one bed! Imagine! That was the only way we could keep warm in [Tom Wallace's] zero flat. Now what in hell is effete Village stuff — or 'party' — in that? Rather it was good old healthy H.H. days back again, and I had a good time — of that kind. The red ink, though, is poison. . . .

"No more lecture letters, please! You never used to be a moralist, and I've never in my life stood for that stuff, even from my Mother. My ethics of life forbid that in any conduct based upon emotional reaction, even Christ or Buddha should tell the lowest slave what he should do. That slave has something actuating him that they can never understand."

Eugene was suffering, it turned out, not so much from his drinking at the Hell Hole as from a severe cold, and for a time the doctor thought he might have fallen victim to a new outbreak of influenza that was spreading. By now he had been in New York two weeks but had been too busy to see a rehearsal. "I'm sick of *Beyond*," he wrote Agnes on the twenty-third, "and convinced that I must forget it. In my judgment there won't be an ounce of Fame or a cent of money in it for us. . . . I'd never go near a rehearsal if I didn't have to — and I'll certainly never see a performance. Those people will never — can never — be my Robert, Ruth, and Andy. . . . Perhaps this is the pessimism of sickness."

Godfrey Tearle, his letter went on, had decided against being in *Chris*, but only because he felt unsuited for the part. The play was to start rehearsing in a few days, with Emmett Corrigan in the title role, for a tryout engagement in Atlantic City in early March. "About your coming down," he said, "all depends on *Beyond*."

The following day, still "marooned" at the hotel, he complained of the weather as "the worst ever with rain and hail — and muck. The 'Flu' is raging as a consequence. . . . So don't speak any more of coming down to this plague spot until the present epidemic is over. Isn't it the curse of the Gods that just as the 'Flu' starts to rage again my first play is to go on! It will put an awful crimp in theater attendance, you know, and place the final touch on the fiasco which will be *Beyond the Horizon*."

He finally saw a rehearsal on Tuesday, the twenty-seventh, and came away depressed. "They all have the possibilities of being very good," he wrote his wife that evening, "and they all just miss it. . . . The characters don't seem to hang together. They all appealed to me to dope out for them the real meaning of what they were trying to do. I tried my best, but I'm no director, God knows, and whether my talking will result in any improvement I don't know. . . . I suppose my feeling of disappointment is my usual one at all rehearsals. God blast 'em, how I hate to see a play in that stage of development!"

Williams planned to test the play with a single performance in nearby Yonkers on Monday afternoon, February 2, and begin the matinee series in New York the following day at the Morosco Theater. "So a week from today," Eugene said, "will be the show-down — and Gawd help us! Williams is doing no advertising and I don't know how people are to know about it. That is his dope on how to get a select, intelligent audience for the first performance. But I'm tired of kicking at his methods."

At his second rehearsal he and Bennett " 'went to the mat' with a loud bang" when the actor, ignoring directions in the text, followed "his own ideas of what he should do." Bennett tried, Eugene wrote Agnes, "to get away with some learned remarks as to the true nature of the hero in tragedy. This was a bad mistake for him because I know more about that than he ever dreamed of and I showed him up before the whole company. . . . He was stung, and resorted to sarcasm anent my inexperience in Broadway productions. But no one can beat me at that game and I came back with a remark about his inexperience in playwriting. Finally, furious, he yelled: 'Will you be responsible for the failure of this scene if we play it your way?' And I said yes, I'd be responsible for its artistic success and that was all I cared about. Then they went over it and he played Robert faithfully . . . as I wanted. After it was over he turned to me enthusiastically and said, 'By God, you're right! Let's have a few more fights and this play'll pick up 100%.' . . .

"For two days now I have occupied that position so unattainable to most playwrights — the only man in the auditorium, director of my own play! And I don't think I've made such a fizzle of it either! They all showed a noticeable improvement today, and also a marked improvement in their respect for me. At the end of each scene Bennett calls 'Suggestions!' and every member of the cast who has been in that scene lines up at the foot lights while I — a lone figure in a vast auditorium — go from one to one, praising or panning, and not excepting Bennett himself.

"Can you imagine! No, you can't — or any one of the P.P. either. For at every one of their rehearsals I was 'pickled' and not myself."

The strain of the final days was telling on him in the form of insomnia. "It's frightful!" he wrote Agnes on the twenty-ninth. "I've never had it before. . . . For the past week I've averaged about 4 hours [of sleep] per night. Last night I took Veronal — with the only result that I didn't get to sleep till 6:30 this A.M.! [Perhaps, since he had used Veronal in his suicide attempt at Jimmy the Priest's, he unconsciously fought the effect of the drug.] Got up at 8:30 — at theater at 10:45 — and then an all day grind. The funniest thing about it is that I don't feel bad, only a bit woozy. . . .

"Rehearsals look better. I think the play has a good chance for artistic success — beyond that, hope nothing!"

His mood changed from one day to the next, if not hourly, and occasionally outside events, intruding on his preoccupation with *Horizon*, affected his state of mind. George Jean Nathan, using a letter from O'Neill as ammunition, attacked the Theater Guild in the February issue of the *Smart Set* for rejecting *The Straw*. Thinking of the "enemies" the article had created for him, Eugene was annoyed with Nathan for printing his letter without his permission, but since he could hardly turn against his champion, vented his feelings on the Guild. "Well," he told his wife, "what the hell! They have always panned me behind my back, anyway, and are no friends of mine. Also what I said in that letter has been proved by the failure of *Silas Lapham* in every way. . . . So it's just as well for them to know I had their number."

Saturday, the thirty-first, was a busy day. After several hours at a rehearsal of *Horizon* he spent the entire afternoon at the Lambs Club with Stanhope going over the script of *Chris*. Several weeks earlier, when Tyler had asked him whether he wanted to make any revisions in *Chris* or *The Straw*, Eugene had said no, feeling that his job was done. But now, he told Agnes, he "found many cuts to make [in *Chris*]. I'm a lot wiser now than when I first went to *Beyond* rehearsals. Honestly, I've learned a tremendous lot that I wouldn't miss for worlds — knowledge that will be of *real* worth to me hereafter. . . . Bennett is really a liberal education all in himself. He has brains and he uses them every second and, outside of some misconceptions, he has really been a great help to the play. And even from his mistakes, I have learned a hell of a lot. I'm a better playwright already, I feel it."

To an author dress rehearsals are the last mile he walks to the electric chair, and O'Neill was no exception. Despite his buoyant mood when he wrote Agnes on Saturday, his spirits plummeted as he watched a runthrough the following day. Conscious of the première fast approaching, he saw all the weaknesses of the performance and the physical production on a magnified scale. The rehearsal started at 1 P.M. Sunday and lasted twelve hours without letup, without a break for dinner. "Toward the end," Eugene told his wife, "I was so tired and deathly sick of hearing and seeing *Beyond* that I wished it were in hell! It all seemed false and rotten and I wondered why the devil I'd ever written it. The sets for the outdoor scenes especially get my goat. To my eye they are the last word in everything they shouldn't be. . . . I couldn't endure the idea of suffering through the Yonkers performance, so I made the excuse that I had to work on *Chris* and so got out of it. . . .

"Well, Wednesday morning will tell the tale. I don't think there's a chance in the world of the play being a financial success, although [Williams], Bennett and other people seem to think there is, but I do hope it will add something to my rep."

A show-wise audience, full of theater people and more critics than had ever attended any previous O'Neill performance, assembled at the Morosco Theater on Tuesday afternoon, February 3. Ella and James were in a box; Eugene, feeling too nervous to remain seated, had intended to take shelter in the rear of the auditorium but, unable to "shake" Williams, found himself "planted" beside the producer. The performance began. Though ONeill had in recent days cut more than a half-hour of running time from the script, it was still overlong compared with the average play, and became even longer in a performance that dragged. The author was in despair, especially as the audience gave no sign of being impressed and, after the customary polite applause at curtain call, filed out quietly.

James O'Neill, who at times during the performance had had tears rolling down his face, congratulated his son, but then, to cover up his state of agitated happiness, added, "It's all right, if that's what you want to do, but people come to the theater to forget their troubles, not to be reminded of them. What are you trying to do — send them home to commit suicide?"

That afternoon found Agnes in Provincetown in a gloomy state; lying down in the bedroom of Happy Home, the thought occurred to her that if she had been told a year ago that she would not be at the opening of

O'Neill in 1921

A scene from Beyond the Horizon, *which launched O'Neill on Broadway. Richard Bennett is second from the right*

Carlotta Monterey

Horizon, she would never have believed it. But now, as she afterward wrote her husband, it appeared doubtful that she would ever see his first Broadway production. The curtain had fallen hours ago, Agnes said, and she was still in the dark as to the audience's response.

Not until the next day did she learn in a wire from him that the play was a "triumph." The letter that followed explained why he had been slow in telling her about it: "The first performance was hell! I suffered tortures. The waits were terrible and the show never ended until ten of six. I went out convinced that *Beyond* was a flivver artistically and every other way. That's why I didn't write you last night — I was too depressed. I dreaded to see this day's papers. When I did — lo and behold, in spite of all the handicaps of a rotten first performance, *Beyond* had won. You never saw such notices! There was not a single dissenting voice — so far, at any rate."

While the reviews were not so rhapsodical as his letter suggests, they were overwhelmingly favorable, with the younger critics tending to be more enthusiastic than the older ones. The latter, it was evident, had had to struggle to take a judicious view of something alien and disturbing in their experience — an American tragedy, stark and unsparing. Where young Alexander Woollcott of the *New York Times* hailed the play as an "absorbing, significant, and memorable tragedy, so full of meat that it makes most of the remaining fare seem like the merest meringue," old J. Rankin Towse of the *Evening Post,* after hemming and hawing, now praising, now damning, pronounced the play an "exceedingly promising juvenile work." Some of the press, qualifying their tributes, complained of the length of the play, with one declaring that the playwright had to learn that, "however minutely he aims to analyze his characters, he must . . . not write his plays in what amounts to six acts." Another said that "an audience goes to the theater to sit for an hour or two, not for a day. Mr. O'Neill seems to think that time is a negligible element in the development of his ideas."

Even his most enthusiastic champions, thinking of the somberness of the work, doubted that it would find much of an audience. After calling *Horizon* "a great play," Robert G. Welsh of the *Evening Telegram* said on February 4 that it was "probably too great to be a popular success." A few critics, unable to find a basis of comparison between O'Neill and other American playwrights, looked abroad. One likened him to Ibsen, another thought his play had "the mood, the austerity and, all in all, the stature of a novel by Thomas Hardy," while a third said *Horizon* "marks the advent of an American realist who promises to go far, quite as far as his Scandinavian, Russian and Irish predecessors in the theater." Perhaps closest to the mark was Kenneth Macgowan of the *Globe* when, viewing O'Neill as *sui generis*, he wrote on February 7 that the playwright "sees life straight and strong. He writes superb natural dialogue. He builds for power . . . always getting down to the big emotional root of things. A man like that will write big plays. . . . His is a genius that seems incorruptible."

Audiences at the Morosco paid their own kind of tribute by watching the play without, in the author's words, "a whisper in the house from start to finish, but many in tears." It would be weeks, because of the theater shortage, until *Beyond the Horizon* found its own home and could settle down for an indefinite run; but the first performance had already told the story. James and Ella's onetime wayward son had at last proven his heritage and, in the process, helped the American stage to come of age. "Before O'Neill," one writer would later sum up, "the U.S. had theater; after O'Neill, it had drama."

Ahead lay the 1920s, the most exciting decade the American theater had ever known and one that for sheer vitality has never yet been equaled, still less surpassed. Not the calendar but *Beyond the Horizon* ushered in that period. Ahead lay, in other words, *What Price Glory?* and *They Knew What They Wanted, Craig's Wife* and *The Silver Cord, In Abraham's Bosom* and *Porgy, Street Scene* and *The Front Page*, the emergence, in short, of George Kelly and Sidney Howard, of Maxwell Anderson, S. N. Behrman and Robert E. Sherwood. But always apart from them and in front of them, pursuing a solitary, unpredictable course, would be O'Neill. Now with tom-toms, now with masks, now with a psychological use of the old "asides," he would set the pace as the most adventurous and gifted of our playwrights. Within the decade he would turn out such diverse and notable works as *The Emperor Jones* and *The Hairy Ape, Desire Under the Elms, The Great God Brown* and *Strange Interlude*. The questing spirit that had possessed him ever since he had lost faith in God and a benevolent universe, the feeling he always had of not "belonging," the great restlessness that had sent him to sea, the dark hungers and forces that had driven him into the depths of Buenos Aires and the New York water front — all this and more would find an outlet, a sublimated voice, in his writings.

NOTES

THE number at the start of each note refers to a page of the narrative. O'Neill's plays, for the identification of quotations from them, are listed alphabetically at the beginning of the Notes; the italic numbers at the end of these listings refer to a page of the play text.

Quite often O'Neill's comments on a particular subject, while made on different occasions, are quoted together, as though one extract, but the several sources are given in the appropriate note. For the sake of smoother reading, elisions in quotations are not always indicated; and liberty has occasionally been taken with the order of a quotation, but never in such a way, it is believed, as to modify its meaning. Whenever someone is quoted without a published source given in the narrative or the Notes, his remarks were in almost all instances obtained through corresponding with or interviewing him; in a few cases, however, the information was obtained from what seemed reliable secondhand sources.

Quotations from O'Neill's Plays

In the play listings, (R.H. v. 1), (R.H. v. 2), and (R.H. v. 3) refer to the three-volume Random House set, while ("Lost") refers to *Ten "Lost" Plays.*

ABORTION ("Lost")

115	"I've always hated," *161.*
149	"Be frank, Dad!" *154.*
149	"I have played the scoundrel," *156.*
278	"We've retained a large portion," *154.*
278	"It was the male beast," *154.*

AH, WILDERNESS! (R.H. v. 2)

106   "I don't believe in this silly," *194.*
107   "Son, if I didn't know," *195.*
233   "dissolute, blasphemous," *201.*

ANNA CHRISTIE (R.H. v. 3)

189   "With his pale, thin," *3.*

BEYOND THE HORIZON (R.H. v. 3)

418   "It's a free beginning," *168.*
418   "I could curse God," *148.*

BOUND EAST FOR CARDIFF (R.H. v. 1)

177   "D'yuh remember the times," *487.*
185   "This sailor life," *486.*
279   "a pretty lady," *489.*
348   "Isn't this your watch," *484.*

"BREAD AND BUTTER" (not paginated)

275   "abnormally large dreamer's eyes," Act I.
276   "remarkably pretty girl," Act I.
276   "I'm always going to start," Act III.
276   "great sickness and lassitude," Act III.
276   "still pretty but has faded," Act IV.

"CHRIS CHRISTOPHERSON"

451   "the kind ought to leave," *6.*

DAYS WITHOUT END (R.H. v. 3)

88   "He grew up," *510.*
88   "Then his mother," *511.*
106   "First it was Atheism," *502.*

DESIRE UNDER THE ELMS (R.H. v. 1)

49   "Two enormous elms," *202.*
50   "Here — it's stones," *204.*
50   "Stones. I picked," *237.*
67   "cold . . . it's oneasy," *238.*

DYNAMO (R.H. v. 3)

67   "not formless," *428.*
67   "I might as well," *429.*
299   "It's so mysterious," *473, 474.*

THE EMPEROR JONES (R.H. v. 3)

151   "The forest is a wall," *187.*

[483]

FOG ("Lost")

271	"big dark eyes," *90.*
271	"Did you ever become so sick," *94.*

THE GREAT GOD BROWN (R.H. v. 3)

67	"full-breasted and wide-hipped," *278.*
94	"Why am I afraid," *264.*
102	"I remember a sweet," *282.*
277	"William Brown's soul," *294.*

THE HAIRY APE (R.H. v. 3)

164	"Oh, to be scudding," *214.*
166	"Hello, Kiddo," *237.*
196	"He seems broader," *208.*

THE ICEMAN COMETH (R.H. v. 3)

171	"the No Chance Saloon," *587.*
336	"tall, raw-boned," *574.*
337	"To hell with the truth!" *578.*

ILE (R.H. v. 1)

385	"He just walks," *536.*
385	"hard man," *578.*
385	"I don't give a damn," *541.*
385	"I guess I was dreaming," *546.*
385	"I used to go down on the beach," *548.*

A LONG DAY'S JOURNEY INTO NIGHT

3	"play of old sorrow," foreword (a dedicatory note from O'Neill to his wife, Carlotta Monterey).
3	"I was so healthy," *87.*
3	"It wasn't until after," *28.*
3	"He has never been happy," *88.*
3	"I was afraid all the time," *88.*
3	"It was in her long sickness," *39.*
4	"born afraid," *111.*
13	"different from all ordinary," *105.*
21	"When you're in agony," *74.*
24	"always getting upset," *110.*
25	"It was a great mistake," *153.*
27	"Twice we were evicted," *147.*
35	"That God-damned play I bought," *149, 150.*
45	"He is by nature," *13.*
50	"big frogs," *43.*
59	"Mamie Burns," *158.*
80	"The Mad Scene," *170.*
80	"Up to take more," *123.*
81	"His quietness fools people," *35.*
89	"It was right after that," *118.*
109	"Land is land," *15.*

Sources Other Than the Plays

For a full listing of sources given in abbreviated form, see Bibliography.

1. APPREHENSIVE MOTHER

4   Ella Quinlan O'Neill's letter: Dated only "Sunday," the letter probably was written 11/2/19. The grandson referred to in the letter, Shane O'Neill, was born Thursday, 10/30/19.
5   "honest old Vermont farmer": New York *Herald*, 10/14/88.
5   "Saved! Mine, the treasures": Clark, *Favorite American Plays*, p. 96.
5   "Excellent performance" and "large house": *Dramatic Mirror*, 10/27/88.
5   "James O'Neill says" and "makes one feel glad": Ibid., 11/3/88.
8   "large and well pleased," "very large house" and "Neither the star": Ibid., 11/3/88.
9   "promotion of and inciting": New York *Sun*, 10/17/88.

10   "Old Irish Problems": New London *Telegraph*, 12/17/00.

10   "One thing that explains": Bowen, "The Black Irishman," *PM*, 11/3/46.

11   "the most rigid seclusion" and "parsimonious in his habits": Nettie Walsh's divorce petition, filed in Superior Court, Chicago, in September 1877.

11   "chaste and virtuous woman": James O'Neill's answer to Miss Walsh's complaint, filed in Superior Court, Chicago, September 1877.

12   "Supper is served": Chicago *Tribune*, 9/9/77.

12   "Oh, Ella, what on earth": Leslie, "Threatens to Desert," Chicago *News*, 7/10/09.

12   Louise Hawthorne's death occurred on 6/28/76 and was widely reported in the Chicago press and the theatrical weeklies.

15   "tall, superb creature": Leslie, "Threatens to Desert."

16   "[James O'Neill] had prospered": *Argonaut*, 3/2/78.

17   "An Actor's Sad Bereavement": Denver *Republican*, 3/5/85.

22   "The increase of the morphine": New London *Telegraph*, 6/21/90.

23   "is the proud father": 11/4/88.

24   "James O'Neill, the celebrated": New London *Telegraph*, 11/5/88.

24   "Usually a child": Pasley, "The Odyssey of Eugene O'Neill," New York *News*, 1/25/32.

24   "I knew it, I knew it": Carlotta Monterey.

2. ACTOR AND PEASANT

26   "Today I remember photographically": O'Neill, James, "Personal Reminiscences," *Theater Magazine*, December 1917.

28   Five sisters: Surviving relation, Miss Mary Keenan of Ludlow, Kentucky.

28   "I know little": O'Neill, Patrick, *James O'Neill*, p. 116.

28   "He was a man of liberal": Patterson, "James O'Neill," *Theater Magazine*, April 1908.

29   "hunger and horror": O'Neill, James, "Personal Reminiscences."

29   "found a few of our clothes": St. Louis *Globe-Democrat*, 1/16/15.

29   "not always to his advantage": Chicago *Tribune*, 4/12/74.

29   "But young Mr. O'Neill": Patterson, "James O'Neill."

29   "Superfluity is": Chicago *Tribune*, 9/6/74.

31   "I worked it out": Patterson, "James O'Neill."

31   "object of probably": Chicago *Tribune*, 4/6/73.

31   "Miss Neilson is fortunate": Ibid., 4/9/73.

31   "most admirable": Ibid., 4/17/73.

31   "deserving of warm": Ibid., 2/25/74.

31   "It is not often": Ibid., 3/7/74.

31   "was wont to bully": New London *Telegraph*, 5/26/90.

31   "such *little* men": William Winter, *Other Days*, p. 158 (New York: Moffat, Yard, 1908).

31   "meeting the demands": Chicago *Tribune*, 10/23/73.

32   "When I played": Brandon Tynan, who costarred with James O'Neill in *Joseph and His Brethren* in 1913. Mr. Tynan presumably heard Miss Neilson's comment from Mr. O'Neill.

32   "That young man": *Locke* scrapbook at New York Public Library, 4/23/05.

32   "work, work": Chicago *Times Herald*, 2/21/97.

33   "the thunders of Sinai": O'Neill, Patrick, *James O'Neill*, p. 66.

33   "I was uncertain": *Dramatic Mirror*, 11/27/80.

34   "My wife likes": Alexander, *Tempering of Eugene O'Neill*, p. 49.

34   "Poor old Salmi!": San Francisco *Call*, 6/15/84.

35   "To O'Neill": New London *Day,* 12/28/97.

35   "I have produced": Winter, *Life of David Belasco,* v. I, p. 125.

35   "It's too bad": Basso, "The Tragic Sense," *New Yorker,* 3/13/48.

36   "Did Fechter": New York *Herald,* 10/16/80.

37   *Monte Cristo* reviews: *Tribune,* 2/19/83; *New York Times,* 2/13/83; *Sun,* 2/13/83.

37   "The critics were": Patterson, "James O'Neill."

37   "Youthful love": *Advertiser,* 4/17/83.

37   "That's what caused": Basso, "The Tragic Sense," 2/28/48.

40   "especially my 'Island' ": EO letter to an unidentified professor at Notre Dame, 9/17/04.

40   "royal blood": *Life,* 3/8/29.

40   "That's good, son!": *New Yorker,* 11/7/31.

41   "Revenge is": Bowen, "The Black Irishman."

41   "Before *Monte Cristo*": *Dramatic Mirror,* 10/20/88.

42   "one of the best": Boston *Home Journal,* 9/15/88.

42   "I hate to see": *Spectator,* 3/16/89.

42   "It was on account": New London *Telegraph,* 4/23/91.

42   "The storming of the Bastille": Boston *Transcript,* 9/30/90.

42   "dreadful nonsense": New York *Post,* 5/5/91.

43   "thoroughly bad actor": *Spirit of the Times,* 5/9/91.

43   "New York does not": *Dramatic Mirror,* 5/23/91.

44   "Almost the first words": Woolf, "Eugene O'Neill Returns," *New York Times,* 9/15/46.

45   "New York City is": New London *Day,* 10/17/98.

3. NEW LONDON SUMMERS

46   "rachitic flair": A case history of O'Neill kept by a doctor who treated him for several years in the 1940's. The physician is not identified at this time as his records will be drawn upon more heavily for the second volume of this biography, and the biographer prefers to postpone naming him.

46   "sort of black" and "routine case": Tyler and Furnas, *Whatever Goes Up,* pp. 91 and 92.

46   "Strenuous childhood": Doctor's case history.

47   "became too small": *Sunday Journal,* 9/2/00.

48   "quaint, picturesque": New London *Day,* 9/1/97.

49   "The truth is": Bowen, "The Black Irishman."

55   "She used to drift": Agnes Boulton.

55   "belongs somehow to the mists": *The King's England/Cornwall,* ed. by Arthur Mee, p. 2 (London: Hodder & Stoughton, 1937).

56   "She had a penchant": Karsner, "Eugene O'Neill at Close Range," New York *Herald Tribune,* 8/8/26.

56   "Mother love": O'Neill probably drew up the diagram in the mid-1920s, when he briefly underwent psychoanalysis. The paper, referred to hereafter in the footnotes as *The Diagram,* is given in its entirety at the end of the Notes.

57   "bashful little boy": Latimer, "Eugene Is Beyond Us," New London *Day,* 2/15/28.

62   "The shells had not": New London *Telegraph,* 6/30/99.

62   "Collegiate exuberance": Ibid., 6/25/08.

64   "O'Neill has acute": Sergeant, *Fire Under the Andes,* p. 88.

4. EUGENE IN EXILE

67   "It was a dream": Boulton, *Part of a Long Story*, p. 67.

69   Line from *Monte Cristo:* There are only a few lines in the play referring to the sea. Most likely the following is the one Eugene used to quote: ". . . a sailor's is a dangerous trade, and the ocean a vast grave. The sea will do my business." Clark, *Favorite American Plays*, p. 72.

71   "of Anita I have": EO to Katherine M. Black, 6/21/31.

72   "I just drifted": Mindil, "Behind the Scenes," New York *Tribune*, 2/22/20.

72   "If I hadn't had": Basso, "The Tragic Sense," 3/13/48.

72   "No, it isn't exactly": O'Neill, J. F., "What a Sanatorium Did," *Journal of the Outdoor Life*, June 1923.

72   "series of sonnets": EO letter to his son Shane, 1/18/40.

73   "Judge Latimer": Clark, *Eugene O'Neill*, p. 24.

73   "Richard Dana Skinner has": Basso, "The Tragic Sense," 3/13/48.

75   "Do you ever think": EO to McCarthy, 9/2/30.

75   "Remember how Sister Mary": EO to Nathan, 5/13/39.

77   *The Following of Christ*, trans. by the Rt. Rev. Richard Challoner, D.D. (New York: Benziger Brothers, 1896): "And when we," p. 49; "If we strove," 49; "Therefore should," 54; "As long as," 56; "Hence it is," 56; "But often," 64.

5. END OF INNOCENCE

78   "Eugene O'Neill has": Sergeant, *Fire Under the Andes*, p. 81.

78   "What made you": Boulton, *Part of a Long Story*, pp. 176–177.

78   "O'Neill is one": Basso, "The Tragic Sense," 3/13/48.

81   "the legend that": Ibid., 3/13/48. Basso ascribed the comparison to Dante to an unidentified friend of O'Neill's, but he told the present biographer that the thought was his own.

84   "I made my way": Boston *Herald*, 5/16/09, rephrased from third-person terminology to the first person.

85   "James O'Neill, Jr., has": *Times-Union*, 4/5/07.

85   "He is a manly": *Leader*, 4/16/07.

86   "mother value": *The Diagram*.

6. BIRTH OF A REBEL

91   "During the evening": "Betts Academy Teacher Recalls Eugene O'Neill," Stamford *Advocate*, 12/26/36, and personal interview with the teacher, Rev. Arthur G. Walter. Walter's other remarks in this chapter are from the same sources.

93   "I was tickled": EO to Betts, 6/7/23.

94   "libidinous laureate" and "unclean fiery": *Selected Poems of Algernon Swinburne*, intro. by Edward Shanks, pp. viii and xxxi (New York: Macmillan, 1950).

96   "After our week was": Basso, "The Tragic Sense," 3/13/48. Since O'Neill was so fond of poetry, it seems likely that his assignment was not *Macbeth* but *The Deserted Village* and that he switched the assignments in recounting the incident for the sake of a better story, especially the final line — "never go on the stage."

96   "We were a very close": Ibid., 3/13/48.

100   "Yes, we are thinking": New London *Telegraph*, 1/9/05.

100   "While other boys": Prideaux, "Most Celebrated U.S. Playwright," *Life*, 10/14/46.

101   "Gene learned sin": Bowen, *Curse of the Misbegotten*, p. 19.
102   "the largest collection": "Only Books That Teach Anarchy" (unsigned), New York *Herald*, 4/12/08.
102   "inner self": Sergeant, *Fire Under the Andes*, p. 90.
102   "an atheist" and "simply unterrified": Sachs, *The Terrible Siren*, pp. 242 and 239.
103   "Neither the ballot": Ishill, *Benjamin R. Tucker*, p. 14.
103   "Tucker did brave": Ibid., foreword.
103   "This journal": Sachs, *The Terrible Siren*, pp. 238–239.
103   "appeared to be in verse": Ishill, *Benjamin R. Tucker*, p. 10.
103   "Aggressive, concise": "Only Books That Teach Anarchy," *Herald*.
104   "very radical preaching": Sachs, *The Terrible Siren*, p. 241.
104   "sure cure" and "the right of the drunkard": Madison, *Critics and Crusaders*, p. 201.
104   "well dressed": "Only Books That Teach Anarchy," *Herald*.
104   Shaw, *Selected Prose of Bernard Shaw*: "Every step," p. 550; "only reductions," 586; "poverty is mainly," 642; "The family," 560.
105   "virtue always triumphed": Woolf, "Eugene O'Neill Returns."
105   "more intense suffering": *Selected Prose of Bernard Shaw*, p. 578.
106   "[The powers that be]": Madison, *Critics and Crusaders*, pp. 220–221.
106   "The hope of humanity": Ibid., p. 210.
107   "Do Long Runs": *Herald*, 3/9/02.
107   "What's the matter": Undated, unidentified article by Rennold Wolf in *Locke* scrapbook, but content suggests it appeared in 1903.
108   "She doesn't act": Boston *Herald*, 4/25/09.
108   "James O'Neill's Pierre": *Dramatic Mirror*, 4/9/04.
108   "Yes, I am going": *Locke* article 6/3/05 but unidentified.
108   "Your dear daddy's"; Tyler to EO, 12/13/20.
108   "There was no": O'Neill, Patrick, *James O'Neill*, p. 117.
110   "Always the gloomy one": Bowen, "The Black Irishman."
110   "I never could get": New London *Telegraph*, 2/8/11.
110   "to the front": *Herald*, 7/24/11.
111   "Mrs. O'Neill's health": *Telegraph*, 3/28/07.
112   "He tells his story": "Chats about James O'Neill" (unsigned), *New York Times*, 7/25/06.

7. PRINCETON UNDERGRADUATE

114   "Princeton was all": EO to William Betts, 6/7/23.
114   "It was not until": Downes, "Playwright Finds His Inspiration," Boston *Post*, 8/29/20.
116   "You could have knocked": The informant prefers anonymity.
116   "the side-shows": Ray Stannard Baker, *Woodrow Wilson*, v. II, p. 218 (Garden City: Doubleday, Page, 1927).
116   "I hold van Dyke": EO to George Jean Nathan, 12/7/31.
117   "on a number of occasions": The informant prefers anonymity.
117   "indelible impression": Downes, "Playwright Finds His Inspiration."
118   "He told us about": F. S. Galey.
118   Wilde, *The Picture of Dorian Gray*: "Conscience," p. 21; "The terror," 33; "Nothing can cure," 36; "When we blame," 116; "Each man," 216; "Children," 85.
118   "Not an old landmark": San Francisco *Call*, 1/6/07.
119   "I can't just decide": Undated note from the instructor in O'Neill's dossier in the Alumni Records Office, Princeton.

120	"Childe Harold's Pilgrimage": *The Poems and Plays of Lord Byron,* v. II, p. 82 (New York: Dutton, Everyman's Library, 1910).
122	"discovered an entire": EO 5/13/38 to a Mr. Olav of the *Norsk Tidende,* a newspaper in Oslo, Norway.
122	"the greatest work": Madison, *Critics and Crusaders,* p. 201.
122	Stirner, *The Ego and His Own:* "What's good," p. 5; "*Everything sacred,*" 216; "I decide," 190; "All things," 366.
122	"Veritable breviary": *The Egoists,* p. 371 (Scribner's, 1910).
122	"The answer to that": "A Eugene O'Neill Miscellany" (unsigned), New York *Sun,* 1/12/28.
123	Nietzsche, *Thus Spake Zarathustra:* "Flee into," p. 68; "But thou," 68; "God is dead," 102; "There is no," 34; "One must still," 32; "And often we attack," 71; "Slow is," 67; "it is the same," 58; "But the worst," 78.
123	"I have known": Ibid., p. 60.
123	"To all those belauded": Ibid., p. 47.
123	"has influenced me": EO to de Casseres, 6/27/27.
123	Nietzsche, *The Portable Nietzsche:* "major work," p. 111; "mature thought," 12; "what we find," 106; "the most important," 103.
124	"general hell-raising": Karsner, "Eugene O'Neill at Close Range."
124	"I think you are": EO to Frank B. Elser, 1/13/32.
125	"I *liked* Woodrow Wilson": Basso, "The Tragic Sense," 2/28/48.
125	"He's the last": Crichton, *Total Recoil,* p. 118.
125	"I'm no good": EO to Ralph Sanborn, 2/2/33.

8. FATHER AND SON

126	"God deliver me": EO to Robert Sisk, 4/24/42.
127	"I object to Broadway": *Locke* article 11/16/02 but unidentified.
127	"Have you ever": O'Neill, Eugene, "A Dramatist's Notebook," *The American Spectator,* January 1933.
128	"Though for the last": New York *Herald,* 9/17/07.
128	"Worse than other": New York *Sun,* 9/17/07.
128	"Yesterday fighting": New York *Globe,* 9/17/07.
128	"Its construction": *Dramatic Mirror,* 9/28/07.
128	"Virginia is": *Sun,* 9/17/07.
128	"James O'Neill, Jr.": Chicago *Tribune,* 2/4/08.
129	"old manor house": O'Neill, Eugene, "Tomorrow," *Seven Arts,* June 1917.
130	James Byth a fraud: To learn more about Byth than O'Neill ever said, the present biographer researched in this country and corresponded with various institutions and official agencies in England, as well as with Reuters and other British news syndicates. The results of the investigation are summarized in Chapters 8, 12 and 13.
131	"When I said": Little, "Haunted by the Ghost of Monte Cristo," Chicago *Record Herald,* 2/9/08. All quotations in this paragraph of the narrative and the following eight are from the same source.
133	"My father's death": EO to Nina Moise, 8/29/20.
133	"My father and I": Basso, "The Tragic Sense," 2/28/48.
133	"More than I should": Sergeant, *Fire Under the Andes,* p. 92.
133	"A-One snob": EO to Brooks Atkinson, 8/16/31.
134	"You can say": George Jean Nathan, "O'Neill," *Vanity Fair,* October 1933.
134	"My nerves": EO to Dr. J. O. Lief, 6/22/29.
135	"sold ten-cent jewelry": Karsner, "Eugene O'Neill at Close Range."
135	"successful debut": *Locke* article 12/7/07 but unidentified.

136	"The dives of New York": Walling, *Recollections of a New York Chief of Police*, pp. 479 and 480–481.
136	Poem "The Haymarket": New London *Telegraph*, 11/21/12.
137	"surrounded by Methodists": *Lonely Americans*, R. W. Brown, p. 153 (New York: Coward-McCann, 1929).
138	"So when we built up": Mantle and Sherwood, *The Best Plays of 1899–1909*, p. 304.
139	"The populace thinks": Downes, "Playwright Finds His Inspiration."
140	"Who knows just what": Ibid.
140	"when my memory": Clark. *Eugene O'Neill*, p. 8.
142	"Crude, melodramatic": St. Louis *Star*, 9/5/08.
142	"Better a thousand": Toledo *Blade*, 10/7/08.
142	"There is many": Indianapolis *News*, 10/5/08.
143	"Bellows and Keefe": EO to his son Shane, 1/18/40.
143	"I used to think": H. C. Beck, *Fare to Midlands*, p. 278 (New York: Dutton, 1939).
143	"used to laugh": Ibid., p. 277.

9. MARRIAGE AND FLIGHT

145	"The woman I gave": Bowen, p. 321.
147	"The audience made up": St. Louis *Star*, 6/21/09.
150	"woman in a thousand": EO letter 11/9/09 to his parents. Unless otherwise specified in the narrative or the Notes, all quoted remarks in the chapter regarding O'Neill's stay in Honduras are from two letters he wrote his parents on 11/9 and 12/25/09. The excerpts are not further identified in the Notes.
151	"The river has lots": Stevens to his sister, 4/8/10.
151	"the early Spaniards": Stevens to his sister, 5/15/10.
154	Nietzsche, *Zarathustra*: "Out of thy poisons," p. 53; "Of all that is," 56; "Creating," 99.
155	"I kept writing": Bowen, "The Black Irishman."
155	"Keep on writing": EO to Patrick O'Neill, 8/18/40.
155	"I looked just like": Basso, "The Tragic Sense," 2/28/48.
155	"Although glad to leave": For some reason difficult to fathom, O'Neill told an interviewer (Fred Pasley, "Odyssey of Eugene O'Neill," 1/25/32) that he was "invalided back to New York via the Panama Canal." The Canal was not opened, however, until 1914, three years after his return from Honduras.
157	"My father was worried": Clark, *Eugene O'Neill*, p. 21.
157	"A courtesy title": Pasley, "Odyssey of Eugene O'Neill," 1/25/32.
157	Excerpts from "The White Sister": Crawford and Hackett, "The White Sister," Act II.
157	"suffered as a retribution": EO to Tyler, 12/9/20.
157	"Life in 60": New London *Day*, 8/14/20, a reprint of a 1909 story from New York *Morning Telegraph*.
158	"one ambition": New York *Sun*, 11/16/09.
158	"The true peace": Conrad, The *"Nigger"* of the Narcissus, pp. 47–48.

10. HOME TO THE SEA

160	"It happened": Downes, "Playwright Finds His Inspiration."
160	"super-tramp": Sergeant, *Fire Under the Andes*, p. 90.
161	"I will sail" and "things that boil": Captain Severin Waage, a son of Captain Gustav Waage.

163   "I can remember": EO to Carlotta Monterey, 11/27/26.

164   Poem "Free": Sanborn and Clark, *Bibliography of the Works of Eugene O'Neill*, pp. 3–4 and 111. First published in the *Pleiades Club Year Book* of 1912, the poem, according to O'Neill, marked his debut in print; but, as recounted in Chapter 11 of this biography, a man in Buenos Aires named Fred Hettman recalls Eugene showing him in 1910 one of his poems from a magazine.

164   "actually written": EO to a Mr. Landon of the Pleiades Club, 3/23/20.

166   "was constantly boasting": Pasley, "Odyssey of Eugene O'Neill," 1/24/32.

167   "They had been strong": Conrad, *Nigger of the Narcissus*, p. 39.

167   "They were fine": Downes, "Playwright Finds His Inspiration."

167   "I liked [seamen]": Mullett, "The Extraordinary Story of Eugene O'Neill," *American Magazine*, November 1922.

168   "something called coffee": Mullett, "The Extraordinary Story."

11. DEPTHS OF BUENOS AIRES

171   "I landed in Buenos Aires": Karsner, "Eugene O'Neill at Close Range."

171   Sixty dollars: In one of Captain Waage's letters to his employer he mentioned that each of the two Americans had deposited $60 with him for safekeeping.

172   "Fifty?" Eugene guessed: Basso, "The Tragic Sense," 2/28/48.

174   "It sure was . . . sober pianist": "Smitty — of S.S. *Glencairn*" (unsigned), New York *World*, 1/6/29.

174   "But somehow a regular": Kalonyme, "O'Neill Lifts the Curtain," *New York Times*, 12/21/24.

175   "He died when": Peck, "Talk with Mrs. O'Neill," *New York Times*, 11/4/56.

176   "Those moving pictures": Kalonyme, "O'Neill Lifts the Curtain."

177   "I wasn't doing": Mindil, "Behind the Scenes," 2/22/20.

177   "That old bucko": Pasley, "Odyssey of Eugene O'Neill, 11/24/32.

177   "Those South American": Downes, "Playwright Finds His Inspiration."

180   "Well, well, so": Basso, "The Tragic Sense," 2/28/48.

180   "I wanted to be": Clark, *Eugene O'Neill*, p. 23.

180   Poem "Submarine": *Masses*, February 1917.

181   "extraordinarily handsome": Kalonyme, "O'Neill Lifts the Curtain."

182   "It was too warm": Ashleigh, "When I First Met Eugene O'Neill," *Bulletin of the American Women's Club*, March 1927.

183   "crazy meeting": Ashleigh letter to the biographer.

183   "tending mules": Clark, *Eugene O'Neill*, p. 10.

184   "start at the bottom": Basso, "The Tragic Sense," 2/28/48.

184   "I didn't do it": Crichton, *Total Recoil*, p. 119.

184   "The stench": Basso, "The Tragic Sense," 2/28/48.

184   "I was then twenty-two": Ibid., 3/13/48.

186   "Preserved how": Crichton, "Mr. O'Neill and The Iceman," *Collier's*, 10/26/46.

186   "The great sorrow": O'Neill, Eugene, "A Letter from O'Neill," *New York Times*, 4/11/20.

12. JIMMY THE PRIEST'S

190   "Jimmy the Priest's . . . was awful," and "The house . . . vermin" Kalonyme, "O'Neill Lifts the Curtain."

190   "One couldn't go . . . by comparison": Sweeney, "Back to the Sources," New York *World*, 11/9/24.

191 "drank too much": Peck, "Talk with Mrs. O'Neill."
192 "hard lot": Pasley, "Odyssey of Eugene O'Neill." 1/24/32.
193 Poem "Shut In": *Telegraph*, 9/1/11.
193 "one of the most elaborate": Ibid., 9/9/11.
194 "ugly, tedious . . . soul his own": Downes, "Playwright Finds His Inspiration."
194 "There was about as much": Mullett, "The Extraordinary Story."
194 "An inferno, all smoke": New London *Telegraph*, 7/13/12.
196 Driscoll's birthplace, age and height: Crew roster of S.S. *St. Louis* in August 1915, his final sailing.
196 "Years ago some Irish": Mullett, "The Extraordinary Story."
196 "giant of a man": Kalonyme, "O'Neill Lifts the Curtain."
197 "box the compass": Downes, "Playwright Finds His Inspiration."
197 "The last one": Pasley, "Odyssey of Eugene O'Neill," 1/24/32.
200 "the eyes that rest": Mann, *Buddenbrooks*, trans. by H. T. Lowe Porter, p. 538 (New York: Knopf, 1959).
201 Poem "Not Understood": *Telegraph*, 11/27/11.
202 "He had followed": Basso, "The Tragic Sense," 3/6/48.
202 "His end . . . in the party": Sweeney, "Back to the Sources."
202 "[He] tottered away": Kalonyme, "O'Neill Lifts the Curtain."
203 The facts of Christopherson's death: A police report, and the death certificate at the New York City Health Department's Bureau of Records.
203 "I looked searchingly": O'Neill, Eugene, "Tomorrow," p. 153.
204 "books of impossible": Ibid., p. 149.
204 "to have a bit": Ibid., p. 160.
204 "Now that I look": Merrill, "Eugene O'Neill, World-Famed Dramatist," Boston *Globe*, 7/8/23.
205 "My early experience": Ibid.

13. RETURN TO LIFE

210 Woollcott's review, 4/4/20.
210 "I was still": Boulton, *Part of a Long Story*, p. 204.
211 "nudges, pokes: Nathan, *Intimate Notebooks of George Jean Nathan*, pp. 35–36.
211 "Beith's suicide": Ibid., p. 35.
214 "As a personal record": EO letter undated, apparently May 1930, to Ralph Sanborn.
214 "After I'd had": Prideaux, "Most Celebrated U.S. Playwright."
215 "The least said": EO to Charles O'Brien Kennedy, 10/29/38.
215 "I am proud": EO to Joseph A. McCarthy, 2/18/31.
215 "silly and hoodlumish": Clark, *Eugene O'Neill*, p. 8.
215 "some kind of misfortune": Charles Webster, last surviving member of the troupe and a chief source of information about the tour. He was the source for "To eat or not" (p. 215); "something was going on" (p. 216).
216 James O'Neill's $40,000 loss: New London *Telegraph*, 10/20/11, and bankruptcy records, Hall of Records, New York City.
216 "That cut-down version": Crichton, "Mr. O'Neill and The Iceman."
216 "very interesting": Cincinnati *Enquirer*, 10/16/11.
216 "has lost none": Memphis *Commercial*, 1/17/12.
217 "A couple of stage": Cincinnati *Post*, 10/16/11.
217 "will set you" and "other funny people": Cincinnati *Commercial-Tribune*, 10/17/11.

217   "one of the most artistic" and "they sing well": Cincinnati *Enquirer*, 10/16/11.
217   " 'Ho, hum,' said James": "James O'Neill Muses" (unsigned), Cincinnati *Times Star*, 10/19/11.
220   "I find that": "Vaudeville Acts Hard on Actors" (unsigned), Memphis *News Scimitar*, 1/17/12.
221   "I wonder just how": Locke, "O'Neill Abandons Vaudeville," Denver *Times*, undated but probably 3/3/12.
221   "Sir, I am not satisfied": Prideaux, "Most Celebrated U.S. Playwright."
221   "Oh, God, those old": Boulton, *Part of a Long Story*, p. 204.

14. THE CUB REPORTER

223   "We hope to have": New York *Herald*, 7/9/12.
226   "Everybody does that": Mullett, "The Extraordinary Story."
226   James O'Neill helped son get job on *Telegraph*: Thompson, "Another Connecticut Yankee," p. 56.
226   "The smell of the rooms": Mollan, "Making Plays with a Tragic Ending," Philadelphia *Public Ledger*, 1/22/22.
227   "night after night": Woodworth, "The World's Worst Reporter," Providence *Journal*, 12/6/31.
227   Woodworth was on the *Day*: Payroll records of the *Day* in 1912.
227   "wonderful insight": Pasley, "Odyssey of Eugene O'Neill," 1/26/32.
228   "He's the first one": Clark, *Eugene O'Neill*, p. 18.
228   "The four things": Ibid., pp. 18–19.
228   "grieve like a stricken . . . wildness of his ideas": Latimer, "Eugene Is Beyond Us."
229   "I thought he": Clark, *Eugene O'Neill*, p. 18.
229   "There was something": Ibid., pp. 19–20.
229   "There is the peaceful": "He Wanted to Know, He Promptly Found Out," 10/24/12.
229   "The men who manned": "Schooner Once Ran Blockade in Cuban War," 10/11/12.
230   Story about the *Maggie Ellen*: "Rowed Twelve Miles in Gale in Open Boat," 11/15/12. Other stories presumably written by O'Neill: "Roosevelt and Dorsey Shake, Crowd Cheers," 8/17/12; "Neighbors Did Not Like Stone Age Methods," 9/27/12; "When Actress Loses Terrier," 9/30/12; "Little Baby Is Locked in Cell with Mother," 10/1/12; "Man About Town in Weird Barroom Fight," 10/3/12; "Still Sure He Saw Deer in Early Morning," 10/14/12; "Candles Used as in Ye Olde Fashion Tyme," 11/19/12.
230   "I. Polsky, a native": "Strike Leaders Are Guiltless, Socialists Say," 9/6/12.
231   "It would be a shame": EO to Francesco Bianco, 2/3/36.
232   "It was a sort": Basso, "The Tragic Sense," 3/6/48.
235   "I spent the summer": Rochester *Post Express*, 9/15/13.

15. BIRTH OF A PLAYWRIGHT

245   "I thought to myself": Mrs. Marion Bridgett.
246   "To an actor's son": O'Neill, J. F., "What a Sanatorium Did."
246   "dose of those germs": EO to Benjamin de Casseres, 8/11/27.
246   "Thanks to a constitution": Ibid.
247   "In the measure": EO to Lyman, 9/2/19.
252   "It was at Gaylord": O'Neill, J. F., "What a Sanatorium Did."

253   "I wish immortality": Winther, "Strindberg and O'Neill," *Scandinavian Studies*, August 1959.
253   "What have I to forgive": Strindberg, *Plays by August Strindberg (The Dream Play)*. p. 32.
253   "You are always": Ibid., p. 33.
253   "My mother": Strindberg, *Six Plays of August Strindberg*, p. 54.
253   "Then he cannot feel": *Plays by August Strindberg*, p. 61.
253   "There is room": Ibid., p. 130.
253   "Well, that is love": Ibid., p. 131.
254   "the healthy heart" and "one of the unfortunate": Lyman to Percy Hammond, 12/3/21.

16. PROLIFIC NOVICE

266   "that winter with you": EO to Rippin family, 8/18/26.
266   "I've never worked harder": EO to Jessica Rippin, 2/4/19.
271   "I looked the lad": Hamilton, "Seen on the Stage," *Vogue*, 4/1/20.
271   "seemed an unobtrusive": Hamilton, "Untold Tales," *Theater Arts*, August 1956.
273   "He did believe": Clark, *Eugene O'Neill*, p. 34.
273   "First five Stations": Inscription dated 12/28/18 in copy O'Neill gave Agnes Boulton.
278   "That's the year": Crichton, "Mr. O'Neill and The Iceman."
278   "Very important from my": R. D. Skinner, *Eugene O'Neill: A Poet's Quest*, p. viii (New York: Longmans, Green, 1935).

17. END OF A LONG NIGHTMARE

284   "I innocently . . . budding aspirations": EO to Hamilton, 4/6/20.
284   "But your advice": EO letter to Hamilton, 4/5/35.
289   "Art of Playwriting": EO to Lyman, undated but summer 1914.
290   "My God! where did": Basso, "The Tragic Sense," 2/28/48.
290   "No manager would": New York *Herald Tribune*, 3/19/33.
290   "satire, light comedy": Eva E. Von Baur, "A Theater of Thrills," *Theater Magazine*, June 1913.
291   "It's funny now": Tyler and Furnas, *Whatever Goes Up*, pp. 90 and 91.
291   "The A-1 collectors' item": EO to Van Doren, 4/27/44.
292   "All my life": Kinne, *George Pierce Baker*, p. 193.
292   "As for my standing": Ibid., p. 194.

18. BAKER'S COURSE

294   "[He] was a man": Thomas Wolfe, *Of Time and the River*, p. 130 (Scribner's, 1935).
295   "There is Dane Hall": Boston *Transcript*, 6/1/33.
296   "He would tell us": E. P. Conkle, "G.P., Some Impressions of a Great Teacher," *Theater Arts*, August 1959.
296   "old stuff": Clark, *Eugene O'Neill*, p. 27.
296   "play at all," "respected his judgment," and "Yes, I did get . . . at that time": Ibid., p. 28.
296   "I learned some": Mullett, "The Extraordinary Story."
296   "He stuck out": Weaver, "I Knew Him When," New York *World*, 2/21/26.
297   "Society is Toyland": "Young Author Satirizes Society" (unsigned), San Francisco *Examiner*, 4/30/12.
299   EO to Miss Boulton, 9/29/27.

301 "We repaired to": Weaver, "I Knew Him When."
302 "stolen from": Clark, *Eugene O'Neill*, p. 28.
303 "By an unofficial": *Telegraph*, 3/4/15.
303 "clever," "a million," and "Perhaps they weren't": EO to Beatrice Ashe, undated.
303 "As my bank roll": EO letter to Doll Rippin, undated but approximately 11/20/14.
305 "for the sake of the company": Gelb, *O'Neill*, p. 257.
307 "I was one of the hardest": Clark, Eugene O'Neill, p. 36.
309 "He showed by the end": Ibid., p. 28.
309 "back in the dark age": Eugene O'Neill, "Professor G. P. Baker," *New York Times*, 1/13/35.

19. THE FILM WRITER

311 "If you have ideas": The advertisement of the National Authors Institute of New York City appeared repeatedly in the New London *Telegraph* in 1912 and 1913.
311 "Film makers are suffering": Ibid., 1/31/14.
313 "You can't imagine": EO to Hamilton, 4/6/20.
314 "I cannot tell you": EO to Susan Glaspell, 1/29/19.
315 "If your play": EO to Elkins, undated, but apparently late June or early July 1915.
315 "I see life": EO to Mary A. Clark, 8/5/23.
317 "Every politician": New London *Day*, 8/28/15.
317 "I hold more . . . a star vehicle": O'Neill, Eugene, "Memoranda on Masks," *American Spectator*, November 1932.
317 "But I anticipate . . . in masked roles": O'Neill, Eugene, "A Dramatist's Notebook," *American Spectator*, January 1933.
318 "the mask is dramatic": O'Neill, "Memoranda on Masks."
318 "Mr. O'Neill does not relish": New London *Day*, 9/2/15.
318 "is holding out": New London *Telegraph*, 10/18/15.
318 "I wanted to [return]": EO to Baker, 6/8/19; Kinne, *George Pierce Baker*, p. 207.
319 "three places I actually": Earl Wilson's column, New York *Post*, 8/2/46.
320 "The authenticity, concreteness": Raleigh, *The Plays of Eugene O'Neill*, pp. 228–229.
321 "its beauty, its coming": Glaspell, *The Road to the Temple*, p. 249.
322 "The American theater": H. K. Moderwell, "Two Interviews," *Theater Magazine*, November 1917.
323 "If the Players": *New York Times*, 2/20/15.
323 "$2 drama for fifty": New York *Herald*, 2/20/15.
323 "The appeal": *Post*, 2/20/15.
323 "Altogether too much dam .": Clark, *Eugene O'Neill*, pp. 42–43.

20. GREENWICH VILLAGE

327 "living among the Villagers": Ware, *Greenwich Village, 1920–1930*, p. 112.
327 "Havel is one": Hapgood, *Victorian in the Modern World*, p. 359.
329 "He promised me": Ibid., p. 318.
329 "passionate reserve": Ibid., p. 427.
330 "realize the dream": Ibid., p. 424.
331 "the female Christ": Harrison Dowd.
332 "smoky quality": Mary Heaton Vorse, "Eugene O'Neill's Pet Saloon Is Gone," New York *World*, 5/4/30.

333   "instrument of brazen": Bodenheim, "Roughneck and Romancer," *New Yorker*, 2/6/26.
334   "He managed to smother": Ibid.
334   "poetry lurks" and "the underworld": Ibid.
335   Date and circumstances of Driscoll's death: Register of Deaths, General Register and Record Office of Shipping and Seamen, Cardiff, Wales.
336   "He frightened me": Luhan, *Movers and Shakers*, p. 269.
336   "[My mother] taught me": Hapgood, *Anarchist Woman*, p. 95.
336   "Ah, that first job!": Ibid., p. 75.
336   "Though we were Catholics": Ibid., pp. 76–77.
337   "I am a remaining product": Ibid., p. 96.
337   "I am driven": Ibid., p. 221.
337   "The kind of prostitution": Ibid., pp. 108–109.
337   "How we do fasten": Ibid., pp. 156–157.
338   "[I have] been suffering": Ibid., p. 308.
339   "I've been doing a little": New York *Sun*, 2/13/16.

21. THEATER ON A WHARF

342   "The great hope": Archer, "Great Contribution of 'Little Theaters' to Our Drama's Future," New York *Post*, 2/24/21.
342   "Those were the early": Glaspell, *Road to the Temple*, p. 250.
343   Date and hour of the Provincetown Players' birth: Letter from Neith Boyce to her father, 7/17/15.
343   Date of *Suppressed Desires* première: A playbill of the Liberal Club performance.
344   "depth and mystery": Vorse, *Time and the Town*, p. 118.
344   "One man cannot produce": Glaspell, *Road to the Temple*, pp. 252–253.
345   "It flashed upon me": Hicks, *John Reed*, p. 123.
345   "I hear that you": Ibid., p. 24.
346   "I have never met": Anderson to Louise Bryant, 9/19/32.
346   "the first person" and "I think I've found": Hicks, *John Reed*, p. 205.
346   "Terry, haven't you": Glaspell, *Road to the Temple*, p. 253.
346   Box marked "Magic Yeast": George Frayme Brown.
347   "He was not left": Glaspell, *Road to the Temple*, pp. 253–254.
347   "There is a bunch": Luhan, *Movers and Shakers*, p. 478.
347   "In utter primitiveness": Philpott, "Laboratory of the Drama," Boston *Globe*, 8/13/16.
348   Date of *Bound East* première: A letter 7/28/16 from Wilbur Daniel Steele to a relation. Though he did not mention *Bound East*, he said that one of his plays was being given that night; the Steele and O'Neill plays were on the same bill.
348   "I may see it": Glaspell, *Road to the Temple*, p. 254.
350   "Dark eyes, what": Boulton, *Part of a Long Story*, p. 114.
350   "You knew more": Vorse, *Time and the Town*, p. 122. The final few words of the quotation have been transposed from the original order.
353   "how clearly I see": Hartley, "Farewell, Charles [Demuth]," an unpublished article, Museum of Modern Art library, New York City.
353   "The children have to": Letter by Phyllis Duganne Given in Provincetown *Advocate*, 9/2/37.
354   "Brave; thin; pure": Glaspell, *Road to the Temple*, p. 17.
354   "The Cabin knew": Ibid., p. 19.
354   "But if you cannot": Ibid., p. 62.
355   "darkly handsome": Eastman, *The Enjoyment of Living*, p. 566.

355   "I have a daemon": Mabel Dodge to Alfred Stieglitz, 9/14/16.
355   "It was a great": Glaspell, *Road to the Temple*, p. 256, with final few words added from an early draft of the book, p. 336, at New York Public Library, Berg Collection.
356   "I'll beat you yet": John Wilcock column, *Village Voice*, 9/5/57.
357   "When we go to": Glaspell, *Road to the Temple*, pp. 257 and 258.
358   "let in the sparkling": Kenton, "The Provincetown Players and the Playwrights Theater, 1915–1922," p. 15.
358   *Bound East*, according to common report, was on the review program, but a playbill of the two performances lists *Thirst*.
358   "Eighty dollars was": Edna Kenton, "The Provincetown Players and the Playwrights' Theater," *Billboard*, 8/5/22. (This article should not be confused with Miss Kenton's unpublished manuscript of similar title, which is quoted extensively in this biography.)
358   "Organization is death": Kenton, "The Provincetown Players," p. 17.
358   "celebrate not only": Ibid., p. 21.
358   "Be it resolved": Ibid., p. 18.
359   "The author shall produce": Ibid., p. 20.
359   "for leasing, equipping": Ibid., p. 22.
359   "Don't worry!": Glaspell, *Road to the Temple*, p. 259.

22. ADVENTURERS ON MACDOUGAL STREET

362   "Even knowing . . . couldn't be done": Glaspell, *Road to the Temple*, p. 261.
362   "You have the police": Ibid., pp. 260–261.
364   "I hope that Gene": Rogers to Louise Bryant, 11/30/16.
364   "The old faithfuls": Louise to Reed, 11/16/16.
364   "Nonnie & Gene had": Louise to Reed, 11/14/16.
364   "unanimously elected": Letter from Provincetown Players to Mr. Francis, 10/14/16.
365   "Harry Kemp left": Cook to Miss Glaspell, 12/11/16.
365   "Please believe me": Louise to Reed, 6/9/17.
365   "Sweetheart, I do hope": Reed to Louise, 6/28/17.
365   "Now, honey, dearest": Louise to Reed, 7/17/17.
366   "We must call Harry": Luhan, *Movers and Shakers*, p. 274.
366   "Jig is so busy": Miss Glaspell to Louise, 12/21/16.
366   "Nord is poisonous": Cook to Miss Glaspell, 12/11/16.
366   "There were those who came": Written by Corley for a booklet when the Provincetown Players moved to the Garrick Theater in 1929.
366   "Yes, yes, I think": Hapgood, *Victorian in the Modern World*, p. 399.
367   "Father and son": Deutsch and Hanau, *The Provincetown*, p. 23.
367   "exaggerated": O'Neill, Patrick, *James O'Neill*, p. 119.
367   "in O'Neill's eyes": Hapgood, *Victorian in the Modern World*, p. 399.
370   "The plays are almost": *Globe*, 1/20/17.
370   "As we understand": *Tribune*, 1/30/17.
372   "We lacked 'strong' ": Kenton, "The Provincetown Players," p. 52.
373   "made me see Mexico": Hicks, *John Reed*, p. 228.
373   "You have perfect": Ibid., p. 134.
373   "Do not be deceived": Ibid., p. 160.
374   "Thou goest to women?": Nietzsche, *Zarathustra*, p. 81.
374   *The Wanderer* reviews: *Sun*, 1/29/17; *New York Times*, 1/29/17; *Life*, 2/15/17.
375   "I accepted the role": *Sun*, 4/1/17.
375   The *Christmas Carol* film: Under Mr. O'Neill's contract with the Webb

Talking Pictures Co. of New York City, he was to get $500 for making three records of dialogue and $250 for the movie. The project was dropped after a test recording proved unsatisfactory and one of the film-makers fell ill.

23. MATURING PLAYWRIGHT

381   "annoyed and rendered": Provincetown *Advocate*, 3/29/17.
382   "I thought it was pretty": EO to Van Doren, 5/12/44.
382   "artists and critics": Oppenheim, "Story of the *Seven Arts*," *American Mercury*, June 1930.
383   "That was my first": Karsner, "Eugene O'Neill at Close Range."
383   "my pet play": EO to Professor Baker, 6/30/19.
383   "When *everybody* likes": Basso, "The Tragic Sense," 3/6/48.
383   "I consider . . . theater as it is": Clark, *Eugene O'Neill*, p. 57.
383   "and *The Moon* . . . finer values": Ibid., p. 59.
384   "Smitty in the . . . insignificance": Ibid., p. 58.
384   "Perhaps [when we meet]": Ibid., p. 59.
385   *Light on the Path*, p. 3. Except that he added exclamation marks, O'Neill retained the wording of the first two sentences, but the original language of the rest of the passage is as follows: "Before the voice can speak in the presence of the Masters it must have lost its power to wound. Before the soul can stand in the presence of the Masters its feet must be washed in the blood of the heart." Characteristically, O'Neill changed "stand" to "fly," and "feet" to "wings." It has been questioned whether he or Terry Carlin painted the lines on the rafters; in a letter 12/14/41 to Silvio Bedini, O'Neill said he was the one.
386   "for minor defects": Letter is undated but probably was written in June or July 1917.
387   "I know what war": Hicks, *John Reed*, p. 231.
387   "I am not a peace-at-any-price": Ibid., p. 234.
389   "In some ways I admire": Hovey to EO, 8/13/18.
389   "the germ idea": Skinner, *Eugene O'Neill: A Poet's Quest*, p. viii.
390   "Less than a year": Hicks, *John Reed*, pp. 249–250.
391   "The idea usually begins": Mullett, "The Extraordinary Story."
391   "What's beyond the ocean?": Pasley, "Odyssey of Eugene O'Neill," 1/24/32. Though doubt has been expressed that such an exchange took place, O'Neill confirmed it in 1946, according to Bowen, "The Black Irishman."

24. GIRL IN THE HELL HOLE

392   "I received a letter": Mullett, "The Extraordinary Story."
392   "most distinguished": Dolmetsch, "History of the *Smart Set* Magazine," p. 100.
393   "are the talked-of": S. Jay Kaufman, New York *Globe*, 11/5/17.
396   "Few people realize": Woolf, "Eugene O'Neill Returns."
396   "I have ideas": Kalonyme, "O'Neill Lifts the Curtain."
397   "as thrilling as a violin": Max Eastman, *Great Companions*, p. 78 (New York: Farrar, Straus & Cudahy, 1959).
397   "Some of the very worst": Kenton, "Unorganized, Amateur, Purely Experimental," Boston *Transcript*, 4/27/18.
397   "anyone fired with an unquenchable": Kreymborg, *Troubadour*, p. 307.
400   "that the stage was": Deutsch and Hanau, *The Provincetown*, p. 29.
400   "Jig Cook's sublime": Ibid., p. 39.
400   "I had a play": Ibid., pp. 41–42.

401   "In the afternoons Christine": Kenton, "The Provincetown Players," p. 78.
402   "This is really a Russian": Hapgood, *Victorian in the Modern World*, p. 442.
402   "They say they'll arrest": Cook letter to Miss Glaspell undated, but fall of 1917.
403   "Many people think that Dorothy Day": Macdonald, "The Foolish Things of the World," *New Yorker*, 10/4/52.
404   "Then I noticed that a man": Boulton, *Part of a Long Story*, p. 16.
405   "so ordinary in some ways": Ibid., p. 18.
405   "What ho!" and "I got lost . . . bad breath!": Ibid., p. 19.
405   "kindly leer . . . telling anybody": Ibid.
406   "I want to spend": Ibid., p. 21.
407   "Turn back the universe": Ibid., p. 32.
407   "No money in milk cows": Ibid., p. 67.
407   "alone and virginal": Ibid., p. 68.
407   "Then I deliberately": Ibid., p. 69.
408   "I am only a dream": Middleton, *Poems and Songs*, "The Artist," p. 98.
408   "began talking and I stood": Boulton, *Part of a Long Story*, p. 59.
409   "Gene! I just finished": Ibid., p. 65.
409   "Again I've gone . . . not you and me, but *us*": Ibid., p. 70.
409   "in an aloneness . . . to act with them": Ibid., p. 68.
409   "And this must . . . on a rock": Ibid., p. 70.
409   "Haven't you got": Ibid., p. 70.
409   "The snow is very deep": Ibid., p. 71.
409   "She will come back": Ibid., p. 72.
411   "came in looking": Hapgood, *Victorian in the Modern World*, pp. 426–427.
411   "Writing is my vacation": EO to Dr. Lyman, 8/18/24.

25. SECOND MARRIAGE

412   "God! My God": Boulton, *Part of a Long Story*, p. 99.
413   "three thousand miles": Ibid., p. 113.
413   "beginning to suffer": Ibid, p. 114.
416   "I've come to see": Ibid., p. 109.
416   "difference — that we had": Ibid., p. 110.
416   "multitude of scenes": All quotations in the paragraph and in the following five are from the same source — O'Neill, Eugene, "A Letter from O'Neill," *New York Times*, 4/11/20.
418   "We should feel exalted": Carol Bird, "Eugene O'Neill — the Inner Man," *Theater Magazine*, June 1924.
419   "The point is that life": Mullett, "The Extraordinary Story."
419   "tragic expression in terms": Quinn, *History of the American Drama*, v. II, p. 199.
419   "One scene is out of doors": Mullett, "The Extraordinary Story."
420   "Instead of tying": New York *Globe*, 2/7/20.
421   "working like the devil": EO to Nina Moise, 4/9/18.
422   "I had been trying": Mindil, "Behind the Scenes," 2/15/20.
422   "I had heard that [O'Neill]": Ibid.
423   *The Rope* reviews: Broun, 4/29/18; *Brooklyn Eagle*, 5/14/18; *Theater Magazine*, June 1918.
423   "I recognized the tone": Boulton, *Part of a Long Story*, p. 130.
424   "I will never, or never have": Ibid., p. 111.
424   "He never seemed to be": Ibid., pp. 156–157.
425   "I will tear . . . on the wine": Ibid., p. 150.
425   "Swallow your poison . . . in your eyeball": Ibid., p. 151.

426   "Where'd the beyond- . . . when he's dead! Ibid., pp. 151–152.
426   "Life's a tragedy . . . sum of money!": Ibid., p. 152.
426   "There is a place": Ibid., p. 153.
428   "completely at ease": Ibid., p. 78.
428   "What ho, kids!": Ibid., p. 168.
429   "Last night, ah yesternight . . . Cynara": Ibid., p. 209.
429   "No, Mr. Jimmy . . . run out — umm!": Ibid., p. 210.
429   "Why don't they leave": Ibid., p. 169.
429   "*he and I* . . . of our own": Ibid., p. 171.
429   "to be alone": Ibid., p. 172.
430   White prostitute as the Dreamy Kid's girl: Cast of characters in *The Dreamy Kid* manuscript, Museum of the City of New York, Theater Collection.
431   Sketch of New York City under bombardment: New London *Telegraph*, 6/11/18.
431   Provincetown port closed: Provincetown *Advocate*, 6/6/18.
432   "I have spells of hating": Cook to his wife, 5/24/18.
432   "Gene was very impressed": Boulton, *Part of a Long Story*, pp. 76–77.
432   "After nearly a year's": EO to Jessica Rippin, 2/4/19.
434   "He felt that he was": Joyce, *Portrait of the Artist as a Young Man*, p. 98.
434   "All the leisure": Ibid., p. 78.
434   "The figure of that dark": Ibid., p. 62.
434   "It is a curious thing": Ibid., p. 240.
434   "This race . . . by those nets": Ibid., p. 203.
434   "To live, to err": Ibid., p. 172.
434   "thoroughly Irish": Ellmann, *James Joyce*, p. 708.
435   Coast Guard station: Originally the Coast Guard was known as the Life-Saving Service, a name that was still in effect when the O'Neills first settled in Provincetown. However, the name better known today, the Coast Guard, is used in the narrative in referring to the service and the old station at Peaked Hill Bars.
435   "This is the house": Boulton, *Part of a Long Story*, p. 182.

26. MOVING DAY ON MACDOUGAL STREET

439   "worked smoothly": Kenton, "The Provincetown Players," pp. 100–101.
439   "Here Pegasus Was": Deutsch and Hanau, *The Provincetown*, p. 45.
440   Ella O'Neill's operation for cancer: One biographer states that she had cancer in 1887, a year before Eugene's birth, and that the O'Neills went abroad that summer to have her operation performed by a foreign specialist. Another writer ascribes the same reason to their European trip in 1906. However, a document recently discovered — a report by a pathologist of St. Vincent's Hospital, dated 3/28/19 — discloses that Mrs. O'Neill's operation for cancer took place "about 6 mo. ago." In March 1919 she had a recurrence of the affliction, a nodule in the breast area, but after this was removed she, so far as can be learned, was not troubled again.
440   "got to his feet": Boulton, *Part of a Long Story*, p. 225.
441   "She's lovely": Ibid., p. 230.
441   "And isn't it wonderful": Ibid., p. 231.
441   "I always wanted a little girl": Ibid., p. 233.
441   "What ho!": Ibid., p. 233.
442   "Haven't I told you": Ibid., p. 234.
442   "one prolonged argument": Kenton, "The Provincetown Players," p. 104.
442   "No. They're rotten": Ibid., p. 105.
443   "one of my best": EO to Nina Moise, 1/17/19.

443 "where did you get": EO to Nathan, 6/20/20.
445 "painted, tried out": Kenton, "The Provincetown Players," p. 112.
445 "just an interlude": New York *Herald*, 12/21/18.
445 "rather pointless tale": New York *Tribune*, 12/25/18.
445 "what with a small": EO to Nina Moise, 1/17/19.
446 "We had breakfast": Boulton, *Part of a Long Story*, p. 275.
446 "Still absorbed in the work": Ibid., p. 276.
449 "A handsome face": Stark Young, "Eugene O'Neill: Notes from a Critic's Diary," *Harper's Magazine*, June, 1957.
450 "What are you doing": Harry Hansen, "The First Reader," New York *World-Telegram*, 9/26/33.
450 "Now you can go home": Boulton, *Part of a Long Story*, p. 297.
450 "I could not tell": Ibid., p. 299.
452 "They looked at last": Ibid., p. 291.
452 "I can't for the life": Goldberg, *The Theater of George Jean Nathan*, p. 77.
452 "extremely shy fellow": Ibid., pp. 76–77.
452 "warm and friendly": Ibid., p. 77.
453 "not so much an imp": Ibid., p. 99.
453 "understanding everything": Ibid., p. 47.
453 "What interests me . . . loveliness": Nathan, *The World in Falseface*, p. x (New York: Knopf, 1923).
453 "Nonsense is the privilege": Nathan, *The Autobiography of an Attitude*, p. 10 (New York: Knopf, 1926).
453 "with all the precision": *The Moon of the Caribbees and Six Other Plays of the Sea*, intro. by Nathan, pp. vii, viii and ix (New York: Modern Library, 1923).
454 "the best of them": Kinne, *George Pierce Baker*, pp. 205 and 206.
454 "I'm glad the stuff": Clark, *Eugene O'Neill*, p. 11.
  Moon of the Caribbees reviews: Broun, 5/4/19; *Review of Reviews*, July 1919; *Nation*, 6/14/19.

27. LAUNCHED ON BROADWAY

456 *The Life-Savers of Cape Cod*, J. W. Dalton, pp. 72–73 (Boston: Barta Press, 1902).
456 "I feel a true kinship": Loving, "Eugene O'Neill," *Bookman*, August 1921.
456 "The sunrises are enormous": Kemp, "O'Neill of Provincetown," *Brentano's Book Chat*, May–June 1929.
457 "only a trifling further": Provincetown *Advocate*, 1/14/17.
457 "Beautiful and unusual": Boulton, *Part of a Long Story*, p. 312.
457 "The stairs are like": Loving, "Eugene O'Neill."
458 "Gene once made one of": Alexander, *Tempering of Eugene O'Neill*, p. 275.
459 "Jig said yesterday": Hapgood letter to his wife undated, but summer 1919.
459 "I wish you would have": Tyler to EO, 7/18/19.
462 "One Man Who Needs": Hicks, *John Reed*, p. 338.
462 "I wish I could stay": Glaspell, *Road to the Temple*, p. 302.
463 "Time was when I": Oliver M. Sayler, "The Real Eugene O'Neill," *Century* magazine, January 1922.
463 "I have been almost off": Tyler to EO, 10/25/19.
464 "The Theater Guild have": EO to Nathan, 11/4/19.
464 "heir to this branch": EO to Tyler, 10/23/19.
464 "spirit which, if it": EO to Tyler, 10/27/19.
465 "I knew we'd forgotten": Boulton, *Part of a Long Story*, p. 330.
466 "wonderful": Tyler to EO, 11/7/19.

466   "A million rousing cheers!": EO to Tyler, 11/13/19.
466   "It looked like a pack rat's": Josephine Johnson.
467   "I already feel": Undated letter but approximately 11/30/19.
467   "The Old Governor": EO letter to Agnes dated only "Monday"; presumably 12/1/19.
468   "Mama knows everyone" and "I decided": Ibid.
469   "Dreamy was a killer": John Lovell, Jr., "Eugene O'Neill's Darker Brother," *Theater Arts* magazine, February 1948.
469   "There was no whiskey": EO letter to Agnes dated only "Tuesday"; presumably 12/2/19.
470   "the hangout of many": Downes, "Playwright Finds His Inspiration."
470   "My firebrand letter": EO letter to Agnes dated only "Monday evening"; presumably 1/5/20.
472   "going to do the O'Neill": Oliver M. Sayler, "Great Gotham," *The Indianan* magazine, 6/19/20.
472   "started to blue pencil": Bennett to Elkins, 11/18/19.
472   "very few beside Williams": Bennett to Elkins, 3/23/20.
473   "if we hadn't had it": EO to Agnes, 1/17/20.
473   "A mine were about": EO to Agnes, 1/14/20.
473   "could work 24 hours" and "to keep both the plays": EO to Agnes, 1/15/20.
473   "quick once-over": EO to Agnes, 1/14/20.
473   "prig," "farewell John," and "worry about": EO to Agnes, 1/17/20.
473   "I'll be home": EO to Agnes, 1/26/20.
473   "I wish I could": EO to Agnes, 1/15/20.
473   "I'd like to lay": EO to Agnes, 1/14/20.
473   "I wish you were": EO to Agnes, 1/17/20.
474   "These sort of letters": EO to Agnes, 1/22/20.
475   " 'went to the mat' ": EO to Agnes, 1/28/20.
476   "Well, what the hell!": EO to Agnes, 1/29/20. (Nathan used an excerpt from O'Neill's letter of 11/4/19, quoted in the narrative on p. 464).
476   "found many cuts" EO to Agnes, 1/31/20.
477   "Toward the end I": EO to Agnes, 2/2/20.
477   "shake" and "planted": EO letter to Agnes, 2/4/20.
477   "It's all right": Basso, "The Tragic Sense," 2/28/48.
480   "The first performance": EO to Agnes, 2/4/20.
480   Woollcott and Towse reviews, 2/4/20.
480   "however minutely he aims": Louis V. De Foe, New York *World*, 2/7/20.
480   "an audience goes": New York *Sun* (unsigned), 2/8/20.
480   O'Neill compared to Ibsen — Welsh; to Thomas Hardy — Woollcott, 2/8/20; to the Scandinavians, etc. — Charles Darnton, *Evening World*, 2/7/20.
481   "a whisper in the house": EO to Agnes, 2/4/20.
481   "Before O'Neill, the U.S.": "Trouble with Brown," *Time*, 12/7/53.

O'Neill's Diagram

THE diagram on the following page, first referred to in Chapter 3 of this biography, was presumably drawn up by O'Neill in an attempt to understand the early forces that had shaped him. The handwriting in the original is so minute that many of the words are almost indecipherable even under a magnifying glass; apparently he tried to assure that no one else could read it, should the paper fall into another's hands.

Except that his words are printed here, for legibility's sake, the transcription is faithful to his sketch.

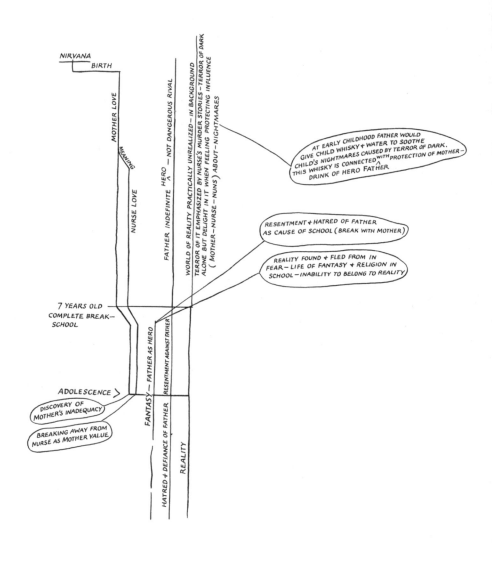

NIRVANA

BIRTH

MOTHER LOVE

MEANING

NURSE LOVE

FATHER INDEFINITE ∧ HERO — NOT DANGEROUS RIVAL

WORLD OF REALITY PRACTICALLY UNREALIZED — IN BACKGROUND
TERROR OF IT EMPHASIZED BY NURSE'S MURDER STORIES — TERROR OF DARK
ALONE BUT DELIGHT IN IT WHEN FEELING PROTECTING INFLUENCE
(MOTHER — NURSE — NUNS) ABOUT — NIGHTMARES

AT EARLY CHILDHOOD FATHER WOULD
GIVE CHILD WHISKY + WATER TO SOOTHE
CHILD'S NIGHTMARES CAUSED BY TERROR OF DARK.
THIS WHISKY IS CONNECTED WITH PROTECTION OF MOTHER —
DRINK OF HERO FATHER ∧

RESENTMENT + HATRED OF FATHER
AS CAUSE OF SCHOOL (BREAK WITH MOTHER)

REALITY FOUND + FLED FROM IN
FEAR — LIFE OF FANTASY + RELIGION IN
SCHOOL — INABILITY TO BELONG TO REALITY

7 YEARS OLD
COMPLETE BREAK —
SCHOOL

FANTASY — FATHER AS HERO

RESENTMENT AGAINST FATHER

ADOLESCENCE ⟩

DISCOVERY OF
MOTHER'S INADEQUACY

BREAKING AWAY FROM
NURSE AS MOTHER VALUE.

HATRED + DEFIANCE OF FATHER

REALITY

Bibliography

Published O'Neill Plays

The page references in the Notes are to the following editions:

Hughie. New Haven: Yale University Press, 1959.

A Long Day's Journey Into Night. New Haven: Yale University Press, 1956.

A Moon for the Misbegotten. New York: Random House, 1952.

More Stately Mansions. New Haven: Yale University Press, 1964.

Ten "Lost" Plays. New York: Random House, 1964. (*Abortion, Fog, The Movie Man, Recklessness, Servitude, The Sniper, Thirst, Warnings, The Web*, and *A Wife for a Life*.)

A Touch of the Poet. New Haven: Yale University Press, 1957.

The Plays of Eugene O'Neill, 3 vols. New York: Random House, 1951. Contains all O'Neill's published plays except those listed above.

Unpublished O'Neill Plays

"Bread and Butter." Four acts. Copyright Division, Library of Congress.

"Chris Christopherson." Three acts. Copyright Division, Library of Congress, and Houghton Library, Harvard University.

"Now I Ask You." Three acts. Houghton Library, Harvard University.

"The Personal Equation." Four acts. Houghton Library, Harvard University.

"Shell Shock." One act. Copyright Division, Library of Congress.

Books, Articles, Unpublished Works

Many sources, particularly articles in newspapers and periodicals, are not listed below but are cited only in the Notes.

Alexander, Doris. *The Tempering of Eugene O'Neill*. New York: Harcourt, Brace & World, 1962.

Asbury, Herbert. *The Gangs of New York*. New York: Knopf, 1927.

Ashleigh, Charles. "When I First Met Eugene O'Neill," *Bulletin of the American Women's Club of Paris*, March 1927.

Basso, Hamilton. "The Tragic Sense," *New Yorker*, February 28, March 6, and March 13, 1948.

Bodenheim, Maxwell. "Roughneck and Romancer," *New Yorker*, February 6, 1926.

Boulton, Agnes. *Part of a Long Story*. Garden City: Doubleday, 1958.

Bowen, Croswell. "The Black Irishman," *PM*, November 3, 1946.

———, with the assistance of Shane O'Neill. *The Curse of the Misbegotten*. New York: McGraw-Hill, 1959.

Brooks, Van Wyck. *The Confident Years: 1885–1915*. New York: Dutton, 1952.

Cargill, Oscar, N. Bryllion Fagin and William J. Fisher, eds. *O'Neill and His Plays*. New York: New York University Press, 1961. Contains a number of newspaper and periodical articles listed here in the Bibliography, as well as a wealth of other material on the subject.

Churchill, Allen. *The Improper Bohemians*. New York: Dutton, 1959.

Clark, Barrett H. *Eugene O'Neill: The Man and His Plays*. New York: Dover, 1947.

———, ed. *Favorite American Plays of the 19th Century*. Princeton, N.J.: Princeton University Press, 1934. Contains the Fechter version of *Monte Cristo*, James O'Neill's perennial vehicle.

Conrad, Joseph. *The Nigger of the Narcissus*. Garden City: Doubleday, 1914.

Crawford, F. Marion, and Walter Hackett. "The White Sister." Unpublished manuscript of a dramatization of Mr. Crawford's novel of the same title. New York Public Library, Lincoln Center Branch, Theater Collection.

Crichton, Kyle. "Mr. O'Neill and The Iceman," *Collier's*, October 26, 1946.

———. *Total Recoil*. Garden City: Doubleday, 1960.

Deutsch, Helen, and Stella Hanau. *The Provincetown, A Story of the Theater.* New York: Farrar & Rinehart, 1931.

Dolmetsch, C. R. "A History of the *Smart Set* Magazine." Unpublished doctoral dissertation, University of Chicago, 1957. New York Public Library, Main Branch.

Downer, Alan S. *Fifty Years of American Drama: 1900–1950.* Chicago: Regnery, 1951.

Downes, Olin. "Playwright Finds His Inspiration on Lonely Sand Dunes by the Sea," Boston *Post*, August 29, 1920.

Dramatic Mirror. In 1889 the New York *Mirror*, a leading theatrical weekly, changed its name to the New York *Dramatic Mirror;* to avoid confusion, its name is always given in the text and the Notes, in its entirety, as the *Dramatic Mirror.*

Eastman, Max. *The Enjoyment of Living.* New York: Harper, 1948.

Ellmann, Richard. *James Joyce.* New York: Oxford University Press, 1959.

Gassner, John, ed. *O'Neill: A Collection of Critical Essays.* Englewood Cliffs, N.J.: Prentice-Hall, 1964.

Gelb, Arthur and Barbara. *O'Neill.* New York: Harper, 1962.

Glaspell, Susan. *The Road to the Temple.* New York: Stokes, 1927.

Goldberg, Isaac. *The Theater of George Jean Nathan.* New York: Simon & Schuster, 1926.

Goldman, Emma. *Living My Life.* New York: Knopf, 1931.

Hamilton, Clayton. *Conversations on Contemporary Drama.* New York: Macmillan, 1925.

———. "Seen on the Stage," *Vogue*, April 1, 1920.

Hamilton, Gladys. "Untold Tales of Eugene O'Neill," *Theater Arts*, August 1956.

Hapgood, Hutchins. *An Anarchist Woman.* New York: Duffield, 1909.

———. *A Victorian in the Modern World.* New York: Harcourt, Brace, 1939.

Hawthorne, Hazel. *Salt House.* New York: Stokes, 1934.

Hicks, Granville. *John Reed: The Making of a Revolutionary.* New York: Macmillan, 1936.

Ishill, Joseph, ed. *Benjamin R. Tucker, a Bibliography.* Berkeley Heights, N.J.: Oriole, 1934.

Joyce, James. *A Portrait of the Artist as a Young Man.* New York: Viking, 1956.

Kalonyme, Louis. "O'Neill Lifts the Curtain on His Early Days," *New York Times*, December 21, 1924.

Karsner, David. "Eugene O'Neill at Close Range in Maine," New York *Herald Tribune*, August 8, 1926.

Kenton, Edna. "The Provincetown Players and the Playwrights' Theater, 1915–1922." Unpublished manuscript.

Kinne, Wisner Payne. *George Pierce Baker and the American Theater.* Cambridge, Mass.: Harvard University Press, 1954.

Kreymborg, Alfred. *Troubadour.* New York: Boni & Liveright, 1925.

Krutch, Joseph Wood. *The American Drama Since 1918.* New York: Braziller, 1957.

———. *"Modernism" in Modern Drama.* New York: Russell & Russell, 1962.

Latimer, Frederick P. "Eugene Is Beyond Us," New London *Day*, February 15, 1928.

Leslie, Amy. "Threatens to Desert," Chicago *News*, July 10, 1909.

Light on the Path (author listed as "M.C."). New York: Theosophical Publishing Co., 1897.

Little, Richard H. "Haunted by the Ghost of Monte Cristo," Chicago *Record Herald*, February 9, 1908.

Locke, Robinson. A scrapbook entitled "James O'Neill" in the Locke Collection, New York Public Library, Lincoln Center Branch, Theater Collection. Some articles in the scrapbook are unidentified as to their publication, or undated, or both; such articles, not fully identified, are designated *Locke* in the Notes.

Loving, Pierre. "Eugene O'Neill," *Bookman*, August 1921.

Luhan, Mabel Dodge. *Movers and Shakers.* New York: Harcourt, Brace, 1936.

Macdonald, Dwight. "The Foolish Things of the World," *New Yorker*, October 4 and 11, 1952.

Madison, Charles A. *Critics and Crusaders.* New York: Holt, 1947–1948.

Mantle, Burns, and Garrison P. Sherwood. *The Best Plays of 1899–1909.* New York: Dodd, Mead, 1944.

McCandless, Marion. *Family Portraits.* Notre Dame, Ind.: St. Mary's College, 1952.

Merrill, Charles A. "Eugene O'Neill, World-Famed Dramatist, and Family Live in Abandoned Coast Guard Station on Cape Cod," Boston *Globe*, July 8, 1923.

Merrill, Flora. "Fierce Oaths and Blushing Complexes Find No Place in Eugene O'Neill's Talk," New York *World*, July 19, 1925.

Middleton, Richard. *Poems and Songs.* London: Unwin, 1912.

Miller, Jordan Y. *Eugene O'Neill and the American Critic.* Hamden, Conn.: Archon, 1962. By far the most complete bibliography of articles and books on O'Neill.

Mindil, Philip. "Behind the Scenes," New York *Tribune*, February 15 and 22, 1920.

Mollan, Malcolm. "Making Plays with a Tragic Ending," Philadelphia *Public Ledger*, January 22, 1922.

Moody, Richard. *Edwin Forrest, First Star of the American Stage.* New York: Knopf, 1960.

Mullett, Mary B. "The Extraordinary Story of Eugene O'Neill," *American Magazine*, November 1922.

Nathan, George Jean. *The Intimate Notebooks of George Jean Nathan.* New York: Knopf, 1932.

New York *Dramatic Mirror.* See *Dramatic Mirror.*

New York *Mirror.* See *Dramatic Mirror.*

Nietzsche, Friedrich. *Thus Spake Zarathustra.* Trans. by Thomas Common. New York: Modern Library, n.d.

———. *The Portable Nietzsche.* Trans., with introduction and prefaces, by Walter Kaufmann. New York: Viking, 1954. Mr. Kaufmann's new translation of *Zarathustra* is clearly superior to that of Mr. Common, but it seemed advisable to quote in the present biography from the earlier version as the one known to O'Neill. Some commentary in the Kaufmann volume is utilized in the text.

O'Neill, Eugene. "A Dramatist's Notebook," *American Spectator*, January 1933.

———. "A Letter from O'Neill," *New York Times*, April 11, 1920.

———. "Memoranda on Masks," *American Spectator*, November 1932.

———. "Second Thoughts," *American Spectator*, December 1932.

———. "Tomorrow," *Seven Arts*, June 1917. The only short story by O'Neill ever published.

O'Neill, J. F. "What a Sanatorium Did for Eugene O'Neill," *Journal of the Outdoor Life*, June 1923.

O'Neill, James. "Personal Reminiscences," *Theater Magazine*, December 1917.

O'Neill, Patrick. *History of the San Francisco Theater, Vol. XX: James O'Neill.* San Francisco: Writers' Program of the WPA in Northern California, 1942.

"Only Books That Teach Anarchy Are Sold in This Sixth Avenue Shop" (unsigned), New York *Herald*, April 12, 1908.

Oppenheim, James. "The Story of the *Seven Arts*," *American Mercury*, June 1930.

Parry, Albert. *Garrets and Pretenders.* New York: Dover, 1960.

Pasley, Fred. "The Odyssey of Eugene O'Neill," New York *News*, January 24–30, 1932.

Patterson, Ada. "James O'Neill — The Actor and the Man," *Theater Magazine*, April 1908.

Peck, Seymour. "Talk with Mrs. O'Neill," *New York Times*, November 4, 1956.

Philpott, A. J. "Laboratory of the Drama on Cape Cod's Farthest Wharf," Boston *Globe*, August 13, 1916.

Prideaux, Tom. "Most Celebrated U.S. Playwright Returns to Theater," *Life*, October 14, 1946.

Quinn, Arthur Hobson. *A History of the American Drama*. New York: Crofts, 1945.

Raleigh, John Henry. *The Plays of Eugene O'Neill*. Carbondale, Ill.: Southern Illinois University Press, 1965.

Ruggles, Eleanor. *Prince of Players, Edwin Booth*. New York: Norton, 1953.

Sachs, Emanie. *The Terrible Siren, Victoria Woodhull*. New York: Harper, 1928.

Sanborn, Ralph, and Barrett H. Clark. *A Bibliography of the Works of Eugene O'Neill*. New York: Random House, 1931. In addition to bibliographical data, the volume contains all the poems O'Neill wrote for the New London *Telegraph* in 1912, as well as other of his verse.

Sergeant, Elizabeth Shepley. *Fire Under the Andes*. New York: Knopf, 1927.

Shaw, George Bernard. *Selected Prose of Bernard Shaw*. Selected by Diarmuid Russell. New York: Dodd, Mead, 1952.

Stirner, Max. *The Ego and His Own*. Trans. by Steven T. Byington. New York: Libertarian Book Club, 1963.

Strindberg, August. *Plays by August Strindberg*. Trans. by Edwin Björkman. New York: Scribner's 1912.

———. *The Road to Damascus*. Trans. by Graham Rawson. New York: Grove, 1960.

———. *Six Plays of August Strindberg*. Trans. by Elizabeth Sprigge. New York: Doubleday, 1955.

Sweeney, Charles P. "Back to the Sources of Plays Written by Eugene O'Neill," New York *World*, November 9, 1924.

Thompson, Charles. "Another Connecticut Yankee." Unpublished autobiography. Author's collection.

"Trouble with Brown" (unsigned), *Time*, December 7, 1953.

Tyler, George C., and J. C. Furnas. *Whatever Goes Up*. Indianapolis: Bobbs-Merrill, 1934.

Vorse, Mary Heaton. *Time and the Town*. New York: Dial, 1942.

Walling, George W. *Recollections of a New York Chief of Police.* New York: Caxton Book Concern, 1888.

Ware, Caroline F. *Greenwich Village, 1920–1930.* Boston: Houghton, Mifflin, 1935.

Weaver, John V. A. "I Knew Him When," New York *World*, February 21, 1926.

Wilde, Oscar. *The Picture of Dorian Gray.* New York: World, 1946.

Winter, William. *The Life of David Belasco.* New York: Moffat, Yard, 1918.

Winther, Sophus Keith. "Strindberg and O'Neill: A Study of Influence," *Scandinavian Studies*, August 1959.

Woodworth, Robert A. "The World's Worst Reporter," Providence *Journal*, December 6, 1931.

Woolf, S. J. "Eugene O'Neill Returns After Twelve Years," *New York Times*, September 15, 1946.

Acknowledgments

THE matter for this book was amassed with the generous help of many persons, libraries, official agencies, and institutions. My debt to all is immeasurable, the extent of my gratitude impossible for me to express adequately. In listing libraries first among the groups, I pay tribute to their being a writer-researcher's indispensable ally and support; practically without exception they responded nobly to my innumerable requests for assistance, and confirmed what I have always suspected: the people who work for libraries are among the worthiest members of our society.

Of the individuals who made this book possible, Carlotta Monterey O'Neill clearly comes first. Besides reminiscing to me at length on numerous occasions about her husband and proving her good will in various other ways — including gifts of photographs and special editions of his works — she kindly gave me permission to quote from his correspondence. I am also beholden for substantial assistance to Jane Rubin, Mrs. O'Neill's literary agent.

Agnes Boulton, O'Neill's second wife, likewise granted me many interviews in which she generously poured out her memories; to her, also, I am greatly indebted. Moreover, the correspondence between her and O'Neill is a prime source of information, and her memoir, *Part of a Long Story*, an essential record of their early years together and of the playwright as he began to win fame. For light on his first marriage, I am indebted to Mrs. Kathleen Pitt-Smith, the first Mrs. O'Neill.

My research would have been far more difficult without the backing of Brooks Atkinson, author, New England gentleman, latter-day Thoreau, and former drama critic of the *New York Times*. Mr. Atkinson, in addition to personal encouragement, lent his considerable prestige by writing a letter endorsing my project, thereby opening doors and winning for me cooperation that might otherwise not have been obtainable.

With the support of Brooks Atkinson, Professor Travis Bogard, John Mason Brown, Malcolm Cowley, Professor Alan S. Downer, Professor Howard E. Hugo, Louis Kronenberger, Kenneth Macgowan, Dr. Whitney J. Oates, Philip Van Doren Stern, and Richard Watts, Jr., I was awarded two Fellowships (1959–1960 and 1962–1963) by the John Simon Guggenheim Memorial Foundation and two grants-in-aid (1960 and 1962) by the American Council of Learned Societies. I am exceedingly grateful both to these sponsors and to the Foundation and the Society.

Since I began working on this biography a number of persons who helped me have died, among them Kenneth Macgowan, a devoted man of the theater and a friend to anyone trying to accomplish something worthwhile. Besides making available his voluminous correspondence from O'Neill, he amiably endured my endless questions. When I visited the West Coast on research, he and Mrs. Macgowan gave me shelter. He was also instrumental in gaining for me — through the kind consent of publisher John Hay Whitney — the use of the reference library of the New York *Herald Tribune*. Robert E. Grayson, head of the library, could not have been more helpful.

The resources of the New York Public Library, especially its excellent Theater Collection, contributed greatly to this biography, and like countless researchers before me, I am much indebted to those dedicated archivists, Paul Myers and the late George Freedley. I am beholden also to the library's manuscript division and the Berg Collection.

As the chief repositories of O'Neill's papers, certain academic libraries were of major assistance. I am particularly grateful to Yale's Beinecke Library and Dr. Donald C. Gallup; to Princeton University Library and Alexander P. Clark; and to Harvard's Houghton Library and Helen D. Willard — not only because of the importance of their O'Neill material but because Miss Willard, Mr. Clark and Dr. Gallup generously extended themselves, beyond the call of duty, to assist me. At Harvard I was helped also by William H. Bond, who gave me permission to use the university's material, and Rodney G. Dennis III; and at Princeton by Marguerite McAneney. For making available the Bella C. Landauer Collection and other papers at Dartmouth, I am indebted to Peter Michael Rainey, Marcus A. McCorison and Elizabeth M. Sherrard; and for access to the O'Neill–George Jean Nathan papers at Cornell University to Stephen A. McCarthy.

The libraries of the following schools and the personnel here mentioned likewise have my gratitude: Columbia University; University of Florida and Fleming Montgomery; Holy Cross College; University of Michigan's Labadie Collection and Edward Weber; New York University's Fales Collection; University of North Carolina and James W.

Patton; Notre Dame University and Dr. Francis D. Lazenby; University of Pennsylvania and Neda M. Westlake; Stanford University and Patricia J. Palmer (particularly for the Wilbur Daniel Steele letter that finally enabled me to pin down the date when *Bound East for Cardiff* was given in Provincetown); Syracuse University and John S. Mayfield; University of Texas and Mary M. Hirth and W. H. Crain.

It would take far more space than I have at my disposal to thank properly all the other libraries, museums, and historical societies that have furthered my research. The list that follows is but an acknowledgment, no real indication, of my great debt to the Library of Congress and Richard S. MacCarteney, David C. Mearns and Robert H. Land; to the Museum of the City of New York and May Davenport Seymour and Sam Pearce; to The Players' Walter Hampden Library and Pat Carroll and Louis A. Bachow; to the Newberry Library and Amy Nyholm; to the Atlanta Public Library and Isabel Erlich; to the Richmond County Library of Augusta (Ga.) and Jean D. Cochran; to the Birmingham Public Library and Fant Hill Thornley; to the Boston Public Library and B. Joseph O'Neil, Mildred C. O'Connor, James Monahan and Michael Venezia; to the Bridgeport Public Library and June K. Csaltko; to the Brockton Public Library and Alice L. Conley; to the Brooklyn Public Library and John C. Frantz; to the Buffalo & Erie County Public Library and Margaret M. Mott; to the Public Library of Canborne, Cornwall, England, and J. R. Burrell.

Also, to the Cincinnati Public Library and Carl G. Marquette, Jr.; to the Cleveland Public Library and Marie Corrigan and Herbert Mansfield; to the Denver Public Library and Alys Freeze; to the Hartford Public Library and Josephine W. Sale; to the Holyoke Public Library and Marjorie L. Marengo; to the Kansas City (Mo.) Public Library and Shirley Mickelson; to the Curtis Memorial Library of Meriden (Conn.), and T. G. Salmon; to the Missouri State Historical Society and Shirley L. Neenan; to the Mobile Public Library and Ruth Warren; to the Newark Public Library and William Urban; to the New London County Historical Society; to the New Orleans Public Library and Margaret Ruckert and E. J. Brin; to the New York State Library and William J. Pringle, Mary V. Jennings and Mary Felix; to the Norfolk Public Library and Virginia H. Pinkerton; to the Otis Library of Norwich (Conn.) and Winifred Hagen.

Also, to the Carnegie Library of Pittsburgh and Mrs. George S. Cunningham and Judith Ondich; to the Providence Public Library and Mary A. Heneghan; to the Richmond Public Library and Gene Harrison Knoop; to the Rochester Public Library and Emma Swift; to the St.

Louis Public Library and Mildred Boatman; to the Salt Lake City Public Library and George M. Hooper; to the City Library Association of Springfield (Mass.) and Margaret Rose; to the Stamford Historical Society and Miss M. E. Plumb; to the Syracuse Public Library and Margaret Bates; to the Texas State Library and James M. Day; to the Toledo Public Library and Irene McCreery; to the Toronto Public Library and Heather McCallum; and to the Worcester Public Library and Louise C. Carruth and James A. Visbeck.

In the course of my research I have made a number of friends, among them Dorothy Berliner Commins; I owe her a special debt of gratitude for her considerable help and her hospitality, and am also indebted to her late husband, Saxe Commins, the noted editor at Random House. Others to whom I am particularly grateful are Hazel Hawthorne Werner for her revealing memories of O'Neill, her extensive research in Provincetown on my behalf, and the loan of her 1934 novel, *Salt House*, which is set partly in the old Coast Guard station at Peaked Hill Bars; C. Waller Barrett for making available his O'Neill papers, which he later presented to the University of Virginia; Peggy Muray and her late husband, Nicholas Muray, the well-known photographer, for a gift of many photographs; Frances Steloff of the Gotham Book Mart for allowing me to copy her O'Neill material; and Marion McCandless, a delightful lady, for the gift of her book, *Family Portraits*, and her flow of letters regarding St. Mary's Academy, the alma mater of O'Neill's mother.

In New London, where I conducted some of my most important research, I was greatly helped by Beatrice Ashe Maher (she and her late husband, Admiral James E. Maher, were gracious hosts), Emily Rippin Griswold, Jessica N. Rippin, Grace Rippin, James Rippin, Jr. (the Rippins were among the first to make me feel at home in O'Neill's home town), Maibelle Scott Beckley, Arthur B. McGinley, Olive Evans Maxson, Arlene Scott Fones, Mabel Reynolds Haynes, Phyllis Bankel of the *Day*, and Frederick W. Edgerton, former head of the New London Public Library. The late Mr. Edgerton kindly gave me free access to the stacks and allowed me to work in the library on weekends, when the place was closed to the public. Special thanks are due Hazel A. Johnson, the librarian of the Connecticut College for Women and a selfless soul; thanks to her unflagging help, I was able to accomplish more in that city than I otherwise could have done.

I am also deeply indebted to Mr. and Mrs. Francis F. McGuire, who were both helpful and warmly hospitable, and to Mr. and Mrs. Lawrence A. White, present owners of the Monte Cristo cottage. Others who contributed to my New London research were Dr. and Mrs. Joseph M.

Ganey, Edward R. Keefe, R. Scott Linsley, Alexander Campbell, Agnes Casey, E. Valentine Chappell, C. C. Comstock, Joseph Corkey, Bernard Cullen, John DeGange, Thomas F. Dorsey, Jr., Mrs. Joseph Ferrini, Charles Doane Greene, Mildred Culver Greene, Alfred H. Gurney, James Hammond, Richard J. Hancock of Lawrence & Memorial Hospitals, Guy Hedlund, Margaret Heyer, Walter Hubbard, Edmund C. Johnson, Louise Johnson, Benjamin King, T. H. Latimer, Mrs. Jacob Linicus, Lucille M. Lohmann, Morris Lubchansky, John McGinley, Margaret Kiley Mead, Richard Meadnis, Frank Mix, Mabel Ramage Mix, Mrs. Malcolm Mollan, Mrs. Julian Moran, Walter Murphy, Frank and Joseph Neilan, Ruth Newcomb, Daniel J. O'Neill, Elizabeth Young Palmer, Helen Ross Palmer, Hattie Parrish, Frank Payne, Coddington Pendleton, Stavros Peterson, Mrs. Daniel F. Porter, Mary E. Raub, Samuel S. Riner, Mrs. G. C. Baxter Rowe, Henkle Scott, Thomas A. Scott, Mrs. Henry Selden, James Shay, Alice L. Sheridan, Bessie M. Sheridan, Philip and Esther Sheridan, Claire Rogers Sherman, Thomas H. Sisk, Lucy Smith, George H. Starr, Dr. Daniel Sullivan, Michael Sullivan, Josephine D. Sutton, Stanley H. Tansey, Mrs. Charles Thompson, Judge and Mrs. Thomas E. Troland, Edna Tyler, Kate Van Emmerick, John Waller, Captain John A. Walsh, Julia Westcott, Henry Whittemore, Arthur Wilkinson, Mrs. George Wood, and Helen Christie and Elizabeth Whitten of the New London Public Library.

Of the many who aided my research none was more willing and interested than Captain Severin Waage of Norway, whose father was master of the *Charles Racine*, on which O'Neill sailed to Buenos Aires. In the course of our correspondence Captain Waage, who made many trips on the barque, must have spent days writing me at length everything he could recall of life aboard the old windjammer; moreover, he supplied me with all the documentary material he could lay his hands on, telling me to keep it as long as I wanted. Others who substantially helped my narrative of O'Neill's voyage were Sigval Bergesen of the shipping line of that name in Stavanger, onetime owner of the *Charles Racine*, and Osmund Christophersen and Rolf Skjørestad, both of whom were on the 1910 voyage. I thank at this point my friends Ruth Grutzner and Colonel Nils L. Nilsen for translating into Norwegian my letters to Christophersen and Skjørestad, and their replies into English. Though Captain Waage had doubts about his ability as a linguist, he expressed himself in English with precision and flavor.

Essentially everything I have said of Captain Waage applies equally to Frederick Hettman in regard to O'Neill's stay in Buenos Aires. Mr. Hettman, who has a remarkable memory for the long ago, has written me in full all he remembers of O'Neill in 1910, and he also took great pains to give a detailed picture of Buenos Aires at the time. Though we have never met, for Mr. Hettman still lives in Argentina, the cordiality of his letters has left me feeling that he, like Captain Waage, is a friend of long standing. Others who contributed to my chapter on Buenos Aires were Charles Ashleigh, Mrs. Hugh Brown, and newspaper executive Joshua B. Powers, an old friend of Mr. Hettman's, whose endorsement of my project won for me Mr. Hettman's all-out cooperation. Also, an American who knew O'Neill in Argentina in 1910 but who prefers anonymity; he is referred to in the narrative under the fictitious name of "Barnes."

For information on O'Neill at St. Aloysius Academy, I am indebted to Sister Mary Florentine, Joseph A. McCarthy, Ewing Philbin, Stephen H. Philbin, M. E. Crane, Dr. F. X. Murray, and Mrs. R. D. Skinner.

At De La Salle Institute: Brother Basil Peter, Ricardo Amezaga, Christopher Campanari, General Tabernilla Dolz, Peter D. Kuser, Hugh Lavery, and Victor F. Ridder.

At Betts Academy: Grace H. Walmsley of the Ferguson Library, Stamford, who generously gave of her time in digging out vital documents on the school; Charlotte E. Betts, Herman A. Burgett, Harry E. Clarke, Henry A. Colver, Allen B. Coon, Matthew Corbett, Ralph J. deGolier, Harold M. Green, Dr. Gordon I. Hislop, Fred C. Iringer, Phyllis Jenkins, Thomson Kingsford, Harold L. Kohler, Charles Mayer, Benjamin M. McLyman, Elliott W. Mott, Laurence D. Oppenheim, José L. Pessino, Mrs. E. Carl Rurode, Reginald Schmidt, William H. Trausneck, Morton C. Treadway, T. G. Treadway, Clarence G. Wadhams, Reverend Arthur G. Walter, and Clarence E. Woodward.

Those who contributed most to my chapter on Princeton were: Warren H. Hastings, Richard F. Weeks, Raymond M. Terry, W. C. Adams, D. C. Benton, Frank D. Brewer, Charles M. Butler, James S. Dennis, James D. Dusenberry, Frank K. Ewing, Frank S. Galey, Ralph Horton, William M. John, Dr. John T. King, Donald S. Olds, Bertram L. Sichelstiel, Homer Tregloan, Rufus J. Trimble, Robert S. Wilson, James S. Wolf, Professor Arthur S. Link, Professor Edward Hubler, and Sarah S. Graham of the Princeton Alumni Records Office.

For material relating to O'Neill's stay in Honduras, I am indebted to Mrs. Earl C. Stevens.

For information on the S.S. *Ikala*, O'Neill's reputed round trip between Buenos Aires and Durban, South Africa, and Driscoll's death, I am indebted to Vice-consul Michael Marshall of the British Embassy in Buenos Aires, Rear Admiral James A. Hirshfield, Captain D. T. Adams, the periodical *Sea Breezes* of Liverpool, F. Carruthers, Stanley Uglow,

S. Denhim, the General Register and Record Office of Shipping and Sea-men, Cardiff, Wales; Lloyd's Register of Shipping, 1910–1911, and the Central Library of Port-of-Spain, Trinidad.

On Jimmy the Priest's (including James Findlater Byth and Chris Christopherson): Mario C. Alessi, John Callan, Christopher Wells of Williams & Wells, John J. Foley of the New York City Medical Examiner's office, Christoffer Holt, Fred Stevens of the New York City Health Department's bureau of records, Dr. Randolph A. Wyman of Bellevue Hospital, Edward H. Michels, Alexander Rains, Dr. George Meade, the New York City Hall of Records' archives, Sidney J. Mason of Reuters, Ltd., the Registrar General's Office, Edinburgh, Scotland; the Edinburgh University Library, King's College, Aberdeen; Glasgow University, Aberdeen University, and the General Register Office, London, England.

On O'Neill's stay in the two tuberculosis sanatoria: Dr. Sterling B. Brinkley, Dr. Edward J. Lynch, Dr. Kirby S. Howlett, Jr., Emma H. Wolodarsky, Clare O'Rourke, Alice V. Murray, Hilmer L. Rosene, Marion Bridgett, George W. MacKay, Colin MacKay, Wilhelmina Stamberger, B. J. Clark, Reba R. Maisonville, E. Scott, Ida Axell, Frank C. Benson, and Oliver Finch.

On O'Neill in Baker's playwriting course at Harvard: Everett Glass, Donald L. Breed, Malcolm Morley, Professor A. R. Ebel, Dr. B. E. Ebel, Dr. Daniel Hiebert, Lingard Loud, Marian Tanner, Corwin Willson, William Laurence, Mrs. George Pierce Baker, and Florence S. Kimball of the Harvard Alumni Records Office.

Of those who helped me in regard to O'Neill in Greenwich Village and Provinceton, I am most indebted to Solveig (Mrs. Harl) Cook and Sirius C. Cook for permission to quote from the personal and published writings of Susan Glaspell and George Cram Cook, including the former's *The Road to the Temple;* to Charles Hapgood for permission to quote from the correspondence and published works of his parents, Neith Boyce and Hutchins Hapgood, including the latter's *An Anarchist Woman* and *A Victorian in the Modern World;* to Harold DePolo for a firsthand account of O'Neill's and his arrest as "German spies," and for his graphic reminiscences in general, to which his wife Helen contributed; to Celia C. Francis for copies of O'Neill's correspondence with her widely loved father, John A. Francis; to Phyllis Duganne Given and Eben Given for help of various kinds; to Nina Moise for the use of her letters from O'Neill and her significant memories of him; to Granville Hicks for reading and criticizing my chapters in which John Reed appears, as well as for permission to quote from his *John Reed, The Making of a Revolutionary;* and to Norma Millay Ellis and Charles Ellis, not only for their reminiscences but particularly for going to the trouble of having Clemens Kalischer photograph Mr. Ellis's painting of leading figures of the Provincetown Players, for inclusion in this book.

Others who contributed substantially to my account of the Greenwich Village–Provincetown period were Peggy Baird, E. J. Ballantine, Forster Batterham, Charles Boni, George Frayme Brown, Susan Jenkins Brown, William C. Bullitt, Dorothy Day, Jasper Deeter, Ida Rauh Eastman, Barney Gallant, Edward Goodman, James Light, Alan MacAteer, Kyra Markham, Robert Allerton Parker, Pauline Turkel, Louise Varese, and Mary Heaton Vorse. Still others to whom I am grateful are Berenice Abbott, Harriet Adams, Egmont Arens, Ozzie Ball, Betty Collins Barnes, Jennie Belardi, Mary Bicknell, Cecil Boulton, Robert Carlton Brown, Lily Burke, Robert Byrne, Holger Cahill, Frank Conroy, Floyd Dell, Mrs. Joseph Dennis, Harrison Dowd, John G. Evans, Jerry Farnsworth, Waldo Frank, Eduard Franz, Hugo Gellert, Carl Glick, Milia Davenport Harkavy, Blanche Hays, Frank Henderson, Inez Hogan, Polly Holladay, Catherine Huntington of the Provincetown Playhouse on the Wharf, Josephine Johnson, John Kelley, Harry Kemp, Ernestine Kettler, Alice King, Maude D. Kivlen, Arthur Lee, Benjamin J. Legere, Mrs. Joseph F. Madeiro, Marie ("Romany Marie") Marchand, James J. Martin, Harold Meltzer, Edwin Justus Mayer, Dr. Margaret Nordfeldt, Gus Perry, Arthur Leonard Ross, Edith Shay, Oscar Snow, Jr., Wilbur Daniel Steele, Helen Swords, Alan Ullman, Alice Woods Ullman, Manuel Zora, and William and Marguerite Zorach.

Concerning other periods and aspects of O'Neill's life, I am much indebted for reminiscences, material and other help to Winfield Aronberg, Silvio Bedini, John Cronin, Russel Crouse, the late Robert Frost, the late John Gassner, Mrs. Clayton Hamilton, Eileen Curran Herron, John O. Hewitt, Gareth Hughes, Philip Kaplan, Charles O'Brien Kennedy, Bella C. Landauer, Julie Haydon Nathan, the Reverend Irving S. Pollard, Windsor Topps, Brandon Tynan, and Charles Webster. Others who earned my gratitude were Mrs. August Belmont, Mrs. Frank Best, Harold Burrows, William R. Castle, Mrs. Barrett H. Clark, John A. S. Cushman, Allen Delano, Jean Detre, Milton I. D. Einstein, Robert W. Farrell, Police Captain Paul Glaser, Dr. James T. Hearin, Ethel Hjul, Mrs. Rhea James, Mary Keenan, Sadie Koenig, Albert Lewis, Theodore Liebler, Jr., Mrs. Richard J. Madden, Professor Ruby Turner Morris, critic Elliot Norton, David F. Perkins, Joseph Plunkett, Marion S. Revett, Jason Robards, Jr., Joan Bennett, for permission to quote from letters of her father, Richard Bennett, and Gilbert W. Kahn and Mrs. John Barry Ryan, for permission to quote from the Otto H. Kahn papers at Princeton University Library.

I am indebted also to St. Ann's Church and Holy Innocents Church (both Roman Catholic churches in New York City), Actors' Equity, the Actors' Fund of America, various departments of the New London (Conn.) Municipal Government, the National Archives, Washington, D.C., and the law firm of Cadawalader, Wickersham & Taft.

"If all the printed sources of history for a certain century had to be destroyed, save one," said Clarence S. Brigham in his *History and Bibliography of American Newspapers*, "that with the greatest value to posterity would be a file of an important newspaper." I am thoroughly in accord with his view, for this book draws heavily upon the newspapers, particularly the New London *Morning Telegraph* (now defunct), the New London *Day*, the *New York Times* and its *Index*, the New York *Herald Tribune* (now, unhappily, also defunct), the New York *Daily News*, and the library of the defunct Brooklyn *Eagle*. I am grateful to George E. Clapp, managing editor, for permission to quote from numerous articles in the *Day*, dating from the 1880s into the 1920s. For use of the following articles — © 1906, 1920, 1924, 1935, 1946, and 1956 — permission was granted by The New York Times Company: "Chats About James O'Neill," July 8, 1906; Alexander Woollcott's review of "Exorcism" April 4, 1920; "A Letter from O'Neill," April 11, 1920; "O'Neill Lifts Curtain on His Early Days," by Louis Kalonyme, December 21, 1924; "Professor G. P. Baker," by Eugene O'Neill, January 13, 1935; "Eugene O'Neill Returns After Twelve Years," by S. J. Woolf, September 15, 1946, and "Talk with Mrs. O'Neill," by Seymour Peck, November 4, 1956. For permission to quote from "Odyssey of Eugene O'Neill," by Fred Pasley, January 24-30, 1932, I am indebted to Floyd Barger, managing editor of the New York *Daily News*. I also thank Arthur Venning of the *Cornish & Devon Post*, Cornwall, England, for information on Sarah Sandy's early background, and the Baltimore *Sun* and Price Day.

Magazines, as well as newspapers, have likewise contributed importantly to this book. I am specially grateful to the *New Yorker* and the authors for permission to quote from "Roughneck and Romancer," by Maxwell Bodenheim, February 6, 1926; "The Tragic Sense," by Hamilton Basso, February 28, March 6 and March 13, 1948, and "The Foolish Things of the World," by Dwight Macdonald, October 4 and 11, 1952. I am also greatly indebted to many other newspapers and magazines for articles which are cited in my Bibliography or Notes, or both.

For permission to quote from books, I am indebted to a number of publishing houses, authors, their heirs, and literary agents. For the use of material from *A Moon for the Misbegotten, Ten "Lost" Plays*, and *The Plays of Eugene O'Neill*, 1951, the standard three-volume set, I am grateful to the Executors of the Eugene O'Neill Estate and to his publishers, Random House and Jonathan Cape Ltd. For permission to quote from his *A Long Day's Journey Into Night* (copyright © 1955 by Carlotta Monterey O'Neill) and *A Touch of the Poet* (copyright © 1957 by Carlotta Monterey O'Neill, I am indebted to Mrs. O'Neill, the Yale University Press, and Jonathan Cape Ltd. Other sources I am particularly indebted to, in addition to those previously mentioned, are: *Part of a Long Story*, by Agnes Boulton (copyright © 1958 by Agnes Boulton Kaufman), quoted by permission of Doubleday & Co., Inc.; *Eugene O'Neill, the Man and His Plays*, by Barrett H. Clark, Dover Publications, Inc., 1947, quoted by permission of the publisher; *Thus Spake Zarathustra*, by Friedrich Nietzsche, translated by Thomas Common, permission to quote given by George Allen and Unwin, Ltd.; *The Provincetown: A Story of the Theater*, by Helen Deutsch and Stella Hanau, permission given by the coauthors, and "The Provincetown Players and the Playwrights' Theater, 1915–1922, by Edna Kenton, unpublished, permission given by Brandt & Brandt. Finally, a great many other books to which I am indebted are cited in my Bibliography or Notes, or both.

In writing this book I was aided inestimably by the informed judgment of Stella Bloch Hanau, who amiably took time from her own editorial work to read and criticize each chapter as it was written. Likewise, this book benefitted substantially from the judicious advice of Iris Rosendahl and Norman Rosten, who read it in galleys. I am greatly indebted also to A. L. Hart, Jr., my editor at Little, Brown, for his sound suggestions and criticism, and to Miss Margaret Mutch for a fine, painstaking job of copy-editing. Portions of this book were read by Hella Bernays, Dr. Florence Halpern, Alberta Harrington, Irma and Roberts Jackson, Hedda Rosten, and Philip Van Doren Stern; I am grateful to them all for their advice. For help in my research and other phases of the work, I thank photographer Jerry Dantzic, Jack Hamilton, Gordon Hyatt, Phyllis Jacobson, Blanche and George Okun, and George Voellmer. Finally, I recall with much pleasure my three stays at Yaddo, where a sizable portion of this book was written, and am deeply grateful to Mrs. Elizabeth Ames and Miss Pauline Hanson for many kindnesses when I was a guest there.

As yet unnamed are many other persons who generously aided my research, but their contributions fall within the scope of the second and final volume of this biography. Their help will be acknowledged at the proper time. — L.S.

INDEX

Moeller, Philip, 320–321, 322, 323, 377, 463
Mohican Hotel, 109
Moise, Nina, 377–378, 394–396, 405, 406, 407, 416, 421–423, 432, 445
Mollan, Malcolm, 226–228
Monsieur, 44
Monte Cristo, 5–6, 17, 35–45 *passim*, 69, 82–83, 86, 107–108, 118, 127–132, 198–199, 375; James, Sr., buys rights to, 18–19; first performance of James, Sr., in, 36–37; newspaper reviews, 37; as source of wealth for James, Sr., 108; effect on Eugene, 200; as vaudeville presentation, 214–221 *passim*; as film, 223–224, 235
Monte Cristo cottage, 20, 48–50
Monterey, Carlotta, 66, 71, 78, 101, 175, 191, 197, 215, 306, 448
Moody, William Vaughn, 259
Moon for the Misbegotten, A: character models, 51, 260–261, 330, 435; Eugene's attitude toward college in, 115; James, Jr., in, 435
Moon of the Caribbees, The, 187, 383–384, 393, 408–409, 438, 443, 445, 452; Eugene's evaluation of, 383–384, 395; published in *Smart Set*, 392; newspaper review, 445, 454
Moon of the Caribbees and Six Other Plays of the Sea, The, 449, 452
Moore, Tommy, 166
More Stately Mansions: insanity as subject, 80; Strindberg's influence, 253–254; character model, 354; autobiographical elements, 354–355
Morgan, J. Pierpont, 110
Morley, Malcolm, 270, 308–309, 316
Morosco Theater, 475
Morris, Clara, 107–108
Morse, Salmi, 32, 34
Moscow Art Players, 205
Mother Earth, 105, 327, 443
Mott, Elliott, 92
Mount St. Vincent, Academy of, xi, 64ff
Mouquin's, 137
Mourning Becomes Electra: influence of James, Sr., 40; New London elements, 51; sea chanteys in, 168; autobiographical elements, 171; sea in, 199; Strindberg's influence, 253–254; concept of sin in, 272; character models, 330; length, 416–417

Movie Man, The, 278
Mrs. Warren's Profession, 104
Murray, Katherine, 247, 248, 255, 257; in *The Straw*, 447
Murray, T. C., 205, 206, 417
Musketeers, The, 75, 82–83, 316
Mystic Wharf, 158, 160

N

Nassau Literary Magazine, 117
Nathan, George Jean, 75, 134, 392, 421, 439, 443, 452–453, 464, 476; and Princeton suspension, 124–125; account of Eugene's suicide attempt, 211; on Eugene's talent, 453
Nation, 452
National Theater, 26, 217
Nazimova, Alla, 121
Neighborhood Playhouse, 372
Neilson, Adelaide, 31
New Central Hotel, 379, 385
New London (Conn.), xi, 19–20, 110–111; Eugene's feeling about, 50–54; residents in Eugene's plays, 50–51; elements of, in plays, 51, 54; the O'Neills' social status in, 57; Boat Day, 59–62; *see also* Monte Cristo cottage
New London *Day*, 227, 229; as biographical source, xi; on Eugene's activities, 198, 318; on Eugene's plays, 304; on Eugene's film writing, 312; on James, Sr., 318, 319, 339
New London Light, 88–89
New London *Telegraph*, 47, 54, 62, 111, 280–281, 381; as biographical source, xi; publishes Eugene's poetry, 193, 201, 230, 231, 235, 239; on career of James, Sr., 199, 223, 258–259; Eugene as reporter on, 226–236 *passim*; on Eugene's tubercular condition, 243, 249–250; on publication of *Thirst and Other One Act Plays*, 290; on Eugene at Harvard, 293; on Eugene's plays, 303; on Eugene's film writing, 311–312; on Eugene's poetry, 313
New Way to Pay Old Debts, A, 132–133
New York (ship), 194–195
New York *Call*, 278, 387, 390, 403
New York–Chicago Supply Co., 135, 141
New York City. See Greenwich Village; Tenderloin district; and specific establishments, such as Hell Hole, Jimmy the Priest's, etc.

OTHER
COOPER SQUARE PRESS
TITLES OF INTEREST

LOVECRAFT AT LAST
The Master of Horror in His Own Words
H. P. Lovecraft and
Willis Conover
New Introduction by
S. T. Joshi
312 pp., 59 b/w illustrations
0-8154-1212-6
$28.95 cloth

D. H. LAWRENCE
A Biography
Jeffrey Meyers
480 pp., 32 b/w photos
0-8154-1230-4
$18.95

KATHERINE MANSFIELD
A Darker View
Jeffrey Meyers
With a new Introduction
344 pp., 29 b/w photos
0-8154-1197-9
$18.95

THE ART DEALERS
The Powers Behind the Scene Tell How the Art World Really Works
Revised and Expanded
Edition
Laura de Coppet and
Alan Jones
496 pp., 160 b/w
illustrations
0-8154-1245-2
$32.00 cloth

RUBENS
A Portrait
Paul Oppenheimer
0-8154-1209-6
432 pp., 17 color plates, 37
b/w illustrations
$32.00 cloth

THE GERTRUDE STEIN READER
The Great American Pioneer of Avant-Garde Letters
Edited with an Introduction
by Richard Kostelanetz
544 pp., 1 b/w photo
0-8154-1246-0
$19.95 paperback
0-8154-1238-X
$29.95 cloth

EDGAR ALLAN POE
His Life and Legacy
Jeffrey Meyers
376 pp., 12 b/w photos
0-8154-1038-7
$18.95

SIR ARTHUR CONAN DOYLE READER
From Sherlock Holmes to Spiritualism
Edited by Jeffrey Meyers and
Valerie Meyers
544 pp., 1 b/w photo
0-8154-1202-9
$28.95 cloth

SHORT NOVELS OF THE MASTERS
EDITED BY CHARLES NEIDER
648 pp.
0-8154-1178-2
$23.95

THE JOY I SEEK
Fragments from *Endymion* by Keats
Preface by Louis Martiz
Introduction and paintings
by David Finn
100 pp., 45 color paintings
1-56833-240-8
$21.95 cloth

GRANITE AND RAINBOW
The Hidden Life of Virginia Woolf
Mitchell Leaska
536 pp., 23 b/w photos
0-8154-1047-6
$18.95

GEORGE ELIOT
The Last Victorian
Kathryn Hughes
416 pp., 33 b/w illustrations
0-8154-1121-9
$19.95

THE GREENWICH VILLAGE READER
Fiction, Poetry, and Reminiscences
Edited by June
Skinner Sawyers
504 pp., 1 map
0-8154-1148-0
$35.00 cloth

AMERICAN WOMEN
ACTIVISTS' WRITINGS
An Anthology, 1637–2001
Edited by Kathryn
Cullen-DuPont
664 pp.
0-8154-1185-5
$37.95 cloth

T. E. LAWRENCE
A Biography
Michael Yardley
304 pp., 71 b/w photos., 5
b/w maps
0-8154-1054-9
$17.95

TOLSTOY
Tales of Courage and Conflict
Edited by Charles Neider
576 pp.
0-8154-1010-7
$19.95

THE TRAVELS OF MARK TWAIN
Edited by Charles Neider
448 pp., 6 b/w line drawings
0-8154-1039-5
$19.95

LIFE AS I FIND IT
A Treasury of Mark Twain Rarities
Edited by Charles Neider
343 pp., 1 b/w photo
0-8154-1027-1
$17.95

THE SELECTED LETTERS
OF MARK TWAIN
Edited by Charles Neider
352 pp., 1 b/w photo
0-8154-1011-5
$16.95

MARK TWAIN: PLYMOUTH ROCK
AND THE PILGRIMS
and Other Essays
Edited by Charles Neider
368 pp.
0-8154-1104-9
$17.95